Advance Praise for *A Red Line in the Sand*

"As we are learning every day, the world is an ever more dangerous place, on a hair trigger from East to West, North to South. David Andelman, one of our most experienced national security journalists, gives us a timely, insightful analysis of the dangers and prospective solutions in this very welcome book." —**Tom Brokaw, senior correspondent, NBC News**

"David Andelman has masterfully accomplished the most difficult possible intellectual exercise: understanding where the balance point lies between war and peace. His work, without a doubt, is an essential landmark for all those who analyze or influence international affairs."
—**Patrick Wajsman, editor-in-chief and publisher of *Politique Internationale***

"In his vital new book, David Andelman deftly marshals a wealth of examples from diplomatic and military history to demonstrate the life-and-death dangers of proclaiming red lines without fully thinking through the consequences. Calling attention to the dizzying web of lines in the sand around the world, Andelman urgently alerts us to the seeds of future conflicts as well as the opportunities for making peace."—**Richard Galant, managing editor, CNN Opinion**

"David Andelman draws on decades of experience as a foreign correspondent to provide a smart, fresh take on the proliferating phenomenon of coercive 'lines in the sand' that world leaders like to draw, often with disastrous consequences."
—**Jacques Leslie, columnist and former foreign correspondent, *The Los Angeles Times***

"Do good fences make good neighbors? Does intervention cost more lives than it saves? From the *Ramayana* to Syria, Andelman takes us on a sweeping tour of every important place where arbitrary borders and diplomatic bluffs intersect. Before deciding on how to tackle North Korea, Russia, Iran, and other hotspots, the next president needs to read this book."
—**Dr. Parag Khanna, managing director of Singapore-based FutureMap and author of *Connectography* and *The Future is Asian***

"David Andelman's book is valuable for specialists, academics and citizens who want to understand not just various conflicts around the globe, but also the origins of these conflicts and how our global political structures make future conflicts almost inevitable. *A Red Line in the Sand* is more than another trip around the world. It probes a dynamic that has become almost ubiquitous in global affairs—red lines that must not be (but often are) crossed—to offer a compelling framework for understanding war and peace in the 21st century."
—**Lincoln A. Mitchell, Arnold A. Saltzman Institute of War and Peace Studies, Columbia University**

"The term 'red line in the sand,' has been used for ages, but with varied, often disastrous results. Examining the history of states using the threat of retaliation to control their neighbors is essential to building a more inclusive and peaceful world. David Andelman offers a powerful testament of how today's world is filled with more 'red lines' than ever before and the dangers they present."

—**Laetitia Garriott de Cayeux, CEO of Global Space Ventures and Fellow at the Truman National Security Project**

"A fantastic work, and an eye opener, vital to understanding past and present red lines that have shaped the world as we know it today. It draws lessons that can help the world become safer and more peaceful. This is especially important in light of the spread of the COVID-19 pandemic, which has not recognized any boundaries or red lines. The recent agreement between the United Arab Emirates and Israel to establish formal diplomatic relations is another example of how eliminating red lines could help the greater good of nations."

—**Dr. Sulaiman Al Hattlan, CEO Hattlan Media, former editor-in-chief** *Forbes Arabia*, **and Nieman Fellow**

"In this important and thoughtful book, David Andelman explores the fascinating story of how red lines have played a decisive, if not always fully understood, role throughout the recorded history of global diplomacy. Andelman traces how leaders have used and abused red line strategies through the centuries with consequences that are often unforeseen, sometimes calamitous, and every once in a while successful. Andelman's detailed study uncovers an aspect of statecraft that, remarkably, has never really been examined before, providing fresh and original insights into the geopolitics of our past and our present."

—**Stephen Schlesinger, Fellow, Century Foundation; former director, World Policy Institute; author,** *Act of Creation*; **coauthor,** *Bitter Fruit*; **co-editor,** *The Letters of Arthur Schlesinger Jr.*

"Andelman's book is both immediate and forward-looking—a sharp analysis of the situation in the many of the hottest areas of our planet. As an historian of the present, his work combines the in-depth research of an historian and the responsiveness of a journalist who has followed the most immediate and compelling global events. He brings to this work contacts at the highest levels he has accumulated over decades and used them in pursuit of his quest. A Michelin Guide to a world of crises, a roadmap of the perils that threaten us all. Read it with open eyes to learn more about the world today, how to react to it, if you can, and where to set foot."

—**Patrice de Beer, former Washington and London Bureau Chief and editorialist for** *Le Monde*

"A look at the world's flash points for conflict, whose number seems to be growing exponentially. The central truth holds: Everywhere around the world, people are digging in, and there's a fight sure to come. If you're taking bets on where the next war will break out, this is essential reading."

—*Kirkus Reviews*

"The failed peace settlement following the Great War of 1914-1918 has been the subject of many fine books. In many respects, David Andelman's *A Shattered Peace* is the best of these."

—Ernest R. May, Charles Warren Professor of American History, Harvard University

"The peace conference in Paris at the end of World War I was the first and last moment of pure hope for peace in the history of world affairs. David Andelman, a classic reporter and story-teller, tells this fascinating tale of hope failing finally and forever on the shoals of naivety and hard-headed cynicism."

—Leslie H. Gelb, former columnist for *The New York Times* and President Emeritus of the Council on Foreign Relations

A RED LINE
IN THE SAND

ALSO BY DAVID A. ANDELMAN

The Peacemakers (1973)

The Fourth World War: Diplomacy and Espionage in the Age of Terrorism (1992)
With the Count Alexandre de Marenches

A Shattered Peace: Versailles 1919 and the Price We Pay Today (2008)
[Centenary Edition: 2014)

An Impossible Dream: Reagan, Gorbachev, and a World Without the Bomb (2019)
By Guillaume Serina [translated by David A. Andelman]

A
RED LINE
IN THE
SAND

Diplomacy, Strategy, and the
History of Wars that Might Still Happen

DAVID A. ANDELMAN

PEGASUS BOOKS
NEW YORK LONDON

A RED LINE IN THE SAND

Pegasus Books, Ltd.
148 West 37th Street, 13th Floor
New York, NY 10018

Copyright © 2021 by David A. Andelman

First Pegasus Books edition January 2021

Interior design by Maria Fernandez

Library of Congress Cataloging-in-Publication Data is available.

ISBN: 978-1-64313-648-6

10 9 8 7 6 5 4 3 2 1

Printed in the United States of America
Distributed by Simon & Schuster
www.pegasusbooks.com

For Pamela . . . ever my treasured and valiant woman.

And Woody . . . in hopes he will help his world become a better one.

CONTENTS

ACKNOWLEDGMENTS

The genesis of this book goes back really to my earliest days traveling the world as a foreign correspondent, first for *The New York Times*, then for CBS News, but I owe an even earlier debt to my studies at Harvard under Ernest R. May, the great diplomatic historian, and Henry A. Kissinger, then the brilliant professor of government and international affairs. Throughout my career, they succeeded in opening my eyes to the reality that today's seismic shifts in red lines and boundaries—geographic, political, or social, enforced by diplomacy, arms or simply states of mind—may be traced to innumerable events I've chronicled personally over the past half century.

When I began my research and compilation of red lines for this project, it began to dawn on me that the numbers, not to mention their reach and impact, were staggering. Effectively, there are more red lines—in all their manifold forms and iterations—in existence today than at any other single moment in history. Some of this is without question a tribute to the lack of any sort of global vision by President Donald Trump, fully prepared to build barricades where none existed previously, cutting America off from a world that so deeply depended on its leadership and example. But under no circumstances should this volume be viewed as an element of the greater anti-Trump literature. On the contrary, since the final changes in this manuscript are taking place at a moment when none of us has any firm idea who will be sworn in as President when this volume reaches your hands, my hope is simply that it may serve as a road map for the next inhabitant of the White House and his successors, as well as policy-makers and influencers around the world.

In the course of researching and writing this book, I've been privileged to have had some extraordinary guides through each of the regions I explore. In the case of China and especially the South China Sea, whose importance I first recognized in the mid-1970s when I served as Southeast Asia Bureau Chief of *The Times*, I owe a special debt to Jan van Tol, one of America's great specialists in the whole region, a retired Navy captain, commander of three warships, and now senior fellow of the Washington think tank Center for Strategic and Budgetary Assessments. For Korea, Evans J. R. Revere, senior fellow at Brookings, who not only played a central role in the diplomacy of North and South Korea while in the State Department, having made innumerable trips to Pyongyang, was of inestimable value, pulling back the curtain on the Kim family and their aspirations for the future of the Korean Peninsula on both sides of the 38th parallel and how we got there. Professor William Taubman, the Pulitzer Prize winning political scientist and historian of Russian studies at Amherst College, was enormously generous with his time and profound understanding of Russian and Soviet government and history. Linas Kojala, director of the Eastern European Studies Center in Vilnius, Lithuania, served as an indispensable guide to the Baltic nations. Gary Sick, the brilliant Columbia University researcher and founder of the Gulf/2000 Project that is an unparalleled resource for anyone dealing with the Middle East or Iran, drew on his vast experience going back to the Iran hostage crisis. At that time he served on President Jimmy Carter's National Security Council and was his principal aide for Persian Gulf Affairs. He was of inestimable help on the entire region. I know of no single Western expert with broader and deeper direct sources in the militias of the Middle East, especially those Shiite groups backed by Iran, than Phillip Smyth, Soref Fellow of the Washington Institute for Near East Policy. He was a priceless guide through the complex thickets of the red lines established by these groups with whom he has maintained close, even personal, relationships unparalleled in the West. On Africa, no one could have had a more attentive and perceptive reader and advisor than Professor Harry Verhoeven of Oxford and the Georgetown School of Foreign Service in Qatar. I am equally indebted to John Campbell, the Ralph Bunche senior fellow for Africa Policy of the Council on Foreign Relations and his extraordinary Nigeria Security Tracker and Sub-Sahara Security Tracker databases, as well as two distinguished French diplomats, François Delattre, Secretary General of the French Ministry of Europe and Foreign Affairs, previously ambassador to the United States and the United Nations, and briefly a student of mine at the École Nationale d'Administration (ÉNA), and his successor at the United Nations, Nicolas de Rivière, whose profound insights were critical to my understanding of red lines of all stripes. Much appreciation, too, to my lifelong friend and fellow correspondent, the veteran *Le Monde* journalist Patrice de Beer.

Finally there are the maps and images. For what work dealing with red lines can possibly ignore the maps and illustrations that define this concept on so many levels? So my profound thanks to the folks at the Asia Maritime Transparency of the Center for Strategic and International Studies, especially Harrison Pretat, for their remarkable before-and-after images of Fiery Cross Reef in the Spratlys; the European Council on

Foreign Relations, particularly Marlene Riedel; the accomplished mapmaker of the early Middle East, Michael Izady and the G-2000 project where I found him; the International Institute for Strategic Studies; Deutsche Welle; the Council on Foreign Relations; and the archives of the Weizmann Institute; *Brill's Journal of the Economic and Social History of the Orient* for its map of the Iron Age in the Levant.

My researcher in the early stages, Noorulain Khawaja, was a talented guide as I established the scope and reach of this book. Two great French journalists and friends, Dominique Bromberger and Pierre Favier, whose original concept of examining the taxonomy of the Obama Syrian red line contributed substantially to that chapter, also helped spark my interest in a broader treatment of the phenomenon. I owe both a debt of deep gratitude.

Then there was my remarkable and innovative agent, Alexis Hurley at Inkwell Management, who has been with me through three books and innumerable ideas large and small, who has read every page of every proposal and every draft, above and beyond her job description, a guidepost through an ever-changing publishing landscape at home and abroad. And it was Alexis who first found for me the incomparable Jessica Case, at Pegasus. No author could be more blessed than to have found an editor and publisher who recognized both the promise and reach of this work from the beginning, and was so meticulous and perceptive in guiding it to its conclusion. My talented and vigilant copy editor, Peter Kranitz and proofreader Daniel O'Conner, held my feet to the fire, rescuing me from myself, while Maria Fernandez was working her magic with our indispensable maps and design. And perhaps my most attentive and vigilant reader, my son Philip Andelman.

Finally, of course, there is my wife, Pamela Title without whose kindness, patience, even brilliance, not to mention her most fastidious final proofreading, none of this would have been possible. Especially in the final fraught months of writing and editing during the height of the coronavirus pandemic when there was just the two of us, isolated in our cabin-in-the-woods in remote northeastern Pennsylvania, she kept me sane, well-nourished, and above all inspired.

CHAPTER ONE

Flashpoints

In August 1983, I arrived in Chad, the sprawling African nation whose territory is divided neatly between the southern reaches of the vast Sahara Desert and the northern reaches of sub-Saharan jungle. A line that could be all but drawn with an X-Acto knife cuts this remarkable nation in two. But that line had existed since geologic time. It was hot that summer, daytime temperatures hovering just below 100 degrees as Chad's capital, N'Djamena, sits just twelve degrees above the equator. My mission for CBS News was to report on a different, more modern danger—the threat by Libyan strongman Colonel Muammar Qaddafi pushing south of his Saharan lands, across a figurative line in the sand that French president François Mitterrand had drawn and pledged, with a number of France's allies in Africa, to defend. The irredentist impulses of an expansionist Qaddafi must be restrained—prevented from breaking out of his boundaries and expanding all but unchecked into the heart of the African continent.

This line, dividing north from south, desert from jungle, the line that Qaddafi must not cross, at least not without paying a substantial cost, was a red line of the most pernicious sort. This book is the story of just such barriers—physical, diplomatic, military, all too often existential—that have proliferated in recent years across every continent and that have reached a toxic apex in numbers and virulence at this very moment in history. There have never been more red lines at any one point in history than today. Some of this responsibility must fall to America's president, Donald Trump. But his too often quixotic approach to international troubles should not be embraced by his foes as the only explanation for many of these pernicious constructions. Their very nature seems to be ill understood by rulers and governments who have brought them to life.

In the past half century, I have visited many such regions on five continents, reported on their anatomies, and the players who animated them. By examining their origins, their structure, their arc, we may have a better sense of those few that have succeeded and all too many that have failed. And we may be able to suggest some guideposts to identify which are most likely to fulfill their mission and which are destined to lead only to noxious outcomes.

—

In the two months I spent in Chad, this beleaguered and suffering land, Qaddafi's warplanes bombed the oasis of Faya-Largeau, deep in the Saharan region of Chad, surrounded by blistering desert, then quickly seized control of the town. But his land forces held back from advancing further south to take on a joint detachment of Chad, French, and Zairian troops who had drawn their own red line they were clearly prepared to defend, even under the most horrific conditions. For a sense of the nature of this contested territory, our Sony and Ikegami electronic cameras were useless in the furnace-like heat of Faya, whose daytime, sheltered temperatures often hit 109 degrees and stayed there, though out in the Sahara itself, daytime temperatures of 136 degrees have been recorded. Erik Durschmied, the freelance film cameraman we dispatched, later told me that if he did not keep his film stock shaded, it became so hot that the emulsion would boil away. Five hundred miles to the south, beyond the furious heat of the Sahara, in a French military cantonment on the outskirts of the capital of N'Djamena, forces of the Foreign Legion set up camp and, with the aim of showing Qaddafi just what he might be facing, had no reservations about parading their armed might before Western journalists. Within days, the bulk of them had moved off into the desert south of Faya to face down Qaddafi's ragtag forces and hold off his further penetration.

On August 20, we got a tip at the wretched, airless hotel where we shared quarters with large beetles that could easily have been saddled and ridden out of the room, that Mobutu was coming to town. American ambassador Peter Moffat learned about the visit only at 6:30 that morning from a radio news broadcast that a worker at the embassy had heard. Mobutu Sese Seko was Africa's ultimate titan. At the point he lurched into my view, he'd already held unchallenged power over the Democratic Republic of the Congo (which he'd renamed Zaire) for nearly a quarter century since he ousted, then arranged the execution of, the democratically elected president Patrice Lumumba. Mobutu would remain in power for another fourteen years after his visit to Chad. Although he was close to China and committed to purging all vestiges of colonial influence from his nation that had until its independence been known as the Belgian Congo, his determinedly anti-Soviet stance endeared him to Belgium and the United States, not to mention France. So, it was hardly surprising that he would suddenly appear in N'Djamena to support a neighboring autocrat—Chad's President Hissène Habré—who was in turn being supported by France's president, but who above all was being challenged by Mobutu's sworn enemy Colonel Qaddafi. After all, the colonel had urged Mobutu's people to rise up and depose their ruler. Qaddafi clearly had designs on the entire region—whether to rule or influence he seemed somewhat indifferent.

Mobutu's DC-10 landed in late morning—the entire exercise clearly timed to make network evening news broadcasts in Europe and the United States. And indeed, from the moment he stepped from the door, garbed in a leopard skin hat and dark tunic with large sunglasses, it was pure television. Waiting at the foot of the stairs after his plane taxied to a stop was Habré, clad head to toe in white. At the end of a long red carpet was Mobutu's huge, personal Jeep, customized with tires taller than myself. The two mounted this elephantine vehicle and it lumbered off slowly toward town. Slowly, because running before it was an honor guard in military camouflage fatigues, chanting rhythmically Mo-BU-tu, Mo-BU-tu, Mo-BU-tu—a chant taken up by crowds that lined his route. Mobutu, standing tall in the Jeep, brandishing an enormous carved staff, unsmiling, raised the staff in salute to his apparently adoring fans.

"I have come to show that Chad does not stand alone," Mobutu declared, standing beside President Habré for their parade through the center of town. Beyond his statement, Mobutu had already shown his support. He'd dispatched some two thousand Zairian troops, who'd joined up with the thousand French legionnaires to set up a defensive perimeter south of Faya, and would represent the furthest advance into the country by Libyan forces. Mobutu spent barely two hours in Chad before heading off to Rome, one of his preferred shopping places, where he was fond of spreading substantial quantities of the billions of dollars he'd looted from his country's treasury.

In the end, Qaddafi beat a retreat to the north of the fifteenth parallel—the line Mitterrand and Mobutu were clearly determined to defend, that was also, by chance, the furthest range Libyan planes could manage in a single sortie. Though the Libyan leader did not hesitate to try again on several occasions to pierce it, the French finally sent the strongest possible signal in 1986 when their own warplanes bombed the Ouadi Doum runway northeast of Faya-Largeau in northern Chad, which Qaddafi had built expressly for his raids. Message sent and received. Throughout, the line held. But these were far simpler times. There were no real global terrorist networks. The few dictators, like Mobutu, had been around long enough to learn the limits of their larcenous power and, apart from Qaddafi, managed to restrain their expansionist urges. Those western nations with long and deep roots in the colonial past were able to continue exerting their paternalism, in this instance for good, and when a red line seemed necessary as in Chad, the geopolitical powers that be were able to identify it, establish it, *and* defend it. And when the need no longer existed, the line was pulled down.

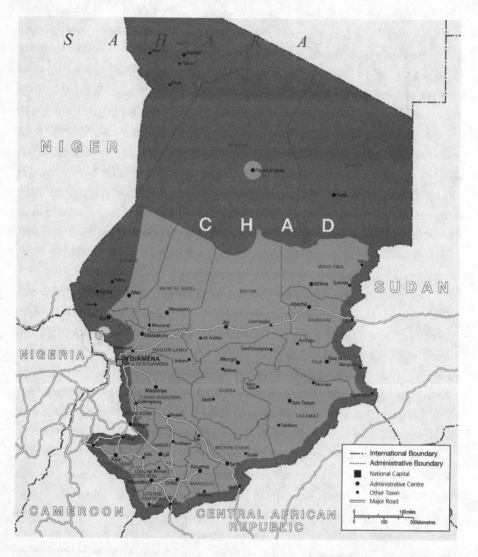

Chad's 15th parallel dividing the nation, roughly, between the Saharan desert lands to the north and sub-Saharan lands to the south, with the oasis of Faya Largeau located in the north.

Thirty years ago, there were, effectively, but two such lines on the African continent. One surrounded Libya and Qaddafi's pernicious regime. President Ronald Reagan ordered American warplanes to bomb Tripoli in 1986 in an ultimately successful attempt to remove Qaddafi's nuclear ambitions after a decade enveloped by a red line policed largely by American forces with British and French assistance. The two lines surrounding Libya and Chad thirty years ago have morphed today into an entire spiderweb, a network of lines, often crisscrossing, through and across a dozen central African nations. At least 2,431,985 square miles and 278,030,000 people are today swathed in red lines that have developed largely since the turn of this millennium and the arrival of a host of terrorist groups. Nigeria has its own collection of barriers across territories where, since 2002, Boko Haram has operated with virtual impunity. All these assorted red lines must be patrolled and sustained—however tenuously—by enormous military forces, leading in 2007 to the creation of AFRICOM, the latest regional US military command structure that encompasses the world's first all-drone military base. This American-run facility is located in Niger, which has become the crossroad of the struggle against African-based jihadists.

The source of these pernicious networks of red lines has come to define the new world order. Propelled too often by the ignorance and hubris of those who laid them out, thousands of miles distant, on maps they hardly recognized, such lines have transformed the lives of vast numbers of people whose languages, rituals, hopes, and aspirations are hardly understood or appreciated by those who have sought to define them. In this respect, at least, they were not unlike the masters of the early twentieth-century universe. These ignorant and poorly advised leaders of the victorious Allies of World War I, as I described in my last book, *A Shattered Peace: Versailles 1919 and the Price We Pay Today*, established the foundations of many of these regions in Paris in 1919, where they drafted the Treaty of Versailles. Some of the lines they drew were real, national boundaries that needed to be patrolled and defended by legions of armed men and women. But many, though they did not call them that, were the red lines that today's statesmen and warriors would easily recognize.

—

If in the past century there has been a single most remarkable and least heralded political and diplomatic gambit, enforced by military dominance and guaranteed by determination and pluck, it is the red line. It is a concept rooted deep in human history, back to Biblical times. The proverbial "line in the sand" has since been drawn increasingly, often with catastrophic results, on virtually every continent. Step across that line—literally or figuratively—and face the consequences. Or not. A line in the sand provoked the first large-scale launch of advanced cruise missiles in history, by Donald Trump, on Syria. Others have led to Russian interventions from the Crimea to the Euphrates. And the threats linger over all heads today—nuclear arsenals, real or anticipated, of North Korea and Iran; Chinese expansion across the South China Sea; Russian lust for lost territories from Ukraine to the Baltics; Afghanistan's violently contested Helmand and Kandahar provinces, across the Hindu Kush into Pakistan; not to mention a broad swath of sub-Saharan Africa where newly arrived terrorists threaten a metastability maintained for centuries by nomadic tribes. Indeed, there are more such red lines, effectively invoked—and largely ineffectual and dangerously ignored—in existence today than at any other single time in history. A conservative accounting suggests at least forty worldwide, and multiplying on every continent. And this horrific geopolitical reality may be laid most directly at the feet of one man: Donald Trump. The American president, whether by ignorance, intolerance, or just plain hubris, has been responsible for the proliferation of such metastable challenges to the world, regional, or local order. Many academics call this "coercive diplomacy." That's a polite term for a loaded gun to the head of someone you want something from, or more often an abstention from an overt action that seems to hold potentially pernicious consequences. But if ill-defined, this inaction may prove to be more ruinous than if the gun had never been held to the head, the red line never established.

To understand the scale of the challenge, we must understand from the beginning the scale of the problem, the density of the webs that exist today, how they have evolved, and especially how many individuals are directly impacted by their establishment. But especially they should be evaluated by their success or failure. Let's examine these region by region and take as our time frame the past thirty-five years, from 1985 to the present.

In 1985, the world was very different from today. It was the final years of Communism versus capitalism as the ultimate driving force, with one superpower as dominant on each side—respectively the Soviet Union and the United States. But at the same time, it was the final years of the Mutually Assured Destruction (MAD) that assured world peace. Mutually Assured Destruction refers to the ability of the nuclear arsenal of one superpower to be in a position to withstand a first strike of nuclear weapons and retaliate, utterly destroying the other. This ultimate red line was drawn from the moment the Soviet Union joined the nuclear club after the United States, until today the only power ever to unleash a nuclear weapon against an enemy. At its peak of power, the Soviet Union and the allied nations of the Warsaw Pact occupied the entire territory from Eastern and Central Europe across Eurasia to the Pacific. NATO occupied much of the remaining European continent and North America. For Winston Churchill, on March 5, 1946, there was an iron curtain: "From Stettin in the Baltic to Trieste in the Adriatic, an iron curtain has fallen across the continent." But what is often ignored about Churchill's commencement address at Westminster College in Fulton, Missouri, was the great British wartime prime minister describing the other challenges that effectively constituted a network of red lines in Europe.

"The United States stands at this time at the pinnacle of world power," Churchill proclaimed. "It is a solemn moment for the American Democracy. For with primacy in power is also joined an awe inspiring accountability to the future." Then, he proceeded to define this future accountability and its challenges, within Europe and beyond:

> Turkey and Persia [Iran] are both profoundly alarmed and disturbed at the claims which are being made upon them and at the pressure being exerted by the Moscow government. An attempt is being made by the Russians in Berlin to build up a quasi-Communist party in their zone of Occupied Germany. . . . In Italy the Communist Party is seriously hampered by having to support the Communist-trained Marshal Tito's claims to former Italian territory at the head of the Adriatic. Nevertheless the future of Italy hangs in the balance. Again one cannot imagine a regenerated Europe without a strong France. All my public life I have worked for a strong France, and I never lost faith in her destiny, even in the darkest hours. I will not lose faith now. However, in a great number of countries, far from the Russian frontiers and throughout the world, Communist fifth columns are established and work in complete unity and absolute obedience to the directions they receive from the Communist center.

Churchill concluded by asserting that he did "not believe that Soviet Russia desires war. What they desire is the fruits of war and the indefinite expansion of their power and doctrines." Then he established what became effectively a regime of lines that NATO and the United States would police henceforth, from that very moment. "Our difficulties and dangers will not be removed by closing our eyes to them. They will not be removed by mere waiting to see what happens; nor will they be removed by a policy of appeasement," he declared. "From what I have seen of our Russian friends and Allies during the war, I am convinced that there is nothing they admire so much as strength, and there is nothing for which they have less respect than for weakness, especially military weakness. For that reason the old doctrine of a balance of power is unsound." Of course, when Churchill spoke, the Soviet Union was still three years away from its first nuclear bomb test. America was the sole nuclear power and apparently the ultimate guarantor of each of the small webs of red lines across Europe.

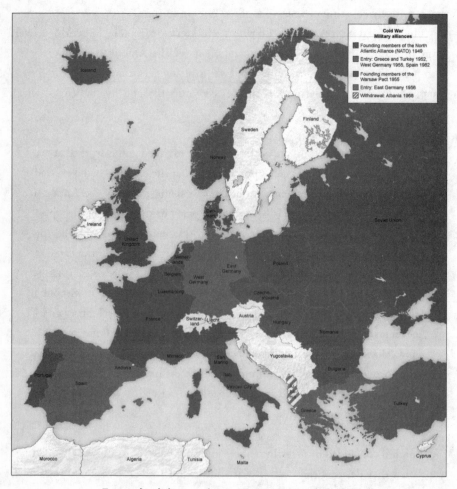

Europe divided east and west, Warsaw Pact and NATO,
where Churchill's iron curtain divided the continent.

To patrol them, Churchill further proposed creation of "an international armed force" under the auspices of the newly created United Nations. Of course, we know today that was utterly fanciful in its presumptive requirement that nations cede control over their armed forces and presumably their national security to any organization beyond that nation's immediate control—in other words relinquishing the heart of their national sovereignty to foreigners.

Beyond the boundaries of NATO, no power has ever had the ability to establish a red line network of comparable power or potential toxicity to that of the Atlantic Alliance. In Asia in 1985, there was the thirty-two-year-old line that divided north from south on the Korean peninsula. There has been a line across the Taiwan Strait since the Nationalists under General Chiang Kai-shek fled to the island of Taiwan from mainland China in 1949, which has served as a flashpoint on numerous occasions since then and remains a point of contention today. There were some scattered localized red lines on the contested Indonesian island of Timor and New Guinea. But even in 1985, China had yet to emerge onto the world, or even the regional stage, as a power seeking to exert the kind of hegemony it is claiming today.

China, in an effort to expand its own territorial horizons, has begun building artificial islands, while fortifying numerous existing islands, atolls, and assorted ocean-born real estate in the South China Sea, each with militarized defensive perimeters across which it dares others to pass. These include the Spratly Islands (less than 490 acres of land scattered across 164,000 square miles of water) and the Paracel Islands (130 small coral islets and reefs with barely three square miles of territory within an area of 5,800 square miles), various locations in the Gulf of Tonkin off Indochina, the Natuna Islands, long claimed by Indonesia which, along with the Philippines, has not been reluctant to establish its own red lines and, with the help of American air and naval forces, police them. Each, by virtue of competing, potentially lethal, Chinese claims, is surrounded or traversed by one or more such lines, depending on which nations might actually be laying claim.

Any one of these could serve as flashpoints, and the United States, by dint of sea and air visitations or repeated fly-bys, has sought to establish red lines at the very same time China is seeking to expand and cement its own sovereignty.

In the Middle East, a similar organic growth of such limits has developed over the past thirty-five years. In 1985, a handful of such clearly-defined lines have persisted since just after World War II. Palestinians and Israelis faced down each other in Gaza and the West Bank. Kurds straddled the frontiers of Turkey, Iraq, and Syria. And since the Iran hostage crisis that ended in 1981 was still a fresh memory for the fifty-two Americans held for 444 days in the American embassy compound in Tehran, Iran was very much a red line unto itself. Today, these lines envelop at least 288 million people across seven countries covering more than 2.2 million square miles across the Middle East.

These lines, often quite literally in the sand, have spawned ongoing wars between Israelis and Palestinians, Yemenis and Houthis (effectively surrogates, respectively, for Saudi Arabia and Iran). The United States and Russia have chosen sides there, as well as in Syria and Iraq, effectively establishing their own limits with lethal impact. In Yemen, more than 70,000 have died since January 2016; as many as 570,000 in Syria; 460,000 in Iraq; in the Palestine-Israeli conflict, at least 1,200 Israelis and 9,500 Palestinians have been killed in clashes just since the year 2000. At the same time, such conflicts have created a vast body of displaced persons and migrants. The United States National Intelligence Council estimated that at least 244 million international migrants have been created in this century alone, 65 million of whom are forcibly displaced persons. Many of these have been compelled to cross any number of red lines, often in direct fear for their lives, to reach any semblance of safety, creating in the process immense burdens on many of the nations that have established or supported building the barriers, real or figurative, that sent them on their journey.

—

So what has changed in this world to draw so many more red lines than a third of a century ago, or to lead so many statesmen, often on an apparent whim, to create such barriers that have left so many dead in their wake? How has the chemistry of the political, diplomatic, or military soil shifted so radically to become more nourishing for such lines to sprout?

In the best cases, each should be a talisman of peace, prosperity, and stability—and, when agreed upon by all parties, have often proved to generate such outcomes. It is a large-scale version of the maxim "good fences make good neighbors." All too often, however, they have simply provided foretastes of ill will, breeding violence and instability. There are, of course, many forces at work in the establishment and enforcement of red lines—some directly relevant, including insurrections, wars between nations, sudden and unexpected seizures of territories, and desire or need for natural resources. Popular opinion, especially in democracies, is often a critical motivator. If the various possible permutations are not clearly visible when the line in the sand is drawn, it may become sharply defined later when it comes to defending it. This was certainly the case with Barack Obama's Syrian line. Obama was a president uniquely sensitive to the drifts and nuances of public opinion. It is what, on several occasions, prevented him from taking action, with horrific results. These same currents of public opinion must be played or resisted when necessary. Often the public cannot see even one move ahead on the geopolitical chessboard. But the pieces are actually moving in three dimensions, multiple moves ahead. The adroit leader is able to play such games deftly. And then there are those who don't even understand the rules of the game, let alone the intricate moves that can lead to success—or worse, who don't care.

Not surprisingly, but often all but unknown even to leaders bent on erecting a red line—or web of them as is more often the case today—there has grown up an entire corpus of international law that should help restrain, moderate, and direct each in a constructive direction toward peace, not war or armed conflict. Yet there are far too many world leaders today who have little knowledge or understanding of such fundamental issues. We will find as we explore the genesis of the red line—back to its first modern invocation at Munich in 1939—that the strongest and most confident world leaders are those most able to carry the concept through to a meaningful conclusion, or at least an end that manages somehow to justify the means. Do keep this fundamental concept in mind as we begin our travels through this land of mirrors and labyrinth of strings.

Today, it would seem, wherever there is a crisis, a military confrontation, men, women, and children under fire and dying, there is a red line: In Asia, from North Korea and the South China Sea, across Pakistan, Kashmir, and the Hindu Kush where the British Empire ended at the Durand Line and today the Taliban and al-Qaeda reign supreme. Across the Middle East, where twenty million have died or been driven from their homes, from Iraq and Syria south to Yemen and west across the Maghreb, sent on endless journeys while the lines remain contested in their wake. Across the Baltics that have so newly won their freedom, yet whose frontiers are still tested daily, down through the Caucuses and Crimea where the redcoats once defended a military line and gave this tactical imperative its name. Africa has its own share of lines in the sand—from Djibouti to Congo and Somalia, then a broad, sweeping arc across the Central African Republic, the vast deserts of Chad, Niger, and Mali, where blowing sands that eradicate most traces of civilization fail to eradicate lines that remain deeply engraved on the minds of these nomads who have dealt with such challenges before any written record. But everywhere today, the United States is present in one form or another at the nexus of so many, all too often of its own making.

America's vast and often pernicious role is hardly surprising. Red lines are defined by power. Established largely by the most powerful nations, they are expected to defend them. When they do not—when they pull back from confrontation or involvement—the structures the red lines were designed to defend or support begin to unravel or disintegrate. Step across the line and pay the price. That line may be geographic, diplomatic, or political, especially military. It may be a concept, a political position, even a trade pact one is expecting an opponent or partner to honor. We will uncover, on our journey, each of these types. Above all, a successful line must be linear. It is not unlike telling a compelling story. Establish right up front the theme or the boundaries of your story, then take the reader gently by the hand and lead him through the maze to the end. Don't bury the lede. The parameters of the line—or the story—must be clear and understood. No sudden, whiplashing turns, no sudden plunges into sinkholes or off cliffs, for you may lose your reader or viewer forever. Clear definitions, clearly arrived at, a reasonably straight trajectory toward an end that is defined from the beginning. Those lines that do not hew to such a formula are inevitably doomed to failure.

One of the most profound questions is whether there is any role here for idealism in what should appear to be quite hard-headed decisions on the defense of policies, territories, or military prerogatives. In other words, can or should red lines be in any fashion established or defended for purely idealistic purposes? Or, for that matter, should there be any underlying, fundamental aim that is itself idealistic. Today, idealism appears to play a very small role, if any, in their creation or maintenance. Perhaps, however, this is what may ultimately lead more directly to the failure of each of these. Red lines that have existed in the past have often had such underpinnings and there have been strong moral reasons for many. As President Barack Obama told Jeffrey Goldberg of *The Atlantic* in 2016, not long after the catastrophic failure of the line he established in Syria by an off-handed remark:

> I am very much the internationalist. And I am also an idealist insofar as I believe that we should be promoting values, like democracy and human rights and norms and values, because not only do they serve our interests the more people adopt values that we share—in the same way that, economically, if people adopt rule of law and property rights and so forth, that is to our advantage—but because it makes the world a better place. And I'm willing to say that in a very corny way, and in a way that probably [Obama's National Security Advisor] Brent Scowcroft would not say.
>
> Having said that, I also believe that the world is a tough, complicated, messy, mean place, and full of hardship and tragedy. And in order to advance both our security interests and those ideals and values that we care about, we've got to be hardheaded at the same time as we're bighearted, and pick and choose our spots, and recognize that there are going to be times where the best that we can do is to shine a spotlight on something that's terrible, but not believe that we can automatically solve it. There are going to be times where our security interests conflict with our concerns about human rights. There are going to be times where we can do something about innocent people being killed, but there are going to be times where we can't.

This is as good a definition of red lines, especially in the modern context, as any I've seen. Sadly, it comes from a person who had allowed one that he established to be breached with all but catastrophic results. Which simply shows each line must be clearly perceived for what it is. As Obama's director of legislative affairs told Senator Carl Levin on April 25, 2013, "Because of our concern about the deteriorating situation in Syria, the president has made it clear that the use of chemical weapons—or the transfer of chemical weapons to terrorist groups—is a red line for the United States of America. The Obama administration has communicated that message publicly and privately to governments around the world including the Assad regime." With this, it was apparent everyone had been put on notice. Obama's challenge should not be in any fashion mistaken for simply a diplomatic or political gambit. And as such, all parties should be prepared to enforce this reality should the line ever be breached.

Yet, subsequently, in his interview with Goldberg, Obama observed that he prefers any sort of military action enforcing red lines to be taken multilaterally with several (hopefully like-minded) partners, since such action "regulates hubris." Quite ironic, considering how deeply he wounded America's staunch ally, France, the very partner who'd agreed to leap to Obama's defense, only to be left swinging alone, hung out to dry when the president suddenly pulled up short and demurred over the launch of cruise missiles hours after they'd been primed and readied by both the French and American armed forces.

There were many at the time who considered it a bluff from the get-go. But when Goldberg asked the president point blank if it was a bluff, he shot back "I'm the president of the United States. I don't bluff." Indeed, he insisted, setting Syria and its chemical weapons aside, he would have attacked Iran's nuclear complex "if I saw them break out." In other words, if they stepped across another of his red lines. There are many to this day who doubt this, and it was never put to the ultimate test.

Yet bluff is at the very heart of some of the most impressive and sustainable red lines. Obama was at least wise enough to recognize, as his deputy national security advisor and confidant, Ben Rhodes, observed in an official White House statement on June 13, 2013: "The United States and the international community have a number of . . . legal, financial, diplomatic and military responses available. We are prepared for all contingences, and we will make decisions on our own timeline. Any future action we take will be consistent with our national interest, and must advance our objectives." This was not seen as a bluff by the president in any sense, though in retrospect it could certainly have been perceived as a bluff that failed. As we shall see, Ben Rhodes also had his own view of the situation that wound up diverging substantially from his boss's.

By contrast, Donald Trump considers himself a master of the bluff, and has said so quite explicitly—which doubtless explains a host of new red lines that have arisen under his administration or which have at least failed to disappear and only hardened under his watch. Many are under constant testing in Ukraine or more or less in suspended animation in regions of the Baltic republics adjacent to Russia, which would dearly love to step across and clasp these nations again into the bosom of the motherland where they each spent quite a miserable half century of servitude under the Soviet Union. But Donald Trump hardly seems to care very much who breaches those red lines. That, at least, is what many Estonians, Latvians, and Lithuanians told me privately during visits to their country. A vivid museum to the Soviet legacy in Vilnius, the aptly named KGB Museum of Occupation and Freedom Fighters is a popular destination for tourists, especially from Russia. Today, the lines drawn by both sides in this nose-to-nose confrontation that still continues unabated are constantly being tested by military maneuvers along their frontiers or cyber challenges in their heartlands.

In the Middle East, red lines have been a desperately immediate reality for centuries, but today are truly omnipresent. Twice the barrier to Syrian use of chemical weapons on civilians has been crossed, in each case leading to diametrically opposite results, but in neither case a satisfactory resolution of any sort. Other red lines have alternately protected and threatened the Kurdish minority that straddles three critical frontiers in Iraq, Syria, and Turkey. Iran has succeeded in breaching lines across the region from Iraq to Yemen, while both Iraq and Saudi Arabia have established many of their own making that the United States has found itself obliged to defend at enormous financial, logistical, and human costs. In Yemen, lines established by Saudi Arabia, backed by American munitions and funding, are crossed every day with catastrophic impunity by both sides in that carnage that passes for war.

Another of Obama's most critical issues was Iran's dash toward a deliverable nuclear weapon, something that the president considered a red line of the highest order. All parties to the Joint Comprehensive Plan of Action—the mullahs of Iran, the five permanent members of the United Nations Security Council (Britain, France, Russia, China, and the United States) plus Germany—agreed to and understood the framework that Iran would respect, curtailing its nuclear weapons program in return for an end to the most stringent economic sanctions. Any deviation from these baselines would lead to dire consequences. Privately, Obama later confessed that he would have been prepared to take military action had Iran not agreed to the establishment of such a red line and respected its architecture. Again, no bluff. Where this came apart was the arrival of a new party to the agreement who had not been in on its establishment. Donald Trump simply established a new and metastable line that none of the other parties agreed to honor—a potentially catastrophic use and abuse of the entire concept to no apparent purpose.

In Asia, the Korean War that ended with a tenuous armistice on July 27, 1953, established the first of what would be a succession of concentric red lines across that peninsula and extending outward toward its major power neighbors, China and Russia, while threatening American allies South Korea and Japan. The rise of China as a major Asian power has itself led to new challenges, vast loops within loops, from the South China Sea to Taiwan, while China's efforts to be perceived as a true superpower have seen it extend its reach to Latin America and especially to sub-Saharan Africa, where it has singlehandedly established new webs from Congo and Djibouti across the continent to the Atlantic Ocean.

In Latin America, America's fifth president, James Monroe, established what was perhaps the United States' first red line in the form of the Monroe Doctrine. From 1817 to 1825, he presided over a nation at its peak in the Era of Good Feelings, yet he could already feel challenges to America's sovereignty brewing from abroad. With the end of the Napoleonic Wars in 1815, the Spanish empire in the New World began to break apart, and freedom fighters managed to win independence for such nations as Argentina, Chile, and Venezuela, and quick recognition from the United States. So in 1823, Monroe declared "the American continents, by the free and independent condition which they have assumed and maintain, are henceforth not to be considered as subjects for future colonization by any European powers," adding "that we should consider any attempt on their part to extend their system to any portion of this hemisphere as dangerous to our peace and safety." Only rarely has the United States been forced to defend this principal, but defend it most resolutely it has—Theodore Roosevelt in Cuba in 1898, and President John F. Kennedy during the Cuban Missile Crisis of 1962. Most recently just as Russia and China seemed prepared to intervene on the side of Venezuela's dictatorial president Nicolás Maduro, Trump's national security advisor John Bolton observed, in intentional or unintentional ignorance of the roots of the doctrine he was invoking, "In this administration, we're not afraid to use the word Monroe Doctrine . . . It's been the objective of American presidents going back to [President] Ronald Reagan to have a completely democratic hemisphere."

A critical question that all these red lines have in common is fundamentally simple. The most viable and sustainable constructions are accompanied by or intricately a part of some comprehensive world view. Henry Kissinger, who was one of my professors at Harvard, was one of the last of such visionary leaders to be paired with a president, Richard Nixon, whose accomplishments in international affairs transcended his overarching personal fail-ings. Kissinger often waxed poetic about the value of such world views, which he loved to call by their historical and most evocative German name, *Weltanschaüng*—the term he brought to Washington and used to shape the future of mankind. At the core of his worldview, as he would put it, was the necessity of eschewing any "foreign policy that is overly guided by moral impulses and crusading ideals." Obama gave the impression of believing in such a concept, but I am persuaded ultimately failed to conceive or follow through with it. Which was why his lines ultimately failed to achieve their goals and left destruction in their wake. Perhaps the problem, as he once expressed it, is that you can't be thinking about things you haven't built. Because what you will then build will be built badly, often simply for the sake of building it in the first place.

With respect to Donald Trump, matters are far worse. For all too rarely does Trump ever give any thought at all to the results of even the most off-handed comment or tweet which can and often does set in motion events that establish red lines that are not only ill-advised, but ill-considered—or more likely not considered at all. Instead, there has developed an approach to global challenges that consists of little more than ping-ponging from crisis to crisis, establishing a principle based almost entirely on what the last person has whispered in his ear. Trump has managed to confound diplomacy with masculinity masquerading as military preparedness and armed might. This often risks smashing a mosquito with a sledgehammer, with all the attendant destruction, while revealing abundant underlying weakness.

On the morning of April 7, 2017, less than three months after taking office, Trump ordered the launch of fifty-nine Tomahawk cruise missiles, targeting the Shayrat Air-base, which the American military believed was the locus of a chemical weapons attack on civilians. It was just the kind of response that Obama had telegraphed, then stepped back from, four years before. The cruise missile strike was an ill-advised and ill-conceived effort to enforce an old red line—one of the very few that Trump had inherited rather than those he would ultimately establish—that Syrian dictator Bashar al-Assad had been stepping across with utter impunity for years. And one that should probably either have been put to rest entirely or enforced with far greater consistency and determination. For within days, Shayrat Airbase was back up and running and Assad was quickly thumbing his nose again at his western foes. A second strike a year later, this time coordinated with another, broader air strike against twice the targets, this time with the participation of Britain under Prime Minister Theresa May and France under President Emmanuel Macron, had equally little long-term impact in terms of dissuading Assad from crossing the chemical weapons red line.

Of course, there are all sorts of other diplomatic niceties inherent in any red line—its establishment, its maintenance, and its success or failure. At the center of this may be the question, as I have suggested, of bluff. How much is bluff and how much real spine and determination? When Obama was going after Iran, there was no bluff. Both sides knew that. The result was a treaty that held to the very moment it was violated by one of its key creators. Trump, however, seems to have embraced the concept of bluff, amalgamated with a not inconsiderable dose of bluster, for each of the lines he has established and sought to defend. And bluff does not go very far when it comes to holding the line.

The United States has enormous wherewithal to enforce any diplomatic, political, military, even economic barrier it may feel it is appropriate to establish or maintain. Its military equipment is without peer on the planet in quantity, quality, or ingenuity. The Air Force has the air lift capacity to get it to any point on earth with speed that no other challenger can match. After Chuck Hegel departed as Obama's third (of four) secretary of defense he recalled that he'd repeatedly made the point in National Security Council meetings that direct confrontation with Moscow was to be avoided at all costs. But, he continued, "I also made the point that the US should be giving more non-lethal equipment to the Ukrainians than we were, at a much faster pace. We had to keep in mind that there was a global leadership optic here," with the world, but especially NATO watching just how we would handle crises. And especially how we would handle red lines. Ukraine, especially eastern Ukraine, was classically mishandled from the moment Vladimir Putin decided he wanted Crimea back for his own. And then, clearly, he wanted Ukraine too. That, as we shall see, is a red line that required both finesse and an iron will to protect.

The origins of this work lie deeply in the roots of its predecessor—*A Shattered Peace: Versailles 1919 and the Price We Pay Today*. There, I examined the horrific price we are paying today for bad decisions, badly arrived at more than a century ago. My fear is that we are well en route to creating a similar set of circumstances today; our successors will look back upon a century hence and wonder at the foolish decisions taken for similar reasons—territorial aggrandizement, control of natural resources, or simply a desire to amass power and leverage that are existentially destabilizing. All of these ill-conceived actions and their consequences, whether intended or not, may in turn be laid directly at the feet of an intricate system of treaties and alliances that have in so many cases been either established or obliterated by Donald Trump, his minions, and his erstwhile friends and allies of varying degrees of capability or culpability. Many have gone virtually unchallenged, too often the product of leaders of autocracies who have sought to pull the strings of power and leverage to their own advantage and profit, or at least maintenance of their power and all the privileges that accompany it. The consequences of today's vast network of red lines, the largest that have ever existed at any single moment, are still to be played out.

Sadly, from none of today's metastasizing lines in the sand and a host of other red lines—from those of Chamberlain at Munich to Kissinger in Vietnam or Trump in Korea, Iran, China, Russia—have we learned any of the most critical and profound lessons that seem likely to determine the future, even the survival, of mankind. We are coming to an end of, indeed have likely blown right through it without even realizing, a rule-based international order that has marked much of the post–World War II world. Such an order was defined by certain rules of law or at least largely universally accepted practices. Now, we must see how best to navigate the new world's proliferation of utterly unpredictable challenges. I am often reminded of action-adventure films where the good guys manage to pick the lock or find their way into the vault room only to find themselves in an unanticipated web of red laser lines crisscrossing in three dimensions and promising, if any of them are broken, to unleash instantly lethal consequences.

The metastasizing of the red line phenomenon may in part be attributable to a host of tectonic shifts. There is the largely unanticipated population explosion in some regions of the world, particularly Africa, which in the next half century is expected to experience more rapid growth in population and density than ever before in human history. There is also climate change, and the slow redistribution of wealth that has left so many regions utterly disenfranchised and seeking some relief, often finding it in religions that preach a violent redistribution of wealth and power. Then there is the rapid spread of new technologies and means of communication that are provoking changes of a scope and rapidity that could previously only have been imagined. Many of these transformations are outside the immediate purview of this work, but must be kept in mind if we are to truly comprehend the concepts we shall be discussing.

Red lines have marked and continue to define many of the critical turning points of history—moments of high drama and desperate confrontation. In many cases, they lay the foundations for the world where we live today. The issues and the moments we will visit represent for now, as well as the future, lessons that can help us deal with today's most profound and often dangerous challenges to our stability and our very way of life. Communism is gone, but terrorism has replaced it. Trade wars threaten again to shake the most firmly planted foundations of our economic health. China, Iran, and North Korea have joined the Kremlin as the major threats to global peace and prosperity. Each of these has forced in one fashion or other the establishment of entire networks of red lines that demand an examination of the larger lessons and compelling narratives each represents. Above all, with non-state actors, terrorist groups, and armed guerrilla bands very often establishing individual lines, the previously clearly defined differences between war and peace also risk being erased. Under such circumstances, regional conflicts quickly and unpredictably may escalate to uncontrollable levels. Carefully tracking the mechanisms and understanding their political and diplomatic underpinnings may be all that can prevent any potential military breaches of these lines provoking uncontrollable escalations.

—

A Red Line in the Sand is an effort to examine the present and draw lessons for the future through the prism of the past.

Throughout my long career as a foreign correspondent, writing and traveling through some eighty-five countries for *The New York Times,* CBS News, and a host of other international news organizations, I chronicled the establishment of many of these red lines and built deep contacts with individuals who then and now helped configure them. We all, collectively, participated in a host of minute-by-minute, nail-biting events that shaped their formation and consequences in Asia, Africa, Europe, and the Middle East.

I hope that upon the conclusion of this book, we will perhaps be a trifle closer to an understanding of how raw political or military power can—and *should*—operate on a global scale. My editor at *The New York Times,* A. M. Rosenthal, refused to dispatch a correspondent to his first overseas post until he'd reached the age of thirty. "You haven't made all your mistakes yet," he told me a few days after I'd turned thirty and he announced he was sending me off to Saigon. "It's one thing to make a mistake in New York. Then you just have the mayor calling me. But in many parts of the world, you can cause a war, a revolution." Yet so many take the reins of power in nations which have made none of these kinds of errors and make them on the job.

We can only speculate about the future, of course. But outlines of the red-lines regime a half century from now are already becoming clear. By then, I am confident, water will have trumped oil as the critical, most desired, often scarcest and most valued commodity. In 2018, the National Intelligence Council saw half the world's population facing existential water shortages by 2035. Today, as of this writing, there are at least six hundred aquifer systems that straddle traditional national boundaries. Any or all of these could serve as flashpoints for conflict in the future. More broadly, resource-poor versus resource-rich nations could well serve as triggers. The amount of arable farmland is one such key reality that is already creating red lines from central Asia to East Africa. Saudi Arabia was among the first to the party, investing more than $3 billion buying rice farms in Ethiopia and Sudan, wheat fields in Ukraine and Poland, ranches in Argentina and Brazil, planting its green crescent flag in a host of countries it must now defend to feed its people effectively as its own arable land shrinks in the face of the ever-warming planet.

There is a danger that the fragmentation of nation-states along ethnic, religious, or cultural lines can only intensify the pressure to develop methods of enforcing the rule of minorities. That this has already become dangerous can be seen in places such as Catalonia and its at times violent efforts to break away from Spain, much as the Basque region did in the last quarter of the twentieth century, and as Scotland seems to be trying to do now in an effort to re-join the European continent post-Brexit. Such aspiring red lines not only weaken the parent governments politically but make it much more difficult to attract investment or strengthen the regions economically.

At the same time, a number of existing nations with aspirations to larger roles in their region or the world, and with a growing economic or military capacity to compel this, are threatening the creation of ever more fault lines in the future. Efforts by demagogues, fully prepared to adopt the methods and behavior of Donald Trump, and other leaders who see opportunities in regional unrest to pursue hegemonic ambitions—China, Iran, Turkey, as well as Saudi Arabia, even Venezuela—risk the establishment of potentially dangerous or destabilizing lines. Each is deeply antithetical to the interests of the people these leaders rule, while at the same time serving to entrench or extend the leaders' own power.

Technology and communications have enabled a host of non-state actors, particularly terrorist groups, to establish their own red lines that they then dare states and others to cross at their own peril. Such was the case with the Islamic State and its leader Abu Bakr al-Baghdadi when, due to some early rapid and unanticipated advances against ill-prepared opponents, they were able to establish a credible caliphate with ever-expanding borders across Syria and Iraq and dared all comers to challenge. Taking down the caliphate merely forced a metamorphosis of the Islamic State into a network of virtual fault lines as its message of violence and destruction spread through Africa and touched off deadly incidents across Europe and Asia.

International institutions will struggle to adapt to the rapid proliferation of these red lines. In most cases, no international body has been involved, or even consulted, when they were established. Nor will they likely be consulted in the future. Britain may have sought Europe's approval for its withdrawal from the European Union when Brexit was first ratified in a referendum of the British electorate, but eventual completion of the process was hardly held hostage to such approval. Instead what we now have is a new, and potentially quite toxic—at least in economic, commercial, and political senses—line that threads its way down the middle of the English Channel.

No international body has succeeded in taming or controlling the deep fractures that are embedded as a way of life between the increasingly nuclearized or militarized nations of India and Pakistan, the two Koreas, Saudi Arabia and Iran—each pair fully aware of the potentially hair-trigger dangers and apocalyptic consequences of the other. Overstepping these lines is controlled only by a profound realization of the existential stakes. Yet none of this awareness has succeeded in halting plans to extend deployment of nuclear weapons and their delivery systems to sea-borne platforms by India or Pakistan, which would nuclearize the Indian Ocean. Nor have the undeniable risks attenuated in any fashion the threat to the South China Sea, where a heavily nuclearized China is seeking utter control.

Enormously interesting and potentially troubling is the prospect of red lines in space—effectively mankind's final frontier. Laying claim to extraterrestrial territory is hardly outside the interests of such players as China, which in 2019 became the first nation to land a satellite on the far side of the moon. There has been considerable success in parceling out territory in the Antarctic: A 1959 treaty is considered among the most effective and broadly observed diplomatic documents in history, establishing effective boundaries. Already, a parallel Treaty on Principles Governing the Activities of States in the Exploration and Use of Outer Space Including the Moon and Other Celestial Bodies was agreed upon in 1967 and remains in force. Still, near-Earth space territories remain open season with surveillance, communications, even weaponized satellites in orbit, each occupying its own protected zone. For the moment, the major space powers have reached a tacit understanding that each nation's devices, whether military or civilian, are effectively sacrosanct. But in times of conflict, all bets are off.

Indeed, red lines themselves are transforming the very nature of future warfare, attenuating the need for large standing armies, forward-deployed around the world, in favor of small, highly mobile, regional forces and high-tech, unmanned weaponry controlled far from the battlefield. Today, even the most primitive tribal force is capable of fielding weaponry of astonishing lethality using basic kits available off the rack at most toy stores and modified by underground bombmakers. So, in May 2019, the United States suddenly moved the aircraft carrier strike group Abraham Lincoln—with at least sixteen support ships and submarines and seventeen aircraft carrier wing fighter squadrons, accompanied by B-52H Stratofortress bombers—and threatened the arrival of a hundred twenty thousand battle-ready ground forces into and around the Persian Gulf. While the excuse was vaguely identified threats from a handful of small Iranian ship-borne missiles, there were those who marveled at the uselessness of this assemblage of lethality in the face of small, mobile terrorist cells. Others marveled at how adept the Iranians were at coming right up to a line without crossing it, while hoping the other side doesn't blink.

Speed of conflicts, increased by the proliferation of hypersonic weapons, means hair-trigger responses to anyone daring to cross a red line are all the more possible with consequences hardly thought through and utterly unforeseeable. Which is precisely what America's allies most fear from the rapidly multiplying Iranian scenarios. For to them, there was no threat that needed additional controls, no matter how definitive the United States might have been. British Major General Chris Ghika, the deputy commander of Operation Inherent Resolve, the US-led coalition fighting the Islamic State in Syria and Iraq, told reporters: "No, there's been no increased threat from Iranian-backed forces in Iraq and Syria."

All of this speaks to the profound danger of proliferating and intersecting lines falling prey to sudden and unexpected miscalculations in an increasingly weaponized world with multiple nuclear deployments. Additionally, there is often the added stress of countries seeking to gain or regain territories and access critical resources, countries which are prepared to ignore traditionally accepted rules of international law. Moreover, with the United States no longer seen in many quarters as the single good and reliable partner it once was, many nations will be seeking new allies—Russia, China, or beyond—each with its own priorities and its own malignant fault lines it will be establishing or defending. And many of these barriers find no basis whatsoever in international law or practice.

—

The legal framework of red lines runs long and deep, encompassing any number of related issues between countries. Beyond simply assuring the respect for international agreements and norms of behavior, there are a host of other issues that cry out to be defined. In August 2017, Emmanuel Macron, in his first major discourse to his nation's ambassadors after taking over the French presidency, observed that his two major priorities for sustaining "*lignes rouges*" were making sure that chemical weapons were not used again in Syria and that humanitarian access be protected in every conflict zone. This "*droit d'accès,*" or right of access, was first proposed by Bernard Kouchner when he headed Médecins Sans Frontières (Doctors Without Borders). After intervention by French President François Mitterrand, the doctrine was enshrined by the United Nations General Assembly as an element of international law under the general umbrella that came to be known as "Responsibility to Protect." Under this doctrine, defined officially as "each state has the responsibility to protect its populations from genocide, war crimes, ethnic cleansing and crimes against humanity," a country or indeed any humanitarian organization does have the right to cross any red line with impunity. Of course, this must be in the interest of seeking to protect the rights, health, and safety of individuals placed in harm's way even by the country that established the line. This concept has been used most effectively, as we shall see, from time to time in critical instances—particularly in the Middle East. Beyond this, however, there is little international law governing the concept of military-diplomatic fault lines.

The big question is: Who actually has the right and power to establish a red line? In the United States, in theory and by law, the president has such authority, though the Constitution does hold that Congress alone has the power to declare war. When the Japanese attacked Pearl Harbor, President Franklin D. Roosevelt went before a joint session of Congress and asked "that the Congress declare that since the unprovoked and dastardly attack by Japan on Sunday, December 7, 1941, a state of war has existed between the United States and the Japanese Empire." However, before making that request, Roosevelt observed, "As Commander in Chief of the Army and Navy I have directed that all measures be taken for our defense." In other words, Roosevelt felt that it was within his right to react immediately, though it was up to Congress to ratify his actions—which it did without hesitation.

The first time Congress officially relinquished its authority to declare war was at the height of the Vietnam War. In 1964, the Gulf of Tonkin Resolution, passed by Congress after a questionable encounter between the American ship *Maddox* and several North Vietnamese torpedo boats in the gulf, gave President Lyndon Johnson blanket power to take any measures he felt necessary to maintain peace and security in Southeast Asia. Cross some ill-defined lines in the Gulf of Tonkin and the American military will rain fire and fury on your nation and your capital without Congress agreeing at all. In 1973, Congress weighed in again with the War Powers Resolution that sought to rein in some of the president's apparently unrestrained ability to bring the American military to bear on any given international confrontation. Under this bill, the president could send in troops for sixty days, by the end of which Congress would need to declare war or the president would have thirty more days to get American forces out of harm's way. Clearly this has not worked very well at all. Red lines continued to be established by presidents who continued to police them with force. Congress has largely remained on the sidelines. Both Barack Obama and Donald Trump have blithely ignored this sixty-thirty edict entirely—if with somewhat more doubts on the part of Obama than Trump. Of course, the establishment—even, for the most part, maintenance—of a red line does not per se require ordering troops into battle. In the best of circumstances, not a single shot should be fired. Still, if there is not a realistic expectation that the red line will be maintained by force, then it can quite quickly turn a light rose, pink, or even fade from effective view entirely.

The best, and most effective, are those actually built on the foundation of carrying out or enforcing existing international law, including responsibility to protect. Indeed, there are international law scholars who believe that red lines, judiciously applied, can be used "to begin brokering consensus around discrete and concrete standards of enforcing existing international laws," as Gabrielle Gould, staff director of the House Foreign Affairs Committee, wrote in a paper for the Georgetown University Law Center. That assumes, of course, that those creating such grids are examining them from what would appear to be a selfless perspective—often hardly the case—and not simply a means of enforcing actions that might be open to challenge on a whole host of levels. It also assumes that there is some international legal or judicial body with the authority to rule on the lines' appropriateness and enforce any such judgment. A worthy concept and one that the United Nations should examine carefully, but to date has shown no interest in pursuing. Instead, the United Nations has simply reacted, case by case, when such lines or the incidents that provoked their establishment are brought before the Security Council. Many that are challenged may fall directly under the UN Charter, and so would appear to be utterly legitimate. Still, with one or another of the Security Council's permanent members having deep stakes in the lines' maintenance or destruction, the veto power has too often been used to neutralize any legitimate enforcement.

Red lines as legitimate expressions of international law are best used to enforce existing international law rather than to create new and questionable law. The seizure or establishment of territories, as China is doing in the South China Sea, each territory with its own protective line that is challenged regularly, does not conform to any international law. To be sure, the lines' effectiveness is not always dependent on their legitimacy. Those solely designed to change states' behavior could wind up having no foundation or basis in international law whatsoever, which is not necessarily dissuasive. Increasing legitimacy often increases their effectiveness, but not always. The threat alone may be enough to deter unwanted behavior whether or not it conforms to accepted internationally recognized standards.

Students of red lines, particularly the French political scientist Bruno Tertrais, have identified at least five different reasons they may fail and six ways to make them work. They fail largely when the basic structures of crossing them are not clear—particularly where and how they are drawn. A national boundary, for instance, is quite clear, as crossing one can certainly be an act of war. But disputed boundaries on the sea or other bodies of water or in the air are somewhat less tangible and more open to misinterpretation. Article V of the NATO treaty is quite clear, by carefully defining every boundary, what constitutes a no-go zone whose violation would cause a reprisal for any potential enemy. It has never been violated by Russia or the Soviet Union, NATO's principal target. At the same time, what constitutes crossing such a boundary is important to know. For instance, no-fly zones such as those the United States have imposed at several points in the Middle East, particularly over Syria, when Russian and Western aircraft were constantly crisscrossing the region, often led to near catastrophes.

The target or targets of any red line must also be persuaded that whoever is establishing it is quite determined to enforce it and that there will be profound consequences for failing to respect it. We can go back to Hitler and the Anglo-French pledge to guarantee Polish independence and that Nazi tanks crossing that frontier would mean war. When Hitler had moved into the Sudetenland in 1938 under the terms of the Munich agreement, then swallowed all of Czechoslovakia in 1939, there was little more than bluster from France and England. So, Hitler thought he was quite free—or at least would suffer minimal damage—if he then rolled his blitzkrieg across the Polish frontier months later. Hitler also clearly believed that the benefit of violating the line established in Munich far outweighed any potential penalty. This was a price worth paying—and has been part of the calculus that has destroyed any number of lines since then. At the same time, the author of any line must assume that it may be tested at any moment. My seven-year-old grandson is a perfect object lesson. Woody will push any issue to the extreme—how far exactly can he go toward reaching his goal before being pulled back or, if he truly crosses the line, being punished? There is also the analogy of the frog. Chuck a frog into a pot of boiling water and he will immediately hop out. But put him in cool water, then gradually raise the temperature degree by degree and he will likely boil to death. Equally, red lines must themselves be carefully tempered. Too firm and they could quickly lead to a violent outcome, too faint and they risk being crossed inadvertently with the dire consequences reserved for their fracture. Finally, such lines must be clearly delineated from the get-go in each of these respects—their nature, intentions, and consequences. Donald Trump has said from the start of his presidency that he does not want to telegraph his punches, but then goes ahead and effectively establishes lines that do just that.

As for the best ways to make them work, the roadmap is fairly clear and should be quite simple, though is rarely followed. First, they must be carefully drawn and well thought out—not an off-the-cuff remark in a press scrum as happened when Barack Obama first proclaimed his red line on Syrian chemical weapons. All the components must be clear from the start, as well as a projection of utter determination to defend it. And be sure to keep it up to date. When the French established their line in Chad, they moved it north from the fifteenth to the sixteenth parallel, closer to Libya's southern border, when military circumstances allowed. But they communicated that intention quite clearly. The military option must never be renounced—something that Trump has taken as a given, but that many of his predecessors have not. Still, that alone is never enough to assure that any particular target won't step across, especially if they undertake a cost-benefit analysis and believe it's worth the risk. Tertrais also believes that whenever possible, it's essential to keep a red line private. I am not fully persuaded. Its very purpose is to call a government or other target to order. So, there may be moments when a strong public statement is essential to call public attention to any who might contemplate violating it and muster support for its defense. Governments, even in autocracies, must worry about the reaction of those they rule. Understanding how close leaders may be to sending their nation into war, placing civilians as well as military in mortal danger, could help sway public opinion and hence the decisions of those contemplating challenging, or even establishing, red lines in the first place. Only when large numbers of body bags began returning to the Soviet Union from Afghanistan did sufficient pressure build showing that defending this line was not in their best, long-term interests. Only then did Soviet troops begin pulling back from that ill-advised conflict.

Moreover, in these days of multiple, often overlapping red lines, can the violation of one avoid touching off a daisy chain of fault lines of unprecedented scope and consequences? All these issues must be taken into consideration.

Sadly, there are more operating today than at any other moment in history—the recurring theme of this volume. There, we've set it up right from the start. In part, it is because most have been hastily drawn with little thought as to their structure or especially their consequences. Not surprisingly, they must constantly be re-drawn and shifted, and not for the better, as was the case with the line the French drew across Chad in the mid-1980s, moving it back closer to its target, drawing it in as their capacity to assure its respect was constantly improving. It has been left to Donald Trump, who has largely by chance or opportunism established such challenges that are for the most part neither stable nor defensible, to create a toxic web that threatens the very foundations of the international order.

While down through history it has become axiomatic that leaders do not act in a vacuum, neither do red lines appear nor are they maintained in a vacuum. Today, however, their foundations all too often appear to waffle between whim and hubris. A dangerous recipe for a world order. As we begin our hopscotch around the world and through time, looking at lines then and now, we must ask what makes one line work, and more frequently, what makes another fail? Such fault lines appear far more prone to failure than to success. Those that are successful can be spectacularly so, though those that have failed are often utter and historic catastrophes.

CHAPTER TWO

Origins

In 1853, Britain, supported by France and the forces of the Ottoman Empire, established a territorial, effectively sacred, red line against the Russian Czar Nicholas I, who was making strong noises about his intention to exercise his own protection over Orthodox subjects of the Ottoman Sultan Abdulmejid I. Of course, there were other issues as well, particularly disputes with Russia over the various privileges of the Russian Orthodox and Roman Catholic churches in the holy sites of Palestine. Each religion had locations deeply sacred to their respective people. The Russians didn't help their case by occupying the Danubian principalities, most of which comprise present-day Romania, but that at one time had been among the further reaches of Ottoman penetration into Europe. As Russian forces moved into these nominally Ottoman lands, the British fleet was ordered to Constantinople, which then and now controlled the Bosporus, the strategic chokepoint from the Mediterranean into the Black Sea. Two weeks after the arrival of the British navy, the sultan declared war on Russia, opening a front in the Danubian provinces to push Russia back across the line the Turks had drawn, and that the British were prepared to defend. The Russian Black Sea fleet promptly engaged Turkish warships just off the coast at Sinop, the furthest northern point of the Ottoman Empire. The Turkish squadron was utterly destroyed, at which point the British and French fleets entered the Black Sea. It was January 4, 1854. Three months later, all three countries formally declare war on Russia. In September, British forces landed in Crimea, then as now a part of Russia, dominating the northern shore of the Black Sea, and laid siege to the Russian fortress at Sevastopol. The first major engagement was fought, largely to a draw, on September 20 at the Alma River.

Dawn on October 25 was brilliantly clear, providing unparalleled visibility to the various forces arrayed for battle, and the ground was a perfect bone-dry, well suited both to cavalry and foot soldiers. The Ottomans held the heights above the harbor of Balaklava, the main supply base of the British army in Crimea. The British manned a series of small forts armed with cannons from the HMS *Diamond*, and held a commanding position over the North Valley, first line of defense of Balaklava harbor. British cavalry held the Sapoune Heights, and what would become the storied Light Brigade was strung out along the valley's western end with the Heavy Brigade in the South Valley. Russian forces had begun moving in the pre-dawn darkness in three prongs. But it was the battalion of 2,500 Russian cavalry who began advancing on the harbor of Balaklava that most concerns us.

In mid-September, a force of British and French armies, accompanied by a small battalion of Turkish troops, had landed on the western coast of the Crimean Peninsula about thirty miles north of Sevastopol. Their goal was to capture this vital city and its naval base that commanded the Black Sea. Then as now, control would assure that the holder could dominate this entire body of water that was the only year-round warm-water outlet for the Russian navy and commercial shipping for the entire southern reaches of that empire. In 1854, Crimea, and especially Sevastopol, was every bit as strategically important to the Russian Empire as it is today to Vladimir Putin and his efforts to expand and defend his concept of Greater Russia and maintain Russian hegemony over the Black Sea. October 25 promised to be a critical day in the war that was already more than half finished and that the British and French were largely winning on behalf of their Ottoman ally.

On the British side were the Ninety-Third Highlanders under Sir Colin Campbell, who had taken refuge from Russian long-range artillery fire behind a crest of the rise they had been commanding. Advancing on the British, though unaware of their exact location, were four Kiev Hussar squadrons. Suddenly, Campbell ordered the Highlanders to show themselves, appearing apparently from nowhere and blocking the entire path of the advancing Hussar cavalry, throwing the Russians into utter confusion.

As it happens, there were two brilliant eye witnesses. One was Fanny Duberly, the fearless wife of Captain Henry Duberly, paymaster of the Eighth Royal Irish Hussars, part of the British light cavalry that took part in the charge of the Light Brigade. She insisted that she be allowed to accompany her husband's unit wherever it went, much to the consternation of the British commander, Lord Lucan. And she kept an impeccable journal of every moment in every engagement. That morning of October 25, feeling "far from well," she'd decided to stay on board the ship where she and her husband had been billeted. But at eight o'clock, "I saw my horse saddled and waiting on the beach, in charge of our soldier-servant on the pony" with a note from her husband that "the battle of Balaklava had begun, and promises to be a hot one." She dressed and mounted her horse, racing to the front. "Not a man stirred," she wrote of that momentous October morning. "They waited until the [Russian] horsemen were within range, and then poured a volley which for a moment hid everything in smoke. A few minutes—as it seemed to me—and all that occupied that lately crowded spot were men and horses, lying strewn upon the ground."

Fanny Duberly, saddled and ready to ride after her husband Henry,
supervising her departure, into the Battle of Balaklava, October 25, 1854.

But it was left to the trained professional, the other on-scene observer—the brilliant wordsmith and foreign correspondent for *The Times* of London William Howard Russell to describe the first battle in defense of the first red line that gave the ancient line-in-the-sand its contemporary name. Russell had landed at Gallipoli on April 5, 1854, and reached Balaklava in time to chronicle the incredible gallantry of the vastly outnumbered and outgunned British forces, which held a defensive line, lined up in their bright red uniforms. He began his narrative:

> The silence was oppressive; between the cannon bursts one could hear the
> champing of bits and the clink of sabers in the valley below. The Russians
> on their left drew breath for a moment, and then in one grand line charged

in towards Balaklava. The ground flew beneath their horses' feet; gathering speed at every stride, they dashed on towards *that thin red streak tipped with a line of steel*. The Turks fired a volley at eight hundred yards and ran. As the Russians came within six hundred yards, down went that line of steel in front, and out rang a rolling volley of Minié musketry. The distance was too great; the Russians were not checked, but still swept onwards through the smoke, with the whole force of horse and man, here and there knocked over by the shot of our batteries above. With breathless suspense every one awaited the bursting of the wave upon the line of Gaelic rock; but 'ere they came within two hundred and fifty yards, another deadly volley flashed from the levelled rifle and carried terror among the Russians. They wheeled about, opened files right and left and fled faster than they came. "Bravo, Highlanders! Well done!" shouted the excited spectators. But . . . the 93rd never altered their formation to receive that tide of horsemen. "No," said Sir Colin Campbell, 'The ordinary British line, two deep, was quite sufficient to repel the attack of these Muscovite cavaliers. (emphasis added)

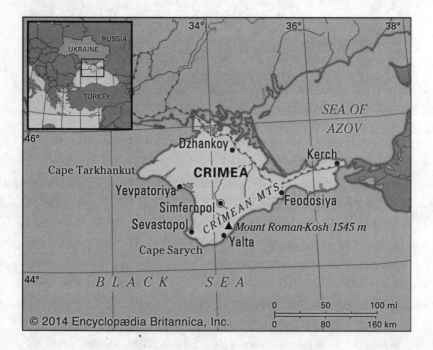

The Crimea Peninsula at the time of William Howard
Russell's dispatches to The Times *of London.*

A footnote in the published collection of Russell's dispatches from the Crimea notes that "this description of the 93rd Highlanders' stand, later misquoted as a 'thin red line', provided the origins of that famous phrase." Cross that line only at your peril, Russell suggested. The Cossacks tried, and few survived. The line had held and entered the legend of warfare and, later, diplomacy. It also forced the Russians to abandon their plans to retake Balaklava. Russia would lose this war and its access to the Black Sea.

Within two years, the Czar surrendered, Turkey reclaimed, for the moment, its Danubian provinces and assured its supremacy over the Orthodox shrines in Palestine, though magnanimously allowed access to Orthodox worshipers.

Fourteen years later, however, now supported by German Chancellor Otto von Bismarck, the Russians renounced the clauses of the armistice dealing with the Black Sea. Since Britain by then found itself unable to enforce this document alone, the Russian fleet returned to the Black Sea, never again to be dislodged. Still, the red line of 1854 was, as it turned out, the first one worth formally defending and, once defended, turned into an opportunity for victory, however transitory or pyrrhic.

The Thin Red Line, *oil-on-canvas painting by Robert Gibb, inspired by Alexander Kinglake's book* The Invasion of the Crimea. *On the left, British infantry forces, with rifles and fixed bayonets, on the right the about-to-be vanquished Russian cavalry beginning their charge on "the thin red streak tipped with a line of steel."*

As we will discover, the role of Russia and the West in Crimea will play an important role in the evolution of red lines as a critical denominator in the equation of Kremlin control over its southern extremities and its efforts to project its power far beyond.

While we can trace the phrase back to the Crimean War, the image of a line-in-the-sand, or a point of no return not to be crossed without potentially lethal consequences, may be found in the earliest human conflicts. In the Book of John in the New Testament, Jesus was said to have drawn a line in the sand when the Pharisees had brought to him an adulteress who under Mosaic law should be stoned to death. Those who were without sin, he dared them, should cross this line and cast the first stone.

But one of the earliest recorded incidents comes in the vast Indian epic *Ramayana*, ascribed to the celebrated poet Valmiki and written somewhere between the fifth century B.C.E. and the first century C.E. It is the story of the Prince Rama from the city of Ayodhya in the kingdom of Kosala, whose wife, Sita, is abducted by the evil Ravana, with ten heads and twenty arms, king of the demons of Lanka. After spotting the beautiful Sita in the forest, and having fallen in love with her, Ravana disguises his servant Maricha as a golden deer to tempt Rama and Sita's brother Lakshmana away from Sita. But before leaving in pursuit of the golden deer, Lakshmana draws a protective line in the dust around Sita, telling her not to step across the line and out of the circle. Anyone other than Rama, Sita, or Lakshmana himself crossing that line would immediately be consumed by flames erupting from that line. Of course, when Ravana disguises himself as an old beggar, asking for food and drink, Sita steps across the line and is promptly abducted. Often invoked even today, the *Lakshman Rekha* refers to a strict line, never to be crossed or broken.

There are references to an actual line being drawn in several historical or legendary military events. As the great Greek historian Polybius describes in his work *The Histories*, in 168 B.C.E., King Antiochus IV of the Seleucid Empire approached and apparently intended to occupy Pelusium, a strategic city and Roman provincial capital on the eastern fringe of the Nile delta, twenty miles southeast of the modern Port Said. Polybius picks up the story:

> Caius Popilius Laenas, the Roman commander, on Antiochus greeting him from a distance and then holding out his hand, handed to the king, as he had it by him, the copy of the *senatus-consultum*, and told him to read it first, not thinking it proper as it seems to me, to make the conventional sign of friendship before he knew if the intentions of him who was greeting him were friendly or hostile. But when the king, after reading it, said he would like to communicate with his friends about this intelligence, Popilius acted in a manner which was thought to be offensive and exceedingly arrogant. He was carrying a stick cut from a vine, and with this he drew a circle round Antiochus and told him he must remain inside this circle until he gave his decision

about the contents of the letter. The king was astonished at this authoritative proceeding, but after a few moment's hesitation, said he would do all that the Romans demanded. Upon this, Popilious and his suite all grasped him by the hand and greeted him warmly. The letter ordered him to put an end at once to the war with [the Roman emperor] Ptolemy. So, as a fixed number of days were allowed to him, he led his army back to Syria, deeply hurt and complaining indeed, but yielding to circumstances for the present.

Clearly, this line in the sand had worked as intended—backed by the might and muscle of the Roman Empire and the clear intention of Popilius to enforce its intentions. But it is quite clear that such red line concepts have been invoked in any number of circumstances on every continent and in every era.

In 1807, the Maoris had been engaged in a series of extended wars among the various tribes that inhabited the north island of what would become New Zealand. The Maoris, natives that British first stumbled upon when they began settling the two islands that would make up their colony, had only recently acquired a handful of muskets and in turn had stepped up the pace and lethality of their intercommunal warfare known as the Maori Wars. Two of these combatants were the Ngati-Whatua and the Ngapuhi who one day clashed viciously near a beach on the west coast of the north island. The New Zealand ethnologist Percy Smith picks up the story as he pieced it together in 1910:

Whilst eating, the [Ngapuhi] were suddenly attacked by Ngati-Whatua and for a time a great scene of confusion ensued, as warriors rushed here and there to secure their weapons. Ngati-Whatua soon drove them to the open beach, where an obstinate fight took place, lasting for some time, as success first favoured one party, then the other. The Nga-Puhi guns stood them in good stead, for Ngati-Whatua had none. It is said that one of the latter was pierced by eight bullets before he fell, and that he eventually recovered. Eventually Ngati-Whatua, incited thereto by Muru-paenga and Taoho, closed on their enemies with a rush, and during the melee, Pokaia received a death-blow from a mere [a jade-tipped cudgel] at the hands of Taoho. Nga-Puhi were panic stricken at the death of their leader, and commenced to flee. At this juncture, Taoho directed Teke, an Uri-o-Hau chief, to get close up to the retreating Nga-Puhi, *and with his weapon draw a deep line on the sandy beach, beyond which none of the Ngati-Whatua were to pass in chase.* The blood relationship of the two opposing parties gave rise to the wish not to finally exterminate the vanquished host. It is said by the victors, that had this not been done, the whole of Nga-Puhi would have been overtaken and slain. As it was, they lost some great chiefs, amongst whom were Pokaia (the leader), Te Waikeri, Tu-karawa, Tohi, Hou-awe, Ti, Hau-moka and others, whilst the celebrated Hong Hika only escaped by his fleetness of foot. Nga-Puhi acknowledged to have lost one hundred and fifty men out of the five hundred that composed the taua. It is said that Taoho was wounded in the mouth by a spear-thrust, that passed right through his head coming out at the back of his neck. Whilst his opponent still held one end of the spear, Taoho drew it towards him and then killed his enemy with a blow from his mere. (emphasis added)

All in all, pretty bloody, but a strategic line in the sand did prevent substantially more bloodshed and far more drastic consequences. It was only the strength and determination of the Uri-o-Hau leader Taoho, and the understanding of the consequences had this line been crossed, that prevented what would otherwise have been an even more horrific massacre. Incidentally, the battle was called Te Kai-a-te-Karoro (the Feast of the Seagulls) because seagulls joined the victors in eating the slain.

The twentieth-century concept of a strategic line as a color may be traced to the period after World War I and the "Red Line Agreement." Signed in 1928 between the largest oil companies of Britain, the United States, and France at the time the Ottoman Empire was being dissolved, this intricate document effectively partitioned what would become the vast oil resources of much of the Middle East. It managed to accomplish what the Treaty of Versailles was designed, and failed, to do. It is especially interesting as the first treaty that dealt specifically with a critical natural resource—in this case, oil, which in the years after the First World War had suddenly begun to emerge as a most valuable commodity. World War I was the first conflict where mechanized vehicles became a definitive force, the first with battles between tanks, troop transport by trucks and trains, in short where the gasoline-fueled internal combustion engine offered an overwhelming strategic advantage; its absence and that of the fuel that powered them, a determinative disadvantage.

In 1908, a British adventurer, George Reynolds, under contract with another Englishman, William D'Arcy, who had a license to explore in Persia, suddenly struck oil at 4 A.M. on May 26—1,180 feet below the sands of Masjid-e-Suleiman, a location so remote it took five days to get word back to London by telegraph. A year later, Reynolds and D'Arcy's organization became the Anglo-Persian Oil Company, the first in what would become a checkerboard of oil companies and wells scattered across Persia, the Ottoman Empire, and down into the great Arabian desert and Saudi Arabia. One of these early enterprises was the Turkish Petroleum Company, formed in 1912 to acquire concessions from the Ottoman Empire and explore for oil in Mesopotamia—what is today Syria and Iraq. The driving force behind TPC was a strange, flamboyant, bearded Turkish-Armenian operator named Calouste Gulbenkian, who'd organized a consortium of European giants—Deutsche Bank, the Anglo-Saxon Petroleum Company (a subsidiary of Royal Dutch Shell), and the British-owned National Bank of Turkey. But the largest single shareholder was Anglo-Persian, which held 50 percent of the shares. TPC managed to acquire a promise of concessions, but the outbreak of war, with the Ottomans on the losing side with Germany and Austria-Hungary, brought the plans of TPC and Gulbenkian to exploit this promise to an abrupt halt.

Gulbenkian was not easily discouraged. By the outbreak of the war, he was forty-five years old and already displaying many of the traits that would ultimately catapult him to the status at his death in 1955, as his *New York Times* obituary put it, of "one of the richest men in the world: oil financier, art collector; lived in obscurity; drove in rented automobile." Gulbenkian had oil in his blood. While the internal combustion engine and the automobile were still some decades in the future, he was born in 1869 in Scutari, a wealthy suburb of Constantinople where his Armenian father was an oil importer and exporter. His father sent him to England to study engineering, then to Baku where his assignment was to study the Russian oil industry. Before the turn of the century, he was in London doing oil deals. So it was hardly surprising when he formed TPC. Already, there were stories running rampant in world oil circles that fabulous oil fields were likely in southern Iraq. Somehow, just before the outbreak of hostilities in 1914, Gulbenkian managed to persuade the Ottoman grand vizier to grant him the concessions TPC needed. Gulbenkian wound up with a 5 percent interest that eventually made him a very wealthy man.

But it was his determination and vision that allowed him to retain this 5 percent. Determination and a red pencil. During and immediately after the war, a complex series of ownership transfers, plus a bit of hard-bargaining blackmail by American officials unwilling to see their country cut out of lucrative deals in territory American arms had helped win, led to the arrival of the likes of Jersey Standard, Socony, Gulf Oil, the Pan American Petroleum and Transport Company, and Atlantic Refining (later Arco). They were, effectively, creating the first oil cartel—a government-backed series of corporations whose immense power balanced on two legs: control of resources, and the muscle to keep all real or imagined interlopers at bay. In short, setting up red lines.

Gulbenkian himself, no doubt unwittingly, certainly impulsively, and most oppor-
tunely, created the first modern-day red line. It encompassed more than physical territory
or defined borders, as the red lines of antiquity did. The very nature of his creation suggests
how the most ill-conceived are arrived at, imposed, then enforced. The issue was precisely
where the TPC, renamed in 1929 the Iraq Petroleum Company, could drill for oil. At a
meeting of the various parties involved, frustrated by the bickering and confusion over the
borders of the Ottoman Empire that the Treaty of Versailles and the subsequent Treaty of
Sèvres in 1920 had long ago fixed, but which none of the interested parties seemed either
able or inclined to recognize, Gulbenkian impulsively snatched up a red pencil. Seizing
the map, he drew, quite arbitrarily, but with reasonable accuracy, these boundaries. This
was then promptly fixed in the agreement that all parties signed. In what became officially
known as the Red Line Agreement, none of the signatories, especially no member of the
Iraq Petroleum consortium, would operate independently inside this defined line. As it
happened, the Arabian Gulf sheikhdom of Bahrain found itself inside the delineated territory. Since IPC had no interest in Bahrain, it sold its stake to Standard Oil of California
(SoCal) for $50,000 ($750,000 in today's money). And with the help of Secretary of
State Henry Stimson, SoCal managed to persuade the British to suspend the agreement
for this one venture. By 1934, Bahrain was producing some 285,000 barrels of oil a day.
Charging first a 14 percent tax, then beginning in 1950 a 50 percent tax, Bahrain found
itself in an enviable position. The line, as adjusted, had worked magnificently and never
had to be defended by military actions.

Stephen Hemsley Longrigg, a long-time IPC employee, noted that "the Red
Line Agreement, variously assessed as a sad case of wrongful cartelization or as an
enlightened example of international cooperation and fair-sharing, was to hold the
field for twenty years and in large measure determined the pattern and tempo of oil
development over a large part of the Middle East." The Agreement lasted until 1948
when two of the American partners broke free, but led to a monopoly for IPC of all
oil exploration inside the line outlined in the original pact twenty years before. Of
course, these boundaries excluded Saudi Arabia, which in 1944 formed Aramco,
assuming control over the vast oil reserves in this portion of the Sahara. But the Red
Line Agreement held as it was first impetuously drafted—a tribute to both to the
financial stakes involved and the disinclination of any of the parties to tempt fate
and risk the billions theoretically in play.

Which only illustrates one critical aspect of a functioning and enforceable red line.
Both parties must recognize the perils and the profits that may accrue to respecting it.
But by the first third of the twentieth century, such lines, or at least the circumstances

leading to their establishment, were becoming a more central part of many diplomatic undertakings. None more so than in the early days of Hitler's all but unchecked rise to power, propelled by his unmatched ability to ignore or circumvent every red line established by the Allies in Europe.

—

On June 28, 1919, in the glittering Hall of Mirrors of the Palace of Versailles, representatives of a defeated Germany signed the Treaty of Versailles, ending what at the time was known as the Great War, but all too soon would be called simply the First World War. Buried in its pages were a series of provisions all but assuring the rise to power of a still unknown Adolf Hitler barely a decade later. One of the key provisions, from our perspective, was the creation of several new nations out of the ruins of the Austro-Hungarian and Ottoman Empires—both allies of a defeated Germany. These newly formed nations, particularly Yugoslavia (nation of the South Slavs) and Czechoslovakia, were the outcomes of a compromise between British Prime Minister David Lloyd George, French Prime Minister Georges Clemenceau, and President Woodrow Wilson. Lloyd George and Clemenceau did not want to deal with a collection of micro-states in what promised to be a most confusing and difficult period of reconstruction in postwar Europe. So, they created a series of crazy-quilt nations—Yugoslavia with six constituent republics, and Czechoslovakia, comprising what would eventually become the Czech Republic and Slovakia. Czechoslovakia was not an utterly unrealistic creation, though both Czechs and Slovaks lobbied fiercely in Paris during the fraught months of the drafting of the treaty for their own individual homelands.

Included in the final configuration, however, were not simply Czechs and Slovaks, but at least three million German speakers, or 24 percent of the total population of Czechoslovakia. These ethnic Germans were largely concentrated in the historical regions of Bohemia and Moravia bordering on Germany and the frontiers of the new nation of Austria. All were carved out of the Austro-Hungarian Empire, which also yielded up the nations of Hungary and Romania. Certainly the Germanic territories, which their people began collectively to call Sudetenland, could have been ceded to Germany, but the drafters of the Treaty of Versailles had little incentive to expand a Germany that they hoped would remain definitively small and defeated. The Sudeten Germans, of course, were not consulted at all as to what they thought their fate should be. They quickly found themselves an underrepresented minority in a nation torn by Czech and Slovak nationalism. By 1935, the Sudeten German Party was founded by a determined Nazi sympathizer, Konrad Henlein. He had grown up in Reichenberg, a hotbed of conflict between the local German community that had lived on these lands for centuries and the Czechs who arrived in the local factories from the countryside prepared to accept wages and working conditions far inferior to the Germans. After World War I, Henlein became deeply involved in the local *völkisch* movement pressing for Sudeten-German nationhood. When Hitler arrived on the scene, it was but a short leap for Henlein to the Nazi cause, joining first the Nazi Party, then the powerful paramilitary SS.

By the time the Sudeten Germans and the Nazis were prepared to move, Hitler had already defied several what we might characterize more accurately as "pink" lines—none carrying the bite or the consequences of the strong red line that was about to be imposed in the case of the Sudetenland. Hitler, born in Austria and working there through young adulthood as a house painter, had strong feelings about the natural affinity of German-speaking Austria and Germany—the union of which had been expressly forbidden by the Treaty of Versailles. It was hardly surprising, then, that Hitler would move first to swallow Austria. It would be a clear violation of the treaty, but Germany, in its press to rearm, had already been violating many of its provisions of the treaty, canceling all payments of German war debt and reparations, reoccupying the Rhineland, and beginning a massive military buildup, all with few consequences. By March 1938, when the Nazi ministry of propaganda began issuing utterly Fake News reports of widespread rioting in Austria and the local population was broadly calling for German troops to restore order, Hitler's forces were primed and ready. On March 11, Hitler sent an ultimatum to Austria's Chancellor Kurt Schuschnigg—hand over all power to the local Nazis, or face invasion. The British ambassador in Berlin went so far as to register a protest against any use of German coercion against Austria. It was as far as Britain would go to defend what had by then become an all but toothless Treaty of Versailles. With the United States failing to sign the treaty or take its place in the League of Nations, it had already become glaringly clear to Hitler that the Western powers would do little to defend most lines that had been erected against Germany in that treaty.

Recognizing that no help to hold the line against a Nazi onslaught was at all likely from France or Britain, Schuschnigg resigned as Austria's chancellor to be replaced by Arthur Seyss-Inquart, ironically a German-speaking lawyer born in Czechoslovakia, but personally chosen by Hitler as Interior Minister. On his elevation to chancellor, he promptly summoned German forces. On March 12, at eight o'clock in the morning, the Wehrmacht's powerful Eighth Army crossed the Austrian frontier and met no resistance, allowing Seyss-Inquart to proclaim Austria the German province of Ostmark. His reign over an independent Austria lasted two days.

Hitler watched for the consequences. In Britain, Prime Minister Neville Chamberlain rose in the House of Commons and proclaimed: "The hard fact is that nothing could have arrested what has actually happened there unless this country and other countries had been prepared to use force." But Chamberlain went further:

> I imagine that according to the temperament of the individual the events which are in our minds to-day will be the cause of regret, of sorrow, perhaps of indignation. They cannot be regarded by His Majesty's Government with indifference or equanimity. They are bound to have *effects which cannot yet be measured.* The immediate result must be to *intensify the sense of uncertainty and insecurity in Europe.* Unfortunately, while *the policy of appeasement* would lead to a relaxation of the economic pressure under which many countries are suffering to-day, what has just occurred must inevitably retard economic recovery and, indeed, increased care will be required to ensure that marked deterioration does not set in. *This is not a moment for hasty decisions or for careless words.* We must consider the new situation quickly, but with cool judgement. . . . As regards *our defence programmes, we have always made it clear that they were flexible and that they would have to be reviewed* from time to time in the light of any development in the international situation. It would be idle to pretend that recent events do not constitute a change of the kind that we had in mind. Accordingly we have decided to make a fresh review, and in due course we shall announce what further steps we may think it necessary to take. (emphasis added)

In short, in a single paragraph, Chamberlain violated every conceivable rule for the establishment of a successful red line and set the stage for the cascade of ever more virulent lines in the sand that would very quickly spiral his country and Europe into the Second World War. First, Chamberlain was quite accurate that the Anschluss—the brazen seizure of Austria by Hitler—would have "effects that can still not be measured." Meaning, once violated, a line of any shade of pink (as the Treaty of Versailles had clearly become) would inevitably lead to consequences "intensify[ing] the sense of uncertainty and insecurity in Europe." Assessing the situation with "cool judgement" is essential for establishment of any political or diplomatic standard. But a "fresh review" of flexible defense programs with an announcement in due course is hardly likely to strike fear into a potential violator. Clearly, the seeds of Hitler's rise had been sown long before, in the Treaty of Versailles and the way World War I had concluded—with retribution rather than reconstruction as the treaty's principal goal. Still, a firm hand a decade later to enforce its provisions, striking before the lines established by the treaty and its aftermath morphed into a pernicious system becoming all the more toxic with time and neglect, could well have suggested to the German people what the true cost of total war might prove. But the reaction of inaction or apathy by Britain and France in particular resulted in ever more flagrant violation of the lines established at the end of the last war.

In France, the government was utterly distracted and made no comment with respect to the Anschluss. The third government of Radical Socialist Prime Minister Camille Chautemps had been forced to step down on March 13, to be succeeded by Front Populaire leader Léon Blum. France was in the midst of a revolving door series of political crises that would drag on through thirty-four governments in nineteen years, plunging the nation into domestic political turmoil at a most inopportune moment. As for the United States, it remained firmly barricaded behind a wall of isolation that would be pierced only by the Japanese attack on Pearl Harbor December 7, 1941, and also demurred.

Clearly, the stage for the twentieth century's most critical red line to date had been set.

It did not take long following his successful Anschluss for Hitler to turn his attention to his next target. The Sudeten Germans had long been agitating for unification with Germany. Their economic and social situation did not help matters. Beginning in late 1929, the Depression that had engulfed the United States spread quickly to Europe and was only accelerated by the deeply protectionist Smoot-Hawley Tariffs, enacted in March 1930, that crippled European manufacturing exports to the United States. The Sudeten Germans, deeply dependent on their export-oriented manufacturing industries, were more profoundly and immediately affected than the rest of the Czechoslovak people. Throughout the 1930s, this crisis only intensified. With the rise of Hitler and the strengthening of the political muscle of the Sudeten Germans, Czechoslovak President Edvard Beneš did his best to appease the Nazi government in Berlin and his own German population at home—even proposing to cede 2,300 square miles of Czech territory if Germany would accept nearly two million Sudeten Germans which Prague would expel. Hitler was unresponsive.

Meanwhile, Britain and France, having seen the effects of the Anschluss in Austria, were frantic to avoid both war and a continuing redrafting of the map of Europe and the expansion of a clearly resurgent Germany that presented an increasingly likely existential threat. France, still in the midst of its perpetual government crises, was desperate not to go to war against Germany, even with the Maginot Line in place, which its military was confident could repel any external aggression. They would all too quickly discover how wrongheaded this assessment was and how easily circumvented the Maginot Line would be by German Panzer divisions simply bypassing it and striking straight for Paris through the utterly undefended Belgian border. But for the moment France turned management of what was rapidly becoming the Sudeten crisis over to Britain and its Conservative prime minister. Neville Chamberlain viewed the Sudeten Germans' grievances as entirely justified. At the same time, he also viewed Hitler's intentions as both honorable and limited.

It was with this context that Chamberlain felt supremely confident in establishing an utterly ill-advised and poorly conceived red line. In fact, this played out in phases that had the untenable effect of moving the goal posts week by week until finally they simply collapsed. The clear object was from the beginning to assure a free and independent Czechoslovakia, even if that meant throwing the Sudetenland overboard to Germany, where most of its residents clearly preferred being in the first place. Britain believed it had effectively established this intention. But it was far from the clear and definitive statement backed by a threat force that might have given Hitler some pause in his still incomplete preparations for total war. Still, the Brits, with the tacit understanding of France's situation, began a process that would only weaken the red line and their barely declared position.

The first attempt was mediation, forced by Chamberlain on Beneš, who accepted only out of fear of abandonment by the French and British. This effort fell afoul of increasingly strident rants by Hitler and provocatively violent demonstrations within Czechoslovakia that allowed Hitler to claim that "his" Sudeten Germans were being persecuted by the Beneš government. To avoid war and the utter breach of what was left of the first line, Chamberlain asked for a face-to-face meeting with Hitler, traveling on September 15, 1938 to Berchtesgaden, barely a dozen miles from the Austrian frontier that Nazi troops had just breached in March. In his lavish mountain retreat, Hitler received Chamberlain with a degree of disdain. As one witness, Sir John Wheeler-Bennett recalled, "Hitler . . . did not even walk down the steps to greet his guest. He waited for him at the top of the stairs." Chamberlain later described his conversation with Hitler in a memorandum:

> He had from his youth been obsessed with the racial theory and he felt that the Germans were one, but he had drawn a distinction between the possible and the impossible and he recognised that there are places where Germans are where it is impossible to bring them into the Reich; but where they are on the frontier, it is a different matter, and he is himself concerned with ten millions of Germans, three millions of whom are in Czechoslovakia. He felt therefore that those Germans should come into the Reich. They wanted to and he was determined that they should come in.

It was impossible that Czechoslovakia should remain like a spearhead in the side of Germany—

So I said, "Hold on a minute; there is one point on which I want to be clear and I will explain why: you say that the three million Sudeten Germans must be included in the Reich; would you be satisfied with that and is there nothing more that you want? I ask because there are many people who think that is not all; that you wish to dismember Czechoslovakia."

He then launched into a long speech; he was out for a racial unity and he did not want a lot of Czechs, all he wanted was Sudeten Germans.

Clearly, Chamberlain was trying to establish just where a line might be drawn with some expectation that it would be respected by Hitler without recourse to war. Hitler suggested where he was coming from:

"I want to get down to realities. Three hundred Sudetens have been killed and things of that kind cannot go on; the thing has got to be settled at once: I am determined to settle it: I do not care whether there is a world war or not: I am determined to settle it and to settle it soon and I am prepared to risk a world war rather than allow this to drag on."

To that [Chamberlain] replied: If the Fuehrer is determined to settle this matter by force without waiting even for a discussion between ourselves to take place what did he let me come here for? I have wasted my time.

But Hitler was hardly one to be played, nor would he prove to have any real interest in respecting any line the Brits might establish. Chamberlain still didn't get that. "I could give him my personal opinion," Chamberlain wrote in his note about their meeting, "which was that on principle I had nothing to say against the separation of the Sudeten Germans from the rest of Czechoslovakia, provided that the practical difficulties could be overcome."

Chamberlain returned to England maintaining his confidence that he'd moved the red line just far enough to avoid war. But a week later, he was back seeing Hitler. In the interim, he'd received a note from General Hastings Ismay, who'd just been named secretary of Britain's Committee of Imperial Defence. It contained several key warnings. First, "German absorption of Czechoslovakia will enhance her military prestige, increase her war potential and probably enable her to dispose of stronger land forces against France and ourselves than she can do at present." At the same time, he warned that "Germany may be able to maintain her lead over the Franco-British Air Forces in air striking power. On the other hand, it is open to us, provided that we make the necessary effort, to catch her up, or at least greatly reduce her lead, in the matter of defence (both active and passive) against air attack." Finally, he concluded that, "from the military point of view, time is in our favour, and that, if war with Germany has to come, it would be better to fight her in say 6–12 months' time, than to accept the present challenge." In other words, move the goal posts to buy more time. As it turned out, a foolish use of this concept. For Germany, going full bore on its own war machine and the arsenal to fuel it, had the same six to twelve months to build an indomitable fighting machine.

Still, Chamberlain was determined to set a line which Hitler might respect. French Prime Minister Édouard Daladier flew to London on September 16 and the British and French settled on a new structure. All Czechoslovak territories with more than 50 percent of ethnic Germans would be ceded to Germany. Britain and France would guarantee the independence of Czechoslovakia. The problem, of course, was that while the line was clearly defined, it remained demonstrably unclear what the consequences might be of any move to overstep this line. Chamberlain still meant to forestall war at what appeared to be any cost. Six days later, Chamberlain returned to Germany. As he was about to board the plane, he told reporters gathered at the steps that "my objective is peace in Europe. I trust this trip is the way to that peace." Not exactly. Still, the Germans welcomed the delegation lavishly. When his plane landed in Cologne, a band played the British anthem, "God Save the King." The entourage was driven to the Hotel Petersburg in Bad Godesberg where flowers and gifts had been placed in the room of each member of the delegation. While Hitler still fumed over the "position of [his] Germans in the Sudetenland," after hours of discussions over two days, Hitler finally calmed down and pitched a concession. As Hitler put it, he was offering "a gift" in thanks for the prime minister's agreement—a retreat on the führer's earlier position that demanded a partition of all of Czechoslovakia. Instead, he was now demanding simply a German takeover of Sudetenland and its German population.

After the delegation's return to London, Chamberlain dispatched a close confidant, Sir Horace Wilson, to Berlin with a personal letter from Chamberlain to Hitler reaffirming that the British and French wanted a peaceful resolution, while clearly indicating that Chamberlain was prepared once again to move the red line, which had clearly become all but meaningless by this time in Hitler's view. The führer gave his response that evening. He would make no further demands on actual Czech territory, but Czechoslovakia must turn over the Sudetenland in its entirety to Germany. Hitler affirmed this new position in a tirade to a packed gathering of some 15,000 at Berlin's sprawling Sportpalast, and, as

The New York Times correspondent Frederick T. Birchall reported, "the German people are listening in by order at loudspeakers all over the land." The next morning, *The Times* ran the entire text of the speech, which took up a full page, together with statements from Beneš, Daladier, and Chamberlain, and the statement of "Britain's decision to join in defending Czechoslovakia in case of attack." Clearly a line had been drawn, though *The Times* clearly believed that war might still be imminent, its six-column lead headline on page one observing BRITAIN PLEDGES AID IF CZECHS ARE ATTACKED; ALSO GUARANTEES SURRENDER OF SUDETEN AREA AS HITLER IN SPEECH KEEPS PEACE DOOR OPEN. But as Birchall pointed out:

> The Czech people escaped vituperation and Herr Hitler addressed soothing phrases to the Poles, Ukrainians, Slovaks, French, British and even Hungarians, all of whom he reminded of his manifested desire to seek no quarrel with them. It was almost as though, knowing himself about to take an action that would be universally reprehended, he sought in advance to create a friendlier atmosphere.

Meanwhile, the Czechoslovak army was mobilizing—a call-up meeting with considerable enthusiasm, with one million men volunteering in twenty-four hours. The Czech military was indeed a formidable, and motivated, force. A survey of their borders suggested that they could withstand some attack, perhaps holding off the Germans long enough for British and French forces to come to the rescue. This would, of course, mean a total breakdown of Chamberlain's red line, for which he had no appetite.

It would all go right down to the wire, especially since now Hitler had effectively drafted his own line, couched in an unbendable ultimatum. In his Sportpalast speech, he had given the Czechs until September 28 at 2 P.M. to turn over the Sudetenland to Germany or there would be war. At 10 A.M., four hours before Hitler's deadline, on Chamberlain's orders, the British ambassador to Italy, Sir Eric Drummond, the seventh Earl of Perth and, earlier, the first secretary-general of the League of Nations, rang Italian foreign minister Galeazzo Ciano to ask for an urgent audience at the Chigi Palace. His message was a request for Benito Mussolini to intercede with Hitler for a twenty-four-hour reprieve. Mussolini agreed and phoned his own ambassador to Germany, Bernardo Attolico, instructing him, "Go to the Führer at once, and tell him that whatever happens I will be at his side, but that I request a twenty-four-hour delay before hostilities begin." Hitler was with the French ambassador and, in an expansive mood, chuckled to his guest, "My good friend Benito Mussolini has asked me to delay for twenty-four hours the marching orders of the German army, and I agreed." Of course, this was not much of a concession, as the invasion date was set for October 1. In return for his intercession with Hitler, Chamberlain asked that Mussolini attend the conference the next morning that would also include Daladier—a request that Hitler seconded. Now, the red line had reversed, and it was Hitler calling the shots, though no one seemed to appreciate that at the time. When President Franklin D. Roosevelt heard of the Munich conference set for the next day, he promptly cabled Chamberlain, "Good man."

Chamberlain embarked on his third and final trip to Germany—to Munich—early on the morning of September 29. The deal was reached late that evening and the Munich Agreement was signed at 1:30 A.M. on September 30 by Hitler, Mussolini, Chamberlain, and Daladier. German troops could begin their occupation October 10, provided Hitler promised to go no further. After they'd agreed on this, Chamberlain took Hitler aside and asked him if he wouldn't mind signing another "joint declaration" which Chamberlain pulled from his pocket. After it was translated on the spot into German for him, Hitler magnanimously said, "absolutely," and the two moved to a nearby table where, after a momentary pause as the inkpot was found to be empty, with a flourish, he signed what would be known in British archives as an "annex." With this one stroke, Chamberlain created yet another line that would all too soon be broken, as Chamberlain asserted that Germany and England desired "never to go war with one another again." Such clear misreading of the ultimate intentions of Hitler by Chamberlain was a direct path toward creation of a red line that was broken from the get-go and a certain path toward World War II. The Czechoslovak red line would last just five months until German troops blithely swooped in and seized the whole country. By then, Beneš was gone, having resigned his office October 5, eventually forming a government-in-exile in London.

Chamberlain's theatrical return from Munich on September 30, 1938, of course, is well known. Stepping off his plane in London, he brandished a paper for the newsreel cameras and declared he had returned with "peace for our time." That very evening, at 7:30 at the Richmond Terrace headquarters of the Ministry of Defence, Chamberlain convened his cabinet. Sir John Simon, chancellor of the exchequer, opened the proceedings by "expressing, on behalf of the whole cabinet [our] profound admiration for the unparalleled effort the Prime Minister had made and for the success that he had achieved." And, he added, he was anxious to say "how proud [we] are to be associated with the Prime Minister as his colleagues at his time."

Not to be outdone, Chamberlain promptly replied that he was "grateful . . . for the support and help which [I have] received from [my] colleagues throughout the crisis," and added that he "appreciated that the journeys undertaken might easily have failed to achieve satisfactory results. As things had turned out . . . we could now safely regard the crisis as ended."

About the only dissenting voice was that of A. Duff Cooper, the first lord of the admiralty, who, with a far clearer understanding of the stakes of all these red lines that were being drawn and redrawn, toward the end of the cabinet session, jumped in to say that he "still felt a considerable uneasiness in regard to the position . . . afraid that [Britain] might get into the position where we were drawn into making further concessions to Herr Hitler."

Cooper was certainly not alone. Winston Churchill, then a backbench member of Parliament, had begun warning of the urgent need of rearming against Germany. Almost alone, Churchill recognized the Munich Agreement for what it was—an ephemeral line that Hitler's Panzer divisions would roll across with impunity six months later, touching off World War II. Hitler, of course, without a moment's hesitation, stepped across this and a succession of subsequent ultimatums made and catastrophically dissolved with utter willfulness—Poland, Belgium, the Soviet Union—each red line established, tested, breached.

Five days after Munich, Churchill rose in the House of Commons to denounce the agreement and warn of its consequences:

> I will begin by saying what every one would like to ignore or forget but which must nevertheless be stated, namely, that we have sustained a total and unmitigated defeat, and that France has suffered even more than we have. . . .
>
> And I will say this, that I believe the Czechs, left to themselves and told they were going to get no help from the Western Powers, would have been able to make better terms than they have got—they could hardly have worse—after all this tremendous perturbation. . . .
>
> I have always held the view that the maintenance of peace depends upon the accumulation of deterrents against the aggressor, coupled with a sincere effort to redress grievances. . . . After [Hitler's] seizure of Austria in March . . . I ventured to appeal to the government . . . to give a pledge that in conjunction with France and other Powers they would guarantee the security of Czechoslovakia while the Sudeten-Deutsch question was being examined either by a League of Nations Commission or some other impartial body, and I still believe that if that course had been followed events would not have fallen into this disastrous state.

Churchill was ever the pragmatist and continued by suggesting that "in the future [a] Czechoslovakian state cannot be maintained as an independent entity. You will find that in a period of time measured only by months, Czechoslovakia will be engulfed in the Nazi régime." While he failed to draw a red line per se, he did observe that Britain's leaders have been engaged in "five years of eager search for the line of least resistance, five years of uninterrupted retreat of British power." The result, he concluded, was his "fear we shall find that we have deeply compromised, and perhaps fatally endangered, the safety and even the independence of Great Britain and France. . . . We have sustained a defeat without a war, the consequences of which will travel far with us along our road. And do not suppose that this is the end. This is only the beginning of the reckoning."

Churchill was, of course, proven absolutely right. Red lines, once established, are never sustained simply by ignoring the obvious. The Czechs would never be told they would receive no help from the British nor the French, let alone the Americans, who continued simply to cheer in a whisper from the sidelines. Any such suggestion to the Beneš government, while it was still in power and could actually do something about the plight into which the Allies had plunged his nation, would have given an immediate and very public lie to this utterly phantasmagoric construction in the first place. And above all, such an admission would have cost Chamberlain enormously in terms of prestige—perhaps even his office of prime minister.

Still, there is ample evidence that Chamberlain may have been well aware of Britain's inability to beat back any immediate German action. Following the Anschluss, Chamberlain asked the British high command for their assessment of a German attack on Czechoslovakia and the Allies ability to thwart any such action. The detailed report came back with a disquieting conclusion:

> No pressure that we and our possible allies can bring to bear, either by sea, or on land, or in the air, could prevent Germany from invading and overrunning Bohemia and from inflicting a decisive defeat on the Czechoslovakian army. We should then be faced with the necessity of undertaking a war against Germany for the purpose of restoring Czechoslovakia's lost integrity and this object would only be achieved by the defeat of Germany and as the outcome of a prolonged struggle.

Secretary of State for War Leslie Hore-Belisha summed it up more colorfully, concluding in his diary, "To take offensive now would be like a man attacking a tiger before he has loaded his gun."

Still, there are others who believe that Hitler was equally ill-prepared at that moment to challenge a determined British effort. Historian Williamson Murray has concluded after examining Luftwaffe records that "In nearly every respect [the Luftwaffe] was unprepared to launch a 'strategic' bombing offensive and so could not have significantly damaged Britain's war effort in spite of weaknesses in British air defenses . . . .and would have had difficulty just in fulfilling its operational commitments to support ground forces operating against Czechoslovakia and the West." But British cabinet records of this period suggest that Chamberlain had no idea of such intelligence. He was going into these negotiations largely in the dark—allowing Hitler effectively to set the terms and force the British prime minister to move the goal posts virtually at will.

—

With this background, the second red line, the "annex" signed privately by Hitler and Chamberlain asserting "the desire of our two peoples never to go to war with one another again," that would last until September 1, 1939, appeared at the time to give Britain some welcome respite from the prospect of a war it could not win—or for that matter, a line that Chamberlain and others knew could not be enforced. In either case, hardly a recipe for success. Indeed, Hitler had been laying the basis for this moment for months, in fact contemplating it for years. Full-fledged preparations for total war by the German general staff were already underway in May 1939, seven months after Hitler had taken the Sudetenland and two months after he had swallowed the remainder of Czechoslovakia, with no Allied reaction. Indeed, the British ambassador to Czechoslovakia, Sir Basil Newton, a week before the Germans seized all of Czechoslovakia, urged Beneš's successor, Emil Hácha, to go to Berlin and meet with Hitler. At the meeting, Hácha suffered a heart attack when Hermann Göring threatened to bomb Prague. Revived, he quickly signed away Czechoslovakia, which Nazi Panzer divisions occupied the next day.

The next, and final, red line, was Poland. France and Britain had guaranteed Poland's independence and Chamberlain felt that his annex had equally guaranteed German forces would never cross their frontier with Poland. But by August 1939, it was clear events were beginning to outstrip assurances—which Chamberlain continued to cling to as a thin and shrinking reed. On April 28, Hitler withdrew from the German-Polish nonaggression pact. Hitler soon learned that the British and French had failed to conclude an alliance with Stalin and that the Soviets might be interested in a similar pact with Germany, which was indeed signed on August 23 by Soviet Foreign Minister Vyacheslav Molotov and German Foreign Minister Joachim von Ribbentrop. The Molotov-Ribbentrop Pact assured Hitler that if France and Britain declared war on Germany, the Soviet Union would not join in.

Hitler was quite convinced by virtue of their behavior on the Sudetenland and his subsequent takeover of all of Czechoslovakia that Britain and France had little appetite or ability to enforce any of the various lines they had established and effectively dared him to step across. A week after the signing of the Molotov-Ribbentrop pact, German forces were fully mobilized and massed on the Polish border. On September 1, 1939, they moved. Two days later, Britain and France declared war on Germany, but, as Hitler anticipated, failed to provide any meaningful support. That same day, Chamberlain brought Churchill back into the cabinet as first lord of the admiralty, the same position he'd held during World War I. The battle for Poland was completed by the end of September. As the journalist and author John Gunther wrote in December, "the German campaign was a masterpiece. Nothing quite like it has been seen in military history." Nor, until then, in diplomatic history. Hitler had proved a master of understanding just what was needed to thwart every diplomatic or military line drawn by his adversaries. Chamberlain managed to cling to power until the moment Hitler turned his armies to the west and began his invasion of the Low Countries—Holland and Belgium—with France clearly in sight, at which point, he went to Buckingham Palace and resigned, urging King George VI to name Churchill as his successor. Then, on May 10, 1940, Chamberlain went on the radio for his farewell address, reminding the British people that "the hour has now come when we are to be put to the test, as the innocent people of Holland, Belgium, and France are being tested already. And you and I must rally behind our new leader, and with our united strength, and with unshakable courage fight, and work until this wild beast, which has sprung out of his lair upon us, has been finally disarmed and overthrown." Queen Elizabeth later told Chamberlain that her daughter Princess Elizabeth wept as she listened to his words.

Chamberlain and his ill-conceived efforts at lame conciliation and toothless challenge certainly played an important role in giving Hitler the license that plunged Europe so quickly into a conflict for which it was so ill-prepared. Red lines, after all, can provide opportunity to prepare for the consequences, provided they are carefully envisioned and resolutely defended. Churchill had warned early on of the futility, indeed the perniciousness, of the lines Chamberlain had been establishing, especially in the face of the utter tyranny against which they were directed. As we shall see, tyranny itself does not by any means guarantee the futility of red lines in thwarting the ambitions of a tyrant.

Yet in this case, each time Chamberlain returned to Germany, it seems he was prepared, indeed eager, to redraw such lines to Hitler's benefit. In this case, the redrafting was more diplomatic than geographic, in contrast to the fifteenth or sixteenth parallel in Chad that Mitterrand had drawn. In the case of the Munich Agreement and the various steps leading up to it, the red line was never moved geographically. It was always the Sudeten border with Germany and the line to the east where Hitler's divisions were pledged to halt, leaving the rest of Czechoslovakia free and independent. At least, that's how it was supposed to work. Such willingness to embrace a geographical reality while ignoring its political and diplomatic underpinnings is clear evidence of how wrong, how utterly malignant, such diplomatic devices can be when used by individuals with little understanding of their mechanics on the one hand and little interest or intent to observe them on the other.

Moreover, the use of red lines to delay the inevitable is only more pernicious in the long run. Britain was no better prepared for war with Germany six months later than at the time of the Munich Agreement. Yet Hitler, with a very clear sense of purpose—and a timeline that his military and industrial leaders had utterly bought into—made very good use of this period.

Munich provided object lessons—for good and for ill—as we entered the Cold War and the post–Cold War eras. This was a reality that President Harry S. Truman clearly recognized, invoking "Munich" to justify his military action at the opening of the Korean War, whose red lines we shall examine next. In a radio and television address to the nation on December 15, 1950, Truman observed, "Our homes, our Nation, all the things we believe in, are in great danger. This danger has been created by the rulers of the Soviet Union. . . . The world learned from Munich that security cannot be bought by appeasement." With Chamberlain's dismal experience, Truman was not about to make the same mistake.

CHAPTER THREE

The Korean Peninsula: Locked & Loaded

The evening of December 15, 1950, President Harry S. Truman addressed the American people from the Oval Office. Every radio and television network carried this address, but most Americans huddled around their radios. There were fewer than four million televisions in the country. Only 10 percent of American households had one. But everyone knew this would be an important message. Six months earlier, waves of North Korean troops had poured across the thirty-eighth parallel that divided the Communist north from the democratic south. They met little resistance from South Korean forces and just a token American contingent from a US Military Advisory Group. Main force units from the United States and, eventually, a handful of other Western nations would take weeks to deploy. But Truman was determined to lay out what the North's invasion of the South meant. The Communists had stepped over a critical boundary set by international agreement, even more blatantly than Hitler when he demanded the Sudetenland and its people for himself. Now, Truman had his own red line and he was not about to make the same mistakes as Chamberlain.

"The future of civilization depends on what we do—on what we do now, and in the months ahead," Truman proclaimed. "We have the strength and we have the courage to overcome the danger that threatens our country. We must act calmly and wisely and resolutely." Then, he proceeded to set out the parameters of just how he intended to enforce this red line:

> First, we will continue to uphold, and if necessary to defend with arms, the principles of the United Nations—the principles of freedom and justice.

Second, we will continue to work with the other free nations to strengthen our combined defenses.

Third, we will build up our own Army, Navy, and Air Force, and make more weapons for ourselves and our allies.

Fourth, we will expand our economy and keep it on an even keel.

Indeed, Truman pledged to triple the size of the military from one million soldiers to three and a half million. And he went before the United Nations Security Council to seek a global agreement on challenging the North Koreans who had the temerity to cross a barrier that had been agreed upon as an integral part of the armistice that ended the Second World War.

For most of its history, the Korean Peninsula has been a single ethnically and linguistically unified nation, utterly free of any frontiers, temporal or virtual. Most, but not all of its history. Indeed, there appear to have been lines crisscrossing the peninsula dating back to the first three centuries of the Common Era, known as the Three Kingdoms period, which actually coalesced from five large tribal groups and the end of the Iron Age in Korea, with even as many as twelve mini-states, each with its own very specific boundaries and rulers. Later, these morphed into the North-South states from the seventh to the tenth centuries, though the North spilled well into what today is a substantial portion of Manchuria, even some of today's Russian Maritime Province. There are mythic stories of splits north and south dating as far back as 2333 B.C.E. and the Gojoseon Kingdom. The boundaries of these states were in constant turmoil, armies coursing back and forth and their frontier lines expanding and contracting. At one point in 427 C.E., Pyongyang became for its first time a national capital. Throughout, Korean rulers were standing steadfast against vast forces from China seeking to overrun their territories, the forces of Sui and Tang emperors sending as many as a million men into vast battles along the frontier separating China from Korea. The Koreans, even with forces vastly inferior in numbers, though not in skills, beat back every incursion.

—

The road to the most recent and in many respects most lasting red line, a millennium or more later, was quite an interesting study in diplomacy. And since it has held, but for this one challenge, longer than any similar line in modern history, its origins are worth exploring. It was established in the blanket document of surrender of the Japanese empire to the Allied nations, signed on the battleship USS *Missouri*, docked in Tokyo Bay, on

September 2, 1945. Present was a host of senior officers of the allied powers headed by General Douglas MacArthur, but including as well, General Hsu Yung-Chang of the Republic of China, which had still not been taken over by Mao Tse-Tung's Communists; Lieutenant General Kuzma Nikolayevich Derevyanko of the USSR; and senior officers of Britain, Australia, Canada, France, the Netherlands, and New Zealand. The document included a detailed section, designated as General Order No. 1, which divided each of the regions Japan had seized in the course of the war among the various victorious allied powers to whom the Japanese would surrender their authority. When it came to Korea, there was a further demarcation, constituting the only one in the entire surrender document:

> (c) The Imperial General Headquarters, its senior commanders, and all ground, sea, air, and auxiliary forces in the main islands of Japan, minor islands adjacent thereto, *Korea south of 38 degrees North,* and the Philippines should surrender to CinCAFPac.
>
> (d) The senior Japanese commanders and all ground, sea, air, and auxiliary forces within Manchuria, *Korea north of 38 degrees North*, Karafuto, and the Kurile Islands would surrender to the Commander-in-Chief of Soviet Forces in the Far East.

In short, the United States, through the Commander-in-Chief, Air Forces Pacific, won control over South Korea, while the Soviet Union took over the north. At that moment, the outlines of what would become the Cold War were only beginning to be understood. It would be another six months before Winston Churchill delivered his Iron Curtain speech in Fulton, Missouri, warning that from "Stettin in the Baltic to Trieste in the Adriatic, an iron curtain has descended across the continent." There was only a passing reference to the fact that a similar curtain was descending across Asia, Churchill observing, "The outlook is also anxious in the Far East and especially in Manchuria." There was no suggestion that the first test of a post–World War II demarcation would actually come on the Korean Peninsula—one that would long outlast the iron curtain that seemed all but impenetrable at the time in Europe. Still, Churchill did point out, "From what I have seen of our Russian friends and Allies during the war, I am convinced that there is nothing they admire so much as strength, and there is nothing for which they have less respect than for weakness, especially military weakness. For that reason the old doctrine of a balance of power is unsound."

How the thirty-eighth parallel was arrived at in the surrender document was a complex series of missteps and misunderstandings—not unlike those plaguing any number of red lines. It all began toward the end of World War II when the Soviet Union was very much an ally of the United States, Britain, and France against the Axis powers of Germany, Italy, and Japan. The matter was first broached at the Cairo Conference in November 1943, when Churchill, Roosevelt, and Generalissimo Chiang Kai-shek of the Republic of China met near the pyramids at the lavish residence of the American ambassador to Egypt, Alexander Kirk. Stalin skipped the event because he feared that meeting Chiang could infuriate the Japanese, with whom the Soviet Union was still not at war. Stalin was most anxious to concentrate his then somewhat limited military might on Germany and seize as much of Central and Eastern Europe as possible at that point. Indeed, the Soviet Union would not declare war on Japan and enter the Asian theater until August 8, 1945, less than a month before the final Japanese surrender and two days after the United States dropped the first atomic bomb on Hiroshima. Still, their entry at that point did allow Soviet forces, together with Mongolian units, enough time to penetrate into Inner Mongolia on the west and the Korean Peninsula on the east, where it abuts the southeastern fringe of Siberia. At the conclusion of the Cairo Conference, the three powers did declare that "in due course, Korea shall become free and independent." And in February 1945, at Yalta, where this time Stalin was present, Roosevelt proposed a joint US-Soviet-Chinese trusteeship over the entire Korean peninsula to last twenty to thirty years. Stalin actually agreed to keep the Korean peninsula intact, though he insisted "the shorter the better." Still, it remained but an oral agreement. In the final document there was no mention of Korea.

By the end of the war, in the first week of August, Soviet forces, many of them redeployed from the western front in Europe, were already punching through Manchuria and entering Korea from the north. Much as their troops had overrun Eastern Europe at the end of World War II, assuring that boots-on-the-ground trumped any diplomatic understanding, the fear in Washington was that there could be a certain equivalence in Asia, with Soviets winding up in firm control of the entire Korean Peninsula.

On the evening of August 10, 1945, a meeting was convened in the Executive Office Building next to the White House. It stretched on into the night. At midnight, two young army lieutenant colonels—Dean Rusk, who'd just joined the State Department's office of United Nations affairs, later to serve as secretary of state under Presidents John F. Kennedy and Lyndon Johnson, and Charles H. "Tic" Bonesteel III, later the US military commander in South Korea, were sent into a small adjoining room and told to come up with a plan of occupation for the peninsula. They settled on a partition, not unlike the partition of Berlin into allied zones. But Korea would be divided north and south. Rusk described that evening in his memoirs nearly a half century later. The two grabbed a

National Geographic map, the only one handy. "Neither Tic nor I was a Korea expert, but it seemed to us that Seoul, the capital, should be in the American sector. We also knew that the U.S. Army opposed an extensive area of occupation." They looked for a good geographic division north of the capital, as the best red lines are those with clear geographic markers. But, Russ continued, "we saw instead the thirty-eighth parallel and decided to recommend that." Why not? After all, it quite neatly divided the peninsula in half and left the capital and principal city of Seoul in the south, though just barely. The Soviets would be allowed to occupy the region to the north. And that's how this was enshrined in General Order No. 1 from a colorful *National Geographic* map. In his memoirs, Rusk disclosed that he'd had no idea that the thirty-ninth parallel had been proposed as a division of the peninsula by Russian Czar Nicholas's negotiators to the Japanese at the conclusion of the Russo-Japanese War in 1905. Otherwise, Rusk wrote, "Had we known, we almost certainly would have chosen another line of demarcation"—possibly the thirty-ninth as well. Of course, it's entirely possible that any such line would not have stood the test of time so firmly.

The first American troops arrived at Inchon in the south on September 8, 1945, to make certain there was an armed American presence and to hold Communist forces above the line agreed upon a month earlier, which was barely twenty miles away from the landing point. In the north, the Soviets quickly installed in Pyongyang a Provisional People's Committee under Kim Il Sung, who had spent the last years of the war with Soviet troops in Manchuria while Japanese forces occupied all of Korea. Kim, succeeded by his son and grandson by the same name, never looked back. From his first months in office, the senior Kim solidified his hold on power, which was completed when the last Soviet troops withdrew from the country entirely in 1948. The line held for five years—throughout the bitter Chinese civil war of 1945 to 1949. But within weeks of the establishment of the People's Republic of China, Kim flew off to Moscow to seek Stalin's blessing to cross the thirty-eighth parallel. It took Kim until the spring of 1950 to win over Stalin, who finally gave his blessing—provided Mao Tse-tung would come up with any reinforcements if needed. They would be essential to the conflict and the North's efforts to break the red line.

What seems quite likely to have given the North a license to cross the thirty-eighth parallel and invade was what seems in retrospect a most intemperate and ill-conceived speech given by Secretary of State Dean Acheson at the National Press Club in Washington on January 12, 1950. In it, he defined a new demarcation line that he described as America's "defensive perimeter" in the Pacific—running through Japan, the Ryukyus, and the Pacific but skirting entirely both South Korea and Taiwan. Truman and Acheson had hoped to build a strong, self-sufficient ally in the south founded on a strong aid bill that was pending before Congress. But the North never gave that any time at all to work. Acheson's feeble attempt at building a new panoramic red line across Asia was poorly constructed, limply enforced, and a simple green light for forces to burst across any such diplomatic or military constructs established by the United States. Ironically, by effectively leaving the two Koreas outside the red line he defined, and the failure of America's defense establishment to staff the Korean Peninsula adequately for fear it was effectively indefensible, Acheson gave license for just the invasion Truman hoped to avoid.

As dawn broke on Sunday, June 25, 1950, North Korean troops swept across the thirty-eighth, and the Korean War was under way. On June 27, the government of President Syngman Rhee was evacuated from Seoul, and the next day, Communist forces rolled in to seize the capital. The first American forces arrived in early July. Truman had no sense that the partition would be challenged by an outright invasion, but feared that it could mean a substantially enlarged war against the Soviet Union and elements of the new Communist Chinese army, freed only recently by their victory over Chiang Kai-shek's Nationalists.

Largely because of two quirks of the Security Council, the United Nations was able to jump in quickly, on June 27, in one of its rare defenses of a militarily guaranteed barrier. China's seat was still being held by Chiang Kai-shek's Republic of China; the Soviet Union, the other power that might conceivably have exercised its veto, had been boycotting the Security Council since January in protest over the disputed Chinese seat. So the council voted seven to one, in a resolution authorizing "members of the United Nations furnish such assistance to the Republic of Korea as may be necessary to repel the armed attack and to restore international peace and security in the area." Two weeks later, a second resolution placed all UN forces under American command.

For three more years, allied forces battled the Communists across the entire length of the peninsula. By September, the North had seized virtually the entire territory, and the UN forces compressed into a tiny sliver of land with a 140-mile perimeter around Pusan, barely 10 percent of the combined territory of North and South Korea. At that point, the United States began to pour in men and matériel to reinforce the defenders of Pusan and to open a second front outside Seoul at Inchon. On September 16, the American Eighth Army began to break out of the Pusan Perimeter. Stalin sent advisors to Kim, warning him to forget Pusan and defend Seoul. It was too late. On September 30, Chinese premier Chou En-lai, now embracing the thirty-eighth parallel, warned that China would intervene if American forces crossed that red line into the North. The next day that's exactly what happened. UN forces pursued the retreating North Koreans, and American commander Douglas MacArthur demanded the North's unconditional surrender. With no response, the Eighth Army captured Pyongyang on October 19. MacArthur, his troops nearing the Chinese frontier, wanted to pursue them north into China. Truman demurred. Nevertheless even the threat of such an action led to a decision on October 18 by Mao and Chou to order three hundred thousand Chinese troops into the war. They crossed the Yalu River in secret by night into North Korea, and twelve days later, Stalin ordered the Soviet air force to provide air cover. The war was fully engaged. With UN forces in retreat again, Truman relieved MacArthur of his command—the general having crossed the thirty-eighth parallel in the mistaken view that China would not enter the war, but threatening to destroy China unless it surrendered. MacArthur clearly had as little understanding of what the thirty-eighth parallel represented as Kim Il Sung. With General Matthew Ridgway in charge now, a stalemate set in, but one that allowed UN forces to advance slowly, but methodically to a new line called the Kansas Line, ten miles above the thirty-eighth parallel at which point armistice negotiations began, first at Kaesong on the north-south Korean border, then at Panmunjom.

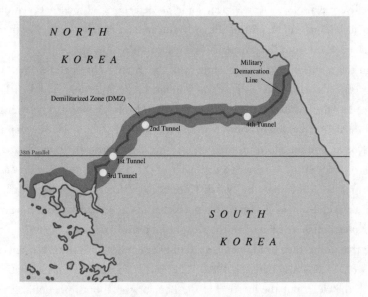

The terrestrial path of the Demilitarized Zone (DMZ) and Military Demarcation Line dividing North and South Korea straddling the 38th parallel.

The armistice, signed on July 27, 1953, set up a new boundary between North and South Korea known as the Military Demarcation Line. Weaving its way along the thirty-eighth parallel, it is a demilitarized zone (DMZ) that stretches one hundred forty-eight miles long and averages two and a half miles wide. It has also been perhaps the single most tested, at times violated, such line in history, and at the age of sixty-five, perhaps the longest-lasting as well.

Every president since the armistice has had to deal with this line in his own fashion. At first, with the North Koreans deeply involved with their own internal problems, with Kim Il Sung making a determined effort to cement his rule, there was little attention paid to the armistice line. By the early 1960s, with the North beginning to test the line at several points, the United States began taking concrete efforts to solidify the armistice line as a defensible red line by fortifying it at various key penetration points.

The largest single test and the most intense set of incidents occurred from 1966 through 1969. This period is often called the Second Korean War and embraced more than fifty incursions and other incidents. The incursions peaked in 1969 from a high of 144, declining to 86 in 1970, 52 in 1971, to just 20 in 1972. Still, over forty thousand South Korean troops were mobilized to deal with the breadth of these challenges to the armistice line and deal with repeated waves of infiltrators testing it at every point. Each year for five years, North Korea spent some 30 percent of its total national budget on building its military might, putting the nation on an increasingly divergent path to penury and in sharp contrast to the prosperity being accumulated by the South.

From the moment of the establishment of the thirty-eighth parallel line, American military officials believed its defense was fundamentally untenable. This belief was only confirmed by the breadth of these attacks launched from the North. These ranged from an attempted assassination of South Korean President Park Chung Hee by an infiltrating North Korean commando team that targeted his residence in the Blue House in Seoul in January 1968 to the seizure two days later of the American spy ship *Pueblo* and her eighty-three crew members by North Korean naval forces operating clearly outside Korean territorial waters. There were reports that it was actually within nine miles of a North Korean offshore island, but the recognized territorial waters extending only three miles at that point (they would not expand to twelve miles until the UN Convention on the Law of Sea was negotiated in 1982). The *Pueblo* was, at least in international legal terms, in the clear. But the location of the Pueblo was all but immaterial. Pyongyang was simply determined to send a message. All these incidents were complicated by the growing American military focus on the Vietnam War, where American involvement was building dramatically. The Tet Offensive—a nationwide uprising of the Vietcong backed by North Vietnamese troops—broke out just a week after the seizure of the *Pueblo*. The crew, who had been beaten and tortured while in captivity, were not freed until eleven months later after extensive negotiations at Panmunjom along the DMZ line. The new, young leader of North Korea, Kim Jong Il, son of founder Kim Il Sung, was described by propaganda pronouncements from Pyongyang of having left the American Congress, Defense, and State Departments "flustered and thrown into confusion," at which point the United States "went up in smoke before the quick moves taken by the Leader," Kim Jong Il. Then in his twenties, Kim was said to have been delighted when President Lyndon Johnson was finally forced to send a letter of apology in order to get the hostage American sailors returned. "US President Johnson lamented that it was the first letter of apology since the birth of the United States," the North Korean government exulted.

The problem posed by many of these incidents is that each developed as a consequence of a major flaw in most red lines when they become replacements for careful international diplomacy and rules of law. As has certainly been the case with Korea, the line has effectively been serving as a proxy for a negotiated peace treaty whose detailed parameters are, if not accepted, at least understood by both sides. The Treaty of Versailles, which took more than six months of herculean diplomatic efforts to draft, may not have been accepted by the various parties to it, but was certainly understood. Red lines are not meant to bring an end to hostilities, nor should they. In most cases they are intended either to prevent them or punish, in some fashion, a hostile act that has taken place, or to fend off such an action that might be anticipated. The best of them are skillfully drawn and quite clear in their intentions. But in the case of Korea, none of this was really the case. At the same time, few efforts were ever made to punish North Korea for repeated violations.

The draft armistice covered no offshore territory of Korea, which led at least in part to the *Pueblo* incident, though much of the disputed territory was off the western coast of Korea rather than the eastern coast where the *Pueblo* had been seized in what were clearly international waters. In fact there are several major disputed islands off the west coast of the Korean Peninsula, particularly five Northwest Islands in the Yellow Sea. At the end of the Korean War, the United Nations actually drew a line of maritime military control (MMC) that continued off the western shore, specifically designating these five islands falling below that line as part of the South's territory though they are, geographically, closer to the west coast of North Korea than South Korea. Drawn up when three miles was the standard offshore limit of national waters, the MMC was never recognized by the North, particularly after twelve miles became the standard limit of offshore territory. So, for years during the 1970s, North Korean fighter jets repeatedly overflew this region, and patrol boats accosted, even fired on vessels, testing the resolve of the South and the Americans.

Kim Il Sung bequeathed to his son, Kim Jong Il, a healthy respect for this red line but an utter determination to challenge and test it at every opportunity. All three Kims have believed, surrounded as they have been by major nuclear powers or their guarantors, that a secure strategic deterrent is the only really viable guarantee that any line, real or virtual, would not be breached. And with the rapid growth and development of North Korean military and intelligence assets, this priority came increasingly into focus. The *Pueblo* incident was described internally as the "first war of brains" (*dunoejeon*), later to morph into a "war of wisdom" (*jihyejeon*) when a nuclear threat became realistic.

The most telling incident, though, with respect to enforcement of the continued division between North and South Korea came as the first major test of Richard Nixon's presidency. At 4 A.M. on April 14, 1969, a US Navy EC-121 electronic spy plane took off from Atsugi Air Base in Japan for a routine surveillance mission off the North Korean coast. The standing instructions for its crew of thirty-one men was to make a series of elliptical passes about one hundred and twenty miles long approaching no closer than forty nautical miles from the coast—substantially outside the recognized three-mile territorial limit. It would then land at Osan Air Base in South Korea. It never got there. Nearly seven hours after takeoff, ninety miles southeast of Chongjin, North Korea, the EC-121, a lumbering four-engine propeller Constellation without any armament, was intercepted over the Sea of Japan by two North Korean MiG fighters that shot it down. No survivors were ever found. News began filtering back to Washington slowly and sporadically, so the crisis took days to gel. As Henry Kissinger, Nixon's national security advisor, put it later, the United States needed "to make high-risk decisions quickly and under pressure. . . . It [was] easier to play safe." Which is precisely what Nixon's new team, barely three months in office, proceeded to do. Kissinger continued: "A crisis casts an immediate glare on men and policies. It illuminates above all those who husband their reputation and those willing to take the heat." As Kissinger described it, the EC-121 had gone down at 11:50 P.M. EST on April 15. The Situation Room in the White House basement received the first word through military channels an hour later. Seventeen minutes after that, Kissinger's military aide, Colonel Alexander Haig (who later, as General Haig, would become Nixon's chief of staff, then Ronald Reagan's secretary of state), received word that there had been an "unconfirmed shootdown." Kissinger chose not to wake the president. Another half hour and Haig and Colonel Robert Pursley, military aide to Melvin Laird, decided not to wake the secretary of defense until there was some certainty. At 2:17 A.M. on April 16, Radio Pyongyang announced that the North had shot down an American military aircraft that had intruded into its airspace—a clear violation of the red line agreement. Except that it hadn't. Radar tracking showed the EC-121 was down ninety miles offshore—a distance that even with the most liberally construed line would suggest was clearly outside any Korean territory. At that point, the entire machinery of government went into slow motion—"nonchalance" as Kissinger put it. Over the next two days, Nixon held a news conference, and Kissinger assembled a first meeting of what would become the Washington Special Actions Group including members from the State and Defense Departments, Joint Chiefs of Staff, and the CIA. "There was no real determination to use force," Kissinger wrote. "All discussions were theoretical, and no concrete operational plan was ever put forward." On August 18, Kissinger told Nixon that "failure to demand some redress or engage in some retaliatory action would make it probable that he would have to act more boldly later on." But Kissinger had to confess that his "judgment was that North Korea would not escalate, though the President should act on the basis that it might." They were meeting in the ornate Treaty Room of the White House residence, but Nixon "never had his heart in a retaliatory attack." He did order a couple of aircraft carriers to steam around the Sea of Japan. That was it. For Kim it was likely enough. He'd read the signal and the new president perfectly. As Kissinger concluded: "We lacked both machinery and conception. We made no demands North Korea could either accept or reject. We assembled no force that could pose a credible threat until so long after the event that it became almost irrelevant."

On the northern side, Kim was clearly doing what his father had done and his son would continue to do—test the resolve of each successive American president to preserve and protect the thirty-eighth parallel line and defend the interests and security of America's client state whose northern border defined that line.

By 1976, the United States already had quite a good sense of just how Kim and the North Koreans were prepared to test the one outstanding red line of that time. But they were utterly unprepared for what happened in August 1976. On August 18, a small squadron of American and South Korean troops were dispatched to prune a tree in the DMZ that was blocking the view of certain key guard posts. They were set upon by North Korean forces, and two American officers were bludgeoned to death with axes. The axe murder incident quickly grew into an international crisis that did not bode well for North Korea, especially in world opinion by virtue of its clearly unprovoked brutality. How this played itself out gives us a sense of just how complex the policing of this division has been through the years. It took some time for details of the incident to filter back to Washington, so it was not until August 25 at 10:30 A.M. that Henry Kissinger convened a meeting of the Washington Special Actions Group in the Situation Room of the White House. At the time, he was serving as secretary of state, having ceded the office of National Security Advisor he'd held simultaneously under President Nixon. At this meeting, though, dealing with "Korea: Possible Military Action," Kissinger brought along the State Department's leading Asia hand, Philip Habib, as well as Deputy Secretary of Defense William Clements, CIA director George H. W. Bush, Air Force General and

Chairman of the Joint Chiefs of Staff George S. Brown, and two senior National Security Council specialists, William Hyland and William Gleysteen. The lead-off subject was guard posts on the two sides of the DMZ. Clements pointed out that US military officers "get treated so badly. They get kicked, spit on, cursed, and we are unable to tell our people to protect themselves. Every morning they have a special meeting where they are told to take abuse and to maximize their restraint." Clements then cited the case of a Navy commander who "got badly kicked [in the throat] in June 1975." Kissinger understood the value of standing up to the North Koreans who seemed to be perpetually testing the DMZ. "Every time I wanted to hit hard at the North Koreans last week I was told that [South Korean President] Park didn't want to take military action." The talk then turned to some form of retaliation, which Clements presented but the details of which are still redacted in the minutes of the session. Still, Kissinger concluded, "No matter how we did it, the North Koreans would charge us with being responsible for it. Then we would be faced with questioning by the Senate Foreign Relations Committee and what would we say to them?" Clements concluded that there had been some "two hundred other such operations and none of these have surfaced." In the end, the United States, probably quite wisely, did nothing. The red line had not been seriously challenged—perhaps in degree a bit more brutally and visibly than elsewhere. But the line stood firm.

Indeed, a report for Congress by the Congressional Research Service listed more than two hundred incursions, including efforts to build at least four tunnels beneath the thirty-eighth parallel from the end of the Korean War through 2003. For more than half a century, loudspeakers broadcast propaganda from both sides until, in 2004 an agreement was finally made to silence them. In 2011, the South Korean defense ministry reported that the North had "violated the armistice 221 times." However, this also included escape attempts by Northern soldiers across the line, offshore attacks on fishing vessels, and several maritime military engagements, though each of these was certainly a violation of the agreement underpinning the physical red line in the form of the Military Demarcation Line. Generally, many of these "engagements" were designed largely to test the resolve of the United States and United Nations forces patrolling the line, to hold it and not give way.

In four months, from October 1973 through February 1974, there were some 219 violations of the Northern Patrol Line among the Northwest Islands, all in theoretical violation of the armistice agreement, with its offshore extensions, none of which was agreed upon by those who established and ratified the onshore line in the pact. The American-led United Nations forces had never really agreed on the offshore extensions—they wanted simply to end hostilities as quickly as possible with the fewest complications. Never a good recipe for a line that will stand the test of time and the test of arms.

And yet it has. Indeed, this very line withstood any number of challenges, large and small, through the years. As many as two hundred incidents, clashes, and at times pitched battles tested nine American presidents, often profoundly, from Dwight Eisenhower through Bill Clinton. But the game, and the nature of the red line, changed dramatically barely two months after Clinton was sworn into office. Today, this line is tested—repeatedly. But the nature and the extent of these tests have expanded dramatically, and toxically.

—

On December 12, 1985, North Korea, anxious to end its status as a global pariah and enter into the community of civilized nations, signed the Treaty on the Non-Proliferation of Nuclear Weapons (NPT) and brought into play another red line, hardly of its own making, yet shaded with the history of its older, terrestrial sibling. This line had been established by global consensus seventeen years earlier, and embraced by 188 nations that ratified the treaty. For both Koreas, this document would quickly supersede in importance the thirty-eighth parallel line that, with the emergence of missile and weapons technology, was rapidly being eclipsed by a new reality. Such lines—politico-military realities—would, as the twentieth century drew to a close and the twenty-first arrived, prove far more ephemeral and far too often more destabilizing than those drawn geographically following natural terrestrial or manmade boundaries.

What is especially curious, however, is that in each phase, as one challenge morphed into the next with what appeared to be increasingly existential outcomes, the American responses were strikingly similar and equally ineffectual. So, today we are left with a half dozen Korea-related red lines replacing the single one established in the truce that ended the Korean War.

North Korea had been lusting after a nuclear weapon since it first became known that the United States had introduced such weapons to the Korean Peninsula in January 1958. In 1963 and 1964, Kim Il Sung had asked first Russia, then China, for their help in developing a nuclear weapon. In both cases, Kim was rebuffed. So in the late 1970s, after South Korea had embarked on its own nuclear weapons development program, North Korea followed suit. By 1991, the United States had withdrawn nuclear weapons from the Korean Peninsula and barred the government in Seoul from building one on its own. About the same time, North Korea had begun hinting that it might have its own nuclear weapons development project under way.

—

On March 12, 1993, a whole new set of red lines, overlaying the thirty-eighth parallel line, came into play when North Korea announced it was withdrawing from the NPT, raising the specter of North Korea eventually developing a significant nuclear capability. Initially, this program was confined narrowly to a small, five-megawatt nuclear reactor. And, it would seem, with little ability to deliver any such weapon to any target beyond its territory. Still, it was quite clear that by the early 1980s, North Korea was producing short-range ballistic missiles based on the Soviet Scud-B model with a range under two hundred miles, carrying a one-ton payload far enough to land on Seoul but not much further. Iran became a major financier and customer, with the first one hundred shipped to Iran in the fall of 1987. By 1991, it was selling the next, newer model to Iran and Syria. Two years later, in late May 1993, the Rodong missile made its first appearance and created quite a little stir. On May 29 and 30, the first four missiles were launched from its test facilities at Musudan-ri in North Hamgyong Province, on the east coast of North Korea directly on the Sea of Japan.

It would take several months for North Korea's withdrawal from the NPT to go into effect. But on June 2, ten days before this deadline, US Assistant Secretary of State Robert Gallucci and North Korea's First Vice Minister of Foreign Affairs Kang Sok-ju opened talks to try to strike some workable deal managing the North's nuclear ambitions. And that, in itself, was the key red line—no nuclear weapons whatsoever for Pyongyang. Kang even admitted, contradicting the aging Kim Il Sung, that the North had the ability to build a nuclear weapon (though had not yet done so). It took just nine days for a "joint statement" to emerge. It contained an agreement in principle that there would be neither any threat or use of nuclear force by the United States and North Korea against the other, and no interference in the "internal affairs" of the other, a key North Korean demand. Most important, the North seemed to recognize the essence of this new tack—it would suspend its withdrawal from the NPT. Moreover, the talks would continue, but with North Korea beginning to make good some of its commitments under the NPT. It shut down a five-megawatt reactor at Yongbyon and said it would allow International Atomic Energy Agency (IAEA) inspectors to monitor the extraction of its nuclear fuel rods. This was a key step to preventing nuclear material from being reprocessed into weapons-grade plutonium, which Defense Secretary William Perry estimated could produce five or six nuclear weapons immediately, and if it moved into full-scale operation, ten or twelve more. Bringing online larger, fifty- or two-hundred-megawatt facilities could lead to production of scores of bombs. Moreover, in such a case, it was not inconceivable for North Korea to begin sale of such horrific weapons to any number of deep-pocketed and utterly malignant customers around the world. A single red line would quickly morph into a toxic and deeply woven blanket that would all but defy any efforts to monitor or control it.

Of course, at this point North Korea still had no actual nuclear device. By the mid-1990s, it had still neither created nor tested an atomic bomb. Its leverage and its challenge consisted only of (conventionally armed) missiles, which it continued to fire into the Sea of Japan on multiple occasions. Talks with the Americans, meanwhile, were not going well. By the next June, the North was already making noises about withdrawing for real from the NPT. At the same time, it was doing burn tests of engines for more potent missiles, while the US was looking at restoring tough sanctions and had dispatched Patriot missile batteries, Apache helicopters, and M-2 infantry fighting vehicles to South Korea. And as a final gesture, the aircraft carrier *Independence* strike group was positioned off the Korean Peninsula in the Sea of Japan. Two weeks before, former President Jimmy Carter, who had as warm a relationship with Kim Jong Il's father as any American leader with a North Korean ruler before or since, paid an unofficial visit to the patriarch and came away with an agreement. In the discussions, both sides pledged to respect the new nuclear norm: North Korea would freeze nuclear development while talks moved forward and allow IAEA inspectors due to be expelled to remain; Carter would recommend the US sell North Korea light water reactors it so desperately wanted to generate much-needed low-cost electric power. In all, a fortuitous moment. Three weeks later Kim Il Sung died of a heart attack on the afternoon of July 8, 1994 and his son, Kim Jong Il was in charge.

It had been clear for some time that the younger Kim was calling the shots, as least as far as military preparedness and challenges to the established rules of North-South relations. The decision by the younger Kim to withdraw from the NPT was not a difficult one to make. It came within days of the demand by the IAEA for on-site inspections of the North Korean nuclear program—a practice that was quite routine for the other 187 signatories to the NPT.

There began another of the perpetual series of sanctions-and-retreat that would mark the next quarter century of relations between the three parties most directly concerned with the two lines dividing the Korean Peninsula. In June 1994, some 80 percent of all Americans supported sanctions and 51 percent supported a military strike against North Korean nuclear facilities if it continued to reject IAEA inspections, while 48 percent even supported all-out war if the stakes were high enough.

In 1997, the United States acquired a new negotiator with North Korea. Evans Revere, a career State Department foreign service officer, was languishing at the US Embassy in New Zealand when a department recruiter asked him if he'd care to take on the role of liaison with North Korea. Within days, he was en route to Seoul for language training.

From Seoul he began a series of little-known trips to Pyongyang where the two countries were deeply into discussions about actually opening liaison offices—one step short of full recognition and the opening of embassies—in each others' capitals. Revere and his team had actually chosen a building in Pyongyang to serve as this liaison office—the former East German embassy—and "we were almost literally measuring the curtains." Revere had even provided for a CIA station out of the liaison office facility. The effort foundered eventually, he continued, since "they were not overwhelmingly interested in having a liaison office in their capital which they saw as a nest of spies." With the collapse of these talks, Revere returned to Washington where he was inserted promptly into what was then and is still known as the New York Channel. North Korea has always maintained a senior diplomat at its United Nations mission in New York whose primary assignment is relations with the United States. As it happens, when Revere arrived, relations had thawed to the extent that they were able to have regular exchanges over a range of matters.

Revere held this job for three more years. The talks, generally conducted in English, though at times in Korean with which Revere had developed considerable fluency, had him on regular flights to New York. The chief delegate, Li Gun, later served as ambassador in Poland, while his deputy, Kim Myong Gil, who later became North Korea's ambassador to Vietnam, in 2019 became the chief nuclear negotiator. Kim Myong Gil replaced Kim Hyok Chol, who was in charge of the relationship at the time of the failed Trump–Kim Jong Il summit in Hanoi and was summarily removed from office for his failed efforts. Not surprisingly, Revere found the official delegates generally accompanied by a "minder," likely a member of North Korean intelligence, whose task seemed to be simply to listen and, eventually, to report back through his own channels to Pyongyang. One of his senior interlocutors was a crusty guy with a mouthful of metal teeth. Still, Revere managed to break through, and it was not impossible for him to have solo discussions with his North Korean counterpart, going for walks in Manhattan or even in a park north of Pyongyang. These discussions twenty years ago were "completely different [then], much more free-wheeling, open and substantive. And unconstrained. . . . Very visionary," Revere recalled, "in terms of what we were trying to achieve." At the same time, he conceded "it was naïve of us to think that we could actually get them on the denuclearization path. But we learned some important things. One of the things that we learned was that they were never going to give up their nukes." This was the ultimate red line that had been well established by the mid-1990s, a time when North Korea had not yet even tested a workable nuclear weapon, nor any sort of missile that might be able to deliver it.

The United States tried every possible form of seduction—removing North Korea from the list of state sponsors of terrorism, even launching North Korean satellites into orbit on American rockets. The North Koreans were interested in just what restoring diplomatic relations might look like—their flag flying over their embassy in Washington, their diplomats able to roam and talk with Americans freely. "He actually asked me, 'we'd be able to do all these things,'" Revere recalled. "And I said, 'Well, why wouldn't you?'"

At the same time, Revere never held back in defining the red lines that were clearly visible from the American side. Decades before Donald Trump began warning of the "fire and fury" that would rain down on North Korea should it threaten the United States, Revere was telling his interlocutors at one of their New York dinners, face-to-face so that there was no misunderstanding, "you certainly are a target of America's nuclear arsenal." Ambassador Li looked back at him and shrugged, "Well, yes, we understand that."

—

It was about this time that nuclear diplomacy suddenly began to acquire a potentially even more lethal overlay. North Korea had begun testing missiles that could travel six hundred miles and carry chemical or nuclear warheads, when these would be sufficiently miniaturized to fit atop a fairly primitive missile. Eventually, it was clear they would inevitably near the point, however, where they could be accurately targeted and withstand the heat of reentry as they fell to their target. In other words, enough range and accuracy to hit Osaka or Hiroshima, perhaps even Tokyo. Now, it would seem, North Korea could be in a position to build such a missile. Syria, Iran, Libya, even Pakistan were said to have expressed interest in this new product. And by 1995 it had begun selling its technology to Iran. But the real fear was closer to home—that this could be another real challenge to the world's newest nuclear red line. The initial armistice line and the DMZ never envisioned the creation of weapons that could vastly pass its boundaries in a matter of seconds. In August 1998, North Korea successfully test-fired a Taepodong-1 missile on a trajectory toward Japan, shocking Japanese officials when portions actually overflew its main island of Honshu, where Tokyo is located. In October 2000, Secretary of State Madeleine Albright paid a visit to Kim Jong Il in Pyongyang, where she met with the North Korean leader for six hours and was invited to a spectacle of military might and tribute to Kim at the sports stadium where she occupied the seat of honor at the right hand of the dictator. It was the closest any American president had come to a visit to the North, and Revere, who helped plan the visit, says that she raised "a range of ideas with Kim Jong Il." Albright left with a commitment only to have experts from both sides meet and what was effectively little more than a wish list: no testing or deployment of missiles of a range of more than 500 kilometers (short of the west coast of Japan), halt all missile sales and exports, and in exchange for \$1 billion in aid, largely food and heavy fuel oil, which was essential for heating during the North's frigid winters, even assistance in building light-water nuclear reactors. There were no concrete pledges and indeed the United States had already been providing fuel oil under an earlier October 1994 formula called The Agreed Framework, and food in response to needs identified by the UN World Food Program. By now, the missile talks had subsumed nuclear negotiations, at least in urgency, and the metaphorical line that now encircled the Japanese islands began to assume paramount importance. Still, a group of experts from both sides did meet in Kuala Lumpur for talks that were intended to lead to a firm agreement on this line, but failed to move forward. What the North Korean negotiators wanted more than anything was a visit by President Clinton to North Korea, and the ultimate photo op—the two presidents grinning and shaking hands. When the American negotiators in Kuala Lumpur would run through their laundry lists of demands, their Korean interlocutors would respond, smiling, "this is something our presidents can discuss." So, Clinton announced he would not be visiting Pyongyang, refusing to meet Kim Jong Il. The last thing Clinton, Albright, or their nego-tiators wanted to reward the Kim family was the credibility of dealing as equals on both sides of the manifold red lines lacing the two nations. Talks ground to a halt—yet again.

In December 2002, matters suddenly got much worse. North Korea announced it would resume building and operating nuclear facilities. A month later, it proclaimed again its withdrawal from the NPT and within weeks let it be known that it had created a functioning nuclear weapon, though no test blast had yet been detected. Six-party talks began in Beijing between North and South Korea, the United States, Japan, China, and Russia—in other words every country that would in theory be within a set of red lines that marked the boundary of territory that North Korea had demonstrated an ability to reach with a missile and the blast radius of any nuclear device it might carry. The talks went nowhere, but did provide tangible evidence of just how many parties now recognized the existence of this next-generation challenge. By now, George W. Bush had succeeded Bill Clinton in the White House, and North Korea was demonstrating an ironclad deter-mination to breach a red line that had been anathema to it from its creation. The United States in turn demonstrated its determination to defend it. "We don't negotiate with evil, we defeat it," asserted Vice President Dick Cheney. He was reflecting the Bush doctrine of the Axis of Evil expressed in the president's State of the Union Address January 29, 2002, singling out Iran, Iraq (under Saddam Hussein), and North Korea. According to Americans who continued to deal sporadically with the North through the New York Channel, the Koreans watched in horror as American forces invaded and took down the potent military force of Saddam Hussein, hunted him down, and invaded Afghanistan with equal equanimity. All these events only cemented their view that their red line was immutable—North Korea would never be deterred from developing a deliverable nuclear weapon.

Three weeks after Bush was sworn in for his second term in January 2005, North Korea officially declared itself "a nuclear weapon state." It would still be another year and a half before North Korea would explode its first nuclear test device, widely considered pretty much a fizzle. Germany's Federal Institute for Geosciences and Natural Resources recorded it at 0.7 kilotons—a fraction of Little Boy, the 12- to 18-kiloton bomb the US dropped on Hiroshima in 1945.

Nevertheless, even this fizzle suggested that North Korea had mastered much of the technology and nuclear production capacity needed to bring it right up against the nuclear red line. So the Bush administration began seeking some way to slow what seemed like Kim's inevitable progression toward nuclear capability. In September 2005, there was a breakthrough of sorts in the six-power talks that had been ongoing in Beijing. The North agreed to shut down and seal its Yongbyon nuclear reactor and reprocessing facility and admit IAEA inspectors again. In return, Western countries would provide fuel for conventional heating and electrical plants and began easing financial sanctions that had virtually shut down Pyongyang's ability to do business with any other bank in the world. It took nearly two years to complete the shutdown process at Yongbyon, but in the interim, the US failed to remove North Korea from the list of "state sponsors of terrorism" which effectively kept Pyongyang firmly pinned outside global trade and financial norms. There followed a host of halfway measures that only served to demonstrate neither side had its heart fully in this process. Bush never really believed Kim had reversed his priorities while Kim continued to believe that the limits set by the United States were intended only to contain its ambitions to the point where they might be thwarted entirely. Still, Kim never gave up hope of renegotiating the armistice that had ended his father's Korean War.

Barack Obama was sworn into office in January 2009. Four months later, on May 25, 2009, North Korea detonated an underground nuclear explosion with a yield estimated at two to five kilotons, still barely a quarter the size of Little Boy, but an indication that they had mastered the concept and much of the engineering needed to produce quite a lethal weapon. This second nuclear detonation had several immediate and long-range effects. First, it removed all doubt—even among the Chinese leadership that had long questioned whether the North really had the capacity to design, build, and explode a viable nuclear device. Second, despite numerous attempts by Japan to build bridges across any potential red line between their two countries, including a visit to Pyongyang by Japanese Prime Minister Junichiro Koizumi in September 2002, the combined improvements of North

Korea's nuclear and missile capabilities had the effect of only hardening barriers that had begun to grow organically between Tokyo and Pyongyang. Indeed, throughout the period from the signing of the armistice and creation of the thirty-eighth parallel in 1954 and the Obama administration, the pace of military advances by the two sides far outstripped any diplomatic maneuverings. Indeed, apparent diplomatic breakthroughs all too often were overtaken by military activities on or off actual battlefields. By the late 1990s, American military intelligence believed that the North had already installed at least 12,000 long-range artillery and multiple rocket launchers on its side of the DMZ—enough to fire at least 500,000 rounds per hour into South Korea.

Eventually, however, North Korea's frequent public demonstrations of its raw, conventional firepower in vast parades through the heart of Pyongyang, designed to display the potential consequences of a breakdown in the truce and evisceration of the red line, were all but subsumed by repeated demonstrations of the North's growing strategic capabilities. Now the North was on the cusp of being able to carry any hostilities to the very heart of America, a tactic never undertaken by North Vietnam at any point during the entire twenty years of the Vietnam War. Since the creation of North Korea, the US believed it could beat the North in any war it might launch. But increasingly the question would become, at what cost? Which remains always a key question—the cost of violation.

In February 2011, North Korea issued a pledge to turn Seoul into "a sea of fire" in response to long-planned joint military exercises of American and South Korean forces, another conventional challenge that had already seen so many efforts to breach it. The pledge of a conventional Armageddon was one of the last major moves by Kim Jong Il, whose health in 2011 was deteriorating rapidly. By December he was gone, and his son Kim Jong Un barely, twenty-eight years old, assumed office on his father's death. It was hoped that the young Kim's education in Switzerland and deep attachment to basketball and especially the National Basketball Association and several of its stars might make him more anxious to have his country shed its identification as a pariah nation and return to the community of responsible powers. That was not at all to be the case. Instead, this Kim chose a different, even more malignant version of the path being followed by his father and grandfather of seeking to break the various red lines that dated to the earliest days of Kim Il Sung's reign.

On February 12, 2013, in the West Tunnel (the South Tunnel having been inundated in a flood the year before), 4,400 feet below the surface of the Punggye-ri test site in northeastern Korea, a nuclear device at least twice as powerful as its 2009 test was detonated. Now the North's nuclear weaponry was approaching the size of the Hiroshima weapon. But this time, of even greater significance, the Korea Central News Agency said that it had been miniaturized—the first step toward developing a device that could be carried by an intercontinental missile. The CIA had no reason to doubt this assessment. "This test makes Pyongyang's nuclear arsenal appear more threatening by taking it one more step closer to possessing a missile-deliverable nuclear weapon," confirmed Siegfried Hecker, former director of Los Alamos National Laboratories, where the first American nuclear weapon was developed and tested in 1945. It was during Hecker's visit to North Korea that his hosts whispered, during a trip through the Yongbyon nuclear facility that they "wanted to show us something." That something was a new, secret enrichment facility just down the road from the offices of the UN monitors who'd had no idea that it was just around the corner. Hecker was utterly trusted by North Korea to convey this information accurately. They'd known him well. He had been the only American to have ever held North Korean plutonium in his hand (when he visited Pyongyang on the invitation of Kim's father some years earlier). Hecker was still able to return to Washington this time with a dollop of reassurance, observing that the North had "still yet to demonstrate that they have developed an intercontinental ballistic missile." That, as it would turn out, was the easy part.

A month later, the UN Security Council unanimously passed Resolution 2094 tightening sanctions on North Korea and adding stiff financial sanctions, including bans on large money transfers and asset freezes of a number of individuals and organizations. In August, turning its back on the UN resolution, the North simply restarted its heavy water reactor at Yongbyon which, after processing, was able to produce weapons-grade plutonium.

For the balance of the Barack Obama administration, there was little progress. The red lines established by each side remained largely untouched, at the same time unchallenged. Obama, Secretary of State John Kerry, and National Security Advisors successively Thomas Donilon and Susan Rice had real crises to deal with—wars in Iraq, Afghanistan, and the Balkans, an Iran that needed to be kept from itself joining the nuclear club. Contact was maintained, largely through desultory conversations along the New York Channel. It was a policy that was very much hands off and that became known as "strategic patience." Basically, let sleeping dogs lie, leave red lines untouched. UN-ratified sanctions remained in place. It was quite clear that North Korea would continue its push toward a deliverable nuclear weapon. Only toward the very end of Obama's second term did matters begin to take a different turn.

On March 7, 2014, a new challenge appeared. On the sidelines of the National People's Congress in Beijing, China's Foreign Minister Wang Yi told reporters: "The Korean peninsula is right on China's doorstep. We have a red line, that is, we will not allow war or instability on the Korean peninsula." Then, he outlined what this meant for China's leadership with remarkable specificity that had been absent from many other such lines, but with quite a clear understanding of what the term he was using meant. All parties, he continued, "must exercise restraint" while "genuine and lasting peace" in Korea was possible only with denuclearization. Of course, he failed to spell out just what that would look like—this being one of the principal sticking points in years of debate over the shape and nature of any such nuclear challenges. In a visit to Beijing the month before, US Secretary of State John Kerry said he'd been pressing China to persuade North Korea to relinquish its nuclear weapons and the missiles that could deliver them to their targets—clearly the American definition of just what such a red line might mean.

Under Kim Jong Un, North Korea seems determined to tie its nuclear and missile programs ever closer to actions taken against what it perceives as its national interests. Effectively, without spelling it out, Kim has begun to establish his own red line directly overlaying those developed by the West in the six decades since the armistice. Throughout 2015, North Korea carried out a succession of test firings of medium-range missiles into the Sea of Japan and underwater-launched missiles off its coast, all with results that ranged from mediocre to outright failure.

But on January 6, 2016 at 1:30 A.M., just as the US presidential campaign was heating up, North Korea announced it had conducted its fourth nuclear test, this time, it claimed, of a hydrogen bomb. The yield, according to seismic evidence, suggested it was North Korea's largest yet—as much as sixteen kilotons. The earliest American thermonuclear devices, however, had yields in the five-megaton range, with the highest yield of an American hydrogen bomb put at twenty-five megatons. North Korea was still very far short of any such threshold.

By September, and the next test, the yield was up to twenty-five kilotons and official announcements said it had been miniaturized to a degree that would allow it to be mounted on a missile. This time, Siegfried Hecker agreed. As *The New York Times* put it the next day: "North Korea's latest test of an atomic weapon leaves the United States with an uncomfortable choice: Stick with a policy of incremental sanctions that has clearly failed to stop the country's nuclear advances, or pick among alternatives that range from the highly risky to the repugnant." Then, the *Times* pointed out the clear break with the past by the North's new ruler. Kim has "made it clear that whatever his grandfather and father intended, his nuclear program is for deterrence and strength, but not a bargaining chip."

This was the state of play when the Obama administration ended. In his first, and last, meeting with his successor in the Oval Office, on November 10, 2016, two days after the election, the president warned Donald Trump that North Korea would be his top national security threat going forward. Eventually, this warning would be mutated by Trump into a declaration that Obama was on the verge of launching a nuclear attack on North Korea. Several of Obama's top national security officials have assured me that he never was.

Instead, Obama had adopted a wait-and-assess doctrine or "strategic patience." Throughout the Obama years, the president found himself repeatedly disappointed by the failure of Kim to understand the value of a return to the club of civilized nations and Kim's inability to grasp the value of agreeing to an NPT embraced by more than 180 other nations. As a candidate in 2008, Obama had pledged to engage positively with the North Koreans—then under the rule of Kim Jong Un's father. Indeed, by contrast with his son, the elder Kim was all but reasonable, if somewhat unpredictable, in his dealings with those arrayed on the other side of the line they had been forced to accept—and respect. Kim Jong Un, however, proved to be utterly unreasonable, though reasonably predictable. He was also the youngest of the three to become supreme leader—at age twenty-eight, in contrast with his father, who was fifty-eight before he could rise to the leadership. Even his grandfather was thirty-six when he became premier (then the top job in North Korea). It was also quite clear that, as was the case with his father and grandfather, the arc of crisis was a response to a set of circumstances directly inherited from his predecessor. And the same was equally true of Donald Trump.

Above all, there was a broader reflection of the Kims' understandings through three generations of just how a red line should function and how it should respond to challenges posed by it.

In 1969, shortly after North Korea downed the American EC-121 reconnaissance aircraft, killing all thirty-one Americans on board, the Soviet Ambassador to Pyongyang, Nikolai Sudarikov, was ordered to explore why such an apparently reckless move had been undertaken, and conveyed intelligence that the action had brought American forces to combat readiness. Late in the evening of April 16, Pak Song Chol, a member of the ruling Communist Party Politburo, met with Sudarikov since "Comrade Kim Il Sung is far from Pyongyang and has charged me with meeting you." In a diplomatic cable to Vasili Kuznetsov, the powerful first deputy minister of foreign affairs and later member of the politburo, Sudarikov detailed Pak's explanation that nicely summarizes the regime's long-standing and deeply held view of red lines and how they must be managed: "It is good for them to know that we will not sit with folded arms," Pak began, an explanation that seems to have motivated every North Korean regime since Kim Il Sung. "We've shot down American planes before, and similar incidents are possible in the future. If the US imperialists continue to violate our border this means that they want to find some pretext to attack us." The concept is especially significant since it was presented from one senior Communist official to another who had a clear channel of communication to the highest ranks of Soviet leadership. Clearly, the successive Kims believed that the United States, with its overwhelmingly superior military power, was unlikely to breach any line, especially one that risked escalating into a nuclear apocalypse or even one that risked tens of thousands of American lives or millions of lives of valued allies.

Each Kim understood the value of red lines but especially the need to test them with each successive American president who had inherited them to see how tenaciously they would hold to them, how likely they might be to modify them, or even whether new, potentially even more toxic or challenging ones might be established. At the same time, each Kim developed his own, quite different, style of confrontation or accommodation in reacting to each successive adversary. In this respect, however, Donald Trump has differed wildly from the rest.

In May 2012, North Korea amended the preamble to its constitution to describe itself as a "nuclear possessing state" (*haekboyuguk* or 핵보유국), carrying the implication that it did possess nuclear weapons. But Obama's legacy to Trump was even more pernicious: repeated talk of the need for regime change or collapse, even plans for assassinating Kim Jong Un, and actual tightening of economic sanctions to the point of targeting particular members of Kim's closest entourage, eventually Kim himself. All this rhetoric, but particularly the new sanctions, only contributed to the bequeathed atmosphere of malignancy and hair-trigger tenseness along the separation between North and South. North Korea called the sanctions a "declaration of war," though in fact the nominal reasons for the tightening had less to do, immediately, with Kim's nuclear and missile programs, but rather his record for vast human rights abuses.

At the same time, Obama also embarked on a clandestine cyberwar designed to slow North Korea's missile and nuclear programs—a war that inevitably continued into the Trump administration as quite a toxic bequest and that hardly served to improve the atmosphere surrounding the transfer of power.

The reality is that by the time Trump arrived in office, North Korea was already claiming to be in virtually full possession of what some feared could become a survivable, second-strike nuclear capability—nuclear warheads sufficiently miniaturized to fit on an intercontinental ballistic missile (ICBM). But it is not yet clear that the KN-08 road-mobile, solid-fueled missile—capable of reaching the United States mainland that could be moved and fired at will with little advance-detection capability—can carry a nuclear warhead able to survive the heat and vibration of reentry, fall, and detonate reliably on a target. At least American intelligence has never seen such a weapon successfully tested. When that becomes a reality, of course, Kim could then threaten the United States with full confidence that if the US struck first, he could rain down unspeakable damage on American territory and critical allies like Japan. What Kim seems to be working toward is the ability, unlike Saddam Hussein and Muammar Qaddafi, to assure himself that regime change involving his forcible removal from power or assassination would be unthinkable.

———

Despite Barack Obama's Oval Office warning, the early days of the Trump administration barely focused on North Korea at all. Still, this is not to say that Trump did not begin by defining a new set of red lines that would seriously impact his relationship to the lines that already existed in legacy form around North Korea. The centerpiece of what would become a toxic network was his extension to Asia of his demand that NATO members devote more financial resources to the alliance and relieve the United State of the burden for their defense. This time, his focus was on South Korea, but especially Japan—both nations directly in the crosshairs of Kim Jong Un and his nuclear-armed missiles. The United States was contractually liable for the defense of both Asian nations. Under the terms of the treaty of surrender at the end of World War II and subsequent agreements at the end of the Korean War, Japan maintained only a "self-defense" force. Yet, by the time Trump arrived in office, Japan had become the world's fourth most potent military force (after the United States, Russia, and China). And South Korea, as a condition of the partition of the Korean Peninsula, understands itself to be under the protective umbrella of the United States, though its military ranks seventh, ahead of NATO members Italy, the UK, Turkey, and Germany. Trump even threatened to remove troops from South Korea, demanding that it assume the bulk of burdens for its own defense, unnerving both that country and Japan, where some 50,000 U.S. troops remain on duty and with an American nuclear force to back them up. On January 26, 2017, Trump had his first phone call with South Korea's interim president Hwang Kyo-ahn, affirming that the alliance between their two countries was "ironclad," but more than two years later, doubts remain.

Concluding that Trump intended little more than an extension of the Obama-era playbook, at 10:55 P.M. on February 11, 2017, North Korea went ahead with its most potentially destabilizing missile test yet—a KN-15/Polaris-2 medium-range ballistic missile with a solid-fuel propellant from a road-mobile launchpad. An utter success, it reached a height of 550 kilometers and splashed down, on target, 500 miles away in the Sea of Japan. This missile was clearly ready for deployment.

There followed a succession of challenges, in a sense testing how close to the line each nation was prepared to bring its various strategic forces. A massive joint US–South

Korean series of military maneuvers in February was followed by a series of launches of North Korea's new Scud missile that managed a down-range splashdown of 1,000 kilometers—twice the range of the KN-15.

Even before he was sworn in as president, Trump embarked on what would eventually escalate to a tweetstorm, defining his ribbon of red lines surrounding the Korean Peninsula. "North Korea has just stated it is in the final stages of developing a nuclear weapon capable of reaching parts of the U.S. It won't happen!" This, American intelligence determined, had already been achieved by the North. Then, a second tweet followed quickly from Trump: "China has been taking out massive amounts of money & wealth from the U.S. in totally one-sided trade, but won't help with North Korea. Nice!" A second line, drawing Beijing into his web.

On April 26, Trump invited Chinese President Xi Jinping to Mar-a-Lago for their first face-to-face meeting. And there, the American president drew for the first time directly for the Chinese leader, with some apparent care and specificity, his own set of red lines—for the first time as president. Trump hoped that what he saw as his natural charm and negotiating ability would win quick acceptance from the cagy Chinese leader. I could not help but be reminded of Woodrow Wilson the first time he dueled with the old foxes of France (Georges Clemenceau) and Britain (David Lloyd George) in Paris at the Versailles peace negotiations. Wilson thought he had right, as well as might, on his side. He never saw what was coming. The leaders of the old Europe, who had been negotiating one-sided treaties for decades, ran rings around Wilson, giving little more than a toothless League of Nations and rewriting the map of the world to their own benefit, creating boundaries and conditions that, as we will see, continue to fester today, a century later. The same was in store for Trump. In the days leading up his summit with Xi, there was a series of leaks promising that Trump was prepared to issue some dire warnings: Get tough with North Korea or face a China utterly surrounded by US missiles and missile defenses targeting Korea but with China only a few longitude adjustments away. Not to mention tough sanctions on China and its enterprises that failed to implement UN and US sanctions against Pyongyang. But Xi arrived, clearly well briefed on how to win over Trump. Flatter the American president, pledge economic cooperation, and explain how little operational leverage China had over North Korea. Add in the reality that red lines in this case simply would not work as Trump might desire. The two went for a long walk, with just their interpreters along. As they strolled through the gardens of Mar-a-Lago, Xi apparently persuaded Trump that bluster and determination would not be effective. There is also no evidence that the American trotted out the kinds of threats he had been mustering in advance. Of course, with no note-takers present, as has been

Trump's preference whenever he deals with tyrants, we will never know for certain what was offered, pledged, or ignored. Still, it turned out to be a huge victory for China. Only gradually would Trump come to realize this, though he continued to preen over the warm, personal relationship he had cultivated with his adversary.

But of perhaps paramount importance was an event that happened as their final dinner was getting underway. Trump had chosen to invoke another red line—with Syria, against use of chemical weapons on its people. He leaned over to Xi and quietly informed him that he had just ordered a launch of fifty-nine Tomahawk cruise missiles against Bashar al-Assad's airfield that was ground zero for the dictator's chemical weapons arsenal. Xi was, reportedly, stunned that his quiet diplomacy had just been upstaged by the actions of an interlocutor that the Chinese leader concluded on the spot was utterly unpredictable, at least partially unhinged, and all but totally unreliable. It would suggest how truly toxic the web Trump was about to spin could be to China's broadest interests, and how carefully their potentially aberrant author must be monitored.

It was left to Trump, however, to establish a whole new web of red lines in Korea and the surrounding nations that would become ever more untenable as time wore on. Still, Van Jackson, a Korea scholar who served in the Obama Pentagon as senior country director for Korea, observed that a Hillary Clinton administration had outlined even more dire plans, "drawing a hard red line against North Korean proliferation of nuclear and missile materials (which could involve preventive attacks)." This, he believed, could also "prioritize extended deterrence for allies, impose maximum pressure on regime elites, and expend whatever political capital was necessary to persuade China to prod North Korea back to the negotiating table." Absent the last item on this toxic laundry list, this was not unlike the playbook that some in the early Trump administration appeared to embrace. Senior members of the Clinton campaign and shadow government ranging from Michèle Flournoy (likely secretary of defense), Mira Rapp-Hooper (Asia policy coordinator), and Wendy Sherman (Obama's undersecretary of state and key Clinton campaign advisor) had largely embraced such scenarios, Van Jackson suggested. That turned out to be a very similar playbook being embraced by Donald Trump and his defense policy minions.

Trump's opening stratagem was not unlike, except perhaps in intensity and unpredictability, the "maximum pressure" concept of the later Obama years.

Trump's first secretary of defense, James Mattis, proffered at least four different scenarios of response, up to and including a preemptive first strike to take out North Korean missiles before they launched, or their capacity to build or stockpile deliverable nuclear warheads. Each scenario was more lethal than the next and each less likely to preserve the new red line that promised some sort of non-nuclear stability and security for the American homeland. But each also contained utterly no recognition of the reality that such metastable realities of any nature do not perform well under either abrupt intensity or, especially, unpredictability. Such lines are not intended to be whipsawed on a whim or a tweet—as Obama saw most immediately, and we will explore in greater detail, when he proclaimed his Syrian red line in an impromptu answer to a question at a press conference.

Still, in April, Trump appeared again with one of his favorite interlocutors, Maria Bartiromo of Fox Business, and puffed, "We're sending an armada. Very powerful. We have submarines, very powerful, far more powerful than [an] aircraft carrier, that I can tell you. And we have the best military people on earth. And I will say this. He [Kim] is doing the wrong thing. He is making a big mistake." As though repeating that would help it sink in and improve prospects for the success of this ill-considered threat. Indeed, it is quite likely that Trump did not in any sense understand North Korean thinking on such matters. The very fact that he had positioned an "armada" off the Korean coast (which was not even correct since, through crossed signals, the aircraft carrier strike group he was referencing was actually steaming toward Australia at the time) could be seen as a preparation by the United States for a preemptive strike. This, in turn, risked a cornered and frightened North Korea striking first. In other words, a challenge and counter would have rendered moot precisely what Trump was threatening. The context was critical as well. It was certainly not lost on Kim that just the week before, Trump had suddenly and without warning launched his Tomahawk cruise missile attack on Syria when it had crossed the long-standing American prohibition on use of chemical weapons. Moreover, with the North Korean dictator warning of "a big event" approaching, Vice President Mike Pence, visiting Seoul as part of a swing across Asia to reassure America's allies, was not reluctant to hammer home Trump's point: "North Korea would do well not to test [Trump's] resolve or the strength of the armed forces of the United States in this region." Standing at the DMZ and looking into North Korea, Pence added, "All options are on the table to achieve the objectives and ensure the stability of the people of this country." And he warned that American military strikes in Syria and Afghanistan were ample demonstrations of Trump's resolve being not open to question.

The New York Times headline observed that PENCE TALKS TOUGH, BUT U.S. STOPS SHORT OF DRAWING A RED LINE. Well, not exactly. In fact, Pence's statements and Trump's actions in fact drew a de facto line that both sides would be forced to deal with going forward. Sadly, from Kim's perspective, the day before, on the anniversary of the birth of his grandfather Kim Il Sung, the "big event" the grandson had boasted—launch of a new ballistic missile—failed as the weapon blew up almost immediately after liftoff. It was a deeply embarrassing effort at a show of force designed to demonstrate for Trump he was not to be trifled with or tested.

It seemed at that moment to be a rather insane race to see how close and how quickly each could crowd right up to those new and ephemeral lines that had been built around their lethal arsenals, their political priorities, and their relationships. This was also the first red line that had been so profoundly personalized by those who drew it and those against whom this line had been targeted. Very early on in their relationship, before the most virulent exchanges of threats of nuclear fire raining down on each other's countries, and before the kiss-and-make-up phase, in August 2017, Trump was asked in a Fox News interview how he would handle Kim's dash for a deliverable nuclear capability. "He's just gotta behave," Trump quipped.

The problem was that a host of different players began operating, or at least commenting, from different playbooks. And no one really understood Kim Jong Un at all. Some suggested that Kim was entirely mad, others that he was utterly rational, simply with a whole different set of priorities or challenges than the Trump administration recognized. The State and Defense Departments and the White House National Security Council each had vastly different perspectives. Not a good way at all to manage the kinds of barriers that the leaders on each side were establishing and preparing to defend. Even Trump himself sought to distinguish Kim, with whom he thought he had a very positive, even friendly, relationship (as he was wont to do with virtually any despot with whom he came in contact), from the North Korean establishment, which he regarded as utterly bent on accumulating a strategic and destabilizing military advantage.

Meanwhile, following the Mar-a-Lago visit and seeking to capitalize on what Trump clearly viewed as the halo effect of his charm offensive, the administration tried to rope China firmly into Trump's vision of the red line that he had established. But Trump was relatively oblivious of the reality that Xi did have his own interests in North Korea. Kim was intent on pursuing his own vision with his larger neighbor and had maintained a relationship with China that varied from chilly to openly hostile since he took power from his father in 2011. By 2017, it was moving toward a more hostile end of the spectrum. North Korea's missile tests were of some considerable concern to Beijing, as those missiles could as easily be directed toward China as toward Japanese or American territory. Kim continued to violate UN Security Council resolutions, including sanctions, which China refused to veto and indeed chose more or less to respect.

Still, Kim kept ploughing ahead, apparently all but totally oblivious to any obstacle that might be standing in the way of his ambition, driven by a toxic mix of paranoia and hubris. In July 2017, Kim twice demonstrated he had attained a missile capability that

Trump, indeed every American president, had identified as an existential no-go zone—a device capable of reaching the US mainland, even potentially Washington, with a nuclear warhead. In short, Kim seemed on a quest for an answer to the ability of the United States to obliterate Pyongyang with nuclear-armed, submarine-launched missiles poised just off the North Korean coast. The difference from all that had gone before was a rhetorical overlay unlike anything President Obama or any other American leader had ever hazarded.

While the red line remained all but unchanged, now the rhetoric had dramatically ratcheted up the danger. In June 2017, James Clapper, the director of national intelligence from 2010 to 2017, had only recently returned from a trip to North Korea where he met two of Kim Jong Un's top security advisors—the director of the Reconnaissance General Bureau and the minister of the interior. They clearly wanted him to come away with certain key and immutable lessons with which he would return to Washington and enlighten the Trump administration. In a speech to the Center for Strategic and International Studies, he delivered the message:

> I was amazed at the magnitude and depth of paranoia, and the overwhelming sense of siege that seems to prevail among the elite leadership in the north. Everywhere they look, as I heard repeatedly, they see enemies who threaten their very existence. They find the Republic's military capability quite formidable, and superior to theirs, and when they then consider the US military force, it compounds the paranoia, and amplifies their siege mentality.
>
> They are NOT going to give up their nuclear weapons. My first White House–issued talking point was to tell the North that they must de-nuclearize. That, I can attest from first-hand experience—is a non-starter; it isn't going to happen. They consider their nuclear capability as their ticket to survival. They went to school on what happened to Gaddafi in Libya. He voluntarily gave up his weapons of mass destruction after negotiating with the US, and they saw how that turned out for him. They understand that if they didn't have their nuclear weapons, no one would pay attention to them, and they would have no viable deterrent. It is about "face," recognition, and leverage. They have none of that without their nuclear weapons.

The takeaway from this, of course, is what most senior Washington figures and intelligence specialists dealing with North Korea had recognized and advised successive presidents, namely that Kim, as was the case with his father and grandfather, saw a nuclear deterrent as the only surefire job guarantee. Only now, Kim had a concrete example of what happens when his own red line is not established and defended at any cost. You wind up slaughtered like an animal in a drainage ditch, as happened to another nuclear aspirant who gave up that dream: Muammar Qaddafi. Or you wind up in a hidey-hole in Baghdad, defending yourself with a shaky hand as you're pried loose by American troops, like Saddam Hussein.

Kim's hoped-for guarantee of self-preservation became a reality when, on July 4, 2017 at 12:40 A.M., North Korea launched its brand-new Hwasong-14 ICBM from a facility near Pyongyang somewhat to the west of the missile force's traditional facilities on the Sea of Japan. This missile also splashed into the Sea of Japan just 933 kilometers away, but not until reaching a height of 2,802 kilometers. Experts at the Center for Nonproliferation Studies of the Nuclear Threat Initiative called it "the first successful test of a North Korean ICBM." It was apparently a two-stage missile and was lofted very high to avoid overflying Japan. But flattening the trajectory could have propelled it much farther. "If North Korea had fired it intending to maximize distance, estimates suggest it could have traveled approximately 7,000 kilometers," the Center observed. "Later analysis and a subsequent test of the missile [three weeks later] increased this range estimate to over 10,000 kilometers which places targets as far into the US as Chicago within range."

That sent the Trump administration racing to the UN Security Council to plead for tightening down sanctions even further. A ban on North Korean coal exports removed with one stroke one of Kim's primary sources of foreign revenue. Neither Russia nor China used its veto, angering North Korea and reinforcing the Trump diktat of no nukes and no means to deliver them to an American target. Of course, it was not lost on either Russia or China how far into their nations such a missile might be directed. Finally, in a totally unscripted remark in the Oval Office during a press gaggle on August 8, Trump let loose, defining what would go down as his most toxic red line yet:

> North Korea best not make any more threats to the United States. They will be met with fire and fury like the world has never seen. [Kim] has been very threatening, beyond a normal statement. And as I said, they will be met with fire, fury, and frankly, power, the likes of which this world has never seen.

Needless to say, like most Trump tweets or off-the-cuff remarks, even those dramatically resetting his growing web of ultimatums, this took everyone—his own staff, not to mention North Korea—utterly by surprise. Especially since North Koreans had not concealed by any means what their reaction would be, most recently in their direct dialogue in Pyongyang with Clapper. Still, to remove any doubt, the North Korean military responded quickly. General Kim Rak Gyom, head of its national strategic forces, suggested "an operational plan for making an enveloping fire at the areas around Guam with medium- to long-range ballistic rocket Hawsong-12." It wouldn't be a direct hit, but he included precise target coordinates corresponding to a circle thirty to forty kilometers around Guam.

A week later, Kim Jong Un appeared to walk back from the precipice when, in a visit to the military command controlling the North's missile arsenal, he pointed out that it was he alone who could give the "go" signal. And he had no intention of doing that just yet. Kim was rewarded with a parallel tweet from Trump: "Kim Jong Un made a very wise and well reasoned decision. The alternative would have been both catastrophic and unacceptable!" As Van Jackson observed, Trump "drew a post hoc red line."

Still, none of this gave Kim any real incentive to pause in his quest for an utterly reliable intercontinental weapon. On August 28, another Hwasong missile was launched, but this time on a trajectory that carried it over the main island of Japan, landing in the north Pacific, but quite far from either Guam or Hawaii. There followed the usual condemnations and threats from the United States, though little from Japan, which continued to hold its collective breath. Japanese leaders prayed quietly they could rely on an utterly unreliable American president who clearly had little understanding of the defensive no-go perimeter that surrounded the Japanese nation and that so far had never been challenged. The challenges, however, kept coming.

On September 3, North Korea unleashed its single most powerful underground nuclear test yet. It was set off in the same Punggye-ri Test Site tunnel as previous weapons, but this was orders of magnitude larger—the Lamont-Doherty Earth Observatory estimating it at 280 kilotons, or at least fifteen times the size of the Hiroshima bomb. A North Korean statement claimed it was the nation's first thermonuclear device, which remains unconfirmed. Still, it was big. And it again crossed a Trump-declared line. With nothing but rhetorical responses, however, both parties settled down on each side of this line and dug in, glaring at each other fiercely. Trump trotted out his nickname for Kim as "Little Rocket Man," which he debuted on the world stage in a speech before the United Nations General Assembly. Kim, of course, retorted, branding Trump a "dotard," which sent journalists and diplomats scurrying to their dictionaries where they found "an old person, especially one who has become physically weak or whose mental faculties have declined." But both leaders remained unwilling to make that last horrific step forward.

The key question in the minds of the few rational players left in Washington at this point was how to keep any avenues of diplomacy open while the leaders in both capitals appeared quite happy to shut them down. Diplomacy seemed to be the only way to restore barriers that both countries were proving quite determined to shred. "Preventive use of force" remained the operative term of choice in military and strategic circles. The phrase by this point certainly most accurately reflected Trump's mood, which admittedly did change from day to day, based on the last person to talk with him.

On November 17, North Korea finally launched an ICBM with a range that, if properly aimed, could strike the entire continental United States, all the way to Washington D.C. Hwasong-15 attained a colossal height of 4,475 kilometers and splashed down in the Sea of Japan 950 kilometers away. Now, North Korean officials began saying, they were ready to engage in diplomacy. This success proved its ability to defend itself and its leaders against whatever the United States could launch. And all this just as discussions began within the Trump administration of inflicting a "bloody nose" as a more palatable alternative to a full-blown nuclear launch, but quite useful in setting or defending limits.

Meanwhile, a new government had arrived in South Korea whose president believed devoutly in conciliation over combat. Moon Jae-in was fully prepared to draw his own defensive perimeter, not with steel, but with an unprecedented diplomatic initiative. Moon's entire life and career had been pointing toward this moment. While Trump and Kim Jong Un were busy building red lines that were founded on their apparently manic capacities for confrontation and belligerence, Moon was looking elsewhere to establish his own countervailing lines that would build bridges rather than walls. The son of parents who fled south during the Korean War, as a baby he rode on his mother's back while she peddled eggs in the port city of Pusan and his father worked in a prisoner-of-war camp. Entering university in 1972 with the intention of becoming a lawyer, he was quickly detoured. Appalled by the authoritative rule of Park Chung Hee, young Moon took to the streets in protest and was jailed. He passed the bar exam while in prison and became a lawyer. Drafted into the South Korean Army, ironically he was sent to the thirty-eighth parallel, where he took part in operations that followed the axe murder by North Korean troops of two US officers that provoked such a reaction from Henry Kissinger. Moon's law partner eventually entered politics. Both had specialized in defending labor rights activists and student demonstrators. When Roh Moo-hyun was elected president of South Korea, he lured Moon to his side as a top aide. South Korea was riddled with corruption at that point. Roh was himself ultimately driven from office and to suicide by accusations of corruption. But Moon chose to stand up for him and on May 9, 2017, was himself elected president of South Korea.

Moon's dream was a true rapprochement with the North, the thirty-eighth parallel melting away while families it divided would be able to reunite and prosper. He dreamed of visiting his ninety-year-old mother's hometown of Hungnam in the north. As it happens,

Kim opened the way forward with a remarkable New Year's speech in January 2018 when he at once swaggered to his people that he had managed to accumulate an arsenal that would protect them from Trumpian militarism, while at the same time extending an olive branch to the South. Kim proposed a truce throughout the period when South Korea would host the Olympic Games the next month. Moon did not hesitate in grasping the branch. The first meetings took place during the games when North and South delegates exhibited unparalleled warmth, while the leader of the American delegation, Vice President Mike Pence, sat stone-faced only steps away from Kim's sister, Kim Yo Jong, who led her nation's delegation.

The new atmosphere on the Korean Peninsula clearly cast a shadow over the Trump administration's continued efforts to maintain its hostile policy of "maximum pressure." Indeed, events were moving quickly and ineluctably in Korea. A high-level delegation from Moon including National Security Advisor Chung Eui-yong and National Intelligence Service Director Suh Hoon spent four hours in a jovial dinner meeting in Pyongyang. Kim even agreed to set up a direct line with the Blue House, Moon's presidential residence, so that even "if working-level talks are deadlocked and our officials act like arrogant blockheads, President Moon can just call me directly and the problem will be solved."

Of paramount importance, however, was the stunning move engineered by both sides. The two South Korean envoys left Pyongyang and flew directly to Washington. They carried with them a pledge from Kim to denuclearize the Korean Peninsula "if the military threat to the North was eliminated and its security guaranteed," and offered "a heartfelt dialogue with the United States on the issues of denuclearization and normalizing relations." As American negotiators, and Trump, to his dismay, would later learn, this locution really signified North Korea's desire to bring an end to the United States' ability to use tactical and strategic nuclear weapons against North Korea, even in the defense of South Korea and Japan as well as the United States. There was one immediate additional sweetener—an offer to release three Americans detained in North Korean prisons.

The two envoys had thought they would be briefing CIA Director Mike Pompeo and National Security Advisor General H. R. McMaster. Instead they were ushered directly into the Oval Office where they found a smiling President Trump, who'd already been given a sense of their mission. The two South Korean envoys presented their statement. Trump spotted an opportunity. He would, he told the two envoys, agree to meet Kim "by May to achieve permanent denuclearization" of the Korean Peninsula. (Of course that would eventually be revealed to be defined as an American withdrawal of all nuclear resources within range of North Korea, including from places like Okinawa and Guam, there being none in Japan itself, which has also been demonstrated to be within range of North Korean missiles.) Trump conveyed that he wanted an immediate meeting but was prepared to hold off until Moon and Kim had a chance to have their first session at Panmunjom. The two South Korean envoys went immediately from the Oval Office to live cameras set up at the stakeout position outside the West Wing to read a statement that detailed all this. They appeared as surprised as the rest of the world. Before they could even get before those cameras, however, Trump, ever the master of reality television, dashed into the White House press room, telling the stunned reporters assembled there that "a major announcement was coming" and that "hopefully you [reporters] will give me credit."

On April 27, the two Korean leaders met for the first time at the DMZ, smiling and talking earnestly, Kim stepping into South Korean territory and Moon, in a first for a South Korean leader, into Northern territory. Over the course of a long day they hammered out a Panmunjom Declaration that pledged to seek peaceful unification and family reunification, embark on joint economic projects including a unified rail system and roads connecting both nations, establish a joint liaison office, build measures of restraint along the DMZ and the Northern Limit Line in the Yellow Sea, sign a peace treaty finally ending the last war, pursue trilateral talks including the United States, and work toward a "common goal of realizing through complete de-nuclearization, a nuclear-free Korean Peninsula." In other words, with the stroke of a pen, they had sought to dismantle a series of red lines built up over six decades of often bitter confrontation. A month later, Moon paid his first visit to Pyongyang and Kim offered "to visit Seoul any time you invite me."

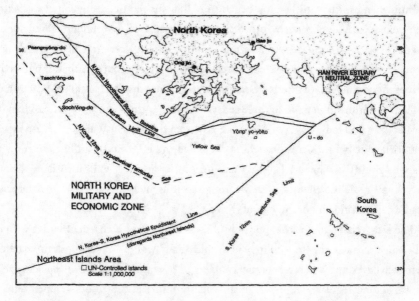

The maritime path of the line dividing North and South Korea
including hypothetical, and often contested, territorial limits.

There were, however, several hiccups along the route to the summit between Trump and Kim—cancellations and repositionings. But since both leaders needed this summit, each for their own reasons, it finally went forward, the two presidents meeting on June 12, 2018, on Singapore's Sentosa Island. Each did get out of it exactly what he wanted or needed. Trump got the photo-op he hoped might mark the first step on a road to the Nobel Peace Prize, in whose aura he delighted in basking, if a trifle prematurely. Kim got his own photo-op, which really went a long way toward affirming the absolute dictator of a small, utterly impoverished Asian nation as an equal to the leader of arguably the world's most affluent, most militarized power.

Neither moved his demands an iota in the lead-up to this meeting or in the weeks and months that followed. Trump had sought to entice Kim with the idea of a nation as rich and prosperous as South Korea or even Switzerland, where Kim spent a part of his youth in a posh boarding school. Kim remained steadfast in his determination to remain a member of the nuclear club. The meeting ended with a communiqué that was thin gruel. Trump committed to "providing security guarantees" for the North. Both agreed to pursue a "peace regime" for the peninsula. Kim reaffirmed his commitment to "the complete denuclearization of the Korean Peninsula" and to return American POW/MIA remains from the Korean War. Both affirmed the Panmunjom Declaration from April 12 and agreed to continue lower-level meetings.

Immediately afterward, Trump began to redraw his red lines. He halted war games with South Korea as needlessly "provocative and expensive," and thought aloud about a campaign pledge to bring all American troops home from Korea for the first time since before the Korean War. Both were impetuous and foolhardy concepts that, if pursued in their entirety, would have utterly destroyed strategic lines that had sustained peace on the Korean Peninsula for more than three generations. In return, Trump got little. A handful of what were said to be bones of American GIs from the Korean War were returned with a flourish. But North Korea has still not rejoined the NPT and continues turning out weapons-grade fissile material and assembling it into warheads, while dispersing the missile systems to deliver them so widely through its hills and valleys that no invader could ever be sure to find and destroy all of them.

The fact is that Kim, by the time of his first summit and his charm offensive with the South, had redrawn the lines entirely to his liking and was in an ideal position to defend them whenever and wherever necessary. He had a workable nuclear arsenal to which he was adding regularly. Many were sufficiently miniaturized to be strapped onto an intercontinental missile with the range to target the entire United States, could be fired at will, and could survive any American first strike—though thus far there has been no single demonstration that the North has achieved the final obstacle: survival of the missile warhead in the heat of reentry to the atmosphere and detonation over a target. Still, unlike Iran, Libya, or Iraq, Kim was a full-fledged member of the nuclear club with an arsenal of thirty to sixty nuclear weapons that could, in some fashion, be delivered somewhere the United States and its allies do not want them to be. No one was going to take that away from him. Now, all that remained was to get rid of those hateful sanctions and his world would be complete. A charm offensive might be just the ticket. And he was more than able to play the long game. After all, he was not yet thirty-five. Absent some catastrophic error, he was president for life without a single whisper of opposition; any real opponent was simply executed. His prime adversary was twice his age, had at best six more years in office, and was deeply challenged at every turn.

As we will see on the Korean Peninsula, as with so many cases around the world, Donald Trump, by his structuring of the challenges, as well as his reaction to each, wound up solving problems largely of his own creation. Certainly such red lines existed before Donald Trump and his administration arrived in Korea—some dated as far back as the ends of the two World Wars, others to the flawed denouement of the Korean War. But none of Trump's predecessors so persistently created more barriers than he was ever able to resolve. Korea will be but one set of legacies to his successor. Trump, by the nature of the individuals he chose to advise him—so many like-minded, of the fire-and-fury variety—and his inability to consider ideas that conflicted with his own often warped view of reality, built diplomatic-military structures too often poised on various brinks of disaster. Most have still not played themselves out and could still serve as trip wires to a conclusion that will serve neither side well.

Finally, there is the ultimate concern of the trip wire. If the goal is to defend one or more red lines, all too often American forces and those of their adversaries must be on very high alert. The battle slogan of American forces in South Korea is "Ready to Fight Tonight." But that could easily be the slogan for virtually any such line the United States is determined to sustain. Misinterpreting the signs of subtle, even unintended moves in one direction or another can have horrific consequences.

Now, Korea's red lines seem to be frozen again in time, yet there remains still the question of just where they should be set. Clearly, the thirty-eighth parallel will not be moving anytime soon, no matter how desperately reunification may be desired on both sides of the Korean Peninsula. There may be growing efforts to bypass or circumvent it, ranging from family unifications, rail, road, and telecom links, and subtle moves toward an easing of sanctions. But the fundamental lines that have been installed by respectively Donald Trump and Kim Jong Un remain immutable. Trump still believes the North must rid itself of its entire nuclear arsenal and the capacity to rebuild it, all policed by international inspectors. The North must make no further effort to test or deploy missiles capable of reaching—in concentric circles—Japan, the Pacific island territories of the United States, and mainland America. At the same time, the United States must begin lifting sanctions on Korea upon demonstrations of good faith and verifiable actions by Kim. What still does not seem to be recognized by Donald Trump, and perhaps most dangerously even by some of his top advisers as well, is that the final red line is immutable. North Korea will never give up its nuclear weapons, under any circumstances.

Red lines are not meant to last forever, nor should they be constructed to endure immutably or eternally. Moreover, they must be flexible, bendable, and in the right circumstances adjusted toward or away from the goal lines. So, it is not unreasonable to expect that North Korea will need, for its own domestic reasons, a sense of self-worth, and a feeling of security, to retain some level of nuclear arsenal. They have seen graphically what happens to nations that relinquish them—Libya, now dismembered and its leader executed; Iraq, dismembered and its demagogue hunted down and executed; Ukraine, invaded and its territory seized by a larger and more powerful neighbor that retained its own mammoth nuclear arsenal and whose ultimate goal is to reclaim the Ukrainian heartland in its entirety. Still, there are problems that are clearly visible if the North retains even a contained and frozen nuclear arsenal as the final solution. More, firmer standards must be established. There can be no horizontal nuclear proliferation. No matter how attractive any offer might be, North Korea can never sell either a weapon or the knowledge of how to build one to any other nation and especially any terrorist group, no matter how attractive the offer. At the same time, there remains the fear of failure by example. Iran and other wannabe nuclear states can easily infer from the Korean example that the only real guarantee of their own safety is to dash toward a nuclear capability that the outside world will be then forced to accept as a *fait accompli*. The first chink in the 188-nation list that signed the NPT could widen like a single thread pulled from an elegant tapestry. None of this can be allowed to happen. This may be the single defensible red line that both sides will be forced to deal with. Another round of tough-guy language and action may still be necessary to get there.

"You need to turn the heat up on the regime using sanctions, covert action, military pressure," Evans Revere says grimly. From his perch at the Brooking Institute, he has been quietly whispering in the ear of any receptive audience, and there are many. What might this look like? He smiles and shrugs enigmatically. But this much is clear. The United States, provided it can bring along willing allies, still has means to squeeze this final endgame of a nuclear freeze. America has still not fully unleashed, for instance, its cyber capacity—on the North's missile or nuclear program, its electrical grid, wherever it might be most damaging and evident. Korea is still not fully isolated from the global banking system. "We seem to have tried everything," Revere continues. "Trump called it maximum pressure. Right. The problem was we never got anywhere near maximum pressure. And now the pressure is being moved. We have tried everything. Putting on sanctions, taking off sanctions. Dialogue, no dialogue. Isolation, no isolation. We've tried all that. The one thing that we have never tried is to attack. The North Koreans are developing nuclear weapons for the preservation of the regime. Yet, we have never put the existence of the regime at risk. I believe the North Koreans are rational actors. They're not crazy. But at the end of the day the North Koreans want one thing above everything. So, if you give North Koreans a choice between preserving the regime and nuclear weapons, I think they will opt for preserving the regime."

Above all, America, as Revere puts it, must "make them stare into the abyss. In that case, I believe as rational actors that they will make the right choice. Yet, the door is rapidly closing on the opportunity to do that. One of the things that Trump has done more than anything is to damage our ability to solve this problem. We must squeeze the North Koreans from every possible angle so that every morning when Kim Jong Un wakes up, he needs to wonder whether his economy will make it through the end of the day. And once again I am convinced he is a rational actor. Persuading the elites we can take their privileges away from them, that is an existential threat to the Kim family's rule."

Effectively, America, and hopefully its allies and China's neighbors, will recognize the necessity of redrawing the latest red lines dramatically, and without North Korea agreeing. So far, playing nice doesn't seem to be working as well now as it ever has in the past.

The best, most sustainable red lines, of course, are those where both sides see a degree of success by their being maintained, or ideally lifted. Moreover, especially in the case of the Koreas, there are other even broader and more toxic stakes involved. Especially in the waters and lands that surround the two Koreas themselves.

CHAPTER FOUR

China:
By the Beautiful Sea

On April 12, 2017, Donald Trump puffed that the Nimitz-class aircraft carrier *Carl Vinson* and its strike group including seventy aircrafts, a guided missile cruiser, two guided-missile destroyers, and support vessels were en route to taking up station in the Sea of Japan off the east coast of the Korean Peninsula to send a message to Kim Jong Un. "We are sending an armada, very powerful, far more powerful than an aircraft carrier," he told Fox Business Network's Maria Bartiromo. "We have the best military people on Earth. And I will say this: he [Kim] is doing the wrong thing." In fact, at that very moment, the USS *Carl Vinson* and its escort vessels were at least three thousand miles away. Having just left Singapore, passed through the Sunda Strait that separates Java from Sumatra in Indonesia, they were steaming resolutely southeast, heading toward a rendezvous with the Australian navy where they were to take part in long-planned exercises. Moreover, the target of those exercises was not North Korea, but a power that then and now looms far larger in strategic thinking of the Asia-Pacific region—China. And particularly the attention China has been paying to its own watery front yard of inestimable strategic and economic value.

This front yard consists of at least 32 islands, 6 banks, 117 reefs, 35 submerged banks, 21 underwater shoals, several hundred rocks, and most recently at least 10 artificial and highly fortified islands. Each is surrounded by its own, often deeply contested, territorial waters and their attendant red lines, and all are enveloped by the "nine-dash line," which is where the next vast, armada-level showdown could well be started over a maritime incident.

In recent decades, China has come to consider itself a world power, certainly on a par with the United States or neighboring Russia. Its population is also on track by 2024 to be surpassed by its southern neighbor, India, whose heavily armed frontier has itself served for decades as a tense and at times deeply conflicted red line. To claim a solid hold on its designation as a global leader, China has recognized that it needs a world-class, blue-water navy. As a first step, it needs to cement its hold over its mare nostrum—the South China Sea. In many respects this is as important to its major power standing as the Black Sea is to Russia. As we shall see, Russia has long been willing to do almost anything to cement its control there—and extend its military, and political, power into the Mediterranean. A solid hold by China over the South China Sea would be only the first step into Beijing's sway over a much broader stretch of the Pacific, into which that sea blends seamlessly and which China also considers its front yard.

The South China Sea is the centerpiece of an oceanic string that connects North and South America via the Pacific to the Indian Ocean, Persian Gulf, the Mediterranean, and Europe. It is perhaps the weakest link, yet for this very reason more and more deeply-drawn red lines crisscross its sea routes, forming a network of potentially toxic barriers to free movement of goods and people, not to mention weapons and matériel of any future conflict. That China is the source of such a vast network of these red lines should be profoundly disturbing not only to the other nations that border it and claim portions as rightfully their own, but also to Western powers, particularly the United States, that fear their own ability to move freely may be persistently challenged. As China develops increasingly sophisticated weapons and the blue-water platforms to move them, its grip over the South China Sea and ability to confront all who challenge its red lines and attempt to pass freely through will become increasingly disturbing.

China has set forth any number of rationales for seeking to establish and guarantee its rightful use of the territory of the South China Sea. But perhaps none was as frank as a 2011 white paper from China's State Council that observed "China has a large population, yet a weak economic base. It has to feed close to 20% of the world's population with 7.9% of the world's farmland and 6.5% of the world's fresh water." The resolution of this conundrum is quite evident—China believes it is not only entitled to the entirety of the seas that comprise its front yard, but needs them for its very survival.

To cement its dominance of the South China Sea, China needs desperately to assert its control over the islands that dot it, and in turn to establish a network of red lines surrounding each of these locations that are utterly pernicious to the other nations that happens to share the sea's borders and transit its waters. As many and as complex as the red lines overlaying the Korean Peninsula, those that overlay China, its neighbors, and vast stretches of ocean that tie them all together are far more intricate, the stakes even larger.

At least a third of all the world's shipping passes through the South China Sea, the principal transit point of traffic linking the Indian Ocean with the Pacific. In total value, this annual trade is estimated to be in excess of $3.4 trillion. This trade is either bound for or originates in a vast array of nations, many far removed from the South China Sea itself. For China, the total annual trade value reaches at least $1.47 trillion, the largest of any nation, followed by South Korea at $249 billion. But the value of trade with Germany follows in fourth place with $215 billion, the United States at $208 billion and even Britain with $124 billion and France with $83.5 billion. These last three are especially significant since at one point or another over the last two centuries, each has played an important role—at times one of ownership—in the lands that border this body of water—and in establishing the first of the red lines that have now multiplied into a tapestry that crisscrosses it.

For at least four thousand years, there have been settlers, or at least navigators, around the islands and through the waters of the South China Sea. They have ranged on the south through the Riau Islands, now part of Indonesia, but whose natives live with little attachment to the outside world; north and east to the islands of the western Philippines; to the west where Malaysia and Brunei contest ownership of small lands off their coasts and especially the richness beneath their waters; and finally to Vietnam on the far north and west. And of course there are any number of deeply contested islands, reefs, even rocks scattered inward from these borders of the sea. Chinese records make reference to early seafarers from the mainland who traced their travels through this region as long ago as the first two centuries of the Common Era with a vigorous sea trade springing up for the succeeding couple of centuries. A sunken shipwreck recently revealed the existence of a brisk trade between China and the Arab world by the ninth century, in the middle of the Tang dynasty. It was only the beginning of broad and deep commerce between Tang merchants and their counterparts in Persia, Arabia, and India, which continued to flourish well into the Song Dynasty. Eventually, caught up in this trade was virtually the entire South China Sea and beyond, including Sumatra, Java, Bali, Borneo, Malaysia, and the Philippines.

This commerce came to an abrupt halt with the invasion of the Mongols from the north and the eventual rise of the Ming dynasty in Beijing. In the centuries that followed, Chinese ships barely existed on the area's waters; there was no sense of ownership. It was common territory for all who dared to venture through the often hazardous, uncharted waters littered with reefs and other obstacles, not to mention the terrors of powerful typhoons and other storms that could arrive all but unheralded and with catastrophic results. So, it was left to the Portuguese and their daring merchant fleets to hold sway, operating without maps, only their sextants and the knowledge of sailors who had gone before, calling on Chinese ports for lucrative trade. Eventually, of course, other great world sea powers would find their way east, particularly the Dutch, who set up shop in Indonesia along the southern fringes of the South China Sea. It was then that the first red lines and the first disputed claims began to appear.

The Portuguese, and later the English, held that right of first arrival gave them at least some degree of exclusivity and the right to use force to protect "their" territory. The great Dutch jurist Hugo Grotius argued that travel over the seas should be utterly free, that no one had the right to lay claim to any portion or establish red lines that would bar ships of any nationality. English lawyer John Selden was forced to take what was apparently a somewhat less persuasive position, that trade and commerce must always take a back seat to ownership rights, which he claimed for the British. *Dominium maris* (dominion of the sea), often known as free passage, does not affect the right of anyone to "own" the sea. Selden, in his extraordinary treatise *Mare Clausum*, effectively laid claim to the entire Atlantic Ocean from Norway and Holland to North America and Greenland, and in Asia across the South China Sea through what were then called the East Indies.

Needless to say, this debate had not been resolved by the time Grotius died in 1645 or Selden nine years later. Eventually, a degree of condominium was reached, allowing ships of all parties to pass through international waters, considered to be anything beyond a cannon-shot from shoreline. Since cannons in those days could rarely pass three miles, the three-mile territorial limit became a recognized standard for half a millennium. Freedom of navigation was guaranteed, at times by force of arms, by the Netherlands, Britain, and eventually the United States. The various tiny islands and reefs within the South China Sea were hardly worth considering and would have to be reserved for another day. Today, though, China itself has come to use a parallel argument to the one Selden first raised—that it has acquired real and effective sovereignty over the islands of the South China Sea by right of discovery, occupation, or construction.

In the interim, however, a new doctrine of international law and diplomacy was to arrive. The Peace of Westphalia, signed in 1648 in Germany, brought an end to the Thirty Years War, but the era it ushered in was far more significant. Effectively, it laid the basis for the future of all relations between modern nations including the base tenet of international law—that each state had exclusive sovereignty over its territory. Yet it failed to delineate just what such territory comprised, nor what sovereignty implied. But it did hold that no nation had the right to interfere in the internal affairs of another. Still, on the high seas, such boundaries could and would become most fluid, spawning so many floating lines and conflicting claims that are so desperately in dispute today, nearly four centuries later.

It was only in the last two hundred years that Westphalian-style borders even came to exist in much of Asia. And most of these boundaries may be directly attributed to the colonial powers that were utter aliens in the first place. Spain and Portugal had already divided up the hemisphere in the Treaty of Saragossa in 1529, which fixed the largely maritime frontier between the Philippines and Indonesia. It would take three more centuries for Britain to weigh in with an agreement establishing a boundary line with the Dutch between Indonesia and Malaya in 1842. Following the Spanish-American War in 1898, the United States and Spain fixed the boundaries of the Philippines, though this border (entirely liquid) would not be confirmed until 1930 by Britain and the United States. In none of these cases did China have a voice, nor did it try to strongarm its way in. Much of this neocolonial process began as an aftermath of the Treaty of Versailles, signed in 1919 which, as we shall see, set up a host of utterly implausible red lines of its own, especially in the Middle East. The major Western powers simply took it on themselves to set borders and red lines they would expect to be respected by all comers.

The first map published by China claiming to denote the limit of lands it believed it controlled in the South China Sea dates back to 1760. Today, Chinese officials cite maps dating even further back into the Qing dynasty to buttress their claims for first discovery indicating lasting entitlements. But there have been successive maps published in 1784, 1866, and 1897 all showing the southern tip of China was really Hainan Island, ten miles off the mainland and nearly two hundred miles northeast of the Paracel group. It was not until 1909 that a Chinese flotilla was dispatched to the Paracels to chart this scattered archipelago and lay claim by virtue of steaming through and around it for several weeks. More recently, China has sought to establish rights to the most important islands or island groups within the South China Sea. Take Huangyan Island, the name China bestowed on Scarborough Shoal. China believes its right of possession of this islet dates to the year 1279 when, during the Yuan dynasty, "Chinese astronomer Guo Shoujing performed surveying of the seas around China for Kublai Khan, and Huangyan Island was chosen as [the empire's southernmost] point in the South China Sea," a 2012 report issued by the Chinese Embassy in the Philippines asserted.

The most widely accepted current name derives from September 1789 when the British East India Company boat *Scarborough*, piloted by Captain Philip d'Auvergne, went aground on one of its rocks before repairing and pushing on to China, though the shoals had apparently been observed by Spanish galleons as much as a century earlier. As a warning to future British captains sailing in that region, *Scarborough* found its way onto Western maps since, as Joseph Huddart wrote in 1809, "The Scarborough

Shoal lies, according to the Spaniards, about 66 leagues to the westward of Luconia; it extends 20 miles from North to South, its southernmost end being in 15°5' north latitude. On this shoal the ship *Scarborough*, Captain D'Auvergne struck, September 12, 1784." Huddart further warned of one of the most dangerous and most contentious aspect of Scarborough, namely that elements of it are hardly visible above the waves, though broaden vastly beneath. "At daylight, the rocks appear frightful," D'Auvergne wrote in his report, "though it pleased the ship was on the sea side of the shoal, which is at left 2 leagues over, and 8 long. On the east side of the shoal the rocks are almost as high as those of Scilly, and a terrible sea breaks over them; on the west side they are no bigger than a boat. . . . On this shoal there are three small rocks above water." The rest of the atoll lies beneath.

Another set of deeply disputed islands are the Spratlys, located some sixty-two miles off the coast of Sarawak on the northern coast of Borneo, inside the exclusive economic zone (EEZ) of Malaysia, and some twelve hundred miles south of mainland China. They are one of the core components of the Spratly Islands, which sprawl across hundreds of square miles in the South China Sea. The Spratlys actually got their names from a nineteenth-century British whaling captain, Richard Spratly, who spent three years crisscrossing the region hunting down enough whales to fill his hold with their highly prized oil, not to mention bones and ivory. This was called simply "dangerous ground" on the charts these whalers carried. But the Royal Navy was sufficiently impressed to bestow his name on these scattered shoals.

During World War II, the entire South China Sea became, effectively, a Japanese lake. No western warships or transports dared venture into these waters that were heavily patrolled by forces of the Imperial Japanese Navy. But after the war was another story indeed. Now, there were new sheriffs in town—China on the north, several newly independent nations (Philippines and Indonesia, eventually Malaysia and Vietnam) on the east, south, and west, and a newly victorious allied navy, largely American with scatterings of Australian, British, and French vessels. By 1946, the Chinese navy dispatched two ships each to the Paracels and the Spratlys, erecting a stone marker on Itu Aba, the largest of the Spratly's islands, claiming it for China, while a year later, France and China pitched their claims on several islands in the Paracels, which are far closer to Vietnam (then a French colony) than China. On October 1, 1949, Mao Tse-tung proclaimed the People's Republic of China, Chiang Kai-Shek's Nationalists had fled to Taiwan, and whatever lines had crisscrossed the South China Sea effectively dissolved ahead of other more pressing terrestrial priorities.

The territories that were and would increasingly be in greatest contention in the South China Sea—at least the natural islands, as opposed to any number of artificial islands we will get to momentarily—are broadly divided into two groups: the Paracels, nearest to mainland China, and the Spratlys. The latter consists of at least 14 islands or islets, 6 banks, 113 submerged reefs, 35 underwater banks and 21 underwater shoals with a land area of under 2 square miles scattered across 158,000 square miles of water. None of these are naturally inhabited or have any recognizably arable land, and few have any potable water. The Paracels include more than 130 small coral islands and reefs scattered across some 5,800 square miles, with a total natural land area of just under three square miles. The largest islands are little more than sand grafted onto submerged, often degrading, coral reefs. This is not to say they lack value, however. Even beyond their strategic location, they also happen to be sitting atop potentially substantial reserves of oil and natural gas, and the large flocks of seabirds have succeeded in depositing vast quantities of guano, a most valuable commodity for agricultural fertilizer for places that do have arable land—like mainland China, the Philippines, Malaysia, and Vietnam.

There is an important question of just how much oil and natural gas lies beneath the South China Sea. The best estimates from the US Energy Information Administration suggest the entire undersea resources total barely 11 billion barrels of crude oil and 190 trillion cubic feet of natural gas, which would rank sixteenth largest in the world for crude oil, after Algeria and marginally ahead of Angola, and ninth largest in terms of natural gas, marginally ahead of all mainland China. Much of these proven reserves are concentrated along the periphery of the sea in the economic zones of these nations, particularly the best-endowed—Vietnam—while many blocks are claimed by China, though remain hotly contested. The US Geological Survey has estimated another 12 billion barrels of oil and 160 trillion cubic feet of natural gas may lie undiscovered—but hardly economically viable at current prices—in the heart of the South China Sea. There have been a host of disputed efforts to tap some of these oil blocks, each of which has largely foundered when it came up against red lines in the form of conflicting claims the other side was prepared to defend by force. This became particularly evident when the United States in May 2016 began lifting long-standing embargos on arms sales to Vietnam. The active process of building sufficient military forces to challenge Chinese claims began to really accelerate when Donald Trump assumed the presidency. The United States gave six forty-five-foot patrol boats to the Vietnamese coast guard, including a Hamilton-class cutter, all de-commissioned US Coast Guard vessels, while Vietnam added the purchase of Boeing ScanEagle drones and radar installations and explored the purchase of F-16 fighter jets and P-3 Orion aircraft for maritime surveillance.

But there are many other reasons beyond oil and natural gas for building what has become the most complex web of conflicting territorial claims anywhere in the world, red lines that snake in and around these at times viciously contested shards of rock and coral. The reasons for these lines, and the means of assuring they are respected, are more directly linked with geopolitical hegemony, national pride, and the ability to command some of the world's most strategically vital waterways in peacetime and especially in war. Now, with the United States and China locked in a bitter trade battle and with scores, if not hundreds, of companies fleeing China to Vietnam, Indonesia, the Philippines, and Malaysia, the stakes in the South China Sea are becoming even higher.

—

The Chinese are not unaccustomed to red lines or deeply-contested boundary disputes. Indeed in one form or another, they have been an integral part of their history as early as the third century B.C.E. when the first elements of the Great Wall were erected. Reaching dramatic heights during the Ming dynasty from the fourteenth through the seventeenth centuries, they were designed for a purpose not unlike France's twentieth-century Maginot Line, and were about as effective—keeping the Mongol hordes and other barbarians from sweeping in on the civilized Hans of central China. Go no further, the Great Wall suggested, just as the red lines crisscrossing the South China Sea are now intended to warn off interlopers.

These red lines first began to coalesce in 1948 around a concept called the "nine-dash line" (or variously, depending on who was drawing it, the ten- or eleven-dash line). Eventually, due to its configuration, this settled into the more generic terminology, "The U-Shaped Line"—the term used by the People's Republic of China (PRC) in its submission in 2009 to the United Nations Commission on the Limits of the Continental Shelf. It was the first time that any country had dared to proclaim vast swaths of open seas as its territory. The backlash against China was immediate and vocal. This line neatly enveloped both the Spratlys and the Paracels—hence, every possible island or rock that might be claimed, quite justifiably, by one or more littoral nations bordering the South China Sea, was claimed by China, which refused to recognize other nations' quite legitimate claims. Particularly alarming: this was the first time evidence had been paraded out in a formal, international context that China intended to claim as its own territorial waters the bulk of the nearly two million square miles that comprise the South China Sea—nearly a third of the total mainland territory of the Peoples Republic of China.

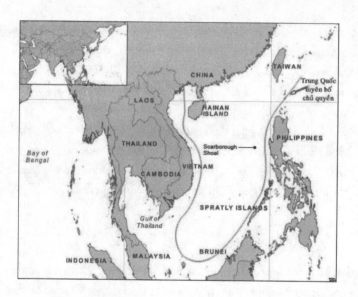

The path of the U-Shaped Line as it knifes through the South China Sea.

Take the Paracels. They lie a little over two hundred miles south of Hainan Island, the recognized southernmost point of China proper, and about the same distance east of Da Nang in Vietnam. Unlike the previously uninhabited, largely rock-strewn debris of the Spratlys, the Paracels actually have a dozen potentially habitable islets including Woody, Rocky, and Tree, as well as South, Middle, North, and Lincoln islands in the Amphitrite group and seven more in the Crescent group a bit south of there. All are in the Paracel group. CIA analysts believe there are a total of "130 small coral islands and reefs . . . a population of over 1,000 Chinese resid[ing] on Woody Island, the largest of the Paracels; there are scattered Chinese garrisons on some other islands." They were first discovered in 1698 by the same French ship that also laid claim to Vietnam, or Indochina (*Indochine*) as it was also known. It is hardly surprising that the government in Hanoi believed the rights to the Paracels went along with their claim to the mainland after the end of the Vietnam War and the reunification of North and South Vietnam. Woody is the largest island—a mile and a quarter long and a half mile wide. At the end of World War II, there were some skirmishes between French and Nationalist Chinese forces that left the main island, Woody, in the hands of China. It promptly claimed the entire group for itself, though the dispute continued throughout the Communist takeover of the mainland and Mao's subsequent preoccupation with cementing his hold. During this period of revolutionary transition, Chinese forces pulled out of Woody and Itu Aba in the Spratlys. This effectively left most of the South China Sea, while legally unclaimed

waters, nominally in control of Britain, France, and the United States, who saw little need
to set up red lines of their own at that point. That would not last very long.

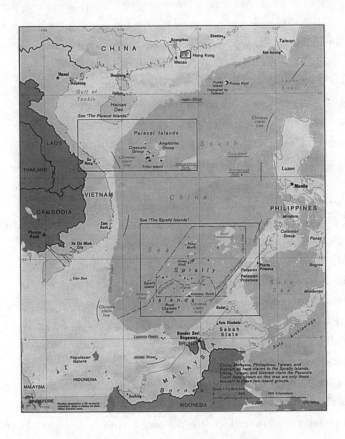

The Paracel Islands and the Spratly Islands.

By 1955, the Communists were back on Woody Island and mining guano to fertilize
rice paddies on the mainland. As for the Spratlys, the Philippines were quick to claim
them as their own, especially when it became clear in the early 1970s that there might be
some significant oil and gas fields beneath the waves. Ferdinand Marcos, then-president
of the Philippines, cemented his hold over the Spratlys later in that decade, occupying at
least nine islands and reefs and sending patrols through much of the remaining territory
to solidify the red line he had drawn around the archipelago.

Oil and gas were an equally powerful reason for Vietnam to draw its own series of
red lines around the Paracels as Exxon Mobil, a Shell subsidiary, and a consortium
of Canadian explorers won bids from South Vietnam in 1973 for blocks off to the south

and east, stretching into the Paracels. Shortly thereafter, Mao put his deputy Deng Xiaoping in charge of China's offshore resources, and the battle was joined. The South Vietnamese assumed the United States' Seventh Fleet would enforce the red lines it had drawn between the Paracels and mainland China. But Kissinger and Nixon had other ideas—an opening to China through Deng to Mao—and they had no interest in lines the South Vietnamese had ginned up that risked throttling those far larger ambitions. So when the Vietnamese decided to force the issue on their own, they found some very determined Chinese forces in their way, defending their own red line, proclaiming, "These islands belong to China since the Ming Dynasty. That cannot be denied." There resulted some substantial exchanges of fire, ultimately damaging two Chinese corvettes but sinking or disabling virtually the entire Vietnamese flotilla. Within days, Vietnam's personnel had been driven from virtually all the habitable Paracels. Kissinger decided to react somewhat passively and sent his deputy Winston Lord to New York with a message for Huang Hua, the veteran Chinese ambassador to the United Nations, to let China know that the United States had no intention of letting some islands in the South China Sea derail a move toward the critical opening to China he'd launched with Nixon. Beijing had protested the intrusion of American warships into the twelve-mile limit that China claimed as its territorial waters around the Paracels it had occupied. The United States would recognize the twelve-mile limit, Lord told Huang, rather than the three-mile limit that was standard at the time and that the United States would continue to use elsewhere as the international standard.

Three miles, twelve miles, and two hundred miles will become the most useful units of measure if we are to examine seaborne red lines. Until 1982, there had been quite uniform acceptance of three miles as the distance a nation could extend its sovereignty out to sea. But in Jamaica that year, a new standard was adopted—the UN Convention for the Law of the Sea (UNCLOS), whose 320 articles covering a wide range of maritime issues came into effect in 1994 after the sixtieth country ratified it. (While the United States has never ratified UNCLOS, it does adhere to its provisions voluntarily.) Twelve miles would become the territorial limit, while an exclusive economic zone (EEZ) could extend beyond that. There was even the possibility of building out further to an "extended continental shelf," though the two-hundred-mile limit was quite sufficient to cause no end of friction in places where bits and pieces of territory—islets, shoals, even rocks—could be used to extend two-hundred-mile red lines all but infinitely and quite overlappingly. The problem ultimately boiled down to definitions. Under UNCLOS, a real island certainly carried with it the ability to envelope itself with a two-hundred-mile EEZ red line. But rocks or some types of shoals carried no EEZ along with them, only the twelve-mile territorial designation. So, a rock could lay claim to barely 420 square miles of ocean, while winning designation as an island could blow out the territory to 125,664 square miles (a circle with a 200-mile radius). Of course, in the twelve years it took to ratify UNCLOS, there was considerable incentive to seize control of territory that would produce utterly legal, and in theory sustainable, red lines that were internationally recognized property lines. China is one of the 164 UN member nations that have signed UNCLOS, though ironically while the United States has signed the treaty and recognizes its provisions as settled international law, it has never ratified it—the Senate having held that it "risks undermining American sovereignty."

As for China, the matter was simple. It ratified the treaty, but where the two-hundred-mile limit failed to protect its claims, China just ignored UNCLOS entirely and reverted to maps dating back to the Ming dynasty to demonstrate Chinese supremacy, especially since long-standing precepts of international law have traditionally recognized explorers and conquerors. China's competitors inevitably default to UNCLOS. China's ultimate goal is quite transparent—eliminate all red lines in the form of other littoral nations' claims, except along the territorial fringes, and recognize that China legitimately controls all of the South China Sea—its rocks, islands, all the mineral and fish wealth that lies beneath, and the skies above. Effectively, China was establishing its own Monroe Doctrine and preparing to defend it on a daily basis, by quite substantial force if it saw the need, as it all too often did. "China has indisputable sovereignty over the South China Sea islands," a foreign ministry spokesman declared archly in December 2007. That could take quite a while to accomplish. Meanwhile, no end of nations—particularly the United States—are determined to prevent that from happening at all costs. Sadly, the way the interim red lines are being constructed and managed by China and every other nation with a claim on por-tions of the South China Sea is hardly conducive to their being defensible or manageable.

Indeed, a number of nations, from China to Brazil, India, Malaysia, the Maldives, and Vietnam, have demanded that all foreign warships passing through their two-hundred-mile exclusive economic zone seek permission for transit. Clearly this could pose an all but insuperable hurdle, especially in times of conflict. Such a requirement would effectively force American warships to circle around the southern reaches of the continent of Australia in order to avoid China's web of red lines crisscrossing the South China Sea, adding thou-sands of miles, precious days, and prohibitive fuel costs to the trip from the Pacific to the Indian Ocean and the Persian Gulf beyond. The ability of the United States to assist allies in and around the South China Sea would be seriously compromised, forcing many of these nations to bend to China's will or face a cutoff of trade and assistance, or ultimately military action. Not surprisingly, American fleets have ignored all such red lines through and around the EEZs of the region, often simply showing up to prove they can and to uphold international legal standards confirmed by extensive litigation. Such operations even have a name, and an acronym: "Freedom of Navigation Operations," or FONOP.

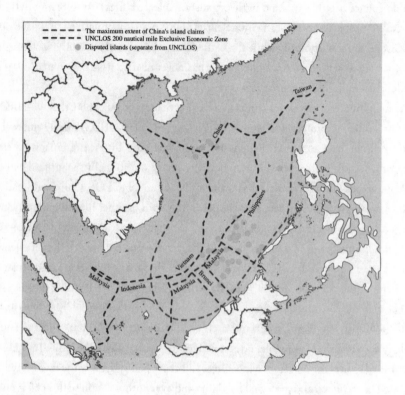

The South China Sea and the nations that lay claim to its waters and islands.

China began its slow but inexorable campaign to solidify its hold over the South China Sea in the more geographically contiguous Paracels, building a military-grade runway and enlarging the harbor on Woody Island. By the mid-1980s, China had also surveyed much of the Spratlys, well within the two-hundred-mile economic zones of the Philippines, Brunei, and Malaysia. And they had begun to build on several of these locations. Take Fiery Cross (Yongshu) Reef. To claim it as Chinese territory, Beijing decided to implant a block house and observation post. The problem is that, even in

1987, before oceans really began rising, most of the reef was almost entirely under water. At high tide, there was a single rock about three feet high at the southern end. The rest was a fifteen-mile-long, four-mile-wide ring of coral. In a little more than a week, Chinese engineers and workers managed to blast through the sharp coral, then dredge enough debris to build an artificial island of eighty-six thousand square feet. They then began broadening their horizons to other nearby underwater mounds, reefs, and banks that had not yet been seized by any of the neighboring countries. Over the years, China has only enlarged and cemented its operations on Fiery Cross into one of the most militarily advanced and lethal artificial islands in the region. Recent aerial photography shows an extended military-grade runway, radar and underground storage facilities, and at least four hardened shelters for missile launchers. All of this material was installed where, in its natural state, Fiery Cross and two neighboring reefs were little more than a handful of protruding rocks that for centuries had been no more than obstacles to shipping.

Nearby Subi Reef started life as circular reef with a narrow entry into a deep lagoon, blues and yellows shimmering in the sun. At least that's how it looked in mid-2012, when the tips of the coral were truly visible only at low tide. Chinese ships began calling at this reef, and two and a half years later five dredges and assorted support ships were working round the clock on the reef and in the waters of the lagoon. By the end of 2015, on reclaimed land, buildings, a jetty, and roads had sprouted. Six months later, some 976 acres of military emplacements had covered the built-up reef with a runway, fuel tanks, weapons silos, surface-to-air missile launchers, radar, and barracks for the Chinese military personnel who staffed it. By now, it is as large as Pearl Harbor.

The Chinese began work on Mischief Reef around the same time with similar results. By the fall of 2015 it had grown to the width of the entire District of Columbia. Personnel stationed there were able to keep close surveillance over Second Thomas Shoal, one of the few that its rightful owners, the Philippine government, were still able to occupy. On Woody Island, the largest in the Paracels, at least a thousand Chinese live, alongside a nine-thousand-foot runway and launch sites for anti-ship cruise missiles with a two-hundred-fifty-mile range, particularly the lethal YJ-12B anti-ship cruise missile. In 2017, a colorful artist's rendering titled "China Dream: Paracel Archipelago—Woody Island future development" showed a vastly expanded Woody Island with skyscrapers, parkland, and a passenger jetliner preparing to land on an extended two-runway airfield.

In all, China has transformed every rock, atoll, or islet it has claimed and occupied into a total of some thirty-two hundred acres of land, each large location well-fortified behind the red line that China has broadened substantially through the years. A May 2019 Pentagon "China Military Power" report identifies at least eight "Chinese-occupied outposts" with sixty other potential outposts in the Spratlys alone. Each, of course, is surrounded as soon as it is occupied by a red line defining a twelve-mile territorial limit that China insists it is prepared to defend. This frequently has led to Chinese protests over violation of their "sovereignty" in regions of the South China Sea that they now claim as theirs and around each of which it established its own twelve-mile red line as the internationally recognized territorial limit. With so many islets and atolls so close to each other, this has led to a tightly woven tapestry of regions where China is prepared to challenge all comers.

*Fiery Cross reef in the Spratlys before China began its major
reclamation and expansion project in August 2014.*

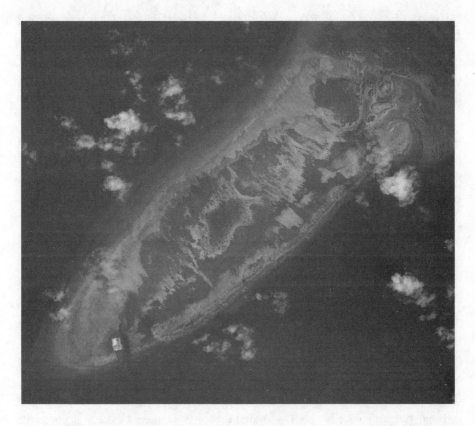

Chinese reclamation is now well underway on Fiery Cross, creating a landmass
9,800 feet long and nearly 1,000 feet wide, increasing the area elevenfold.

The neighbors have, of course, become furious—especially the Philippines, Vietnam, and Malaysia. Chinese naval forces had managed somehow to build naval bases as close as one hundred thirty miles from the Philippines in areas that were prime fishing territory, not to mention potentially valuable oil and gas fields. Fellow members of the Association of Southeast Asian Nations (ASEAN), Malaysia, Indonesia, and Brunei, felt equally threatened. But ASEAN has never been a military alliance, though it has been facing down a heavily armed and highly trained Chinese maritime force that has only been growing. By the late 1990s, these three ASEAN nations began holding joint military exercises in regions that extended into the southern Spratlys, with Chinese warships hovering around the periphery—just observing, for the moment.

Malaysia alone claims at least twelve of the components (rocks, shoals, atolls, or islands) of the Spratly Group and occupies five of them. James Shoal certainly lies within

Malaysia's EEZ and indeed it has names in each of the claimants' languages—Beting Serupai in Bahasa Malaysia or Zengmu Ansha in Chinese. All the features claimed by Malaysia are within China's U-shaped line. So, China has designated James Shoal—most of whose territory lies at least seventy feet below the ocean's surface and a thousand miles from mainland China—as the southernmost boundary of its nation. Chinese naval vessels have stopped at the shoal to reinforce this claim, and Malaysia hardly has the naval power to challenge China if it came to a direct confrontation. So far, it hasn't. China sees Malaysia as hardly worth spending any diplomatic or military capital on defying in a major confrontation. Moreover, China represents both the largest market for Malaysian exports and the largest supplier in terms of imports, two-way trade in 2017 totaling some $80 billion—hardly a figure that Malaysian officials would want to place in jeopardy.

About the only power laying claim to any part of the Spratlys that might be willing and able to challenge China is Vietnam. It has taken over Richard Spratly's prime discovery, what is called today Truong Sa Lon, its highest natural point being little more than eight feet above the waves. It has now been enveloped by a narrow, sandy beach and poured concrete wall topped by solar-powered floodlights and windmills and accompanied by antennae and satellite dishes—all this serviced by a military-grade runway able to accept flights from the mainland some three hundred miles to the northwest. It houses a small community, most of whose food must come from Vietnam by ship or plane. There's even a Buddhist pagoda. But there is also a formidable military presence of tanks, long-range guns, and a substantial garrison. Vietnam, too, has a red line around the few possessions it can still claim in the South China Sea. What it wants particularly from these possessions are the oil and gas that are believed to lie in the territorial waters around them. China, however, has hardly stood idly by. In 2011, a leading Chinese military official, Long Tao, believed to be pseudonym for Air Force Colonel Dai Xu, published an "opinion" piece in China's *Global Times*, warning "There are more than 1,000 oil and gas wells, plus four airports and numerous other facilities in the area, but none of them is built by China. Everything will be burned to the ground should a military conflict break out. Who'll suffer most when Western oil giants withdraw? But out there could just be an ideal place to punish them. Such punishment should be restricted only to the Philippines and Vietnam, who have been acting extremely aggressive these days." As for America's role in the region, "US pressure in the South China Sea should not be taken seriously, at least for now," he concluded.

Other parts of the Spratlys have been seized by other nations. China launched the process, laying claim in 1956 to the largest island, Itu Aba (or Taiping), when China was ruled by the Nationalists. It is still claimed by both the government of Taiwan and Beijing. With a four-thousand-foot runway completed in 2008, it is heavily fortified with heavy mortar and sea-gun emplacements. More recently, mainland China has managed to seize control of nine reefs in the Spratlys, but their ability to implant artificial structures has turned each of them into substantial, defensible islands, much to the consternation of a host of other nations whose mainland territories are located far closer or whose shipping must pass within range of heavily fortified bases. These Chinese islands are meant to withstand military attack, but especially to control the sea and shipping lanes that surround them. And all come with readily manufactured and utterly defensible red lines. The Philippines have taken over at least seven of the more substantial natural islands plus dozens of reefs and shoals, managing to hold onto them—for the moment. Some have at most just a handful of settlers or defenders. None could really withstand a determined Chinese effort to expel them and seize control: the total population of this group, known collectively as the Kalayaans was 184 in the official Philippine census of 2016.

—

Beijing is inclined to accept red lines that are barely pink provided they pose no threat to its broader priorities of dominance of the sea lanes and protecting the artificial islands it has implanted. What Beijing seems especially anxious to prevent is any concerted effort by all of the Southeast Asian nations from banding together with a unified policy toward the South China Sea and China's role in its strategic character. Hu Jintao, China's president for a decade, set the stage for an acceleration of its efforts to cement control of the South China Sea when, five months before the end of his rule, he told the landmark eighteenth Communist Party Congress in what was effectively his farewell address, that China's number one priority was to "Improve development of China's geographical space." This included a mandate to "enhance our capacity for exploiting marine resources, develop the marine economy, protect the marine ecological environment, resolutely safeguard China's maritime rights and interests, and build China into a maritime power." Fateful words. For embedded within them was the clear intent to build and defend a network of red lines across the South China Sea. It was at this same party congress that Xi Jinping was elected to serve a term that would ultimately be morphed into "president for life." And if there was anyone even more determined to enforce, even multiply these red lines in the interest of turning the South China Sea into his nation's backyard pool, it was Xi.

Chinese efforts at maintaining and legitimizing the red lines it alone has established have been a centerpiece of China's relationship with Southeast Asia and the ten member states of ASEAN since at least 2003, and in reality back to 1995 when China occupied the Spratly's Mischief Reef, long claimed by the Philippines, and first began drawing its own versions of today's red lines in the region. "As events transpired, differences among ASEAN states over how to manage territorial disputes in the South China Sea emerged as a litmus test of their ability to achieve an ASEAN Political-Security Community by 2015," observed Carlyle Thayer, a leading Australian military scholar. In a remarkable piece, punctuated by Thayer's access to the notes of one of the key participants, he details how China manipulated a critical summit of the ASEAN nations to arrive at what was effectively a "no-contest" conclusion that left China in all but total charge of the region, with no group of nations prepared to stand up against Beijing. "It is clear that Chinese influence played a major role," Thayer concluded, and to date, ASEAN has utterly failed to unite in opposition to Chinese expansion across the Spratlys, Paracels, and the seas that lie between and around these groups.

This has allowed China to treat all this territory as very much its personal property. On a Thursday afternoon, March 2, 2017, under bright, sunny skies and a balmy seventy-two degrees, a new luxury Chinese luxury cruise ship, the *Changle Princess* set sail from Sanya on the southern Chinese island of Hainan, bound on its maiden voyage to the Paracels. On board for the four-day voyage were 308 passengers, though the ship could hold 499 people in 82 guest suites, as well as entertainment, shopping, and medical and postal services. Their destination was three utterly disputed islands in the Crescent Group of the Paracels. It was all part of a much grander master plan for the mini-archipelago that would include hotels, villas, and shops, eventually turning many of these groups into a string of Maldives-style resorts, though no foreigners have yet been allowed to visit. The tour company said it also planned to expand its offerings to air tours, calculated only to irritate Vietnam even further, which nearly three decades earlier had already established its own red lines around the Paracels. Xiao Jie, mayor of Sansha on Hainan Island, which administers all disputed islands in the South China Sea, told the *South China Morning Post* that "one of our priorities is to strengthen our administrative authority starting from grassroots organizations," and that ten residential communities had been set up across the Paracels, including the largest, Woody Island, where a heavily armed Chinese military camp was already established.

The Hainan Provincial Marine Fishing Industry Group pulls no punches in describing its mission—"protecting sovereignty" and "emphasizing presence" in the South China Sea where Beijing has drawn its red lines that need protecting. "Grasp the principles of 'being both military and commercial, both soldiers and civilians, combining war and peacetime and civilian-military dual use' to organize a Spratly fisheries supply fleet," the Group's website proudly proclaims. "We will organize and drive the fishermen masses to go to the Spratlys on a large scale and open up new fishing grounds, 'catching government fish and casting nets of sovereignty' to display sovereignty and let the Chinese flag wave over waters in the Spratlys." Bold words, that very much throw down the gauntlet.

In April 2013, China's Ministry of National Defense had laid the basis for much of this colonization, producing a major white paper "Supporting National Economic and Social Development." When it came to the South China Sea, the paper was quite direct:

> China is a major maritime as well as land country. The seas and oceans provide immense space and abundant resources for China's sustainable development, and thus are of vital importance to the people's well being and China's future. It is an essential national development strategy to exploit, utilize and protect the seas and oceans, and build China into a maritime power. It is an important duty for the PLA [Peoples' Liberation Army] to resolutely safeguard China's maritime rights and interests. . . .
>
> With the gradual integration of China's economy into the world economic system, overseas interests have become an integral component of China's national interests. Security issues are increasingly prominent, involving overseas energy and resources, strategic sea lines of communication (SLOCs), and Chinese nationals and legal persons overseas.

This was implemented in May 2013 when the first "rights protection" expedition left the port of Baimajing on Hainan Island bound for the Spratlys. Some thirty one-hundred-ton trawlers, led by a four-thousand-ton command ship and fifteen-hundred-ton cargo ship set off on a forty-day swing through the Spratlys. Challenged at one point by a pair of Philippine patrol vessels, the Chinese apparently backed off without incident—the first of a host of ever-larger fishery operations with the dual purpose of asserting China's red line prerogatives.

With all this proceeding in seas so clearly claimed by the Philippines, President Benigno Aquino finally decided to put the entire question of just who had what rights to what property in the South China Sea to the ultimate arbiter—the Permanent Court of Arbitration in the Hague, operating under authority of UNCLOS, which both nations had ratified. The immediate question concerned Scarborough Shoal, most of whose rocks are visible barely six feet above the waves at high tide, surrounding a small lagoon. Both countries claimed Scarborough, but it lies just 150 miles west of the Philippines (well within its 200 miles EEZ), but more than 600 miles southeast of China. A remarkable photograph taken in 1997 shows Philippine congressman Roque Ablan and four companions planting a Philippine flag on a rock at the heart of Scarborough Shoal, which at low tide is scarcely large enough to allow all five to gain a foothold.

The defining claim over the red line China had built around Scarborough began on April 8, 2012, when a Philippine surveillance plane spotted eight Chinese fishing vessels circling in the vicinity of the reef. Dispatching one of its few serviceable ships, an obsolete US Coast Guard cutter renamed the *Gregorio del Pilar*, they found a huge haul of illegally taken and highly endangered giant clams, corals, and live sharks on board. Neither the surveillance plane nor officers on board the *Gregorio del Pilar* spotted Chinese Coast Guard ships nearby who descended on the scene to prevent the arrest of the fishermen. The ships from the two nations quickly squared off, the small Philippine contingent quickly outnumbered by the vastly larger number of Chinese vessels. Philippine authorities had quickly roped off the mouth of the huge C-shaped lagoon. Some Chinese fishermen were trapped inside the lagoon, then allowed to exit and were not permitted to return. Main force ships of the Chinese Navy meanwhile hovered just beyond the horizon as the standoff intensified. Philippine President Benigno Aquino was enraged. "At what point do you say, 'Enough is enough'?" Aquino asked *The New York Times*. "Well, the world has to say it—remember that the Sudetenland was given in an attempt to appease Hitler to prevent World War II." Yet again, the model of Neville Chamberlain's red line with Hitler is invoked in desperate circumstances. Aquino recognized how poorly that had been managed. For him, it was a genuine red line issue.

Aquino's first action was to fly to Washington to present his case in person to President Obama, pleading with his only major-power ally to send in the US Navy to defend his country's red line. But Obama was at that moment more interested in roping China firmly into talks for a global climate agreement that were beginning outside Paris. No red lines or small atolls half a world away would be allowed to derail these critical negotiations.

Aquino began to warn Asia and the world of the consequences of American inaction, again invoking Neville Chamberlain. "If the United States, which is the superpower, says 'We are not interested,' perhaps there is no brake to ambitions of other countries," Aquino warned during a visit to Japan. "If somebody said stop to Hitler at that point in time, or to Germany at that time, could we have avoided World War Two?" Aquino clearly recognized he was pushing against a locked door. Instead, during his visit he opened negotiations with Japan for the transfer of defense equipment and technology, which Prime Minister Shinzo Abe was eager to pursue in an effort to block China's more overt activities along some of his country's key shipping channels in the South and East China Seas.

Meanwhile, as the Hague panel began to deliberate, and China remained free to defend its red line, asserting its control over Scarborough Shoal all but unhindered. Early on in the dispute, it announced it would be carefully inspecting large shipments of Philippine bananas, rotting on Chinese docks, and began barring Chinese tourists from visiting the Philippines. It also began to emblazon the U-shaped line in every passport it issued, prompting the Philippines and Vietnam to announce they would no longer stamp their visas into any Chinese passport decorated with this map.

And, hardly surprising, China refused to participate in the complex proceedings of the Hague arbitration action that dragged on for more than three years. Finally, on July 12, 2016, the five-member panel issued its ruling—a blistering and all but total condemnation of China's activities across the region. The final ruling went far beyond the immediate case of Scarborough and was devastating in its apparent effort to sweep away every Chinese-imposed red line in the South China Sea.

There were two primary issues—China's expansive claim to sovereignty, and its construction, wherever it desired, of artificial islands, no matter the impact on fisheries, oil and gas exploration rights, or even free passage of ships. In each instance, the court utterly rejected every Chinese claim and action, beginning with its foundational claim that it enjoyed historical rights over this entire territory. Perhaps most immediately damaging were the tribune's findings that China had violated basic international law by establishing its own red lines, creating artificial islands on reefs and shoals, which the ruling observed, had done "irreparable harm" to the maritime environment. Not surprisingly, China both rejected the tribune's findings and reverted to its claim that the South China Sea had been its property "since ancient times." The tribunal's ruling "selectively strips the islands and reefs from the macro-geographical background of the South China Sea Islands and subjectively and imaginatively interprets and applies the [UNCLOS] Convention," the foreign ministry said. "China's territorial sovereignty and maritime rights in the South China Sea are not affected by arbitral awards under any circumstances."

The very evening of the Hague tribunal's decision, China's ruling State Council issued its reply. It began by enumerating "China's territorial sovereignty and maritime rights and interests in the South China Sea," listing the various island groups it expected the world to recognize, due to "the activities of the Chinese people in the South China Sea dat[ing] back to over 2,000 years ago . . . and the first to have exercised sovereignty and jurisdiction over them continuously, peacefully and effectively."

The day after the ruling, the first two passenger aircraft from state-owned China Southern and Hainan Airlines took off from Haikou on the northern side of Hainan

Island. One landed on Mischief Reef, an atoll surrounding a large lagoon 150 miles west of Palawan in the Philippines, well within its EEZ. The second landed on Subi Reef, barely fifteen miles southwest of Philippine-occupied Thitu Island. Both reefs were defended by Chinese anti-aircraft guns and close-in weapons systems to protect against strikes by cruise missiles, not to mention aircraft landing strips capable of supporting fighter aircraft. Many of the Chinese reefs and artificial islands were already being tied to the mainland by undersea fiber-optic cables and satellite uplink facilities.

Fiery Cross reef today, complete with military-grade air strip, radar, underground storage, and four hardened silos for missile launchers.

At the same time, China seems to be investing in the kinds of advanced new capabilities that will give it an important advantage in any challenges to the red lines it has erected. The authoritative SIPRI Military Expenditure Database points out that Chinese military outlays more than doubled in the decade ending in 2018, settling in at $239.2 billion, four times the level of India, sixty times the level of Vietnam, and seventy-five times the level of the Philippines. In the aggregate, China spent nearly twice as much on their defense as all of their South China Sea neighbors combined. Hardly surprising, since the South China Sea has become a major focus of China's military, much as Hu Jintao envisioned in his final months in office and as Xi Jinping has regularly asserted ever since. In April 2016, China's top military commander, General Fan Changlong, vice chairman of the Central Military Commission, out-ranked only by Chairman Xi, visited the Spratlys, the first visit ever paid by such a high-ranking officer. The purpose? "To offer good wishes to offices and personnel stationed there, and also to understand the construction of facilities on the islands," according to a brief Ministry of Defense statement.

Quietly, as it has been expanding dramatically across the South China Sea, China has also managed to construct the world's largest navy. The US Naval War College's analysis of the Chinese fleet lists more than 300 vessels, and the US Office of Naval Intelligence believes it will soon have 313 to 342 warships. As of August 2019, the current Navy Demographics Report showed 291 "deployable battle force ships." It also has one ex-Soviet aircraft carrier, is building two more, and is said to be planning five or six to be deployed by the start of the next decade. While in terms of aircraft carriers, this is fewer than the United States, it has not sought to deploy its naval resources globally. China's Coast Guard alone—the world's largest—has another 225 ships over 500 tons capable of operating throughout the South China Sea and more than 1,100 others confined to its coastal waters—outnumbering the coast guards of all its neighbors combined, including Japan's 80 ships and South Korea's 45.

By 2030, Andrew Erickson, of the US Naval War College in Newport, Rhode Island, one of America's leading experts in the Chinese navy, estimates that China's Coast Guard will have more than 1,300 ships, including 260 "monster" warships and two Zhaotou-class patrol ships—at 10,000 tons and 541 feet long, the world's largest. With a range of 15,000 nautical miles, each Zhaotou-class ship is capable of operating anywhere on the planet. The newest Zhaogao-class patrol ships are equipped with four diesel engines and four propeller shafts, able to reach top speeds nearing thirty knots with a range five thousand miles. Some of the smaller patrol boats can range up to ten thousand miles. Many are armed with thirty-millimeter and seventy-six-millimeter guns, smoke grenade launchers, and high-pressure water cannons. Some have helicopter decks as well. Most of the newest models have quick-launch boat ramps on their sterns that allow rapid launching and recovery of thirty-foot fast interceptor boats that can reach top speeds of fifty miles per hour to facilitate boarding, search, and seizure of target vessels or platforms.

In 2014, Vietnamese military ships challenged Chinese efforts to implant a major oil rig belonging to the China National Offshore Oil Corporation in the Paracels, which Vietnam claimed as part of its Exclusive Economic Zone. A flotilla of as many as 140 Chinese ships surrounded the oil rig, forming a circle as far as 10 miles out, hosing the bridges of the arriving Vietnamese vessels with water cannons, destroying navigational equipment and sending high powered water jets cascading down their exhaust funnels.

As a precautionary measure, China is believed to have stationed at least one interceptor boat at each of the South China Sea islands it has claimed or built. And in April 2019, it unveiled a stunning new armored amphibious drone boat called the "Marine Lizard" that can reach top speeds of fifty knots on water and twelve miles per hour on land and is expected to be deployed on some of the more remote South China Sea islands. At the same time, China has not hesitated to test, in full deployment conditions, some of its most advanced weapons in the heart of its red line network, which it has called its "blue territory." In June 2019, American defense intelligence officials reported that China was conducting a series of tests of advanced anti-ship ballistic missile systems it had deployed more than a year earlier on Fiery Cross, Subi, and Mischief Reefs.

There are thousands more vessels—reinforced fishing boats and trawlers—in the so-called maritime militia which enforces Chinese hegemony over the South China Sea, effectively serving as the day-to-day enforcement mechanism or trip wire for its network of red lines. In Congressional testimony, Erickson observed that "China—drawing on the world's largest fishing fleet—has deployed the world's largest Maritime Militia; and the only one charged with advancing disputed maritime claims. These Chinese 'Little Blue Men' are roughly equivalent at sea to Putin's 'Little Green Men' on land. . . . In recent years, it has used its Maritime Militia against civilian ships and crews of its immediate neighbors and the United States—with no direct public response from any of them. . . . These are state-organized, -developed, and -controlled forces operating under a direct military chain of command."

United Nations figures confirm China's maritime power—both civilian and military. It is the world's largest ship-owning nation, with 5,512 commercial ships over 1,000 gross tons. And this margin is only expected to widen. In 2018, China accounted for 41.6 percent of all shipbuilding tonnage under construction—nearly double the level of South Korea or Japan. Seven of the world's top ten cargo ports are in China. Of the world's top twenty container ports, eight are in China, only one (Los Angeles) is in the United States. As far as China is concerned, all of this—shipping, transit routes and ports—must be protected no matter what the cost. Erickson has estimated that each of China's three maritime forces—the regular navy, coast guard, and maritime police (or Maritime Law Enforcement)—has more ships than any of its counterparts, including the United States—a gap that will only widen going forward.

China's South China Sea fleet heads out for exercises—the aircraft carrier Liaoning *escorted by frigates and submarines.*

All this, of course, is just the immediate close-in challenge China has mounted to secure its red lines across the South and East China Seas. There is also the full-blown challenge of the Chinese navy, suddenly becoming for the first time in its history a true blue-water adversary. This means a robust complement of naval and maritime capabilities including cruise and ballistic missiles capable of mounting sustained and effective attacks against foreign bases and naval forces up to and including aircraft carrier battle groups and their support facilities from Okinawa to Guam, even Hawaii. Then, of course, there are space-based and cyber capabilities which China is mastering as well or better than most other nations. Even Chinese fishing boats, closely tied to naval and coast guard bases, are being equipped with highly effective satellite communications equipment useful for surveillance and reconnaissance purposes.

China has hardly been reluctant to make use of these resources, often in violation of any number of international treaties or standards of practice. Coast guard and militia ships have often been involved in cases of bumping, ramming, or shouldering out of the way, even turning water cannons on fishing, exploration, or cargo vessels of neighbors, particularly Vietnamese vessels, that crossed China's self-established red lines. Much of this is in utter violation of the 1972 Convention on the International Regulations for Preventing Collisions at Sea.

China has set forth in considerable detail the actions that just might trigger a "police response"—violations of its red lines, from its vast nine-dash line periphery (the bulk of the waters of the South China Sea) down to the narrower red lines around each of its claimed "properties." Such "violations" include "illegally" stopping at or anchoring near a Chinese-held island, conducting propaganda operations threatening Chinese security or hegemony, fishing, and of course putting down any roots including floating oil plat- forms or other means of exploiting resources that China considers its own. Any foreign ships (including American vessels) involved in such activities are potentially subject to being stopped, boarded, inspected, and having their crews detained. The vessels may be shouldered out of the way, forced to change course, or compelled to leave declared Chinese waters on penalty of having these ships seized and impounded.

———

For years, the US Navy has been examining potential responses to any such challenges posed by China that reverberate especially around the red lines it has drawn in the South China Sea. At the Office of Net Assessment (the Pentagon's internal think tank), the Center for Strategic and Budgetary Assessments, and the US Naval War College in Newport, Rhode Island, and its China Maritime Studies Institute, the Navy has been examining just how to deal resolutely with these Chinese red lines that are all contrary to established international law. Many of the potential responses take into account new and ever more advanced weaponry, with increasing reliability and lethality, that is being fielded by the Chinese military.

One set of Pentagon answers is included in the classified and unclassified versions of a white paper from the Air-Sea Battle Office called "Air Sea-Battle: Service Collaboration to Address Anti-Access & Area Denial Challenges." It begins most straightforwardly: "The Department of Defense recognizes the need to explore and develop options that will preserve U.S. ability to project power and maintain freedom of action in the global commons." Startlingly, the document contains not a single mention of "China," though it gets quickly to the heart of matter observing that "anti-access/area denial capabilities . . . challenge and threatened the ability for U.S. and allied forces to both get to the fight and to fight effectively while there."

In a separate document, Andrew Erickson ties this theme more directly to the Chinese challenge: "The United States has effectively defended its rights as a seafaring state. It has done so by operating wherever international law allows and daring Beijing to stop it." In short, the United States has refused to accept any of the red lines that China has erected outside the limits allowed under the UNCLOS convention. The question is how long the United States will be in a position to challenge these red lines in the face of an undeniable and explosive Chinese buildup. "U.S. policymakers should consider a more direct role for American sea power by empowering it to use nonlethal methods to defend allies' rights to use and administer waters that fall unambiguously under their jurisdiction. Doing so would involve greater risk of tension with China, but the risk is manageable and ultimately is a necessary element of any effective response to China's expansion." Already, the United States has lost considerable credibility throughout the region for its failure to stand up to China's bold, successful, and utterly determined efforts to implant itself firm on every likely or unlikely piece of real estate (even a rock, for that matter) in the South China Sea.

The Chinese have shown a most determined effort to enforce their red lines and their declared prerogatives across the region. Moreover, they have hardly been reluctant to employ any number of measures short of outright war in their efforts. China's activities have been among the most adroit and effective in patrolling red lines and an object lesson of how to carefully straddle the fine divides between war and peace that are inherent in so many red line scenarios. Effectively, Chinese warships and closely linked civilian activity in the South China Sea have marginalized or neutralized virtually every player on the other side of their carefully calibrated red lines, while assuring their domination within the "blue territories" delineated by these often virtual but no less clearly understood barriers.

Thus far, China has not sought to enforce the entire area of the South China Sea as its own national territory, though its more advanced naval and coast guard vessels certainly have the ability to deal with any vessel engaged in any manner of "violations." China has insisted in some international forums that it does believe in freedom of naval and air navigation across this territory. Blanket hegemony, however, does still hang like a sword of Damocles over the South China Sea, as it has hung inside each of the twelve-mile territorial limit red lines that China has established around each of its claimed islands, reefs, and atolls. In 2015, a Chinese official, speaking anonymously to a *Newsweek* reporter, singled out 209 land features that were still unoccupied in this region. "We could seize them all," he pointed out. "And we could build on them in 18 months."

The key question that remains is the viability of policing these red lines going forward. Clearly, China is moving rapidly to build a navy that is capable of enforcing its will virtually anywhere it wishes to establish it. In the meantime, the United States is continuing its regular surveillance missions over the entirety of the South China Sea and monitoring Chinese progress there. In May 2015, CNN's Jim Sciutto went along on an overflight of the three Spratly reefs—Subi, Mischief, and Fiery Cross—in an advanced P-8A Poseidon electronic surveillance plane. Replete with antennas, cones, and camera wells, and capable of being armed with Harpoon all-weather, over-the-horizon, anti-ship missiles and anti-submarine torpedoes, it was loaded for action. First pass was over Subi Reef, where more than two dozen Chinese dredges blanketed the internal lagoon, lifting huge plumes of sand from the ocean floor to build the artificial island that would hold an air field and a host of military installations. On the approach, a voice came over the radio relay, in Chinese-accented English proclaiming, "This is the Chinese Navy. This is the Chinese Navy. . . . Please leave immediately to avoid misunderstanding." The American pilot recited from his carefully prepared script that the US plane was traversing international airspace over international waters. The energy of the Chinese voice began to rise, ending in a screeched, "You go!" It was a warning repeated eight times until finally a nearby Delta Airlines pilot on the same frequency broke in to ask what was going on, ratcheting down the tension. Over Fiery Cross and Mischief, the approach was at an even lower altitude, diving to 15,000 feet. At times, the Chinese air force has been known to scramble fighters, even approaching dangerously close to the Poseidons. The only known collision came in 2001, when a Chinese jet collided with a Poseidon precursor, an EP-3E, over Hainan Island, with the American plane barely able to limp to a landing on Chinese territory. In every case, however, China continues to insist "its" islands are sovereign territory, despite the United States maintaining they are international waters and airspace.

Another central question is just how large China will see its global ambitions and how far it is prepared to extend its red line networks. It is increasingly expecting to be regarded as a major power, with all the perquisites accompanying such status—especially the ability to establish any red lines where it sees its interests lying and expecting that these lines will be respected without question, allowing itself a veto over all external activity that threatens any breach of its sovereignty.

As for its reach, there are already a host of Chinese deployments as far as the Indian Ocean and the Horn of Africa, operations in the Persian Gulf and Strait of Hormuz, and even the Mediterranean and the Baltic Seas—a couple of Chinese warships participating in a joint Chinese-Russian exercise in the Baltic Sea in 2017.

Sometimes known as the "string of pearls," China has invested in multiple efforts to build port and basing facilities along the entire periphery of the Indian Ocean, much as the United States sought to do in and around the Caribbean, effectively since the time of the Monroe Doctrine, its own *mare nostrum*. Already, China has financed shipping facilities in Hambantota, Sri Lanka, and a deep-water port in Gwadar, Pakistan, near the foot of the Persian Gulf. In Hambantota, Sri Lanka had little choice. It had racked up more than $8 billion worth of debts to China that it quickly found itself unable to service. So it signed over to China a 70 percent stake in the port on a ninety-nine year lease. Even more distant, China has established a base in Djibouti—a tiny nation barely the size of Vermont, but which occupies a strategic corner of Africa overlooking the Gulf of Aden, through which some 12.5 percent to 20 percent of global trade passes each year—much of it en route through the South China Sea. The United States military operates Camp Lemonnier in Djibouti with 4,000 personnel stationed in what the Navy describes as "the primary base of operations for US Africa Command in the Horn of Africa." As it happens, Camp Lemonnier is located not far from a new, massive, billion-dollar Doraleh Container Terminal complex that also includes roads and a hotel, all built by Dubai-based DP World, the mammoth owner and operator of ports and related facilities in nearly fifty countries. In 2017, China opened its first overseas military base next door. Several months later, armed Djibouti troops, without any warning, seized control of the DP World facility and claimed it for Djibouti's government, which quickly ceded it to Beijing. With 85 percent of its GDP committed to servicing its debt to China, there was little choice. And as soon as China implanted itself, a sharp red line went up around the facility.

China's activities increasingly far from home are not unlike the behavior of the United States and the United Kingdom in previous decades and in much the same type of locations. The island of Diego Garcia is in the heart of the Indian Ocean, commanding sea lanes where global shipping and aircraft carrier groups can take the shortest route to and from Asia. The largest of sixty islands in the Chagos Archipelago, it was transferred to the British after the Napoleonic Wars—until 1965 when it became the heart of the British Indian Ocean Territory (BIOT). The population then was barely nine hundred souls, mostly working coconut plantations—until they were summarily uprooted and moved to Mauritius and the Seychelles.

There, on Diego Garcia, Americans built their largest air and naval base east of Africa and west of Asia. In 1977, with a few colleagues, I became one of the few journalists to visit this facility barely a decade after it was opened. When I stepped off a C-135 transport after a ten-hour flight from Singapore, a very British officer with short khakis, a swagger stick, and an inkpad demanded my passport. He opened it, and promptly stamped it with the visa "BIOT—valid for one day." It was quite a day. The base was preparing to receive an entire aircraft carrier battle group at the single longest docking facility I'd ever seen. The island teemed with antennae, radar domes and other 1970s-vintage equipment that I suspect has been updated today. Beyond the military personnel, the only other living creatures were a herd of Sicilian donkeys, the feral dogs that had roamed the island having been ordered exterminated some years earlier. Diego Garcia was, effectively, a South China Sea island writ large—a template for future efforts by China to protect its own red lines and the territories where they believed the future security of their nation was most in jeopardy. Indeed, in 2010, at the peak of China's efforts to defend the entire South China Sea as its home waters, Britain established at Chagos a vast 210,000 square mile area, larger than the territory of the Spratlys and twice the size of the UK, enclosed by a red line—a Marine Protected Area (MPA), with Diego Garcia at its epicenter. Britain, on behalf of its American tenant, was asserting its sovereignty. The BBC observed at the time that "the conditions of the MPA are expected to be enforced by the territory's patrol vessel." Just like the Philippines, Mauritius took its case to the Permanent Court of Arbitration, which duly ruled against Britain. Unlike the Chinese, Britain said it actually accepted the decision—but rarely respected it. British warships continued to intercept fishing boats that entered the zone. The difference? Neither Britain nor the United States has sought to extend its operations or influence beyond this zone, nor build, new or artificial islands within it.

—

Essentially, China has been taking a leaf out of the Western, particularly the American, playbook dating back centuries. From its own over-the-horizon bases around the Indian Ocean and on the Persian Gulf, China has also been able to keep close guard over its security interests along global sea lanes and the tankers transporting oil to the homeland. These deterrent strategies were perhaps the single most challenging aspect of maintaining a red line regime without jeopardizing its image as a significant nation of international standing. Sadly, it is still not clear how any self-awareness, at least with respect to its military and diplomatic ability to influence actions of neighbors or perceived foes even in its own backyard, might be affected by its growing power and confidence. A deep understanding of the emergence of a new China by American or other Western forces anxious to protect free movement through China's red lines is essential if untoward surprises are to be avoided. In the Spratlys, China has been engaged for some time in what some analysts have called a "classical salami-slicing strategy." If each slice is thin enough, would you really notice that the salami (or tiny atolls in the South China Sea) were disappearing until suddenly, one day, they were all gone? The United States, acting as proxy or guarantor for any number of small, free nations with interests in and claims over these very territories, must understand just what it takes to prevent China from ever so gradually extending its red lines that it intends to defend. Until there is no longer a need for any red lines, China will simply control it all. This may be the ultimate denouement of red lines, cementing *de facto* control into *de jure* control beyond anyone's abilities to challenge them.

The United States has been far less clear than China in defining what it sees as that nation's overplaying its hand. Challenging such a red line regime also involves a clear understanding of how far America (with its allies) might be prepared to go to enforce what it sees as its mission in guarding against an overly aggressive or invasive Chinese maritime network. As Bruce M. Russett, the Dean Acheson Professor of Political Science at Yale and for thirty-seven years editor of *The Journal of Conflict Resolution*, one of the great scholars of deterrence, wrote in 1963:

> Deterrence fails when the attacker decides that the defender's threat is not likely to be fulfilled. In this sense it is equally a failure whether the defender really does intend to fight but is unable to communicate that intention to the attacker, or whether he is merely bluffing.

Apparently, China has been most successful in using its salami-slicing techniques to convey to the United States that its threat in any given location or moment in time is not likely to be fulfilled—or, for that matter, worth going to war over. Suddenly American and any number of Southeast Asian forces now find themselves utterly bound up in bright red lines that are metastasizing to a degree that even the most powerful is unable to break through, at least given the amount of force it is prepared to commit. After all, China's red lines could all be simply an elaborate bluff. Or not.

In reality, a number of asymmetric issues are at work here. America, from its birth, has been very much a seafaring nation. It was settled entirely by sea and is one of the rare nations on earth surrounded by three major seas (the Atlantic, Pacific, and Caribbean), over which it has sought to hold sway for centuries. Still, it would seem today that the United States is all too often thinking twice before risking any escalation over a simple water canon attack by a Chinese Coast Guard vessel on a Vietnamese oil platform, if at risk may be delicate trade talks between the two countries or a tightening of sanctions to contain North Korea's nuclear weapon program. In such a case, China may very well be in a position to take a few more slices off the salami, especially due to its proximity to potentially existential challenges.

In May 2017, the destroyer USS *Dewey* conducted a "freedom of navigation operation" maneuver inside the twelve-mile limit of Mischief Reef, where China had emplaced multiple military systems on the artificial island it had constructed. Two Chinese guided-missile-armed warships had warned the American vessel out of the area and were ignored. "The ship's actions demonstrated that Mischief Reef is not entitled to its own territorial sea regardless of whether an artificial island has been built on top of it," a US Navy official told Reuters. It was the first indication that President Trump had elected to break with President Obama and effectively draft his own set of red lines in the South China Sea, separate from those the Chinese believed had been tacitly accepted (by omission) for years. It was an arguably aggressive, dangerous, but likely essential maneuver. The image of a massive US destroyer operating freely in what settled law has established as international waters while Chinese warships hover on the horizon? Priceless. For if the United States won't stand up anywhere in the world for settled international law, let alone red lines some of its most loyal, and defenseless, allies are desperate to erase—then who will?

To put this in a deeply historical perspective, it is not unreasonable to equate China's South China Sea red lines with the those established by President James Monroe in 1823, when he enunciated the Monroe Doctrine—effectively drawing his own red line, or nine-dash line, around the entire Western Hemisphere—barring interlopers from asserting any unwanted hegemony, seizing territory, or planting their flag on territories inside that line. Today, in the South China Sea, the goal is for America to assure each of its allies that they are prepared to defend international law and custom and territorial integrity, which China, with its own maps, has sought to smash, while at the same time America is eschewing any territorial ambitions of its own.

Certainly, there are analogues with other red lines imposed or violated by other authoritarian powers. In in his confirmation hearing for secretary of state in January 2017, Rex Tillerson, grilled about the red line that Russia crossed in its seizure of Crimea, warned China equally that "your access to those islands will not be allowed." So far, China has not seen fit to tighten the nooses its red lines could represent to global shipping or even impede the movement of armed force across what it sees as its home waters. But its little blue men—an Asian analogue to the Kremlin's little green men—have certainly become omnipresent across the South China Sea. Both sides may simply have a credibility problem. The only difference is that China has assembled a powerful fortress, one small atoll at a time.

CHAPTER FIVE

From Soviet Union to Russian Empire

In Dominic, the small, dark but elegant restaurant with a world-class wine list on the fringe of Tallinn's medieval Old Town, two well-dressed Estonian gentlemen sat across from each other, whispering in Russian. One a cancer surgeon, the other an importer-exporter, they explained they were whispering because the Russian language—and all it represents—is hardly well-received in this Baltic nation that shares a 183-mile border with Russia, was once a vassal of the Soviet Union, and still sees an existential threat from across the frontier that has become among the world's most fraught, but least recognized, red lines. I first mentioned the two gentlemen in my CNN column that was headlined COULD WORLD WAR III START HERE? And my answer then, three days before Donald Trump was elected president four thousand miles away, was indeed it could. And that impression has only intensified since.

In my three-week swing through the three Baltic republics—Estonia, Latvia, and Lithuania—in the final weeks leading up to the 2016 elections, it was quite clear that the greatest fear, from the nations' leaders to the most humble workers, was what might happen if Trump did win the election—placing Vladimir Putin in an even more empowered position to work his will on their nations. For the Russian minority, however—those ethnic Russians who arrived as occupiers in the previous century and learned the language from their parents and grandparents—an even more empowered Kremlin is still not unwelcome, though the sentiment is a close-guarded secret to be discussed fervently in their own households and only rarely admitted to strangers who might strike up a casual conversation. Still, when a visitor manages to win a bit of their confidence, they are not unwilling to concede that they admire the Russian leader.

"He is strong," the cancer surgeon confides. "And he never tells us anything but the truth." Clearly a true believer.

The next morning, I drove out to the Tallinn airport to meet Marju Lauristin, Estonia's representative to the European Parliament, who was just returning from that body's latest session in Strasbourg. At a café in the airport terminal, until we were shooed outside by leather-booted Estonian troops responding to what turned out to be an ephemeral terrorism threat, Marju talked about her country's history with Russia. "We have been a neighbor of Russia not for one hundred years but one thousand years," Marju began. She understood profoundly just what those years meant to Estonia, as she put it, effectively enslaved so long by the nation that loomed over its history, culture, and the freedoms Estonians cherish but were rarely able to enjoy until the Soviet Union broke apart. Ironically, Marju comes from a family deeply enmeshed in Estonian Communism. Both her parents, Johannes and Olga, were leaders of the Communist Party of Estonia. It was the only real way to succeed in any tangible fashion in the Baltics of the Soviet era. Her fields were journalism and sociology, and she completed her doctorate in journalism at Moscow State University when Communism still held sway across the region. Her dissertation, focusing on content analysis of Russian newspaper texts, gave her a full-blown taste of the hypocrisy of the Soviet state and how it spoon-fed propaganda to its people. So, nursing her horror of this system for two decades, in 1988 she leapt at the chance to break the bonds that enslaved her and her people. Together with Edgar Savisaar and several colleagues, she launched Rahvarinne (the Popular Front in Support of Perestroika)—a mass popular movement that had attracted some sixty thousand members within weeks of its debut. In a year, its mission had morphed from an effort to build more autonomy within a still-functioning Soviet red line to agitation for full-blown independence. In 1989, marking the fiftieth anniversary of the Molotov-Ribbentrop Pact that aligned the Soviet Union with Nazi Germany, Marju was a leader of the Baltic Way, uniting the popular fronts of all three Baltic republics—each lusting for a total break from the Soviet empire and for full independence. On August 23, at 7 P.M. local time, nearly two million people joined hands for fifteen minutes to form what was then history's longest human chain—their own red line of sorts—spanning 420 miles across all three Baltic nations starting at Pikk Hermann in Tallinn's Old Town, winding through villages, up hills and down valleys, across three open frontiers, to its terminus at Gediminas' Tower in Vilnius, Lithuania. It was a stunning visual and emotional image for the Soviet Union, which promptly dismissed it as "nationalist hysteria." But within seven months, Lithuania became the first of the Baltic republics t o declare its freedom. By the end of 1991, all three had declared their independence, and Western nations recognized their emancipated status. Effectively the red line that the Soviet Union had built around Estonia, Latvia, and Lithuania had been replaced by a new one surrounding Russia, with the three new nations on the outside. Suddenly—with a single stroke—Russia had found itself on the other side of any number of red lines not of its own construction or mediation around the entire periphery of the Russian republic.

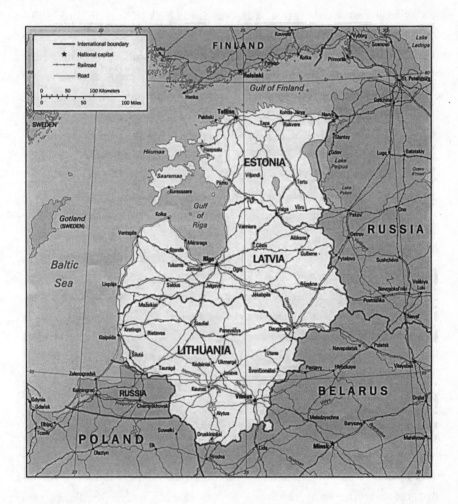

The three Baltic states of Estonia, Lithuania, and Latvia, in a fraught neighborhood.

How those red lines came to be established—snaking 183 miles along the frontier with Estonia, 141 miles along the Lithuanian frontier, and 133 miles with Latvia—is a lesson both in the morphology of red lines and the most sharply drawn possible contrast between democracy and autocracy. Marju was quite right in pointing out that there has been a thousand years of history in the boundary of her nation, and indeed all the Baltics, and Russia. In many respects, there is little in common between the three Baltic peoples. Estonians speak a language that is of the Finno-Ugric family, having more in common with the Finns to the north and west and Hungary. It has few links to the languages of Latvia and especially Lithuania, whose tongue is considered by linguists to be the oldest surviving Indo-European language with roots dating back to Sanskrit, thanks to vast migrations across northern Europe beginning in the thirteenth century B.C.E., or even earlier. The first inhabitants of the Baltics are believed to have arrived as early as 9,000 B.C.E., though the first written mention of an Estonian people dates to Tacitus in the first century C.E., who talked briefly of the Aestii in his landmark work *Germania*:

> The Suevic sea, on its eastern shore, washes the tribes of the Aestii, whose rites and fashions and style of dress are those of the Suevi while their language is more like the British. They worship the mother of the gods, and wear as a religious symbol the image of a wild boar. This serves as armor, and as a universal defense, rendering the votary of the goddess safe even amidst enemies. They often use clubs, but seldom iron weapons. They are more patient in cultivating corn and other produce than might be expected from the general indolence of the Germans. But they also search the deep, and are the only people who gather amber (which they call "glesum"), in the shallows, and also on the shore itself. Barbarians as they are they have not investigated or discovered what natural cause or process produces it. Nay, it even lay amid the sea's other refuse, till our luxury gave it a name. To them it is utterly useless; they gather it in its raw state, bring it to us in shapeless lumps, and marvel at the price which they receive.

At that point, there seemed to be more ties with the Germanic tribes to the west, some of whom overran their lands, than to the Russians. Indeed, much of the Baltics spent the ensuing millennium under Swedish rule as well as a succession of Polish rulers. Still, by the sixteenth century, "Muscovy" in the person of Czar Ivan the Terrible sought to take over some of these territories while the Grand Principality of Lithuania united with the Kingdom of Poland under the legendary Stefan Batory. The real turn for most of the Baltics, however, took place in the Great Northern War, a twenty-one-year holocaust that erupted in 1700 and continued in a succession of bloody battles punctuated by recurrent bouts of the plague that ran rampant through Swedish forces until the fall of Riga, Latvia, in 1710. By 1721, Russia had managed to emerge dominant across the

Baltics, and with the defeat of Sweden emerged as a new, major, pan-European power. But of greatest significance, Russia had managed to win its ultimate goal from this entire series of hostilities—one that still motivates it to this day: Russia gained critical strategic access to the Baltic Sea. For the next three centuries, similar drives to acquire access to seas led to the red lines Russia would attempt to impose or restore along many fringes of its empire—access to the sea, whether in the frozen reaches of the Baltic or a year-round, warm-water outlet through the Black Sea to the Mediterranean.

As the October Revolution of 1917 brought an end to imperial rule in Russia and the Versailles Treaty redrew the boundaries of Europe after World War I, the three Baltic republics, along with Finland, took the opportunity to declare their independence. Together, they formed the northern limits of what French Prime Minister Georges Clemenceau called his *cordon sanitaire*—Europe's longest red line rimming Bolshevik Russia from Romania on the south through Czechoslovakia, Hungary, Poland, and on to the Baltics in the north. All were nations created expressly for the purpose of containing Russia, but even more importantly, inoculating the rest of Europe from the spread westward of the scourge of Bolshevism. This red line or *cordon sanitaire* had only limited success. While it did certainly contain Lenin's armies from any western advance, it was somewhat more porous when it came to the ideology of Communism. Across Germany, France, and Italy, communist parties, of varying degree of loyalty to Moscow, took root and began to grow in the fertile soil of a deep economic depression that began in 1929 and spread across the continent.

At home, the Bolsheviks were at work expanding and cementing their own revolution, spreading it across any number of national fragments ignored by the mapmakers of Versailles, whose handiwork we will explore in even greater detail when we visit the Middle East and the disintegrating Ottoman Empire. Russia's civil war ended in various stages from 1920 to 1923 across what would become the Soviet Union, which gradually began to take form. In 1922, the Soviets won large territories of Belarus and Ukraine—an essential acquisition, since Ukraine has always been Russia's breadbasket. The Baltics managed, for the moment, to retain their independence. Armenia, Azerbaijan, Byelorussia, Ukraine, and Georgia all joined Russia with the creation of the Soviet Union in 1922. Eventually, between 1924 and 1936, the various 'Stans joined, spreading the Soviet Union across Central Asia.

During World War II, Soviet armies were able to overrun the Baltic republics and sweep up Moldova (Bessarabia), completing the final configuration of what should have been at least fifteen independent nations combined into a single autocracy. Instead of a multiplicity of red lines, there was one. Heavily patrolled by heavily armed troops and isolating the region's 8.65 million square miles and 293 million people from the outside world, this was the longest and most meticulously protected red line in history.

It took another seven decades and what was this time a bloodless revolution for this red line to be shattered with the collapse and dismemberment of the Soviet Union. In the 1970s, when my beat for *The New York Times* was the so-called "satellite nations" of Central and Eastern Europe, the Warsaw Pact monolith looked not unlike the "thousand-year Reich" at the peak of Hitler's power when he launched Operation Barbarossa, the catastrophic invasion of the Soviet Union in June 1941. The Soviet Union in the 1970s seemed equally invincible—utterly capable of enforcing the red line that Churchill had dubbed the Iron Curtain. But already the seeds of its destruction were being laid. There was much discontent on the fringes—the Hungarian Revolution of 1956 and the Prague Spring of 1968 were both brutally suppressed by Soviet armor as object lessons that their frontiers were not a red line to be trifled with.

During this period, Vladimir Putin was learning the value of red lines when they functioned according to their design and were properly policed and maintained. In East Germany, where he served mostly in Dresden, as a KGB agent, the Berlin Wall was an extension of the Iron Curtain red line that had been established a generation earlier at the February 1945 conference in Yalta between Franklin D. Roosevelt, Winston Churchill, and Joseph Stalin. The Yalta Conference was called to discuss the mechanisms of granting self-determination to the newly freed peoples of Nazi-controlled Europe. But the conference had really been undercut by an earlier conference in Moscow between Churchill and Stalin alone. Codenamed "Tolstoy," it would ultimately enable Stalin to establish the red line that was the Iron Curtain. Roosevelt was not present. The US ambassador to Moscow, Averell Harriman, hung around as an observer, along with the head of the American military mission in Moscow, General John Deane. British Foreign Secretary Anthony Eden and his Soviet counterpart, Vyacheslav Molotov, were also present. The official goal of the meeting was to set a timetable for Russia to enter the war in the Far East against Japan. But the most lasting and pernicious outcome was a casual gesture by Churchill. Stalin's price for sending his forces into war against Imperial Japan was a significant postwar role in the Balkans. Churchill seized a scrap of paper and scribbled on it what he was prepared to cede to Stalin: 90 percent of Romania, 10 percent of Greece, half of Yugoslavia, half of Hungary, and three-quarters of Bulgaria. Eden and Molotov had arrived at the percentages after some tendentious haggling, which Churchill approved when Stalin agreed that British troops could occupy Greece. Stalin reached over and put a blue checkmark on the paper and the deed was done. Poland was left up in the air—Churchill proposing a meeting between the London-based head of the Polish government-in-exile and the Soviets to fix his country's frontier. None of this, of course, meant very much at all after Soviet troops rolled through Poland, Hungary, Romania, and Bulgaria, while the Communist-inclined leader of Yugoslavia, Josip Broz Tito, seized power there. Boots on the ground were the device that established the red line the Soviet Union would defend for half a century. When I asked Milovan Djilas, a top counselor to Tito and later the leading Yugoslav dissident, about Tolstoy and its results, he sent me to his memoir, *Conversations with Stalin*, where he wrote: "This war is not as in the past: whoever occupies a territory also imposes on it his own social system. Everyone imposes his own system as far as his army can reach." Which really pretty much defines how so many red lines are in fact established and maintained, especially today.

Which is not to say that this Soviet red line was not tested by both sides on innumerable occasions since then. The Soviets wanted to extend its reach as much as the West, particularly the United States, wanted to shrink it. Berlin proved to be one of the earliest and most definitive tests of these aims. At the end of World War II, Germany was divided into four sectors—Soviet, American, British and French. While Berlin was situated one hundred miles deep within the Soviet zone, as the capital of Hitler's Germany it too was divided into four quarters. The allies quickly decided that the best course was simply to unify their three zones into a single West Germany and a single West Berlin. This vast, glittering metropolis was closely tied to a grim, dour, gray, Communist East Berlin. East Berliners, in those years before the actual wall went up between the sectors, were able to ride the U-Bahn freely into the West. It quickly became quite clear whose economic and social system was winning. The hyperinflated eastern Reichsmark was but a pale shadow of the powerful western Deutschemark that could buy so much more in the amply stocked markets and vibrant economy of the western sector. All this deeply rankled Stalin, who finally decided the only way to eradicate a pernicious, capitalist cancer deep within the territory that his red line had defined was simply to starve out the Western allies from their zone of West Berlin, ceding the entire city.

So, on June 15, 1948, Soviet authorities announced that the Autobahn, the one road linking West Berlin with West Germany, would be closed entirely and indefinitely for unspecified "repairs." On June 21, all barge traffic was halted, and rail traffic from the west two days later. The Allies would not be deterred. Nor did President Harry Truman want to provoke a war with the Soviet Union that could easily "go nuclear." Instead, as air corridors remained open, the Allies began a colossal effort to supply the entire city of West Berlin and its two million residents, by planes. On June 26, the first Air Force C-54 transport, followed by a succession of British Dakotas, Yorks, Sunderland Flying Boats, and Hastings landed four minutes apart, day and night at three Berlin airfields. On April 16, 1949, the peak was reached just before Easter when 12,940 tons of cargo arrive on 1,398 air sorties. Food, clothing, coal during the winter months, and medical supplies followed. On May 12, 1949, the Soviets finally admitted defeat and lifted the blockade, though it took until September for all supply routes by road, rail, and barge to return to normal. In all, some 2.4 million tons of supplies were delivered on 300,000 flights. But the airlift and Western activities only cemented Soviet determination to maintain a tight rein over their German territories. East Germany and its capital of East Berlin became the single most tightly controlled of Moscow's satellites—the Stasi, the most brutal and intrusive of the various police operations, assured conformity with Kremlin-established norms across eastern Europe in East Germany.

With the building of the Berlin Wall in 1961, the red line was firmly in place. Until then, at least in Berlin, it had been a line that was only barely pink. Each day, East Berliners crossed into the western sector to work, play, and attend sporting events and concerts that were banned in the austere precincts of the impoverished East. At the same time, West Berliners would cross into the East for cheap haircuts, clothes, and a variety of services that were a fraction of the price they were in the West. These contrasts led to a constant drain of East Berliners who decided to flee, fed up with the little Communism seemed to offer. Eventually, some 15 percent of the population left, never to return, a tide whose pace only swelled. In the first seven months of 1961, over 150,000 made the one-way trip. Finally, the Soviets were moved to action. Truman had demonstrated that he would not let go of West Berlin. But there were other means of securing this porous red line. Late in the evening of August 12, 1961, swarms of VoPos, the East Berlin police, descended on the entire length of the border, sealing it with twenty-five miles worth of carefully stockpiled barbed wire. The U-Bahn metro was frozen. Residents of apartments located along the wall threw themselves out of windows in frantic efforts to reach a West from which they suddenly realized they were being excluded forever. As dawn arrived on August 13, the border was complete. Within weeks, the first concrete slabs began moving into place. By 1965 it had become a fortress and by the time I first traversed it twenty years later, vast interlocking segments of steel and concrete were firmly implanted. The frontier of the rest of East Germany was similarly reinforced, punctuated by some three hundred watch towers, anti-vehicle ditches, and concrete bunkers—all patrolled by hundreds of dogs and a force of ten thousand heavily armed guards.

By 1984, during my first and only penetration of the Berlin Wall, it had reached its powerful and intimidating apex. The only authorized entry through that fortress the Soviets had erected was at Checkpoint Charlie—the third letter in the phonetic NATO alphabet (entries to East Germany named Alpha and Bravo were located along the Autobahn). I went through Charlie with a CBS television crew and producer to meet an East German "handler," likely an agent of the Stasi. We'd been given permission to shoot one of the many showcases of East German progress, under careful escort. At the end of our day, I gathered the videotape cassettes. I was to head back to the western side so that I could begin writing the script and prepare the piece for transmission that evening for the CBS Evening News. I didn't think much of what was ahead as I entered the wall through a large metal gate that clanged behind me. It's essential to understand what this red line, or wall, comprised. A simple barbed wire fence had morphed into a true fortress. The path through the wall wound down heavily armored, windowless corridors. There were East German border police throughout. To make certain that total control could be exercised, the complex was built entirely on East Berlin ground. It occurred to me only after the gate had closed behind me that there was no way for me to get any word to the outside world. In those days there were no cell phones—not that any would have worked inside this metal tomb. The cassettes also could easily have been seized, and I had no "minder" to reassure the guards I was an official guest of the German Democratic Republic (GDR)—Communist East Germany. So, when I came upon the first checkpoint, I must have looked panicked and utterly guilty to the grim-faced border agent who examined my American passport with suspicion, then turned with it still in hand and walked behind a mirrored door. After an interminable moment, he reappeared. No smile. He handed it back to me and gestured with an outstretched arm to another door, which I opened and walked through into the bright lights and chattering crowds of a West Berlin evening.

Few East Germans ever had that opportunity. But that is not to say they did not know what life was like on the other side of this red line. West German television and radio was easily captured in apartments in the eastern sector, though consumed only with dark-drawn curtains and the volume lowered to a whisper to make sure that no neighboring informants for the Stasi could eavesdrop, leading to a quick and frightening trip to a concentration camp.

In August 1978, I visited another point along the Soviet-controlled red line just west of the village of Szombathely, less than ten miles from the Hungarian frontier with the free state of Austria. Along the border were tall guard posts spaced closely enough so each could see the next one in line. Every morning, a broad swath of care-fully groomed earth along the entire border was carefully raked so that footprints of anyone foolhardy enough to have sought an escape across the tall barbed wire frontier would be clearly visible. In the gymnasium of the local teachers' college, a few students wandered in. I asked them if they read the local newspaper. Religiously, every day they assured me. But not for its Communist propaganda. Recently it had begun printing lists of the programs on Austrian television. The red line was becoming dangerously porous. What tanks or armored cars could not pierce, ideas could.

Quietly, this was the case along much of the red line that separated east from west in Europe. Increasingly, the mechanism the Kremlin had erected at the borders was being tested in a myriad of fashions. Vladimir Putin, to his credit, learned firsthand just how such red lines might or might not function. Putin had worked in the KGB for ten years, learning German at university before he was posted to the German Democratic Republic. He was based in Dresden and lived in a building that housed the Stasi. "The work was political intelligence," he would say later, "obtaining information about political figures and the plans of potential opponents." Materially, life was better in Dresden than in Moscow where "there were lines and shortages, and in the GDR there was always plenty of everything," his ex-wife Lyudmila later told an interviewer. "Four years passed, and in four years a foreign country and a foreign city can become almost like your own. When the Berlin Wall fell and it was clear this was the end, we had the horrible feeling that the country that had almost become our home would no longer exist." When this happened, Putin and his fellow agents, as described, "destroyed everything, all our communications, our lists of contacts and our agents' networks." Then he continued:

I personally burned a huge amount of material. We burned so much stuff that the furnace burst. We burned papers night and day. All the most valuable items were hauled away to Moscow. But it no longer meant anything in terms of operations. All of the contacts were cut off. Work with the information sources was stopped for security reasons. The materials were destroyed or sent into the archives. Amen!

In 1989, when they began to break into the directorate of the Ministry of Security in the GDR, we were afraid they would come for us, too. I stood in the crowd and watched it happen. People were breaking into the Ministry of Security (MGB). . . . I understood those people—they were tired of being watched by the MGB, especially because the surveillance was so totally inva-sive. They saw the MGB as a monster. But the MGB was also part of society. It was infected with the same sicknesses. There were all kinds of people who worked there, but the people I knew were decent people. I was friends with many of them, and I think that the way they are now being castigated isn't right. . . .

I called our group of forces and explained the situation. And I was told: "We cannot do anything without orders from Moscow. And Moscow is silent." After a few hours, our military people did finally get there. And the crowd dispersed. But that business of "Moscow is silent"—I got the feeling then that the country no longer existed. That it had disappeared. It was clear that the Soviet Union was ailing. And it had a terminal disease without a cure—a paralysis of power.

In a sense, the GDR was a real eye-opener for me. I thought I was going to an Eastern European country, to the center of Europe. It was already the end of the 1980s. And suddenly, when I talked with people from the MGB, I realized that both they themselves and the GDR were going through something the Soviet Union had gone through many years before.

It was hard to imagine that such abrupt changes could take hold in the GDR. No one could have ever imagined it! And we didn't know how it would end.

Putin, one of the few world leaders with direct, personal up-front contact with red lines and their consequences, believed deeply in the Soviet myth. "Whoever does not miss the Soviet Union has no heart," he was fond of saying. But then, ever the realist he quickly qualified that by adding, "whoever wants it back has no brain." Still, since assuming power, he seems to have behaved as if his life's mission would be to reassemble it again as best he could. When he served as deputy mayor of St. Petersburg, he hung proudly on the wall a portrait of Peter the Great, whose command of an entire, unitary Russian empire he openly avowed to have admired. This would, of course, mean a substantial redrawing of decades-old red lines—albeit with often catastrophic results.

Red lines of varying shades and traits—real or illusory, threatening or anodyne—have long existed between Russia and many of the nations with which this nation shares frontiers spanning eleven time zones. From the very moment the transition began from a monolithic Soviet Union into a splintered collection of fifteen independent republics (and two contested locations—Chechnya, officially the Chechen Republic, and the disputed territory of Nagorno-Karabakh), each has been a subject of metastable red lines of their own, often defining a discrete, often tense, at times deeply subservient relationship with the mothership, the Russian Federation.

With most of the former Warsaw Pact nations of Eastern Europe, plus such former Soviet republics as Estonia, Latvia, and Lithuania, all joining NATO, Article Five of the NATO treaty presents both a challenge and a barrier to Russia's twenty-first century ambitions. This article provides that an attack on one NATO member is an attack on all. Not surprisingly, Vladimir Putin has chosen to test the West's resolves only at the margins. He has not yet tested Article Five. But across other red lines that define Russia's borders, he has not hesitated to mount some quite muscular challenges.

For more than a decade after the dissolution of the Soviet Union, the new frontiers Russia shared with many of its former republics remained largely untested as Putin seized, then cemented, power of his own within the new Russian Federation. While his predecessor, Boris Yeltsin managed in his own fashion to bring many of the former Soviet states back together into an organization known as the Commonwealth of Independent States, Putin used it to his own purposes, recognizing it, no doubt, as somewhat of an oxymoron. At least nine of them were ruled by despots that served as utter toadies to Putin, who had wisely left them pretty much alone to rape and pillage their nations in the name of "democracy." Russia, in turn, guaranteed it would establish and maintain red lines of security enveloping each of their nations that the Kremlin would police, provided their leaders toed lines of ideological purity and supplied what Russia needed in terms of trade, labor, raw materials, and food. At times, this even meant forced labor bordering on slavery, as has routinely been the case with Uzbekistan and its efforts to mobilize more than a million workers, some as young as eleven years old, to harvest its vast cotton crop, much of it for consumption in Russia.

By the early twenty-first century, with oil prices soaring and the rising power Russia derived from its newfound petro-wealth, Putin began to envision testing some of the red lines that had been so carefully crafted by him, but especially those he saw erected against his interests. The first was with Estonia. In April 2007, the Estonian government had the temerity to remove a World War II–vintage Soviet memorial known as *The Bronze Soldier of Tallinn*, whose original name was *Monument to the Liberators of Tallinn*, from its long-standing location in a small park, known in Soviet days as "Liberator Square," in the center of the Estonian capital on the site of several Russian war graves. The monument consisted of a six-and-a-half-foot tall bronze statue of a soldier in a Soviet Red Army uniform surrounded by a stone wall of dolomite. The entire monument was seen by the nation's more than one million native Estonians as an affront to Estonia and a tribute to a half century of Soviet "occupation" by troops that the monument characterized as "liberators." Nazi troops had largely withdrawn from the country before Soviet forces even entered Tallinn and seized it, and a flag of an independent Estonia had been clearly flying over the capital. To the three hundred thousand ethnic Russians who still lived there, however, this war memorial still represented all Soviet soldiers everywhere who'd given their lives fighting for their country. So, in an effort to avoid any outburst, before dawn on April 26, the entire memorial and its graves were quietly uprooted and moved into storage in preparation for a transfer to the Tallinn Military Cemetery on the outskirts of the city. There, it was restored to an earlier name: *Monument to the Fallen in the Second World War*. When Estonia's Russian population awoke to the disappearance of their beloved monument, they took to the streets. As western reporters described it, "violent clashes" broke out. "Demonstrators threw rocks and bottles at the police, who responded with stun grenades. One man was stabbed to death and at least 12 police officers and 44 protesters were injured. Around 300 people were arrested amid widespread vandalism and looting in the worst riots since Estonia declared its independence from the Soviet Union in 1991," one observer reported. The Russian foreign ministry quickly weighed in, with spokesman Mikhail Kamynin, later ambassador to Portugal and Cuba, describing "the actions of official Tallinn as sacrilegious and inhuman." A member of the Russian parliament even suggested that this could be cause for war. Would Estonia's red line hold?

Putin was not happy by what he saw as a clear slight. His foreign minister, Sergei Lavrov, warned darkly that Russia could move against its tiny, but apparently quite independent, neighbor. "We must react without hysteria but also take serious steps which would demonstrate our true attitude to this inhuman action," Lavrov added. That didn't take long.

Russia was clearly locked and loaded. On April 27, a viciously coordinated series of attacks whipsawed the entire Internet system of a nation that was among the world's most highly networked. An after-conflict report from the NATO Cooperative Cyber Defence Centre of Excellence, which happens to be located in an old brick fortress on the fringes of downtown Tallinn, described the actions:

> They were unparalleled in size and variety compared to a country the size of Estonia. . . . A wide scale attack on the availability of public digital services has a significant effect on the way of life of ordinary citizens and businesses alike. Therefore, these cyber attacks can not be disregarded as mere annoyances but should be considered a threat to national security.

The barrage continued for twenty-two days. The NATO report observed that the "malicious traffic often contained clear indications of political motivation and a clear indication of Russian language background." It pointed to malware lines of code that included *ANSIP_PIDOR=FASCIST.* Pidor was the name of the Estonian prime minister and his personal website and e-mail that were all but totally shut down by the massive DDoS (Distributed Denial of Service) attacks by the Russian "invaders." For that was precisely the nature and intent of the Russian cyber operation. Effectively it comprised a three-week electronic carpet-bombing of an entire nation. The campaign had breached what Estonians and other Balkan leaders believed was an utterly unbreachable red line, but without any of the consequences of a conventional armored assault across the frontier that might have led to a united NATO military response. Estonia, as a full member of the alliance, was sheltered under the Article Five umbrella. In this fashion, the Baltics' red lines were unique with respect to those that surround the rest of the Russian Federation.

NATO's "principle of collective defense" was invoked for the only time in its history after the 9/11 terrorist attack. As a result, NATO forces became heavily involved in the invasion of Afghanistan to root out al Qaeda and the Taliban who shielded them. But in the case of Estonia, which had joined NATO only three years before the Russian cyber onslaught, Article Five was not invoked.

But there were also other, softer underbellies neighboring the Russian Federation where Putin might strike in his effort to expand the Russian red line and seek to reestablish a semblance of the old Soviet Union.

———

Late in the night of August 7, 2008, and into the pre-dawn hours of August 8, Georgian forces launched an extensive artillery barrage centered on the village of Tskhinvali in the province of South Ossetia. Russian forces had already quietly infiltrated the Russo-Georgian frontier and advanced into South Ossetia, coming to the aid of South Ossetian irregulars who'd begun shelling Georgian villagers. It was a dangerous and fraught moment that ultimately tilted into the first full-scale shooting war in Europe in the twenty-first century.

The roots of this exchange had been growing for nearly two decades since a strong red line went up between Georgia and Russia with the disintegration of the Soviet Union. In fact, however, Georgia itself has had a long and proud history of its own, utterly distinct from Russia, even before it first embraced the kingdom of Georgia at the turn of the nineteenth century. The first traces of mankind appeared in this region in the Paleolithic era, while the world's oldest wine jars, dating back some 8,000 years, suggest that wine was being produced there by Georgians of the Neolithic period. Romans and Greeks made their way to Georgia, said to be the site of the Golden Fleece sought by Jason and the Argonauts, from the region's western stretches neighboring the Black Sea. Indeed, it is this location, commanding a stretch of the eastern shore that has long made it attractive to Russians who were also seeking warm water ports in Crimea and southeastern Ukraine. Early converts to Christianity, Georgians were subject to Muslim invaders by the seventh century, while further centuries of internecine warfare split the region. The Kingdom of Abkhazia assumed dominance in the early Middle Ages, to be succeeded by the Kingdom of Georgia during what became known as the Georgian Renaissance. Art, architecture, and literature flourished, including the writing of the poem *The Knight in the Panther's Skin*, a national epic that still is part of a dowry of many traditional Georgian brides. Eventually, a succession of invasions—beginning with the Mongols, concluding with Tamerlane and eventually a succession of Persian rulers—led to the kingdom fragmenting into a collection of tiny kingdoms and principalities. By 1801, Russia had pledged to take Georgia as a protectorate, but wound up simply seizing much of the territory after driving off Iranian forces in the nine-year-long Russo-Persian War. The rest of Georgia was eventually absorbed into imperial Russia in the course of the nineteenth century.

Georgia had a brief flirtation with independence after the collapse of imperial Russia during the Russian Revolution. But by February 1921, the Red Army, rolling south in the civil war that brought the Soviet Union into existence, swept into the Georgian capital of Tbilisi. In 1922, it was incorporated into the nascent Soviet Union. Stalin was a proud Georgian, but following his death in 1953, the republic's Communist leadership spiraled into blatant corruption and cruel belligerence toward its people. Not surprisingly, in the late 1980s Georgia became one of the first of the Soviet republics to agitate for independence. Once won, this quickly turned into answered prayers as Russia seemed most reluctant to let go. Georgia declared its full independence from Russia on April 9, 1991. But serious questions remained, ones unlike the issues surrounding most of the Soviet republics that largely picked up where Communism left off, including rule by the same corrupt and autocratic sovereigns. Georgia faced other, more existential issues. Just what was Georgia, what comprised its borders, and what red lines would be established and defended by the fledgling Georgian military force against Russian pressure?

The central issues revolved around the two provinces of Abkhazia and South Ossetia—both at various times in the long history of Georgia, dating back to the kingdoms, part of or independent from the remainder of the territory. Under the Soviets, they were quasi-independent "oblasts," or administrative districts. So where would they come to rest, once the parts split up? In fact, today's Georgia is a stewpot, with more than eighty ethnic groups living within its boundaries. Abkhaz and South Ossetians are among the largest of these groups, and are generally confined to their own narrow regions. When the Soviet Union broke apart, many wanted to remain within the new, core Russian Federation, fearing their rights and distinct heritages would be trampled by the majority Georgians. North Ossetia, the ethnic group's real historic homeland, achieved and remains a semi-autonomous republic of Russia. But when Georgia achieved a real independent status, it took along with it both Abkhazia and South Ossetia, and despite often armed resistance, succeeded in incorporating both regions into the nation ruled by Georgians from Tbilisi. An implicit, but quite clear, red line was then drawn between Russia and the at least tenuously united nation of Georgia. There was a degree of peace during the eleven-year rule of Eduard Shevardnadze, the former foreign minister of the USSR but an ethnic Georgian. Yet there were some violent interludes, especially in 1993 when the Abkhaz rebelled and three hundred thousand Georgians were forced to flee to Georgia from Abkhazia, while in South Ossetia a hundred thousand Ossetians fled north into North Ossetia.

An uneasy red line between Russia and Georgia held for more than a decade, policed by various international agreements and United Nations resolutions. But with the replacement of Shevardnadze in 2004 by a new, thirty-seven-year-old, liberal, pro-Western president, Mikheil Saakashvili, Russia began to grow uneasy. Suddenly, the Kremlin feared the arrival of NATO and a new red line that conformed more to NATO norms than to Russian, as it had seen on its northern boundaries with the new Baltic states. Not to mention Article Five. Vladimir Putin feared another former Soviet republic slipping from his goal of reassembling the empire.

It took four more years, though, for it all to come apart—which it did in April 2008. The trigger, as with so many such red line conflicts, was an apparently trivial incident—a Georgian unarmed drone shot down over Abkhazia, not far from the Russian frontier. The Georgian defense ministry released a video the next day which appeared to show a Russian MiG-29 downing the drone. The Kremlin promptly issued a denial, in turn accusing Georgia of violating the decade-old ceasefire agreement and UN resolution by flying a drone across this red line in the first place. The issue scaled up quickly as Russia beefed up the troops it maintained in the UN peacekeeping force in Abkhazia and more Georgian drones were downed. On August 8, Georgian troops moved in force on Abkhazia, while Russian forces poured into Abkhazia and South Ossetia. For four days pitched battles opened on land, sea, and air, with Russian naval vessels beating back forces of the Georgian Navy in the Black Sea and Russian bombers striking deep into Georgia. Finally, breaking a ceasefire, Russian columns moved into the heart of Georgia, taking the cities of Poti and Gori without a fight as the Georgian military fell back to defend the capital, Tbilisi.

Viewing this as very much a European conflict, French president Nicolas Sarkozy, as president of the European Union, stepped in to negotiate a ceasefire on August 12. Backed by Russian forces, however, South Ossetian irregulars embarked on a program of ethnic cleansing of Georgians from many of their villages. On August 26, Russia recognized the independence of Abkhazia and South Ossetia, and began withdrawal of its forces from Georgia. Only five countries—Russia, Venezuela, Nicaragua, Nauru, and Syria—recognized Abkhazia or South Ossetia, all effectively quid pro quos with Russia to whom each looked for civilian or military aid. The international community still refers to these red lines as "Administration Boundary Lines."

And the problems really began in 2015 when South Ossetians, with the encouragement of their Russian patrons, began grabbing land that was actually Georgian territory. The Ossetians believed they were merely clarifying and consolidating ancestral borders, but it really came down concretely to the maps of the region. Farmers had been using old tax maps, while most maps in Georgia were drawn by Soviet General Staff cartographers dating to World War II and were of questionable reliability themselves. All too often, the Georgian farmers would stray into territory of Russian-occupied South Ossetia. Moreover, since the Georgian government never recognized a separate South Ossetia, there was no real way to negotiate a defined and stable red line that would serve as a frontier. John Durnin, the longtime spokesman for the European Union Monitoring Mission (EUMM) in Georgia, still on duty more than a decade after hostilities, e-mailed me in mid-2019:

> This led to a great deal of public unrest because farmers felt that their land was being "grabbed" by the Russian FSB troops [successors to the KGB] on behalf of the South Ossetian authorities. The latter claimed they were merely clarifying a situation that already existed. However, the situation led to a major crisis at a national (and even international) level when not only were actual farms and homesteads being divided, but the Green Signs which marked the "border" were placed within 400 meters of the main highway which crosses east-west across Georgia, south of the village of Khurvaleti, in the Orchosani-Tsitelubani area; and simultaneously "grabbed" part of the BP Baku-Supsa oil pipeline which also crosses Georgia.

> The EUMM's view at the time, and I am sure still is, that the Russian policy of "borderisation" creates obstacles to freedom of movement and the livelihoods of the local population.

Indeed, the day after Russia became the first power to recognize the breakaway territories as nations, Swedish foreign minister Carl Bildt told the *Financial Times*: "South Ossetian independence is a joke. We are talking about a smuggler's paradise of 60,000 people financed by the Russian security services. No one can seriously consider that as an independent state." But even more importantly, Bildt observed that Russia was "opening up a Pandora's box of questions that will be extremely difficult to answer. If you are interested in the stability of the Caucasus—and Russia is more interested in that than anyone else—you should be very careful with borders. . . . They have fought two wars in Chechnya."

A year after the hot-war conflict, the European Union published a three-volume study by its Independent International Fact-Finding Mission on the Conflict in Georgia. None of its researchers were either Russian or Georgian. It was "the first fact-finding mission of its kind in the history of the EU," the report began. After spending some time detailing the roots and the battle itself, the EU observed, "Both South Ossetians and Abkhaz consider their right to self-determination as the legal basis for their quest for sovereignty and independence of the respective territories. However, international law does not recognize a right to unilaterally create a new state based on the principle of self-determination outside the colonial context and apartheid."

The report demonstrates quite convincingly that there were repeated violations of human rights by military forces, largely of the Russian federation, along with Abkhaz and South Ossetian irregulars. Bordering at times on genocide, the conflict certainly involved ethnic cleansing as all sides sought to reorder their territories, often putting tens of thousands on the road to regions far from their long-standing homes. But this has little to do with the question of any respect for or defense of red lines. When red lines are established to defend or support ethnic, religious, even tribal interests, there will inevitably be abuses that transcend any concrete geopolitical, diplomatic, or military motive for establishing the lines in the first place. Indeed, the European report points out that "[t]here is a clear need to address the current human rights/discrimination issues following the conflict in conjunction with the previously existing human rights concerns, many of them related to the conflict in the 1990s. It is critical to adopt a comprehensive approach in order for the settlement of those issues to be part of a lasting solution." But such human rights issues have hardly subsumed the basic reality of ill-conceived boundaries maintained in poor faith.

What Russia sought to do once the hot war had morphed into a quasi-stable armistice was simply to redraw the red lines of the region to its own advantage and then seek to defend them—politically, diplomatically, even at times militarily. It was and remains an approach virtually unique to the Putin model of international law and relationships. In practice, this simply overlays the red lines established and recognized by the rest of the world with consequences that Russia, as we shall see when we turn to Crimea and Ukraine, may transcend in the value of the territory or concept being defended.

As to just what a red line looks like in this remote part of the world, it would be useful to turn to the experience of two Columbia researchers from the Harriman Institute, each fluent in Russian, if not Abkhaz, who in 2010, I, as editor of *World Policy Journal*, sent across what existed of the frontier between Georgia and Abkhazia. Alexander Cooley and Lincoln Mitchell headed out by car from Tbilisi to Abkhazia and eventually came to the border:

> At the [Georgian] checkpoint, Gocha, our dependable and easygoing driver, heads back to Zugdidi, the nearest city on the Georgian side. We walk 200 yards towards the guards, carrying our passports and a printout of a permit to visit Abkhazia, secured through a visa agency in Toronto. The Georgian soldiers take a cursory glance at our passports before waving us through. They're chatting in Mingrelian, a west-Georgian dialect. We set off up the road towards the Abkhaz checkpoint and after about half-a-mile we find two more Georgian Russians; we continue. A bedraggled donkey stands hitched to a jerry-rigged cart. The cart is built from discarded farm equipment and the wheels of an old Soviet Lada sedan. A few feet away sits the driver, anxiously waiting to make a few rubles ferrying travelers across this no man's land between the checkpoints. We turn down the donkey cart and walk over a concrete bridge designed for truck traffic. Spanning the scenic Inguri River, it marks the boundary of the breakaway territory. The bridge is pock-marked and full of deep puddles. It has had few repairs since the USSR collapsed.
>
> On the Abkhaz side, the checkpoint consists of a series of rundown shacks surrounded by a few kiosks selling cigarettes, water and liquor. There's an empty restaurant that smells of barbecued meat. Though the checkpoint is manned by Abkhaz troops, there is no question who is in charge here. A substantial Russian military camp lies a few hundred yards away, a Russian flag flying over the entrance, just a few feet from a large election campaign billboard promoting the presidential candidacy of Sergei Bagapsh, Abhkazia's recently reelected leader.

A minor clerical error by the visa agency in Toronto threatens to destroy our plans and force us to turn back, but the Abkhaz soldiers make a few calls to our contacts in Sukhumi and tell us to wait. We can't call because Georgian cell phones don't reach Abkhaz territory, presumably because they are being jammed by Russia, or Georgia, or both. We settle in, eating energy bars and sipping water. From our previous trip to Abkhazia we learned to bring our own food—there are few stores and restaurants, even in the capital.

At least 100 people pass in both directions. All are locals, ethnic Georgians who live in southern Abkhazia. In the decades since conflicts began, Abkhaz leadership has allowed about 30,000 Georgian residents from border villages around Gali to return to their homes. The Georgians refer to them as "spontaneous returns." Most have roots in Gali, but friends in Georgia. We watch them carry large bags of goods, presumably taking advantage of the trade opportunities on either side. Taxis and Abkhaz *martshutkas*, the local minibuses, wait at the checkpoint and gradually fill up before departing for points further into Abkhazia. One smiling taxi driver approaches every 10 minutes, reminding us that if our ride doesn't come he would gladly take us to Sukhumi.

While we wait, we are approached by a chatty Russian soldier, educated, well-armed and clearly with the Federal Security Service (FSB), the successor to the Soviet-era KGB. We answer his questions cheerily, explaining that the error in our paperwork was not our own, and agree with him that all people in the world should live in peace and friendship. A few minutes later we are allowed across the checkpoint, as a large Russian helicopter flies above us at low altitude, patrolling the northern bank of the Inguri.

Even today, one side or the other has been known suddenly to close down this frontier on a whim, making routine crossings a matter of life or death, as each side eyes the other through a heavily armed prism.

At the same time, on both the Abkhaz and South Ossetian sides of Georgia, red lines are not only still in place, but Russia continues to engage in red line creep, often with quite bizarre, but at times quite profitable and strategic, effect. Andrew North, a British correspondent writing for *The Guardian*, who's lived in Georgia for years, observed in 2015 that Russia had quietly set up new markings defining just such a new frontier in South Ossetia. They were cleverly designed to seize a mile-long stretch of the BP-operated Baku-Supsa oil pipeline—and a swath of Georgian territory as well. Farmers suddenly found themselves with Russian troops on their farmland as much as a mile inside the internationally recognized boundary. "I went to bed in Georgia and woke up in South Ossetia," one farmer told North, peering through a stretch of barbed wire that had replaced the old boundary delineated by a line of wrecked cars across the rolling farmland. "We've lost most of our fields. The Russians said we are no longer allowed [into what they were now calling] occupied territory." The EU monitoring mission for South Ossetia reported that one new border sign had been placed 980 feet south of the previous location in Orochosani and another nearly a mile south in Tsitelubani. EU official John Durnin described it as yet another step in Russia's "borderization" policy, which "creates obstacles to freedom of movement and the livelihoods of the local population." New signs in Russian and Ossetian (though not Georgian) dotted the new line which approached to within a few hundred yards of Georgia's main east-west highway that links Tbilisi with Turkey and with the Black Sea ports where the pipeline terminates. It was the same road taken by Russian tanks in the push to within twelve miles of the capital during the 2008 war. The pipeline is an especially strategic resource as it links the Caspian oil fields of Azerbaijan—a thoroughly Russian-allied nation—with Georgia's Supsa oil terminal on the Black Sea.

Georgia, with Abkhazia and South Ossetia, its much-disputed border
traversing the Caucuses, and the conventional boundary of Europe and Asia.

As to just why such a red line has been established and apparently so diligently defended, at least by one party, in such an utterly god-forsaken corner of the confluence of Europe and Asia can only be explained by a complex amalgam of hubris and venality. With respect to the Georgian region, the value to Russia would appear to be at least materially and geographically minimal. There is the small outlet to the Black Sea, though Crimea and Ukraine would be far more substantial and appropriate outlets—more direct shots north to the Moscow and the Russian heartland. A few miles up the coast is the resort town of Sochi, site of the 2014 Winter Olympics. At the time, it appeared that one of Putin's central objectives was to safeguard the Olympics and build another tourist destination that the Kremlin could control. That never happened. There was never a boom, or even a boomlet, in Abkhazia, and since then it has sunk bank into its historic torpor and desuetude. So, we are left with hubris—perhaps the least viable or sustainable excuse for establishing or maintaining a red line. Part must be attributed to Putin's territorial ambitions and the goal of restoring the old Soviet empire. Perhaps at some point, Abkhazia and South Ossetia could again serve as a bridgehead for a push into or through Georgia. But his experience in Crimea and eastern Ukraine should hardly suggest this will be in any fashion an easy or fruitful path—particularly if he were to balance costs against benefits. Russia is still buried by the sanctions against this more recent adventure.

—

In 2015, General Martin Dempsey, retiring chairman of the US Joint Chiefs of Staff, in his farewell statement on military strategy, warned of the toxic effects of these Russian tactics that he labeled "hybrid conflict," which, he continued, "serve to increase ambiguity, complicate decision-making, and slow the coordination of effective responses."

"Russia also has repeatedly demonstrated that it does not respect the sovereignty of its neighbors and it is willing to use force to achieve its goals," Dempsey continued. He then proceeded to outline the playbook that Russia would use in its next target of opportunity and expansion—Crimea, and eventually Ukraine: "state and non-state actors working together toward shared objectives, employing a wide range of weapons." Vladimir Putin had been preparing for just such an action for a long time. For Ukraine was Russia's ultimate prize. If ever there was a red line worth shattering, the one between these two nations was it.

*Ukraine in the eighteenth century, crushed between a powerful
Polish-Lithuanian Commonwealth and the Russian Empire.*

Ukraine, and its preceding iterations, back to the vibrant Kievan Rus, has been a signficant civilization straddling Europe and Asia for a thousand years. In the tenth century, the prince of Kiev had the audacity to invade the powerful Byzantine Empire. While defeated in this endeavor, within a century Ukraine had expanded its boundaries to make it the largest state in Europe, including in its territory vast stretches of Russia and Poland. Rising as a major trading hub connecting Europe, Constantinople, and Baghdad—capitals respectively of Byzantium and the powerful Abassid Muslim empire—Kiev was one of the most lavishly appointed cities in Europe. At its peak in 1200 C.E., its population of fifty thousand was equal to that of Paris and nearly double that of London. Vladimir the Great, married to a Byzantine princess, converted his nation to Christianity, and under his successor, Iaroslav the Wise, communities of Jews, Greeks, Armenians, Italians, and Russians grew, along with the trading opportunities they'd opened. But none of this glory was destined to last. Eventually, other empires were on the rise—Lithuania, Poland, and Muscovy, the precursor of modern Russia, took over large swaths of Ukraine, not by massive invasions but simply by creeping settlement and expansion. Lithuania and Poland, both nations of rising power—the former with its princes and boyars, the latter with its noble families—confronted Muscovy and the Khanate of Crimea. Ukraine was gradually ground down between these powers, its own rulers ill-equipped to master far-flung regions and retain their hold. Conventional red lines played little role here as inexorable demographic forces placed these regions in constant, often centrifugal motion. Russia at first played the role of protector, then conqueror under Catherine the Great.

For all of its neighbors, Ukraine was a wealthy and fabulous prize. In 1654, Ukraine formally united with Russia. By 1700, vast estates were dominating the fertile Ukrainian heartland. Then, as now, ethnically Ukraine was divided east and west. The wealthiest Ukrainian of Polish origin, Jeremi Wiśniowiecki, owned 7,500 estates in the province of Kiev. A quarter million of his serfs worked landholdings unlike any in Europe. Although Jeremi himself was known to have lived somewhat austerely, many others built soaring palaces with walls lined with paintings by Dutch masters and carpets from Byzantium, maintained vast private armies to guarantee their security and boundaries, and established laws of their own. Their red lines remained unchallenged, even by the nation's nominal rulers.

Eventually, Ukraine would all but disappear into Russian and Polish spheres of influence—large noble families from each side controlling the landscapes and the lines that defined them. Particularly under Czar Peter the Great, Russia proved indispensable to what remained of Ukraine in resisting the hated Poles and preventing them from encroaching further on Ukrainian territory. Peter, in turn, as eager in his own way as is Putin today, was anxious to eliminate red lines wherever possible and simply absorb or consolidate even the most far-flung regions under his power. This was perhaps suggested most clearly by Peter's not inconsiderable full, royal title as translated from the Russian:

> By the grace of God, the most excellent and great sovereign emperor Pyotr Alekseevich the ruler of all the Russias: of Moscow, of Kiev, of Vladimir, of Novgorod, Tsar of Kazan, Tsar of Astrakhan, and Tsar of Siberia, sovereign of Pskov, great prince of Smolensk, of Tver, of Yugorsk, of Perm, of Vyatka, of Bulgaria and others, sovereign and great prince of the Novgorod Lower lands, of Chernigov, of Ryazan, of Rostov, of Yaroslavl, of Belozersk, of Udora, of Kondia and the sovereign of all the northern lands, and the sovereign of the Iverian lands, of the Kartlian and Georgian Kings, of the Kabardin lands, of the Circassian and Mountain princes and many other states and lands western and eastern here and there and the successor and sovereign and ruler.

Following World War II, Ukraine assumed its contemporary shape within the Soviet Union, with Crimea the final piece, arriving in 1954. The insert shows how Ukraine swelled in the course of 300 years beginning in 1654.

In 1462, the Muscovite nation-state comprised barely 9,200 square miles. In 1914 at the outbreak of World War I and the final days of the czars' rule, that had grown to more than five million square miles, or one-sixth of the world's land surface. At its peak, it was expanding at an average rate of three square miles per day. Much of that expansion was in the same direction as today—south toward the warm waters of the Black Sea and its year-round ports and the world trade the czars were able to access freely and efficiently. But along the way, of special value, were the fertile steppes of Ukraine—vast rolling acres, millions of them, with soil ever more fertile the more southerly the czars' armies were able to push. Wheat for the bread of Russia and its exploding population was the preferred crop. Corn and potatoes were eventually introduced, along with more than three thousand water mills and twelve thousand windmills in the most fertile regions. And then, of course, were the thousands of distilleries to turn out wheat-based spirits.

It was largely through the efforts of Russians, and especially under Peter's rule, that the richest black earth—a third of the entire territory of Ukraine—was opened to cultivation in the first place. The population to work the land surged tenfold in the middle third of the eighteenth century with labor imported from as far as Serbia. By the time Catherine the Great, wife of Peter the Great's grandson, ascended the throne to reign for thirty-four glorious years, Ukraine, now virtually a province of Russia, had been restored to much of its previous glory. This province, if it were an independent nation, would have been, after Russia, Europe's largest in land area. When an imperial official in Ukraine had a medal struck in Catherine's honor in 1793 marking thirty years of her reign on the Russian throne, it bore the inscription "I have recovered what was torn away." Throughout the nineteenth century, as hundreds of the czar's garrisons and outposts of the imperial bureaucracy sprang up across the country to make sure that Russian rule and frontiers were respected, Ukraine was drawn ever deeper into the Russian orbit.

After the serfs were freed in 1862, there was more labor to work the fields. By the early twentieth century, wheat was the main export of the Russian Empire, accounting for 90 percent of the nation's foreign trade. Indeed, Ukraine accounted for more than 40 percent of the world's entire barley crop, a fifth of its wheat, and 10 percent of its corn. But sugar beets eventually became the main cash crop and the main source of sugar for European tables. At the same time, indispensable industry grew up in the Donets River Basin, where massive deposits of coal and iron ore were uncovered. Remember that name, Donets, and its region, the Donbas. Russia was beginning to recognize that Ukraine was essential to the prosperity, the very life, of the motherland itself. In 1914, before boarding his train in Switzerland for St. Petersburg's Finland Station and the start of the Russian Revolution, Vladimir Ilyich Lenin delivered a speech pointing out that Ukraine "has become for Russia what Ireland was for England: exploited in the extreme and receiving nothing in return." This changed little when Lenin's Bolsheviks seized power. The Soviet-era editions of Lenin's complete works eliminated this speech altogether. Instead, the Bolsheviks reflect uniformly the czarist-era view of Ukraine as an integral part of the Russian heartland.

The end of World War I brought a brief flirtation with independence for Ukraine, which collapsed in a series of violent internal struggles and two invasions of Bolshevik forces that were dispatched to establish a viable and unitary Union of Soviet Socialist Republics into which, from the beginning in 1922, Ukraine was incorporated. The great Canadian-Ukrainian scholar of Ukrainian history Orest Subtelny observed:

> In 1919, total chaos engulfed Ukraine. Indeed, in the modern history of
> Europe no country experienced such complete anarchy, bitter civil strife,
> and total collapse of authority as did Ukraine at this time. Six different
> armies—those of the Ukrainians, the Bolsheviks, the Whites, the Entente
> [French], the Poles and the anarchists—operated on its territory. Kiev changed
> hands five times in less than a year. Cities and regions were cut off from each
> other by the numerous fronts. Communications with the outside world broke

down almost completely. The starving cities emptied as people moved into the countryside in their search for food.

Eventually, order was restored, but not by Ukrainians. As Subtelny asks, "At a time [after World War I] when empires collapsed and almost all the peoples of Eastern Europe, including such small subject nations of the tsars as the Finns, Estonians, Latvians and Lithuanians, gained their independence, why was it that the 30 million Ukrainians did not? . . . [Moreover] the Ukrainians probably fought longer for independence and paid a higher price in lives than any other East European nation." The answer was simple. Ukraine had never managed to build an independent nation, let alone a state. For centuries, it had been and would remain a province of Russia. And in the mind of Vladimir Putin, it no doubt still is.

None of the events of the rest of the twentieth century would reverse that perception—beginning with a series of famines. The first, in the harsh winter of 1921 to 1922, took several hundred thousand lives. And then there was the Holodomor. It took three years and an unforeseen drought to build to what was effectively a Ukrainian holocaust. Enforced collectivization by Josef Stalin, who, despite his Georgian origins, had no sense of what agriculture was like, led to this catastrophe. Stalin desperately needed Ukraine's grain to feed his urban workforce throughout Russia. Federal troops and secret police forces stormed through villages across Ukraine seizing every morsel of grain, even seed grain for next year's crop. The result was a famine of unparalleled proportions in the horrific winter of 1932 to 1933. Many of those who did not die of famine were executed, often for stealing from a silo a handful of grain that had been destined for Russia. Subtelny describes how "lacking bread, peasants ate pets, rats, bark, leaves, and garbage from the well-provisioned kitchens of party members. There were numerous cases of cannibalization." Whole villages died and still Russia continued to seize whatever grain the exhausted and barren fields could disgorge. Census takers were ordered shot by Stalin as the consequences of his madness against Ukraine began filtering out. There may never be a truly accurate figure, but estimates place the death toll in Ukraine at between three million and six million people. *New York Times* correspondent Walter Duranty, eager to win Stalin's favor and access, repeatedly filed dispatches denying the building evidence of famine while privately estimating that as many as ten million people may have died. Duranty won the Pulitzer Prize in 1932 for his "profundity, impartiality, sound judgment and exceptional clarity." In 1937, Stalin quietly decided to exterminate the entire leadership of the Ukrainian government and Communist Party—more than one hundred seventy thousand individuals, including entire families. Not surprisingly, the Holodomar has been permanently seared into the DNA of Ukrainians to this day.

World War II all but completed the horrors of the Holodomar. Some 5.3 million Ukrainians died in the conflict and its aftermath, while 2.3 million were shipped to Germany for forced labor. In all, nearly a fifth of the population had been wiped out, another 10 million rendered homeless as over 700 towns and 28,000 villages were destroyed or heavily damaged. For a time, the Nazis would destroy and execute the inhabitants of two hundred and fifty Ukrainian villages for every one that met a similar fate in France or Czechoslovakia. At the end of the war, Khrushchev, who had been appointed viceroy of the region by Stalin, returned to his duties in Ukraine and sought to make amends. Part of his task involved bringing Western Ukraine—long ruled in parts by Poland or Austria—and Soviet-controlled Eastern Ukraine together into a single Soviet republic.

It was an economically and politically worthwhile endeavor. Ukraine was to become, after Russia itself, the most significant component of the Soviet Union, with four times the output of the next-ranking republic, according to the Central Intelligence Agency. Diversified agriculture on rich, black soil and a range of mineral mining and heavy industry supplied respectively food, raw materials, and industrial output to the rest of the Soviet Union.

Khrushchev had deep roots in the region. Though an ethnic Russian, he was born in Kalinovka, a village seven miles east of the Ukrainian border with Russia. At the age of sixteen, he arrived in Donetsk to work the coal mines. His wife, Nina, was born into a Ukrainian family in what was then Western Ukraine, now Poland. He understood the depths of horror to which this land had been subjected and tried, at least in some ways, to right that wrong. In 1949, Khrushchev returned to Moscow and, following a brief power struggle after Stalin's death in 1953, emerged as the leader of the Soviet Union.

So it was hardly surprising that one of the new Soviet leader's earliest moves was one that would echo loudly a half-century later. On February 27, 1954, Khrushchev made a present to Ukraine of one strategically critical region of the Russian republic—Crimea. *The New York Times* clearly recognized the historical significance of this action, positioning the story by its star Moscow bureau chief, Harrison E. Salisbury, at the top of the front page with a two-column headline and a map that demonstrated graphically the position of the peninsula. You will recall that it was here, a century earlier, that Russian forces came upon the red line of British soldiers at the height of the Crimean War. Now, the decision was made to shift ownership rights of Crimea to Ukraine, effectively as a means of "further strengthening the brotherly ties between the Ukrainian and Russian peoples." In the Soviet parliament, M. P. Tarasov, member of the presidium, rose to explain the unusual action.

> The entire Crimean Peninsula territorially adjoins the Ukrainian Republic, and is a sort of natural continuation of the southern steppes of Ukraine. The economy of the Crimean Oblast is closely tied to the economy of the Ukrainian SSR. The transfer of the Crimean Oblast to the fraternal Ukrainian Republic is advisable and meets the common interests of the Soviet state for geographic and economic considerations. The Ukrainian people have tied their fate with the Russian people since olden times. For many centuries they fought against common enemies—tsarism, serf owners, and capitalists, and also against foreign invaders. The centuries-long friendship of the Ukrainian and Russian peoples and the economic and cultural link between Crimea and Ukraine were consolidated still further with the victory of the Great October Socialist Revolution. The issue of the transfer of the Crimean Oblast to the Ukrainian Republic is being examined in days when the peoples of the Soviet Union are marking a notable event, the 300th anniversary of the reunion of Ukraine with Russia, which played an enormous progressive role in the political, economic, and cultural development of the Ukrainian and Russian peoples. The transfer of the Crimean Oblast to the Ukrainian Republic meets the interests of strengthening the friendship of the peoples of the great Soviet Union, and will promote the further strengthening of the fraternal link between the Ukrainian and Russian peoples and the still greater prosperity of Soviet Ukraine, the development to which our party and government have always devoted great attention.

There was, of course, much more to this decision than simply a bit of bureaucratic legerdemain or whatever quite appropriate historic antecedents might be unearthed. At the time, Khrushchev was in the process of shoring up his standing within the leadership of the Central Committee of the Soviet Communist as first secretary and Stalin's successor. Bulking up Ukraine with Crimea was an easy gesture to the powerful leader of Ukraine's Communist Party, Alexei Kirichenko. Over the next half century, the Ukrainian party leadership did its best to preserve and expand the integration of Ukraine into the Russian empire. Russian became the language to use if one wanted to advance in life, to the point where some two million Ukrainians came to embrace Russian as their mother tongue. At the same time, millions of Russians arrived in Ukraine to work the mines and factories, especially in the Donbas region of eastern Ukraine. Barely a third ever bothered to learn Ukrainian. In 1926, there were three million Russians in Ukraine; by 1959, that number had risen to seven million, and to ten million in 1979. At the same time, large numbers of Ukrainians were encouraged to migrate to other parts of the Soviet Union. This, then, was Ukraine when the Soviet Union finally came apart between 1989 and 1991.

Ukraine today, its "Autonomous Republic of Crimea," now a hardly autonomous component of Putin's Russia.

There were any number of critical consequences—or loose ends, depending on your perspective—for both Russia and Ukraine. First, and in many respects paramount, was the reality that the red lines that once surrounded all of the Soviet Union were sharply and dramatically shrunk to encompass simply the Russian Federation and, to a large degree, the small, still-Stalinist neighbor of Belarus next door. Many of the 'Stans, too, could be seen to fall within this newly drawn network of red lines, as well as the likes of Armenia and Azerbaijan. But far more definitively on the outside now was Ukraine—and its fertile farmlands, mineral resources, and the outlet to the Black Sea represented by Nikita Khrushchev's forty-year-old gift, Crimea.

The second loose end that remained was the vast arsenal of intercontinental missiles and their nuclear warheads that still lay beneath the ground in Ukraine, now an independent nation largely outside the Kremlin's control. Both Russia and the West had every motivation not to allow these to escape the hands of responsible—and especially accountable—governments. Missiles, particularly those carrying nuclear weapons, have long been subjects of red lines as to their use or deployment, certainly the threat they carried. Several of these red lines have been quite clear—most notably between the nuclear-armed nations of India and Pakistan, whose missiles remain targeted on each other. Between the United States and Russia these lines have been equally clear, though the closest any two nations have come to breaching it—the Cuban Missile Crisis, when Nikita Khrushchev sought to introduce nuclear missiles into Cuba in defiance of a young and inexperienced President John F. Kennedy—came within hours of utter catastrophe. But the concept of Mutually Assured Destruction has prevented this ultimate red line from ever being breached. Now, however, with the collapse of the Soviet Union and liberation of Ukraine, what was to be done with at least five thousand such weapons and virtually no control over their use or abuse? Effectively, Ukraine had control of the single largest nuclear arsenal in the world: one hundred and thirty SS-19 ICBMs, each carrying six nuclear warheads; forty-six SS-24s, with ten nukes; six hundred air-launched nuclear missiles; and more than three thousand tactical nukes. On January 14, 1994, Ukraine agreed to return this entire arsenal to Russia for reprocessing or destruction. The agreement, signed by the United States, Russia, and Ukraine, in turn provided one hundred tons of nuclear fuel for the new nation's power plants. Effectively, Russia succeeded in reinforcing its own red line while eviscerating the ability of a neighbor to enforce any red lines of its own that it might decide to erect. Which is precisely what would happen two decades later.

Putin, like centuries of Russian rulers that preceded him, and certainly every leader of the Soviet Union, saw Ukraine as an integral part of the Russian heartland. The modern reality of a newly independent nation was simply the result of an accident of history, or an aberration. This temporary separation would ultimately be corrected, and there was no time like the present to begin the process of erasing what Russian leaders saw as an artificial and ill-placed red line. "Little Russians," as they liked to call Ukrainians, would ultimately lose those distinguishing features that set them apart and become again True Russians. Certainly, this would be the case in Crimea and in eastern regions like the Donbas, where such a new reality would be accelerated by the "little green men" speaking Russian rather than Ukrainian.

This was the situation in February 2014 when Putin decided the red line that had kept Ukraine separate and independent from Russia for the preceding quarter century was moveable. At the time, Ukraine was deeply divided along the same ethnic, cultural, and linguistic lines as it had been prior to its independence, when throughout the decades of Soviet rule, its irredentist tendencies had been smothered and, on the rare occasions when they surfaced, quickly suppressed. For much of the post-Soviet period, Ukraine and its province of Crimea had remained in more or less reliable hands from the Kremlin's point of view. While there were flirtations with membership in the European Union or even NATO, none of the six presidents to hold office there had taken irreversible steps toward such acts, which were utter red lines to Vladimir Putin. Bringing NATO to some remote Baltic frontiers of Russia was one thing. Bringing the alliance to the doorsteps of the old Soviet Union's heartland was quite another. But by early 2014, matters had begun to get out of hand.

In February 2010, Viktor Yanukovych managed to snatch a victory from what was declared a free and fair election against his opponent, Prime Minister Yulia Tymoshenko. This was a sharp contrast to the previous time Yanukovych sought the office in 2004, when he was declared the winner over former Prime Minister Viktor Yushchenko, the corrupt balloting sending thousands of protestors into the streets of Kiev and other cities in what was hailed as the Orange Revolution. The result in 2004 was a ruling by Ukraine's Supreme Court nullifying the vote and ordering a new election, which Yanukovych lost. That would not happen this time.

Yanukovych had an interesting past, which no doubt played an important role in cementing a relationship with Putin. Born in Donetsk, then known as Stalino Oblast, in 1950, his mother was a Russian nurse, his father a Belarusian locomotive driver. Both parents died as he entered his teens. He was raised by grandparents who were Lithuanian Poles—descended from the time when Lithuania ruled over large swaths of Ukraine. Yanukovych had a rough-and-tumble youth and was twice sentenced to prison for robbery and assault. Finally he became a member of the Soviet Communist Party and a transportation company manager. By 1996 he had risen to the top ranks of the Donetsk regional administration, and his political career was launched.

Donetsk, of course, was one of two regions of Ukraine that the Kremlin saw as being, effectively, within the natural red line that defined Russia's intellectual and military, if not its legal, geographical border. So, when in February 2010, Yanukovych managed to eke out a 48.95 percent to 45.47 percent win over Yulia Tymoshenko, the Kremlin could hardly have been unhappy. The Patriarch Kirill of Moscow and All Rus' conducted a public prayer service at his inauguration, along with European Union Foreign Secretary

Catherine Ashton, US National Security Advisor James Jones, and Speaker of the Russian Duma Boris Gryzlov. Yanukovych promptly set visits for his first week in office to Moscow and Brussels. Within a year, though, it had become clear that Yanukovych's rule would hardly be evenhanded. The reality of the Russian red line emerged as far more important than any challenge that might be mounted on the other side by Ukraine or any of its friends in the West. But, by 2012, polls showed Yanukovych's popularity had plunged to a low of 13 percent.

Yanukovych's path toward an early exit from power began November 21, 2013, with a small protest in Kiev's Independence Square. The trigger for that protest was set that morning in Vilnius, Lithuania, when Yanukovych walked out of a meeting where he was to have signed a long-negotiated Association Agreement with the European Union—a first step toward Ukraine becoming the newest EU member state. At a minimum, the nation would have been allowed by early 2014 to export goods duty free to the European Union, the largest tariff-free market in the world. Anders Åslund of the Peterson Institute estimated that such a pact could have added as much as 12 percent to the nation's GDP and boosted exports by 46 percent. But leading up to that day, Yanukovych had already begun pivoting sharply away from the EU and toward new and stronger economic ties with Russia. Putin, it seems, had pulled out his own economic incentive, though he still held in check the military muscle that was very much available if needed to protect what he saw as a critical red line he was anxious to establish. He had no interest whatsoever in any Ukrainian leader dragging Ukraine across his red line and into the arms of the European Union. As Reuters headlined, RUSSIA STEALS "UKRAINIAN BRIDE" AT THE ALTAR.

Well, actually, somewhat before the altar. Yanukovych arrived in Lithuania with his mind already made up. This red line with Russia was unbreachable. Ukraine would remain firmly within the Russian orbit. Putin was prepared to demonstrate that quite clearly. On November 9, Yanukovych had traveled to Russia to meet with Putin. In the Kremlin, Putin held out a carrot, a pretty rotten one in comparison to what the EU was holding out for Ukraine: join a Russian-led customs union and you'll get cheaper gas from Russia and avoid trade sanctions. The meeting lasted until five o'clock in the morning, with Yanukovych winning one concession—that the meeting would be kept secret. Meanwhile, Russia began to deliver a little foretaste of what life would be like if the red line did not hold. Armed Russian customs officers began arbitrary border checks on Ukrainian trucks crossing the frontier. Yanukovych, a transport expert from his early years, understood the economic cost of such tactics—not to mention the military threat from a Russian armed force far superior to any that Ukraine might field. To reinforce its threats, Russian state gas monopoly Gazprom presented Ukraine with an outstanding bill for $882 million, while Russian officials began warning the country that it would face bankruptcy long before any EU trade and tariff pact could begin producing concrete results.

So, on November 21, Yanukovych suddenly and unexpectedly backed out of the "association" deal with the European Union, effectively throwing in his lot with Russia. It was quite clear on which side of Russia's red line the Ukrainian president was prepared to make his stand. Within hours, even before Yanukovych could make his way back to Kiev, a small group had gathered on Independence Square in the center of the capital to make their views known. It took a week for this small protest to blossom into a violent, national uprising, known as Euromaidan (literally "European Square"). By early December, protests had spread across all of western Ukraine, attracting more than a million people to Independence Square alone, where protestors quickly erected barriers. The price for their leaving? Freedom for all imprisoned demonstrators, signing the EU association pact, and the resignation of Yanukovych.

Yanukovych managed to hold on to power until February 21, when, a virtual civil war having broken out, he was forced from office by a massive parliamentary majority. By then, at least 104 had died in the Euromaidan protests and 2,500 had been injured, according to Ukrainian prosecutors. Abandoning his lavish, 350-acre estate of Mezhyhirya, with its private zoo, airstrip, and orangery, which he'd been leasing for less than $40 a month, the sixty-three-year-old Yanukovych fled in the dead of night. As *The New York Times*'s Alison Smale described it, he traveled light, in a three-car caravan that included one old business crony, Andriy Klyuyev, a handful of guards and his thirty-nine-year-old girlfriend, Lyubov Polezhay. Finding themselves blocked from helicopters and planes by government security forces, they were believed to have boarded a Russian ship on the Black Sea, eventually emerging in Russia, which received him with open arms.

Across the Black Sea in Sochi, Putin was waiting for the end of the Winter Olympic Games before launching his next move. A year later, in an interview for Russian television, he described, in some remarkable detail, the process that took place, beginning late on the evening of February 22 and stretching into the morning of February 23. "We ended at about seven in the morning," Putin recalled. "When we were parting, I said to my colleagues: we must start working on returning Crimea to Russia." He was also consulting with a number of interested parties. German Chancellor Angela Merkel was favored with a phone call. A German official said they'd agreed that the "territorial integrity of Ukraine must be preserved." That didn't last for long. Foreign Minister Sergei Lavrov talked with US Secretary of State John Kerry twice in two days. But Putin pressed on, recalling his ambassador to Ukraine just as Kerry was urging him to back the transition underway in

Kiev. Ukrainians did not help matters much, with Parliament quickly passing a measure restricting the use of the Russian language in Ukrainian schools.

By February 27, unidentified soldiers in fatigues with no unit markings had seized and occupied the local parliament building in Simferopol, and the deputies, quite literally with guns to their head, spent little time voting in a new government utterly sympathetic to the Putin agenda. At the same time, Russia was mobilizing a major military exercise of ground and air forces on its western border with Ukraine—tens of thousands of troops were ordered on full alert for an exercise to last until March 3. Twenty-five miles outside Sevastopol, men in blue uniforms and others with green camouflage stopped and inspected every vehicle, while in downtown Simferopol an instant demonstration was ginned up with protestors from the region's Russian majority population, shouting "Crimea is Russian." Many believed it was past the time to reverse the historic injustice done to them by Khrushchev when he turned their homeland over to Ukraine. Local Crimean Tatars, meanwhile, were lining up behind the pro-Ukrainian forces, determined to demonstrate their determination to carve out an enclave, having survived and returned to their homes following the mass deportations their ancestors had suffered under Stalin.

Amid such passions, Russian military forces, their identities carefully concealed with their units' identifying insignia removed from their uniforms, swarmed through the streets of the province, surrounding government buildings, closing the main airport, and seizing all communications facilities. A squadron of such troops, wearing face masks, camouflage fatigues, and silencer-equipped Kalashnikov assault rifles, stormed a hotel in Simferopol occupied largely by foreign journalists, with Ministry of the Interior officials later arriving to claim it was a "training exercise." Though Ukrainian forces had been ordered to "full combat readiness" by the government of Oleksandr V. Turchynov, the acting president who'd replaced Yanukovych in Kiev, Russia clearly had the upper hand in Crimea. Putin formally convened Parliament in Moscow to grant him authority to use whatever force was necessary to protect ethnic Russians, not only in Crimea but across Ukraine. Having pushed his red line back to the Crimea-Ukraine boundary, Putin seemed prepared to go much further. He had not counted on the degree of the backlash from the West.

On March 18, with the full annexation by Moscow formally consummated first by proclamation, then by a somewhat specious referendum, the consequences began to unfold for Putin. As in the case of most red lines, though the consequences must be fully weighed, at times they may be utterly unforeseen. In the case of Ukraine and Crimea, they were clear from the first moment. Putin was hardly unfamiliar with the nature and potential cost of sanctions. In 2012, the United States had already imposed a catalogue of sanctions on Russian individuals and entities under the Magnitsky Act in response to human rights abuses and the suspicious death of Sergei Magnitsky, a leading civil rights attorney, in a Russian prison. Now, in the wake of the Russian seizure of Crimea and threats to eastern Ukraine, the United States was quickly joined by the European Union. Some 650 individuals, corporations, and even ships were sanctioned—quite specifically for events surrounding the invasion of Crimea. This included a series of ever-widening circles of Russian officials and business executives, ranging from the minister of internal affairs to the secretary of the security council; directors of the Foreign Intelligence Service (formerly the KGB) and National Guard Troops; the chairs of both houses of parliament; and the chief executive officers of state-owned oil company Rosneft, gas company Gazprom, defense and technology conglomerate Rostec, and banks VTB and Gazprombank. Others sanctioned were private individuals including a number of oligarchs—eleven of Russia's wealthiest hundred, including two of the top ten, all billionaires according to *Forbes*. Companies included privately held banks and financial services companies (e.g., SMP Bank and the Volga Group); private aluminum company RUSAL; gas pipeline construction company Stroygazmontazh; construction company Stroytransgaz; electric company EuroSibEnergo; vehicle manufacturer GAZ Group; United Shipbuilding Corporation; air defense system and missile manufacturer Almaz-Antey; tank and other military equipment manufacturer Uralvagonzavod; missile and rocket manufacturer NPO Mashinostroyenia; and several subsidiaries of state-owned defense and hi-tech conglomerate Rostec, including its Kalashnikov Group, maker of the renowned assault rifle.

Eventually, these sanctions would begin to bite, but by then Putin had made two critical moves. First, he had fully reabsorbed Crimea as a portion of Russia, the red line surrounding it firmly in place and all but uncontested, certainly in any military terms. But of potentially even greater long-term value, Putin had positioned this new economic reality as an attack by a jealous West on Russia's growing power and influence. In an annual call-in talk show in June 2019, Putin warned his Russian listeners that America's aim was to "contain the development of China as a global power," after which he was quick to add, "The same thing is happening with regard to Russia and it will keep going, so if we want to win a place under the sun we simply need to get stronger, primarily in the economic sphere."

Indeed, there is some considerable question as to just how badly Russia has fared under the sanctions. In terms of long-term growth, there may be some penalties. But by the time those begin to bite, Putin may even be gone from his presidency that seems increasingly to match Xi Jinping's presidency-for-life. And he's made some efforts to inoculate his economy against some of the more immediate impacts. In 2018, he embarked on an experiment of diversifying the country's still substantial foreign currency holdings—at least $530 billion in the third quarter of 2019—away from the dollar. This effort at diversification cost the treasury nearly $8 billion in gains as the dollar appreciated in value.

In fact, the Russian economy has not done so badly under the sanctions, which have been designed intentionally to hurt the government, leadership, and oligarchs more than ordinary folks. The sanctions were first levied in 2014 when Russia was just beginning its longest recession in two decades, a tribute more to plummeting oil prices, which fell from $115 to $35 a barrel. Since oil revenues comprise half the government budget and nearly a third of the nation's GDP, when they began to rebound in 2016, so did the economy, though sanctions by then had kicked in seriously. Slow growth returned, unemployment neared historic lows, and the stock market boomed, though ordinary Russians still found life difficult. The sanctions also helped Putin achieve some of his most closely held priorities, particularly persuading a number of oligarchs to repatriate at least some of their assets to avoid having them frozen abroad. At most, the sanctions may have shaved 1 to 1.5 percent from the nation's output.

Meanwhile, they seem to have had little appreciable impact on where Putin placed his red lines around Crimea and Ukraine and how he was prepared to enforce, or even extend, them. Two years after the Russian takeover of Crimea, it began construction of a mammoth, twelve-mile-long bridge spanning the Kerch Strait that cost nearly $4 billion. In 2018, when it was inaugurated, Ukrainian president Petro Poroshenko observed that it would be useful for "Russian occupants when they have to leave the Ukrainian peninsula," which doesn't seem likely any time soon. Effectively, the bridge cements Crimea to Russia and avoids any need to pass by land around the entire periphery of the Sea of Azov or enter any part of south or southeastern Ukraine, much of which remains heavily disputed territory, crisscrossed with red lines that are among the most deeply contested in the world on a daily basis. They remain the subject of some of the most costly sanctions ever enacted and enforced.

Meanwhile, for the five years since Russia established a firm red line around Crimea, it has been trying with varying degrees of desperation and concealment to press it westward as deeply into the ethnic Russian–dominated regions of Ukraine as possible. Much of this effort has been undertaken by soldiers equipped with the identical weaponry and uniforms of Russian special operations (Spetsnaz) forces. Few Western organizations understand these forces better than the Finnish military, which, much like its Baltic neighbors, has for decades been carefully monitoring their Russian foes across the red line they share. *Soldier of Finland* magazine identifies the forces "with a high probability" as belonging to the "45th Guards Separate Reconnaissance Regiment of VDV" based at Kubinka outside Moscow, though all insignia that would identify their origins has been carefully removed from their uniforms. Photos of these soldiers show them in new EMR camouflage combat uniforms, 6S112 tactical vests, and 6B27 composite helmets, with 7.62 mm PKP machine guns and Russian 5.45 mm AK-74M assault rifles. An observer mission of the Organization for Security and Cooperation in Europe reported that at just two Russian border crossing points they were able to monitor, Gukovo and Donetsk, they "observed more than 30,000 individuals in military-style dress crossing," concluding "Imagine, colleagues, what is crossing where we can't see." These forces quickly became known as a "ghost army" as they fanned out across the region, acquiring and supplying local allies. This has forced Ukraine to mount a red line defense that has caused innumerable casualties—and required significant military aid from the West. When large quantities of this aid were held hostage by President Trump on the condition of Kiev's willingness to mount an attack on the Biden family, the potential lethality of this position and how deeply it plays into Russian military strategy becomes graphically clear. UN officials have placed the death toll at more than ten thousand, with another one million displaced from their homes by the fighting that Ukrainian officials are careful to call an invasion rather than a civil war. By October 2019, Ambassador William B. Taylor, America's veteran chargé d'affaires in Kiev, was testifying before Congress that more than 13,000 Ukrainians had been killed in the conflict and were continuing to die at the pace of at least one or two every week. Taylor added that he had traveled to "the front line in northern Donbas [where he] could see the armed and hostile Russian-led forces on the other side of the damaged bridge across the line of contact." In short, Russia was continuing to apply serious military pressure along the entire red line that Putin had established and was prepared to press—but that was hundreds of miles to the west of the red line recognized by the entire Western world as the legitimate frontier between the two countries.

So, there seems to be little incentive for Ukraine to engage in serious negotiations that could result in any adjustment to the red line, since that exists on the eastern frontier of Ukraine and encompasses all the territory so deeply coveted by Putin. It is equally unclear just how much further Putin might be willing or able to press his red line into Ukraine. Ukrainian forces are prepared, though they still rely heavily on Western military aid to be able to engage in the defense of this critical line. Holding this line is essential if Putin is to be discouraged from even more pernicious activities in red lines surrounding his nation and further afield. For at least four years the red line surrounding the regions of Donbas and Luhansk where rebels with heavy Russian backing have held sway have been unable to cement their control or advance definitively the Western-recognized red line that has long existed along the actual frontier that separates Ukraine from Russia. But in October 2019, Ukrainian President Volodymyr Zelensky signaled his willingness to at least consider a pullback of Ukrainian troops along the 250-mile frontline, where mortars and machine gun fire continues to be exchanged, sporadically but often quite lethally. There have been ongoing efforts by France and Germany to broker some sort of permanent cease-fire, but there also seems to be little motivation on the part of Putin to pull back or even recognize these Western efforts at a brokered peace or cease-fire. Clearly, the Russian leader sees advancing his red line would provide him with enormous strategic advantages and little downside risk beyond what has already been built into the status quo. Military specialists are calling the Ukraine battlefield a classic example of a "hybrid" conflict, as the US National Military Strategy 2015 observes "military forces assuming a non-state identity as Russia did in Crimea." This utterly prescient concept was advanced in June 2015, when it was not yet clear that Putin had transferred precisely the same tactics used in Crimea to eastern Ukraine and the Donbas.

By October 2020, many of Russia's red lines that Putin had thought would firmly define his frontiers were suddenly becoming increasingly fraught, if not fluid, boundaries that risk becoming quite costly indeed to defend. Belarus, Azerbaijan, Armenia, Kyrgyzstan, theoretically independent states since the breakup of the Soviet Union, but long seen by Putin as firmly within his Russian envelope, suddenly began showing new signs of restlessness. Revolts by their people against rulers, remnants of the Soviet era like Alexander Lukashenko in Belarus and Sooronbay Jeenbekov in Kyrgyzstan, as well as the on-again, off-again war between Azerbaijan and Armenia, all demonstrated the necessity of people within artificially-established red lines to buy into their core concepts. And fewer than ever among these peoples now seem prepared to do that.

Putin's efforts to establish and maintain such lines close to home would test his ability to establish and maintain red lines further afield. And that would put him directly in the middle of the world's most intricate and deadly web of red lines, which has proliferated across the Middle East, a network where Russia would emerge to control a series of lines which the United States, having long established and defended, was suddenly in danger of losing control. And just as America's control over a complex and dangerous series of lines was slipping away as well in another region that had become profoundly important to Western interests.

CHAPTER SIX

Mesopotamia:
Crime & Punishment

For half a millennium, the most immutable, most sacred, if at times most contested, but highly defended, and above all universally recognized of history's red lines is the boundary between the peoples, at times the empires, of the Persian and Arab worlds. It was a line first drawn even before the time of Mohammed, dropped by Tamerlane and the Mongols who poured in to conquer the region, but which reappeared with the arrival of the first modern Persian shah, Ismail I, who established the powerful Safavid Dynasty in 1501. Through at least four successive Persian dynasties this line has remained in force—at times tested but never truly breached until today. In the next two chapters, we will examine this line from both sides—first from the Arab, then from the Iranian perspective. From the Arab side, a multiplicity of red lines has also been created within the region itself, which, more open to waves of invasion and conquest, has seen today a larger concentration of such barriers than in any other corner of the world.

—

Red lines have crisscrossed the Arabian Middle East since biblical times. Joshua and the Israelites fought the mythical battle of Jericho in an effort to pierce the walls of that city, today the town of Tell es-Sultan, a mile north of the center of modern Jericho on the Israeli West Bank, and where excavations have cast doubt on whether this military operation ever actually took place. Still, the Book of Joshua describers how the Israelites launched their campaign against Canaan by sending two spies into Jericho, the city that was the first obstacle to their mission of conquest of the Holy Land, then marched seven times around the wall, carrying the Ark of the Covenant and blowing their rams horns, at which point the walls just came tumbling down. One way to do away with a red line.

It took more than two millennia before the prophet Mohammed would launch the religion of Islam and the accompanying concept of *jihad*, or holy war. Less than a century later, Muslim warriors of the Umayyad Caliphate would extend the boundaries of Islam across three continents with a passion that has yet to be extinguished today. Above all, however, his followers took this religion into the Persian heartland, where in its own peculiar form it took strong and deep roots. The Islamic armies had already fought a series of battles among themselves in the year immediately following Mohammed's death in 632. As it happens, many of these early battles were waged along an almost identical frontier as the one that consumed both Iraq and Iran in their nearly ten-year war beginning in 1980. As a leading historian of this era, Michael G. Morony of UCLA, described it:

> The Persians were totally routed, and fugitive Persian soldiers were pursued and killed in the villages, reed thickets, and river banks. Some 4,000 Iranian soldiers (the Ḥamrāʾ) joined the Muslim army at Qādesīya, shared equally in the booty, and participated in the subsequent campaign; the fate of the Sawād was settled. . . .
>
> The Muslim conquest of Iran meant the eclipse of Iranian monarchic traditions except to the extent that these were adopted by Muslim Arab rulers and the loss of political support for Zoroastrians. . . .
>
> The conquest also brought Muslim Arab settlers to Iran, initially as garrisons to ensure the payment of tribute, and tended to concentrate them in frontier regions. Because the conquest of most of Iran turned out to be permanent, Islam eventually spread among Iranians, and Arabic became the language of religion, literature, and science in Iran. In this respect the Muslim Arab conquest marks a major turning point in the history of Iran.

The Umayyad Caliphate—the first real Islamic dynasty—in 661 established its capital in Damascus. At its peak, the territory of totaled 4.3 million square miles, larger than either the United States or China today. From these early days, the Islamic warriors came to understand deeply the value of red lines in maintaining their hegemony over territories won or held, ultimately extending these territories, victory by victory. Eventually, Islam would also penetrate to the gates of Budapest on the east. On the west, its armies crossed the Pyrenees into France, penetrating as far as a point between the towns of Tours and Poitier where only Charles Martel's brilliant military maneuvers held an early red line, defeating the Umayyad army of Abd al-Rahman ibn Abd Allah al-Ghafiqi, who was forced to retreat, eventually into Spain. There, he and his descendants managed to establish and defend their Caliphate of Córdoba until at least the time of the first European crusaders, who were determined to penetrate the lines drawn by the Islamic armies of the east.

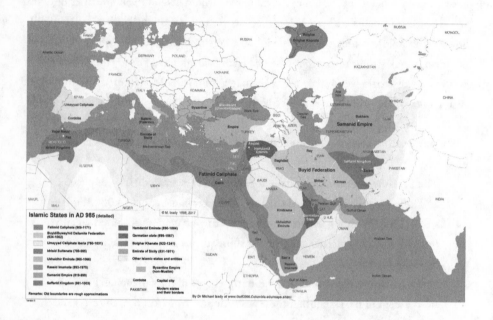

Islam expands, 350 years after the death of Mohammed.

Beginning some three centuries after the first Muslim armies entered Europe across the Strait of Gibraltar, the first European crusaders did not have quite so easy a time in their efforts to pierce the lines the Ottoman Turks had erected in their push north and west from Damascus and Jerusalem. The idea of taking and holding Jerusalem for Christianity was really the brainchild of Pope Urban II as the eleventh century was drawing to a close. His call was for a "holy war" on Islam that would not only cleanse the souls of those who undertook this First Crusade, but also take down the red lines the Muslims had erected around the lands Christendom considered holy.

In the early fall of 1097, the warriors of the First Crusade entered what was then northern Syria, arriving at the walls of the great Seljuk metropolis of Antioch, now the town of Antakya, twelve miles north of the current border between Turkey and Syria. Antioch was the beginning of a string of fortresses that sustained a defensive line southward along the Mediterranean coast. The Franks, the heart of the First Crusade, sought to break this red line to reach their goal of reclaiming Jerusalem for the Vatican and Christianity. They succeeded in reaching the great biblical city and occupying it, but only for a moment in historical terms. By the time of the Third Crusade, the most memorable as it involved three notable royals—Richard the Lionhearted, Philip II of France, and Yusuf ibn Ayyub, known in the West as Saladin—the concept of accretion of territory followed by settling lines to defend these territories had been well established. Eventually, the crusaders built a thin defensive perimeter that ran along the Mediterranean coast. They never succeeded in expanding inland as far as Jerusalem, though Richard did manage to advance twice to within a day's march of the holy city. Eventually, he ran out of resources to capture the city and establish a defendable boundary.

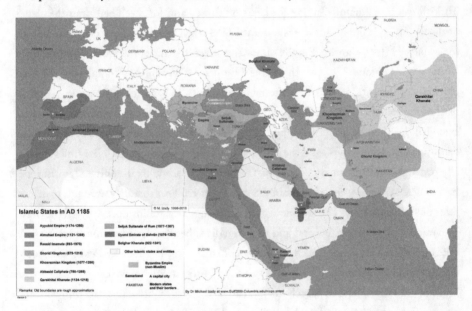

By the time of the Crusades, Islam expands across northern Africa and into fringes of Europe.

Six more Crusades would follow over the next century, ending with the final collapse of the thin line of Christian states along the Mediterranean coasts of what would become Libya and Palestine. In the end, the fall of Tripoli and Acre (on the coast north of Haifa, barely a hundred miles from Jerusalem) suggests that the Europeans were not terribly adept at either creating or defending any red lines—or alternatively that they did not mean very much at all to them. For the crusaders, territorial conquest and aggrandizement was far more important. Such a policy, especially in as fluid a region as the Middle East, has always been anathema to the successful construction and maintenance of viable red lines.

I am persuaded that much of this was and remains due to something deep inside the Arab soul—springing from the nomadic roots at the core of many of these cultures. Certainly, this has been the case deeper within the Arabian region. Saudi Arabia did not coalesce as a real nation until 1744 with the emergence of the Al Saud dynasty in central Arabia, and even then, it remained a patchwork of tribal rulers and their often nomadic people.

By around 1300, the Seljuk dynasty had begun to disintegrate as it was pressured by Mongol invaders from the east pouring in through Persia. Coupled with the inability to hold onto some of its more remote regions, the Muslim empire began to disintegrate into small *beyliks*, or principalities. Eventually, several began to coalesce into the early Ottoman state, and that empire was born. In 1299, Osman I took over leadership of a large group of Turkish tribes in Anatolia, today the heart of Turkey and for seven centuries the center of the Ottoman Empire. But it was not until 1453 when Mehmed the Conqueror and his forces pierced the Byzantine Empire's lines and seized the ancient city of Constantinople, whose origins date to 324 with the Roman Emperor Constantine's conquest of the even older city of Byzantium, that the Ottoman Empire would begin to approach its zenith. It reached its peak after a succession of sultans, climaxing with Suleiman the Magnificent, who extended the lines defining the Empire to include Syria, Lebanon, stretches of the Arabian Peninsula, Palestine, Egypt, and the entire coastal strip of North Africa. His armies eventually penetrated into Hungary, Romania, Greece, and Macedonia in southeastern Europe. Everywhere his forces went, they established their own red lines that they were able to defend more or less successfully. The red line across Northern Africa, for instance, hugged the coast. The impenetrable deserts beyond and the nomadic tribes that traveled from oasis to oasis were incapable of being controlled or circumscribed. As was the case with Persia: this would remain outside the Ottoman boundaries and the Christian lines as well.

These red lines—Islam largely to the east and south, Christianity to the west and north—for the most part held until the Treaty of Versailles upset the entire structure of the Middle East. These lines, at times challenged but rarely successfully, represented centuries of boundaries—geographic, political, social, and spiritual. Until that watershed year of 1919. Then, most were upset, with a host of new, largely geographic red lines ignorantly redrawn during a horrific and ill-informed six months in Paris at the beginning of 1919. Here, the framework was set for the multiplicity of such lines that crisscross the region today. The goals of the peacemakers who came to Paris—France, Britain, Italy, and the United States, collectively the allied victors of World War I—were to dismantle the old empires of Germany, Austria-Hungary, and the Ottomans, and to make certain that their successor states would be in no position ever again to wreak havoc on world order. This had, after all, been described and fought as the war-to-end-all-wars.

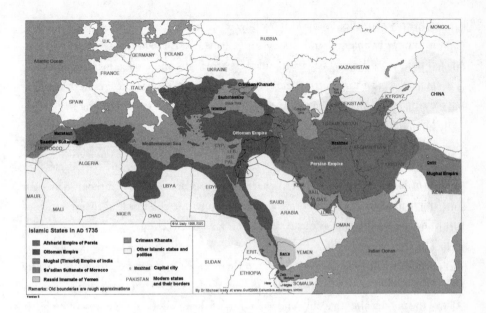

In 1735, the Persian and Ottoman Empires near the peak of their reach and influence.

The fundamental problem was that none of those drafting the articles of peace had any idea what their new boundaries and new lines of demarcation meant to those tens of millions of people who would be forced live within them. But above all, these Western statesmen had barely any idea of the consequences of their edicts. The goal, especially of British Prime Minister David Lloyd George and his French counterpart, Georges Clemenceau, was to create nations small enough that they would pose no real challenge to the major powers, yet large enough that the West would not be troubled by dealing with a whole host of fractious statelets. In the Middle East, in particular, the nations—initially protectorates of one or another of the major powers—were designed to allow unfettered access to a land route from the Mediterranean to the British colonies on the Indian subcontinent and the French colony of Indochina. But no one had any real idea what these lines they were drafting meant. Take, for instance, the diary entry of a young counselor on the British delegation, Harold Nicolson, who would later go on to considerable fame as a diplomat, member of parliament, author, and especially husband of Vita Sackville-West. Nicolson, who was dismayed by the ill-informed decisions being made by his superiors, was hovering in the anteroom of American President Woodrow Wilson's townhouse near the Place du Trocadéro, passing the time with Oscar Wilde's *The Picture of Dorian Gray*, when suddenly the ornate doors to the salon flew open and he was summoned inside:

A heavily furnished study with my huge map on the carpet . . . bending over
it, bubble bubble toil and trouble, are Clemenceau, Lloyd George and PW
[President Wilson]. They have pulled up armchairs and crouch low over the
map. . . . They are cutting the Baghdad railway. Clemenceau says nothing
during all of this. He sits at the edge of his chair and leans over the map.
More than ever does he look like a gorilla of yellow ivory. . . . It is appalling
that these ignorant and irresponsible men should be cutting Asia Minor
to bits as if they were dividing a cake. . . . Isn't it terrible, the happiness
of millions being discarded in that way? Their decisions are immoral and
impracticable. . . . These three ignorant men with a child to lead them. . . .
The child, I suppose, is me. Anyhow, it is an anxious child.

"Cutting the Baghdad railway" was the final stage in creating the new and largely
artificial nation of Iraq. So truly, Nicolson had much to be anxious about. For openers,
none of the peacemakers had any understanding of the profound differences, often bitter
and hostile animosities, between Shiite and Sunni Muslims, or especially the Kurds. Wilson's chief Middle East advisor was Professor William Westermann of the University of
Wisconsin, later Columbia, whose specialty was the pre-Ottoman Middle East, largely the
Greco-Roman era and the Crusades, meaning that his real experience ended somewhere
in the vicinity of 1300 with the Ninth Crusade. Still, other members of Wilson's brain
trust, The Inquiry, whom he brought to Paris, were hardly better informed. Arthur I.
Andrews, a Tufts professor who specialized in the Transcaucasus, would describe "the
Koords" [sic] in racial and generalized terms that, though today highly discomfiting,
would have informed decades of policy.

Then, as now, the Kurds were scattered across the new nation of Iraq as well as Iran,
Turkey, and Syria—all of whose boundary lines, with the exception of Iran's, were
in the process of being redrawn in Paris in 1919. A small adjustment to each of these
lines—carving a small slice off Turkey, off Syria, and off what would become the multi-
religious nation of Iraq, could easily have created a separate nation for the Kurds, as the
peacemakers did for the Jews in setting up their homeland in British-overseen Palestine.

Clearly what was happening already in 1919 was the establishing of new and artificially created boundaries of these nations—created on the carpet of Wilson's Trocadéro
townhouse, in conference rooms of the Quai d'Orsay, Clemenceau's townhouse in the
16th arrondissement, and in other venues across Paris. On the ground in the Middle East,
however, still utterly invisible to these peacemakers but no less real and eventually utterly
toxic, were the red lines of Sunni versus Shiite, especially in Iraq where the majority Shiites

were concentrated in the oil-rich regions across the south of the country, the entirety ruled by the minority Sunnis who occupied the north and the region around Baghdad. This nation survived decades of British occupation, finally winning its independence in 1932.

This complex web would only truly come into focus at the moment in 1990 when the Iraqi dictator, Saddam Hussein, decided he was entitled to Kuwait and quite simply came in and took it. For centuries, Kuwait had been an integral part of the Ottoman province of Basra. In 1899, the ruling family of the emirate of Kuwait negotiated a treaty with Britain that made it effectively a protectorate of the United Kingdom, which assumed all control over its foreign affairs. When Iraq was created in the Versailles Treaty and a subsequent document, the Treaty of Sèvres, the province of Basra was simply divided in half—leaving Iraq utterly landlocked and Kuwait with a large part of the vast oil reserves beneath the desert that straddles both borders. Iraq never really recognized that boundary as legitimate. Eventually, Saddam Hussein acted to erase it, invading Kuwait in a blitzkrieg two-day operation launched August 2, 1990.

Eventually, the United States and some Kuwaiti neighbors, particularly the Kingdom of Saudi Arabia, as well as French and British forces, moved in and embarked on the First Gulf War. The big mistake was in its conclusion, yet again demonstrating how badly drafted and ill-enforced red lines can prove utterly toxic. The conclusion of the First Gulf War came just as the commanding general, Norman Schwarzkopf, was poised to roll into Baghdad, presumably bringing down Saddam Hussein. Instead, with American forces barely 150 miles from the Iraqi capital, President George H. W. Bush declared a unilateral ceasefire. Bush, then eventually his son President George W. Bush, would effectively ratify the red lines established by the Saddam regime.

The First Gulf War was in many respects less important for any physical red lines established—effectively they were simply designed to restore national boundaries, more or less poorly drawn in the first place, of course—than for drawing some critical, if more ephemeral and less clearly defined, diplomatic or politico-military boundaries. Most of these revolved around the possession or use of weapons of mass destruction—nuclear, chemical, or biological. Such red lines would play a central role in the outbreak or containment of future conflicts and efforts to maintain security across the region.

Saddam Hussein had built his entire regime on challenging red lines. On September 22, 1980, Iraqi forces crossed the frontier into Iran. Saddam feared, perhaps with some justification, that Iran's newly resurgent Shiite majority, which had just assumed control of the country little more than a year earlier, was intending to assume dominance over the entire Persian Gulf region. That fear was only stoked by Ayatollah Ruhollah Khomeini's call, some months after seizing power, for Iraqis to rise up and throw off the

Ba'athist (Sunni) government of Saddam. This was simply a follow-through to the ayatollah's incendiary message as he stepped off an Air France jet in Tehran on February 1,
ending a fifteen-year exile and igniting a furiously Islamist state. "Our final victory will
come when all foreigners are out of the country," he proclaimed. "I beg God to cut off
the hand of all evil foreigners and all their helpers." A landmark speech by Saddam on
July 17, 1979, holding out an olive branch, praising the Iranian Revolution, and calling
for mutual respect of their frontier and each nation's internal affairs, was effectively
slapped aside by Khomeini, who responded by calling even more stridently for outright
revolution in Iraq. Saddam, forty-four years old, had just officially assumed the reins of
power as president from his sixty-eight-year-old predecessor, Ahmed Hassan al-Bakr,
the veteran Ba'ath Party leader, though Saddam had already been running the country
for at least three years.

Al-Bakr and Saddam had long considered the boundary between their country and the
Shah's Iran all but untouchable—a true red line that both parties respected and upheld.
By contrast, Khomeini had no interest in any red lines beyond those that defined the
peripheries of the Shiite religion, and which therefor extended well into Iraq, particularly
its oil-rich southern regions, which Shiites dominated, and extending to the eastern region
of Saudi Arabia. The deep concern of the Saudis to preserve their national frontier intact
and free of any ideologic, religious, or certainly military encroachment by Iran meant
constant vigilance, internal and external, and close attention paid to the actions of Iraq.

As for Iraq, it was fully prepared to try to get along with the new regime in Iran. That
would quickly prove to be utterly unrealistic, particularly in the wake of Khomeini's
earliest pronouncements. Still, Saddam quite rightly feared some of the ayatollah's most
vicious pronouncements. So, on September 4, 1980, he sent a detachment of ten thousand
troops to seize ninety square miles of territory along the strategic Shatt al-Arab waterway
to secure a particularly strategic stretch of the border. The waterway, Saddam proclaimed,
now belonged fully to Iraq. He had effectively crossed a red line that Iran could not easily
ignore. By September 20, the two sides seemed to be edging toward full engagement along
some 900 miles of the frontier—a line that had by now all but totally collapsed.

There ensued eight years of bitter fighting, World War I–style trench warfare with
barbed wire strung along miles of fortified defenses, and even chemical weapons
deployed by Saddam's forces. At least 500,000 troops died during the bitter hostilities,
punctuated by suicide attacks—human waves of Iranian soldiers operating under a "cult
of the martyr" fanned by Shiite clerics in the holy city of Qom. Hostilities were finally
brought to an end by a UN-brokered ceasefire, and the resulting truce line, marked by
the geographical boundaries of the two nations, remained all but unchanged.

On his own side of this red line, however, Saddam continued to build his strength, rebuilding a military and internal security team designed to make certain that no force, internal or external, would be in any position to challenge him or his iron-like grip on his nation. Still, he was ill-prepared for the consequences. With George W. Bush seeking some easily identified scapegoat for 9/11, and with Saddam clearly eager to promote his invincibility in the region as a credible deterrent to guarantee an impregnable frontier, it was but a short leap of faith to the belief that he was in possession of a "weapon of mass destruction" that needed to be taken out. And so the Second Iraq War—a conflict far bloodier, far more destabilizing in virtually every way than the one that followed Saddam's adventure into Kuwait. This time, the resulting power vacuum would leave open a path toward a whole new configuration of red lines across the region.

Operation Iraqi Freedom was ill-conceived, poorly executed, and based largely on manipulated intelligence. Saddam never had the nuclear weapon he was said to have been on the verge of deploying. Nor did his people rise up spontaneously against his villainous rule as American forces poured across his borders. Nor were any of these invading forces in any position to establish or enforce any red line regime of their own. All they were remotely able to accomplish was to set up a puppet regime that was itself utterly ill-prepared to hold at bay the inevitable insurgency that promptly developed. A bloody stalemate set in—no red lines, only a constantly shifting kaleidoscope of violence and mayhem. Eventually, there was a handoff—from George Bush to Barack Obama, who had pledged in his presidential campaign to end the war at all cost, which would not happen until three years after he assumed office in January 2009.

Through much of the first decade of the twenty-first century, American forces operated effectively as an occupying army, as many Iraqis increasingly came to see it. The only red line that they were monitoring was an evanescent one of restoring stability to a nation that had effectively a new and utterly unfamiliar form of government forced on it—an American-style democracy. At the occupation's peak in September through November of 2007, 168,000 American troops were based and operating in Iraq. On December 14, 2008, President Bush, by then a lame-duck president, flew to Baghdad to sign the Strategic Framework Agreement and the Security Agreement with Prime Minister Nouri al-Maliki. It was a unique moment. These documents provided for a final and definitive withdrawal of American forces from Iraq in three years. Asked at a press conference that accompanied the signing if he considered this a "victory lap," Bush replied, "No, I consider it an important step . . . on the road toward an Iraq that can sustain itself, govern itself and defend itself." Not everyone agreed, especially one audacious journalist who, in the ultimate Arab insult, hurled both his shoes at Bush and Maliki. "This is a gift from the Iraqis. This is a farewell kiss, you dog," Muntadhar al-Zaidi, a twenty-eight-year old reporter for Egyptian-based Al-Baghdadia Television, shouted as he hurled his first shoe. Then as he hurled his second he added, "This is from the widows, the orphans and those who were killed in Iraq." Later, Bush told reporters, "I don't think you can take one guy throwing shoes and say this represents a broad movement in Iraq." Only it did. And this was just the beginning. The first suggestion of red lines began appearing as soon as the first American troops began their withdrawal.

Bush considered that what tenuous red lines al-Qaeda terrorists had established within Iraq were already coming down. As he put it at the signing ceremony: "Violence is down dramatically. Al Qaeda is driven from its safe havens. Sunnis, Shia, and Kurds are sitting together at the same table to peacefully chart the future of this country." Little of this was either true or particularly relevant.

For in January 2009, Barack Obama was sworn in as president, and his goal was a sharp turn in America's entire relationship with the Middle East, establishing his own, new construct with little apparent understanding of the old order on which stability had been based. On June 4, Obama flew to Cairo to deliver a major address to the Arab world. He chose the American University of Cairo, a venue he recognized as "a beacon of Islamic learning," as well as an acknowledgment of the rising power of both Arab youth and the Arab street. A new set of boundaries, he believed, were being built—all but unrecognized by the West, but not for long. "America is not—and will never be—at war with Islam," he proclaimed to an audience watching on live television across the Arab world. Then, he turned to Iraq:

> America has a dual responsibility: to help Iraq forge a better future—and to leave Iraq to Iraqis. I have made it clear to the Iraqi people that we pursue no bases, and no claim on their territory or resources. Iraq's sovereignty is its own. That is why I ordered the removal of our combat brigades by next August. That is why we will honor our agreement with Iraq's democratically-elected government to remove combat troops from Iraqi cities by July, and to remove all our troops from Iraq by 2012.

Obama went on to touch on a number of points central to what he saw, quite accurately, as Arab aspirations that could be contiguous with American interests—democracy, religious freedom, women's rights, economic development, and opportunity. The problem is that most of what Obama saw as shared aspirations were hardly shared by the vast majority of the autocratic rulers of most of these Arab nations, who had erected their own internal red lines designed to maintain singlehanded control over their nations. But from Tunisia to Syria, their hold was about to be challenged. It did not take long for the Arab street—the young activist street in particular—to react.

On December 17, 2010, a twenty-six-year-old Arab street vendor, Mohammed Bouazizi, poured flammable paint fluid over himself outside the municipal building in the village of Sidi Bouzid, Tunisia, where he'd been harassed and humiliated, his wooden vegetable cart and scale confiscated. Then, he set himself on fire in the ultimate act of protest. The flame he ignited quickly spread from this tiny market town a hundred thirty miles from the capital to Tunis and quickly across the Middle East. On January 14, 2011, the government was overthrown in Tunisia. Eleven days later, vast throngs surged into Tahrir Square in Cairo, demanding the resignation of Egyptian president Hosni Mubarak, which took place on February 11. Four days after that, the first protests broke out in Benghazi against Muammar Qaddafi's rule in Libya. By August, rebel forces had overrun Tripoli, the Libyan capital. On October 20, Qaddafi was captured, hiding in a drainage pipe in Sirte, and killed by rebels.

It was on March 15, 2011, however, that the most consequential rebellion began in Syria—one that would lead to the establishment of an unrelenting multiplication of new and utterly unimagined red lines crisscrossing that country and neighboring Iraq. By July, the Free Syrian Army had been organized by a group of seven defecting officers from President Bashar al-Assad's own military, with the stated objective "to work with the people to bring down the system; to protect the people from the armed killing machine of the system." What began was a complex and utterly lethal competition for territory that, with the arrival of the Islamic State would turn into an elaborate game of three-dimensional chess.

One of the principal reasons for the long-term American occupation of Iraq was to neutralize the organization built initially by Abu Musab al-Zarqawi, a Jordanian Sunni and close ally of the Saudi-born Sunni terrorist leader Osama bin Laden. While bin Laden was leading his jihad against the United States from the mountains of Afghanistan, climaxing in the 9/11 attacks on the World Trade Center and the Pentagon, al-Zarqawi was moving from the terrorist training camp he'd being running for bin Laden in Herat, Afghanistan's third largest city, to Iraq. There, he began building his al-Qaeda-in-Iraq organization, challenging American forces. By October 2003, al-Zarqawi and his murderous regime were well established, his personnel reinforced by a network of ratlines for foreign fighters to join him in his crusade, and accounting for some 42 percent of all suicide bombings in Iraq. From the start, however, al-Zarqawi appeared little interested in establishing any real red lines. His goal was indiscriminate carnage designed to spread terror and fear with a global audience—hence his early embrace of televised beheadings of carefully selected individuals, staged for maximum dramatic effect. If there was any red line in any of this, it was al-Zarqawi's self-perception as the leader of the defenders of the Holy Land against the infidel invaders of the Crusades. The territory he was defending was much of Mesopotamia. Or, as he put it in a letter in 2005: "We do not fight for a fistful of dust or the boundaries drawn by Sykes-Picot," referring to the secret Anglo-French agreement to carve up and establish boundaries in the Middle East and ratified, rather unthinkingly, in the Versailles Treaty of 1919. Inevitably, though, al-Zarqawi had a target on his back. In 2006, even before the American military presence in Iraq had peaked, al-Zarqawi was tracked to an isolated safehouse thirty miles outside of Baghdad, where two US Air Force F-16s dropped two five-hundred-pound laser-guided bombs.

But what al-Zarqawi left behind was an organization that would ultimately form and test some of the most pernicious red lines of the modern era. A succession of individuals followed al-Zarqawi as leaders of the al-Qaeda-in-Iraq organization and then, beginning in October 2006, the Islamic State in Iraq. How complex this overlapping set of directorates and organizations had become is indicated by an "At War: Notes From the Front Lines" dispatch in May 2010 from *The New York Times* Baghdad bureau that described "the Islamic State of Iraq [as] the insurgent group that serves as a front for al-Qaeda in Iraq." The brief, eleven-paragraph piece then went on to note, as an aside, that "the group had named Abu Bakr al-Baghdadi al-Husseini al-Qurashi as the new leader after consultations with the group's leaders, influential people and 'opinion-makers.'" The group's perfunctory announcement statement concluded, "We implore God to help them make the right decisions."

Over the next four years, those decisions would cause the transformation of the Islamic State of Iraq from a front for al-Qaeda in Iraq into the murderous caliphate known as the Islamic State of Iraq and Syria (ISIS). Its initially unchecked expansion would begin in March 2013 with the capture of Raqqa.

Raqqa is the capital of an eponymous governorate, strategically situated on the banks of the Euphrates River. Back in the earliest days of Islam, it had served as the capital of the Abbasid Caliphate from 796 to 809 c.e. Just one hundred miles east of the Syrian financial capital of Aleppo and twenty-five miles east of the Tabqa Dam, Syria's largest, it would also come to serve as the epicenter of a constantly expanding red line that defined the Islamic State. For the long-suffering citizens of Raqqa, this meant great visibility and misery as the forces of the Free Syrian Army seized the city from Assad's troops and were in turn displaced by force of arms by the terrorists of ISIS. It was here that al-Baghdadi established the capital of his self-styled caliphate—a model of brutal dictatorship devoted to the practice of an extreme form of sharia law, enforced by imprisonment, torture, and beatings in the street with thick leather straps, punishments meted out even to women not considered adequately covered up and fathers photographing their families. Summary justice extended from amputation of a hand for simple theft to routine public beheadings.

Al-Baghdadi was able to begin expanding the territory controlled by his own red line largely because of a conscious decision by Bashar al-Assad that his resources, particularly his air power, could more profitably be spent attacking the Free Syrian Army that he saw as the principal challenge to his control over his own territory in what had rapidly turned into a full-blown civil war. But it was not purely air power that Assad was prepared to call on. And this was where his hubris ran up against a red line defined by global consensus but that he had never really taken very seriously at all. That red line was the use of chemical weapons, outlawed by the world at the Geneva Convention of 1925 after their indiscriminate use in the First World War had so horrified global sensibilities.

—

The red line that is most often invoked today as the contemporary paradigm of the concept is a tribute as much to an offhand remark by an American president as to any carefully thought through policy or plan. And the process began unspooling at the very moment al-Baghdadi was plotting his rampage through Mesopotamia. Since the Syrian red line of Barack Obama has become the touchstone by which so many have been patterned, it would be worthwhile to examine in some detail just how all this played out, especially for the very few winners and the many losers.

On August 20, 2012, it was a bit cloudy and, for Washington, a rather temperate seventy-seven degrees outside, when Jay Carney, the rather boyish-looking press secretary for President Barack Obama, stepped to the podium in the Press Briefing Room of the White House West Wing to observe, "looks like there's a surprise guest here." It was, spontaneously, the president himself who'd decided to take over the daily briefing that day, observing lightly, "Jay tells me that you guys have been missing me. So, I thought I'd come by and just say hello." He plunged right into what was top of mind—Medicare and the impact his new healthcare law was having on America's elderly, then the presidential race where he was pitted against the Republican candidate, Mitt Romney. It wasn't until the president paused for questions and turned to NBC anchor Chuck Todd that Syria and the Middle East came into focus.

Todd wanted to know the president's "latest thinking of where you think things are in Syria, and in particular, whether you envision using U.S. military, if simply for nothing else, the safe keeping of the chemical weapons, and if you're confident that the chemical weapons are safe?"

Obama provided an answer, on the fly, apparently without having given it very much deep thought beyond the baseline ethics:

> Obviously, this is a very tough issue. I have indicated repeatedly that President al-Assad has lost legitimacy, that he needs to step down. So far, he hasn't gotten the message, and instead has double downed in violence on his own people. The international community has sent a clear message that rather than drag his country into civil war he should move in the direction of a political transition. But at this point, the likelihood of a soft landing seems pretty distant. . . . We want to make sure that the hundreds of thousands of refugees that are fleeing the mayhem, that they don't end up creating—or being in a terrible situation, or also destabilizing some of Syria's neighbors.
>
> The second thing we've done is we said that we would provide, in consultation with the international community, some assistance to the opposition in thinking about how would a political transition take place, and what are the principles that should be upheld in terms of looking out for minority rights and human rights. And that consultation is taking place.
>
> I have, at this point, not ordered military engagement in the situation. But the point that you made about chemical and biological weapons is critical. That's an issue that doesn't just concern Syria; it concerns our close allies in the region, including Israel. It concerns us. We cannot have a situation where chemical or biological weapons are falling into the hands of the wrong people. We have been very clear to the Assad regime, but also to other players on the ground, that *a red line* for us is we start seeing a whole bunch of chemical weapons moving around or being utilized. That would change my calculus. That would change my equation.
>
> Q: So you're confident it's somehow under—it's safe?
>
> THE PRESIDENT: In a situation this volatile, I wouldn't say that I am absolutely confident. What I'm saying is we're monitoring that situation very carefully. We have put together a range of contingency plans. We have communicated in no uncertain terms with every player in the region that that's a red line for us and that there would be enormous consequences if we start seeing movement on the chemical weapons front or the use of chemical weapons. That would change my calculations significantly.
>
> All right, thank you, everybody. (emphasis added)

Then he turned and left. At this impromptu Monday afternoon news conference, Obama had tossed off a line that much of the world would come to regret, and that would, as had so many red lines before, alter the course of history in this strategic corner of the world where so many Americans had already lost their lives and that Obama had pledged to quit militarily. None of the principal attributes of a successfully established and defended red line, with intended outcomes, was remotely in place. Assad had never really at all "been told clearly," at least in terms he could understand, indeed most of America's leading allies were utterly blindsided. Nor was the American military in any position to establish and police such a line reliably and, if not eternally, at least through to a defined end. But above all, his "range of contingency plans" was all but utterly ephemeral. Certainly, Western intelligence had already seen any numbers of chemical weapons being moved around virtually at will in Syria. A year later everything would change.

On the ground in Syria was the locus of this red line that Obama had never actually seen or, clearly, very deeply understood, except as it would play out on some grainy cell-phone video.

In Damascus, it was 2:25 in the morning, August 21, 2013—one year and six hours since Obama had defined the red line in his answer to NBC's Chuck Todd. The Syrian capital never really sleeps. The rebels held most of the suburbs, including the plain of Ghouta, the vegetable garden that surrounds the city. The old town was within reach of artillery. The highway leading to the international airport was under fire from rebel snipers, so traffic on the road was negligible. For forty-eight hours, supporters of the regime had been nervous. Their security services learned that the Free Syrian Army, still the main force of military opposition to the Assad family, was preparing an offensive. The troops assigned to defend the city, including the renowned Republican Guard, were on the highest alert. The stormy, stifling night was punctuated by sporadic exchanges of artillery. The regime's general staff had been summoned late in the evening of August 20 by Maher al-Assad, Bashar's younger brother, who commanded the fourth division, the regime's shield. Ali Mamlouk, the president's most trusted security advisor, confirmed that the Free Syrian Army was ready to launch a new assault on the capital.

Maher began questioning the various corps leaders. The atmosphere was gloomy. The very existence of the regime was being threatened. Bashar's forces must strike a blow terrorizing the enemy. The head of the chemical forces understood instantly what he had to do and affirmed his units were ready.

That night, as had been routine since the beginning of the insurrection, Maher did not sleep. Bashar, the president, went to bed early. Between 10 P.M. and 6 A.M., Maher, whom his men had begun calling "president of the night," assumed command from his headquarters, attached to the barracks of the Fourth Division atop Mount Qasioun, dominating the city and offering a unique vantage point.

For forty-eight hours, Western intelligence services, particularly the American and French, had observed unusual movements around the complex where they were confident chemical weapons were stored. United Nations inspectors landed thirty-six hours earlier to investigate their scattered use four times in the north of the country weeks before. Before there was any definitive announcement, samples taken by rebels and transmitted to France and the United States still had to be verified by international inspectors making on-the-scene checks. Both the government and rebels had been accused of using these gases. Although they accepted the arrival of the investigators in Syria, the government had not allowed them direct access to the sites. They remained pinned in their hotel in Damascus.

Now, shortly after two o'clock in the morning, a dozen rockets began falling in a five-hundred-yard radius on the eastern side of the densely populated Damascus suburb of Ghouta. The barrage was quite precise, yet after touching the ground, the warheads produced only small explosions. On the spot, observers of the Free Syrian Army noticed a heavy white smoke spreading over the houses. It took barely a moment to understand that it was gas. But at this hour, the neighborhood was asleep. Some 1,400 persons, including more than 600 children, would never wake up. At 6 A.M., images of convulsed bodies began circulating on social networks. In Paris, London, and Washington, senior officials were alerted, and horrified. "We cannot stand still without reacting," observed French Defense Minister Jean-Yves Le Drian. He quickly assembled his brain trust, whose members universally expressed their astonishment that Bashar would so flagrantly cross this quite clearly defined red line. But had it been so clearly defined? Had the consequences, if not the horror, ever been truly spelled out? A senior official who was at the session confided later to French journalist Pierre Favier: "We were stunned that Bashar dared to cross this Red Line. We received this news as a break with all precedent, an utterly flagrant action. For doing this, Bashar must be even crazier than we ever imagined. We all thought, it cannot be allowed to pass without a reaction." As soon as he became aware of the gas attack, Admiral Édouard Guillaud, chief of the general staff of the armed forces, warned General Benoît Puga, chief of staff for President François Hollande.

"Some minutes later," Guillaud recalled, "Puga reminded me: 'Prepare yourself seriously, we will do something.' It was already clear that military action was an option. I determined to examine potential targets, what we knew and the means we had to target them." At the Quai d'Orsay, Foreign Minister Laurent Fabius, alerted immediately, did what every good French minister would do—assembled a task force. But the central question was how the Americans would react. For a year to the day, Obama had maintained a strict policy of nonintervention in what he had determined was a civil war. In international diplomacy and strategy, civil wars have no red lines. But then, there was that red line that he had apparently defined a year before.

The military were the first to consult with each other. Admiral Guillaud, General Martin Dempsey, chairman of the US Joint Chiefs of Staff, and General David Richards, chief of the British Defense Staff, confirmed their readiness to support civilian authorities if the decision was made for a strike and began assembling targeting lists. François Hollande also demanded before any decision was presented to him that a smoking gun be identified. "Sarin gas particles break down very fast," said a senior Ministry of Defense official. "We asked our services to bring in samples of contaminated material, and to do that, they took enormous risks."

As the day began in Washington, Fabius contacted Secretary of State John Kerry. Their first conversations dealt with coordinated reactions of their two countries. In the evening, French intelligence communicated its provisional conclusion that the convulsions of the victims on the early videos were characteristic of poisoning by sarin gas. The British government promptly demanded a meeting of the UN Security Council. Bashar al-Assad denied his forces had used gas, branding the attack the work of the rebels.

Fabius was quickly able to assure Hollande that the Brits and Americans were determined to react. The next morning, August 22, James Clapper, US Director of National Intelligence, interrupted the President's daily CIA briefing with the news that "the information we have received on the use of sarin gas is solid even if not totally without doubt." Obama ordered the Pentagon to identify a targeting list. Five US Arleigh Burke–class cruise missile destroyers began moving into position in the eastern Mediterranean. In France, Le Drian assured Hollande that operations could be carried out without endangering French military personnel. Rafale fighter jets, armed with SCALP cruise missiles, and based in Djibouti and Abu Dhabi would be in a position to launch as far as two hundred miles from their targets.

"The targets were related to the division of labor among allies, which depended on the capabilities of each," Admiral Guillaud told Favier. "The President [Hollande] had demanded that only facilities and units related to the chemical weapons attack be considered." As it happens, the French military still maintained close ties with the most senior Syrian military officers, back from the days when Syria was a French protectorate and its officers would come to study at the École Militaire in Paris—particularly Ali Mamlouk, the head of all Syrian military intelligence and the author of many of the most profound atrocities of the Assad regime. So it's hardly surprising that the French had the best intelligence on Syria's military chemical complex—the other, critical side of Obama's red line and where the French were light-years ahead.

On the 24th, David Cameron summoned the British Parliament back into session to endorse the operation—what turned out to be a foolhardy move.

On the 25th, French, English, and American researchers were in a position to compare their soil samples taken from Ghouta. The French were the first to reveal the presence of the deadly agent sarin, though in small quantities: one nanogram per milligram of gas. British samples contained a higher proportion of the lethal agent. French intelligence services would say only that they had proof that the use of gas was decided at the highest level of the Syrian government. Bashar al-Assad had, at a minimum, given his tacit agreement.

A high-level meeting of the French Defense Council was convened that same morning at the Élysée, in the ornate conference room adjacent to Hollande's private office. By tradition, the president opened with a statement that in this case emphasized the gravity of the crime committed four days earlier. Then he turned over the meeting to the minister for foreign affairs. Laurent Fabius presented the resolution drafted by France and its two allies. With respect to the British, however, he could not conceal that there was some doubt. Cameron had no obligation to seek the approval of his Parliament. But that's just what he was about to do. The British prime minister was quite determined to attack, but public opinion in Britain had still not recovered from being dragged into the Iraq adventure a decade earlier by Obama's predecessor, George W. Bush, who'd persuaded Tony Blair, on the flimsiest evidence, of the presence in Iraq of weapons of mass destruction that never existed. So now it was entirely possible that Parliament would refuse to follow Cameron's lead.

Le Drian then took the floor. As his chief of staff said later: "We quickly concluded that the use of chemical weapons on Ghouta had been decided at the highest level of the Syrian state. We were well aware of the organization of the chemical army, its military units, its research, manufacturing and command centers. It was a vertical structure where all decisions went back to the Presidency. If a strike were authorized, there were three levels of intensity. Attacking one or more communications centers would be nothing more than a warning not to do it again. The next strongest action would be to bomb one or more command centers. This would show that our countries intended to enforce international law." Nobody, apparently, suggested that day the extreme option of targeting Assad himself in Damascus.

The choice of such options has always been the responsibility of the French president alone, though in this case he had every intention of operating in tandem with his American and British allies. Hollande insisted again at his Defense Council session that the strikes must be most carefully targeted so that the meaning of the military intervention would be perfectly clear. It was not under any circumstance, however, to be a question of overthrowing the regime. The minister of defense then turned to his chief of staff, who revealed the attack plans. Three squadrons of three Rafale fighter-bombers would leave Saint-Dizier, Djibouti, and Abu Dhabi, supported by a squadron of tanker aircraft from Istres. The Rafales would launch their SCALP cruise missiles 120 miles from the target. It was without major risk to the pilots, and the targeting would be more precise than the cruise missiles deployed from further away by American or British ships.

Across the Atlantic, the tone was ratcheting up as well. "Those responsible will have to pay the price for their crime," John Kerry told reporters on the 26th. That evening, the principles and the broad outlines of a common response appeared fixed. But in Damascus, Syrian leaders were doing what they could to ensure that UN inspectors had no access to the scene of this crime. When the Syrian government finally give permission for them to go there, their convoy was attacked by sniper fire. They were forced to turn around.

In Moscow, Vladimir Putin feared for his Syrian ally. "If there is evidence of the involvement of the Damascus regime, let us see it," he proclaimed. "If we cannot, it's because there is none." And to impress the West with his determination, he deployed his naval assets in an arc across the Mediterranean, circling the Syrian coast. Russian submarines patrolled beneath allied ships to make their presence known. Observers noted, however, that the deployment of the Russian Navy was close to its Tartus base and the submarine commanders had routinely greeted the captains of the Allied fleet in a friendly manner. The NATO officers in the region concluded there was no risk of extension of the conflict. In this crisis, or at least for the moment, Russia was acting simply to protect its property. The Kremlin was not yet prepared to defend the regime of Bashar al-Assad unquestioningly, Paris quite rightly concluded.

The day after his Defense Council session, and in a clear effort to sway opinion in Britain and put some steel in the backbone of President Obama, Hollande, asserted: "The massacre of Damascus cannot remain unanswered. Those responsible will have to pay the price."

On the 29th in London, David Cameron summoned the newly convened House of Commons for a full debate and vote. There appeared to be little doubt, at least on the official level, that the world was heading toward an armed operation.

Meanwhile, in Syria, the UN inspectors, more briefly than they preferred, finally managed their first visit to Zamalka and Ain Tarma in Ghouta. It was understood that if there was no new activity, they would leave Syria on Sunday, September 1. Reports begin circulating that the Allied military operation could be triggered on their departure.

UN High Representative for Disarmament Affairs Angela Kane left Syria. In Damascus, with her departure, panic seized the ruling class, and beginning on August 28, hundreds of 4x4 trucks loaded with families of security forces crossed the border into neighboring Lebanon. Yet public opinion in the West, which at least officially subscribed to Obama's red line, remained largely opposed to any military reaction enforcing the mandate.

Many French leaders began to fear the British were about to drop out. In the name of socialist solidarity, Laurent Fabius embarked on a campaign to mobilize his Labour Party counterparts, in particular the shadow foreign secretary, Ed Miliband. Hollande, however, remained quite determined, telling one of his relatives: "Even if the British snort, we go." At the same time, the foreign ministry and the Élysée were receiving from their ambassador in Washington some decidedly mixed signals. Ambassador François Delattre was a singularly accomplished member of the French diplomatic corps. A graduate of Sciences Po and the most distinguished of the French *grands écoles*, the École Nationale d'Administration (ENA) [where he was a student of the author], he'd served at the French embassy in Germany, at the Quai d'Orsay as deputy chef de cabinet of the foreign minister, as consul general in New York, and ambassador to Canada before arriving in February 2011 as ambassador in Washington where he'd earlier served as press attaché. He was as plugged in as any diplomat in the capital to the elites of American media, diplomacy, and politics—uniquely equipped to provide guidance to his masters back home, but equally equipped to serve as a sounding board for those on Obama's senior staff who were attempting to guide their president.

"We knew the message of caution," Delattre told me five years later, "the fact that Obama was very cautious on Syria. That was really one of my key messages to Paris all along. In the end, the last mile leading to a decision of Obama on the red line and his decision not to go was really managed for the most part directly between Paris and Washington. But our line all along was a line of caution considering that Obama never wanted to be engaged in Syria, never wanted to own the problem as he told me personally."

Still, much of the decision-making was undertaken by both leaders directly. This effectively removed many who understood even better than the decision-makers the broader stakes involved. "That last mile leading to the decision, that was really a direct Paris-Washington channel of communication by our military—to the point where they were very specific with respect to the targets, who does what. So, this was by definition, very much a Paris-Washington direct line," Delattre observed.

What Delattre and his counterparts in Paris could have injected into the equation, had anyone paid attention, was the profound consequences if the crossing of this red line were not avenged. A very high price—in diplomatic, political, and military terms—would be paid for failing to punish its cavalier flaunting. This is the ultimate lesson of the Syrian red line that none of the parties directly involved in the decision-making ever really seemed to appreciate or even take into account, but that certainly should have been a central part of the deliberations. Had any of these principals also understood the consequences of earlier failures to respect or punish the crossing of red lines, this quintessential experience in Syria might very well have gone differently, as well as all the outcomes flowing directly and indirectly from it.

Meanwhile, still under the blind illusion that his two NATO partners remained fully on board, Hollande convened yet another Defense Council at the Élysée. It formalized France's response to events. The minutes of the session evoke "the reality of a gas attack recognized by all parties [and] the responsibility of the regime." It was decided to "prepare a punitive attack, coordinated with the United Kingdom and the United States, which could be launched quickly from French territory, sending cruise missiles targeting Syrian military sites tied to its chemical capabilities." The minutes still evoked a "firm and proportionate response."

In Washington, Obama announced that the United States had confirmed the guilt of the Damascus regime. American plans involved launching as many as 100 to 150 cruise missiles. Positioning this large number of missiles was in response to the possibility of a second strike if needed. The cost of a single American Tomahawk cruise missile is upward of $1.4 million. The numbers deployed by France would be more modest. At the Élysée, the size of the strike force that had been described in the previous session of the cabinet was confirmed, along with long-range tanker planes that would be launched from Corsica. All would complete their pre-flight setup at 15:00 (Paris time). The tankers would take off at 20:00. The Rafales would take off from their bases at different times depending on their distance from the target. Those originating in the Emirates would attack from the east over Jordan, while the Rafales based in Saint-Dizier and Djibouti would operate from the west, releasing their missiles over the Mediterranean. It would not be necessary for any to enter either Syrian or Turkish airspace. The three squadrons would launch their SCALP missiles at exactly the same time, 02:30 Paris time. These missiles would reach their targets, the command centers of the chemical army, half an hour later, 03:00 in Paris, 04:00 in Damascus. The three squadrons of three Rafales could not fire more than twenty missiles. But the French boasted of being most precise.

On August 29 came the first shock. The House of Commons, by a slim 285 to 272 vote, after a bitter debate that began at 2:30 P.M. and lasted until past 10:30 that evening, broadcast in its entirety by the BBC, failed to authorize armed action by British forces—a humiliating defeat for David Cameron. At the height of the debate, the prime minister rose to defend his position that intervention was indispensable, no matter what the previous history might be with ill-considered American actions and their consequences for Britain when it had been suckered into accompanying the United States into the ill-conceived war in Iraq:

> The President of the United States, Barack Obama, is a man who opposed the action in Iraq. No one could in any way describe him as a President who wants to involve America in more wars in the Middle East, but he profoundly believes that an important red line has been crossed in an appalling way, and that is why he supports action in this case. When I spoke to President Obama last weekend I said we shared his view about the despicable nature of this use of chemical weapons and that we must not stand aside, but I also explained to him that, because of the damage done to public confidence by Iraq, we would have to follow a series of incremental steps, including at the United Nations, to build public confidence and ensure the maximum possible legitimacy for any action. These steps are all set out in the motion before the House today.
>
> I remember 2003. I was sitting two rows from the back on the Opposition Benches. It was just after my son had been born and he was not well, but I was determined to be here. I wanted to listen to the man who was standing right here and believe everything that he told me. We are not here to debate those issues today, but one thing is indisputable: the well of public opinion was well and truly poisoned by the Iraq episode and we need to understand the public skepticism.

But it was left to Dr. Liam Fox, a backbench Conservative MP from North Somerset, who had earlier served as secretary of state for defense, to help Parliament and the world understand the broader consequences if this Syrian action went unpunished:

> I believe that if we do not take action—and that probably means military action—the credibility of the international community will be greatly damaged. What value would red lines have in the future if we are unwilling to implement those that already exist?

Backers of Cameron observed that if this Middle East red line were breached with impunity, other similar and potentially more lethal consequences might well follow. "Inaction now that red lines have been crossed would send a message to Iran that it has little to fear if it continued to develop nuclear weapons," observed Conservative MP Peter Lilley. But, he warned that while "that is a legitimate and powerful reason, it can have difficult consequences." He added that he would be prepared to back his party leader, the prime minister, if he carefully circumscribed the limits of British intervention and "say, 'So far, but no further.'" While that was Cameron's pledge, he still did not carry the day. Other, opposition MPs observed simply that whatever they might believe about the value of red lines in the abstract, Obama's red line was ill-considered, and Britain had no need to follow him over this precipice. "Is not the real reason we are here today not the horror at these weapons—if that horror exists—but as a result of the American President having foolishly drawn a red line, so that he is now in the position of either having to attack or face humiliation? Is that not why we are being drawn into war?" asked Paul Flynn during the debate.

Later, in the wake of Parliament's inaction, Cameron's chancellor of the exchequer, George Osborne, told Radio 4 in an interview that Britain would now be forced to embark on "a national soul searching about our role in the world. I hope this doesn't become a moment when we turn our back in all of the world's problems." In fact, it effectively did. It was a true moment when Britain turned inward, leading eventually to Brexit and its withdrawal from the European Union more than six years later.

At the same time, French officials in Paris, who remained in close contact with their American counterparts, were convinced that nothing had changed in the plans they'd developed with Washington. This was what Fabius told François Hollande after the foreign minister held his latest conversation with John Kerry on the phone, ignoring quite clear and definitive reporting from his own ambassador in Washington. The entire entourage of the president of the United States seemed very determined—everyone but the one man who counted the most.

Still, the United Nations Security Council, in possession now of the UN arms inspectors' preliminary report, also failed to act—paralyzed by the veto power of the Russian ambassador. Putin very much understood the value of currying favor with his counterpart in Damascus in this, Assad's hour of greatest need. Obama quickly condemned the impotence of the UN Security Council, calling on the world not to be blind to criminals or their crimes. In fact, he announced a key speech by John Kerry for the next day.

Meanwhile, a week had passed and the Syrian regime, aware of the danger, had begun saturation bombing the entire Ghouta neighborhood—doing their best to erase as much as possible the traces of the crime against humanity that had so horrified the world.

Friday morning, August 30, 2013, dawned bright and blistering in Washington, eighty-eight degrees with humidity hitting a tropical 80 percent. At noon, American and foreign journalists, alerted that Secretary of State John Kerry would deliver an important address, crowded into the State Department's robin's egg blue oval Treaty Room with its white lacquered columns. That morning, *The New York Times* in the lead headline on its front page highlighted the full breadth of what seemed likely as a response to the Syrian action: OBAMA SET FOR LIMITED STRIKE ON SYRIA AS BRITISH VOTE NO. That was the conventional wisdom around Washington, and John Kerry was always reluctant to disabuse anyone of conventional wisdom

The secretary of state entered the Treaty Room and walked directly to the podium, carefully positioned under the watchful gaze of previous holders of that office, whose portraits line the walls. Kerry looked grim. Twenty-four times, he pronounced the words "We know"—who was responsible for the massacre, that there was a specific order, where the rockets were fired, that sarin gas was used. In all, it was a carefully documented indictment of the leaders of Syria, and especially its head of state, Bashar al-Assad. Then Kerry concluded: "If the Syrian regime can get away with it, it will endanger the peace of the world and our own security. What happened last week is a crime against conscience, a crime against humanity. Our choice has great consequences. That counts for the credibility of the United States and our national security."

These last words erased the final doubts. How could any nation change course after such a speech and fail to punish the clearly flagrant breach of a red line that now most believed was unequivocal? Kerry had already told Fabius that the British parliamentary vote against armed intervention the evening before would not change the American position, that Obama asked him "to prepare public opinion for the strikes." Susan Rice, the president's national security advisor, was a little less dogmatic, telling Paul Jean-Ortiz, her counterpart at the Élysée, that Obama was "almost ready to go"—reinforcing Jean-Ortiz's suspicions that the American commitment was not quite as definitive as Kerry was leading the public to believe.

And indeed, in the late morning of August 30, Obama, who was receiving the presidents of the three Baltic states, wanted to add a few words on Syria to the traditional welcome. His final decision to attack was not made, he insisted, but even so, he added: "It is important for us to recognize that when more than a thousand people, including hundreds of innocent children, are killed by a weapon which 98 percent to 99 percent of humanity believes should never be used, would be sending a message that international standards do not mean much. This would be a danger to our national security . . . We are studying any form of military action that does not include the intervention of troops on the ground."

In the entourage of Barack Obama, his national security team, Susan Rice and Ben Rhodes, breathed a sigh of relief. He has finally taken the plunge, they thought. Clearly, they had not heard one key phrase in those remarks: "we are studying." Not words spoken for a full-throated defense of an utterly unbreachable red line that had so very clearly been breached.

In Paris, the counselors of the French president, meeting in a Defense Council session in the Élysée palace conference room, had received a cable from the French embassy in Washington describing how Kerry's speech earlier that day had actually been written by Ben Rhodes himself. It was difficult to imagine that this would not correspond directly to the thinking of the president. Rhodes was very close to Obama. But Rhodes had not written those words that Obama had spoken himself when he greeted the Baltic leaders.

Meanwhile, in Paris, while waiting for the call from the White House, François Hollande consulted again the timeline developed by his own military—a nighttime attack, which could help avoid collateral damage or casualties. The day before the operation, French attack fighters, Rafales based in Abu Dhabi, Djibouti, and metropolitan France, would complete their final checks, and at 15:00 hours Paris time, take off from their bases, preparing to launch their SCALP cruise missiles at 02:30. The missiles would reach their targets half an hour later, at 3 A.M. in Paris, 4 A.M. in Damascus. These missiles would not overfly Turkey—a NATO member that was becoming increasingly close to Syria and ever more prickly. Holland's military leaders had told the strike force commanders that they must minimize civilian damage and rely on an element of surprise to prevent the Syrian high command from redeploying the targeted units that had conducted the gas attacks.

On Friday, August 30, when Obama had scheduled a talk with Hollande for Sunday, it was almost 1 P.M. in Washington, 7 P.M. in Paris. François Hollande had convened his session of the Defense Council. Prime Minister Jean-Marc Ayrault, Fabius, Le Drian, Admiral Guillaud, and General Puga all gathered at the Élysée. At the start of the last weekend of August, when most of Paris had long since emptied for the annual summer holidays, government offices were largely empty, except the teeming Ministry of Defense. In Washington, Obama had the whole afternoon in front of him to think. It was during these hours, in the stifling heat of the American capital and the all but absolute vacuum of Paris, that the future of the Middle East and the design of the great Franco-American misunderstanding began playing to its tragic dénouement.

The French president was thoughtful. He told his staff, "The problem in Syria is that the Americans do not have a long-term strategy for the Middle East." Hollande was not wrong, but if the Americans had never implemented a clear strategy, it was because their president could not bring himself to act. From his earliest days in office, Obama had no Middle East policy. It was not for lack of desire. Obama recognized that the regional strategy of his predecessor—George W. Bush and his militant vice president, Dick

Cheney—emerged from the barrel of a gun. This was anything but Obama's style. Four years earlier, he had tried to turn his back suddenly and definitively on the Bush vision of the Middle East in his "A New Beginning" speech at the American University in Cairo, a message founded on peace and an end to violent extremism. It was received in France and across the region with acclaim as indeed foreshadowing a new beginning. With one problem. The morning after, he boarded Air Force One and promptly did whatever he could to forget this region and its utterly intractable problems, except when, as in the case of Assad's barbaric chemical attack on his people, they intruded directly on his consciousness and his conscience. But clearly there was little real sense of the hard choices that would be necessary to enforce his message or the challenges he himself had laid down. This time would be no different. In Paris, the general belief was that everything was in place, but on Friday, August 30, Obama began to think seriously about suspending the operation.

Obama was troubled. Since the day before, he had been feeling that events were escaping him. Kerry's speech set a direction he had not chosen himself. Susan Rice, his director of the National Security Council, shared the identical view of Ben Rhodes and Kerry. The president himself, however, was careful to say that he had not yet decided anything. He was beginning to feel the trap closing in on him. Obama never liked feeling trapped.

To get some fresh air, Obama began wandering the corridors of the West Wing. His first stop was the office of Valerie Jarrett, an old friend of Michelle and himself. He'd provided her with an office a stone's throw from his own and a vague title of Senior Advisor and Assistant to the President for Public Engagement. She was the person to whom he could at key moments, or simply out of boredom, confide his doubts and his feelings. Jarrett, who was about to leave for Chicago, wished him a good Labor Day weekend. He said it was a difficult time, and he was always happy to talk to her. The conversation only lasted a few minutes.

Although he knew the position of his NSC officials, all in favor of the intervention, Obama decided to consult them on one aspect of the problem that especially troubled him. He had in mind a project that was more critical, he believed, on the international stage—more central to what he was beginning to see as his eventual legacy—an agreement with Iran to prevent the mullahs and their out-of-control Revolutionary Guard from acquiring nuclear weapons. Israel had threatened to bomb Iran's nuclear enrichment sites. But there were indications that he had a good chance of achieving his goal with Hassan Rouhani, the newly elected Iranian president, without resorting to military action, which in the long run he believed would prove a vast mistake and utterly fruitless. Obama already had effectively established a red line with respect to Iran's quest for a nuclear weapon, as we will see in the next chapter.

It was here that these red lines were poised on the brink of a toxic overlap. Iran was an ally of Syria. Would an American strike on the Damascus regime jeopardize these other, critical negotiations? His national security advisors were forced to concede, with Iranian Pasdarans joining Bashar's troops, a major strike on Syria and its chemical arsenal would put Rouhani in a delicate position. Rouhani would condemn any such actions against Syria by America and its allies. That would not facilitate any such negotiations on the broader nuclear issue, particularly with France and Britain.

This admission by his national security staff that there might be a broader price attached to any military action against Syria only reinforced the president's reluctance to move forward. As soon as his conference with his national security team was over, Obama asked the Pentagon if a delay in the schedule of the operation would make it less effective. Secretary of Defense Chuck Hagel and the military officers around him had reservations from the beginning over the use of force in Syria, even to send a warning signal that this red line was still intact and inviolable. Their answer now was what the president wanted to hear: for the moment, we can delay without damage—the opposite of the view from Paris. A rapid strike, the French believed, would be seen as punishment for the use of chemical weapons, just as any delay would be seen as a desire to embark on a far broader campaign for total regime change, hardening the determination of Assad to hang tough and perhaps use chemical weapons again in the future.

So, the clock was ticking, and Obama's concern was growing. Like Paris, Washington was emptying out. Already, officials, lawyers, and lobbyists, who make up a good part of the population, had left their offices for the Labor Day holiday, just as Congress would close for its recess. For nine days the Capitol would be empty of anyone to whom Obama's aides could explain the White House's position. Kerry's speech suggesting an imminent strike threatened to become the doctrine of the Administration. Republican leaders had become menacing. As loudly as they had applauded the invasion of Iraq, now, with a Democrat in charge, they did not want to hear of a strike on the Damascus regime. The president must ask permission from Congress, they insisted. The word impeachment was even pronounced by some. He must, very quickly, loosen the cage where he'd allowed himself to be locked by his closest advisors and his own procrastination.

For help, Obama turned to Denis McDonough, his chief of staff. Shortly after 5 P.M., the two began a long walk alone in the Rose Garden of the White House. His choice of a companion was hardly random. McDonough was the most cautious of his advisors, the only one who had been reluctant and even opposed to military intervention. Still, he was the one seated two seats from Obama in the White House situation room in May 2011 when Navy SEALS took down Osama bin Laden in that daring night time raid in Pakistan. Now, as they strolled through the gardens, the president laid out his reservations: Assad using civilians as human shields; the difficulty of the strikes; targeting chemical weapons raising the risk of releasing into the atmosphere agents which had already done considerable damage. They had to reach the units that used them. But the manufacturing plants that produced and weaponized the gas were never among the targets. At the same time, Obama feared too much success. If the regime collapsed, would it not be the jihadists who would seize power? Obama never believed either the Free Syrian Army or the Syrian National Coalition could lead the country. That's why he had never provided them with significant help, even in the form of offensive weapons, let alone on-the-ground American advisors.

In his conversation with McDonough, he pointed out how difficult it would be at this juncture, especially, to get his way. He avoided a central point. It was the red line he himself had drawn that had now unquestionably been crossed and was at the heart of the dilemma he was now so reluctantly facing. Kerry quite rightly had told the world that the very credibility of the United States was at stake. It would be necessary to strike the Damascus regime, the president told McDonough. Still, he quickly added, it may be impossible at this moment: He would not have the agreement of the UN Security Council, did not even have a coalition of nations (utterly forgetting France, which clearly did not weigh very heavily in his eyes). And he believed American opinion was largely opposed to the intervention. With that comment, an idea occurred to him. He must seek the authorization of Congress. Nothing in the Constitution imposes such a requirement, not even the War Powers Act. But without the support of public opinion, at least the consent of Congress was essential. Did Obama realize that he would likely never get this consent? If nothing else, he was a most savvy political operative. All the president knew with certainty was that Congress would be on vacation for nine days, thus requiring a new delay. Perhaps the whole question would simply evaporate.

On returning to his office fifty minutes after leaving it, he summoned a meeting of his closest personal advisers for seven o'clock. The scene, as it appeared on the photo taken by the president's official photographer said it all—Barack Obama sitting on a chair in front of the Oval Office fireplace, the only one in shirtsleeves, the rest respectful of a minimum of decorum, wearing jackets. The body language spoke volumes. The president slouched on a chair while his guests, settled on sofas, sat back. Only one of them leaned toward the president. Listening to his boss, Ben Rhodes did not try to hide his skepticism. Denis McDonough, on the other hand, remained standing as if his job was to supervise the class. For two hours, the president of the United States faced criticism from his team. The exchanges were "robust" according to one participant. All were afraid to believe that the operation might not take place. It did not matter. "One nay, twelve yays," summed up President Lincoln in an often-cited historical reference, "the nays have it."

Early the next morning Saturday, August 31, another principals meeting was convened, this time in the White House situation room. Key members of the NSC, the vice president, secretary of defense, chairman of the Joint Chiefs of Staff, and secretary of state were invited to hear the president repeat what he'd announced the day before to his smaller group of close advisers in the Oval Office. The official photo testifies that once again the atmosphere was tense. John Kerry seemed totally confused. Only Secretary of Defense Chuck Hagel, dressed in sportswear, seemed relaxed, perhaps relieved.

Immediately after this session, the White House informed the Élysée that there would be a small change in the program: President Obama would call President Hollande around 9 A.M. Washington time, mid-afternoon in Paris. This sudden change of the calendar astonished Paul Jean-Ortiz when he was apprised of it on his arrival at the Élysée. At the Ministry of Defense and the Quai d'Orsay, officials believed there would be an acceleration of the timetable and a green light from the American president. A defense council was summoned, as the day before, in the room adjacent to where Hollande would take the phone call from Obama. The French continued to believe the operation was on schedule, indeed might even be accelerated. As a precaution, the military launched a countdown to the operation. The time of the phone call to Paris was changed again, twice.

American advisers, immediately contacted by their counterparts at the Élysées and Quai d'Orsay, continued to talk and behave as if nothing had changed. It was true that so far, the news had not yet been made public. But Obama's first concern that morning was to send envoys to Congress to explain to any members still in town that the decision no longer was the one they'd anticipated.

When Obama finally placed his call to Holland, he tone was most determined. He began by exploring several options with Hollande. The two were in agreement on the principal of a limited intervention. However, without the support of the British and without a UN Security Council resolution, Obama had decided to seek congressional support. The operation was "neither canceled nor stopped," simply "postponed." But, while Obama continued to express his determination to move forward, his assurances of his "firmness" and "determination" recalled to Hollande the trauma provoked by weak-willed failures of previous American assurances. Obama reminded the French leader that he'd been elected to end wars, another suggestion of how unlikely now any intervention was to take place, which Hollande heard as an expression of how unlikely Obama would be to enforce his own red line. Hollande underscored the operational difficulties that would result from any delay. Obama agreed that it could be done very quickly "or," he suggested immediately, "after the G-20 of St. Petersburg." Hollande was stunned. Did Obama intend to make a final diplomatic attempt at the annual summit of world leaders in St. Petersburg? Hollande insisted a quick action would have the advantage of avoiding a redeployment and dispersal of the military forces of the Syrian regime, which had been identified as the targets of the attack. The French president ended by trying to pin down his American counterpart on the length of the delay. "About 15 days," responded Obama. An eternity in politico-military terms.

The French leader was astonished, disappointed, almost humbled by what he had just learned. France had no say, and had no choice but to agree. To his Defense Council waiting in the adjoining room for word, Hollande explained that it was necessary to halt the operation forthwith, even as some Mirages had already begun warming their engines at airbases in metropolitan France.

At 4:30 P.M. in Washington, Barack Obama spoke to his nation and the world from the Rose Garden with Vice President Joe Biden at his side, his face frozen. The tone of the president was one of stern resolve:

> This [chemical weapons] assault is an attack on human dignity. It also pres-
> ents a serious danger to our national security . . . It risks making a mockery
> of the global prohibition on the use of chemical weapons. It endangers our
> friends and our partners along Syria's borders, including Israel, Jordan, Turkey,
> Lebanon and Iraq. It could lead to escalating use of chemical weapons, or
> their proliferation to terrorist groups who would do our people harm. In a
> world with many dangers, this menace must be confronted. Now, after careful
> deliberation, I have decided that the United States should take military action
> against Syrian regime targets. . . .
>
> But having made my decision as Commander-in-Chief based on what I
> am convinced is our national security interests, I'm also mindful that I'm the
> President of the world's oldest constitutional democracy. I've long believed
> that our power is rooted not just in our military might, but in our example
> as a government of the people, by the people, and for the people. And that's
> why I've made a second decision: I will seek authorization for the use of force
> from the American people's representatives in Congress. . . .

While I believe I have the authority to carry out this military action without specific congressional authorization, I know that the country will be stronger if we take this course, and our actions will be even more effective. . . .

Make no mistake—this has implications beyond chemical warfare. If we won't enforce accountability in the face of this heinous act, what does it say about our resolve to stand up to others who flout fundamental international rules? To governments who would choose to build nuclear arms? To terrorist who would spread biological weapons? To armies who carry out genocide?

Obama was quite right in at least one respect. This decision did indeed have profound "implications beyond chemical warfare." He had utterly failed to recognize the blow he had dealt to the effective establishment and utility of virtually any red line in modern diplomacy and warfare. It was, many members of his administration conceded to me, perhaps Barack Obama's single greatest failure of international diplomacy.

American opinion largely closed ranks behind its president. Disapproving a military intervention, most were delighted that Obama was asking for an agreement they hoped Congress would never provide. Still, it took the Editorial Board of *The New York Times* two days before it would weigh in. When it did, it gave Obama all the backing he needed:

Debating the Case for Force

President Obama made the right decision to seek Congressional authorization for his announced plan to order unilateral military strikes against Syria for using chemical weapons. There has to be a vigorous and honest public debate on the use of military force, which could have huge consequences even if it is limited in scope and duration.

If he is to win Congressional support, Mr. Obama and his top aides will have to explain in greater detail why they are so confident that the kind of military strikes that administration officials have described would deter President Bashar al-Assad of Syria from gassing his people again (American officials say more than 1,400 were killed on Aug. 21) rather than provoke him to unleash even greater atrocities.

They will also have to explain how they can keep the United States from becoming mired in the Syrian civil war—something Mr. Obama, for sound reasons, has long resisted—and how military action will advance the cause of a political settlement: the only rational solution to the war.

However, in reaching this conclusion, the Editorial Board called attention to the failure of Obama's entire red line concept, challenging its structure and his ill-considered motivations for establishing it:

> It is unfortunate that Mr. Obama, who has been thoughtful and cautious about putting America into the Syrian conflict, has created a political situation in which his credibility could be challenged. He did that by publicly declaring that the use of chemical weapons would cross a red line that would result in an American response. Regardless, he should have long ago put in place, with our allies and partners, a plan for international action—starting with tough sanctions—if Mr. Assad used chemical weapons. It is alarming that Mr. Obama did not.

If there was a lesson for this particular iteration of a red line, it is contained in *The Times*'s single most astute observation: *If you're going to establish such a challenge, to draw such a line in the first place, make terribly clear right up front and in exquisite detail the costs that will accrue to any who step across it.* This Obama never did. It cost him dearly—not to mention the price paid by his allies and all who sought an end to what has turned into a charnel house in Syria and beyond.

The French government persisted in believing, and would continue to believe for several more days, despite all evidence to the contrary and repeated cables from its embassy in Washington, that the operation would take place. The Obama team was making real efforts to rally Congress, so the thinking in Paris went. Arizona's Republican Senator John McCain, a leading Congressional hawk and former prisoner of war during the Vietnam conflict, was leading the support for an attack. But to limited effect.

Indeed, many in the press continued to characterize the kabuki dance being engineered by the White House as an "aggressive push for Congressional approval of an attack on Syria," as the *Times* national security team described it on September 2. McCain emerged from an hour-long meeting with Obama to announce to the waiting press corps that the president had given general support to doing more for the Syrian rebels. Which of course Obama had no intention ever of doing. But later in a private interview with the *Times*, McCain, himself no fool, confessed, "There was no concrete agreement. OK we got a deal. Like a lot of things, the devil is in the details."

In Paris, aides to Le Drian at the Ministry of Defense, who had been the most ardent supporters of an attack, were the first to understand. They went home feeling helpless. They had planned nothing else for that time late Saturday night and Sunday morning when it all fell apart. Their only anticipated mission had been to manage the consequences of an intervention that would never come.

Over that Labor Day weekend, the Élysée published a record of the French intelligence services, hitherto classified, which underlined the responsibility of the Syrian regime for the chemical attack. Afterward, a third meeting of the Defense Council was convened at the Élysée, this time without the military. If the operation was to take place later, without the impact of surprise and after Obama had consulted the United States Congress, President Hollande would at least need to inform the French parliament, the Assemblée nationale. There was no need to ask for a vote. But in this hours-long debate with his senior advisors, opinions began to converge: if there were a majority, it would be quite narrow. The impact on public opinion would be negative. So, instead, there would be a simple statement by the government, followed by a debate.

An extraordinary meeting of parliament was called on September 4. The prime minister and the minister of defense rose to speak. Prime Minister Jean-Marc Ayrault repeated several times, to demonstrate the guilt of the Syrian regime, the phrase: "We are certain." The members of the Assemblée nationale erupted in a storm of protest, with right-wing deputies opposing any military intervention, just like most Republicans in Congress.

Rumors of imminent war persisted until September 5—the opening of the G-20 summit in St. Petersburg. But as the days passed, it became increasingly clear that Congress would not approve the intervention. Vladimir Putin remained persuaded the United States would strike. The American, Russian, and French navies continued visibly on station in the Mediterranean. In St. Petersburg, on the evening of September 5, during the opening dinner of the summit, Obama failed to win approval of a motion calling for the condemnation of the Syrian regime for having used nerve gas against its people. The American and the Russian presidents had a brief and icy talk, Putin surfacing the idea of dismantling Syrian chemical weapons. This proved to be key, allowing Putin to rescue his protégé, Bashar al-Assad, cementing his standing as a reliable ally of a keystone nation in the Middle East. It was at the same time a chance for Russia to reenter the region for the first time since the fall of Communism and to reassert the power of Russia in a part of the world where it had once been a central player. If Obama could establish his own red line in Syria, it was now clear that Assad had assembled quite an adequate counterweight to push back.

Perhaps most intriguing was the origin of a Russian initiative—in Israel in the immediate aftermath of the gas attack on Ghouta—in the wake of the collapse of the red line in Syria. In a meeting between Israeli Minister of Intelligence and Strategic Affairs Yuval Steinitz and a senior emissary of Vladimir Putin, the Israelis suggested the disarmament plan as a means of ensuring there would be no armed intervention against its immediate neighbor. The Russian official was intrigued. In September at the G-20, this idea suddenly emerged, since it appeared to meet the requirements of nearly all the protagonists. It allowed Barack Obama to avoid, in an almost honorable fashion, the consequences of failing to exact any penalty for a quite flagrant violation of the red line he had so impulsively and thoughtlessly established. It also allowed Russia to save the Syrian regime, and enabled Israel to retain in Damascus a partner it had demonstrably little reason to fear—and win its gratitude as well.

At the G-20, Obama confided to Hollande: "In Congress, there are difficulties." On September 7, John Kerry, visiting Paris, referred to "a new Munich" as a result of the inaction. At least this one senior American official understood how fragile and potentially hazardous red lines—especially those ill-conceived and ill-defended—can be. That same day, Russian Foreign Minister Sergei Lavrov seized the opportunity, summoning Walid Muallem, the Syrian minister of foreign affairs, to Moscow, urging him to accept the offer "suggested" by Obama, which Assad did not for a moment hesitate to embrace.

Events now moved rapidly toward a resolution. Working quickly, Russian and American diplomats began drafting a treaty, though on September 10, during a final conversation on the subject, Hollande and Obama agreed to keep all options open. Behind their commitment were diametrically opposing intentions. For Hollande, the possibility of intervention remained. For Obama, delighted to see a peaceful outcome, his only pressure was on Moscow to accelerate the process—and incidentally rope Russia into a long-term solution to the Iranian nuclear red line. On September 14, Russians and Americans agreed on a plan to eliminate Syrian chemical weapons—removing 1,300 tons of nerve gas from more than forty-five sites scattered across the country. Those were the ones that the West knew about, at any rate. During the signing ceremony, John Kerry publicly thanked the Syrian government for its cooperation. Only fifteen days had passed since August 30, when cruise missiles were on standby to enforce this red line.

What had not been mentioned in the conversations between Obama and his advisers were the consequences of this decision—particularly the lessons the Russian president would draw from the decline of American resolve. Vladimir Putin had long believed that Barack Obama would invariably avoid the use of force at any cost. It would now take the Russian president only a few months to conclude he could, with impunity, intervene in Ukraine and annex Crimea. And barely two more years to believe that he could, with equal impunity, bomb the positions of Syrian rebels and play a pivotal role in the victory of Bashar al-Assad over his opponents.

What Obama also preferred to ignore was the dismay of the Syrian people and especially pro-Western rebels at their apparently total abandonment by the West. A few days after Obama's clear capitulation, units of the Free Syrian Army that had held Raqqa disbanded. Some of the activists even passed through lines drawn by the Islamic State, which had taken control of the city as the capital of its self-styled caliphate. Similar actions occurred with frightening regularity elsewhere in Syria as the Islamic State continued its all but unchecked expansion.

The costs to America's allies in the collapse of the chemical red lines were no less apocalyptic, but especially for French President François Hollande, who had gone all-in to defend a red line he had no role in drawing. At the time Assad's forces launched its chemical attack, Hollande's popularity stood at an unenviable but hardly catastrophic 33 percent. By November, his indecision and bad choices, coupled with his utter abandonment by Obama, drove that number down to 20 percent. A year later it fell to a record low of 13 percent of the French electorate that were satisfied with his performance. By the time he decided not to seek a second term, this figure stood at a dismal 4 percent. While other failures certainly contributed to such a historic collapse, many members of his entourage traced the real start of this plunge to Obama's cavalier and insensitive treatment of Hollande and the French.

Obama's red line was quite clearly the nadir of his administration's foreign policy, and for most of those in his entourage still remains the one incident few want to revisit. But there are object lessons here that are profound—and link this red line to its antecedents in Munich and ahead to a host of similar lines drawn in the sand by Donald Trump. But if there was a watershed, Syria and sarin gas are the ultimate pivot. For if we have not learned this lesson, there were many more—even more potentially lethal ones—to come.

———

While Obama and much of the West were utterly preoccupied with the red line of Assad's use of chemical weapons, al-Baghdadi and ISIS were in the process of all but unchecked expansion of the Islamic State. It was a process that its highly mobile and utterly brutal forces undertook in a series of lightning advances and strikes across northern Syria, crossing rapidly into Iraq. Their stated goal was to fulfill, as the formal pronouncement of its creation promised, "the Promise of Allah"—creating a caliphate with al-Baghdadi as "the Caliph for Muslims everywhere." By the time of this proclamation, on June 29, 2014, the caliphate and the rapidly expanding red line that defined the extent of its control was about to reach its murderous peak. The RAND Corporation estimates that at that moment, the Islamic State encompassed more than thirty-eight thousand square miles—more than triple the size of Massachusetts—with eleven million people scattered across Syria and Iraq. Its reach had penetrated from the outskirts of Aleppo on the northwest through the all but eradicated frontier with Iraq, through Mosul, Tikrit, Ramadi, and Fallujah, nearly to the suburbs of Baghdad. The boundaries of this self-proclaimed caliphate were ill-defined by al-Baghdadi and his people only because they were in a constant state of flux—hardly a prescription for a defensible red line. But their leaders were proud that they were in the process of eradicating the artificial boundaries established by the Treaty of Versailles a century ago.

Along the way, al-Baghdadi established within these lines a real nation, complete with ministries, schools, oil fields it had seized and whose product it sold in complex black market transactions, and a complex mechanism of justice and retribution. At its peak in 2015, it had amassed a revenue stream that passed $2 billion a year—with $500 million a year from oil and gas, $360 million from extortion and taxation especially from the *zakat* (an Islamic tax of 2.5 percent on net worth), and $500 million from the looting of bank vaults in overrun towns. Over it all ruled a bizarre and utterly perverted Islamic philosophy expressed and inspired by the black flag, hoisted everywhere and carried into battle, emblazoned with the white Arabic *Shahada*: "There is no god but Allah, and Mohammed is His messenger." In many ways, al-Baghdadi's red lines strategy was not unlike that of the Ottomans or the early Umayyads on which he claimed to pattern this latter-day caliphate: amass territories, establish a red line, then expand it at the first opportunity. That could, of course, apply equally to China and its strategy in the South China Sea. One fundamental difference, and in the case of al-Baghdadi the fatal flaw, was a first lesson for students of any red line. As zealously and attentively guarded as they might be, as wealthy as their managers might become, each such boundary is never more stable or sustainable than the support generated by those it encompasses. And this was never more acutely demonstrated than by how quickly the red lines of the caliphate, hollowed out from within by those it oppressed, so easily collapsed from without by a determined land and air assault. China, of course, benefits from the inverse—most of the islands it has occupied or manufactured have no indigenous people, beyond those utter loyalists it brings to build or occupy them.

In the case of the Islamic Caliphate, eventually, beginning with a determined assault by allied forces and a motivated Kurdish army that recognized its people risked extermination, the forces arrayed against it were able to demonstrate how easily a determined offense, with heavy air support, could begin to shrink a territory whose people were also quite ill-disposed to assist in the maintenance or expansion of its borders.

On June 25, 2014, Barack Obama ordered American forces back into Iraq, two and a half years after he'd ordered the last such forces out, and seven years after George W. Bush had initiated the withdrawal process, effectively clearing the way for ISIS's surge into Iraqi territory. It took nearly a year after the forces' return in 2014 as "advisors" to build sufficient forces and alliances in the region as ISIS continued to grow and proclaimed the existence of its caliphate. But eventually, the newly drawn and policed American-Iraqi red line began to expand westward under what the Pentagon dubbed Operation Inherent Resolve—quite an apt description of the tangible intentions of this new line that the United States began to enforce. The results were quite symmetrical. ISIS's red line of control began shrinking just as American and allied troops—largely Kurdish Peshmerga together with participants from nine other countries—began their push westward. By April 13, 2015, the Pentagon was in a position to announce that "some 25 to 30 percent of Iraqi territory has been taken back" from ISIS control. That translated into a contraction of the ISIS red line by "approximately 5,000 square miles to 6,000 square miles [of Iraqi territory] since the peak of [ISIS] territorial influence in Iraq," according to US Army Colonel Steve Warren.

By March 2019, ISIS's last redoubt in Baghouz, Syria, had been penetrated, the city and its vast network of tunnels effectively reduced to rubble, and thousands of ISIS fighters seized by Syrian Democratic Forces and Kurdish troops. There is one final caveat, however, in tracing the arc of the Islamic State. Its territory and the physical red lines that defined it are gone, but a vast network of virtual red lines remains. RAND Corporation analysts believe that the Islamic State's investments in legitimate businesses continue to throw off large amounts of cash for use globally in its terrorist activities, whose bases, as we shall see, have only been transferred abroad—largely to unstable territories in sub-Saharan Africa. RAND analysts believe it remains "a caliphate of the mind," adding that "if the Islamic State is planning a comeback, which we assess it is, the group will stick with what works—diversifying its financial portfolio to maintain steady access to financing."

Still, as Trump would discover, it was not so easy to give the final American "warriors" a warm welcome home—nor in the process establish defensible red lines that work to the advantage of the United States and not to any of the other malignant forces in the region—Syria, Russia, Iran, Turkey, and the remains of ISIS.

In the four years after Bashar al-Assad escaped the consequences for violating Barack Obama's chemical red line in 2013, the Syrian dictator had grown confident and more than a little cocky. He managed to maintain his iron hold on power, pushing back domestic opposition forces relentlessly. But there still remained much work to be done to reclaim full control over his entire nation and establish a defensible line that would keep all his enemies at bay. In January 2017, Donald Trump succeeded Barack Obama as president of the United States, determined to reverse most, if not all, of the international priorities established by his predecessor. But some things had not changed.

Bashar al-Assad was still determined to reestablish unchallenged borders and reassert his utter control over his own people. With ISIS now on the run, Assad could turn his attention to reclaiming some of the far corners of Syria that had still not been wrapped within his authoritarian red line. One of these territories was in still rebel-held Idlib Province, two hours by car from Ghouta and just southeast of Aleppo, the important commercial center in the far north of Syria. Before dawn on Tuesday April 4, 2017, the same scenario that played out in Ghouta unspooled in Khan Sheikhoun—shells landing, puffs then fumes of smoke, and within minutes, men, woman, and children gasping for breath, foaming at the mouth as the deadly sarin gas spread through the houses and shops of the town.

This time the action spooled out at a compressed speed. By 10:30 that morning in Washington (5:30 in the evening in Khan Sheikhoun), President Trump was seeing the first searing images of the suffering of small children and babies, writhing from the attack in their final death throes. The president was deeply moved. By 8 p.m., staff aides were reviewing options, and through the next morning, as the president's national security advisor, General H. R. McMaster, recalled, "the confidence level has just continued to grow" that Assad was responsible, rather than the rebel groups that the Syrian dictator was already beginning to blame. By noon, the president, with reporters pressing him on how he might respond, was uncharacteristically taciturn, saying only, "You will see." In the early afternoon, Trump visited in the White House with King Abdullah II of Jordan, whose warplanes had been flying sorties over Syria for at least five years. At a press conference, with the king at his side, Trump expressed his horror over the images that the world had already been seeing, adding that his "attitude toward Syria and Assad has changed very much." Then, in a clear, if perhaps unintended gesture to Obama and his Syrian red line, Trump established his own, suggesting that Assad's attack "crossed a lot of lines for me. When you kill innocent children, innocent babies, little babies, with a chemical gas that was so lethal [then that] crosses many lines beyond a red line, many many lines." He pledged that, now having responsibility, "I will carry it very proudly."

By late Wednesday, the focus in the Situation Room had been narrowed to a "proportional" response that would be unlikely to provoke an escalation. Thursday afternoon, flying through great turbulence en route to Mar-a-Lago in Florida and a summit with China's Xi Jinping, Trump, still driven by the emotions provoked by the images of the gas attack victims, convened a virtual National Security Council meeting. By the time he landed at Palm Beach, Trump had decided on a surgical strike using Tomahawk cruise missiles on Shayrat airfield, where US intelligence had determined the planes carrying the sarin weapons had been based. At 7:40 P.M. (2:40 A.M. Friday in Syria), US destroyers *Porter* and *Ross*, on station in the eastern Mediterranean, launched fifty-nine Tomahawks at the airfield. An hour later, they begin arriving at their targets in and around Shayrat—aircraft, hardened shelters, radar installations, an air defense system, ammunition bunkers, and fuel storage facilities. Avoided were locations where chemical agents might be stored, as release of their toxins could lead to untold more innocent casualties. But the strike didn't work.

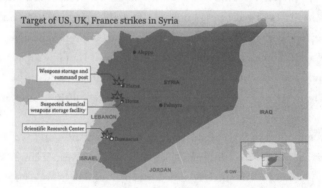

First joint strikes at Syrian chemical weapons facilities
have little impact, even in the short-term.

The problem was that Assad quite simply never recognized the existence of any red line surrounding his arsenal of chemical weapons, or for that matter any red line that would restrict his ability to secure the territory within the broader red line he had established, defining his nation's frontiers. Moreover, that Tomahawk cruise missiles could pierce any red line in Syria with impunity was largely irrelevant—they would not be targeting him. His personal safety was assured by Executive Order 11905 issued by President Gerald Ford in 1976 that prohibited "political assassination" by any US government agency.

The irrelevance of the attack was quite clear within hours. Assad's air forces, operating from that same Shayrat airbase, mounted a defiant series of bombing raids on seven rebel-held towns in eastern Homs province as well as—in an utterly in-your-face gesture—on

Khan Sheikhoun, the same village the initial gas attack had targeted. Within days, Russia had also pledged to bulk up Syria's air defense systems, while mocking the ineffectiveness of the attack. So much for Trump leaping to the defense of Barack Obama's indefensible red line. This incident by no means discouraged Trump from either recognizing or establishing his own lines, or respecting those established by other leaders with goals utterly antithetical to American values—and in each case, with little real understanding of how they worked or the dangers they might pose.

From the beginning of the Syrian civil war in 2011, the United States maintained varying degrees of active or passive military involvement, largely on the side of rebel forces and quite often, as we have seen, to control the spread of ISIS and the extension of its red lines. Effectively, this meant active or passive respect for, and even establishment of, new sets of red lines. But when Donald Trump arrived on January 17, 2017, a whole new configuration of these lines began taking shape across the region, especially in Syria. Some expressed his intention to limit Iran's influence or expansion of its influence and presence in the region, which we'll examine in the next chapter. But quite a number of these lines involved actors previously utterly extraneous to Syria in particular.

Russia's involvement in Syria began not long after the end of World War II. The Soviet Union first recognized Syria's independence in 1944, two years before French troops were forced to withdraw from their Middle East colonies. On February 15, 1946, Soviet Vice Foreign Commissar Andrei Y. Vyshinsky told the UN Security Council meeting in London, "We must meet the demands put forward by the Governments of Syria and Lebanon. These demands are just and have the full support of the Soviet delegation. The Council must pronounce that there is no ground for the presence of these foreign troops on the soil of Syria and Lebanon and that these troops should be withdrawn within a time to be fixed by the Security Council." By April 17, French troops had left, and throughout the Cold War, Syria remained a close and unwavering ally of the Soviet Union, indeed, as Dmitri Trenin, director of the Moscow Center of the Carnegie Endowment for International Peace put it, "the centrepiece of the entire Soviet position in the region, remaining so throughout the Cold War." A coup d'état in 1970, thoroughly backed by the Soviet Union, brought to power Hafez al-Assad, father of Bashar. Grateful for the Kremlin's support, he allowed the Soviet military to open its naval base in Tartus, giving it not only a major military presence in the Middle East, but fulfilling a dream nourished since Peter the Great of a presence on the Mediterranean. The Soviet Union and Russia continued to demonstrate unflinching support of the Assad dynasty, wielding without hesitation their veto in the UN Security Council through the years. This support became indispensable as Bashar al-Assad confronted a host of challenges and enemies seeking to unseat him.

The intricate set of contemporary major power red lines in Syria really dates to the arrival of Russian air power in 2015 and the sudden need to deconflict with existing forces—particularly American and NATO air power—that were already operating in the region. The major Russian buildup began with a request from Assad for broader support against both ISIS and rebel forces that together had seized vast swaths of Syrian territory at the peak of the caliphate's expansion. It was a request that Putin was thoroughly open to for several reasons—preeminently because he quite rightly saw Syria as his only tangible chance for a solid foothold anywhere in the region. But at the same time, Obama's defense secretary, Ash Carter, adopted the utterly boneheaded rejection of a joint operations center including Russian officers in Jordan for the war against ISIS, then refused even to take a call from his counterpart, Sergei Shoigu, and persuaded Obama to go along with his decision. The Carnegie Endowment for International Peace called it "the worst of both worlds," giving the "Russians an implicit green light to intensify operations in regions where US-backed Syrian opposition forces were concentrated or held an upper hand." It also led directly to a major buildup of Russian forces in the region and Russian overtures, as we shall see, to other players that would result in a proliferation or extension of truly toxic red lines.

By September 2015, artillery units, along with seven of Russia's most advanced main battle tank, the T-90, had arrived at the Syrian airbase of Khmeimim, which had been turned over to Russian control outside Latakia on the Mediterranean, fifty miles up the coast from the naval facility at Tartus. At the same time, Russian Sukhoi Su-24M bombers, Sukhoi Su-25 ground-support fighters, cutting-edge Sukhoi Su-34 bombers, Mil Mi-24 gunship helicopters, Mil Mi-8 support choppers, a pair of the air force's most advanced model, the Su-57 fighter-bomber, armed with cruise missiles and smart bombs, the super-jumbo Antonov An-124, as well as Ruslan and Tupolev Tu-76 transport aircrafts were stationed at the base that Russian media reported had bays for more than fifty military aircraft. It was clear from Russian reporters who visited the facility that their military forces—numbering at their peak at least six thousand—were dug in for a long time, with a bakery for fresh-baked bread, central kitchen, air conditioned barracks, even a Russian sauna. All of this was protected by an umbrella of S-300 and S-400 missile systems that effectively established a no-go, or aerial denial, zone of considerable presence.

This posed a significant risk of red lines overlapping, potentially with lethal consequences. For at least four years, Russian and American warplanes played a dangerous
game of tag in the skies over Syria, mirroring the fortunes below of the ground forces
of the Syrian government and its Russian allies and the opposing Free Army, Kurdish
fighters, and American "advisors." A kaleidoscope of constantly shifting red lines quickly
emerged as the fortunes of rebels and the government ebbed and flowed. At various times,
Russians and Syrians sought to establish red lines along the Euphrates River or in various
locations in northern and eastern Syria with varying degrees of success and little sustain-
ability, since they were recognized by neither American nor Free Syrian forces. Of course,
American warplanes, cruise missiles, even drones had the ability to take out Russian air
defense missile systems in a heartbeat, placing many of their ground forces in great peril,
but that would have raised the stakes and tensions in the region geometrically. Neither
side had any real appetite to test that.

Instead, the structure of the Russian-American red line emerged in a fashion characteristic of the Obama chemical line—a deconfliction line in the skies. In late September
2015, Obama and Putin met at the UN General Assembly fall session in New York.
Although Syria and Russia's newly expanded presence there never really came up, the
next day a three-star Russian general appeared in the office of the US defense attaché in
Baghdad and announced that Russia was launching air missions over Syria and demanded
that American operations cease. By October, with both sides clearly aware of the stakes,
a "memorandum of understanding on air safety in Syria" was announced by Pentagon
spokesman Peter Cook. The memorandum included "specific safety protocols for air-
crews to follow, including maintaining professional airmanship at all times, the use of
specific communication frequencies and the establishment of a communication line on
the ground. The U.S. and Russia will form a working group to discuss any implementation issues that follow." In other words, a clearly delineated red line that both sides
understood and accepted—the best possible in battlefield conditions. Cook elaborated
that the agreement "does not establish zones of cooperation, intelligence sharing or
any sharing of target information in Syria. The discussions through which this [agree-
ment] has developed do not constitute U.S. cooperation or support for Russia's policy
or actions in Syria." This channel defining and policing the Russian-American red line
eventually became highly structured, with a twenty-four-hour hotline connecting mid-
level American officers at the Combined Air Operations Center located in Qatar with
equivalent Russian officers at their Khmeimim Air Base. There was an overlay as well
at the three-star general level between the Joint Chiefs of Staff's director for strategic
plans and policy and his Russian General Staff equivalent, as well as a direct channel

in the region between the commander of Operation Inherent Resolve and his Russian counterpart at Khmeimim.

Over the next four years, these lines would ebb and flow as the Assad regime and its Russian backers continued to press their struggle with the Syrian Free Army and as efforts of Kurds and American advisors against ISIS peaked. In 2017, a ground component was added to the system of deconfliction as the ground war on both sides of the red lines intensified. This system remained in effect for four years, until suddenly, with the appearance of a major new player, the red lines shifted again—quite dramatically.

Enter Turkey. This adds, if not a new red line, certainly a third dimension to what had been effectively a two-dimensional chess game. This should hardly have been an entirely unexpected development. As we have seen, the peacemakers at Versailles utterly failed to take into consideration the fortunes or aspirations of the Kurds with the creation of modern Iraq, Syria, and Turkey. The Kurds have been anxious to create their own proper homeland, and able and willing to fight for it. This has led to any number of terrorist attacks undertaken by Kurdish freedom-fighters within Turkey, and a desire by Turkey to undertake hot pursuit, some would say ethnic cleansing, even extermination, of Kurds in Syria and Iraq. Faced with a somewhat unsympathetic attitude in Washington, Turkey's autocratic president, Recep Tayyip Erdogan, began to look elsewhere for like-minded leaders and friends.

Turkey had grown increasingly frustrated over more than three decades of failure in its bid to win a coveted and lucrative membership in the European Union. It watched, frustrated, as Greece, its arch-rival across the Bosporus, was welcomed into the EU in 1981, the passport-free Schengen Area in 2000, and the coveted eurocurrency zone in 2001. By the arrival of the Trump administration, Turkey's fortunes had hardly changed. A host of issues, from its turn toward autocracy and virulent human right abuses, combined with slowing economic growth, only compounded long-standing reservations about welcoming the nation, 95 percent of whose territory actually lies outside the continent of Europe. At the same time, closer to home, Turkey's own southern border was being overrun by Syrian refugees fleeing the civil war, and the Kurds had hardly moderated their attacks. So, Turkey looked to new horizons and new friends.

Throughout the early years of the Trump presidency, Erdogan had grown increasingly strident in his recitation of America's failures in the region. Its military intervention in Syria had failed to bring the civil war to an end, stem the flow of refugees, or bring a halt to Kurdish attacks in his own country. But Russia and Iran held out some serious promises. Iran we will examine in the next chapter. Russia, however, was even more seductive and held out more immediate lures. In 2013, Turkey announced its intention to purchase China's long-range air-defense missile system at a cost of $3.4 billion. It was a truly in-your-face slap to its NATO allies, which had installed uniformly American or European systems—Patriot or SAMP/T Aster. After a firestorm of complaints, Turkey scrapped the China deal and blithely turned to Russian S-400s in 2017, which made more sense as the same Russian systems were already securing the Kremlin's red line just across the frontier in Syria. Two years later the first Russian systems arrived in Turkey.

But there was much more in store. It had quickly become clear that Putin had much grander ideas than simply the sale of a Russian missile system to a NATO member—which was still the first time the Kremlin had managed to insert its military nose past the hitherto impenetrable NATO red line of defense systems. Putin had every intention of using Erdogan's close personal relationship with Donald Trump to enlarge and cement the red line he was building in Syria, his bridgehead into the Middle East and the Mediterranean.

On October 6, 2019, Sunday afternoon in Istanbul, morning in Washington eight time zones to the west, Erdogan picked up the phone and dialed the White House. As Trump has put it, the two had been "very good friends almost from day one." The Turkish president was, in Trump's view, "a hell of a leader." We are embarking on a full-scale push into Syria with our Russian allies, Erdogan began. Why don't you get your forces out of harm's way? Trump clearly had no problem with Erdogan suddenly redrawing the red line that had marked the Turkish-Syrian frontier for nearly a century. Within minutes, he tweeted out what would become his orders to an utterly horrified Pentagon. Several hours later, facing a host of protests at home and abroad, Press Secretary Stephanie Grisham issued a somewhat sanitized readout of the conversation between the two presidents:

> Today, President Donald J. Trump spoke with President Recep Tayyip Erdogan of Turkey by telephone. Turkey will soon be moving forward with its long-planned operation into Northern Syria. The United States Armed Forces will not support or be involved in the operation, and United States forces, having defeated the ISIS territorial "Caliphate," will no longer be in the immediate area.

It all sounded depressingly familiar, especially to those who recalled George W. Bush standing on the deck of the aircraft carrier *Abraham Lincoln* on May 1, 2003, beneath a banner proclaiming "Mission Accomplished" in Iraq just six weeks after the invasion, announcing that "major combat operations in Iraq have ended. . . . In the battle of Iraq, the United States and our allies have prevailed." That was seven years before Barack Obama pulled the final American combat unit out of Iraq.

But now, under presidential orders, the last American troops in northern Syria began a precipitous withdrawal. The morning after his conversation with Erdogan, Trump was in an urgently defensive posture over his decision to abandon the red line the United States had held for years with its loyal Kurdish allies. "The Kurds fought with us, but were paid massive amounts of money and equipment to do so," Trump tweeted. "They have been fighting Turkey for decades. I held off this fight for almost three years, but it is time for us to get out of these ridiculous endless wars, many of them tribal, and bring our soldiers home. We will fight where it is to our benefit, and only fight to win." There is no question that most viable and sustainable red lines are based on the principle that they benefit those who establish them. But it is essential when establishing and defending them that their long-term interests and strategic value are clearly in focus. Trump had in many respects as myopic a view of the strategic situation in Syria as Bush had in Iraq sixteen years before. On October 10, 2019, in a gaggle with White House reporters on the South Lawn as he was preparing to board the Marine One helicopter, Trump offered his own Mission Accomplished moment: "Look, we have no soldiers in Syria. We've won. We've beat ISIS. And we've beat them badly and decisively. We have no soldiers [there]." Which seemed to be Trump's rather naïve view of victory.

The day before, following a long night of aerial bombardment of border towns by Turkish jets, the first Turkish troops crossed the border into Syria, joined by units of Assad's army. They fanned out to begin what would prove to be a barbaric ethnic cleansing of Kurdish territories, pushing the new red line from the border at least twenty miles into Syrian territory. From the beginning, Trump insisted he had a red line established in his mind that governed how deep this penetration could go, how barbaric it could be, and how long the battle to establish a defensible line from the Turkish side could last. From the Kurdish perspective, however, there was never any real doubt. The Kurdish website Rudaw, from its base in Erbil, Iraq, offered its view of how Turkey intended to structure its newest line:

> Turkish jets and artillery are being used to sow panic in the cities to cause a major displacement of civilians before launching a concentrated ground offensive into Tal Abyad, known as Gire Spi to the Kurds.
>
> Tal Abyad is an Arab-majority area that was captured by the Syrian Kurdish People's Protection Units (YPG) from the Islamic State (ISIS) in 2015. It is situated directly between the two primary Syrian Kurdish cantons, or regions, Kobane and Jazira.

If Turkey focuses on capturing this region then it will have effectively sev-
ered direct routes between Kobane and Jazira. If this is the focus of Operation
Peace Spring, then this operation may be another tactical phase in Turkey's
long-term strategic plan to carve-up and conquer Syrian Kurdistan (Rojava).

All of Turkey's Syrian operations to date have had the same objective of
dividing Rojava's different regions and then invading them. Turkish officials
invariably claimed that Turkey's actions in Syria are solely directed at preventing a "terror corridor" from spreading along the length of the Syria-Turkey
border, hence a contiguous Rojava.

Trump quickly concluded that standing utterly isolated at home and abroad by virtue of
his withdrawal from Syria was not working. So, he dispatched Vice President Mike Pence
and Secretary of State Mike Pompeo to Ankara, Turkey, to arrange a ceasefire. After hours
of intense negotiations, Pence emerged to report that a 120-hour ceasefire had been arranged
"to allow for the withdrawal of YPG [Kurdish armed] forces from the safe zone," adding
that "Operation Peace Spring will be halted entirely on completion of the withdrawal."
Of course, there was no sense that the Kurds had any intention of withdrawing and abandoning the ancestral villages where their families had lived for centuries. Pence added
that there was also an "agreement by Turkey to engage in no military action against the
community of Kobani," which was the center of Kurdish Syria. Pence was barely back in
Washington when Turkish forces launched a full-blown assault on Kobani. This time,
Russian units went along. Within days, as American forces pulled back, abandoning a
succession of outposts that had secured the red line across northern Syria, Russian forces
moved in. Outside Raqqa, in the strategic crossroads village of Tal Samin, the Russian
news agency Tass quoted Arman Mambetov, a Russian military policeman, saying that
his units had seized and were patrolling the entire surrounding area. It was the third
abandoned American facility Russian forces had seized since the Turkish invasion.
On October 22, a Russian Defense Ministry video showed its helicopters landing at the
abandoned Tabqa military airfield. On November 15, the Russian Ministry of Defense
television channel Zvezda showed Russian attack helicopters and troops landing at a
sprawling air base abandoned by American forces in Aleppo province.

On October 22, Erdogan travelled to Putin's Black Sea retreat at Sochi for six hours
of meetings about how to divide up Syria. No Americans were present; no Syrians either.
But at the end, it was quite clear who was in charge. Putin saw to it that Erdogan got his
way, to a degree—a buffer zone free of all Kurds, whether exterminated or driven away
seemed to be somewhat immaterial. But the Turkish leader had to "share" control with

the forces of Putin and Assad. Effectively, Putin had simply ratified a fait accompli in Syria and, with his standing with Assad very much intact, had also managed to structure the new red line very much to both of their advantages. Effectively, now Russia and Syria had free rein to complete the destruction of Syria's remaining rebel forces in their last strongholds and return to Assad full control of his country. His gratitude to Putin would presumably have no bounds. And Trump no longer had a single red line he needed to guarantee in Syria. Instead, there was an entirely new red line regime that the United States and the West would have no choice but to observe.

By October 14, *The New York Times* had already published a map demonstrating quite graphically how and where Russian ground forces, accompanied, often, by Turkish and Syrian regular army brigades, were strung out in a nearly straight line following the M4 highway that runs across northern Syria at least twenty miles inside the internationally recognized frontier with Turkey. In the final push into the last rebel-held territory in Idlib in December 2019, at least 235,000 civilians were forced to leave, according to the UN Office for the Coordination of Human Affairs, as Russian air and artillery strikes reduced the city quite literally to rubble. One such refugee, Abu al-Majd Nasser, who fled to the border with his family from the town of Telmanas, told a Reuters correspondent that Vladimir Putin "wants to kill every Syrian who opposes the regime." Indeed, by the end even Erdogan began to seem concerned by what he had unleashed, warning that Turkey could not support the newest wave of immigrants forced across the border, and that Europe would begin to feel the impact if it did not put sufficient pressure on Putin and Assad to halt the carnage. Such warnings, now too late, seem to have fallen on deaf ears. The red line Erdogan had so desperately desired was now firmly, perhaps ineradicably, in place.

But even more ominously, as the final days of the decade ran down, the navies of Russia, China, and Iran staged their first joint naval exercise in the northern Indian Ocean, extending as far as the Sea of Oman. Hardly surprising, but certainly troubling for stability in the region, for the third dimension of this series of red lines across Mesopotamia is the product of an increasingly assertive Iran. Emboldened by American indecision and failures that it observed closely in nearby Iraq, encouraged by its growing closeness to neighbors Russia—a traditional foe with hegemonic intentions—and Turkey—no longer a loyal member of a NATO alliance long anathema to the ayatollahs—suddenly an expanding Shiite Middle East seemed within the grasp of the rulers of Tehran and Qom.

CHAPTER SEVEN

Iran to Persia and Back

For nearly two thousand years, Persia, or Iran, has survived, and for long periods even thrived, behind perhaps the world's longest-standing and most impregnable red line—the borders it has maintained with a constantly shifting kaleidoscope of civilizations. Then suddenly, at the very debut of the third decade of the twenty-first century, in a single ill-considered stroke that represented the combined hubris and miscalculation of two leaders—one American, the other Persian, each virtually incapable of reading the other—the region, perhaps much of the world, found itself teetering on the precipice of another world war.

Late in the night of January 3, 2020, General Qasem Soleimani—commander of the Iranian revolutionary Quds Force, considered the second most powerful man in Iran after the Supreme Leader, Ayatollah Ali Khamenei—chose to cross his nation's frontier into Iraq in what was viewed by some as a victory lap. Donald Trump chose to terminate him with a single strike from an unmanned drone. With both these moves, a host of red lines were crossed, indeed crushed. There was the bloody red line between Iran and Iraq, as we have seen in the previous chapter; and the red line that Gerald Ford established by executive order in 1976 that no foreign leader would be assassinated by American arms. Then there were red lines established to counter the rampant spread of terrorism across the region, patrolled by American forces whose energies and focus were suddenly redirected to protecting American facilities or avenging apparent wrongs that were nothing of the sort. Finally, there was the red line of a nuclear-armed Iran, which this single episode seemed to destroy as the nation's leadership announced its first retaliatory move—a rapid opening toward a self-sufficient nuclear fuel cycle, a giant step toward development of a deliverable and sustainable nuclear weapon.

—

If we are to examine just the origins of how all this went suddenly careening off the rails, we must necessarily travel back as many as six millennia or more into the past. The village of Susa in what would become Khuzestan Province has been identified as perhaps the oldest organized human settlement, dating back at least to 4300 B.C.E., with some evidence of habitation there dating even further—to the eighth millennium before the Common Era. Dating to the late forty-fourth century B.C.E., the Susa Acropolis shows evidence of "monumental brick platforms with an apparent temple on top," according to University of Chicago archaeologist Gil J. Stein. It is mentioned in the Bible in the Books of Daniel, Ezra, Nehemiah, and Esther, and was said to be the home of both Nehemiah and Daniel. Above all, it was the heart of the Fertile Crescent, considered by many anthropologists as the birthplace of human civilization. In the book of Daniel, this is the place where he was said to have received his vision, and there is evidence of numerous places of worship where early human faith began. There are even early histories of red lines destroyed by invasions of Assyrians from nearby Mesopotamia, the Assyrian King Ashurbanipal sacking Susa as he overran the entire region as far as the Persian Gulf. By 671 B.C.E., his Neo-Assyrian Empire dwarfed the Greek city-states and had absorbed the Egyptian kingdom. Twelve centuries before the birth of Mohammed, maps of Assyria show a kingdom that would rival that of the Umayyads or the Ottomans, but with its epicenter in Nineveh on the banks of the Tigris in Northern Iraq, outside what is today Mosul.

Persia came into its own again under the rule of Cyrus II, more often known as Cyrus the Great, who in the course of his nearly thirty-year reign as king of Persia beginning in 559 B.C.E., founded the first Persian (or Achaemenid) Empire. He was known in full as "King of Persia, King of Anshan, King of Media, King of Babylon, King of Sumer and Akkad, and King of the Four Corners of the World"—hardly an exaggeration. The full red lines he established covered the largest surface area on the planet in history. According to the *Guinness Book of World Records*, at its peak in 480 B.C.E., "By share of population . . . the Achaemenid Empire, better known as the Persian Empire, accounted for approximately 49.4 million of the world's 112.4 million people—an astonishing 44 percent," the largest empire by percentage of any single nation. "Originating in modern-day Iran," Guinness continues, "the empire was first established by Cyrus the Great and included parts of Central Asia, the Mediterranean, North Africa, and even European territories such as ancient Thrace and Macedonia." It must be remembered, of course, that this was still nearly a millennium before the birth of Mohammed. Cyrus's wars were little more than territorial conquests. There was no true sense of mission or proselytizing.

Still, this was the first Persian Empire, and it did encompass a large slice of the known world. The first Iranian shah, Ardashir I, came along in 224 c.e. with the advent of the Sasanian Empire, which eventually encompassed today's territories of Iran, Iraq, Azerbaijan, Armenia, Georgia, Avkhazia, Dagestan, Lebanon, Jordan, Palestine, Israel, Turkey, Syria, and swaths of Pakistan, Central Asia, Eastern Asia, Eastern Arabia, Egypt, and Afghanistan. For a host of reasons, one of which was the agility of the mounted forces of Ardashir and his successors in contrast with the bulked-up foot soldiers of the Roman Empire and Byzantium, none of these external forces ever managed to cross the Sasanian's frontiers. For a sense of scale, Persians were in a virtually constant state of conflict with the Roman Empire and the Byzantines for some six hundred years, or nearly the amount of time between Christopher Columbus discovering the New World and the present.

But then, along came the Umar and Islam. As the historian Bernard Lewis put it:

> Iran was indeed Islamized, but it was not Arabized. Persians remained Persians. And after an interval of silence, Iran reemerged as a separate, different and distinctive element within Islam, eventually adding a new element even to Islam itself. Culturally, politically, and most remarkable of all even religiously, the Iranian contribution to this new Islamic civilization is of immense importance. The work of Iranians can be seen in every field of cultural endeavor, including Arabic poetry, to which poets of Iranian origin composing their poems in Arabic made a very significant contribution. In a sense, Iranian Islam is a second advent of Islam itself. . . . It was this Persian Islam, rather than the original Arab Islam, that was brought to new areas and new peoples: to the Turks, first in Central Asia and then in the Middle East in the country which came to be called Turkey, and of course to India. The Ottoman Turks brought a form of Iranian civilization to the walls of Vienna.

By the mid-seventh century, Persian rule was effectively restored for half a millennium—ending only in 1258 when an invading Mongolian army swept through the land on its way west. Beyond a penchant for pillaging every land through which they passed, the Mongols were responsible for introducing a new form of warfare to Persia and eventually to Europe. Gunpowder had been develop by regiments of Chinese technicians who traveled with the armies of the heirs of Genghis Khan, throwing gunpowder bombs using trebuchets, or catapults capable of lobbing missiles large distances—at least in medieval terms—with surprising accuracy, as they laid siege to much of Persia in the decade of the 1250s.

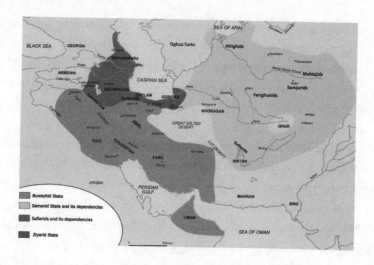

Iran at the dawn of the second millennium (1000 AD).

Modern Iran was really born, however, with the emergence in Persia of the Safavid dynasty, which ruled the nation from 1501 to 1722. Persian became the single language of choice and law, replacing Arabic even among the masses and the theocracy. And the entire nation, previously all too often networks of roving nomadic tribes, was unified under a single leader—the shah. Eventually, the unification of this empire was cemented by the choice of Shiism as the principal religious sect—at about the time that the Ottomans, the principal military and political force outside the firm Persian boundaries, was choosing Sunnism as their theology of choice. Eventually, the two empires would come to deep and lasting blows in the middle of the sixteenth century, though the massive Turkish victory at the Battle of Chaldiran in 1514 led to a suggestion that perhaps there was less to the divinity of the shah and his successors than had been attributed to them. Eventually, Persia was forced to relinquish Azerbaijan, Karabakh, Shirvan, Dagestan, and Baghdad, as well as parts of Kurdistan and Lorestan, to the Ottomans, retaining the core Persian territory that comprises the heartland of Iran today. Some of these territories and the red lines that went along with them seesawed back and forth for a century or so, particularly Kurdistan and parts of Iraq. But there was one overwhelming priority, as Middle Eastern historian Rudi Matthee put it so well, describing the rule of Shah Abbas I (from 1588 to 1629), often called Abbas the Great, the strongest ruler of the Safavid dynasty:

Regaining Persia and securing its borders was intimately linked to Shah Abbās' main objective, that of maximizing personal control and

centralizing power. Abbās ended the practice of appointing the crown
prince as governor of Khorasan, and other sons to various provincial
governorates under the tutelage of Qezelbāš guardians. Instead, in order
to forestall rebellion and premature claims to the throne, he killed one of
his sons and blinded two more.

Incidentally, he also locked up all his grandchildren in the harem and had his own
tutor assassinated as a potential rival to the throne. Still, Abbas was very much a builder
of infrastructure and networks that would solidify Persia's prosperity, its ability to
maintain its social and political cohesion, guarantee its frontiers, and above all preserve
his mastery of the throne. So a network of roads, new trading centers, and industries,
particularly the manufacture and export of fine silks, were all part of his master plan. At
the same time, he extended the empire's southern reaches to the Persian Gulf, allowing
unfettered access to the Indian Ocean and beyond, without need to pass through any
Ottoman lands. All these are quite modern themes that define the red lines and boundaries of contemporary Iran.

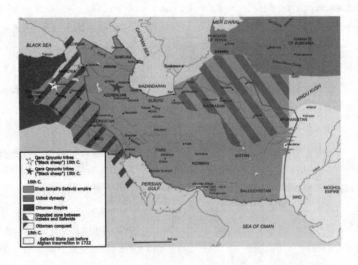

Three centuries of Iranian expansion and evolution (Safavid Persia).

Eventually, a succession of weak rulers led the Safavid regime to begin crumbling by
the early eighteenth century—an opening for Ottomans from the west, but especially
Russians from the north under Czar Peter the Great to begin testing, then penetrating, the

Persian boundaries and seizing territory. As Persia's red lines began to shrink, Russia's expanded, beginning two centuries of alternating conflict and alliances, extending to the present. For twelve years, from 1804 to 1813 and 1826 to 1828, Russia and Persia fought the Russo-Persian Wars. In both cases, and hardly surprisingly, the powerful empire of the czars came out on top. In the first case, urged on by his British allies and backed by a call for jihad by the ulema religious leaders, the shah's forces attacked on a long line across Armenia into Baku. At first, Russia was hobbled by the invasion of Napoleon's armies, and Persia felt empowered by its first battles against a major Western military force. Eventually, in a string of battles, Russia cemented its hold over the Caucasus and the Black Sea. The first war ended effectively in a draw, though Russia managed to retain the Caucasus, which then as now it so desperately wanted in order to assure control of the Black Sea and access to a year-round port. By the time of the second Russo-Persian War, the balance of power had clearly tipped. As Russian forces rolled through Armenia and Azerbaijan, then turned toward Tehran itself, Persia was forced to sue for peace. The red line that formed the frontier between the two empires, which was defined in the Treaty of Turkmenchay and was signed on February 22, 1826, would last, virtually immutable, through the Bolshevik Revolution and formation of the Soviet Union, through two World Wars, the Cold War, and the dissolution of the Soviet Union. Only Russia was allowed to maintain a navy on the Caspian Sea, though both parties could use it for commercial purposes. And the shah had to empty his treasury to pay Russia the humiliating tribute of 20 million rubles in reparations. Feelings ran quite high over the humiliations of this treaty. In 1829, the thirty-five-year-old Russian ambassador Alexander Griboyedov, also a virtuoso poet and playwright, together with his entire embassy staff, was murdered by a mob. It had been incited by a leading Muslim cleric when a rumor spread that the young ambassador had seized two Georgian women from the harem of a leading aristocrat and forced them to renounce Islam. Throughout the rest of the nineteenth century, as the Great Game played out between major powers, Iran and its strategic geopolitical position became a critical pawn, with Britain anxious to preserve the integrity of Iran's borders to make sure its colony of India did not become tempting prey for the Russian czars. With both Russia and Britain anxious to maintain an independent and nonaligned Iran, it managed to fend off becoming a colony of any outside force. During the wars of the nineteenth and early twentieth centuries, however, Russia and the Ottomans eventually divided much of what was then the outreaches of northern Persia, largely territories of Armenia and Azerbaijan, later republics of the Soviet Union, that had never truly been part of the Iranian heartland.

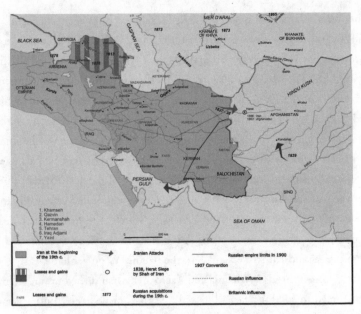

*Iran by 1900 begins to assume its present form as Russia
and Britain press their claims and interests.*

During World War I, Iran steadfastly maintained its neutrality, though German, Ottoman, Imperial Russian, and British troops threaded their way through the country, the czar's forces even entering the holy city of Qom. The Bolshevik Revolution ended all of this, the provisional government ordering the withdrawal of all Russian forces from Iran, the frontiers restored to prewar levels. With the end of World War I came the end of the Qajars who had ruled Persia since 1789. In 1921, Minister of War Colonel Reza Khan deposed Ahmad Shah, the last of the Qajars, in a bloodless coup when the shah was on a sybaritic European tour. The parliament (Majlis) proclaimed Reza Khan as shah, and the Pahlavi dynasty was born.

One key constant remained throughout these periods, however. Shiism was thoroughly ensconced as the religion of the people, not to mention the court, of Persia. Also particularly important as antecedents to the lines that prevail today across the region were the long periods during Safavid rule when Baghdad, as well as eastern and southern Iraq, were firmly under Persian, hence Shiite, control. Not surprisingly, descendants of these Shiites continue to form the majority of Iraq's people, though Baghdad and the nation remain nominally under Sunni control—another legacy of the Ottoman Empire.

Still, the first of the Pahlavis, Reza Khan, known after his coronation as Reza Shah Pahlavi, and his successors understood better than any of the dynasties that preceded them the value of maintaining their borders as an impenetrable red line to be defended to the utmost of their military might and their political and diplomatic dexterity. Reza embarked on a determined campaign of Persianization of Iran and, while maintaining the unitary role of Shiism, adopted a host of modern customs—eliminating the chador for women, welcoming women into universities, even changing his nation's name from Persia to Iran. The clash with Iran's clergy was only the first step toward their eventual outright hostility toward the Pahlavis. Still, despite Iran's official neutrality, World War II was marked by the utter collapse of Iran's borders as military forces of the Soviet Union and Britain moved into the country to prevent Germany from taking over critical oil resources. On September 17, 1941, the Red Army entered Tehran with British backing. Reza Shah fled into exile, and his son Crown Prince Mohammad Reza Pahlavi assumed the throne as the second and last shah of the Pahlavi dynasty. His was a tumultuous reign, but for our purposes here, one of relatively steady rule. Iran's frontiers had long been fixed and effectively guaranteed by its neighbors and by the Allied powers that remade the Middle East for a second time, preserving the vast bulk of the national outlines established after the First World War—certainly the outlines of Iran.

The problem was that a number of the Western powers, particularly the United States and Britain, failed to recognize the foundations of postwar Iran's sovereignty. By 1951, the West was deeply into the Cold War with the Soviet Union and its proxies, one of whom, at least some Americans believed, was Mohammad Mosaddegh. The shah, installed by the allies, followed the will of the Majlis. Fearing an uprising by opponents of his increasingly absolutist rule, he appointed this veteran center-left politician as prime minister. Mosaddegh came from a venerable Persian family, his father having served as a finance minister under the Qajar dynasty before the Pahlavis came to power. When he finally assumed office he acted quickly to limit the supremacy of the Shah and increase the influence of the people, as expressed through the Majlis. With the economy worsening and unrest spreading, Mosadddegh was forced briefly into retirement, then returned when the Shah and his interim prime minister failed to quell spreading revolts. This time, having gained favor with most of the left and center elements in parliament, Mosaddegh demanded and won emergency powers. Among his most loyal supporters was the Tudeh Party, the communist party of Iran. When Mosaddegh nationalized the Anglo-Iranian Oil Company, Britain launched a series of sanctions against the already-strapped nation. Britain was becoming increasingly anxious to depose Mosaddegh. So, with the arrival of the determinedly anticommunist Dwight Eisenhower as president of the United States, a joint CIA-MI6 operation was launched. Kermit Roosevelt, head of the CIA's Middle East division, traveled to Tehran to take charge. The local CIA station chief, who opposed a coup, was promptly replaced. On November 1, the British emptied their embassy in Tehran, and a large convoy headed to Beirut by road. It was a complex plot, which in the end revolved around the shah, whom the Americans promised to support for life in a style to which he'd become accustomed should the coup fail. The shah signed a series of *firmans*, or royal decrees, removing Mosaddegh. A number of fake pro-Tudeh demonstrations were launched, using American funds. At the same time, the military was enlisted to support Mosaddegh's replacement, Fazlollah Zahedi, a veteran Iranian general and politician, trained in the Cossack Brigade, who, anointed by the British and Americans, promptly assumed the office of prime minister and restored the rule of the shah. In turn, to prevent the possibility of any further antiroyalist plots, SAVAK, the secret police, was given terrifying powers that only built throughout the fifties and sixties until their control over the nation was absolute. Meanwhile, the shah himself was building a court that rivaled the opulence of those of the greatest monarchs of Europe centuries in the past. So it would not be long before the efforts to preserve American and British control over Iran's actions would prove utterly, indeed catastrophically, misguided.

In October 1971, in the ancient center of Persepolis, the shah celebrated the 2,500th anniversary of continuous Persian monarchy since Cyrus the Great founded the Achaemenid Empire. As Charlotte Curtis reported on the flamboyant festivities in *The New York Times*, "presidents, prime ministers, assorted royalty and highly placed commoners from 63 countries [were] due here for the national celebration." Virtually every major nation came to pay tribute and guarantee the shah that the sanctity of his lands would be eternally free from challenge from abroad. He had bought and paid for his security behind the lines he had established. Beginning in 1950 until he was deposed in 1979, the shah purchased some $33 billion worth of arms and military equipment, much of it from the United States. Iran in those years was the second largest importer of arms from abroad after Germany, according to the Stockholm International Peace Research Institute. The shah thought he had adequately protected all his flanks. In the end, though, the real challenge to his regime came both from abroad and at home—from the radical Shiite fringe and a dissident cleric, Ayatollah Ruhollah Khomeini. From his places of exile, first in the Shiite holy city of Najaf, then from Neauphle-le-Château, a leafy suburb twenty-five miles west of Paris, this wise and savvy revolutionary realized that he could penetrate the red lines with which the shah had surrounded himself. And only at the final moment was it even necessary for him to set foot anywhere near them. Each morning, under an apple tree in the small villa where he'd installed himself, he would preach his revolutionary wisdom to a small coterie of acolytes and a tape recorder. These cassettes, smuggled into Iran and then duplicated by the hundreds of thousands, were his trebuchets into the very heart of the shah's empire. Even the utterly barbaric SAVAK seemed incapable of thwarting this intellectual invasion of its ruler's lands and especially his people. You will recall, my research has suggested that red lines are most effectively maintained and defended when the people who lie within their boundaries have bought into the viability, even necessity, of them. If there was ever that feeling in Pahlavi-era Iran, it had all but evaporated by the time the ayatollah's cassettes and his preaching began arriving. They found a broad and deep audience in an Iran whose people had been impoverished and oppressed by the shah's confiscatory policies and the brutality of his security apparatus—effectively disappointed reversal of rising expectations. The cassettes and a number of foolish and intemperate initiatives of the shah—including abolition of the traditional Iranian calendar and substitution of one whose year-zero was the investiture of Cyrus the Great—led to a growing belief that the shah and all he represented had to go.

Khomeini's triumphal return to Iran was on board a chartered Air France jet, accompanied by 120 journalists. The aging but quite vigorous grand ayatollah was met on arrival at Tehran Airport and at his every appearance by mobs of adoring followers often numbering in the millions. The shape of the new red lines of Iran quickly became quite clear and largely impregnable. And they encompassed multiple levels—spiritual as well as temporal. From his earliest days in power, Khomeini's goal was to draw new lines of demarcation across the Middle East and beyond—wherever men worshipped and made war, particularly in defense of Shiites, for whom he immediately anointed himself and his nation their leader and protector. The vast American-trained security machinery of the shah could make no headway against the faith of millions in the streets. They were fighting a different set of wars, battling to control a different set of red lines. The shah, in his efforts to "modernize," had all but totally lost touch with his people, who had little or no interest in modernizing, especially if the price was remaining under the sway of the monsters of SAVAK.

In retrospect, anyone who'd paid any real attention to Khomeini and his thinking, even setting aside his mesmeric charisma, could have seen this coming. But few did. The world, if not the Persian population at large, was way too caught up in the euphoria of the moment and the aura the shah had established to explore the nature of the system that from his earliest days as a scholar-in-exile the ayatollah had been preaching. But it was all there for any who were prepared to look. Especially in his book *Islamic Government: Governance of the Jurist (Velayat-e Faqih)*, Khomeini made his case directly and without a scintilla of qualification, the title justifying the rule of the clergy as supreme over the state:

Since the Most Noble Messenger [Mohammed] promulgated the divine command through his act of appointing a successor, he also, implicitly stated the necessity for establishing a government. It is self-evident that the necessity for enactment of the law, which necessitated the formation of a government by the Prophet, was confined or restricted to his time, but continues after his departure from this world. According to one of the noble verses of the Qur'an, the ordinances of Islam are not limited with respect to time or place; they are permanent and must be enacted until the end of time. . . .

The only way to prevent the emergence of anarchy and disorder and to protect society from corruption is to form a government and thus impart order to all the affairs of the country. Both reason and divine law, then, demonstrate the necessity in our time for what was necessary during the lifetime of the Prophet and the age of the Commander of the Faithful—namely the formation of a government and the establishment of executive and administrative organs.

Which is precisely what Khomeini proceeded to do. This was Karl Marx's *The Communist Manifesto* or Adolph Hitler's *Mein Kampf* for an Islamic audience. Few actually read these works, but for those who did, neither the Bolshevik revolution nor the Nazi state should have come as a major surprise in terms of their shape, their texture, or the vast red line networks their leaders contemplated and began to draw with their devoted legions. For Khomeini and his followers, even—or especially—if it meant returning to a seventh century political, social, and judicial system, even the most malignant outcome would be powerfully and morally justified. Almost immediately, his followers began preparing the way—taking down, often quite violently, the modern institutions the shah had sought to graft onto Shiite Iran—burning to the ground banks that charged interest banned in the Koran, as well as liquor stores, theaters, and brothels. Mobs even deconstructed a brewery in Tehran brick by brick. Each such action, albeit a short-lived burst of total destruction, was seen as vital to the imam's mission and that of his followers.

By the time a ragtag collection of university students, members of the "Moslem Student Followers of the Imam's Line," seized 52 American hostages and barricaded themselves for 444 days in the US embassy in Tehran from November 4, 1979 (nine months after Khomeini's return from exile), until January 20, 1981, the outlines of this Islamic state had been well established. President Jimmy Carter should have recognized this when he tried his ill-fated mission to penetrate these lines and rescue the hostages. Equally, Iraq's President Saddam Hussein should have recognized the fanaticism that drove the waves of suicide attackers against his forces during the eight years of war that raged across their borders. Khomeini and his regime seemed to have little trouble establishing or defending their red lines on multiple fronts. At the same moment Iranian college students were confronting American opprobrium and all efforts to regain control over the embassy and freeing the hostages, Khomeini was also forced to take on the major military power in the region—Saddam Hussein's Iraq—when he was lured into a catastrophic conflict by reports of Iran's post-revolutionary vulnerability.

We've already examined from the Iraqi side the perception of just how territorial this eight-year conflict was. From the Iranian side, however, there was little question of Khomeini relinquishing control of a single square meter of his territory, nor for that matter a single Shiite believer. From his perspective, there was also the broader question of Islamic revolution and the desire to bring within Iran's spiritual, Shiite red line the 60 percent of Iraq's population that was suffering under the bootheel of that country's minority Sunni leaders. The Iranian forces had several major shortcomings. Many of the most accomplished and experienced officers of Iran's armed forces had been trained by Americans and served the shah loyally. They were among the first targets of Khomeini when he assumed office, and were purged and often summarily executed. Still, Khomeini did have the power of summoning tens of thousands of the faithful to arms with a single edict. The Pasdaran—better known as the Islamic Revolutionary Guard Corps (IRGC)—and its infamous paramilitary Home Guard the Basij numbered some 200,000 men by the end of November 1980, whom Khomeini was able to dispatch to the front against Iraq; the ayatollah called them his "Army of Twenty Million." Many carried their own shrouds into battle, anticipating martyrdom. It took eight years of horrific bloodshed, but eventually it was nominally—at least under the terms of the United Nations–facilitated truce—a draw, with about equal losses from each side. The real outcome, however, was quite uneven. Iranians and especially Ayatollah Khomeini saw themselves as the winners, though the cost has been estimated at as much as $645 billion plus 250,000 Iranian deaths and a million casualties on both sides.

Still, in terms of their broader mission and looking back over the previous decade, Khomeini had accumulated some considerable success. He'd defeated the Great Satan, the United States, seizing its embassy and holding fifty-two of its people hostage for a year. The shah of Iran had been exiled, then died in Egypt from a cancer that the greatest American doctors were unable to stem. Jimmy Carter was swept from office, giving way to Ronald Reagan, the Great Conciliator. Saddam Hussein had sustained some crippling losses and won no victory in the end. What could be better? The answer was simple—utter defeat of America and banishing its forces from the Middle East. And cementing control over the world's Shiites and Iran's own near-abroad.

Indeed, Iran, and the powerful red line it established and exhibited every intention of defending to the last man, was never really threatened by the United States or the American military. But Shiites remained in many locations in dire peril. It quickly became clear that Iran was fully prepared to establish and defend to their greatest ability lines around every Shiite community in the region—and beyond.

The ceasefire of the Iran-Iraq War took effect on August 20, 1988, with 307 military observers and a squadron of Canadian signals officers fanning out in 51 patrols along the entire border. Both sides began withdrawing their forces immediately, which would appear simply to have released some vast military resources for Saddam's invasion of Kuwait, which began on August 2, 1990, two years later. Five months after that, Operation Desert Storm was launched by thirty-five nations led by the United States. Iran promptly convened its National Security Council. It was an extraordinary session, particularly with the sudden and unheralded entrance by the Ayatollah Ali Khamenei, who had taken over the role of supreme leader barely a year earlier upon the death on June 3, 1989, of Ayatollah Khomeini. It was clear that Ayatollah Khamenei held powers commensurate with his predecessor. Karim Sadjadpour of the Carnegie Endowment for International Peace wrote in a 2009 study that Khomeini's successor as supreme leader, Ayatollah Ali Khamenei, developed a relationship with the IRGC that was "increasingly symbiotic, politically expedient for the Leader and economically expedient for the guards," helping compensate for the fact that he lacks Khomeini's authority. "He is their commander in chief and appoints their senior commanders, who, in turn, are publicly deferential to him and increasingly reap benefits by playing a more active role in political decision making and economic activity," Sadjadpour wrote.

On June 4, 1989, the Assembly of Experts—the highest spiritual and secular body in Iran, the only arbiter of who will become supreme leader—had chosen Ayatollah Ali Khamenei. As two Chatham House researchers, Sanam Vakil and Hossein Rassam, put it, "A 50-year-old midranking cleric at the time, Khamenei lacked Khomeini's towering stature. But at a meeting on June 4, 1989, the day after Khomeini's death, [Akbar Hashemi] Rafsanjani, a close confidant of Khomeini, told the assembly that Khomeini had considered Khamenei qualified for the job. The group elected Khamenei by a vote of 60 to 14." Even with the apparent ratification from beyond the grave of Ayatollah Khomeini, this was not enough to assure a unanimous vote for the new grand ayatollah. Still, this system was one that had been cemented by Khomeini and enshrined in his seminal work, *Governance of the Jurist (Velayat-e Faqeeh)*. What is especially interesting is the fact that even at the very moment of his election, there were already chinks in the armor. This consisted of two powerful strains that continue to divide Iran and become more or less distinct depending on the intensity with which the nation's internal well-being and its dominance in the region may be challenged. More moderate jurists have long held that the power of the supreme leader derives from the people, through the elected Assembly. The conservative strain, dominated by Khamenei, believes simply that the Assembly, through divine intervention, discovers the right individual, who should then rule unchecked until the end of his days. At which time, the process repeats.

A very savvy Khamenei, from the moment of his elevation, took great pains to cement his relationship with the elements of state security, particularly the IRGC, as well as the judiciary and the media, all of which he controls under the Khomeini-era constitution. He also appoints the twelve members of the Guardian Council, which has the power to veto any candidate for elected office at any level that does not meet its standards, and has the right as well to veto any parliamentary decision, without appeal. Khamenei also decides how all oil revenues are spent and ascertains that all government units adhere to the strictest Islamic standards, which he sets. Finally, he is guardian of the fundamental principles of the Khomeini revolution. To facilitate all this, he appoints the leading jurists, the heads of state radio and television, the regular armed forces, and his own IRGC, which by reporting directly to him is able to operate virtually without restraint. As a result, over the last twenty years, the IRGC has accumulated considerable wealth and power, establishing a fortress of their own red lines around their prerogatives, so much so that when they do commit some error that might otherwise be considered unpardonable, they are quickly absolved and move on.

Always keep in mind this theme: that Iran's supreme end is to make certain that the red line of the Persian nation—little challenged and rarely broken during three millennia of existence—is maintained and that, by extension, the supremacy of the Shiite branch of Islam is also preserved within its boundaries or expanded to include wherever Shiites are scattered abroad. This, of course, is somewhat of a fantasy, particularly since the Shiites are vastly outnumbered by Sunnis throughout the Islamic world. Nearly 90 percent of all Muslims are Sunnis, with the balance of Shiites concentrated in Iran, Iraq, and Pakistan, where they are dominant, as well as portions of India, where they chose to remain after the British departure and the split-off of Muslim-dominant Pakistan.

What Iran did do, however, virtually from the day of the return of Ayatollah Khomeini from exile, was to begin building out a web of red lines among terrorist groups and other dissident or opposition forces in neighboring countries carefully designed at once to reinforce Iran's own security and protect its fellow Shiites. Or so the mullahs would have their followers believe. Indeed, while terrorists were certainly a component of this structure, the Shia of the region, as far off as Pakistan and India, were also natural constituents, indeed had been regarded as protected even under the Shah. By virtue of the mullahs' all but absolute control over the media and local political infrastructure, they succeeded in persuading the vast majority of their people that following their lead was essential to the health and welfare of the Persian nation.

The network the grand ayatollahs succeeded in building may be divided into several key zones and, much like the web of red lines the Chinese established around the islands that are only marginally theirs by law or claim, have become integral to the Iranian Shiite sense of well-being, even survival. Having large numbers of Sunnis, or a substantial Sunni-controlled nation, on its borders could only be seen as ultimately threatening the rule of the Iranian mullahs. Iran needed desperately control over a near-abroad. The first and clearest target would necessarily be Iraq, where some 65 to 70 percent of the population (19 to 22 million people) is Shiite, yet the nation's rulers are dominantly Sunni—one of the remnants of the old Ottoman bureaucracy, perpetuated by the Ba'ath party, which brought Saddam Hussein to power. It was quite clear from the futile and enervating eight-year war that Iran fought to a draw with Iraq that as long as Saddam Hussein remained in power, Shiites in Iraq would remain a repressed majority in their own land. Nevertheless, even after the American invasion and the death of Saddam, the United States was forced to rely on many of the established institutions, and particularly the still Sunni-dominated bureaucracy, that continued to function. What was left of the military or state security was also incapable of containing the rise of Shiite militias that Iran was eager to finance from their earliest days. "Iran is competing with its neighbors, asserting an arc of influence and instability while vying for regional hegemony, using state-sponsored terrorist activities, a growing network of proxies, and its missile program to achieve its objectives," the US National Defense Strategy reported in 2018, with little effort to apply any nuance that could provide context. A year later, the *Worldwide Threat Assessment of the US Intelligence Community* added that "Iran-supported Popular Mobilization Committee-affiliated Shia militias remain the primary threat to US personnel, and we expect that threat to increase as the threat ISIS poses to the militias recedes."

Today, as many as two hundred such Iranian-supported militias or their offshoots, comprising as many as 200,000 fighters, thrive in the border regions of Iraq and Syria and as far afield as Afghanistan and Pakistan—a figure that has more than doubled since 2014 when the umbrella *al-Hashd al-Shaabi* (Popular Mobilization Forces) was launched by Iran in Iraq and Syria. Phillip Smyth, who has made his career monitoring the anatomy and taxonomy of these militias at the Washington Institute for Near East Policy, has compiled an interactive map and what is effectively a family tree of these utterly toxic organizations. As to why so many often overlapping and highly competitive groups have not only been tolerated, but even encouraged by Iran, the answer has many levels. This confusion often enables deniability by Iran for their more virulent operations. At the same time, competition offers incentives. Many compete with one another for favor, recognition, funding, and arms from Tehran, but particularly from the IRGC and its international terrorist-oriented offshoot, the Quds Force, both of which report directly to Supreme Leader Ali Khamenei. The mandate of the Quds Force is particularly central to this narrative since its mission from the moment of its founding was to implant resistance operations globally. And it has proven itself quite successful, initially in Iran's near-abroad of Iraq and Syria, but eventually extending its immediate red lines concentrically to Lebanon, Saudi Arabia, and Yemen, and ever more broadly to Afghanistan, Central Asia, Africa, even Latin America. Quds Force's most advanced weaponry has been used against Iran's opponents, particularly American troops as far afield as Afghanistan, according to Congressional testimony. In 2008, General David Petraeus, then a commander of American forces in Iraq battling Shiite militia, was handed a cell phone with a chilling message: "General Petraeus, you should know that I, Qasem Soleimani, control the policy for Iran with respect to Iraq, Lebanon, Gaza, and Afghanistan. And indeed, the [Iranian] ambassador in Baghdad is a Quds Force member. The individual who's going to replace him is a Quds Force member." Actually, three consecutive ambassadors to Iraq beginning in 2005 have been members. Until the assassination of General Soleimani in January 2020, Iran had paid little price for the actions of the Quds Force wherever it operated. Yet until his death, this Iranian general from a tiny, impoverished village in Kerman Province reigned as "the most powerful man in Iraq, no question," as Iraq's former national security minister Mowaffak al-Rubaie observed. Much of his power was due to the resources commanded by the IRGC and its Quds Forces.

And central to the entire operation is financing. A RAND Corporation study reported in 2009 that "from laser eye surgery and construction to automobile manufacturing and real estate, the IRGC has extended its influence into virtually every sector of the Iranian market. Perhaps more than any other area of its domestic involvement, its business activities represent the multidimensional nature of the institution. The commercialization of the IRGC has the potential to broaden the circle of its popular support by co-opting existing financial elites into its constellation of subsidiary companies and subcontractors." Indeed, as Columbia University researcher Gary Sick, founder of the Gulf-2000 network, observes, "expansion of the IRGC into the domestic economy of Iran is directly related to the imposition of U.S. sanctions. As we closed off legitimate sources of financing and trade, the IRGC was given increasing responsibility." One IRGC-linked organization, Khatam al-Anbia, is the sole contractor for Iran's lucrative gas industry, having been awarded no-bid contracts worth billions of dollars. Directly or through a parallel network of foundations, or *bonyads*, most run by former IRGC commanders, these organizations have participated in Iran and abroad on mammoth construction projects and trading contracts, while at home cementing their political position in the most remote villages with more than 270 million rials of low-interest home loans to families of martyrs more than twenty years ago. Those numbers have only multiplied since then. At the same time, IRGC-supported organizations have also been singled out, even by members of the Majlis, as engaging in illegal smuggling activities, trafficking in alcohol and narcotic drugs, all of which are banned and for which penalties for sale or use can include execution. These same Majlis members suggest that smuggling nets the organization as much as $12 billion a year.

Above all, this provides the Iranian regime with resources to establish and maintain a vast network of Shiite militias across the Middle East and beyond, no matter how tightly the United States or Western powers may tighten sanctions. Amnesty International has reported that Shiite militias "source a proportion of their arms and ammunition directly from Iran, either in the form of gifts or sales," a comment that could of course, be mirrored with respect to other regional groups like the Kurds, who until the later Trump years were recipients of comparable American largesse. These militia groups, however, have been the primary vehicle for expanding Iran's red lines into an even vaster territory than any contemplated or realized by Cyrus the Great or Assyria's King Ashurbanipal before him. Not that any of these pre-Islamic potentates would have carried much weight in the thinking of the supreme leaders of contemporary Iran, but eradicating the lines established by the drafters of the Treaty of Versailles has been expressed as an aspiration, and indeed today they are well along their way to achieving this singular goal.

—

Contemporary Iran, together with its brutal extensions, is an empire built at once on faith and force of arms. Over the first four decades of its existence, it has succeeded in building a continuously fluid network—groups and subgroups that have each claimed and established a vast web of lines that morph and shift by the year, often by the week or day. Iran's contribution has been on a variety of levels. At its most basic, Iran has provided an ever-broadening stream of funding for arms and munitions, as well as complex killing machines—missiles, rockets, and drones, shaped charges capable of penetrating armored vehicles and sophisticated IEDs (improvised explosive devices). More fundamentally, the IRGC and Quds Force helped finance the religious establishment's desire to cement the vast red lines it was building abroad and staff the militias that were prepared to defend them at all costs.

The nature and structure of these forces have evolved on a host of levels beginning in the earliest days of the Khomeini regime in Iran, expanding with the arrival of his successor, Ayatollah Ali Khamenei, as supreme leader in 1989, not long after the end of the Iran-Iraq War. The efforts of Khamenei only accelerated in the wake of the chaos created by the American invasion of Iraq and the toppling of Saddam Hussein in 2003. In 2007, the Popular Mobilization Forces were formed as clones of the Iranian-supported Lebanese Hezbollah and began operating throughout Iraq alongside the Badr Organization, which also began building a number of sectarian death squads.

Just how tightly Iran controls these forces on any number of levels is striking. Their methods are quite distinct from many others used by major state actors that have deployed red lines and defended them, yet no less effective. Iran's functions are both decentralized organizationally yet tightly controlled ideologically and with respect to the final goals and political interests across a broad spectrum. The ideology is founded on the concept of *velayat-e-faqih*, as first expressed in Ayatollah Khomeini's work of political and moral philosophy. It grants the supreme leader absolute authority, derived from God and Mohammed. That authority passed definitionally to Ali Khamenei when he assumed that position. And this absolute subservience is demanded of and accepted by virtually all the Shiite militia operating throughout Mesopotamia and beyond. Not surprisingly, this means that Iran controls far more—and more tightly—Shiite militias operating in Syria than either Assad or Vladimir Putin, not to mention Turkey's leader, Recep Erdogan. And it means Iran, by extension, has established utterly defensible red lines across this region—lines it cannot afford to abandon or shrink. These red lines include military, political, and ultimately religious varieties. The military variety are quite clear and often encompass barbaric acts of torture, assassination, and even beheadings. They also formed the backbone of Iran's efforts to shrink the red lines established by the heavily Sunni Islamic State. Eventually, with that threat extinguished, many—particularly the Kata'ib al-Imam Ali (Imam Ali Brigade)—turned their efforts to ridding the region of American forces. A number of Iraqi militias were smuggled into Iran for advanced training in use of advanced weapons and techniques used in roadside bombings and other operations often directed at American forces, especially before the Obama-era troops withdrawals. Equally, militias were being supplied with advanced weaponry that could only have originated in Iran.

The political lines continue to be constructed and maintained by a number of Shiite militia soldiers and leaders who have shed their uniforms and stood for parliament, especially in Iraq and now even in Syria as the civil war winds down toward an Assad victory. Now these individuals have accumulated a critical mass that allows them considerable ability to influence policy. A number have assimilated so deeply into the Iraqi infrastructure that Iran no longer needs to maintain separate logistical or storage facilities for their military units within Iraq; they are simply allowed to co-locate on Iraqi bases. Many former militia officers, elected as members of parliament, even played a major role in the unanimous vote by the Iraqi parliament in January 2020 to demand American troops leave Iraq following the assassination of Soleimani in the drone attack ordered by President Trump. Indeed, Shebl al-Zaidi, the Kata'ib al-Imam Ali leader, had been photographed with General Soleimani as early as early as June 2014, shortly after he formed his Imam Ali brigade. Suggesting his group's closeness with the Iraq regular army and how far it has been coopted by the extension of Iranian influence into its neighbor, Zaidi has also been photographed being transported in an Iraqi military helicopter, though of course any number of other individuals including western journalists have also availed themselves of such resources.

In March 2018, Haider al-Abadi, the Shiite prime minister of Iraq, formalized all these arrangements, issuing an order to the armed forces detailing how militia members should be organized and comport themselves. This strikingly detailed document describes everything from the qualifications for a young recruit joining the popular militia—his age and education, being "of good morals, good reputation and behavior"—down to the "distinctive identification board with a specific color and shape indicating [their rank] attached to the right side of the chest." Each of these militia members would receive the "same entitlements as are their peers in the Ministry of Defense." This included "financial entitlements," transferring much of the cost burdens from Iran to the Iraqi treasury. For the 122,000-strong militia forces, the Iraqi government budgeted $2.16 billion in 2019, some 20 percent higher than a year earlier—a burden that an increasingly cash-strapped Iran, reeling under the ever-tightening American sanctions, would be relieved from bearing. There was also now little doubt that large numbers of Iraqi militia forces, most of whom owed their true allegiance to Ali Khamenei under the doctrine of *velayat-e-faqih*, would be an integral part of the Iraqi army.

The first and most deeply integrated Iranian enterprise abroad—and the one that has managed the deepest penetration into the national society, politics, and psyche, is in Lebanon. Hezbollah, from its birth following the 1982 invasion by Israel, has been a creature of, by, and about Iran and its Shiite ambitions across the region. Its name, The Party of God, was defined by its link to the Islamic clerics of Iran, and the organization is funded by them and takes its orders largely from them. At the same time, its organizational structure has been cloned in militias across Mesopotamia, and within Lebanon has become a potent political as well as military force. "Hezbollah was once a state within the Lebanese state, but now Lebanon is a state within Hezbollah's state," said Hanin Ghaddar of the Washington Institute. On January 23, 2019, the website Arab News proclaimed that the "new government [in Lebanon] shows Hezbollah 'takeover of Lebanon is complete.'"

But in fact, the situation on the ground has gone much further. "Tehran has also used Hezbollah and other militias to build a land bridge across portions of Iraq, Syria, and Lebanon," Ghaddar suggested. "This corridor has three purposes: (1) providing cheap transport of weapons from Iran to the Mediterranean Sea; (2) establishing an alternate supply route in case Israel bombs airfields during the next war with Hezbollah or its allies; and (3) reaffirming militant Shia identity in the region." Lebanese Hezbollah has also been quite useful in training radical Shiite militants in the fine points of guerrilla warfare, bomb making, and the use of advanced weapons, including missiles—all supplied by Iran. Indeed, the International Institute for Strategic Studies has estimated that the longest-range precision targeted missile, the Soumar, can reach 2,500 kilometers, or as far as eastern Libya on the west; Ethiopia on the south; all of Ukraine, Romania, and Russia as far as Moscow on the north; and all of India and Pakistan, the other 'Stans, and stretches of western China on the east.

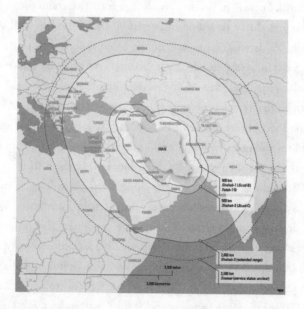

Iranian regional missile reach: selected ballistic and cruise missiles. Sources: International Institute for Strategic Studies. Note: Maximum missile ranges assuming standard payload and most forward deployment. Distances shown are approximate.

In 2018, Iran launched six medium-range ballistic missiles across Iraq, landing with precision on the headquarters of the Islamic State group in Syria's eastern Euphrates River valley, the IRGC celebrating that "many *takfiris* (apostates) . . . were killed and wounded by the missiles." Already, in December 2017, Iranian missiles had been launched by Houthi rebels in Yemen targeting Riyadh's international airport and even the royal palace of King Salman, though Saudi air defenses were said to have intercepted them.

Iran's interest in neighboring Syria and control over Assad as the end of his brutal civil war approached was especially striking since it suggests Iran's enormous interest in expending its southern and western red lines into Syria, at the same moment Russia and Turkey are both interested in planting their own flags—and outposts—there.

Iran's particular interest in Syria dates back to 2012 when Iran began tasking Lebanon's Hezbollah with training groups of Shiite fighters based in Syria operating in the capital, Damascus, and in the regions around the major provincial capitals of Homs and Aleppo. These militias' activities were aimed at both the expanding Sunni-dominated Islamic State and the Syrian rebel forces operating in the civil war against Bashar al-Assad's government. The numbers of fighters assembled by these Shiite militia grew steadily until, at their peak, they reached at least five thousand domestic Syrian Shia and as many as thirty thousand imported by Iran from Iraq and as far afield as Afghanistan and Pakistan. The nature of the often quite sophisticated recruitment techniques suggests how vast and deeply implanted Iran's red lines have become across the region. Unlike the lines created and maintained by governments from Russia to China to North Korea, Iran has no system of military service at the national level, certainly not beyond its borders. Even within, the vast majority of IRGC and Quds Force military are Shiites volunteering out of profound conviction, prepared to give their lives at a moment's notice for their cause. By extension, among the militia network abroad, it takes only a little effort to establish tents along Shiite pilgrimage routes to yield vast numbers of recruits to the cause. Moreover, each atrocity committed against a Shiite cleric, leader, or—even more effectively—shrine, is filmed and immediately posted to the Internet along with a vast number of social media sites. As early as 1999, when Saddam Hussein ordered the assassination of the Iraq's Grand Ayatollah Mohammed Sadiq al-Sadr, the website of Asa'ib Ahl al-Haq used the ayatollah's image along with that of Iran's Ali Khamenei to promote the Shiite cause and act as a potent recruiting tool. Indeed, recruits' utter loyalty to Khamenei, the Shiite religion, and the Iranian cause, in whatever order, is always immutable and never in question, to the point of martyrdom whenever and wherever necessary. Martyrdom and martyr videos are used as powerful recruiting tools. Take that of Mohammed Baqir Al-Bahadly, a young militia soldier who apparently died on the battlefield in 2014. The four-minute, eleven-second video of his life and funeral that includes shots of him in his softball uniform and in battle fatigues armed to the hilt, followed by shots of his funeral procession and his gravesite, accompanied by images of Ayatollah Khamenei smiling down benevolently on his photograph, all overlaid with inspirational, martial music, was viewed thousands of times on YouTube along with comments from viewers along these lines:

> A thousand thousand have mercy on his kind soul, Mohammed Baqir Al-Bahadly, the jealous hero of his homeland, and the family of Mohammed and the family of Mohammed and Zainab al-Hawra.

This degree of faith is rare even among the most devoted supporters of red lines that other major powers in Asia, Europe, or Africa have erected and defended, and renders Iran's all that much more toxic. Facebook pages—established for even the most minor militia splinter group—show tough, determined fighters posing with formidable weaponry, even tanks, accompanied by inspirational notes like, "The fighters of the Zulfikar Brigade continue their fight in Adra and insist on victory," and comments like, "God willing on the enemies of God." These are often accompanied by phone numbers of recruiting hotlines and links to the encrypted Telegram messaging app—all useful tools for recruiting Shiites deeply loyal to Ali Khamenei and the concept of *velayat-e-faqih*. For those who man recruiting hotlines, there are careful scripts to be used with each caller, centering first on identifying true Shiites ("name all the martyred sons of Shiite Imam Hussein or Imam Ali's children," for instance), then whether they are truly prepared to defend the faith and the Shiite shrines. This concludes with a promise that the recruit would "learn to defeat the villainous force," as one such recruiter told Phillip Smyth.

At the same time, Iranian leaders demonize Sunnis, and even Shiites who refused to accept the concept of *velayat-e-faqih*, as *takfiris* or apostate Muslims—those declared impure. And there has been no hesitation in using such a designation to extend Iran's geographical and political grasp into neighboring nations, branding even the earliest Syrian revolutionaries who rebelled against Bashar al-Assad as *takfiris*. While there has been no fatwa declared by the Ayatollah Khamenei, the militia activities on behalf of Assad and the Syrian forces have been declared, collectively, a jihad, or holy war. Equally, they have branded as *takfiri* even the most devout Wahhabis, the ultra-conservative Sunni sect that rules Saudi Arabia, who in turn of course regard all Shia as deserving nothing but death. Such religious zealotry has motivated much of Iran's activities in Yemen backing the largely Shiite Houthi rebels against the regime supported by Saudi Arabia's ruling Sunnis.

—

In 2012, civil war broke out in Yemen. In fact, it was less a true civil war—in the sense of Syria, where the rebels sought an end to the Assad dictatorship and the installation of a democratic, secular government. Here, it was more a war between Sunnis and Shiites as was effectively the case in the Iran-Iraq War, at least from the Iranian perspective, where a large bulk of troops went into battle fully expecting to martyr themselves for their faith. But in this case, in Yemen, it was the two religious behemoths—Shiite Iran and Sunni Saudi Arabia—battling to the death by proxy in this country that has found itself in the unfortunate position of being trapped between these two diametrically opposed theocracies, armed to the hilt and prepared to fight to the last Yemeni. The envisioned end result would be the establishment of a new red line, or at least a dramatic enlargement of an existing one. And for this goal, any amount of blood would willingly be spilled by both sides. Saudi Arabia, in mortal fear of being surrounded by Shiites, leaped into the fray, contributing unlimited resources—arms, munitions, aerial support—of its own and increasingly its American supporters. Iran called in its Iraqi Shiite militias, who declared themselves willing to fight alongside their Houthi brethren.

In just one graphic example, a leading Iraqi-based brigade announced online that it would be willing to enter the fray in no uncertain terms. Accompanied by a photograph of a phalanx of determined, fatigue-clad troops, their arms uplifted in closed-fisted Hitlerian salutes, Abu Walaa al-Walai, secretary general of the Kata'ib Sayyid al-Shuhada of the Popular Mobilization of Iraq, which never hid its ties to the IRGC, made his declaration: "I announce my volunteering as a young soldier who is at the disposal of Mr. Abdul-Malik Al-Houthi [organizer and spiritual leader of the Houthi rebellion]. I declare that the Brigades of the Master of the Martyrs, who is one of the factions of the state, is one of your factions, O Ansar Allah, so the invaders will not be safe." An interesting turn of phrase. In fact, the Houthis had driven the more or less legitimate government out of Yemen's capital, Sanaa, occupied it, then tried their best to oust the government from Aden, the other major Yemeni city. At one point, Aden had been the capital of the People's Democratic Republic of Yemen, until its unification in 1990 with the Yemen Arab Republic. At that point the capital of the new nation became the Arab Republic's original capital, Sanaa. Now it was all being torn apart, effectively, in the name of religion.

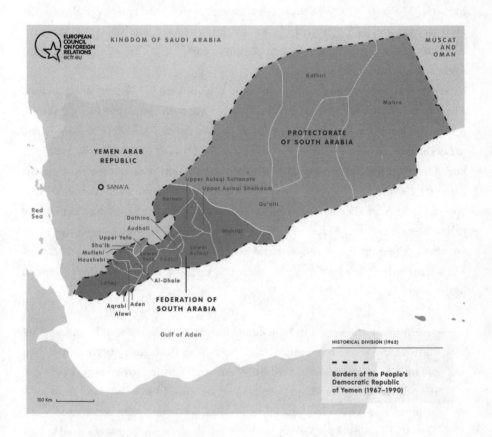

Yemen, a nation carved out of some of the most strategic fragments of the Arabian peninsula.

Some believe that Cain and Abel are buried in Aden, even that this was the location of the Garden of Eden. Today, however, Yemen is the antithesis of the Garden of Eden—much of it a hot, dry, largely lifeless landscape of deserts in the north that blend away across the largely unmarked frontier into the forbidding Empty Quarter of Saudi Arabia. Still, these largely barren lands have been fought over for centuries, a tribute to Yemen's strategic location dominating the southern Red Sea and the Gulf of Aden. This point, where Asia meets Africa, overlooks some of the world's most vital shipping lanes and especially the Bab al-Mandeb choke point. For nearly two millennia—beginning in 200—six successive rival civilizations have vied for control of the area, including Jews, early Christians, who arrived in the fourth century, and finally Islam, which arrived in 630 C.E. when Mohammed sent his cousin Ali to Sanaa. Mohammed proclaimed to his entourage that the Yemeni people "are the most amiable and gentle hearted of men. Faith is of Yemen, and wisdom is Yemeni." Amiable, perhaps, but Yemeni troops played an early, central role in the expansion of the boundaries of Islam.

Yemen has always been a tribal culture, not unlike neighboring Saudi Arabia, where nomadic Bedouins ruled until the early twentieth century before a cohesive nation was established there. That kind of peace has been elusive in Yemen, where today the line between Houthis and tribes like the Hajours remains a deadly powder keg. The Houthis claim a virtually direct descent from Mohammed through his daughter Fatima and identify today as Shiites. At the same time, many of their opponents' tribes hailed from coastal areas that had converted to Sunni, explaining their closeness to Saudi Arabia. The battles between these two opposing forces today are among the most lethal and barbaric in the world. By 2019, the United Nations was warning that the resulting series of crises could also become "the worst famine in the world in 100 years":

> The humanitarian crisis in Yemen remains the worst in the world. . . . [as] conflict and severe economic decline are driving the country to the brink of famine and exacerbating needs in all sectors. An estimated 80 per cent of the population—24 million people—require some form of humanitarian or protection assistance, including 14.3 million who are in acute need. Severity of needs is deepening, with the number of people in acute need a staggering 27 per cent higher than last year. Two-thirds of all districts in the country are already pre-famine, and one-third face a convergence of multiple acute vulnerabilities. The escalation of the conflict since March 2015 has dramatically aggravated the protection crisis in which millions face risks to their safety and basic rights.

In any event, it did not take long for the civil war to be truly joined. America's inevitable entry on the side of the Saudis would cement even more firmly in Iran's mind Washington's alliance with the Sunni faith in the global war of religion that had been touched off when Khomeini landed in Tehran in 1979.

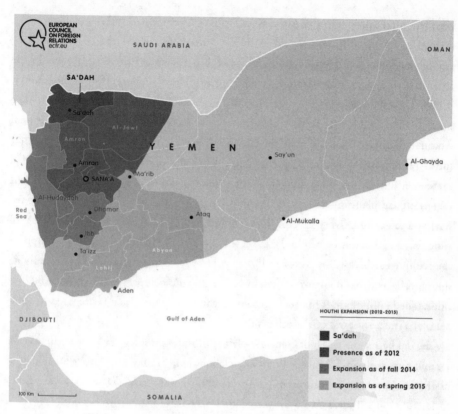

The Iranian-backed Houthi expansion of its lines of control across
Yemen is a great threat to neighboring Saudi Arabia.

Behind their red lines, each side has dug in firmly and in quite deadly style. From the start of major combat in 2015 through the early days of 2020, at least 100,394 persons have been killed in the fighting in Yemen, of whom 12,405 were civilians, often the product of indiscriminate bombing or flawed targeting, according to the Armed Conflict Location & Event Data Project. At the same time, some 85,000 children have starved to death, according to Save the Children, with at least 17,000 others living in areas cut off from resources by the war. UN data suggests that 14 million people, or half the entire population of Yemen, are at risk of famine.

With this number of military casualties alone, it is clear that a constant stream of new fighters is necessary on both sides—many, especially on the Houthi side, from proxy militias. Iran and the IRGC/Quds Force are hardly prepared to leave the management or oversight of this critical conflict entirely to proxies. On January 2, 2020, the same day an American drone killed General Qasem Soleimani in Iraq, another, unsuccessful attempt was made on the life of General Abdul Reza Shahla'i, a key IRGC/Quds Force commander in charge of Unit 400, one of two main force units comprising the Iranian military mission in Sanaa, the Houthi-controlled capital in Yemen. At the time, he was in the command compound where Iran was managing its military support effort in the country.

The United States has viewed the red lines established in Yemen as a critical strategic element that needs to be dealt with. Ambassador Robert O'Brien, Trump's national security advisor, told Chuck Todd on *Meet the Press* on January 12, 2020, ten days after the assassination of General Soleimani and the attempt on the life of General Shahla'i in Yemen, "What I will say, and what the president has said, is if there are folks out there that are planning to kill, maim, and harm Americans, that's a red line for us. And you've got to be very careful. If you're out, trying to attack the United States of America, you'd better be careful." Yet these American are in Yemen entirely to support the red line established by Saudi Arabia to protect its own interests, and especially its southern flank, from being overtaken by Shiites. It would appear, however, that neither side of the red line that right now runs down the middle of Yemen is prepared to see it dissolved in the interest of the other side.

Ten days after the death of General Soleimani, Iran's president Hassan Rouhani told a cabinet meeting in Tehran, without any elaboration, "Today, the American soldier is in danger, tomorrow the European soldier could be in danger. We want you to leave this region, but not with war. We want you to go wisely. It is to your own benefit."

⸺

Rouhani's oblique reference was to the decision Britain, France, and Germany had taken the day before to trigger a dispute mechanism that was one of the foundations of the agreement these three powers, together with Russia, China, and the United States, had concluded with Iran in 2015 to prevent Iran from building and deploying a nuclear weapon. This was the ultimate red line that the West had established, and that Iran had, however reluctantly, agreed to respect—that it would not acquire the bomb. Until that moment, Iran had seemed to be dashing toward a nuclear red line of its own making.

Throughout, however, there were many who believed that Iran's deeply religious faith would prevent it from acquiring the ultimate weapon of mass destruction. The rest of the world did not believe it could bet the future of mankind on the faith that Iran's ever more expansive jihad was not prepared to stretch its frontiers by whatever means necessary. After all, if the ayatollahs of Qom could go to war and their soldiers accept martyrdom with utter equanimity simply to guarantee that the minority Shiite sect could dominate a neighboring country, what would prevent Iran from acquiring the ultimate weapon of defense, or offense, for that matter.

If we are going to examine nuclear red lines, however, we need to go considerably further back than the Joint Comprehensive Plan of Action, agreed upon in July 2015, adopted in October 2015, and implemented three months later. The starting point should probably be the signing of the Nuclear Non-Proliferation Treaty (NPT), opened for signature in 1968, entering into force two years later. To date, 191 states have joined as parties to the agreement, including six nations possessing nuclear weapons—the US, Russia, China, Britain, France, and North Korea. India and Pakistan have not signed it, though both have acknowledged possessing nuclear weapons, and neither has Israel, which is considered a nuclear power. This agreement represents the ultimate nuclear red line—the vast bulk of the world recognizing that proliferation of nuclear weapons can only lead to deadly consequences, particularly if they should fall into the hands of any non-state actors with few constraints on their behavior and little respect for any red lines. Sadly, there are few enforcement mechanisms in the agreement. What it does include is a mechanism, administered by the UN's International Atomic Energy Agency, whose inspectors are dedicated to ensuring that "safeguards . . . can verify that a State is living up to its international commitments not to use nuclear programmes for nuclear-weapons purposes." But apart from naming-and-shaming, there is little that can be done to enforce whatever red line may be implicit in this accord. Of course, the IAEA can bring before the UN Security Council its fears over gross violations by any country, which the Council can then penalize—provided a veto is not invoked by one of the five permanent members.

Iran has long had a nuclear program, dating back to 1953 when President Dwight Eisenhower launched the Atoms for Peace initiative, telling the United Nations that "if a danger exists in the world, it is a danger shared by all; and equally, that if hope exists in the mind of one nation, that hope should be shared by all." What Eisenhower hoped to do was to build peaceful nuclear reactors in nations that would, a quarter century before the NPT, agree to a quid pro quo. In exchange for the bounty of what then seemed to be a boundless supply of nuclear energy to be used for electrical generation and other peaceful purposes, each country would agree to assure the United States that nuclear material was not diverted to production of weapons. Under this program, the US built nuclear reactors in Pakistan, Israel, and, in 1957, began a nuclear research program in Tehran. (Ironically, Pakistan and Israel would eventually join the nuclear weapons club, though Israel has never admitted as much.) Ten years after the Atoms for Peace program was launched, the United States supplied Iran with a five-megawatt nuclear research reactor along with highly enriched uranium as fuel. The reactor, at the Tehran Nuclear Research Center (TNRC) at the University of Tehran was able to produce some six hundred grams of plutonium each year as a spent-fuel byproduct. When Ayatollah Khomeini took over Iran in 1979, that program was in full flower and by the early 1990s had begun chemically extracting and stockpiling plutonium and small amounts of polonium-210, which could be used to ignite a nuclear weapon. Iran insisted this as being used, instead, for research into the production of neutron sources for medical and other radioisotope purposes, not weapons. This was still far removed from the intention of the original Atoms for Peace intiative. Iran seemed to be en route to establishing its own nuclear red line. By then, the United States had ended its nuclear collaboration with Iran and halted its supplies of fuel. Iran was hardly deterred. Pakistan's nuclear weapons guru, A. Q. Khan, was the first person Iran turned to for advice, technology, and eventually fuel. China stepped in as well, supplying Iran with a research reactor capable of producing plutonium and two Qinshan power reactors. Russia also stepped up with offers of reactors and enrichment technology.

What Iran really needed was the technology and know-how to build nuclear gas centrifuges to enrich uranium to the point where it could used in a sustained nuclear reaction. Of course, it was only one short—if complex—step toward the even more highly enriched uranium to build a bomb. In October 1988, Iran's parliament speaker, Akbar Hashemi Rafsanjani, who a year later would become president of Iran for eight years, told the Majlis that the nation's recently concluded experiences in the Iran-Iraq War only reinforced his belief that the nation needed to develop nuclear and other nonconventional weapons. Already, the year before Rafsanjani's speech A. Q. Khan had quietly begun supplying Iran with technical drawings for a P-1 centrifuge and some of the key component parts. The IAEA reported in 2004 that "the centrifuge R&D programme had been situated at TNRC between 1988 and 1995, and had been moved to the Kalaye Electric Company workshop in 1995. According to Iran, the centrifuge R&D activities were carried out at the Kalaye Electric Company workshop between 1995 and 2003, and were moved to Natanz in 2003." Still, it was by no means clear even at this point that the clerics who ran the country were prepared to go that final extra step toward production of a nuclear weapon.

The road to the point where Iran was prepared to establish its own nuclear red line really began in 2006 when it embarked on a major program of uranium enrichment, nearing a critical level of 20 percent by 2010. There was considerable jockeying throughout this period, with Iran testing just how far it could push this idea of becoming a nuclear power—with or without an actual weapon. But by 2011, the situation was becoming what appeared, at least from the outside, to be desperate. Russia and China were opposing any Security Council resolution that would constrain Iran's nuclear ambitions. Barack

Obama, together with American allies in the European Union, chose to push forward in a different direction.

In the summer of 2009, not long before Congress approved the first sanctions on Iran, I had some long conversations with Kayhan Barzegar, director of the Institute for Middle East Strategic Studies in Tehran and at the time also a research fellow at Harvard's Belfer Center for Science and International Affairs. At the time, Barzegar believed that "Iran [was seeking] an 'independent nuclear fuel cycle,' the domestic capacity to produce enriched uranium and plutonium to fuel nuclear reactors for electricity generation." He did note that there were divisions within the Iranian elite, and he concluded with a warning: "If the West continues to stall, not only will Tehran's nuclear program continue, but there is a distinct possibility that the current Iranian dilemma whether to choose between civilian capability and weaponization will be settled simply by the course of events." Barzegar was prescient. It did take another six years before the West was able to come together sufficiently to arrive at a consensus agreement with Iran. And by then, a consensus had been largely arrived at that eventually the nation would have to become a nuclear power.

On October 1, 2012, I sat down with Ali Akbar Salehi in the elaborately decorated townhouse on Fifth Avenue in New York that served as the residence of Iran's ambasssador to the United Nations. Salehi had earned his PhD in nuclear engineering at MIT, but when we spoke, he was halfway through a three-year term as Iran's foreign minister. So when I launched immediately into the nuclear question, he was very much at home with the vocabulary, and still adhering to the Barzegar line. Iran, he emphasized, had already acquired the entire suite of nuclear technology, from mining uranium to turning it into fuel rods, running the product through centrifuges for enrichment. "There's nothing in the nuclear field that we have not really achieved, and the technology is within our reach," he smiled broadly, but then added the key caveat, that if Iran had wanted a bomb, "we would have detached ourselves from the NPT. There is in the treaty an article which says whoever is in the NPT, if they wish, they can get out of it with three months' notice, and then free of the NPT, we could do whatever we wanted to do." But the NPT he described as "in our interest," since "the stronger the NPT becomes, the more immune we become to possible proliferation of nuclear weapons in the region and in other places in the world." The supreme leader, he concluded, "has issued a fatwa, which says the production, accumulation, and the use of weapons of mass destruction including nuclear weapons is forbidden and is against [our] religion."

Less than a year later, Salehi was out. Ayatollah Khamenei had, quite rightly, decided he was far better suited, by education and temperament, to serve as the head of Iran's Atomic Energy Organization. He took over from Fereydoon Abbasi-Davani, an Iranian nuclear scientist and member of the IRGC who'd been seriously wounded in an assassination attempt. Salehi was replaced by Mohammad Javad Zarif, another American-educated academic who'd served for five years as Iran's UN ambassador. Zarif's first visitor as foreign minister was the sultan of Oman, Qaboos bin Said al-Said. Ten days after assuming office, Zarif went personally to Tehran's Mehrabad Airport to welcome the sultan, who had ruled over his Persian Gulf emirate for nearly half a century. The sultan maintained close ties to virtually every important faction in the Middle East. Though there are more Sunnis than Shiites in his nation, which borders both Saudi Arabia and Yemen, the dominant sect and that of its ruler is Ibadi, which actually pre-dates the seventh century split between the two larger branches of Islam. Its adherents have been known as peace-makers for much of their existence. And they felt threatened by the turmoil in Yemen, not to mention a potential nuclear arms race in the Middle East should Iran develop such a weapon. So, their sultan sought to do all within his power as a ruler whose sway vastly transcended the power of a nation smaller than the state of Kansas. An emissary of the sultan, Salem Ben Nasser al-Ismaily, first made contact with Barack Obama shortly after he took office in 2009. Nearly three years later, in December 2011, Salem first met John Kerry, who at the time was chairman of the Senate Foreign Relations Committee. Kerry immediately recognized his value and that of the sultan's vast understanding of the lines of power and stress in his region. Inviting Kerry to Oman, the Sultan turned on all the charm—drinks on the veranda of his palace, lunchtime serenades of American songs by the royal orchestra, a Middle East feast—and expanded on the opportunity represented at that moment by Salehi's appointment as foreign minister in Iran. The supreme leader clearly trusted him, as a nuclear scientist, to safeguard the nation's nuclear ambitions and the rapidly developing nuclear red line. But, the sultan counseled Kerry, "If the Iranians feel bullied or condescended to, they will walk away at once."

Before any significant movement could begin, however, Zarif had replaced Salehi as foreign minister and John Kerry had become secretary of state. The fear was that the supreme leader had replaced Salehi with a harder-line, more inflexible clone. So it was with some trepidation that Kerry and Zarif held their first face-to-face meeting in a tiny, austere conference room next to the Security Council chamber at the United Nations. It was the beginning of a beautiful friendship—or at least a meeting of minds—vital at a moment when IAEA inspectors learned that Iran had installed some 27,000 centrifuges to produce enough highly enriched uranium to fuel at least eight to ten bombs.

Six countries, known as the P-5+1—the five permanent members of the UN Security Council (Britain, France, Russia, China, and the United States) plus Germany—had been following Iran's progress with varying degrees of unease. The United States was the last of these powers, which would ultimately sign the nuclear limitation pact with Iran, to come around to the need to allow enrichment of uranium on a limited basis—Barzegar's "independent nuclear fuel cycle." The process toward an agreement began to accelerate largely as a result of two key developments—the first heavy sanctions regime leveled at the Iranian government and the arrival of a new president after national elections in Iran. The new president, Hassan Rouhani, was considered by most in the West as a liberal (at least in Iranian terms) replacement for Mahmoud Ahmadinejad.

So now the real talks got underway in Geneva. It took more than a year simply to agree on a framework for discussions, which went into effect in January 2014. The Joint Plan of Action had Iran buying into an agreement to freeze production of highly enriched uranium and to halt the installation of centrifuges and the development of a heavy-water reactor near Arak. In return, some $4.2 billion of Iran's money, frozen in banks around the world, would be unblocked. But there was still no agreement from Iran on a freeze of the processes that could lead to a quick dash to a bomb. Yet in the West, this was a firm red line that could not be crossed, and that Iran was still not prepared to relinquish without some serious quid pro quo.

In the end, it came down to the length of "breakout time" and what Iran could get in return—good old-fashioned diplomatic horse-trading, with potentially existential impact. Kerry, Obama, and the rest of the P-5+1 identified one year as a reasonable period—enough time, as Kerry put it in his memoir, "for the United States and our allies to pursue 'alternative' (read: military) means of preventing a nuclear-armed Iran." In the end, it was Salehi and his MIT-educated American counterpart, Secretary of Energy Ernest Moniz, who provided the necessary compromise. All the delegations assembled at the grand, lakeside Hotel Beau-Rivage, where ironically the Treaty of Lausanne, the last of the Versailles treaties, had broken up the Ottoman Empire in 1923. Each of the six P-5+1 delegations plus the EU and Iran, had suites in the hotel as offices. The Americans converted a small tent into a highly secure video conference center where NSA advisor Susan Rice, Treasury Secretary Jack Lew, and finally Barack Obama could be briefed every evening (afternoon in Washington). The negotiations were hardly simple and went on at times all night until past dawn the next day, followed by two or three hours of sleep, then back at it again. On April 2, 2015, an agreement was fixed, the shape of the new red line established—though the praise it immediately began winning in the American press frightened the Iranians. Three months later came the final round at the 1840s-vintage Palais Coburg that sits atop the Brown Bastion, part of Vienna's defenses since 1555, but by then a five-star hotel with thirty-three sprawling suites off long, mazelike corridors. Here, though the sketchy air conditioning was ill-equipped to handle the heat of an Austrian summer, the final touches were put on what would become the Joint Cooperative Plan of Action (JCPOA). What finally got negotiations over the hump was a last-ditch offer by the United States to remove a dozen mid-level Iranians from the list of those still under sanctions.

So what was the shape of this new red line that both sides now seemed to have accepted and prepared to live up to? There were at least fifty-three key provisions that fixed the small number of centrifuges Iran could still operate, the research allowed at some sites, the disabling of reactor cores, and detailed monitoring and verification throughout the various terms of this agreement. On the Iranian side, for twenty-five years the IAEA would be able to monitor all of Iran's uranium mines and mills. For twenty years it could monitor all centrifuge operations, and for fifteen years access all nuclear sites including those Iran had not disclosed. There would be no reprocessing of spent fuel, nor any heavy water reactors. Enriched uranium stockpiles would have to remain under 200 kilograms, enrichment capped at 3.67 percent. Finally, for ten years, no additional centrifuge production. These terms would render Iran incapable of "breaking out" to produce or stockpile enough material to assemble any sort of viable nuclear weapons arsenal in any less than a year. In return, the Unites States ended all sanctions against Iran's oil and banking sector and its citizens, allowed sale of commercial passenger jets, and pledged to remove all nuclear-related sanctions when the IAEA would conclude all Iran's nuclear activities were peaceful. But the US would maintain all sanctions targeting human rights, terrorism, and missile activities. The European Union and UN did similarly with respect to sanctions. There was one further note: that after ten years, the "UN will cease to be seized of Iran's nuclear file." It had taken two years and the good will of six nations, all with substantial stakes in the shape of this agreement to arrive at its conclusions.

It took a single statement by Barack Obama's successor to unravel it all four years later. Until then, the firm red line that Europe, Russia, China, America, and Iran had so carefully and exquisitely constructed held, and had given every indication of holding for at least a decade. It was, effectively, the most perfect red line existing in the world—the least challenged, the most effective for all parties concerned. Each side deeply understood what it comprised and the horrific stakes of violating it. All parties agreed that a perfect starting point was the axiom that Iran must never have a nuclear weapon. How to achieve that required a profound sensitivity to the history, background, and deeply held sensibilities and beliefs of each side. Yet, what Donald Trump based his withdrawal on was a caricature of diplomatic shorthand:

> The Iranian regime is the leading state sponsor of terror. It exports dangerous missiles, fuels conflicts across the Middle East, and supports terrorist proxies and militias such as Hezbollah, Hamas, the Taliban, and al Qaeda.

Over the years, Iran and its proxies have bombed American embassies and military installations, murdered hundreds of American servicemembers, and kidnapped, imprisoned, and tortured American citizens. The Iranian regime has funded its long reign of chaos and terror by plundering the wealth of its own people.

No action taken by the regime has been more dangerous than its pursuit of nuclear weapons and the means of delivering them. . . .

In theory, the so-called "Iran deal" was supposed to protect the United States and our allies from the lunacy of an Iranian nuclear bomb, a weapon that will only endanger the survival of the Iranian regime. In fact, the deal allowed Iran to continue enriching uranium and, over time, reach the brink of a nuclear breakout.

The deal lifted crippling economic sanctions on Iran in exchange for very weak limits on the regime's nuclear activity, and no limits at all on its other malign behavior, including its sinister activities in Syria, Yemen, and other places all around the world.

In other words, at the point when the United States had maximum leverage, this disastrous deal gave this regime—and it's a regime of great terror—many billions of dollars, some of it in actual cash—a great embarrassment to me as a citizen and to all citizens of the United States.

A constructive deal could easily have been struck at the time, but it wasn't. At the heart of the Iran deal was a giant fiction that a murderous regime desired only a peaceful nuclear energy program.

There ensued an elaborate two-year dance involving Europe, Russia, and China in an effort to salvage what Trump seemed so anxious to destroy, with the United States on the sidelines and Iran struggling to cope with the ever-tightening American sanctions regime. Struggling desperately to keep the nuclear agreement alive—at least to the extent of discouraging Iran from bolting across the red line toward rapid development of a nuclear weapon—France, Germany, and Britain cobbled together a barter system known as INSTEX, or Instrument in Support of Trade Exchanges, headquartered in Paris. Effectively, it established a new red line, sidestepping the line that Trump was doing his best to hold onto unilaterally. INSTEX and other ad hoc mechanisms were designed to allow Iran to sell oil and import products and services, bypassing the US dollar system, whose clearing functions had been barred for use by Iran or any of its trading partners. In November 2019, Belgium, Denmark, Finland, the Netherlands, Norway, and Sweden joined the INSTEX system. The fact is that sanctions have rarely succeeded in sustaining red lines without a critical mass of nations buying into the mechanism. They do not work alone. Indeed, reacting to the continued tightening of the sanction restrictions, Iran continued to inch further back from the accord, without actually fracturing it or breaking out toward development of a nuclear device. Still, it began edging ever closer to the line. In July 2019, Zarif announced Iran had allowed its stockpiles of low-enriched uranium to pass the agreement's 300 kilogram (660 pound) maximum threshold, and the IAEA confirmed the cap had been breached. A week later, Iran announced its intention to begin enriching uranium above the 3.7 percent level that is reasonable to fuel a commercial nuclear plant. That's still far from the 90 percent enrichment need for a bomb, but once a 20 percent level is reached, the time needed to reach 90 percent is cut in half.

With the agreement clearly beginning to slip away, the Europeans continued expressing their view of the pact—namely that its structure had bought at least a decade of a nuclear-free Middle East. (Or at least a nuclear-free Arab world. It was widely understood that Israel had long since built a nuclear arsenal that it had never officially acknowledged.) During this ten-year interregnum, a host of different scenarios could play out. But above all, a new, reinforced, perhaps permanent red line regime could provide Iran with a sense of security that its interests and its faith were secure, and that there was a real future and safety for Shiite believers beyond Iran's borders. Instead, with the nuclear accord coming apart, it became clear that all the guardrails had been loosened and quickly began to fail.

Trump's national security advisor, John Bolton, on a visit to Israel, which opposed the JCPOA from its first negotiation stage, told reporters that President Trump still welcomed "real" negotiations, adding "all that Iran needs to do is walk through that open door." The problem was that neither Iran nor most in Washington or in any of the other capitals that had signed the JCPOA had any real understanding of just what lay on the other side of that door or even if Trump had any idea what, realistically might lie there. Clearly, Iran would never declare itself a nuclear-free zone in the sense that Trump appeared to desire—a similar framework that he had been urging on North Korea. Neither Iran nor Kim Jong Un is ever likely to declare their nation nuclear free. That is an utterly implausible construct for a red line in either location. Not surprisingly, there continued to be a host of highly destabilizing exchanges of invective and incidents along the new lines that marked the divide between Iran and the United States. In a Twitter tirade, the president threatened Iran with "obliteration," warning as he had cautioned Kim, "any attack by Iran on anything American will be met with great and overwhelming force. In some areas, overwhelming will mean obliteration," pointing out that "the USA is by far the most powerful military force in the world, with $1.5tn invested over the last two years alone." This invective followed Iranian attacks on two oil tankers in the Gulf of Oman, one month after similar attacks on four tankers.

The final round of escalations began with the US drone assassination of General Qasem Soleimani at Baghdad Airport shortly after midnight on January 3, 2020. Commander of the IRGC Quds Force, Soleimani was the closest military officer to the supreme leader. Certainly he was the principal liaison between Tehran and militias from Palestine to Pakistan and beyond. And indeed he was, more or less directly, responsible for the deaths of hundreds of American soldiers at the hands of the irregular forces he had armed and unleashed. Still, in climbing the ladder of escalation, Trump was nearing the final rungs, while having little apparent understanding of the passions he had unleashed. Iran's President Hassan Rouhani began privately and publicly warning European leaders—who still desperately wanted rapid deescalation in the interests of salvaging the JCPOA—that they needed to get their forces out of the region. Iran needed to respond. But especially interesting, in terms of red lines, was precisely the kind and scale of the response Iran unleashed. The ayatollahs understood by now that Trump clearly had a red line of his own, that he might not even have identified, or had even defined with any precision within his own administration. The problem, of course, is that throughout the ensuing process there has never been any sense that having taken down the powerful and universally respected red line of the JCPOA, how a new line might be installed. And what might it even look like?

Instead, what began was a ladder of escalation, with the United States testing just how far it could push Iran's economy to the wall and, on the other side of the line, Iran testing the American appetite for total war. Some scattered mines directed at tankers in the Persian Gulf escalated to a devastating attack in the pre-dawn hours of September 14, 2019, by ten drones on two key oil installations inside Saudi Arabia, damaging Aramco facilities that process much of that nation's crude oil output. Houthis initially claimed responsibility, but there seemed little doubt that the scale and sophistication of the action could only have been conducted with full Iranian complicity.

Neither the United States nor Saudi Arabia made any visible response to what was effectively an act of war. The Iranians began to understand something quite profound with respect to Trump—he was all bluster. He can tweet with bravado that he has at his command "by far the most powerful military force in the world, with $1.5tn invested." But he doesn't really want to go to war. He sees what it did for his predecessors Bush and Obama, who were prepared to launch or sustain conflicts where Americans died in large numbers. He did not want Americans coming home in body bags to an airport where he would have to console weeping parents and answer to his own political base, which would be disproportionally impacted by his actions. Ironically, Vladimir Putin has a similar internal red line, though it perhaps goes a bit deeper. He saw the horrors of Afghanistan and the thousands of Soviet soldiers returning dead—a reality that he quite rightly saw as an important contributor to the fall of Communism and disintegration of the Soviet Union.

So Iran's immediate response to the assassination of Soleimani was significant: the launch on January 7 of sixteen missiles at two American airbases in Iraq—Al-Asad west of Baghdad and Erbil in northern Iraq—eleven striking their intended targets while one went astray and four malfunctioned. There was ample warning to get Americans out of the way, so there were no deaths. These missiles were the first launched by Iran against any American military target. They had two primary messages.

First, we have the capability to precision-target where we want, whenever we want, with as little or as much warning as we might desire. Furthermore, this salvo was only a small fraction of the more than two thousand ballistic missiles Iran is believed to have stockpiled. "One must fight America like a goat fights a predator wolf," Ayatollah Ahmad Alamolhoda told his Friday worship service in the city of Mashhad on January 17, ten days after the attack. One of the most conservative senior ayatollahs, he is a member of the Assembly of Experts and confidant of the supreme leader. He went on to talk about just what the Iranian military had demonstrated—the precision accuracy of the Iranian response: "What is the meaning of an accurate missile? It means that if it is sent to hit the palace of a certain emir, sultan, or king of a country where there is an [American] military base, it will hit that exact spot. That is the meaning of an accurate missile. Iran has long-range accurate missile[s] of this kind. So wherever there is an American base, that is a source of danger for that country." The lessons of Iran's growing missile capabilities were not lost on the Saudis, other Gulf states, even Israel.

The second message was equally clear. This was the end, for the moment. No one died. No escalation required. This showed a deepening understanding by Iran of American red lines and a message that Iran had red lines of its own. Moreover, the vacuum left by the United States in its withdrawal from Syria and the winding down of its presence in Iraq and Afghanistan "has allowed Iran to test (and successively breach) perceived international red lines," the International Institute for Strategic Studies concluded. "The absence of red lines risked Iran and the West stumbling into conflict as a result of increasingly aggressive Iranian and Iranian-proxy actions. Instead, regional states have seemingly grown accustomed to conventional military operations instigated by Iran, but limited to front-line states."

What Iran may have failed to factor into any such equation was an especially grim reality on the other side of these lines—that there has been little deep understanding of any of the morphology of these red lines, nor any real understanding of the mind of the ayatollahs and their minions who control them. Iran, particularly Ayatollah Khamenei and his two key allies—Foreign Minister Zarif on the political and diplomatic side and, until his assassination, General Soleimani on the military—have been able to construct, expand, and, most importantly, defend a network of red lines vital to their survival even in the face of apparently existential challenges. Yet Donald Trump has never understood that to establish or break a red line, one must without fail establish very clear structures and, in the case of what should be just temporary lines in this region, have an exit strategy clearly in view. He had none, it would appear. Or at least none short of the utterly unrealistic one of total regime change in Tehran. But for that to happen would mean shattering two millennia of faith among a people not known to crumble easily before any provocation—a regime whose very existence is founded on the perpetuation of such faith.

In many respects, this is not unlike the case of Russia and its near-abroad, or China and its islands. Each is a dominant regional power establishing red lines far enough from its heartland to guarantee its safety. In the case of Iran, it is doing its best to solidify a fully Shiite vassal state in Yemen, a direct challenge to Saudi Arabia, a strategic stretch of the Arabian Peninsula dominating the Red Sea, the Gulf of Aden, and Africa beyond. Moreover, if there were ever any doubt that Iraq has now effectively become itself a vassal of Iran, serving as an existential buffer, that doubt was erased by Ayatollah Alamolhoda. In a sermon at Friday prayers on September 20, 2019, broadcast this time on Khorasan TV, the ayatollah explained:

> Today's Iran is not just Iran. It is not limited by geographical borders. Today, the PMU [Peoples' Militia] in Iraq is Iran. Hezbollah in Lebanon is Iran. Ansar Allah [Houthis] in Yemen is Iran. The national front in Syria is Iran. The Islamic Jihad and Hamas in Palestine are Iran. They have all become Iran. Iran is no longer just us. The *sayyed* of the Resistance [Nasrallah] has announced that the resistance in the region has one imam and that this imam is the honorable leader of Iran's Islamic Revolution. . . .
>
> Today, Iran is the resistance in the region. This means that if you trespass our border, Israel will turn into dust in half a day.

The audience promptly responded:

> Allah Akbar! Allah Akbar! Allah Akbar! Khamenei is the leader! Death to those who oppose the Rule of the Jurisprudent! Salutations upon the warriors

of Islam! Peace be upon the martyrs! Death to America! Death to England! Death to the hypocrites and the infidels! Death to Israel!

At which point the ayatollah concluded:

Do you even understand where Iran is? Do you look to see where it is? Isn't south Lebanon Iran? Isn't Hezbolla Iran? The Yemeni-sent drones that caused such damage to Saudi Arabia—wasn't Iran there? You say that [the drones] came from the north and not from the south. South or north—what difference does it make? Iran is both to your south and to your north.

And to the west, an entire continent—Africa—is now suddenly in play and up for grabs, with a vast web of red lines unlike those that any other continent has ever experienced.

CHAPTER EIGHT

Africa:
Cradle of Lines

With 1 billion people packed into 54 countries scattered across more than 11.7 million square miles, Africa has been a fertile breeding ground of more red lines than any other continent. Centuries of colonial conquest and occupation only accelerated a trend that was long pending and, today, never more toxic. For Africa is where all the world's red lines and conflicts are converging in an intensely overlapping tapestry. It is here that Russia, China, the United States, and Europe, Sunnis and Shiites, terrorists of every stripe, are all doing battle for the hearts and minds—but especially the vast mineral and agricultural wealth—of Africa.

Africa's people, as diverse as all of humanity, have fought interminable, internecine wars. These conflicts gave birth to the Punic Wars between Rome and Carthage, slave wars that stretched across West Africa from Angola to Benin, Senegal to the Gambia, and deep into the interior, all fueling the American slave trade, the repercussions of which still reverberate today. Later on, there were the Boer Wars, genocides from Idi Amin's Uganda to the Congo, where between three and six million died in the Congo Wars; south Sudan, where two million people were massacred; and Rwanda, where one million Tutsis and moderate Hutus were slaughtered between April and June in 1994. Today terrorist groups that have threatened world order far beyond their borders have established a presence in a dozen or more African countries.

The result of much of this conflict is that all major world powers have developed significant interests in establishing red lines of influence to protect and assure access to what is important to them. For China and Russia, it is important raw materials, ranging from diamonds to rare earth minerals, not to mention access to the world's fastest-growing group of consumers. For the United States and many West European countries, it is oil and gas, particularly along broad stretches of West Africa. Saudi Arabia has begun amassing arable lands that can, potentially, be used to help feed that desert kingdom. But to understand the roots of all these overlapping interests, it's essential to go back far into the past, as we have in every other region of the world where red lines have taken a firm root.

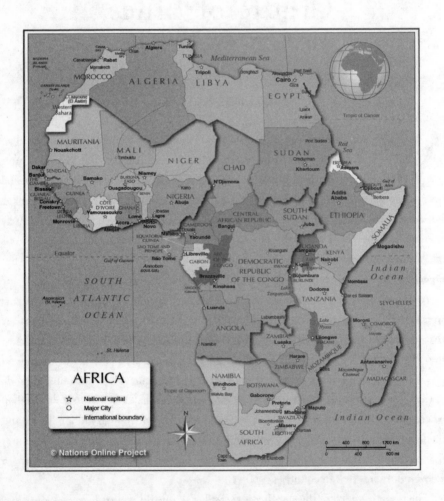

Africa today

—

Africa was not always this nexus of globally induced strife. Indeed, most historians and anthropologists believe that the first *homo sapiens* were African. "Barely more than fifty thousand years ago, the ancestors of every single human being alive today lived in Africa," said Christopher Ehret, Distinguished Research Professor in the Department of History at the University of California at Los Angeles. But then, he added a most important clarification. "Just because a few Africans left the continent around fifty thousand years ago and began to expand across the rest of the globe, history did not come to a halt in Africa." Those who stayed behind "passed through the same great transitions of human history . . . *in the same broad periods of time* as did people elsewhere in the world."

It did not take long for agriculture—beginning with the cultivation of grains, black-eyed peas, and groundnuts—to develop, along with at least three major linguistic groups. But any real nations were very far in the future and indeed there was so much migration across many of the key African regions that it is hard to see anything resembling lines or boundaries beginning to coalesce earlier than the first millennium of the Common Era. Eventually, however, some key nationalities, or at least major tribal agglomerations, did begin to appear.

In many respects, Africa is unlike most of the other regions we've examined. Here, red lines were defined early on by geographic and climatic zones more than any political or military reality. On the north, beginning at the southern shores of the Mediterranean and across the Sahara, is the desert zone. That stretches into the savannah as vegetation begins to appear, then the tropical zone, defined by Oxford Professor Richard J. Reid as a band between the fifteenth degree of latitude on either sides of the equator, or roughly a line that bisects Mali, Niger, Chad, and Sudan to the north, and Angola, Zambia, Malawi, and Mozambique to the south. Within this zone lie many of today's principal population regions—Nigeria, the two Congos, Central African Republic, Kenya, and Tanzania. At the turn of the Common Era, none of these nations existed. What has always marked this area, however, is its infestation with the tsetse fly, carrier of *trypanosomiasis*, or sleeping sickness. It is frequently fatal to humans, but invariably lethal to animals. What this means, Professor Reid observes, is that "between the Sahara and the Kalahari, horses and other pack animals are almost completely absent, feasible only in isolated zones. Cavalry forces are therefore confined to the Sahel belt and the adjacent Sahara." War could be made only on foot—use of cavalry was utterly impracticable—while vast hordes of porters were necessary to transport supplies and munitions wherever battle might be necessary. There are other transitional zones between desert and jungle or savannah. And they have, as Reid concludes, "long constituted some of Africa's most volatile and militarized frontiers." Some of this began to change, of course, beginning in the early twentieth century with the arrival of mechanized transport, which first arrived with colonial powers.

Especially striking is that these frontiers are unlike those in any other part of the world we have examined. Across much of Asia, eastern and central Europe, and the Middle East, the climate and environment are relatively uniform within and across each region, if subject to seasonal variations, but largely similar on both sides of any red line that might be established. In Africa, this was different. Chad, for instance, is almost perfectly bisected into desert and jungle.

Nomadism was a central reason for the localization and stunted development of red line networks, at least in the early days when urbanization was only just beginning. As Reid suggests: "The roots of urbanization lie in itinerant royal camps comprising armies and their entourages, whereas in other circumstances they have come together in fortified urban clusters for protection." The scattered defensive lines established in these cases would have been the first primitive use in Africa of such devices, particularly among either the Yoruba or Nyamwezi people.

The Yoruba today live largely in western Nigeria, though as far back as the eleventh century were spread more widely. They were among the earliest to establish thoroughly urbanized communities, governed by an *oba* (or king) in city-states that were well-fortified against intrusions. Their elaborate civil and military bureaucracies maintained potent lines of defense, recognized within and without for their effectiveness in safeguarding their people and the wealth they succeeded in developing. One of these leading kingdoms, which reached its apex between the twelfth and thirteenth centuries, was Oyo, the absolute power of whose ruler and the sanctity of whose borders were preserved and defended by a military leader known as the *are-ona-kakanfo*. It would appear that such a powerful community was not easily challenged, allowing the growth of a substantial and creative culture and society with art forms in clay, bronze, and terracotta that have been preserved even today.

What especially marked the evolution of Africa, at least until the period of European colonial occupation starting in the late nineteenth century, was the constant sense of expansion, contraction, and division that resulted in the difficulty of establishing or defending red lines in broad stretches of the continent. Often, communities that had been successfully organized would, amoeba-like, suddenly split apart as elements of the population moved off in a migratory fashion to establish new communities that would eventually split again. It must be remembered that only quite recently have large stretches of Africa became at all densely populated. The entire continent is believed to have had no more than 35 million people at the beginning of the Common Era, rising to barely 50 million at the year 1000, and 87 million in 1500. By 1700 it had reached 100 million—by comparison with today's 1.3 billion. Nigeria alone has twice the population today of all of Africa in 1700 and is projected to be the fastest growing country in the world in the next half century. Before the Common Era, Egypt was the only region to have engaged in fixed agriculture, the entire rest of the continent remaining largely hunter-gatherers for at least four thousand years. In the eighteenth and nineteenth centuries, populations were decimated by the dispatch of slaves to North America and Europe; some demographers estimate that without that depletion, the population might have tripled. With such a drain on resources, of course, much of the continent was in a constant state of turmoil, with little ability to establish any stable red lines or defenses.

The Soninke people were among the earliest to coalesce into a real empire, and by the eighth century had formed the early kingdom of Ghana, which eventually built a formidable army at least 200,000 strong to defend its boundaries. Over five centuries, on the strength of the reserves of gold that it mined and sent north across the Sahara, Ghana rose in power and reach. But eventually, unable to defend its furthest frontiers, neighboring Mali emerged to dissolve the boundaries between the two kingdoms and absorb it. These were centuries-long transformations of red lines that formed, were defended, dissolved, then re-formed again along the entire length of the western savannah and the southern fringe where desert gave way to jungle. In sub-Saharan Africa for at least the first millennium of the Common Era, there was a constant ebb and flow of populations. Improving weapons, including iron-tipped arrows and spears, allowed these Bantu-speaking peoples to build communities with boundaries they could defend—effectively the first African red lines. One of the earliest and most powerful was the kingdom of Mali, which eventually stretched from the Atlantic across the Niger River into the heartland of Africa, peaking in the fourteenth century. It was during this period that Islam arrived with Berber caravans crossing the desert as traders spread this new religion and its monotheistic values that eventually led to widespread conversions. By the tenth century, Islam had begun a push not only south from the Maghreb but was a well-entrenched feature of societies westward from the Red Sea through what is today Somalia, Djibouti, Eritrea, and even into Ethiopia, which had already been Christianized. As Islam arrived, it began to establish the first spiritually based red lines as it pressed westward.

More closely held and contested frontiers between communities and states led to more battles to pierce or defend them, with successful invaders often burning down entire villages. Some engaged in what are believed to have been important battles, including sieges, especially in western Africa. There, the powerful and disciplined forces of the Oba of Benin often sent forces against neighbors to add land, labor, or resources. Archaeologists have concluded that Benin's colossal defensive earthworks, dating from as early as the eleventh century and peaking in the fifteenth century, were "the world's largest earthworks carried out prior to the mechanical era," according to the 1974 *Guinness Book of Records*.

Though representing more than a thousand years of military history and effectively serving as the first sustained African red line, these barricades were destroyed by invading British colonial forces in 1897 in what became known as the "Punitive Expedition." At their peak, however, they comprised some fifteen kilometers surrounding downtown Benin City and extended out into the surrounding jealously protected and fertile countryside for a total of some 16,000 kilometers of wall. This would have been twice the length of the Great Wall of China and, according to Fred Pearce of *New Scientist,* were built with a hundred times more material than the great Pyramid of Cheops. They may have taken 150 million man-hours to construct. One of the early Western visitors, Portuguese ship captain Lourenco Pinto, described central Benin as larger than Lisbon, and a "wealthy and industrious city" where the people "live in such security that they have no doors to their houses."

For centuries, beginning early in the second millennium, from the Congo region to Mozambique, between the Limpopo and Zambezi rivers, and in the southern stretches of what is today Nigeria, states emerged with important stocks of cattle to be jealously protected and border lines to be defended by the emerging military classes. Perhaps the most significant religious-based red line collapse took place in the Horn of Africa in early sixteenth century Ethiopia when Islamic forces bearing Ottoman firearms swept west and south in a jihad, led by Imam Ahmad ibn Ibrahim al-Ghazi, known as "The Left-Handed," who sought to expand his Adal Sultanate, one of the Indian Ocean's most powerful states. In the defining Battle of Shimbra Kure, outside what is today Addis Ababa, his forces pummeled the Ethiopian Christian forces and occupied much of the ancient Abyssinian kingdom, establishing his own defensive perimeter to defend his new realm. It would turn out to be a brief rule as, aided by Portuguese reinforcements, Christian forces managed to retake the lands they had abandoned a decade earlier as the Islamic sultanate was weakened by internal divisions.

Slowly at first, then ever more rapidly, Islam was making its way, at times by force of arms, often simply through the proselytizing of determined disciples, across the continent. Sweeping south out of the Sahel and eastward from the eastern shores, it would eventually encompass nearly 250 million people in the sub-Saharan region, growing by as much as 30 percent in some decades, so that by 2030 it is now projected to reach at least 385 million individuals—nearly a third of the continent's population, according to the Pew Research Center's Religion & Public Life program. By 2030, 17.6 percent of the world's Muslims are projected to be living across the continent. In West Africa alone, Muslims already constitute a majority—concentrated in Nigeria and at least six other smaller but utterly Muslim-dominated nations—Niger, Mali, Burkina Faso, Senegal, and Guinea. Here, as we shall see, is where jihadist terrorism is very much putting down roots today.

These waves of invasion, pillaging, revival, and recapture, some with religious motives, others to expand into needed lands or in search of water and other resources, were to mark much of the history of the African continent until suddenly the arrival of Europeans would change it all. Through at least a millennium, Africa contained the seeds of red lines unlike those on virtually any other continent. Often, many of these lands were prey to wild swings in climate and especially the availability of water that required large-scale movements of people, many of whom effectively took with them their red lines of protection as well as equally fragile lines of commerce and trade. Large stretches of the continent were then, and to a degree still are, the province of nomadic tribes such as the Tuareg of the lower Sahara, in what are today the states of Mali and Niger.

From the thirteenth to the fifteenth centuries, there was a plateau on which sat Great Zimbabwe, capital of the eponymous kingdom buried in the southeastern hills and stretching across 1,800 acres near Lake Mutirikwi, guarded by fortifications 36 feet tall and 820 feet long—the largest such structure south of the Sahara—designed not even as much for defense as to mark a territorial line that was not to be crossed. Efforts, all unsuccessful, but often sharp and brutal, to penetrate its frontiers, erupted from time to time. Still, Great Zimbabwe marked the starting point of a far longer line that tied together one of the continent's most lucrative trade routes between the gold mines of Zimbabwe and the bustling port of Kilwa on the Swahili Coast. This strategic town was founded by Ali ibn al-Hassan Shirazi. One of seven sons of a ruler of Shiraz, Persia, he was driven out by his brothers, winding up in Africa with his entourage and his religion. Both took root there, building a center for trade of gold with the interior, and eventually slaves, until finally a succession of Portuguese armadas arrived to break through and take over these lucrative commodities from the fifteenth century onward. The result was a most successful form of red line that emerged and confined the Portuguese largely to the coast—a not entirely irrational fear of the often predatory Zimba on the east coast of Africa and the Imbangala on the Atlantic Coast—both tribes that practiced cannibalism. Of course, it also had the effect of preserving the trade monopoly of Portuguese merchants who happily stayed in their coastal fortresses and could source whatever they needed from the hinterland through intermediaries.

These were only the first colonial interlopers, whose pace of arrival began accelerating later in the fifteenth century, led by forces of Portugal's Prince Henry the Navigator. Initially planting their flag on offshore islands, these forces were eventually joined on the mainland by two Italian explorers from Genoa and Venice, hired by Prince Henry to push inland along the east coast of Africa up the Gambia River into Senegal. But it was left to Diego Cáo to first learn of the existence of the great kingdom of Kongo and begin to work his way up the Congo River into the mainland of Africa in 1485. These early explorers were not in any sense conquerors. Beyond planting the odd stone *padrão*, or pillar, attesting to their passage, they made little efforts to penetrate the boundaries claimed by the Congo and its king (*mutinù*). The first such mutinù, who effectively established the limits of the early empire, was Lukeni lua Nimi. Lukeni began expanding his kingdom largely by conquest, pushing out its boundaries as it succeeded in expanding the "protective" arrangements that were effectively colonial subjugations. By the time Diego Cáo arrived on the scene, its population is estimated to have reached three million—quite a substantial number since the population of the entire continent at that time is generally believed to have been under fifty million.

Over the next century and a half, the Portuguese expanded their involvement in affairs of the Kongo, converting the kingdom to Christianity in 1495, then helping to expand its territory by dismantling resistance of the neighboring territory of Ndongo. Its Queen Nzinga resisted gamely, but in the end unsuccessfully, since her ability to defend her boundaries was circumscribed by domestic unrest and an unsuccessful attempt at an alliance with Dutch forces that had also begun to push inland through what is now Angola. Still, today she is remembered and revered as the Mother of Angola.

The Dutch, who followed the Portuguese, implanted more than a dozen forts down the west coast of Africa, especially in South Africa, that it adopted as bases for its forays into East Asia and supports for its colonies as far as Indonesia. The Dutch founded Cape Town in 1652, its fort designed to protect the Cape of Good Hope and the straits rounding the southern tip of the continent at L'Agulhas.

It would appear that the earliest colonizers sought to work with those leaders who had managed to establish and maintain by force of arms red lines that guaranteed their rule over vast areas of the continent that interested the early explorers, especially land, gold, and eventually slaves. By 1750, some ten thousand slaves a year—but possibly more—were passing through the single port of Luanda in Angola. This was treasure to be maintained at any cost. At the same time, each of the emerging states of Europe sought to plant their own flags and defend, often by force of arms, their colonial rights against all comers while expanding their control from the littoral on both sides of the continent into the interior. Each established a distinct relationship with leaders of the Dahomey, Oyo, Asante, Segu, and Lunda people.

The slave trade became the chief reason for establishing and defending outposts, and in turn lured new arrivals, beginning with the British in 1530. Later, in the seventeenth century, the Brits established themselves at Fort James, upriver from the mouth of the Gambia River. The French arrived in Africa and began establishing trading posts along the coast of Senegal in 1624 with an armed contingent and by 1678 had managed to break the Dutch hold over Senegal. Belgium would become an important force in Africa, particularly over the Congo, but only after it managed to win its own independence from the Netherlands in 1830.

For nearly three centuries, the slave trade played a major role in establishing the first networks of centralized states and the red lines that would delineate them—forming the basis of colonial empires and ultimately the modern Africa of today.

—

Throughout the centuries-long period of state building and colonization, Africa was in the process of establishing a vast web of boundaries. Initially these were fault lines between tribes and agglomerations that gathered together eventually into kingdoms whose frontiers were established at the very extremity of what the ruler could maintain and police given his resources and organizational capabilities. Richard J. Reid describes the potent centrifugal forces of "armed, mobile frontiers which witnessed the production and reproduction of polities over the long term . . . as true for the continent's deeper pre-colonial past as it is for the post-colonial era, with its anti-colonial revolts, revolutionary guerrilla insurgencies, and diamond-smuggling warlords."

What became known as the "Scramble for Africa" was actually quite a confined but intense moment in the continent's history—from a breakout in 1881 until its effective conclusion with the start of the First World War in 1914. When this period began, barely 10 percent of the continent was under substantial control of any European power, but in less than four decades, some 90 percent of Africa had fallen into the grasp of one European nation or another. It was in this period that a succession of firm, carefully delineated lines was created. Their creation effectively began with the Berlin Conference that took place between November 1884 and February 1885 and was probably responsible for creating more defined and accepted red lines over a broader geographical area than any other single conference, with the possible exception of the Treaty of Versailles. Though Versailles redrew the maps of at least two continents, in Berlin none of the interested parties were invited to contribute a single thought to its outcome, nor did a single African nation (not even proudly independent Ethiopia, which would be the only major polity surviving the Scramble with its sovereignty intact) participate in the drafting or signature of the ultimate document. On the wall of the Reich Chancellery in Berlin, the delegates assembled beneath a sixteen-foot tall map of Africa, with few frontiers, few red lines, drawn on it. That would not remain the case for long.

The Berlin Conference: carving up a continent few have ever seen.

Every major European power was in attendance—Britain, France, Germany, Belgium, Spain, Portugal, Italy, the Netherlands, the Austro-Hungarian Empire, as well as nations with only the most marginal on-the-ground interests at the time: Sweden, Norway, Denmark, the Russian and Ottoman Empires, even the United States. In the end, however, America never subscribed to the subscribed to the document or played any real colonial role on the continent, much of any such direct role it played having largely evaporated with the end of the slave trade decades earlier. At the same time, the United States did play a crucial diplomatic role in recognizing the Belgian King Leopold II's personal rule over what is today Congo, where he established a regime of terror to extract rubber and other valuable commodities.

The result of the Berlin Conference was a desperately ignorant redrawing of a map for a place that few remotely understood or had even visited, and the establishment of a vast network of red lines that would exist, often quite toxically, until today. The reality, recognized in the concluding document, was that until the Berlin Conference and the Scramble for Africa there were really no effective boundaries at all on much of the continent. At least, beyond some fixed barriers like the fifteenth century Benin earthworks, there were none that had not been in a constant state of flux. So, the first networks that would be laid down as today's national frontiers, often so jealously and perniciously guarded, and so brazenly flouted by terrorists and adventurers, did not develop in any concrete sense until the Western powers began their scramble.

Immediately after the conference, Britain, and Germany divided East Africa between them—Britain laying claim to vast territories in Kenya and Uganda, Germany seizing lands to the south including Mount Kilimanjaro and what would become Zanzibar, part of today's Tanzania. France moved largely into western Africa—enormous stretches of what would become Mali, Niger, Dahomey (now Benin), Upper Volta (now Burkina Faso), Ivory Coast, Guinea, Mauritania, and Senegal.

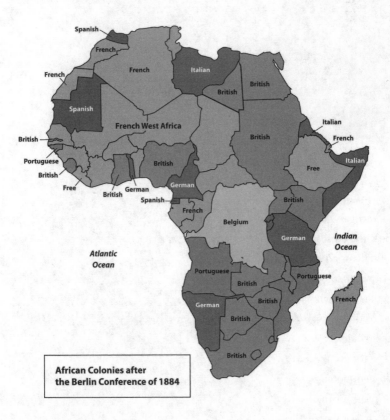

African Colonies after
the Berlin Conference of 1884

Europe sets up its lines across the continent.

A large number of diplomats, military officials, commercial travelers, and soldiers of fortune were involved in what would turn out to be a confusing, erratic, and often violent scramble. A handful of these individuals were particularly colorful and instrumental in establishing the continent's new anatomy. In 1870, when the "scramble" began, the map of Africa was all but a blank slate as far as boundaries and lines were concerned.

"We have behaved like madmen," French President Félix Faure lamented in 1898. The scramble was nearing an end that would be marked by the opening salvos of World War I. But by then, Africa had become a neatly drawn plaid of many colors, reflecting a host of red lines that were being defended as never before by vast colonial armies of the major powers and the African chieftains and their forces they had conquered or bought:

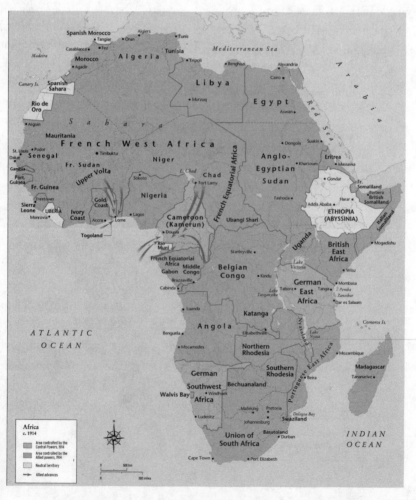

As World War I begins, African nations, most still colonies, begin to take shape.

In 1870, Europeans held sway over barely 10 percent of the continent. Thirty years later, they'd seized and divvied up some 90 percent, with France geographically taking the largest slice, followed by Britain. Drawn with little attention to on-the-ground realities, the lines were to be crossed often only with force of arms. Examine the map of any other continent. None will have the geometrically straight lines that mark many of Africa's often artificial borders, laid out or negotiated with little understanding of the tribes, nationalities, linguistic groups, or heritage of the people who live between them. Britain and Portugal, for example, differed sharply on just how to define the line between Angola (a long-time Portuguese territory) and Northern Rhodesia, much of which would become Zambia. In 1891, the two countries agreed that the line should follow the western border of the kingdom of the Barotse, but few could agree on just where this stretch of Barotseland actually lay. The two European disputants submitted their problem to the king of Italy, who knew as little about this remote region as did the leaders of Britain or Portugal. King Victor Emmanuel III had a simple answer: the boundaries to Barotseland consisted simply of the effective authority of the ruler of Barotseland. "Any precise delimitation is impossible," he observed in his far from Solomonic ruling, since there was an "imperfect knowledge of localities . . . [and] the notorious instability of the tribes and frequent overlappings." So he simply decided to mark an arbitrary and geometrically straight line, and there it stands today. Would that all red lines could be so nicely defined. The north-south line in Korea is perhaps the only one in existence outside Africa. Professor Elliott Green has studied African lines and population density extensively and concludes that "pre-colonial population density has a significant relationship with state shape," adding that "the higher the density of pre-colonial population, the less artificial are the contemporary state's borders."

Ironically, as we shall see momentarily, today's terrorists operating across vast stretches of this continent are effectively returning Africa to pre-colonial times, with little respect for traditional red lines or any other boundaries—and little understanding of where these lines should be drawn or have been drawn and little incentive to uphold them. Each is as porous, and as lethal, as the terrorists' weapons and their transports can make them. Moreover, many of the West African lands with the most lethal terrorist networks are those with the straightest-lined boundaries—Mali and Niger in particular—and the least dense populations.

Many of the late nineteenth and early twentieth century treaties that defined the boundaries of today's African states were questionable, some outright forgeries and utterly fraudulent. Often, they were signed by an individual who was not even the real chief of the village or region, the victim of ill-prepared or venal interpreters. The one individual responsible for more of these documents—at times real, other times barely so—was a colorful character, Frederick John Dealtry Lugard, the first Baron Lugard.

Frederick John Dealtry Lugard, the first Baron Lugard, as
Governor-General of Nigeria, with Lady Lugard, Flora Shaw.

Born in Madras, India, in 1858, he began his career as a soldier, passed five years as governor of Hong Kong (then a British colony) and wound up as governor-general of Nigeria (another British colony). But it was his long stint as a soldier of fortune, explorer of Africa, and sometime diplomat that left its most lasting mark on the continent. Lugard was responsible for more treaties covering a broader swath of Africa than any other single individual. Contemporary accounts suggest that he was a deeply persuasive man of action, whose piercing eyes, above a vast handlebar mustache, could bore into a subject and persuade almost anyone to do whatever his bidding might be. And that bidding was invariably in the interest of the British crown to establish lucrative lines of provenance across

Africa. It was said that the borders of northern Nigeria were set by how far Lugard could walk before he had to rest. Saadia Touval, one of the great students of international mediation, based at Tel Aviv University for three decades, believed one of the most exemplary such negotiations revolved around the treaty at Nikki that was to establish its frontier with Nigeria. It seems Lugard was the first to arrive in Nikki and signed a treaty. Some weeks later, the French arrived and signed their own, then promptly challenged Lugard's document as having been signed by individuals who did not at all represent the king of Nikki. Indeed, the king himself issued a statement that the Muslim community in the town had improperly used his name without any authorization, and the name on the treaty was not even the king's real name. Moreover, Lugard had even used a form marked "For Moslems" though the king was not a Muslim. It gets worse. It seems the man who presented himself as king, speaking through Lugard's interpreter, was concealed behind a screen. Lugard never laid eyes on him. In the end, Nikki went to France, the region became the French colony of Dahomey and is today the independent, though still francophone, nation of Benin. Moreover, as one Dutch anthropologist, Johannes Fabian, observed, many of the explorers, not to mention the soldiers of fortune, were quite literally out of their minds much of the time with alcohol, drugs, and khat, which they chewed with some abandon before, during, and after their treaty negotiations, with equally stimulated rulers and their henchmen.

Lugard rarely pulled any punches when he came to describe some of the potentates he encountered. On September 17, 1894, Lugard arrived in Jebba, a Yoruba city in western Nigeria, where he'd come to meet the local potentate:

> In the afternoon, a summons came from the King about 4 P.M. . . . We were kept waiting in the sun for nearly a half hour. I got terribly out of patience. It is a radical mistake, this abasement of the European before *very* petty African chieflets. I would not be treated so at any Government Department in England. I brought the scarlet coat emblazoned with gold lace and stars and foolery, but I wrapped it up in a towel and only put it on at the door. I detest this mummery, it is more irksome to me to dress myself up like a Punch and Judy show than to visit a dentist. The King of all the Bussas turned out to be a specially dirty and mean-looking savage, seated on a filthy and greasy carpet and Musnud, surrounded by a group of ordinary savages. . . . And this man is subsidized by the Royal Niger Company to the tune of £50 a year.

What especially astonished Lugard was that "even a petty chief like Bussa gets a small subsidy—how then could Frenchmen secure important treaties for nothing at all?" His conclusion? "If the French want to come into the country with which they have made a treaty they invariably have to fight, which shews that the treaty was Nil."

At other times, there were more direct inducements. In 1888, representatives of Cecil Rhodes, the South African–based entrepreneur (for whom Rhodesia was later named), managed to win a written concession from King Lobengula of Matabeleland (a region today of Zimbabwe) for lucrative mining rights in return for £100 a month, a thousand breech-loading rifles, and an armed steamboat for the Zambezi River, as well as a pledge of maintaining his frontiers against encroachment by Fulani forces. Lugard went one better on another of his agreements. The Brits wanted Sekgoma, chief of the Tawana in Ngamiland (now in the nation of Botswana), to improve their mineral concession with the British West Charterland Company. The offer was a simple one: support the chief's boundary claims against the rival British South Africa Company, plus sweeteners of a writing case and nifty notepaper imprinted "Ngamiland." Done deal. Touval quite rightly concludes that a host of similar deals arranged with local potentates was not a tribute to their ignorance or venality, nor as Lugard often expresses in his diaries, that African rulers really did not understand very many of the documents he and others presented them to sign. Rather, like today, this region was highly unstable, with conflicts between south and north, Muslims and pagans, slave-raiders and weaker tribes. The rulers, rather than being bamboozled, had carefully calculated the price of maintaining their lines of authority and defense. An agreement with a clearly overwhelming outside military power that could offer protection and a degree of prestige, not to mention guns and ammunition, would be very much to their advantage. The mineral rights they were signing away were a small price to pay for such clear objectives, since without external customers and guarantees of the safety of the routes to get these resources to market in Europe, they were effectively worthless anyway. It's worth pointing out that many pre-colonial, or certainly pre-treaty, agglomerations did not necessarily hew to neat ethnic, tribal, or linguistic threads. Many rulers assembled their kingdoms or chiefdoms through conquest or simply through need for new arable soil or sources of water; in other words, they grew organically.

When European armies began arriving in Africa to lay claim to the vast territories allocated to them in Berlin, they were not always met with a warm welcome. Instead, French, British, Italian, and Portuguese forces were met with long wars of attrition. Most, but particularly the French, made difficult, often deadly progress mile by mile through the dense jungles of what they would call the Cote d'Ivoire, as well as vast stretches of Gabon, Middle Congo, and Ubangi-Shari (eventually the French Congo, followed by the Central African Empire led by the utterly insane dictator and self-crowned emperor Jean-Bédel Bokassa, today the still metastable Central African Republic). The British were forced to fight their way inland through the forbidding Niger delta. In the Belgian Congo, the Belgian crown shrewdly ceded pacification of vast, dense jungle territories to the rubber companies and their private militia units that used scorched earth tactics to establish their lines of authority. Most existing lines of demarcation dissolved in chaos, leading to fractured societies. The proliferation of mercenary bands gave the arriving *colons* arms and legs to cement the authority that their European sense of order and the demarcations settled in Berlin would bring to the continent. For the French, there were the *Tirailleurs Sénégalais*, or Senegalese Riflemen, who made their first appearance in Senegal, French West Africa, in 1857 and spread across French colonial territories, eventually providing troops for various fronts in World War I and World War II. For the British, there was the Royal West African Frontier Force, which helped enforce British red lines in the colonies of Nigeria, Sierra Leone, and Gambia in western Africa. The King's African Rifles, assembled in 1902, lasted until Britain's East African colonies were finally liberated in the 1960s. They became infamous for the atrocities they committed during the Mau Mau uprisings in Kenya in the 1950s. Germany had its *Schutztruppe* in German West Africa, southwest Africa, and Togoland. Belgium, the other major colonial power, had their *Force Publique* in the Belgian Congo, which became the Congolese National Army (*Armée Nationale Congolaise*). This came into its own under Mobutu, who began his career as a sergeant in the Force Publique, and who used it most effectively to cement his control over what he would call Zaire. Today, it is the continually dysfunctional Democratic Republic of the Congo, large stretches of which, as we shall see, are all but out of control of the central government.

In most cases, these were tiny, though professional, forces that were able to maintain a hold over the often tenuous lines established only by their discipline, drilled into their ranks by their colonial military officer corps, and well supplied with the most modern armaments of their time. A British force of some 3,000 African soldiers managed to police the boundaries of vast northern Nigeria, while all its military forces in Africa numbered barely 11,000, and the King's African Rifles rarely passed 2,500 men under arms. Professor Richard J. Reid points out notably that most of these indigenous forces "hailed from distant frontiers and peripheries, having little in common with the people over whom they watched," even their languages being different. The French, for instance, preferred to make use of the Bambara (which actually means "unbeliever" or "infidel"), a group of nomads with a common language found in Mali, Burkina Faso, Senegal, and Cote d'Ivoire. Though their language hardly matched that of many locals, Bambara did become the patois of the Tirailleurs Sénégalais forces. Such linguistic and cultural independence allowed many of these colonial forces to operate with greater impunity and focus their total regard only on their mission of safeguarding the periphery and maintaining order within.

After World War I, many of the colonial red lines began to disappear. The mandate system of the Treaty of Versailles created a vast, unitary British African empire. German colonies, effectively seized under this system, were amalgamated with long-standing British colonies, creating the British dream of a single British African empire stretching from Cape Town to Cairo. This dream would turn all too quickly into a nightmare. Some of these components were run in London from the Foreign Office, the Colonial Office, and the India Office, each of which ran different portions of the African possessions. The first to win a semblance of autonomy were Kenya and Southern Rhodesia, which became self-governing in 1923, though still ruled in the final analysis from London. But it took another world war and uprisings like the Mau Mau Rebellion in the 1950s to bring a definitive end to this system of governance from Europe.

On August 3, 1941, aboard the heavy cruiser *Augusta* deployed off the coast of New-foundland, President Franklin D. Roosevelt met for four days with British Prime Minister Winston Churchill. This was still four months before the Japanese air force would attack Pearl Harbor, catapulting the United States into a war that Churchill was desperate to have America enter. At the end of their session, he was well on his way toward his objective as the pair negotiated an agreement known as the Atlantic Charter. For Africa, it was the beginning of a long road toward independence for scores of colonies. The core principles of the document held that Britain and America "respect the right of all peoples to choose the form of government under which they will live; and they wish to see sovereign rights and self-government restored to those who have been forcibly deprived of them." And it concluded that after victory over the Nazis, "they hope to see established a peace which will afford to all nations the means of dwelling in safety within their own boundaries." This would prove to be the foundation document for NATO, but it also appeared to spell an end to the principles that underwrote much of the British empire. Indeed, Churchill would have second thoughts about the imperial elements of this pact. Nearly a year after America had entered the war, in a speech at the Lord Mayor of London's luncheon at Mansion House in London, Churchill observed:

> I have not become the King's First Minister in order to preside over the liq-uidation of the British Empire. . . . I am proud to be a member of that vast commonwealth and society of nations and communities gathered in and around the ancient British monarchy, without which the good cause might

well have perished from the face of the earth. Here we are, and here we stand, a veritable rock of salvation in this drifting world.

But Churchill, at least in this respect, was very much behind the times. The world had begun moving with unrelenting speed and inevitability toward establishing new nations with their own very clear ideas of sovereignty and boundaries—quite apart from the British Empire.

The final map of Africa with the lines that correspond most directly with those that are being defended today, often at great cost, really emerged between 1950 and 1980—the great period of decolonization. These three epiphanal decades left a continent that looks very much like this:

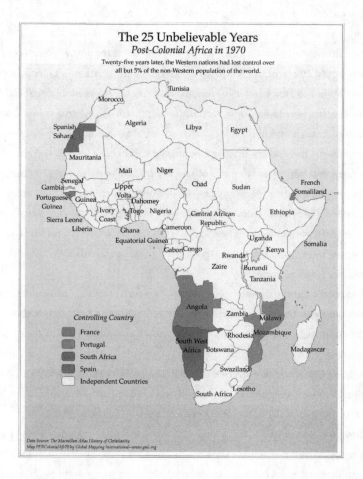

The West pulls out, new lines are drawn, and nations emerge.

By that time, Africa was already changing dramatically, particularly its urban areas. In 1950, Lagos had a population of 325,000; ten years later, when Nigeria won its independence from Britain, that figure had more than doubled to 762,000. Then its real growth spurt began—10 percent or more per year for a decade—until today its population stands at 14.4 million. But it still was only the eighth fastest growing city in Africa. Clearly, such rapid growth and the accompanying demands represented an insuperable burden on the colonial powers flattened by the Second World War. Africa would need to stand on its own—each nation fending for itself, guaranteeing its own borders—perhaps the most stinging legacy of the colonial period. Between 1950 and 1980, fifty-one African colonies won their freedom—nineteen each previously governed by Britain and France, five each by Portugal and Spain, and three by Belgium; and Tanganyika, the portion of the colony of German East Africa that Britain seized in 1922 as a mandate colony after World War I, joined with the offshore archipelago of Zanzibar, another British colony, in 1964 to form the state of Tanzania. In short, a staggering number for three often tumultuous decades. Again, this would represent unprecedented turmoil on any continent, especially since each country would now be responsible for maintaining its own frontiers against neighbors and internal forces that were not always especially content with the existing colonial structures.

At the same time, a host of outside powers, anxious to maintain or attain a new foothold on this continent, made their first significant appearances. These years represented the height of the Cold War. Russia and China were especially anxious to slide into vacuums created by the departure of Western nations—who competed with each other, too, not least the United States and France—and that were themselves hardly anxious to relinquish the resources and populations to their Cold War foes. A pattern would begin developing here, affecting political, diplomatic, and military lines and alliances across Africa long after the Cold War had ended.

When it came time for many of these post-colonial regimes to begin establishing their own defensive positions to maintain the red lines and boundaries they inherited from their colonial masters back in Berlin a century and a half earlier, they turned, not surprisingly, to many of the same military forces used by the colonizers, now under their control. Now they were overseen by African officers trained by colonial advisors. Eventually, the most imaginative of these officers recognized the value of trading their uniforms for mufti and using their deep understandings of the workings of power. Many moved into positions of influence in their countries. All too frequently, some took short-cuts to the top. Military-backed takeovers became an increasingly dominant feature of the African landscape. So between 1946 and 2019 there were seventy-eight "successful" coups in thirty-nine different countries in Africa, according to statistics compiled by the

Center for Systemic Peace, with many countries experiencing multiple forced changes in leadership. Nigeria alone has had six successful coups and nine more that failed in one stage or another. But three more nations—Benin, Burkina Faso, and Ghana—each had five successful coups. The compilers define success as meaning, "coup leaders must seize and hold central authority for at least one week."

Just one example from Nigeria. In December 1983, relations between the Nigerian military and the nation's president, Shehu Shagari, had reached a breaking point, at least in part because of the disintegrating boundary with neighboring Chad that was itself in a state of utter chaos. The boundary, a critical red line as far as the Nigerian military was concerned, was finally sealed by the Third Armored Division's First Armored Brigade, commanded by Brigadier General Mohammedu Buhari. On December 31, Buhari, facing strong pushback from Lagos, finally led a coup that resulted in one casualty when the president's Brigade of Guards chose to stage an unanticipated defense of the presidential villa when the plotters came to unseat him. I was in Paris at that moment, but on New Year's Day 1984, CBS News hustled me onto a chartered jet with producer and camera crew, bound for Lagos. After taking off from a refueling stop at the oasis village of Tamanrasset in the southern Algerian desert, our pilot received word that all Nigerian airspace had been closed. We diverted next door to Benin, where we found that all land borders to Nigeria had also been sealed, particularly the border with Benin, for four days. There was no love lost with Benin, which at the time was a determinedly pro-Soviet Communist dictatorship, its government the product of a coup by Major Mathieu Kérékou, who, determined to shed his colonial past, changed its name from Dahomey to the People's Republic of Benin. That land frontier never opened up while we waited patiently. But Buhari was well-positioned as an authority figure. Twice he would become president of Nigeria—this first time through a coup, then thirty years later after a more conventional presidential election in a time of utter crisis.

Beyond the attempts to seize central power in these countries, there were repeated efforts to redraw ancestral red lines—at times along ethnic or tribal boundaries, at times simply to seize control and hive off regions or localities with particularly attractive, that is to say profitable, natural resources. Among the most lethal was in Congo, which had won its independence from Belgium on June 30, 1960 and promptly faced a mutiny by its armed forces. Amid the chaos, an effort was launched by Moïse Tshombe, to separate the mineral-rich province of Katanga, under protection of Belgian troops that remained in the territory, and effectively allow the Union Minière du Haut Katanga, a Belgian mining company to continue to dominate the economy. Congo's prime minister, Patrice Lumumba, promptly appealed to the United Nations for help in maintaining the integrity of his nation—the beginning of a bloody conflict that would wind up killing Lumumba himself. When Secretary General Dag Hammarskjöld flew to break the stalemate and negotiate a truce in 1961, his DC-6 plane was downed as it was approaching Ndola Airport in what is now Zambia. An extensive UN investigation was never able to establish a definitive cause. Still Hammarskjöld is widely believed to have been the victim of an assassination. Eventually, UN troops overran Katanga when foreign support was largely removed and the revolt ended. Katanga was reincorporated into Congo. Unrest, however, continued with a powerful American-backed army officer, Joseph Mobutu, seizing power in 1965 and ruling until he was finally deposed thirty years later. His legacy, as we shall see, continues to destabilize the entire region.

Many of these coup leaders arrived in power with commendable aims that included improving the lives of their people, while having at times the tertiary effect of defending the boundaries that had effectively been established by their colonial predecessors. Sadly, however, most morphed quickly into vicious kleptocrats that held their people hostage. The result in all too many cases was that this set the stage for any number of external and internal forces dedicated to establishing their own lines of authority and power. More recently, the role models of such destabilizing actors have become outside terrorist organizations, largely of Middle Eastern origin, with a thin overlay of African cultural, societal, even religious paraphernalia.

Sadly, Africa has known a large number of horrific leaders, from Idi Amin in Uganda to the self-styled Emperor Jean-Bédel Bokassa in what he called the Central African Empire. He was ultimately deposed in an elaborate coup d'état backed by French President Valéry Giscard d'Estaing and engineered by Alexandre de Marenches, leader of the French special services the Direction Générale de la Sécurité Extérieure (DGSE), the equivalent of the CIA. In one deftly engineered event, a planeload of DGSE agents in camouflage fatigues landed at Bangui Airport in the dead of night, pulled out a wad of cash to pay the military guards there the months' worth of back pay they were owed, then waited while a second plane landed with the nation's previous, elected leader, David Dacko. The contingent waited until dawn, when Dacko was officially reinstalled in the presidential palace, then flew off quietly into the dawn.

A succession of French presidents immersed themselves deeply in African politics, stationing large forces of French troops in Rwanda, Cote d'Ivoire, Mali, and Niger, as well as Zaire, to make certain that their leaders remained firmly in the Western (especially pro-French) camp and their frontiers secured. Indeed, they remained that way largely until terrorist groups with no fixed roots and alien ideologies found their way to these nations with utterly porous frontiers and vast, largely unpatrolled wilderness tracts.

The problem across the continent is one that has been largely absent from virtually every other place where red lines have sprouted, following national borders, natural geographical realities, or political, diplomatic, or military prerogatives, not to mention religious, cultural, or linguistic imperatives. But in the case of Africa, the British, French, Belgian, German, or Portuguese colonies therein had little of the natural coherence that marked these nations' European homelands. The colonial powers had little understanding or real interest, for the most part, in preserving any historic roots in their African colonies. It was all done for material motives. And thus the boundaries they established enclosed states with few real missions, little national unity, or pride. The result: many are desperately vulnerable, internally and externally. And it is to these realities that we should turn now to examine how today's red lines have been established and how likely they are to lead to growth and stability that can allow them to become important and constructive contributors to global security and prosperity.

Certainly, the growth, at least after 2003, has picked up. The African continent as a whole is growing faster today than any other region of the world. Of the top twenty-five fastest growing nations by population, twenty-three are in Africa, while twenty-three of the top fifty countries by GDP growth are African, their annual growth rates ranging from 5 percent to 11.9 percent. Still, not surprisingly, Africa also has thirty-five of the world's fifty most impoverished nations by percentage of their population who are living on less than $1.90 a day. All this has layered innumerable pressures on already severely taxed societies and people. So while terrorism has thrived in other parts of the world where red lines have been established for religious reasons or simply out of hubris and a desire for territorial aggrandizement, in Africa the reasons for these barriers are often quite simply a desperate cry for existence under horrific conditions. As a toxic lubricant, vast stocks of weaponry have also found their way to Africa for use both during and especially after the Cold War, much of it falling eventually into the hands of the terrorist groups that would cross borders to destroy long-established lines that had assured stability—if at a stiff price in terms of horrific slaughter and mayhem.

In Chad, and radiating outward, the lethal "technicals" wreak havoc. These Toyota four-wheel-drive vehicles carry heavy machine guns, even anti-aircraft guns or powerful anti-tank weapons mounted on the back, are manned by soldiers at times as young as seven years old, armed with floods of AK-47 assault rifles. These highly mobile technicals have become the nomads' mounts of choice and are far more lethal than the horse- or camel-mounted forces that surged across the deserts in the past. With this mobility came the capacity to push red lines of control further and faster than ever. Weaponry and transports, even anti-aircraft missiles of Russian and eventually Cuban and Chinese origin found their way to rebel forces including FRELIMO (Mozambique), ZANU-PF (Zimbabwe), MPLA (Angola), ZAPU (Zimbabwe), EPLF (Eritrea), NRA (Uganda), EPRDF (Ethiopia), RPF (Rwanda), and NPFL (Liberia), and in South Africa the more political ANC and SWAPO. All very quickly challenged increasingly armed and deadly frontiers with their forces and new ideologies acquired during long stints of political and military training in Marxist countries. Africanist historian Richard J. Reid has described the targets of many of these groups as "fault lines of conflict dating back to the nineteenth century or earlier," adding, "all of them belong to a tradition in African warfare of organizing on the frontier and proceeding to march to the center."

What this means in Africa's all but unique setting is that red lines are as much targets and battle lines as firm boundaries—advancing as the conflicts expand and contract, effectively living, breathing organisms. Early on, even today, many rebel groups also established actual "liberated zones," increasingly large enclaves that often cross ancestral, national frontiers and whose boundary lines the rebel groups protect viciously against all efforts to penetrate them. As we shall see, today's terrorists have replaced yesterday's freedom fighters, provoking even greater challenges to governments seeking to reestablish and defend firm red lines of national frontiers. The costs are all too often frighteningly high.

The major colonial powers were rarely induced by force or persuasion to give up their colonies and the lines that defined them until well into the twentieth century. Nor did many conquered territories buckle gently down and accept the new lines of power brought by European forces. So for the British, there were the Bambatha uprisings among the Zulus and others in Rhodesia by the Shona and Ndebele. The Germans had to deal with the Maji Maji, who rebelled in German East Africa shortly after the end of the nineteenth century. Many of these uprisings took the form of attacks against isolated outposts that had been intended to hold long, thin lines defining the territories they had simply seized. But often, as was the case in German East Africa, the revolts were repressed by utterly ruthless actions that led to vast stretches of scorched earth and widespread famine that killed hundreds of thousands of natives.

What marked these early colonial-era battles was the vastly disparate clash of cultures on both sides of the red lines the colonial powers were establishing. Europeans arrived with an *idée fixe*—that the vast bulk of Africa constituted a dark continent populated by savages whose brutality too often descended to the point of cannibalism. These views—namely that their establishment of new regimes was accompanied by an essential element of civilization they were bestowing on those who would ultimately come to appreciate their benevolence at bayonet-point—helped salve whatever conscience remained among the occupiers. Never was there any real attempt to understand the profoundly creative cultures and societies they were making every effort to dismantle.

On the ground, the European forces brought to bear greater mobility, far more sub-stantial resources, and hence more potent firepower. Many of the existing African red lines melted away before the advancing colonial troops, which in turn were only happy to restore them directly behind them as they advanced, though on their own terms—so that little really changed, except the nationality and skin color of those who would now enforce these lines. Lines were set up a continent away by statesmen and officers who often had never visited the territories they were creating.

Some of the earliest terrorists consisted of self-styled independence movements at key turning points of the colonial period. Many represented any number of ethnic, cultural, linguistic, and religious groups that formed their own carefully delineated zones they were prepared to defend with zeal and determination. Some could trace their origins to the time of the slave trade and continued on in fits and starts into the twentieth century. In some cases lines were drawn to defend critical resources such as access to water, especially in areas of critical shortages including Ethiopia and Sudan, portions of Kenya, and northern stretches of West Africa, where the desert continues its encroachment every year.

Many of these sub-nations were effectively states-within-states, establishing and main-taining their own red lines and ties with foreign powers that supplied arms and training. In 1989, for instance, when Samuel Doe established his bloody autocracy in Liberia, rebel troops under Charles Taylor formed the National Patriotic Front of Liberia (NPFL). They were armed by Russia with AK-47s and rocket-propelled grenades and controlled large stretches of the country, replete with their own radio station and government offices. Taylor finally managed to take over the federal government in 1997, but this time other, now oppositional, forces set up their own enclave, expanding into neighboring Sierra Leone. Financed by the large-scale sale of illicit (blood) diamonds and dragooning child-soldiers, they maintained their own red lines of horrific brutality.

—

For decades, African nations have grappled with the question of just what constitutes a terrorist. The African Union has been at the forefront of establishing such guidelines and indeed it has a long history of fighting for an independent and sovereign Africa. Attempting to cope with groups that were growing in power and reach and increasingly showing no respect for long-standing lines that defined frontiers dating back a century or more; in 1999 the Union's predecessor, Organization of African Unity, promulgated a Convention on the Prevention and Combating of Terrorism. This represented the first such pan-African attempt to come to grips with a phenomenon that in many parts of the continent was spiraling out of control, even if it also arose from the self-interest of incumbents, especially autocrats, who sought to criminalize any opposition.

In 2009 alone, the Jane's Terrorism and Insurgency Centre identified 171 terrorist attacks that left 541 fatalities across Africa. Six years later that volume had exploded to 738 attacks leaving 4,600 dead. Most were the product of militant Islamic groups. "We have seen a dramatic rise in the number of attacks carried out by militant Islamist non-state armed groups across the African continent," said Matthew Henman, head of the Jane's organization. "Boko Haram, Al-Qaeda in the Islamic Maghreb, and Al-Shabab were the most active groups, but there are new trends emerging that could mean attacks will further intensify." Since 2015 the attacks have mushroomed even further. The Jane's database shows that in 2018 some 1,552 terrorist attacks left at least 3,231 dead. Overall, at least 15,000 are estimated to have been killed in Boko Haram–generated violence alone, which has displaced at least 2.8 million people from the Lake Chad region and cut humanitarian assistance to at least 3 million more. Hardly a single African nation has been immune, but a number of contiguous countries have seen the bulk of this activity as terrorist groups effectively transcended any of the traditional boundaries and roamed across vast stretches of the continent. The deadliest groups are more or less linked to Middle East groups that have been successfully neutered in their home region and have found sanctuary in the vast and sparsely populated stretches of Africa—several of the Al-Qaeda franchises being particularly appropriate cases. Some have successfully linked up with existing organizations, forming what are effectively sovereign territories or at least no-go zones that straddle multiple frontiers.

The Jane's incident mapping of their activities suggests exactly where long-standing red lines as national frontiers are most challenged by unrest and violence. This map is from 2015. In the following five years, the activities of these terrorists multiplied, particularly across Mali, Niger, Chad, and down into Cameroon, which today ranks as one of the top ten of the world's most violent nations by attacks, alongside Somalia and the DRC.

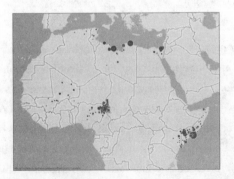

Terrorism begins to metastasize.

But most modern terrorist activity has been concentrated in a natural band of territory that reflects the spread of Islam, stretching across the midline of Africa south of the
Sahara and known as the Sudanic Belt.

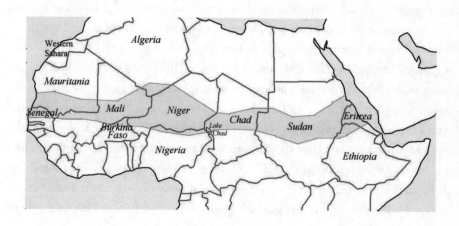

The Sudanic belt bisects Africa.

For centuries, this did define an effective red line or network of lines where Islam was
a common denominator. Now, it also defines the centers of activity of Islamic terrorists
who have chosen Africa as their new base of activity. Their alliances with local terrorist
organizations challenging embedded norms have only magnified the danger and enlarged
the web of red lines that have long been operative across this region.

—

Islam first arrived in what today is Nigeria in the eleventh century, spreading southward
from its entry point in Borno in the northeast. Today this sprawling nation has the largest
Muslim population in West Africa, accounting for at least half the country's population.
Most Nigerian Muslims are Sunni, but there is a significant Shiite population in the
northern states of Nigeria that operate under their own form of sharia law, not sanctioned
by the Nigerian state—a relatively new phenomenon of the last few decades.

In 2002, in Maiduguri, capital of the state of Borno, where Islam first appeared, a self-
styled Islamic "scholar," Mohammed Yusuf, opened a religious prayer room and school
that quickly attracted a broad variety of students from impoverished Muslim families.
He preached the idea that his version of Islam makes it *haram* (forbidden) to take

part in any activity that might be in any fashion associated with Western society. And since half of Nigeria is Christian, including, at that moment, its particularly devout president, Yusuf believed it was necessary to push back and establish his own society with its own very strict boundaries and declare war on the larger state that surrounded him—purified of Christians and Muslims whom he considered insufficiently pious and conversative. He called his organization Society of the People of the Sunnah for Propagation and Jihad. More popularly, it became known as Boko Haram, which not surprisingly means "Western education is forbidden." In December 2003, Boko Haram militants attacked and occupied police stations in the state of Yobe near the border with Niger, raising the flag of the Afghan Taliban, whose ascetic and radical goals appeared most contiguous with their own—despite no evidence of formal contact between the movements. The militants had already formed their own state that they called Al Sunna Wal Jamma (Followers of the Prophet's Teachings). Their goals now were running parallel with those of the Islamic State, formed as an offshoot of al-Qaeda-in-Iraq founded by Abu Musab al-Zarqawi two years after Mohammed Yusuf opened his prayer room and school in Nigeria.

Boko Haram draws a brutal red line bisecting Nigeria.

Boko Haram spread slowly until the summer of 2009 when, following a series of attacks on police stations and government facilities, the Nigerian military retaliated in force, leaving some seven hundred dead in the fighting. Yusuf was seized and died in police custody—the government claiming he was killed while trying to escape. The group, driven underground, reorganized. By 2010, it had a reemergence under Yusuf's deputy, Abubakar Shekau. The scope and intensity of Boko Haram's attacks began to rise exponentially as the group also began to cooperate with al-Qaeda in the Islamic Maghreb. The contested election of Goodluck Jonathan, the devout Christian from southern Nigeria, as Nigeria's president only infuriated the Boko Haram leadership even further. In May 2011, during the president's inauguration, it carried out a series of bombings.

Over the next three years, Boko Haram began expanding its caliphate and its operations to neighboring nations, crossing frontiers with apparent impunity and amalgamating forces from Chad, Somalia, Sudan, and Niger, where it began to run rampant. It also linked up with Abu Bakar al-Baghdadi and his Islamic State, which had begun to enlarge its domain. In both cases, these radical Islamic leaders succeeded in establishing significant red lines that official military forces from the traditional nations where they'd set up their self-styled caliphates seemed powerless to penetrate. Perhaps the most dramatic evidence of Boko Haram's growing power was the April 2014 invasion in southern Borno of a secular school in Chibok, the terrorists having already seized control of the township. The insurgent forces promptly kidnapped three hundred young girls from the school. Some fifty managed to escape quickly, but for the rest, there began a years-long ordeal punctuated by a dramatic video from Shekau showing the remaining girls seated, shrouded in black from head to toe including their faces and hair. The narrator claimed that all had been "converted" to Islam and "married off" to Boko Haram fighters.

Efforts, often quite successful, to expand the effective borders of its caliphate continued to multiply as Boko Haram extended its control over the towns of Baga and Doron Baga in the state of Borno before finally mounting an attack on the state capital that was only narrowly repulsed by federal troops. By 2015, Boko Haram had expanded its activities broadly enough to compel the African Union to assemble a joint military task force of some 7,500 counterterrorism troops from Nigeria, Chad, Cameroon, Niger, and Benin to patrol the broader Lake Chad region and deploy into Nigeria in an effort to thwart the group's expansion. Air strikes from Nigeria and Chad did succeed in driving Boko Haram out of some of its strongholds, but touched off prompt retaliation by Boko Haram across the Chadian basin, the group torching houses and kidnapping civilians. By that time, estimates put the size of this caliphate, that existed with none of the theological underpinnings of ISIS, at more than 20,000 square miles, or nearly the size of Belgium and the Netherlands combined. Its territory is home to some thirty million people, at least five million in desperate need of emergency food aid, which has largely been blocked by Boko Haram operations. Two thousand schools have closed, depriving a million or more children of any education. Simultaneously, Boko Haram rebranded itself as "Islamic State's West Africa Province"—emphasizing its increasingly trans-national, trans-border character. While ISIS has been forced underground, its vast territories and red lines in the Middle East largely destroyed, this is its new incarnation—and with much of the same DNA as the original. What Boko Haram has, with some success, accomplished, and what the Islamic State was never really able to effect, is to force a recognition of its own red lines without in any fashion recognizing those of its opponents. Over the long term, such a practice has only resulted in the ultimate destruction of any toxic interloper. The problem in this case is that the interim can stretch into a very long and quite deadly present. In this case, it is a reality approaching two decades and growing.

With Boko Haram's expansion across the Lake Chad basin and on into neighboring Cameroon, Chad, Mali, and Niger, its home nation of Nigeria has proven itself incapable of response. The United States eventually came to the realization that this is one reality it could not afford to ignore. In November 2013, the State Department finally added Boko Haram to its list of foreign terrorist organizations. Six years earlier, President George W. Bush had agreed to the creation of a joint Africa Command to be based at America's European military headquarters in Stuttgart. AFRICOM was designed to unify all American military operations on the African continent. At the same time, Congress authorized $500 million for a new Trans-Sahara Counterterrorism Partnership. The most ambitious and potentially effective move, though, was the opening of the world's largest drone base just outside Agadez in Niger. The construction alone was a challenge—plagued by sandstorms and locust swarms, as well as its remote desert location. "We are working with our African and international partners to counter security threats in West Africa," said General Stephen Townsend, head of AFRICOM. "The construction of this base demonstrates our investment in our African partners and mutual security interests in the region." Up to a point.

In 2018, the government of Niger granted American forces the authority to carry out armed drone operations over its territory after an October 2017 ambush in Niger by an Islamic offshoot of Boko Haram that left four American servicemen dead. It was not until November 2019, however, that the first drone strike was launched from what was dubbed simply Niger Air Base 201. Three months later, Donald Trump disclosed he was planning to pull American forces out of West Africa, even to shutter the drone base entirely and end all American aid to French forces that are struggling to shut down these terrorists in Mali, Niger, and Burkina Faso—hardly an appropriate way to approach the increasingly desperate need to dismantle the growing network of red lines surrounding terrorist-held territory across much of central and western Africa.

And there were any number of new such lines and their overseers fanning out across the region. Beginning in January 2013, al-Qaeda in the Islamic Maghreb (AQIM) made a major push through the southern Sahara into Mali, where French and Malian security forces promptly began to push back against AQIM's expansion. While none of these local terrorist bands wanted to trigger the kind of reaction that accompanied ISIS's proclamation of a caliphate in Syria, they certainly gave every evidence of mounting land grabs that would suggest concrete territorial ambitions. AQIM began spreading its activities into urban areas of Mali, particularly Bamako, where it hit the Radisson Blue Hotel in November 2015, followed two months later by an attack on the Cappuccino Café and Splendid Hotel in the Burkina Faso capital, Ouagadougou. Three months later, it expanded into Côte d'Ivoire, hitting the seaside resort of Grand Bassam outside Abidjan, leaving nineteen dead. "The attacks mark a distinct change for AQIM from the period between 2007 and the first half of 2015, when the group struggled to carry out large-scale attacks, predominantly acted in northern Mali, and rarely attracted significant media attention," said Jane's expert Henman. "During this period the group had suffered from numerous defections and a strong counter-terrorism drive by Algerian and French forces, which considerably reduced its operational capacity." The fact is that these groups have been proliferating, splintering, and re-forming faster even than the State Department's terrorist list has been able to recognize.

Al-Mourabitoun (The Sentinels) was formed in 2013 in a merger of al-Mulathamun Battalion (The Masked Men) and the Movement for Unity and Jihad in West Africa—all splinter groups of the larger al-Qaeda in the Islamic Maghreb. Al-Mourabitoun's announced aim was to implement strict sharia law throughout its area of operations of Mali, Niger, and southern Libya, where it established a liaison with some local tribes. It has inaugurated effectively a shadow government headed by an "emir." French forces, which number some 4,500 troops throughout the region, have been most diligent in their pursuit of al-Mourabitoun and its leaders in an effort to neutralize its aim of broadening its base of support and the territory it controls. But it remains a serious challenge.

Ansar al-Dine (AAD) operates in the same region of Mali and is closely affili-ated with AQIM, which suggests the broad overlap of these organizations, their regions of operation, and control, as well as the complex nature of interwoven boundaries and effective red lines. At the peak of AAD's power and reach in 2013, it had captured and held the towns of Aguelhok (where it executed eighty-two Malian soldiers and kidnaped thirty more), Tessalit, Kidal, Gao, even the ancient city of Timbuktu—a center of African Islamic culture going back six centuries and, with AAD's operations there, designated a UNESCO World Heritage in Danger Site. In each of the territories it seized—and amalgamated into its effective territory—locals who failed to observe and pay tribute to AAD's medieval laws and prescriptions faced harassment, torture, even summary execution. All are leaves lifted directly from the ISIS caliphate's playbook.

Across the continent, Al-Shabab ("The Youth") has been a perennial source of mayhem and death in Somalia, an all but dysfunctional state that has spawned pirates in the Red Sea and terrorist activities in neighboring Kenya extending even into the capital, Nairobi. The group has been closely affiliated with al-Qaeda since its first appearance as an independent entity in 2007. Antecedents of al-Shabab trace back to the 1993 Battle of Mogadishu, the infamous Black Hawk Down catastrophe where an American Ranger Delta Force unit was pinned down and massacred after their Black Hawk attack helicopters were downed by shoulder-launched, rocket-propelled grenades. Osama bin-Laden eventually claimed responsibility for training the Somali gunmen who took part in the attack—a claim many Somalis regard with deep suspicion.

From its beginning, al-Shabab has maintained as its mission the same as those of other leading African jihadists—to control territory, establishing ever-expanding red lines within Somalia, all leading to a society based on a rigid form of sharia law. The movement sprang from a nationalist backlash against the 2006, American-sanctioned Ethiopian invasion of Somalia, which united many of the country's historically divided clans into a religious-nationalist insurgency against the foreign occupier. Al-Shabab, which until then had been a relatively minor (if lethal) militia, was able to recruit thousands of young unemployed men to fight Ethiopia and its allies and established control over large swaths of the territory. Over the next decade, under pressure from a pan-African military force, the regions al-Shabab actually controlled began shrinking. But the group itself only morphed into a more lethal organization as it broadened its attacks in Somalia and abroad. In 2010, during the final match of the FIFA World Cup in Uganda, it mounted a suicide bomb attack on a restaurant in Kampala that killed seventy-four people. In an effort to force the Kenyan government to withdraw its military forces from Somalia (which had entered the country a few months earlier), al-Shabab attacked Nairobi's vast Westgate Mall in 2011, killing sixty-eight people in a bloody four-day siege. It kept up the .pressure, invading the campus of Kenya's Garissa University in 2015, killing 147. Meanwhile, it maintained its bloody campaign at home, in 2017 setting off two truck bombs in central Mogadishu, killing more than five hundred Somalis. The African Union Mission to Somalia (AMISOM) was preparing to withdraw its forces from Somalia by 2020, though it appeared that the Somali government was ill-prepared to stave off al-Shabab's efforts to reclaim the territory it had gained, then lost, more than a decade earlier.

The Trump administration identified al-Shabab as a particular target of opportunity in Africa—a focus of its attempts across the continent to stem the spread of territories controlled by terrorists and ripping through their red line barricades. Sadly, this entire operation has been thrown into jeopardy by President Trump's ill-considered pledge to withdraw entirely from the continent. While US forces were active, and in scattered regions even somewhat effective, their military activities also led to increasing pushback by the terrorists seeking to maintain or even expand their zones of control. Al-Shabab was particularly determined. In January 2019, in a mirror-image of its Westgate Mall invasion of 2011, the terrorist group seized Nairobi's five-star DusitD2 Hotel and surrounding office buildings and held at least seven hundred people hostage for nineteen hours, leaving twenty-one dead. In its statement, al-Shabab said its action was "a response to the witless remarks of U.S. president, Donald Trump, and his declaration of al-Quds [Jerusalem] as the capital of Israel." Beginning in 2017, American forces based in Somalia launched thirty-one unmanned drone strikes against al-Shabab, escalating to forty-seven in 2018, killing sixty-two of its fighters in December alone. In all, the military said it had killed more than three hundred terrorists in Somalia in 2018.

In January 2020, Lauren Ploch Blanchard, the Africa specialist for the nonpartisan Congressional Research Service, summarized the findings of many local Somali researchers when she wrote that al-Shabab "still controls parts of the country [Somalia], earning revenue through 'taxes,' including of the illicit trades in charcoal and sugar. Experts warn of 'mafia-style' extortion by the group in government areas, including Mogadishu." Blanchard observed that al-Shabab's control lines were continuing to expand: "Complex assaults [by al-Shabab] on AMISOM [African Union military force in Somalia] bases have killed hundreds of troops and prompted the mission to realign forces, pulling back from some areas that insurgents have since reoccupied." This suggests that American or African force attacks have had little impact in redrawing or erasing al-Shabab red lines and seizing the territories that lie within.

Within this mix, there is a collection of non-Islamic, but no less lethal and challenging, terrorist organizations that have seized vast territories in Central Africa and effectively established their own sub-national states that have on several occasions threatened at least regional order. The most frightening web of such red lines, and among the longest lasting, were established and are still maintained in the far northeastern stretches of the Democratic Republic of the Congo (DRC). According to the authoritative New York University team at the Congo Research Group (CRG), today there are at least 130 armed insurgent groups operating in North Kivu and South Kivu provinces alone, up from 70 in 2015 and 120 in 2017. A few have Islamist ties, others are little more than armed bandit gangs. But each has its own red lines it defends, and a number spill across the porous borders into equally lawless regions of Uganda and Burundi. "One can draw a line between Eringeti town in the far north of North Kivu and Baraka in the far south of South Kivu that encompasses a large majority of all violence in the two provinces," the CRG reported in August 2019. This stretch of territory may actually be the most lethal and least penetrated by forces of order anywhere in Africa. According to the Council on Foreign Relations Nigeria Tracker, the death rate from Boko Haram activities was 6.87 per 100,000 people in 2018, while the Yemen Data Project registered 4.13 deaths per 100,000. In the Kivu provinces, the death rate according to the CRG was 8.38 per 100,000. Some 3,015 armed attacks left 6,555 dead from 2017 to 2019 in this region of the DRC.

This has not historically been a major area for Islamist activity, but recently that may have begun to shift. With ISIS seeking an increasingly broad footprint in the region, there have been growing indications that the unrest and all but utter breakdown in government control of the vast northeastern portion of the DRC has given ISIS a potentially useful entry point. The leading agglomeration of subversive forces for at least fifteen years, beginning in 1995, was the Allied Democratic Forces (ADF). With origins on the eastern side of the all but meaningless official border in Uganda, its leadership and troops fled into North Kivu territory of the DRC when Ugandan military forces finally managed to mount a sufficiently potent offensive to break through their lines and drive them out of their traditional stronghold. At about that time, as ISIS was finding its way into other vacuums across western Africa, it also arrived in the DRC with some first tenuous feelers. Its leaders seemed especially attracted to the ADF as it found an entire network of quasi-governmental institutions the ADF had established in North Kivu, ranging from prisons, schools, banks, and health centers to broad and deep ties with smaller, like-minded groups. This seemed to mirror precisely what ISIS, at the peak of its power and reach, had succeeded in establishing in the conquered territories of Syria and Iraq it characterized as a caliphate. In the DRC, all of this structure has been able to thrive and expand in the absence of any central authority from the DRC's corrupt, autocratic government in Kinshasa and the inability of its military to make much headway throughout eastern and northern DRC. The Congo Research Group has found that the combined organization has adopted an even more resolutely militant Islamic posture.

The density and complexity of the territorial red lines and lines of activity and authority in this part of Africa are all but unique and a tribute to the unique character of the insurgency here. In addition to the ADF, there are several varieties of Mai-Mai terrorists operating particularly in North Kivu. Moreover, taking advantage of the vacuum in any armed suppression or rule of law, substantial numbers of insurgents forming the National Council for Renewal and Democracy, a breakaway splinter group from the Democratic Forces for the Liberation of Rwanda, meandered across that nation's frontier into the highland areas of South Kivu province—at least two waves of five thousand or more warriors along with women and children. Human Rights Watch and DRC judicial officials documented numerous cases involving child soldiers across this region. The fear is that fighting could break out between these forces and other groups that have long held onto this territory as their own.

But of special interest beyond the confines of the DRC is that this is the heart of Africa's central Ebola-belt. It is here that this horrific disease originally emerged, nearly morphing into a pandemic in 2018 due largely to the inability of outside health specialists and caregivers to reach the sources of the epidemic due to persistent attacks by armed insurgents. In December 2019, the Congo Research Group reported that Mai-Mai forces had staged at least four attacks on Ebola response facilities, setting afire two disease control units, attacking a health center in the village of Mandelya, destroying medical equipment, and kidnapping a nurse, who was freed the next day after a ransom was paid. In July 2019, the World Health Organization reported more than 2,700 Ebola cases had resulted in 1,800 deaths—a staggering 67 percent mortality rate (compared with a 3.4 percent mortality rate for COVID-19, which originated in China in 2019).

Finally, not to be ignored is another virulent and determinedly non-Islamic terrorist movement that has terrorized a vast territory and whose red lines are as pernicious as any established by Islamic-linked organizations. The Lord's Resistance Army (LRA) is a successor to the Holy Spirit Mobile Force Christian cult formed in late 1986. Political scientist Christopher R. Day has catalogued at least fifty insurgent groups or splinter organizations that have operated at various times since 1986 in Uganda though he quite rightly singles out eight as providing "organized, violent challenges to incumbent rule." The leading, and most successful in seizing territory and establishing red lines it has successfully defended, has been the LRA. Its foundations were laid by the utterly mad preacher and spirit medium Alice Auma Lakwena. Her name derived from an Italian army captain named Lakwena, meaning "Messenger," who drowned in the Nile during World War I. Alice defined him as a primary spirit she channeled as a manifestation of the Christian Holy Spirit which took possession of her at the age of twenty-seven on May 25, 1985. After a major military success commanding rebel forces a year later, she attracted a considerable armed cult following of as many as ten thousand, calling on witches and evil spirits who came to her in visions. Each fighter was smeared with a mixture of shea nut oil and red soil (*pala*) which she promised would provide an armored shield against any enemy bullets. At her peak, her Holy Mobile Forces overran much of the region encompassing the Acholi in Uganda. This did not last long. A series of defeats sent her fleeing into exile in Kenya, where she appeared to have gone completely mad. Taking her place was a cousin, Joseph Kony, a high school dropout and altar boy at the local Catholic church. With Alice disgraced and in exile, it was not a long stretch for Kony, a charismatic figure, to assume control of her Lord's Resistance Army. Kony was able to persuade her followers that the Acholi people—long the subject of prejudices and tropes that warned against their inherent barbarism—were about to be targets of genocide. The enemy was the government of Yoweri Museveni, who had just begun his thirty-four-year rule over Uganda and remains in power today. Kony needed to establish an area his forces could control and from which they might ultimately challenge the government in Kampala. That never happened. At the same time, neighboring Sudan was at first quietly, then quite overtly, providing substantial military assistance to Kony and his forces—flying in land mines and anti-personnel mines and training recruits in four facilities.

Over the next quarter century, the LRA has become one of the most enduring and lethal plagues inflicted consistently on any region of the world. Emphasizing the supremacy of the Ten Commandments, the LRA was the Christian and African ante-cedent of the Islamic State in many of its attributes—most notoriously its brutality, including horrific mutilations, mass executions of civilians, and the violent indoctrination of youngsters. More than 67,000 youths, including 30,000 small children, have been abducted and pressed into service as fighters, sex slaves, and porters. Kony himself and a number of his top commanders succeeded in developing an elaborate and lucrative trade in gold, blood diamonds, and ivory from the mass slaughter of elephants in the Garamba National Park in eastern Congo, where the group maintains a sanctuary outside its immediate target zone in western Uganda. More than 100,000 civilians have died during the LRA's reign—including the brutal counterinsurgency waged by the Ugandan army, which was scarcely kinder to the civilian population squeezed in between. A multinational force of the African Union has had little success in penetrating the LRA's resolutely defended perimeters.

In March 2017, a high-ranking LRA commander, Michael Omona, surrendered to American military forces in the Central African Republic. A month later, however, with the LRA hardly broken, in one of the first acts of the Trump administration, and an early indication of how the United States intended to manage or control terrorist activities in Africa, the Pentagon withdrew its counter-LRA units. The mission had been launched in 2011 when President Barack Obama dispatched one hundred Special Forces troops to help the Ugandan army locate Kony. Operation Observant Compass never succeeded in capturing Kony, though it did have some success in trimming the size of the terrorist forces. Still, monitoring groups like Human Rights Watch believe that that the LRA infrastructure remains intact and a threat to civilians in their strongholds in Uganda and especially the Central African Republic, where it remains yet another virulent terrorist group in that lawless region. The indictment of Kony by the International Criminal Court in the Hague on twenty-one counts of war crimes and crimes against humanity as well as an Interpol red notice remain open.

———

The aftermath of the withdrawal of the small Observant Compass force in 2017 has not been an encouraging indication of what lies in store if the Trump administration embarks on its next and most dramatic abandonment of red line defense across much of the most besieged stretches of the African continent.

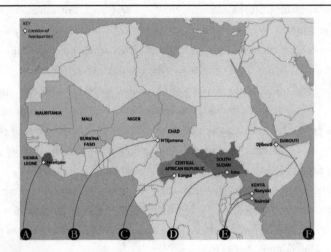

Ⓐ British based in Freetown. The British military and advisory centre; International Military Assistance and Training Team (IMATT). Began in 2002. **Ⓑ French based in N'Djamena.** Mission of 3,500 French Servicemen primarily based in N'Djamena, with troops in Mauritania, Mali, Burkina Faso, Niger, and Chad. The group is commonly referred to as the "G-5 Sahel." Began in 2014. **Ⓒ French based in Bangui.** Mission of 1,700 french servicemen under "Operation Sangaris," began in 2013. **Ⓓ Chinese based in Juba.** Earlier this year, the Chinese deployed a 700-man force as part of a UN peacekeeping mission. **Ⓔ British based in Nairobi and Nanyuki.** The base for the British Peace Support Team (BPST) located next to Nairobi international airport, and the British Army Training Unity Kenya (BATUK) based in Nanyuki, with a small rear element just outside Nairobi. **Ⓕ US and French based in Djibouti.** The primary base for US and coalition forces, called Camp Lemonnier, currently housing 4,500 American and 1,700 French military personnel. Active since 2001.

The threat, pending for years since Trump first took office, gained momentum in late 2019. General Mark Milley, the new chairman of the Joint Chiefs of Staff, told *The New York Times* that the United Sates needed to reexamine its military force deployments in Africa, the Middle East, and Latin America, especially given new challenges from China. Milley, a veteran Army commander before being elevated to chairman of the Joint Chiefs of Staff by President Trump, is a determined believer in the ability of American forces to master any situation. He also has a profound understanding of the limitations of the United States to respond to a given challenge and the number of such simultaneous challenges it could handle—or red lines it could patrol—at any given moment with the resources available. He once told me in a conversation, when he was serving as army chief, that "you tell me what victory looks like and I will tell you what I need to get there." I had been asking him specifically about Afghanistan at the time, but this concept could be equally applied virtually anywhere American forces are deployed—especially in perhaps the single most complex theater of all: Africa.

The withdrawal, particularly from West Africa, would also involve, at least in theory, shuttering the massive drone base in Niger that had just begun to prove its value in searching for and interdicting activities of terrorists operating in Niger, Mali, and the entire Lake Chad basin region. Effectively this would leave the route clear for many of these terrorist groups to reinforce or expand red lines they had long sought to defend but that joint American and African operations were finally placing in some jeopardy. As I suggested in a commentary in February 2020, even before the decision was taken, any substantial withdrawal of American forces from Africa would send the wrong signal at precisely the worst time. Not only are malevolent forces in the region sensing an opportunity with Western attention focused elsewhere, but they have also begun receiving substantial reinforcements in terms of men, matériel, and especially ideology and backbone from elements of ISIS and al-Qaeda, whose operations and red lines the United States and its allies have successfully dismantled, for the most part, in the Middle East.

What America's allies, particularly the French, fear may be even worse. Trump wants to withdraw and leave Africans to establish and defend lines that are totally beyond their ability to sustain. And France, which has long shouldered the lion's share of the burden of intelligence, advanced weaponry, training, and manpower, is reaching the limits of its not inconsiderable power. Any substantial American pullout would also effectively eviscerate the carefully crafted and assembled AFRICOM that the African Union has quietly come to rely upon for sustaining their lines of authority and security.

France's roots in the region as provider of last resort of security and, today, anti-terrorist activities across broad swaths of Africa stretch back deep into the colonial era. French is still the mother tongue for many of these nations—and the language of their militaries as well. In January 2020, in the midst of a nationwide transit strike that was paralyzing French society, President Emmanuel Macron flew in for a sudden visit to West Africa to preside over a Sahel summit with five West African leaders and visit some of the French troops deployed there. "We will keep up the fight against jihadist terrorists. We will continue to do so with our African partners and with our European and international partners," Macron told the assembled troops. "Because if we let the threat flourish, it will impact us too." At a news conference after the summit, he was even more pointed. The ordinarily calm and unflappable French president let his anger boil over: "I know who is dying for the citizens of Niger, Mali and Burkina Faso. It's French soldiers." Macron had summoned the leaders of the five frontline Francophone nations in the battle against the terrorist red lines that were shredding their countries to read them the riot act at a time when the United States was turning its back on them. He was even prepared, he suggested, to mirror what the Trump administration was doing and withdraw France's 4,500 troops. He was lit up, he said, by the spreading anti-French activities by many of their people who have taken the unthinkable action of burning the French tricolor flag in the streets. "I can't have French troops on the ground in the Sahel when there is ambiguity toward anti-French movements and sometimes comments made by politicians and ministers." France's top military leader, General François Lecointre, who rarely stands for an interview, was even more blunt with journalist Jean-Pierre Elkabbach in November 2019, asserting that if French forces did withdraw from the Sahel nations of West Africa, each would collapse from within, causing unchecked terrorism and in some ways a more desperate threat—unchecked migration to Europe. Still, the French military is making a major effort to find some way of carrying on—ordering additional C-130 transport planes, even Reaper drones, while their special forces are already stepping into the key vacuum of training African militaries in specialized techniques of coping with the terrorist threats.

As it happens, all these American maneuvers are especially shortsighted given the fundamental rationale that has been defined as underpinning the withdrawal—to refocus America's priorities on confrontation with what are perceived to be its primary military challenges: Russia and China. For it seems that with the American withdrawal through the back door, Trump has left the way free for Russian and Chinese influence to come rushing in through the front to fill this impending vacuum. China, in particular, has a huge presence across Africa, where it has built large dams and other infrastructure projects in exchange for access to valuable mineral resources, but especially in East Africa where it has managed to establish its first extra-territorial naval base.

Both major powers have lusted after Africa for decades and sought any number of toeholds, alliances ranging from the smallest terrorist groups to entire nations prepared to demonstrate anti-Western tendencies. During the Cold War a handful of countries lined up with the Soviet Union. Stalin had little interest in Africa, but he'd died by the time decolonization was ramping up, and Nikita Khrushchev was determined to win African hearts and minds. He had an open field, because of the long-standing association between "Western" and "colonial." Soviet aid went to the MPLA freedom fighters in Angola, Patrice Lumumba (the CIA's passionate foe) in Congo, and General Mengistu in Ethiopia, where Marxism-Leninism was installed as the official ideology. Indeed, when I landed with our CBS crew in Benin in 1983, it was resolutely aligned with the Soviet Union.

But it happened that the American ambassador was a drinking buddy of the minister of the interior, so when we landed they were both at the airport to greet us. We sat in the thatched-roof terminal and sipped very nice French brandy on the veranda, then, when we promised to produce no American propaganda, were allowed in.

China had established some toeholds in Africa in the Cold War era. Zhou Enlai made a grand tour of sympathetic African nations in 1966 and was warmly received by a number of national leaders, particularly one of the luminaries of African independence movements, Ghana's Kwame Nkrumah.

The end of Africa's colonial period was messy, brutal, and left behind a legacy of metastable red lines that are reflected today in repeated efforts by foreign powers who never had a shred of colonial presence in Africa to establish their own. But, in the post-Communist era, relations of Russia and China with Africa broadened and deepened to the point where today they represent political, diplomatic, and especially military challenges to American or French dominance in much of the continent. In a number of countries, they have proved themselves willing partners either with the national leaderships or insurgent and terrorist groups. China has sought to build trade and financial bridges across Africa, to the extent that London's *Financial Times* described this relationship even in 2008 as "Drawing contours of a new world order." Since then, that relationship has only broadened and deepened. China has passed the United States as Africa's largest trading partner, with some $148 billion in two-way trade in 2017—three times the level of trade with the US—continuing to grow to $102 billion in the first half of 2019 alone. Of even greater importance in terms of cementing long-term ties is the volume of Chinese trade, investment and construction in Africa, which has reached by some estimates as much as $2 trillion since 2005. Much of this, however, has been concentrated in dams and other facilities that are spectacular but have proved to be of marginal economic utility. Still, they have tied each such country in a debt spiral that has all too often been resolved in favor of China, which has quietly but resolutely begun to stake its own territory and establish its own red lines across Africa.

In Djibouti, at a strategic choke-point entrance to the Red Sea, where 20 percent of the world's commerce passes en route to and from the Suez Canal, China persuaded the government to take over the main port facility from Dubai's DP World, then to allow China to build its first overseas naval base right next door. As it happens, on other side of the port is Camp Lemonnier, a US Naval Expeditionary Base, home of the Combined Joint Task Force—Horn of Africa. It also happens to be a centerpiece of an American secret intelligence operation across a network of air bases strung along the continent to spy on terrorists' hideouts. Russia, too, is eyeing a strategic location for its own first military base on the African continent, in the port of Berbera on the coast of the Gulf of Aden in Somalia—just down the coast from the American and Chinese facilities in Djibouti.

A number of African nations are hedging their bets in the event that Western powers, particularly the United States or France, do lose interest and pull out. All of the frontline sub-Saharan nations confronting Islamist terrorism threats—Malik, Niger, Chad, Burkina Faso, and Mauritania—have appealed for military help from Russia. Still unclear is what the future might bring for such operations if Trump carries through with his plan to move American forces out of Africa. What is clear is that it could not happen soon enough for Vladimir Putin and Xi Jinping. While Trump has made not a single visit to Africa, indeed has barely devoted a moment to cultivating relationships there, Putin hosted a lavish African summit at his Black Sea resort of Sochi in October 2019, inviting forty African heads of state to preview military hardware that would be available for a simple exchange of oil, gas, diamonds, and a host of precious minerals, not to mention treaties of friendship and cooperation. Each leader had an opportunity to heft some of the most advanced Russian weaponry in a lavish display of military power and engineering. Not to be outdone, Xi Jinping invited high-ranking military officers from some fifty African states to Beijing for two weeks to take part in the first China-African Defense and Security Forum in 2018. On a more personal basis, he has also visited six leading African countries where China is eager to build or cement relationships—Republic of Congo, Rwanda, Tanzania, Zimbabwe, Mauritius, and South Africa three times.

What all this adds up to is simple. The United States has never sought in any similarly systematic fashion to build lines of communications and support to African nations that China and Russia both clearly see as central components of their future security and prosperity. The Trump administration has set itself in an even less appropriate direction. In December 2018, National Security Advisor John Bolton unveiled the Trump administration's new Africa policy based in a fundamental thesis that is the precise antithesis of the themes Russia and China have been enunciating: what's good for America is good for Africa. "Every decision we make, every policy we pursue, and every dollar of aid we spend will further U.S. priorities," Bolton began. "All U.S. aid on the continent will advance U.S. interests." Now this may well be how Moscow and Beijing view matters privately, but they have had the good sense not to pronounce or act in any such a fashion.

While no outside power may, in the final analysis, ever be able to build red lines of their own on this continent, those who are able to help Africa establish or maintain their own enduring barriers against destabilization from without or disruption at home will certainly have made an important step toward securing the resources and friendship of the world's fastest growing region. None of these are eternal red lines. As we have seen,

Africa's red lines have throughout their history been more or less successfully established or manipulated by Africans themselves. But as Russia and China, themselves architects as we have seen of largely pernicious red lines, implant themselves ever deeper in this growing web across this critical continent, it is vital for the United States also to remain deeply involved. It is essential that America establish a presence equally dynamic in its own fashion to create and maintain a system that could serve as an important model as we bring our entire tour of red lines around the world to a close.

CHAPTER NINE

Eternal Lines

I n 1884, the raj, the British rulers of India, which comprised the entire subcontinent including what is today India, Pakistan, Bangladesh, and large stretches of
Afghanistan, came to the conclusion that they no longer wanted responsibility for
the wild territories of the Hindu Kush and what lay beyond to the west and south. These
lands stretch from the impenetrable mountains they straddle on the north, where they
merge with the Karakoram Range, the Pamirs, and the eternally tense point where China,
Pakistan, and Afghanistan converge, and onward to the south, where they connect with
the Spin Ghar Range near the Kabul River.

There have been tribes in these forbidding hills of Afghanistan for 2,000 years
or more. The Greek historian Herodotus wrote in 440 B.C.E. of the Pactrians, one
of the "wandering tribes" that occasionally helped comprise armies of Persia. These
were the Pashtuns of the time of the raj, who still dominate much of the mountains,
caves, and valleys of Afghanistan and the North-West Frontier Province of Pakistan.

When the British assumed control over this vast region, there was resistance. Twice
in the last quarter of the nineteenth century, British troops battled forces of the emir of
Afghanistan. The first began in November 1878 when forces moved quickly into the emir's
territory, defeating his army and forcing the emir to flee. The British envoy, Sir Pierre
Louis Napoleon Cavagnari, and his entire mission that had arrived in Kabul on July 24,
1879, were massacred to the last man on September 3, touching off the second Afghan
campaign. This ended a year later when the British overran the entire army of Emir Ayub
Khan outside Kandahar in southeastern Afghanistan, not far from the frontier that was
about to be established. These wars, the diplomacy, maneuvers, and experience dealing
with the Afghan people whom the British encountered, persuaded the raj that the price for
retaining control was simply far higher than it was willing under any circumstances to pay.

So in 1884, Lord Frederick Hamilton-Temple-Blackwood, the Marquess of Dufferin, viceroy and governor of India, named Henry Mortimer Durand a member of the Afghan Boundary Commission. This was a critical post on at least two different levels. First, Russia was also beginning what would turn out to be a succession of attempts to push its own frontiers down into Afghanistan. Afghanistan was seen by the Russians, then the Soviets, then the Russians again, as a buffer against encroachment from the British Empire of that period, and against the potentially hostile and disruptive tensions on the subcontinent today. Ironically, Britain of the 1880s viewed Afghanistan through a similar prism—potentially a firm line that could not be crossed and that would keep the wild mountain tribes and the legions of Russians at bay. Durand headed off into the tribal lands of the North-West Frontier Province, beyond which lay Afghanistan. In 1885, a Russian delegation appeared as well at a neutral meeting place—the Zulfikar Pass. On July 16, 1885, *The New York Times* published a "special dispatch from Jagdorabatem via Meshed" telling of a "reported advance to Zulfikar Pass" that comprised "a large number of Russian reinforcement [that] has arrived at Merv and Pul-i-Khisti during the past fortnight." At the same time, "the British Frontier Commission [was] moving nearer to Herat—the Afghans determined to resist invasion."

If this sounds sadly, desperately familiar, it is because it was. History has never failed to repeat itself in this part of the world. Durand and his commission did finally succeed in arranging a truce and, most importantly, an agreement to establish a line to which his name was quickly attached and has persisted in some fashion or other until today. The Russians agreed to its provisions since it allowed their forces to control the sources of several critical canals. But it would be some years before any of this became reality. First, it was up to the emir of Afghanistan to agree. In April 1885, the British viceroy, Lord Dufferin, gave a lavish banquet in Rawalpindi where the emir praised the friendship between the two countries, as well as Durand. The viceroy promptly named Durand his foreign secretary, the youngest in the history of the British Empire. Over the next eight years, Durand traveled frequently to the hostile lands along the frontier, which he and his British colleagues saw as populated by "absolute barbarians . . . avaricious, thievish and predatory to the last degree." In 1893, Durand planted himself permanently at the frontier, sitting day after day with the bearded emir, a series of rudimentary maps spread out before them to carve out the line that would define their mutual border. The one last sticking point was Waziristan—then, as now, a sprawling, provocative, and unsettled territory on the fringes of two empires. This was one stretch that Britain wanted very much to retain, largely as a buffer. Durand could hardly understand the emir's apparently desperate desire to retain a place that "had so little population and wealth." Why? Durand asked.

A simple one-word explanation. "Honor," the emir responded. This was easily satisfied by tripling the emir's annual "subsidy" from the British Empire from six to eighteen lakh rupees ($8,000 to $24,000). On November 12, 1893, the agreement was signed, though the emir really had no idea what he was signing since the original was written in English, which he neither spoke nor read.

The Durand line establishes what is even today the boundary between Afghanistan and Pakistan.

Sir Olaf Caroe, who served as the last governor of the North-West Frontier Province in what was then India, and a firsthand expert on the Durand Line, which defined the western border of the territory he governed, observed that "the Agreement did not describe the line as the boundary of India, but as the frontier of the Amir's [Abd-ur-Rahman] domain and the line beyond which neither side would exercise influence. This was because the British government did not intend to absorb the tribes into their administrative system, only to extend their own [British], and to exclude the Amir's authority from the territory east and south of the line. . . . The Amir had renounced sovereignty beyond the line." But a host of would-be interlopers, from Soviet invaders to Taliban freedom fighters to al-Qaeda terrorists, not to mention American forces and their NATO allies, never fully came to appreciate that reality.

Afghanistan still refuses to recognize this line, which effectively defines the border today, describing it as a colonial mandate imposed by force of will, though Pakistan freely accepts it as part of the legacy inherited, along with its freedom, at the time of the British exit from the subcontinent. It remains one of the longest-standing and firmest of such red lines, while also being utterly violent, unsettled, and, admittedly, quite porous.

But it is only one of three.

A second is in the Holy Land. For more than 5,000 years, from the time of the early Bronze Age, Jews and Arabs, or their antecedents, have lived side by side, dividing the Holy Land between them, initially with Jews against non-Jewish Canaanites, many of whom eventually embraced Christianity then, half a millennium later, Islam. By the late Bronze Age, Israeli tribes began to appear. By the late Iron Age, in the second millennium before the Common Era, there were already city-states in the Levant, what is today Israel and the Palestinian territories, many controlled by Egypt at the time. Maps of the Levant in the Iron Age already show quite well-defined areas of Israel, Judah, Moab, Edom, and Ammon (where Amman, Jordan is now located). Moreover, by the tenth century B.C.E., the time of Kings David and Solomon, walled cities, like Megiddo, were already flourishing, containing within their walls entire palaces.

The capital city of the region was already Jerusalem. By the year 850 B.C.E., there is also clear evidence of having been Israeli and Judean states, suggesting that even then, lines were being established not unlike those that exist, in a far more toxic fashion, today. The Jewish state of Israel was effectively destroyed by a sweep of Assyrian forces in 721 B.C.E. A century later, the Babylonian King Nebuchadnezzar II completed the process, scattering Jews in what became known as the Babylonian exile, though many were able to return and build the Second Temple in Jerusalem in the mid-sixth century B.C.E. All this is to say that for nearly two thousand years, Jews and Arabs were living side by side in some fashion in what would become the Holy Land, each with their own very clearly defined lines of demarcation. Eventually, of course, Romans would conquer and overlay much of this region. Christianity would arrive, and, by the sixth century, Islam. But in each case, distinct communities with their own lines of authority that they were prepared to defend at all costs would emerge and managed to coexist until the modern era. Many were perhaps the oldest red lines of all.

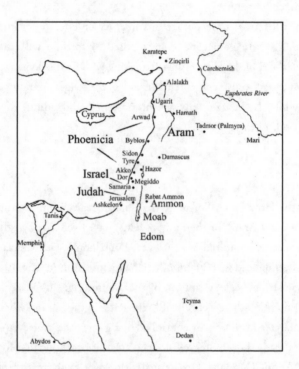

The Levant during the Iron Age. A millennium before Christ.

Equally immutable, if less venerable, is the last of three unchanging, if not utterly unchallenged, red lines—the one that surrounds NATO, established by the Western alliance as a bulwark against all comers. First were the Soviets and their Warsaw Pact allies during the Cold War. Today, there is Russia and its outlying satrapies of Central Asia, the 'Stans, and a handful of outposts managed by the Kremlin from Moldava to Belarus. The origins of the NATO red line are those meetings of Roosevelt and Churchill in August 1941 on board the United States cruiser *August* and British battleship *Prince of Wales* anchored together off the coast of Newfoundland that we introduced in Chapter Eight. Initially, the document that emerged from what was a pre-war discussion (the United States still four months away from entering World War II) encompassed only Britain and the United States. But the eight points of what would become known as the Atlantic Charter included self-determination for all people without any "aggrandizement, territorial or other," free trade, full economic collaboration, and abandonment of all use of force. This eighth and final provision was the most important for the future:

> Since no future peace can be maintained if land, sea, or air armaments continue to be employed by nations which threaten, or may threaten, aggression outside of their frontiers, they believe, pending the establishment of a wider and permanent system of general security, that the disarmament of such nations is essential.

Both Churchill and Roosevelt returned to their respective capitals, each to a hero's welcome. As *New York Times* correspondent James MacDonald reported: "Bronzed by the sun and sea breezes enjoyed during his historic trip for conferences with President Roosevelt, Prime Minister Winston Churchill arrived back in London amid vociferous cheers from an admiring populace." It was, clearly the most singularly important moment for these two countries, which together would be responsible for building an impregnable line around themselves and their allies. Any doubt about the historic nature of this meeting was dispelled by the collection of dignitaries who met Churchill at King's Cross Station when the train from the British coast arrived—Clement Attlee, Lord Privy Seal; Anthony Eden, foreign secretary; and Albert V. Alexander, first lord of the admiralty. Churchill's speech to the British people describing the conference the following Sunday would be carried across the United States as well "by national networks."

Eight years later, the document drafted by the two leaders, and particularly this final provision, would form the foundation for the NATO alliance. Its twelve founding nations pledged a common goal:

> Its purpose was to secure peace in Europe, to promote cooperation among its members and to guard their freedom—all of this in the context of countering the threat posed at the time by the Soviet Union. The Alliance's founding

treaty was signed in Washington in 1949 by a dozen European and North American countries. It commits the Allies to democracy, individual liberty and the rule of law, as well as to peaceful resolution of disputes. Importantly, the treaty sets out the idea of collective defence, meaning that an attack against one Ally is considered as an attack against all Allies. The North Atlantic Treaty Organization—or NATO—ensures that the security of its European member countries is inseparably linked to that of its North American member countries.

The critical issue, and the heart of NATO's virtual boundary lines, is the final one—detailed in Article Five of the alliance's charter: one-for-all and all-for-one.

Over the next six years, the Soviet Union watched the growing unity of NATO with anxiety, along with the expansion of American forces in the nations that surrounded the Soviets' European territories. Finally, in 1955, six years after NATO was created, and timed for the moment when West Germany joined the alliance, the Soviet Union created its own organization uniting its client states across Eastern Europe—Poland, Hungary, Czechoslovakia, Romania, Bulgaria, and Albania (until it withdrew in 1961 when it broke with Moscow and allied itself with China). Known as the Warsaw Pact, its boundary with the West was as inviolable as NATO's boundaries with the East. There was one paramount difference. While the same concept of "an attack on one is an attack on all" was implicit in its nature, in fact this was not a mutual defense pact. No Warsaw Pact member was in any position militarily to confront a massive incursion from outside without the immediate involvement of the Soviet Union. While Britain and France each maintained its own independent nuclear arsenal, no Warsaw Pact nation other than the Soviet Union possessed any nuclear weapon. At the same time, as was demonstrated twice in its first fifteen years, forces of the Warsaw Pact, largely Soviet armored columns, were fully prepared to invade other members of the pact to enforce precise ideological adherence to the Kremlin line. In 1956 in Hungary and again in 1968 in Czechoslovakia, Soviet-backed Warsaw Pact forces rolled through these countries. In the first case, they violently suppressed the Hungarian Revolution, the second brought an end to the Prague Spring that threatened unchecked pluralism and criticism of Soviet domination of Eastern Europe. In short, all other elements of the Atlantic Charter—self-determination and freedom of choice in particular—had no place in the document that created the Warsaw Pact.

As a succession of other nations was added to the initial NATO dozen following the breakup of the Soviet Union, including all the founding members of the Warsaw Pact as well as the three Baltic Soviet republics (Estonia, Lithuania, and Latvia), the red line that surrounded NATO expanded to fit. There has never been an overt effort to penetrate that line, as there was no effort to penetrate the boundaries of the Warsaw Pact when it existed. This effective red line has been as inviolable as any in the world. But as we shall see, not without being tested.

—

These three sets of red lines—the Durand Line, the lines that separate Jews and Arabs in the Holy Land today, and the boundaries of NATO—are what I would suggest are the intractable lines. These immutables are not, in the final analysis, red lines, but rather black ones. Each is a hard line that is likely never to be breached. We must find a way to live with them. For attempts to destroy them or erase them may be as pernicious and dangerous to the world order as allowing them simply to fulfill, yes, even at times exhaust, their intentions by allowing them to remain in place.

—

There has been no end of challenges to the Durand Line virtually from the day of its creation. Pakistan ultimately inherited the Durand Line and all the territories it guaranteed to the east and south when its nation was created from the partition of India in 1947 when Britain departed and the two nations gained their freedom. But the Pashtuns, who straddled this line, were given only two alternatives—join India, or join Pakistan. Neither the Pashtuns, nor the central government in Kabul, ever really recognized the 1,500-mile Durand Line as an international boundary. And in cultural, social, and especially tribal terms, it was not. It was, rather, an international no-man's-land that has been all but immutable for its very failure to gain legitimacy by any of the real parties. Effectively, a red line recognized by neither side can be as indelible as one that is deeply contested by one party or another. Today, it is still tribal allegiances and realities that define this line and what lies on both sides of it. And the Pashtuns are the core of these problems.

On October 7, 2001, less than a month after the 9/11 terrorist attack on the United States, a plot masterminded in the mountainous region bisected by the Durand Line, American forces, joined by a smattering of NATO troops, invaded Afghanistan. Their principal goal was immediately successful—forcing the Taliban from power in Kabul, if not from much of the rest of the country and certainly not from the mountain ranges that straddle the Durand Line.

As it happens, *Taliban* means "student" in the Pashto language. The Pashtuns, collectively at least sixty tribes and upward of four hundred sub-tribes, are an immensely proud people—especially proud of their three-thousand-year history of never having been conquered by an invader (except perhaps briefly by Mongols sweeping through en route from Asia to the Middle East and Europe in the thirteenth and fourteenth centuries). Pashtun folklore suggests the entire nationality sprang from a single ancestor, most commonly referred to as Baba Khaled—Khalid ibn al-Walid, the storied warrior of the prophet Mohammed. Today, Pashtuns number upward of forty million people who have managed to resist a succession of invading forces even in the last century that have sought to rule or control them. They managed to defeat the entire armored power of the Soviet Union, which in December 1979 launched a full-fledged Prague-Spring-style invasion of Afghanistan, which borders the southern reaches of the then-Soviet republics of Turkmenistan, Uzbekistan, and Tajikistan.

The real reason for the Soviet invasion did not come to light until years later. It was not the fear of the potential for terrorism that motivated the Kremlin to launch its ill-conceived and ill-fated action. Instead, it was really the same fear that motivated their actions in Hungary in 1956, Czechoslovakia in 1968, and later Georgia and Ukraine in the post-Soviet period. They worried that Afghanistan was on the verge of shifting its loyalties to the West. The last thing the Kremlin wanted was a member of NATO directly on its southern flank. It wanted a determinedly neutral power, or ideally one that was solidly pro-Soviet. If not a member of the Warsaw Pact, then certainly not a member of the NATO alliance.

What started out as a simple police action did not go well at all for the Soviets from the beginning. The Afghan resistance was all but immune to the Soviet military's massive armor and air power, an army unaccustomed to fighting any sort of real guerrilla-style tactics. The Taliban, which came to full flower under the aegis of Pakistan's ISI (Inter-Services Intelligence) and the American CIA, launched a fully declared jihad and began receiving major Western-style matériel, especially shoulder-launched ground-to-air missiles. The Soviet advantage of massive helicopter-borne assaults melted away. Scores of helicopters and their crews went down in flames. Body bags began returning to Russia in waves. And eventually it became impossible for even the awesome Soviet propaganda machinery to successfully deny the reality. The Soviets were losing. It took ten years for this truly to hit home. But finally, by February 1989 they were gone. The agreement had been signed nearly a year earlier by Soviet leader Mikhail Gorbachev. The United States was a party to the agreement—pledging to end its support for the Taliban resistance. Of course, within two years Gorbachev was deposed and the Soviet Union dissolved. Without a doubt, the ill-fated Afghanistan adventure played an important, if not a singlehanded, role in this event.

The third signatory to the withdrawal document was Pakistan, which had played its own part in the Soviets' defeat and agreed to end its interference in Afghanistan's internal affairs. This worked, certainly for Pakistan, at least from the moment the Taliban assumed power in Kabul. That took seven tumultuous years—from the end of the Soviet departure in 1989 until 1996—and involved more unsettling tribal conflicts. A host of rival mujahideen groups vying for power and territory surged back and forth across Afghanistan—only confirming the fundamental reason for the original Durand Line. Finally, in 1996 the Taliban rolled into Kabul, seizing the capital and deposing the corrupt president, Burhanuddin Rabbani, who happened to be a Tajik, a tribe that served as a principal foe of the Pashtun people. Pakistan and the ISI were back in control. Their intention—which has held firm to the present day—has been to maintain the security of the Pakistani nation, whose western boundary continues to be defined by the Durand Line. Largely, this has led to the ISI's determination to assist the Taliban at every turn. This meant also, from the get-go, an all-out effort to thwart the will of the American and allied forces that had invaded the country and unseated the Taliban in order to install a pro-Western government in Kabul. Pro-Western is inevitably anti-Taliban and, definitionally, anti-Pashtun.

I'll dispense with the sad and sorry history of Western forces in Afghanistan—more than 2,000 American and 1,100 allied lives lost. The Costs of War Project of Brown University's Watson Institute has documented at least 157,000 people who've died in Afghanistan since the American invasion in 2001. Nearly 2.4 million Afghans were effectively exiled as of February 2020, according to the United Nations High Commisioner for Refugees. The pace of this carnage has barely relented. In July 2019, the UN Assistance Mission in Afghanistan recorded the highest number of civilian casualties ever recorded in a single month since its activities began ten years earlier. Long before this, the Afghan War had already become the United States's longest conflict, eclipsing even Vietnam and World War II. And for what end? The various lines have held. The Pashtun are on the verge of reclaiming the entirety of their home territory, and then some.

So, what then? Throughout, there has never been much sympathy at all to dismantling the Durand Line and all it has represented. Beginning with the presidency of Barack Obama and accelerating under Donald Trump, there have been repeated efforts to reach some sort of condominium with the Taliban, if there is even any such unitary organization that can be addressed. Certainly, there is what is known as the Quetta Shura, reflecting the town of Quetta in Pakistan where the long-time Taliban leader Mullah Omar sought refuge after the Western invasion. The concept of a *shura*, Arabic for "consultation" dates back to Mohammed and the Quran, encouraging all Muslims to consult all those who would be impacted by decisions that might be taken on their behalf. The membership of the Quetta Shura includes leaders of a number of Taliban factions, particularly the deadly Haqqani Network that maintains close ties with Pakistan's ISI and al-Qaeda, raising the specter of a return of the same rabidly anti-American terrorist organizations that launched 9/11, but are even more toxic today. Effectively, these Taliban have established an entire shadow government with every intention of reinstalling the same horrific power structure that terrorized women and girls who were deprived of any rights or education, destroyed historic monuments, and held the entire nation in the sway of a militant version of sharia justice underpinning one of the world's most despicable dictatorships.

When the Trump administration decided it wanted out of this region whose lines it no longer had the remotest ability to control, it began a long series of negotiations with putative representatives of this very Taliban organization. From the start, however, there was never any real assurance that the Taliban with whom they were dealing represented the factions of the Quetta Shura most committed to total victory in any fashion. Nor was there any real assurance that all the shura's members represented the entirety of the mujahideen battling American forces in the field or setting off deadly terrorist bombings in Kabul. At the same time, there were other separate diplomatic initiatives that threatened all such efforts to end the war and stem the Taliban's march toward full control again of Afghanistan. Foremost among these moves was Trump's own effort to cement a warm and deep friendship with India's right-wing leader, Narendra Modi, climaxing in a whirlwind visit by Trump that all but utterly ignored Pakistan and its leader. Pakistan and India have had a fraught relationship since the moment of their partition following the British departure in 1947. Each has raised substantial nuclear arsenals, targeted primarily on each other. And while India has tried its best to cement a close relationship with the pro-American government in Kabul, Pakistan and especially the ISI have found it both necessary and opportune to cement their relationships with the Taliban and Pashtuns. What possible motive could there be for the Taliban to conclude any meaningful agreement with the United States that would build friendly forces on either sides of the historic Durand Line that would be antipathetic to their ultimate goals of a return to power?

In fact, there is one real motive for any diplomatic discussions: getting American forces out of Afghanistan. This would inevitably allow the Taliban to reassert its control over both sides of the Durand Line—precisely what would most likely happen after the conclusion of any agreement that appeared to be successful from the American perspective.

Effectively, for the first time in its century and a half of existence, the Durand Line would cease, functionally, to exist. The results would be catastrophic for those who lived on both sides. With the Taliban and the ISI firmly in power, Afghanistan would revert to the medieval Islamic state it had become during the years prior to 9/11 and the American invasion. Yet President Trump was determined to go down as the individual who brought his troops home and ended the loss of American lives.

Trump was hardly the first to have attempted such an endeavor. As early as September 2007, Afghanistan's president at the time, Hamid Karzai, offered to open discussions with the Taliban while George W. Bush, who launched the war, was still America's president. Not surprisingly, the Taliban, still riding high and believing in their ultimate victory, rejected the overture out of hand. "Karzai government is a dummy government. It has no authority so why should we waste our time and effort," Taliban spokesman Qari Mohammed Yousuf told Reuters. "Until American and NATO troops are out of Afghanistan, talks with Karzai government are not possible."

Still, Karzai did not give up. In 2009, in a televised speech following his reelection, he told his people: "We call on our Taliban brothers to come home and embrace their land." Mullah Omar was still very much in charge of the Taliban. He had no interest. The Taliban saw themselves then, and still do today, as a group with a very long time horizon and a font of human resources far broader and deeper in their lands than anything America or its allies might bring. Like the Vietcong and North Vietnamese before them, they could simply wait it out. Still, a June 2019 report from the UN Security Council observed that "one of the most significant developments of the past 12 months has been increasing pressure from ordinary Afghans to bring an end to the fighting." This was a product of the latest of a string of unsuccessful ceasefires, from June 15 to 17, 2018, when some 25,000 to 30,000 Taliban "entered government-controlled cities, towns and villages. These Taliban engaged in direct peaceful contact . . . with government officials and members of the Afghan National Defence and Security Forces in an unprecedented display of good will." The Taliban leadership panicked at this exercise and the potential outcome. By the second day, Taliban leaders called such behavior by their forces "treasonous" and ordered it to cease, a day later demanding that all its fighters "leave government-controlled areas by sunset of the same day and resume *jihad* against the Afghan government." This reminded me enormously of the interaction between the Khmer Rouge and the Cambodian people in the final days of the war in Cambodia in 1975. Many Cambodians, including my interpreter and photographer, Dith Pran, wanted desperately for the war to be over at any price, even a Khmer Rouge "victory." "Afterwards," Pran would tell me before the final victory of the insurgents, "we will all find ways to live together in peace.

After all, we are all Khmers." How wrong that turned out to be. The Khmer Rouge, living apart from the vast mass of their people for so many years, engaged in desperate struggles against overwhelming forces of foreigners or locals backed by foreign armies, were determined to establish an utterly dissonant society. They were not "all Khmers" except in the language they spoke. There were the victors and the vanquished. The Taliban, I fear, have the same mentality. The Taliban leadership, according to the Security Council report, "took action to carry out a systematic replacement of all Taliban commanders believed to have shown reluctance in preventing their fighters from fraternizing with Afghan citizens in government-controlled areas. Those commanders relieved of their positions were replaced by more hardline Taliban, often from other provinces, or supported by the Haqqani Network."

At the same time, the Taliban do not lack for resources. They maintain a vast annual income from a host of activities, which the UN singles out as "narcotics, illicit mineral and other resource extraction, taxation, extortion, the sale of commercial and government services and property, and donations from abroad." They cultivate at least 263,000 hectares of poppy production (650,000 acres, more than 1,000 square miles, or nearly the size of the state of Rhode Island), exporting some $400 million worth of product.

Indeed, the Taliban has effectively been operating an entire nation in parallel with that of the government based in the capital of Kabul and established in elections that really encompass only the fraction of the geography and people of Afghanistan it controls. The new empire the Taliban will establish and the lines they will draw will be simply a reversion—even a more toxic version—of the one they had already established more than two decades ago. They have had all this time to understand more deeply the errors they made and that will not be repeated. There will be no tolerance, no sensitivity. Certainly, no democracy.

Still, America pressed ahead. Meetings in the last half of 2019 everywhere from Brussels to Moscow including Pakistan, France, Germany, Italy, Norway, Britain, the European Union, Russia, even China were intended to find some way forward. It finally all came together in Qatar. This Persian Gulf emirate has long sought to punch beyond its weight, and succeeded. It is in Doha that Al Jazeera, the Arab world's leading television news network, was born and remains headquartered. Qatar has also served as the site and source of a host of important efforts at mediation from the moment in 1995 when Emir Hamad bin Khalifa Al Thani assumed the throne of the tiny emirate. Early on, he served as a neutral party among a host of factions in Lebanon, where the emir cultivated close relationships with Hezbollah. He arranged for peace in Darfur, rallied the Arab League for interventions from Libya to Syria, even provided financing for Egypt's

Muslim Brotherhood in the days following the Arab Spring. So, it was hardly surprising that the Taliban looked to Qatar when they were considering where to establish their first mission abroad. Qatar provided a most hospitable environment—comfortable homes, an entire lifestyle underwritten by the Qataris, even as the delegation's numbers in Qatar grew from a handful to dozens.

The first talks began in 2010 and after two desultory years, sputtered as they focused on prisoner exchanges that seemed non-starters. The delegations included the insurgent group led by Mullah Omar and later his successors, traveling to Qatar via Pakistan. Still, there were other, especially toxic Taliban, most based in Afghanistan and scattered elements in Pakistan, who had never played a role in negotiations. In 2013, however, talks resumed in Qatar, and the following year, these Taliban negotiators won the release of five of their number who'd been imprisoned for thirteen years in Guantanamo Bay, Cuba, in exchange for the freedom of Sergeant Bowe Bergdahl, who'd been seized after wandering off from his unit in Afghanistan five years earlier. The Taliban Five, as they became known, were flown to Qatar, where under terms of the agreement they were to be held for one year.

Five years later, they were still in Qatar. Talks continued on and off. But Donald Trump, who arrived in office in January 2017, was determined to go down in history as the person who ended America's longest war. In September 2018, Trump named Zalmay Khalilzad, who'd served as ambassador to Afghanistan under George W. Bush, as special envoy to Afghanistan and the peace process. As it happens, Khalilzad, a Sunni Muslim, is himself an ethnic Pashtun, or at least claims Pashtun origins. Talks began shortly after his appointment. Across the table were Taliban leaders and, quite pointedly, the Taliban Five. On February 29, 2020, a peace deal was signed in Qatar in the convention hall of an opulent hotel by Khalilzad and Mullah Abdul Ghani Baradar, described as the deputy leader of the Taliban. What has never been perfectly clear is precisely what that meant. Which Taliban did he represent? As a witness to the signing was Secretary of State Mike Pompeo, who called the moment "historic." The Taliban said they hoped it would lead to a "permanent solution" to the violence in Afghanistan. But even that seemed an open question. A precondition for the signing was a seven-day period of "reduction in violence" by all sides—American, Afghan, and Taliban forces who pledged no offensive operations. The calm appeared to hold. Just barely. Indeed, the Taliban's spokesman in Qatar observed that with the signing, the period of reduced violence that was to last for a week had "ended." The agreement also called for the Taliban to break with al-Qaeda. And intra-Afghan talks including representatives of the government in Kabul were to begin in ten days. Within 135 days, the United States also pledged a first withdrawal of

8,600 troops to be accompanied by a proportional draw down of other allied and coalition forces. From Washington, Trump issued a statement that contained considerable hope, perhaps more than might ultimately be warranted:

> If the Taliban and the government of Afghanistan live up to these commit-
> ments, we will have a powerful path forward to end the war in Afghanistan
> and bring our troops home. These commitments represent an important step
> to a lasting peace in a new Afghanistan, free from Al Qaeda, ISIS, and any
> other terrorist group that would seek to bring us harm. Ultimately it will be
> up to the people of Afghanistan to work out their future. We, therefore, urge
> the Afghan people to seize this opportunity for peace and a new future for
> their country.

There was way more in this statement than was contained in the agreement. The hope was that this pact would return the region to much the same historic status promised by the Durand Line nearly a century and a half before. Still, there is the suggestion in its language of much of the lasting power behind any red line. "Ultimately it will be up to the people of Afghanistan to work out their future," the President said. Indeed, any red line is in the final analysis no stronger than the will of the people on both sides to accept it.

The people on both sides of the Durand Line played little role in its establishment. But for generations they have learned how to live with it. Since at least 85 percent of the 1,640-mile-long line follows natural boundaries, from rivers to mountain crests, it bisects ancestral Pashtun tribal holdings and communities. More than forty million Pashtuns in the region would love to be united in a single nation, taking down the Durand Line and creating a nation of Pashtunistan, which would include some forty thousand square miles of territory inside Pakistan. That is unlikely ever to happen. But across a dozen or more mountain passes, the tribes have managed to maintain their identity and accept each reality that's been presented.

Whether this can be accomplished peacefully now is another question entirely. Within three weeks of the signing of this agreement, it was already unravelling. In March 2020, Secretary of State Mike Pompeo flew to Kabul on an urgent "diplomatic rescue mission," which failed to produce any path forward. To complicate matters, a deeply disputed Afghanistan election left the nation with two feuding presidents and their respective governments, each vying for control of whatever territory the Taliban does not control in whole or in part. On his way out of the country, Pompeo slashed $1 billion of some

$4.5 billion in annual American military and political aid, threatening a repeat next year. His final stop, in Qatar, proved equally disappointing. The Taliban there pledged to avoid attacks on US forces, but in the three weeks after the agreement was signed, more than a hundred Afghan troops and civilians died in escalating violence.

"I went there to try and—I'm sorry," Pompeo told the press traveling with him as he flew out of his final meeting in Doha. "Look, there's places where progress has been made. The reduction of violence is real. It's not perfect, but it's in a place that's pretty good. We're continuing to honor our commitment that says that we will engage only when we are attacked. There haven't been attacks on American forces since the peace agreement was signed, what, three weeks ago now, three and a half weeks ago." And then he tossed off perhaps the most trenchant comment since the process began, and which bodes least well for the future: "There's a long history," said Pompeo, who at times seems to have a grasp of history, having graduated first in his class from West Point. "There are lots of power centers in Afghanistan." And he concluded, "These are the expectations that we have, that the Afghans themselves will lead this path forward. Their leaders need to do that, all of their various leaders."

What is especially telling is that at no time did Pompeo or any senior American official make contact with any official at a high level in Pakistan. In the case of any red line there must be buy-ins from both sides if it is to work and achieve long-term stability with any degree of peace. There is no sense that there is any real buy-in from Pakistan, especially its most independent-minded ISI. Nor is there any real indication of a buy-in from Taliban fighters out in the maquis, many of whom have been and will continue receiving help and support from Pakistani elements devoted to preserving Taliban loyalty to their anti-Indian agenda. Moreover, even if those negotiating do represent a body of the fighting force, there is no sense that Western negotiators will ever be in a position to sit down across a table from the most obdurate, those most committed to an armed solution to the entire problem. These remain utterly committed to waiting as long as it takes to arrive at one. Such complications will inevitably transcend any agreement that may be signed in Kabul, Doha, or any other location.

And the question of peace on two sides of an intractable red line is the same dilemma that has confronted Palestinians and Jews two thousand miles to the west.

—

As we have seen, Jews have been an integral part of the Holy Land for at least two millennia, living side by side with a host of conquerors and indigenous non-Jews—first with

Arab Christians after the first century c.e. and, eventually, after the arrival of Mohammed five centuries later, with Islamized Arabs. They were subsumed into the Ottoman Empire, where they managed to coexist for four hundred years with the Islamic rulers of Constantinople as key elements of the province of Syria. By 1896, they had become a majority in the city of Jerusalem. Four years earlier, Chaim Weizmann, born in Belarus, part of the Russian Empire, left for Germany to pursue his studies as a chemist, working as a Hebrew teacher at a Jewish boarding school to earn a meager living. He'd already embraced Zionism and by the time he moved to England as a brilliant young chemist, he was fully committed to turning Palestine into the Jewish homeland. Shortly after his arrival as a professor at the University of Manchester, Weizmann met Arthur Balfour, the local MP and later foreign secretary during World War I. At the same time, however, Weizmann was pursuing his experimental work in chemistry. And shortly before the outbreak of hostilities, discovered a way of artificially creating acetone, a critical component in making the cordite explosives integral to bombs. At about that time, Britain was also seeking a way to weaken the Ottoman Empire and build its own influence in the Middle East. Weizmann had developed this pitch:

> Should Palestine fall within the British sphere of influence and should Britain encourage a Jewish settlement there, as a British dependency, we could have in twenty to thirty years a million Jews out there, perhaps more; they would develop the country, bring back civilization to it, form a very effective guard for the Suez Canal.

His pitch contained three central and powerful elements for British politicians of the time that would lead to the creation, three decades later, of the State of Israel: Palestine for the British, development and modernization of a desert wasteland, and a loyal and powerful ally prepared to do battle in defense of the Suez Canal—the fastest and most direct route to India and the East. Britain's indebtedness to this brilliant young chemist and its own self-interest in building its presence in the Middle East and protecting the Suez Canal, while at the same time weakening the Ottoman enemy, were a decisive and politically potent cocktail. David Lloyd George would later tell friends that he had "rewarded" Weizmann with a Jewish homeland in Palestine for his donation of the formula to produce vast quantities of acetone. In fact, the political and diplomatic pirouette that led to this homeland was a trifle more complex. The route wound through a friendship that had developed between Weizmann and Sir Mark Sykes, chief secretary of the war cabinet who, with his French counterpart, François

Georges-Picot, drafted the secret Sykes-Picot Agreement dividing the Middle East between the two allied powers. This pact rewarded a large swath of Palestine to the French, though the war cabinet, even Sykes himself, believed Britain had every right to much of Palestine, Greater Syria, and Iraq, which the agreement had awarded to France. Weizmann lobbied mightily for the position that France should have rights that did not extend beyond "Syria, as far as Beyrouth [since] the so-called French influence which is merely spiritual and religious, is predominant in Syria. In Palestine, there is very little of it. . . . The only work which may be termed civilizing pioneer work has been carried out by the Jews."

On November 18, 1917, with Weizmann waiting outside the door, the War Cabinet met, with Lord Balfour presenting a text. Minutes later, Sykes emerged, waving the document, proclaiming, "Dr. Weizmann, it's a boy." In fact, it was the Balfour Declaration, framed as a letter from Balfour to the powerful leader of the British Jewish community Lord Lionel de Rothschild:

> His Majesty's Government view with favour the establishment in Palestine of a National Home for the Jewish people, and will use their best endeavors to facilitate the achievement of this object, it being clearly understood that nothing shall be done which may prejudice the civil and religious rights of the existing non-Jewish communities in Palestine or the rights and political status enjoyed by Jews of any other country.

Chaim Weizmann meets Faisal bin Hussein (Aqaba, Jordan).

Weizmann promptly set off on a trip to Palestine for a meeting in the desert, arranged by T. E. Lawrence, with the Arab leader Faisal bin Hussein, third son of the grand sharif of Mecca. Lawrence believed the Jews could do much to advance the Arab agenda in the region—namely ridding themselves of their Ottoman overlords. The result was a two-hour conference in which the Zionist leader explained that the Jews intended "to do everything in our power to allay Arab fears and susceptibilities, and our hope that he would lend his powerful moral support." Over thick, sweet coffee and tea there was very much a meeting of minds, so much so that Faisal insisted that a remarkable photo be taken of them outside his tent, Weizmann donning the traditional Arab headdress atop his three-piece white linen suit, Faisal in the robes of a Bedouin warrior.

Of course, there was much work left before the Jewish state of Israel would be created three decades later. In 1922, a British census showed the total population of Palestine as 757,182 people, "of whom 590,890 were Mohammedans, 83,794 Jews and 82,498 Christians and others." Then the Jewish migration began. By 1930, there were 162,059 Jews and 692,195 Muslims, though the birthrate was higher among the Muslim population. When the Jews came, they were prepared to pay for Arab lands where they might settle, though in 1922 they held barely 14 percent of the total arable land. The same British census document observed:

> The Arabs have regarded with suspicion measures taken by the Government with the best intentions. The transfer of land ordinance [of] 1920, which requires that the consent of the Government must be obtained to all dispositions of immovable property, and forbids transfer to other than residents in Palestine, they regard as having been introduced to keep down the price of land and to throw land which is in the market into the hands of the Jews at a low price.

The basis was being laid for future problems between the Jews and the Arabs, who would see themselves as increasingly disenfranchised and impoverished. In the course of the 1930s, the trickle of Jews to Palestine rose dramatically—from 3,265 in 1930 to a peak of 61,458 in 1937. At the same time, the mix was beginning to swing as well—Jews with 17 percent and Arabs 74 percent of the population in 1931 to 30 percent and 60 percent respectively by the end of the decade. By the time of the creation of the State of Israel in 1948, Jews outnumbered Arabs 716,700 to 156,000.

The physical boundaries of the State of Israel were effectively drawn and little changed by the British in the course of their mandate over Palestine. This included what is today considered the Palestinian territory of Gaza (a theoretically self-governing territory of Israel) and the lands along the West Bank of the Jordan River. From the moment of its creation, Israel was challenged by massive armed reactions from Arab armies. At least three times over the next half century—the Arab-Israeli War of 1948, the Six-Day War of June 1967, and the Yom Kippur War of October 1973—Arab forces attempted to force their way past the red line that was Israel's fiercely defended boundary.

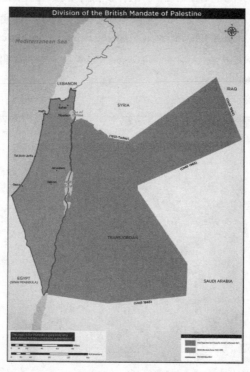

The British mandate over Palestine: the Jewish settlements west of the Jordan River and the eastern region, closed to Jewish settlements beginning in 1921.

Each time, Israel fended off these attacks from the outside, even managing to expand its frontiers, in the face often of all but unanimous condemnation by the outside world, including the United Nations and its Security Council. After the 1948 war, with the Green Line border—a red line that held for nineteen years until the Six-Day War—Israel retained territories that included East Jerusalem, the West Bank, Gaza Strip, Golan Heights, and Sinai Peninsula. Little of this territory was part of the original boundary established by Britain when it allowed the creation of the Jewish state. But Israeli leaders believed that retaining and expanding the nation's red lines provided vital buffers against further challenges, including the expansion of Israel's "narrow waist" that could be used to divide Israel in half. Palestinians and their organizations, particularly the Palestine Liberation Organization (PLO), had by that time seized on the Gaza Strip and the West Bank as their future homeland, though Israel still considered them as having been absorbed into its newly expanded home. Following the Six-Day War, Israel seized the Golan Heights, but as part of the truce agreed to return the Sinai Peninsula to Egypt and the Golan to Syria. It retained the Gaza Strip and the West Bank—which put Israel in direct conflict with the view of the UN Security Council, which voted unanimously on November 22, 1967, to approve Resolution 242 introduced by the British representative, Lord Caradon. It called for Israel to relinquish these territories and even drew a map of what it viewed as the nation's new red line.

Firm lines begin to be drawn, all too often at the tip of a spear.

Six years later came the Yom Kippur War, a joint surprise attack by a coalition of Arab armies on the holiest day of the year in Judaism. Egyptian forces crossed the Suez Canal and advanced through the Sinai, while Syria struck from the Golan Heights. The Israeli military retaliated by air and land on all fronts, and within two weeks of the invasion had utterly humiliated the entire Arab armed force. Finally, US Secretary of State Henry Kissinger called a news conference at the State Department, proclaiming:

> Our position is that . . . the conditions that produced this war were clearly intolerable to the Arab nations and that in the process of negotiations it will be necessary to make substantial concessions. The problem will be to relate the Arab concern for the sovereignty over the territories to the Israeli concern for secure boundaries. We believe that the process of negotiations between the parties is an essential component of this. . . . We will make a major effort to bring about a solution that is considered just by all parties.

Kissinger recognized that the Palestinians needed some hope of a future homeland, perhaps outside of the Israeli envelope. "Palestinian interests and aspirations are a reality, and the U.S. has recognized publicly that no settlement is possible without taking them into account," Kissinger wrote in a "top secret/eyes only" cable to General Vernon Walters, who was in touch with Palestinian leaders. "In the context of a settlement, the U.S. would be more than eager to contribute to the well-being and progress of the Palestinian people."

Since the Yom Kippur War, the last full-scale conflict between Israel and any external armed force, there have been a host of efforts by internal and outside parties and military groups to breach or shrink the red line that Israel has long maintained and sought to expand. Two intifadas, or large-scale Palestinian uprisings against Israel in Gaza and the West Bank, were accompanied by a war in southern Lebanon that Israel launched in an effort to break down the paramilitary forces of Hezbollah. In between, there were innumerable actions by Israel against Palestinian forces and the militant organization Hamas, now the de facto governing authority of the Gaza Strip—often efforts to halt rocket and other attacks on Israeli border settlements.

A number of diplomatic initiatives were launched with the same end in view. Six months after the Yom Kippur War, Henry Kissinger, Secretary of State and National Security Adviser to President Richard Nixon, embarked on two extended sets of "shuttle diplomacy"—traveling, with a team of aides and a phalanx of journalists, between Cairo and Jerusalem in January and again in May of 1974. He was accompanied by his principal deputy, Peter W. Rodman, who helped Kissinger chronicle this extensively in *Years of Upheaval* and for the Office of the Historian of the State Department.

His first trip brought an end to the uneasy truce between Israel and Egypt and staged a withdrawal by Israel from the Sinai Peninsula, shrinking the red line that had expanded exponentially at the end of hostilities. In eight vigorous days, Kissinger bludgeoned both sides into a first pullback, and in September 1975, a second disengagement that would have the effect of removing Israel largely from the Sinai Peninsula. Its red line retreated up the Gulf of Aqaba to the southern tip of Jordan, where it remains today. It would also leave Egypt in control of the vital Suez Canal and the Gulf of Suez, though it would guarantee the right of Israeli shipping to transit the Canal, the Straits of Tiran, and the Bab el-Mandeb.

In May 1974, Kissinger tried his same magic on Syria with another round of shuttle diplomacy between Jerusalem and Damascus, with the added hope that an agreement on that front would persuade OPEC to lift the embargo on oil shipments to the United States that was crippling the American economy. On May 31, the two countries signed an agreement and Israel pulled out of the Golan. The Israeli red lines had effectively returned to the *status quo ante bellum*, where they remain today.

A succession of future peace negotiations, some more or less successful, had little or no impact on the configuration of the red lines that divided Israelis from their Arab neighbors. Jimmy Carter, his National Security Advisor Zbigniew Brzezinski, and Secretary of State Cyrus Vance engineered the Camp David Accords after bringing Israeli Prime Minister Menachem Begin together with Egyptian President Anwar Sadat for twelve days in 1978. It was, in many ways, the most consequential of a host of such peace negotiations, though in the end the United Nations refused to recognize it. The Camp David agreement did result in, as Jimmy Carter would later put it, "Arab recognition of Israel's right to exist in peace," effectively recognizing the red lines surrounding the Jewish state that had existed at least since its creation in 1948. Israel also pledged "withdrawal from the occupied territories, with exceptions to be negotiated for Israel's security." The pact also established, as Carter put it, "a contiguous, or Palestinian state, with—to use Prime Minister Begin's phrase, 'full autonomy for the Palestinians' or to use his more precise phrase, 'Palestinian Arabs'—because he maintained to me that Israeli Jews were also Palestinians." The final provision was "an undivided Jerusalem" which was in the end deleted from the final document. And, as Carter conceded twenty-five years later, "those were the basic elements for peace, but obviously, peace was not achieved."

What is critical for this discussion, however, is not the issue of a lasting or especially comprehensive peace but rather the nature of the territory and the boundaries that were left behind. The land of Palestine—Gaza and the West Bank—remained from the Israeli point of view within the borders of Israel, as it recognized the envelope of its frontiers. Under the Camp David Accords, the Palestinians were given the right to establish a "self-governing authority," which has done little to change any of the boundaries involved. The United Nations General Assembly quickly and definitively refused to recognize the Accords since neither the UN nor the PLO (then under the leadership of Yasser Arafat) participated in the negotiations and the Palestinians did not win the "right of return," self-determination, or national independence and sovereignty, as was available to Jews and Israelis. Effectively that would have meant dramatically redrawing Israel's red lines, very much endangering the viability of these lines and the security of the Israeli heartland.

Twenty years later, in September 1995, President Bill Clinton tried again, bringing Israeli Prime Minister Yitzhak Rabin and PLO chairman Yasser Arafat together in Washington to conclude a new agreement. This time the negotiations would include the Palestinians. The resulting document detailed the establishment of Palestinian entities on the West Bank and Gaza, particularly the Palestinian Council and an "elected Ra'ees of the Executive Authority" to govern both areas. Sadly, it did little to ease the ongoing levels of tension, all too often erupting into violence in both areas that continues now and likely well into the future along the lines of demarcation that were established, only with some largely unworkable elasticity.

At the same time, this only elevated what is effectively an existential debate that has continued as a *basso continuo* to Israeli politics for much of Israel's existence—a one-state versus a two-state solution to the Palestinian question. Should Palestinians and their Gaza and West Bank territories be simply incorporated into the State of Israel and all Palestinians become full-fledged Israeli citizens? Or should Gaza and the West Bank become a separate, recognized Palestinian nation? There is a fundamental problem.

The land area of Israel and the two Palestinian territories is wildly unbalanced—respectively 21,671 square kilometers versus 5,506 square kilometers. But the Palestinian population has been increasing at a dramatically faster rate than the Jewish population. In March 2018, Colonel Uri Mendes of the military-run civil administration of the West Bank and Gaza told the Knesset (the Israeli parliament) that West Bank territories' population alone totaled "between 2.5 million and 2.7 million," though he conceded that a Palestinian census showed that number as closer to 3 million. Add in 2 million that Avi Dichter, former head of the Shin Bet internal security force, estimates live in Gaza and you have nearly 5 million Palestinians. Combined with 1.84 million Arabs living inside Israel, you arrive at nearly 7 million Arabs, as well as a small number of Christians, all within what would be the boundaries of a single, unified Israeli state. According to the Israeli Census Bureau, that is nearly the same as the number of Jews living in the State of Israel. Moreover, Palestinian families are averaging five children (down from seven, twenty years ago), outpacing Jewish population growth. This means that within the next decade, Jews would become a minority in their own land. The situation could well become not unlike that of South Africa under apartheid, when a white minority was governing an oppressed and disenfranchised majority—becoming a global pariah among nations as it sought to defend its own utterly indefensible (on moral, political, and diplomatic grounds) red lines. Or, alternatively, a Jewish minority would be governed—if the same democratic model of government were maintained—by a Palestinian majority. Israel's red line frontiers, then, would become all but meaningless. None of this seems very likely to happen. A two-state solution would seem to be the only viable formula for maintaining the seven-decade-old red line of the Israeli frontier.

Effectively, however, for nearly two decades, Prime Minister Benjamin Netanyahu has been endeavoring, through a creeping red line, to resolve this problem without another full-scale war, but at the same time without enfranchising the Palestinians. Netanyahu has led Israel for some fourteen years over two separate stints that straddled two centuries. Three months into his second term, in June 2009, the prime minister announced the road map for his version of a two-state solution: immediate renewal of talks with the Palestinian Authority for self-government, as long as that doesn't endanger Israel; West Bank settlements would not be "an obstacle to peace." But even then, it became clear that the train was poised to go imminently off the rails. A freeze on new construction of settlements on the West Bank was nothing more than a pledge—at least for a certain limited time—and with no enforcement mechanism. Barack Obama, whose special envoy George Mitchell was in charge of talks with the Israeli government, was never happy at all with the pace or direction of negotiations on such a freeze, which turned out to be utterly ephemeral.

Over the next dozen years, settlements continued to mushroom, stretching the eastern red line of Israel recognized by UN fiat and international law far into areas nominally Palestinian but, in reality, firmly behind the Israelis' intended red line. In March 2020, Israel's defense minister, Naftali Bennett, even approved a master project, called "Sovereignty Road," designed to separate Palestinian and Israeli motorists, as one Israeli journalist put it, "to enable construction of settlements of a highly sensitive area . . . near East Jerusalem." Such a project had been frozen for nearly a decade. Now it was full speed ahead.

All this was happening just as Donald Trump was unveiling his own, stillborn peace plan for Israel. Early in his presidency, Trump put his Jewish son-in-law, Jared Kushner, in charge of this delicate, highly fraught subject. The then thirty-six-year-old New York real estate developer had no diplomatic experience and for much of the early gestation of this project was even denied top secret security status that seemed indispensable for his success. Moreover, if there were ever an opportunity for either side to come together on such an agreement, that possibility ended a month after Kushner's appointment with the decision announced on December 6, 2017, by Trump to move the American embassy in Israel from Tel Aviv to Jerusalem. The status of this city, it must be remembered, has never been fully adjudicated between Jews, Muslims, and Christians, since all the major religions have important claims on parts of the Holy City. Palestinians were outraged. Five months later, on May 13, 2018, when the ceremony of transfer was held, more than 10,000 Palestinians protested along the border fence with Gaza, leaving 2,700 injured, with at least 1,350 wounded by Israeli military gunfire and 58 killed, including several teenagers. Jared Kushner attended the opening ceremony, standing in front of a huge American flag and embassy seal as a video message from his father-in-law played to the gathering. The president pledged the United States "remains fully committed to facilitating a lasting peace agreement."

There followed two years of frantic settlement building across the West Bank. "Netanyahu has chosen to cross the red lines and take us all with them," Nir Hasson, a columnist for the leading Israeli daily *Haaretz*, wrote in February 2020. Construction on the West Bank, he continued, "makes a future Palestinian state unimaginable." Still, desultory discussions continued between Kushner and Israeli officials, since the Palestinians declined even to receive Kushner or any other American as long as the embassy remained in Jerusalem.

Then, on January 28, 2020, President Trump, joined by Netanyahu at the White House, unveiled the peace plan. The outlines of the full 181-page plan were simple. The most critical issue, for this discussion, is the precise boundaries of the "new" Israel and the territories identified as Palestinian. As many commentators in both the United States and Israel observed, "The maps show Israel, the West Bank and Gaza Strip as a single unit, a series of numbered 'Israeli enclave communities' in what is today the West Bank." The fifteen carefully named and numbered "Israeli enclave communities" are settlements that Netanyahu managed to have established before the map was printed. Some sort of tunnel is also shown running beneath Israel and connecting the two enclaves—Gaza and the West Bank.

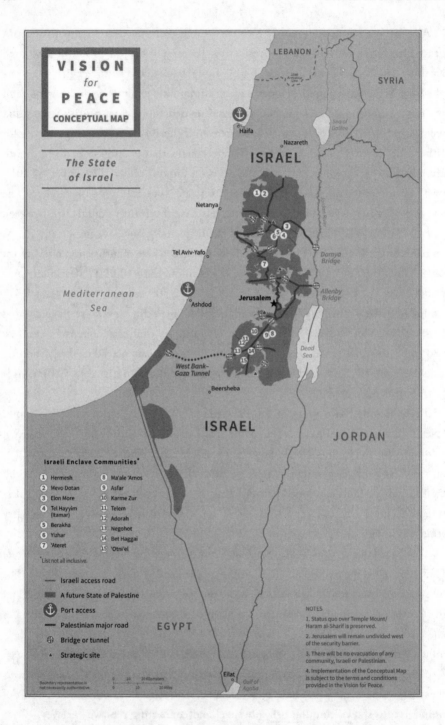

Jared Kushner's "Vision for Peace" . . . conceptually.

The Palestinian authority promptly labeled the entire deal "utterly unacceptable and grossly unjust." Indeed, the "talking points," which Kushner and the State Department cabled to all American embassies, a copy of which was obtained by *Politico*, were all but ludicrous in many of their claims:

- This is the first time Israel has ever agreed to a public map detailing the borders of a two-state solution.
- For the first time, the State of Israel has agreed to recognize a future State of Palestine, based on a map that is included in the Vision.
- This Vision ensures the future State of Palestine is viable, connected, and reasonably comparable in size to the territory of the West Bank and Gaza pre-1967.
- Israel has agreed to comport its policies to this Vision for at least four years, including freezing all settlement activity in the West Bank in areas that this Vision designates for the future State of Palestine.
- The status quo is not acceptable.

On August 13, 2020, Trump triumphantly announced, in a tweet, a first major breakthrough toward redrawing at least a portion of the century's worth of red lines that had threatened to harden irrevocably in this region:

HUGE breakthrough today! Historic Peace Agreement between our two GREAT friends, Israel and the United Arab Emirates!

The United Arab Emirates agreed to establish formal diplomatic relations with Israel. Trump credited his son-in-law, though it is likely that other forces were at work—especially a fear of Iran's growing reach and hostility that screamed out for a more united and coherent response across the region. But of greater importance to the geography of red lines was the quid pro quo to which Israel agreed. As the White House put it:

As a result of this diplomatic breakthrough and at the request of President Trump with the support of the United Arab Emirates, Israel will suspend declaring sovereignty over areas outlined in the President's Vision for Peace and focus its efforts now on expanding ties with other countries in the Arab and Muslim world.

There were certain red flags immediately visible in this statement. First, Israel had only agreed to "suspend" declaring sovereignty over the new territories. It had done so before and quickly regressed. Second, there appeared to be a certain conditionality that ties with other Arab nations might be necessary before there was any permanent Israeli agreement to establish firm new lines with these territories in Palestinian hands.

Sheikh Mohammed bin Zayed Al Nahyan, crown prince of Abu Dhabi and deputy supreme commander the UAE armed forces has long served as a major power broker in the region. If the pact with the UAE could be cemented—the first with a major Arab nation since Israel and Jordan signed a peace agreement in October 1994—then it is not inconceivable that similar agreements could be concluded with Saudi Arabia or other regional powers that could force Israel really to adhere to the boundaries agreed upon in the UAE accord.

Of course, there have been any number of maps delimiting red lines, the boundaries of Israel, the extent of its penetration into conquered territories, and its willingness to withdraw over the past seventy years. In the Kushner peace map delineating the new boundaries of Israel and Palestine, there is a host of other problems. The tunnel that appears to link Gaza with the West Bank territories is itself stunningly ill-conceived. Would Israel ever let a tunnel be built entirely under its land that could be a focal point of attacks on Israeli territory above? It has done its best to dismantle a number of tunnels built into Gaza, for instance, that have been used to smuggle arms and explosives into this Palestinian territory from Egypt. Freezing settlement activity on the West Bank, of course, has never happened at all, as the map accompanying the "Vision" so graphically demonstrates.

About all that is accurate in these talking points is the final one. The status quo is indeed not acceptable, not even tenable in the final analysis. Does that mean, however, that this—one of our three intractable red lines—is in danger of dissolution? Not at all. Creeping red lines—for this is precisely the nature of the lines delimiting Israel's liquid frontiers—may hold for a very long time if there is a surfeit of power on one side. But in the long run, they will never work. What is essential is for a brilliant, well-intentioned outside arbiter with no clear agenda to find a way of making these lines permanent, or drawing them in a fashion where everyone on both sides can live and prosper.

Two decades ago, I had lunch in New York with an Israeli minister of finance. He had an interesting idea. Why not, he posited, help the Palestinians really understand the value of a cooperative arrangement that could reach across this red line, the failings of which he understood with profound clarity. He'd begun already, in fact, to establish a fund that would finance, using Israeli and American private and public funds, new and vibrant Palestinian businesses. By seeing graphic demonstrations of what was possible—jobs, growth, prosperity, and peace—might his adversaries not appreciate the real, human, and material value of a bridge? It seemed like a brilliant and utterly worthwhile idea. Two months later, he was ousted in one of the innumerable cabinet shuffles that have made Israeli politics and its revolving-door democracy so problematic in the pursuit of peace and a stable red line regime. His idea died with him.

—

Vladimir Putin has never been very happy about the extension of the immutable line that defines the peripheries of NATO, especially as the alliance expanded dramatically with the addition of former Warsaw Pact allies, even former Soviet republics, as his beloved Soviet Union came unglued. He has repeatedly poked and prodded it, testing it at every perceived vulnerable point. Putin came to power at a particularly tumultuous moment in Russia's history. Russia was on the verge of collapse. In the midst of a vicious war in the breakaway province of Chechnya, a series of bombings of massive apartment blocks in Moscow, Buynaksk, and Volgodonsk, left more than three hundred dead and a thousand injured, spreading fear across the country. The economy, too, was collapsing. A decaying, alcoholic president, Boris Yeltsin, named former KGB officer Vladimir Putin as his prime minister. Putin went to work. On December 31, 1999, Yeltsin resigned and Putin took over. For the next five years, Putin focused on bolstering the impoverished nation, building on the support of a host of oligarchs, and quickly strengthening Russia's armed forces.

By 2007, Putin was ready. His first direct target was the former Soviet republic, now independent nation, of Estonia. As detailed in Chapter Five, Moscow embarked on a full-scale, eventually crippling, cyberattack that lasted three weeks and was quickly traced to Russian sources. Estonia had become a member of NATO just three years earlier along with the two other Baltic republics, Latvia and Lithuania. Several years later, when I visited Estonia, I asked its foreign minister at the time, Urmas Paet, why his nation had not invoked Article Five of the NATO charter, which holds that an attack on one member is an attack on all. There were no actual casualties of this war, Paet told me. That was his red line. Unlike the 9/11 attack—the only time in history that Article Five has been invoked—this one had not led to any loss of life. What it did accomplish, however, was the creation in May 2008 of the NATO Cooperative Cyber Defence Centre. Located in an old Soviet-era brick military post on the outskirts of Tallinn, it has been transformed into a bulwark against large-scale attacks on NATO by any power, with Russia clearly the leading target. Indeed, the Kremlin seems to have learned that lesson. NATO's cyber red line has never been tested again in any such systematic fashion. Even the Russian attack on the United States' 2016 election processes never rose to the level of virtual invasion as the across-the-board attack on Estonia's entire infrastructure and government. Putin has clearly learned, at least in this respect, how far he could go.

One of Putin's objectives is to reassemble, wherever possible, the Soviet empire, which in his heart he believed had been torn apart unreasonably. Following in Yeltsin's footsteps at least in this one respect, Putin has had some success in retaining a number of former Soviet republics, particularly the Asian 'Stans. Putin's efforts have succeeded in several respects. Effectively, he has been building his own new red line in opposition to NATO and with a nod to the old Warsaw Pact. Forming the Commonwealth of Independent States (CIS), each member state, with the exception of Moldova, signed the Collective Security Treaty, known as the Tashkent Pact, though Uzbekistan has since withdrawn. Like the Warsaw Pact before it, the military forces of the various members have held periodic maneuvers to "boost [their] joint defense capabilities," according to Russian news dispatches. Moreover, the FSB, the successor security service to the Soviet-era KGB, maintains close ties with the security services of most of these states, particularly in the Central Asian regions, according to two Russian investigative journalists, Andrei Soldatov and Irina Borogan, who have made a career out of chronicling the work of the FSB at home and abroad. In 2000, the year Putin came to power in Moscow, "Russia backed the establishment of a CIS Antiterrorist Center, headquartered in Moscow with a Central Asia branch in Bishkek, Kyrgyzstan," Soldatov and Borogan wrote, adding that its "mandate was to create a database for intelligence sharing among the security services of all member countries."

All of these nations are Putin's "near abroad," and he has been determined to make certain that he holds his friends close and any potential enemies closer. Clearly, the Baltic republics were a difficult loss. But having been gathered behind the NATO red line, reclaiming them was just one step too challenging. Not surprisingly, Putin's next two adventures were against Georgia in 2008 and Crimea, followed by Ukraine itself, in 2014. These two adventures have proven to be substantial victories for Putin. His seizure of Crimea and prompt incorporation of this strategic region into the Russian nation was the first substantial redrawing of Russian boundaries since the collapse of the Soviet Union itself. But the rest of these adventures also had some profound successes in that they had the effect of redrawing psychological red lines that are equally strategic to Putin and, conversely should be equally disappointing to NATO. Neither Georgia nor Ukraine—despite their election of pro-Western leaders in recent years—have taken any significant steps toward joining NATO. In December 2017, at a NATO foreign ministers meeting, the alliance's secretary general observed broadly, "The Alliance is fully committed to providing Georgia with the advice and tools it needs to advance toward eventual NATO membership." The operative word, no doubt hardly lost on the Kremlin, was "eventual." Two years later, Russian Foreign Minister Sergei Lavrov pointed out on the occasion of resumption of direct flights between Russia and Tbilisi, "I confirm that we do not want to see NATO near us," adding that if Georgia did accept an offer of NATO membership "we will not start a war, but such conduct will undermine our relations with NATO and with countries who are eager to enter the alliance."

This has hardly exhausted Russia's efforts to test NATO's red lines, or its patience. Russia has repeatedly sought to flex its muscles in and around NATO's borders, particularly on the oceans and in air spaces around the northern NATO periphery. Among the most blatant such actions took place in August 2019 in the Norwegian Sea. Some thirty ships of the Russian navy including the *Severomorsk*, a 535-foot guided-missile destroyer, and the 4,500-ton frigate *Admiral Gorshkov*, armed with cruise missiles, together with submarines and supply vessels as well as anti-submarine and strategic aircraft, undertook what Norway's Chief of Defense Haakon Bruun-Hanssen called "a very complex operation" designed to demonstrate Russia's ability to block NATO's access to the Baltic Sea, North Sea, and Norwegian Sea—NATO's entire northern flank that includes the three Baltic states as well as Scandinavia and Germany. "This is an exercise where Russia seeks to protect its territory and its interests by deploying highly capable ships, submarines and aircraft with the purpose of preventing NATO of operating in there," said Bruun-Hanssen. "Any allied attempt to strengthen Norway becomes very difficult." And this was only the latest such operation, the commander observed.

Six months later, British monitoring picked up seven Russian warships that were "lingering" in the English Channel, forcing the Royal Navy to deploy nine of its own ships to monitor them as they lingered off the coast. "The navy has completed a concentrated operation to shadow the Russian warships after unusually high levels of activity in the English Channel and North Sea," a navy statement said. "Type 23 frigates HMS Kent, HMS Sutherland, HMS Argyll and HMS Richmond joined offshore patrol vessels HMS Tyne and HMS Mersey along with RFA Tideforce, RFA Tidespring and HMS Echo for the large-scale operation with support from NATO allies." Russian warships often travel through the channel to and from the Baltic and the Mediterranean. This time, they just hung around. Too long. The naval activity followed two incidents when RAF Typhoon jets scrambled to intercept Russian TU-142 Bearcat bombers north of the Shetland Islands and heading into transatlantic passenger airline routes.

In all of these cases, NATO forces have succeeded in standing firm and Russia has not been tempted to go further in its provocative acts. But red lines that can fracture the

NATO alliance from within may in many respects prove to be more toxic to the long-standing and immutable red lines of the alliance than any external threat. These challenges from within have grown increasingly proximate and threatening since the arrival of Donald Trump as president. Trump had long believed most NATO member countries were not paying enough for their defense and the upkeep of the alliance. In July 2018, he decided to force the issue. At an emergency summit in Brussels, Trump warned that if every country did not begin spending at least 2 percent of its GDP on defense by January (barely six months away), he would "do his own thing." At that same summit he also conflated his demand for greater spending with Germany's purchase of vital natural gas from Russia. Such transactions, he held, weaken the alliance from within. They foster, Trump believes, reliance on an external power for a strategic resource that, at a crisis moment, could be used for some sort of blackmail, or worse—indeed could prove to be as toxic to his concept of NATO as insufficient defense spending. To a degree, he even got his way at this session, with members pledging $266 billion in new military outlays by 2024, though that would still leave some members shy of the 2 percent threshold. Trump, however, could not grasp what success seemed to be his for the taking. He promptly upped the ante to a demand for 4 percent of GDP across the board by each NATO nation, more even than the United States spent at the time.

The Bulgarian president, Rumen Radev, described what immediately followed. "This summit is very important because it needs to make proof of unity, solidarity and decisiveness," Radev began. "Unfortunately, the questions turned out to be more numerous than the answers. President Trump, who spoke first, raised the issue, not only the 2 percent to be attained as of today, but raised the bar higher—at 4 percent," after which Trump promptly turned tail and left. Radev took the floor and asked NATO Secretary General Jens Stoltenberg to react. "I asked [Stoltenberg] about the 'what if' scenarios. What happens with the transatlantic link, which is the backbone of NATO, if we don't reach the 2 percent target, not speaking of a 4 percent target," Radev said. "I asked my question, and there was silence."

Many NATO nations did raise their defense spending in response. But there were others whose fragile economies simply would not allow any such dramatic boost. Some began to fear what might happen were they ever attacked. How firmly was NATO, and especially its American military backbone, committed to recognizing Article Five, particularly if a nation below the 2 percent threshold were threatened? Not surprisingly, European partners began to think about themselves. After all, Donald Trump's nationalist operating philosophy appeared very much to be "America First." Two days before Trump was due to arrive in France in November 2018 to celebrate the centenary of the armistice that ended

World War I, Macron proposed a European Defense Force, suggesting that Europe could no longer rely unequivocally on the United States, or by extension NATO, to assure its defense. Trump, furious, promptly shot back that the French "were starting to learn German in Paris before the U.S. came along," referring to the early days of both world wars. A thirst for gratitude seemed to be taking a front-row seat over strategy. NATO had never before seemed to be so firmly on the ropes. Fortunately, other issues distracted Trump. And several countries did raise their military spending substantially.

A year later, Stoltenberg paid a fence-mending trip to the White House, thanking Trump for his "strong leadership and commitment to the Alliance." As he left, he talked briefly with a gaggle of American and European reporters gathered outside the West Wing entrance, emphasizing:

> The Allies are stepping up, investing more and by the end of next year will have added $100 billion extra in defense spending across Europe and Canada. This shows that the clear message from President Trump is having a real impact, is making NATO stronger.
>
> Question: What about [French President] Macron's statement that NATO is brain dead?
>
> Stoltenberg: NATO is strong and NATO has implemented the biggest reinforcement of collective defense since the end of the Cold War. Despite the differences on issues like trade, climate change or the Iran nuclear deal, North America and Europe are doing more together than they have done in many, many years.

All this, of course, has allowed Trump to crow repeatedly that without him, NATO would never have had such resources. Indeed, he never seems to have understood that the "resources" he claimed to have won for NATO were in fact committed by the individual members to their own defense. Still, all this *sturm und drang* has left NATO intact, though the European Defense initiative has not died either.

What has died, it would seem, is a bit of the internal comity that did preserve the NATO red lines so definitively through its first three-quarters of a century of existence. The unanimity of thought and action were beginning to evaporate, but the external red line remained. Still, Turkey, a NATO member and guardian of its southeastern flank, seemed to feel itself free to purchase an advanced anti-missile defense system from Russia, then join Russia in a joint operation in northeastern Syria that forced the US to pull back its forces. Later, US Secretary of State Mike Pompeo blithely chose to bludgeon the G-7 nations, six of whom are NATO members, at the height of the coronavirus crisis, to dub the virus "the Wuhan Virus." The G-7 was horrified, resulting in separate statements from a body whose unanimous voice was indispensable to deal with one of mankind's most existential challenges. "What the State Department has suggested is a red line," one European diplomat told CNN. "You cannot agree with this branding of this virus and trying to communicate this." The World Health Organization has uniformly referred to the cause of the pandemic as COVID-19 or coronavirus.

—

In the end, internal challenges to the alliance, to the indispensable unanimity of voices, cannot be ignored. As I have sought to convey repeatedly, any red line is only as strong as the determination of those who live on either side to accept or defend it.

You will recall from Chapter Five that in August 1978, I visited the village of Szombathely, less than ten miles from the Hungarian frontier with Austria. It was one of the most carefully patrolled red lines in Europe—at the time a most direct point of contact between the Warsaw Pact and the West. Tall guard posts were spaced close enough so that each could be seen from the next. There were some strands of wire well inside the actual frontier. And carefully raked earth made certain to identify a single footprint of anyone foolish enough to sprint to the border—and freedom. Today, barbed wire is going up again. Along Hungary's 180-mile border with Serbia, a fellow member of NATO and the European Union, Hungarian Prime Minister Viktor Orban ordered a $500 million fence built. It is even more elaborate, more high-tech, even more secure than the barrier the Soviets once built along their red line with the West. Viktor Orban's fence is double-hung with razor wire. There are loudspeakers that announce if someone is approaching too close. It is heavily patrolled.

CBS *60 Minutes* correspondent Jon Wertheim and producer Michael Gavshon spoke to Laszlo Toroczkai, mayor of the small border town of Ásotthalom. His was among the voices most insistent that the Hungarian government build the wall. "This is about preserving, we keep hearing, 'European values,'" Wertheim said to Toroczkai. "What does that mean?"

"For me, the European culture, the European values are the classical music. Mozart. Beethoven. Tchaikovsky," Toroczkai said. It goes beyond pleasures of the ear, though. He also objects to mixing tastes, or it would seem almost anything else. "The foods, the European foods," he continued. "For example, the *doner kebab*, in Berlin, Budapest? No, I would like to eat the *doner kebab* in Istanbul."

"You're spending a half a billion dollars on a fence to keep out *doner kebabs?*" Wertheim asked.

"You know—we need this border fence to preserve our safe country," Toroczkai said.

There is one fundamental difference between now and the '70s, however. This new red line that Hungary's nationalist prime minister has ordered up has a different purpose. The Soviet red line was designed to keep people in, and ideas out. It was designed to make sure that no one escaped the gulag, while at the same time assuring that the inmates had no real sense of just what democracy held on the other side of this barrier. Viktor Orban's red line, and those of other nations in Europe flooded by immigrants that threaten not only their security but their way of life, is designed to keep people out. Ideas seem to be immaterial. At the same time, by holding at bay the tsunami of immigrants from the wars and poverty of the Middle East and Africa, all anxious to find a home in Europe where freedom and prosperity has been for most of them an impossible dream, the Orban line is also keeping ideas out. Ideas that could suggest the role compassion and promise can play in improving the human condition on all sides. Red lines can sustain that purpose, or when misguided, destroy it.

In the end, red lines are most deeply dependent on or reflective of where you are coming from and where you are going.

Coda

In these pages, I have sought to shine a bright light into some of the darker corners of our human existence, to show their historical antecedents and the positions, often barely tenable, where they have placed us. So perhaps, dear reader, you will now indulge me for a final moment in some reflections of where we might be going, as so many of these red lines have interlocking consequences often far removed from their locations in our world today.

I am no soothsayer, but history can often provide us with a useful roadmap, and there are many cautionary tales buried in these pages. Beware, above all, of leaders who have learned none of these lessons of the past, but who seek instead to blaze their own way to a dark future. Bludgeoning past or forming new red lines, many are charting their own blinkered paths to a world that would, they believe, reward their missteps with applause and accolades. And now, there arrives the new coronavirus.

"Like climate change, the COVID-19 pandemic is a perfect example of why we need multilateralism in a globalized world," former Australian Prime Minister Kevin Rudd observed at an early peak of the pandemic in March 2020. "Rather than resorting to thinly veiled racism and isolationist policies, global leaders—particularly the United States—should have started organizing a collective response weeks ago. In times of international crisis, playing the nationalist card is the easiest and crudest form of domestic politics. But in the cold light of day, it doesn't fix a single problem. Only effective global coordination can do that."

In some cases, some red lines may utterly disappear, others may appear. A globally existential event, of which there have been only a handful in each millennium, can transform this entire construction. COVID-19 and its consequences have proven to be one such collective event. As such, each such an event can and often will transcend all red lines. A virus knows no boundaries, natural or manmade. The vital question to explore, of course, will be whether those lines that have worked in the past can, or should, be restored once this crisis has passed. The red lines that were natural boundaries of Europe—frontiers born from centuries of strife or comity that had disappeared over the past half century in the interest of creating a single European Union, even the individual red lines of defense that were subsumed by the NATO umbrella—all became questionable in the face of COVID-19, which itself has posed an existential challenge, crossing national boundaries and natural red lines across Asia, Africa, and the Americas as well as Europe.

So, what I would like to examine in these final pages is just where on the continuum of human history and social and political interactions the worst, certainly most universal, global crisis in a century has left us. The last time there was a global event that threatened the entire world community was the Spanish Flu epidemic of 1917 to 1920, caused by a variant of the H1N1 avian flu virus. As it happens, it was overlaid in part by the First World War. Still, some 500 million people are estimated to have become infected with it, or at the time nearly a third of the world's population of some 1.6 billion. Extrapolating to today's population of 7.8 billion, that would mean at least 2.6 billion (or nearly twice the entire world's population in 1918) would fall ill from COVID-19. But of greater concern is the mortality. At least 50 million people worldwide and 675,000 in the United States (whose population was 103 million) died from the Spanish flu, which would translate to at least 2 million American deaths today. As it happens, World War I, which left at least 40 million people dead, military and civilian, has vastly overshadowed our perception of that era. The vast bulk of these wartime deaths were concentrated on a single continent—Europe. But India recorded at least 12.5 million deaths from the flu out of a population of barely 320 million. One of the largest single concentrations of illness due to the Spanish flu was in Africa, where it ran all but unchecked through vast stretches of the continent, especially in its most lethal second wave of mid-August through September 1918.

The disease entered the continent through three seaports. In Freeport, Liberia, a Royal Navy warship brought the disease in the person of 124 stricken sailors who infected 70 percent of the town's entire population in two weeks, the governor reporting: "the disease spread with devastating rapidity, disorganizing everything. Everybody was attacked almost at once." From Freeport, two ships returning African troops home from the war in Europe traveled onward, spreading the pandemic to Cape Town in South Africa. As the soldiers headed home into the interior, the disease traveled with them at a catastrophic pace. From Mombasa, members of the demobilized military units of the Kenyan Carrier Corps fanned out from that port across Kenya, traveling upcountry, carrying the virus with them by rail, road, and river. A King's African Rifles Regiment spread a similar arc of infection and death from the coast of Tanganyika inland to Nyasaland, one official finding the road they followed "strewed with dead and dying." Infected workers, largely men, breaking out of the diamond mines and other labor centers, fled into the interior. Planting, harvesting, milking all came to a halt, raising the prospects of famine. Swept before these diseases were many red lines of colonial Africa. Still, behind them, those left untouched or recovered and immune from reinfection managed to restore the boundaries that existed before this epidemic. After all, in Africa, disease was hardly an unknown, as cholera, malaria, and a host of other tropical ailments had long plagued vast stretches of the continent. And still the red lines survived.

We can by no means be as sanguine today. We have seen other pressures coming to bear that have affected the nature and structure—not to mention the stresses—of red lines. And today's COVID-19 epidemic threatens to be longer, more lethal, more universal than any in the past, and is perhaps a harbinger of other existential, global threats on the horizon, like climate change. It would thus be useful to take a quick tour around the world we have already explored in some detail to suggest what it may look like when we emerge on the other side of the coronavirus.

Europe

Europe was already finding itself challenged. In a half century, this continent managed to rid itself of ancestral red lines that were its national frontiers and that had led in the twentieth century alone to two world wars. In the process of disassembling more than two dozen national boundaries, a single European Union had been created, surrounded by a single, all-encompassing protective shield. But there were already serious centrifugal forces at play even before the arrival of COVID-19. Britain managed to hive itself off from the continent through the process known as Brexit. Millions of refugees from conflicts and poverty that swept across Africa from the Middle East began knocking on Europe's doors. In nations from Greece and Hungary to Germany, Italy, and France, there was growing pressure to turn back these immigrants who threatened to strain already overburdened social and fiscal safety nets, and who at the same time carried with them risks of expanded terrorist activities.

While the vast mechanism of border crossings that dotted all of Europe's major highways had long been disassembled and passport controls eliminated in the entire Schengen Area, there was still a residual recollection of what life was like before the arrival of a unitary European passport. The agreement that brought this about was signed by ten European nations in the Luxembourg town of Schengen in 1985. Ultimately the single passport, effectively creating a Europe without internal borders, was embraced by twenty-six nations from Britain on the west to Greece on the east, and all of Scandinavia on the north to Spain, Portugal, and Malta on the south. Most recently, in March 2020, the EU even opened negotiations with Albania and North Macedonia (the former Yugoslav Republic of Macedonia) to join as the twenty-seventh and twenty-eighth members, just as North Macedonia became the thirtieth member of NATO. The whole concept was to provide free movement of goods and people between all twenty-six nations. But it also allowed free movement of guns, munitions, and eventually viruses as well. Though there was considerable effort expended in constraining guns and terrorism, a single virus turned out to be far more lethal than any terrorist and led to a more extreme balkanization of a region that had been speaking and acting with an all but unitary voice.

When the coronavirus hit, first and most catastrophically in Italy, starting in Lombardy in the north, then inexorably spreading south, and with new outbreaks or "clusters" suddenly appearing from Spain across France and eventually into Germany, the pressure to isolate intensified. Initially, the isolation was confined to individual regions, then within countries, then makeshift controls began going up at long-ignored frontiers. In mid-March, Germany shut its borders with France, Austria, and Switzerland. Spain followed suit, though its principal frontier was simply with France, which had already closed its borders, especially with Italy. This led to some bizarre and quite imaginative efforts to return to a united Europe. Patrick Kingsley of *The New York Times* found a couple, Karsten Tüchsen Hansen, eighty-nine, a retired German farmer, and Inga Rasmussen, eighty-five, a Danish caterer, who each cycle daily from their respective homes on each side of the German-Danish border to a remote stretch of farmland to hold hands across a card table they put there, straddling the border of their two countries, which they are legally prevented from crossing. "We're here because of love," Karsten explained. "Love is the best thing in the world."

On April 13, French President Emmanuel Macron, who aspired to assume the mantle of leader of a single, united Europe after German Chancellor Angela Merkel left office, announced that, while schools and some businesses would begin to open on May 11, France's frontiers would remain closed "indefinitely." In each country, this involved national police setting up checkpoints at the borders, turning back non-nationals. Germans were still allowed to enter Germany, the French to return to France. Indeed, every other European country declined to bar the return of their own nationals, many of whom brought the virus along with them.

At the same time, the existential emergency did seem only to accentuate tendencies of some countries and their rulers. Hungary's Viktor Orban, already displaying distinct autocratic and xenophobic qualities, turned into an evil caricature of himself. Hungary's parliament, controlled by Orban's Fidesz party, granted him sweeping powers in the form of an indefinite state of emergency, allowing him to rule by decree and suspending all elections that could have removed him from office. Since Fidesz also owns or controls most of the nation's media, there was little dissent, and little understanding of how the nation might continue to fit into the European Union, whose fundamental tenets were still deeply democratic. This Hungarian red line seems likely only to intensify the longer the viral crisis continues. Indeed, US Representative Eliot Engel, chairman of the House Foreign Affairs Committee, issued a frantic statement shortly after the Hungarian parliament's move to grant Orban sweeping powers:

> Prime Minister Orban is making a blatant power grab in the face of the worst global health crisis in recent history. This legislation marginalizes the Hungarian parliament and allows Prime Minister Orban to rule by decree like a dictator. It limits the parliament's oversight authority and judicial review and it imposes draconian punishments on citizens for COVID-related offenses that are vaguely defined and overly broad. Worse, there is no sunset clause or end date for when these powers would be terminated; that decision would be made solely by the Prime Minister.
>
> This is just the latest overreach by Prime Minister Orban, who has tightened his grip on power for years. The legislation solidifies his position as the incontestable ruler of a non-democratic Hungary. Such a serious affront to democracy anywhere is outrageous, and particularly within a NATO ally and EU member. Those organizations are founded on their members' shared respect for freedom and democratic values.

The question of what would happen after the coronavirus ceased to be a problem began to arise across Europe. Britain had already chosen to sever its ties with the continent when, after years of angst, it finally managed to implement Brexit and leave the European Union only months before the coronavirus hit. There had been discussion, even before the COVID-19 outbreak, of Poland being forced out of the EU over changes in its judicial system that clashed with the European community's rules for fair and impartial administration of justice. At the same time, there was no suggestion that the firm red line surrounding NATO (both Hungary and Poland, former Warsaw Pact members, are now members of the Atlantic Alliance) was in any danger of being breached or either nation being expelled. Still, the first chinks have begun to appear. Accusations have flown back and forth across the continent of certain countries or enterprises hoarding critical medical equipment or profiteering from the outbreak. Landlocked Switzerland and Austria accused Germany of blocking deliveries of vital material destined for their countries. Other cases involved stolen cargos and defective medical masks.

A fully united and barrier-free Europe has been undergoing its biggest test since it first began moving toward unity a half century ago. "Never in the history of the IMF, we have witnessed the world economy coming to a standstill," Kristalina Georgieva, executive director of the International Monetary Fund told a World Health Organization briefing in April 2020. "It is way worse than the global financial crisis and it is a crisis that requires all of us to come together." The problem is that in this crisis there has also been an unprecedented reversion to nationalism—a return to ancestral barriers, especially in the developed world. The barriers began going up or intensifying not only between nations in Europe, but between regions as well. The traditional gulf between the wealthy northern European nations and their poorer southern European brethren began widening even further. A half billion euros of emergency lending early in the crisis period was quickly exhausted as Germany and the Netherlands failed to come to the aid of hard-hit Italy in terms of medical supplies, as well as any financial relief. One opinion poll found 70 percent of Italians believed Germany was seeking to "strangle" Italy, while barely 16 percent disagreed with that sentiment.

"Even ardent Europeanists normally appreciative of open borders joined the deafening calls to end freedom of movement across Europe's national borders—a longstanding demand of nationalists," said Yanis Varoufakis, former Greek finance minister and cofounder of the Democracy in Europe Movement. Sadly, this was the one moment when a global, or at least a regional, pan-European or hemispheric response was more vital than ever. The preeminent question was whether the reversion to the norm of the human spirit is represented by globalism or nationalism—the destruction or building of red lines or borders.

It seemed, at least for the moment, that coherence and comity had evaporated in large stretches of the continent with the return of pernicious red lines that are far more destabilizing than leveling. In the midst of the pandemic, the sourcing of food and medical supplies and the efficiencies of a broad, unitary market became increasingly problematic with the gradual reappearance of twenty-six fragmented, even competitive, economies and the multiplicity of markets that service them. In these times of war, said French President Emmanuel Macron, nourishing the French people has become a mission of public service.

Assuring the viability of this mission could make life far more dangerous, certainly more expensive, across a Europe barricaded behind these new red lines that sprang from containment of viral clusters, followed by competition for scarce medical equipment and devices, ultimately hobbling entire transcontinental routes of supply and demand.

At the same time, as the progress of COVID-19 continues, it is beginning to remind a growing body of citizens across Europe of the value of a common, cross-border approach. The artificial frontiers that rose early on—routes patrolled by national police searching for foreigners potentially carrying disease—were simply futile in halting the spread of a virus that knows no red lines. The value, instead, of all players acting in concert is a far more useful currency for assuring the rapid return to a degree of normalcy in economic, social, medical, and interpersonal terms than isolation and balkanization.

By July 2020, much of Europe had begun to reopen, lifting newly-imposed national boundaries, returning to the red-line-free zone it had been for previous quarter century. The result was that France recorded just 697 new cases of Covid-19 on July 18 and 14 deaths in the entire country, according to World Health Organization figures, compared with 71,484 cases and 921 deaths that same day in the United States. The United States has five times France's population but registered more than 100 times the number of infected and 65 times the number of deaths. These rates of infection were very much the case across the European Union, with the exception of Sweden, which prided itself on its economy never closing down and recorded surges in cases and especially deaths. But by the end of September a new, second wave seemed to be taking hold across the continent, Europe as a whole reporting a weekly 5 percent increase in new cases. France alone registered more than 82,000 new cases, the highest on the continent, and 7,700 new deaths, leading President Macron to contemplate a restoration of lockdown provisions, closing bars and restaurants, from Paris to Marseilles.

In the end, the continent managed to come together, returning to a boundary-free region where the well-endowed help the more fragile and impoverished. This Herculean effort, however, in five tense days of the longest summit conference of European leaders in two decades, while agreeing on a €1.8 trillion rescue package, did reveal new fault lines and tensions—North and South, rich and poor. There was a clique known as the "frugal four" (Sweden, Denmark, Austria and led by the Netherlands) that balked at underwriting the poor southern states, particularly Italy and Spain whose economies were decimated by the early weeks of the pandemic. Germany and France, especially Angela Merkel and Emmanuel Macron, stepped up to the leadership role each was accustomed to play. As President Macron said when it was all over at 5:30 A.M. on the morning of the fifth marathon day, "This long negotiation was marked by difficulties. Sometimes by disagreements—different conceptions of Europe." But these differing conceptions nevertheless did leave a more or less single unit, intact and powerful.

Covid had by no means been defeated, as a proven vaccine was still very much on the far horizon. But the continent began to chart a path toward a future that contained many of the most promising avenues of the past—rebuilding a continent-wide environmentally-conscious economic and social system, responding nimbly in a coordinated, barrier-free fashion to global health challenges. At the same time, it showed a determination to hold at bay other countries, especially the United States, that failed to recognize the new shape and requirements of the post-Covid world.

Middle East

By early April 2020, the coronavirus pandemic had begun spreading across both divides of the Middle East—dramatically in Iran and simultaneously in Iraq and Syria, though all three countries appeared to be catastrophically underestimating the full extent of their exposure. Of course, none of this seemed to have taken the edges off the ongoing and lethal battles being pursued by Iran and its proxies in Syria and Iraq or the endgame of the civil war being waged by the government of Syria against its insurgents.

In early April, Donald Trump was warning of a "sneak attack on U.S. troops and/or assets in Iraq," as well as plots by Iranian-backed militias. At his regular daily White House briefing on the coronavirus on April 1, Trump huffed that his "response will be bigger" this time than when he ordered the assassination of Iranian Revolutionary Guards commander General Qasem Soleimani. But as it would turn out, the coronavirus would wreak greater havoc than any weapon that either side had been able to deploy through decades of strife and conflict.

No nation in the region was hit harder by COVID-19 than Iran. But no nation was more determinedly isolated—less by its own choice than that of much of the world, led by the United States under Donald Trump. Of the ten countries with the highest number of recorded and acknowledged cases of COVID-19 (and there was a long-held feeling that Iran was only acknowledging the tip of the iceberg with respect to the true extent of the spread), Iran was the poorest in terms of economic growth and inflation. From the beginning, Iranian authorities were laying the rapid spread of the virus at the feet of Donald Trump and his refusal to ease sanctions even as thousands were dying and tens of thousands sickening across Iran. The mayor of Tehran, Pirouz Hanachi, highlighted his people's dilemma as the virus developed a stranglehold on his city in the spring of 2020:

In Iran, urban administrators are left facing an unprecedented public health crisis. Figures show that 3,160 had died from the disease by 2 April and there are more than 50,000 cases of infection. The rate of infections is not yet slowing, and many of them are in Tehran, the city of which I am mayor.

Doubtless there are things that we could do differently, like every country in the world. But we are operating against the backdrop of the most extreme sanctions regime in history. The US embargo not only prohibits American companies and individuals from conducting lawful trade with Iranian counterparts, but given that the sanctions are extra-territorial, all other countries and companies are also bullied into refraining from doing legitimate business with Iranians, even the selling of medicines.

As a result, the ability of my colleagues and I to provide the health, logistical and other essential infrastructure necessary to combat the disease has been drastically reduced. We experience this loss every day, and it can be counted in people that would not have died.

An outstretched hand rather than the back of a fist could have paid enormous dividends for Trump and the world at this moment. For the open hand of friendship would have been an enormous indication that secular charity and democracy together comprise a far more viable system than a hardline, primitive, clerical dictatorship. For a people on the cusp of standing up to such a religious dictatorship, the foundations of which were already trembling, they might only have needed a nudge to topple it as thousands of their countrymen lay dying and with no supreme being or grand ayatollah in any position to stay the inexorable hand of a deadly pestilence.

Early on, Iraq officially cut itself off from Iran, canceling all air connections and sealing its border, at least as effectively as it was able. None of which really seems to have stayed the willingness of Iranian leaders to wage jihad. And their minions among the Iraqi militias continued, even expanded, their activities. Phillip Smyth, the brilliantly sourced Shiite researcher at the Washington Institute for Near East Policy, maintained his contacts with scores of militia leaders throughout this period. Many took the opportunity of relaxed enforcement and interdiction on their side of the Iran-Iraq red line to ramp up social activities, cleaning villages and towns, offering vital medicines and food to local populations, and filling in where the government was unwilling, unable, or just too scared to make good. Iraq had already been for months in a critical state. The country, as Steven Cook of the Council on Foreign Relations put it, was "already in terminal collapse, doesn't really have a government, doesn't have much in the way of resources."

Even before the arrival of the coronavirus, Iran had already become cash-strapped as Western, especially American, sanctions had begun to bite and prices for whatever oil Iran was able to sell plummeted. But even during the pandemic, when this cash crisis only intensified, the militias were undaunted in pursuing their activities. "'Go big, or go home,'" Smyth quotes militia leaders. "They still believe in theocratic rule and they are trying to impose God's will on earth." Effectively, this was the time to up the ante, to take that major push finally to eradicate the red lines established at such high cost by America and its allies over so many years. Now that one side, utterly distracted by the raging pandemic, had taken its eye off the ball, this was the time to erase these pernicious red lines and cement Iran's hold over Iraq, its people, and especially its oil reserves that were still unencumbered by sanctions. Erasing the Shiite-Sunni, Iran-Iraq red line that has been the cause of so much unrest and bloodshed in Persia and Mesopotamia may be the ultimate, indeed ultimately–positive, outcome of COVID-19 in this entire region. Effectively, the virus was reversing one of many colossal errors committed by the drafters of the Treaty of Versailles a century earlier. By creating a new nation of Iraq dominated and ruled by Shiites in the stretches where they predominate, together with a small, Sunni-dominated state around Baghdad and eventually a Kurdistan in the north, there would emerge an outcome that the First World War and the peace that followed had been unable to assure: a far greater sense of stability throughout this region. Such a new configuration would allow Iran and Saudi Arabia to manage what was effectively a godfather status for two religiously congruent nation-states in what was once greater Iraq. Moves in that direction, coupled with a devout belief in respectively God-given missions, only accelerated the perforation of the always porous red line between Iran and Iraq. It would be wise for the United States and its allies to recognize reality and get out of the path of the progress of history.

For many in Iran, and quite seamlessly across a host of militia groups, there was a growing feeling that these may be The End Times. "Well, we want to be on the right side of our version of history," Smyth observed wryly, quoting militia contacts, adding their belief that "the Islamic Republic will survive because it's an ordained rule of government." Indeed, Iran has sought to double down on its self-sufficiency, even as a number of leaders embraced the view of UN Secretary General António Guterres, who told the G-20, "This is the time for solidarity not exclusion. Let us remember that we are only as strong as the weakest health system in our interconnected world." There was a rising chorus of voices urging relief from sanctions in an effort to preserve the political, military and social status quo.

As the United States seems to have bludgeoned much of the world into continuing to ignore statements such as those from Guterres, many of the feelings of insularity and defensiveness clearly on display by Donald Trump have been reflected in recent pronouncements from the supreme leader, the Grand Ayatollah Ali Khamenei himself, particularly in his seminal televised address on the festivals of Nowruz and Eid al-Mab'ath:

> The country should become strong. Strengthening the country is one of our goals . . . The Quran says, "Against them make ready your strength to the utmost of your power, including steeds of war." It means that we should increase our power as much as we can. At first glance, power might seem to mean "military power", but its scope is much wider than military power. Power has very broad dimensions. It has economic, scientific, political—it is political independence which prepares the ground for political power—and promotional dimensions. With the passage of time, there will be other arenas for strengthening the country and the nation.

Khamenei added that he was rejecting the proffered hand of friendship from the United States that might have helped restrain the pandemic, adding that "your medication might become an instrument for further spreading the disease. You have no credibility and you are not trustworthy. The medicines that you prescribe or export into our country might make the virus last even longer or prevent it from being controlled." The only hint of concern among the leadership was Khamenei's radical decision to broadcast the message from an isolated room—no live audience, no cheering crowds at the Imam Reza shrine as in years past. Comfort in God and total self-sufficiency was all that was needed to overcome Iran's enemies. A message that could easily have come from Donald Trump himself in this age of nationalism. Indeed, as the spring turned to summer in the Middle East, the virus only continued its spread. By July, Iran, which began loosening all restraints two months earlier, was posting its highest case numbers and daily death toll since the start of the outbreak, with some 164,500 cases and 13,400 deaths, at 5 percent, the highest mortality rate in the world. By late September, Iran and Iraq were still the two leading covid hot spots in the region, each posting more than 25,000 new cases a week and Iran registering more than 1,200 deaths.

As for Iran's other principal antagonist in the region, Saudi Arabia, it has been forced—its back to the wall—to pull down some of its own long-standing red lines. The coronavirus struck the kingdom with unanticipated ferocity, reporting some 240,000 cases by July—half again as many as Iran in a nation little more than a third of its foe's size. By early April 2020, as many as 150 members of the ruling House of Saud, many of them senior princes, fell victim to the coronavirus, striking to the heart of its ability to rule and govern with impunity and maintain the red lines it had established to protect its right to govern as it wished.

So, on April 8, the Saudi government ordered a unilateral ceasefire in Yemen, seeking an end to the catastrophic war that had divided this nation—a misguided effort to maintain a Sunni redline against encroachment by Shiite Iran.

The kingdom of Saudi Arabia was already suffering. Its vast oil reserves that had served to support its economy through good times and bad, allowing it to maintain a strong barrier against all outside forces, was suddenly under attack from two quarters—the coronavirus that was drying up oil demand worldwide and hammering prices, and a Russian leadership that was prepared to do all in its power to wreak havoc on the Saudi and American oil industries by allowing prices to plunge all but unchecked as it ramped up its own output. Since much of the geopolitical power of both nations derives largely from oil, this mad oil crush, compounded by the COVID challenge, sent both careening toward potential existential crises. The open question was how long Saudi Arabia, but especially the royal family, could hold out to challenges across multiple fronts. Clearly its move to end the fighting in Yemen was early evidence that time might be running out. A sudden ceasefire in the first week of April 2020 was an indication of just how profoundly Saudi Arabia was hurting. But not just Saudi Arabia.

Russia and its Empire

The other side of this oil trade was Russia. For Russia, and Vladimir Putin, the coronavirus did appear, at first blush, to be an opportunity of a lifetime. Russia, as we have seen, has been increasingly tied to the Middle East since the arrival in power of Vladimir Putin. Now, in the age of the pandemic, his actions were proving increasingly toxic. Oil had been the lubricant enabling all varieties of Russian adventures and efforts to expand or solidify red lines critical to Putin's strategic vision in the near abroad and further afield as well. This had worked well until suddenly a succession of seismic shifts threw much of Russia's stability off balance.

With the global shutdown of business, travel and all varieties of economic activity, the need for oil began to dry up as well. Prices began to plummet, from a high of $63 a barrel in January 2020 to $20 three months later. By early April, the pain had become so intense that Russia and Saudi Arabia agreed to substantial oil production cutbacks and OPEC quickly ratified the action, all in an effort to restore some equilibrium in supply and demand and return oil prices to some vestige of pre-pandemic levels.

At the same time, the coronavirus began to bite to an extent that Putin was finally forced to postpone the nationwide vote for a change in the Russian constitution that would effectively allow him to serve as president for life. Eventually, he would win this vote, but there was a big price. Russia was forced to take similar measures to those most of his West European neighbors were adopting, sealing borders to outsiders. And on April 10 he described how he'd opened a regular dialogue with Donald Trump on best methods for containing the spread of the virus and its economic impact. That hardly worked well. By September 27, Russia had already counted 1,151,438 cases, the highest in Europe, and more than 20,000 deaths. Each day Russia was vastly outpacing every other European nation in cases and deaths with no apparent strategy of controlling the spread, especially in the vast territories outside of Moscow. Much of this was a tribute to one of the core tenets of Putin's governance, or as I suggested in mid-May of 2020, "the president [was] clearly stepping back from what rapidly seems to be turning into the greatest single challenge to his presidency, placing administration of the crisis in the hands of governors and mayors, most of whom owe their job to him in any event." In short, Putin was setting up his own internal red lines designed to insulate him from the most catastrophic turns of the pandemic that was sweeping, all but out of control, across his nation.

All this would appear to suggest that outside adventurism by Putin would have to be curbed, but in fact it was not—in large part due to years of coping with sanctions and fiscal isolation that Russia's economy was in relatively good shape. Already unable to borrow abroad, its largest corporations were all but debt-free, their coffers bulging with cash they could not spend fast enough. And Russia was virtually self-sufficient in agricultural output. Indeed, when Saudi Arabia proposed the cutback in oil production by OPEC countries, Russia (not a full OPEC member) was able to thumb its nose and raise production, though this action sent oil prices plummeting globally. While oil and natural gas comprise more than 60 percent of all Russian exports, its companies and state hard currency reserves were hardly impacted. Indeed, Putin saw the COVID-19 crisis in the Middle East as an opportunity to expand his reach and operations in the region. In mid-March, Russian Defense Minister Sergei Shoigu traveled to Damascus "on President Putin's instructions" to meet with Syrian President Bashar al-Assad. Help with the burgeoning coronavirus crisis in Syria was high on the agenda. Syria's official request included test kits, personal protection equipment, and medical devices including ventilators. Two days later, countries already under various sanctions (Russia, China, Iran, Syria, Venezuela, North Korea, and Nicaragua) appealed to UN Secretary General António Guterres to ease up, in an effort to halt the spread of the pandemic in their nations. There was no response to the plea.

Still, Putin continued on the offensive, discussing how Russia might come to the aid of Turkish president Recep Tayyip Erdogan, Iranian prime minister Hassan Rouhani, even Israeli prime minister Benjamin Netanyahu. Deputy Foreign Minister Mikhail Bogdanov talked by phone with Ismail Haniyeh, head of Hamas's political bureau. At the same time in early April, Russia began reaching into territories of potential NATO expansion, deploying chemical, biological, radiological, and nuclear defense military units to Serbia to help in decontamination and disinfection efforts against the spread of COVID-19. Serbia had been toying with NATO membership. And Russia has been cementing relations with such near-beyond states as Armenia and Kazakhstan, offering similar help.

Of course, there are two ways of looking at all such efforts. One is that rulers like Putin are using this opportunity to enlarge or embed even more firmly red lines that are in their own basest interests. The glass-is-half-full perspective is that the pandemic has forced dictators like Putin to restrain their appetites and adjust their goals while they deal with a virus that respects no edict, no fist, no matter how firmly clenched.

Asia

In the strategic shipping lanes that crisscross the South China Sea that once carried a third of the world's shipping, traffic plunged 20 to 30 percent by early April 2020, less than three months into the beginning of the pandemic. In one week, ship cancellations surged to 212 from 45, with the bulk of the shrinking capacity on Asia-Europe routes which go directly through the South China Sea. At least 338 container ships with a capacity of at least 3 million containers were idle by the end of April.

Hardly idle was the Chinese navy, which remained intent on enforcing, if not expanding, the red lines the nation had built painstakingly for years. In early April, a Chinese coastguard ship rammed a Vietnamese fishing vessel in the Paracel Islands, which US State Department Spokesperson Morgan Ortagus described as "the latest in a long string of PRC actions to assert unlawful maritime claims and disadvantage its Southeast Asian neighbors in the South China Sea." In the period following the outbreak of the coronavirus pandemic in Wuhan, China, the government announced it was establishing new research stations on military bases at Fiery Cross Reef and Subi Reef in the Spratlys, which China calls Yongshu and Zhubi, respectively, but which are claimed by Vietnam and the Philippines. Still, there is an overlay of opportunism that has allowed China to move directly into a region that had previously been much more directly contested by the United States, which had been defending the rights and claims of the surrounding littoral nations. Suddenly, the vast resources of China were being deployed to polish Beijing's image in many of these countries that have fallen prey to the coronavirus. In March, China delivered a vast trove of N-95 masks and other protective gear and two hundred ventilators to Malaysia, that country's foreign minister promptly returning thanks, saying, "We really, truly know our friends in times of crisis." Zack Cooper, research fellow at the American Enterprise Institute, observed that "these countries don't have a lot of options on how to contest these claims. The Chinese are confident that the status quo is stable in the South China Sea, and trending in their favor in the long term."

The Chinese are adept at playing the long game, and the pandemic has only strengthened their hand. The powerful USS *Theodore Roosevelt* aircraft carrier group was taken out of service at the height of the pandemic and beached at Guam when the virus spread through the crew of the carrier and the captain was sacked for demanding action to protect his sailors. Other US navy ships, the super-carriers *Ronald Reagan*, *Carl Vinson*, and *Nimitz*, also deployed in the region, had sailors testing positive with COVID-19. To fill this vacuum, China promptly dispatched its first aircraft carrier, the *Liaoning*, and a five-warship escort through the Miyako Strait between Japan's Ryukyu Islands and the Bashi Channel east of Taiwan toward the South China Sea.

Still, Xi Jinping's plans for world domination, though hardly abandoned, have been substantially upended by the pandemic, particularly in the wake of its origins in China, the delayed avowals of the extent of the danger, and ultimately the reaction in various countries abroad to China's responses. A host of issues combined to puncture Beijing's efforts to extend its red lines and dominance beyond the immediate confines of East Asia and the South China Sea. China's embassy in France posted an incendiary text on its website entitled "Observations of a Chinese diplomat posted to Paris," sharply criticizing the delayed response from the West to the spreading coronavirus, even accusing workers at French nursing homes of "abandoning their posts overnight . . . and leaving their residents to die of hunger and disease." French Foreign Minister Jean-Yves Le Drian summoned the Chinese Ambassador to the Quai d'Orsay for a tongue-lashing, forcing China's foreign ministry spokesman Zhao Lijian to repudiate quickly the embassy's remarks.

At the same time, a number of countries China had spent years courting found that its largesse too often took the form of medical equipment and supplies that were more or less defective. The Netherlands found 600,000 face masks were unusable; Spain, Turkey, and the Czech Republic found hundreds of thousands of test kits were unable to yield any accurate results. At the same time, reports began accelerating that the actual origin of the virus, rather than a wet market selling exotic fish, was instead the Wuhan Institute of

Virology laboratory that for years had been studying coronaviruses in bats, with suggestions that the real mission extended to development of a biological weapon. And all this with insufficient high-level safeguards to prevent the escape of virulent strains. China in turn sought to blunt the impact of these reports by suggesting that the US Army was the source of the pandemic, having first spread the coronavirus in China. These converging patterns of apparent weakness or incompetence only paralyzed Chinese efforts to expand their influence or their boundaries of dominance.

Still, the clear and continuing absence of the United States from the world stage at this critical turning point, the increasingly apparent ineptitude of Donald Trump in dealing with it, and his aversion to any sort of global engagement, highlighted by his withdrawal of all financial support from the World Health Organization that he accused of tilting toward China, gave Xi Jinping just the opening he was seeking. In the midst of the greatest single challenge to his leadership of the nation, Xi took this opening of American retrenchment to expand his efforts toward greater global leadership.

At first, it appeared as though China and North Korea had been too shattered by the pandemic and its aftermath that they could not help but change their behavior. And indeed, while North Korea launched a handful of short-range ballistic missiles (all under three hundred miles), none posed any substantial threat. Both nations seem to have been more focused on their domestic challenges posed by COVID-19. China, however, recovered quickly and decisively, becoming effectively a model for much of the world. What this did allow it to do was to continue to reinforce and defend the red lines it had built, especially in its own back yard of the South China Sea.

Which was not to say they went unchallenged. Indeed, in early July, China and the United States went nose-to-nose, China staging five days of large-scale air and naval exercises around the Paracel Islands at the same moment the Trump administration sent in two aircraft carrier strike groups—the USS Ronald Reagan and USS Nimitz for their own air and naval maneuvers. "The purpose is to show an unambiguous signal to our partners and allies that we are committed to regional security and stability," said Rear Admiral George Wikoff, the operation's commander, adding that the maneuvers would include "round-the-clock flights testing the striking ability of carrier-based aircraft." Indeed, Secretary of State Mike Pompeo tweeted a week before exercises opened, "China cannot be allowed to treat the SCS [South China Sea] as its maritime empire."

Moreover, China is doing its best to build its attack forces with potentially global reach, far outside its immediate red lines and posing what could prove to be an enormous series of challenges should it opt to extend these boundaries dramatically. In 2020 Chinese shipyards launched the nation's first two major amphibious assault ships, the core of a projected expeditionary force that will allow the projection of power of a force of 25,000 to 35,000 marines—nearly triple the number just three years earlier. Massive landings on South China Sea islands or even Taiwan could become difficult and costly to repel. Suddenly, China's red lines seemed to be deepening.

The ultimate challenge, however, for both China and North Korea, as well as the broader Asian region in the age of pandemic has been economic. Even at the very beginning of the spread of COVID-19, the International Monetary Fund was already forecasting zero economic growth or worse across the region—the bleakest performance in sixty years. Even in the depths of the Great Recession of 2008–2009, Asia registered a growth rate of 4.7 percent, and the previous financial crisis in the region in 1997 never saw pan-Asiatic growth fall below 1.3 percent. That reality has constrained any shift in the anatomy of red lines established by major powers across the region. China's economy was the one bright spot, though still decidedly bleak, with Asia's only projection of positive growth, or 1.2 percent, hardly enough to give any serious lift to its activities or its ability to maintain substantial aid to its neighbors or beyond—especially Africa.

Africa

In the Spanish Flu pandemic of 1918–1920, more than two million people died in Africa, triple the number who died in North America. That widely accepted mortality number could be barely half the actual number, as the most precise recent estimates suggest. At the time, however, the entire population of the continent was barely 150 million. Today, Africa's population is approaching 1.2 billion which, extrapolating, could put the death toll for a comparable viral pandemic at 16 million or more. On March 28, 2020, Dr. Denis Mukwege warned readers of the French daily *Le Monde* that "we must react most quickly if we want to avoid a massacre." Mukwege is a surgeon in the Democratic Republic of the Congo, the source of Ebola, the last major pandemic to sweep out of Africa. In 2018, he won the Nobel Peace Prize for his work in the most violent areas of that nation. At the time he was urging rapid action to prevent a holocaust, some forty-three of fifty-four African countries had been swept by the coronavirus, with few tools available to halt its spread. The contagion and lethality of COVID-19 threatened to eclipse the more traditional influenza that had cut through these same nations a century earlier. Above all, as in much of the rest of the world, the coronavirus respected none of the long-established red lines which we have seen overlie much of the map of Africa.

This was a "break the glass moment," Ghana's finance minister Ken Ofori-Atta told David Pilling of the *Financial Times* at the end of March 2020. One immediate fear, echoed by Bill Gates, whose Bill and Melinda Gates Foundation has been on the front lines of disease treatment especially in the developing world, is that the coronavirus could find in Africa a fertile seeding ground for retransmission to the rest of the world. Most pandemic experts have focused on the continent as a whole rather than any specific zone, since common failures of health care and mitigation cut across a broad swath of the continent.

As it happens, the pandemic erased red lines and boundaries across the continent as the capacity of containment, the availability of lifesaving equipment, and the prevalence of trained medical personnel was equally dismal in virtually every corner of sub-Saharan Africa. The World Health Organization identified fewer than two thousand ventilators in forty-one of fifty-four African countries that reported their figures. Somalia had none; Central African Republic had three; South Sudan, four. Nigeria, the continent's largest nation by population, with two-thirds that of the United States, had fewer than one hundred ventilators. Somalia had just 4 intensive care unit beds and 116 confirmed cases at the very debut of the pandemic. "We are now failing. Let me use that word deliberately," Mahad Hassan, one of Somalia's few epidemiologists and a member of the government's coronavirus task force, told the *Washington Post*. "At our main treatment center, almost nothing is there. Last time I visited, beds, only beds. No oxygen, no ventilators." Abdirizak Yusuf, the thirty-five-year-old official put in charge of the Somali government response, believed at the time when there were 116 officially confirmed cases that there could be "even a million cases we are missing in Somalia. My colleagues are even testing positive. Our ministry people are testing positive. Most of the people we are testing are testing positive."

There have been a host of efforts to address Africa's multiplicity of coronavirus-related problems on a global basis, since it was clear from the get-go that there were no longer any boundaries to be respected or enforced. French President Emmanuel Macron proposed a debt moratorium for forty countries in sub-Saharan Africa, as well as thirty-six other impoverished nations. "We absolutely must help Africa bolster its capacity for the shock to its health system," Macron said in a nationally televised address to the French people that was also carried across Africa. "Furthermore, we must help the continent on the economic front to respond to this crisis that's already there. It's our moral and human duty." Economic relief, he said, should be accompanied by emergency funding for the establishment of intensive care beds and accompanying supplies of respiratory units.

At the same time, China continued to knock on Africa's doors—outdistancing in its response both the United States and Russia, the other two major power competitors for hearts and minds on the continent. Jack Ma, the founding chairman of Chinese Internet titan Alibaba and a close confidant of President Xi Jinping, used his charitable foundation to dispatch planeloads of equipment and supplies that included five hundred ventilators, as well as personal protective equipment and coronavirus test kits for distribution across fifty-four African nations. Chinese state media were on hand to chronicle every step of the way. At the same time, just as the need for outside equipment and expertise was becoming clear across the continent, Secretary of State Mike Pompeo ordered the US Agency for International Development (USAID) to confine American aid largely to funding rather than to the critically needed supplies or expertise that Africa would have to find elsewhere. By contrast, during the Ebola epidemic of 2014 to 2016 that originated in the Democratic Republic of the Congo and spread across the continent, USAID played a central role in containment. Health officials in both the United States and Africa are deeply aware that if Africa, which would arrive late to the vast worldwide spread of the pandemic, were to become fully engulfed, the continent could seed a virulent second wave around the world. It is also a region where social distancing and traditional methods of controlling viral spread are all but impossible, with crowded millions living from hand-to-mouth, feeding themselves in crowded open-air markets. A reader of the *Financial Times* living in Sierra Leone added in a commentary, "Though our population is young, they (and many African populations) are severely immunocompromised due to HIV, malaria, general poor health etc. It is unlikely that demographics will be favorable." Dr. Matshidiso Moeti, regional director for Africa of the World Health Organization, summarized the challenges from Brazzaville in the Republic of the Congo:

There is no doubt that social distancing is difficult in some settings, especially when we consider that component of asking people to stay indoors and not go out in some settings, the way people are living, is simply not going to be possible. If we take into consideration the size of buildings, the size of families, the weather, the climate in some cases is going to be very difficult. So, it is important that it be applied in ways that are contextualized for the reality of people. But it also needs to be supported and enabled. For example, when people are going to the type of places where we go shopping in an African setting, the markets where we buy our food, it is very difficult to keep people apart. These are informal settings where if you are the person running a store, you are not going to be reminding your potential clients to stay away from each other, because in this way you might disadvantage what you are going to earn that particular day. I don't think we should give up on this altogether, but we also need to understand it is not possible for the police to enforce staying indoors where it is not feasible for families to do that.

Then, Dr. Moeti turned to a critical aspect of attenuating the spread of the disease in many parts of the continent where terrorist or revolutionary activity has established isolated communities outside any medical delivery systems:

> Other conditions of course that might affect this are the conflict situations where simply the presence of interveners is going to be a challenge and being able to put in place some of these measures in a systematic way is going to be difficult.

Still, Africa remained one of the world's real bright spots, nine months into the pandemic. Just 26,945 new cases were reported in the last week of September across the entire continent, barely a third as many as France alone and six percent of Europe's total. And while Europe's cases were surging by 5 pecent, in Africa, the caseloads were shrinking by 7 percent.

The very need for such measures, however, could be a mitigating factor in bringing down some of the more pernicious red lines and establishing a common effort across borders, piercing lines long established and enforced by terrorist groups whose activities will be seen as counterproductive to restraining the spread of this pandemic. A recognition of this reality is an encouraging, though very preliminary, first step.

———

The great evolutionary biologist Lynn Margulis believed that human beings have been, as her chronicler Charles C. Mann puts it, "unusually successful" as a species. "Of course," he quotes her telling him in a chance encounter on the street in the town of Amherst, where they both lived, "the fate of every successful species is to wipe itself out." Margulis herself put it even more directly:

> The species of some of the protoctists [single-celled amoebae] are 542 million years old. Mammal species have a mean lifetime in the fossil record of about 3 million years. And humans? You know what the index fossil of *Homo*

sapiens in the recent fossil record is going to be? The squashed remains of the automobile. There will be a layer in the fossil record where you're going to know people were here because of the automobiles. It will be a very thin layer. . . . Look, there are nearly 7,000 million people on earth today and there are 10,000 chimps, and the numbers are getting fewer every day because we're destroying their habitat. Reg Morrison, who wrote a wonderful book called *The Spirit in the Gene*, says that although we're 99 percent genetically in common with chimps, that 1 percent makes a huge difference. Why? Because it makes us believe that we're the best on earth. But there is lots of evidence that we are "mammalian weeds." Like many mammals, we overgrow our habitats and that leads to poverty, misery, and wars.

Certainly pandemics and, ultimately, she might suggest, extinction. Our social organization, unlike that of any other species, has managed until now to prevent such a calamity. Part of this organization has been in the form of lines and boundaries, whether physical, social, diplomatic, economic, religious, or military. As we have seen in these pages, the most effective red lines through the ages have had a purpose, an organization, often for the good, and at times malevolent.

The United States has traditionally in times of crisis taken the lead on establishing and maintaining many of these red lines, at times leading global efforts to remove unwelcome or toxic barriers. This has included engineering environmental preservation and climate change initiatives like the COP 21 Paris Agreement; neutralizing nuclear threats from the Soviet Union, North Korea, Iran, and beyond; restraining the expansion of terrorism and transnational criminal activities; and orchestrating a host of humanitarian efforts to eradicate poverty, deal with enforced migration, and treat hunger and disease.

Yet from the very beginning of the pandemic crisis, Donald Trump has congratulated himself on his ill-considered decisions to cut the United States off abruptly from much of the planet, pulling up and securing the national drawbridge resolutely and definitively. Beyond the step taken by many other countries of banning immigration, he withdrew from the World Health Organization, the one global body charged with preserving the world's health and stability; slashed aid to much of the world's most disadvantaged nations; and proclaimed again at every turn it was the time for "America First." These new red lines were ill-conceived and utterly counterproductive. Fortunately, the rest of the world had more sense. When the Group of Twenty agreed to inject up to $5 trillion into the global economy and establish a worldwide effort to find an effective vaccine against COVID-19, the United States retreated to the sidelines. This was an unaccustomed and, for many Americans and their traditional allies and friends, an uncomfortable, deeply troubling, certainly unwelcome position at home and abroad. As Gilles Paris, the veteran Washington correspondent for the French daily *Le Monde* put it, "The health crisis . . . risks accentuating the insular reflex developed over the past three years by the administration of Donald Trump, further excluded Washington from the role of metronome of an international order of which it has been, for decades, the main beneficiary."

The coronavirus pandemic was the first moment in a century when the entire globe found itself plunged into a common, existential threat to our species not unlike that posed by our cavalier treatment of the environment and the air we breathe, the water we drink. And beyond the immediate threat from the virus, there is a host of attendant threats, not the least being famine as production and distribution of food is deeply disrupted. "The world is on the brink of a hunger pandemic," World Food Program Executive Director David Beasley warned the UN Security Council in April 2020. But rather than decades or centuries, this entire set of existential challenges has been compressed into a single year or less. The red lines of the past may give way to needs of potable water, arable land, and livable temperatures.

The only way, perhaps, to avoid extinction at the hands of such threats, which seem more likely to be exacerbated as our planet becomes more crowded, more complex, is to band together. We must understand that for us to survive as a species it is essential to act and behave in unison, using our inherent, collective intelligence, greater than any single individual's. Certainly, our minds are more advanced than those of any other species that at one point or another in our planet's history seemed to dominate, then ultimately fade into extinction.

None of this is to say that all our societal organizations—red lines included—need to be destroyed with a single stroke. Many will prove to be the useful, even indispensable organizational tools that was intended when they were established in that very different pre-pandemic world. We now have a unique opportunity to choose our own direction. We must seize the opportunity, not squander it in balkanization and fearful retreat into ourselves. If we can manage this, perhaps we may find the means of coming together on other longer-term existential issues: an end to nuclear weapons and to environmental excesses, all with the capacity of extinguishing life on earth. We have seen here what has divided us. Now we must learn how to unite and come together.

At the same time, none of this will be possible without some visionary leaders able to look beyond their own frontiers and self-interests to understand that the greater good is far more rewarding than any parochial ends or means. An end to American exceptionalism and leadership already appears to be a most serious consequence. But this is the challenge to the next American president. He, or she, may find the United States no longer in a position to dictate or structure red lines or define their dynamics. This has happened before, as we have seen, at certain inflection points of history. But the United States and those who would lead it and the world must understand the new reality. Others already have. French President Emmanuel Macron, seizing the reins of Europe while guiding his own nation deftly through its existential crisis, is a prime example. As I wrote, in mid-April 2020, he was even at that moment, given the absence of any leadership from America, prepared to assume a global role out of all proportion to the size of his nation, but utterly appropriate in a time of peril. Urging a global ceasefire—a truce stretching from Afghanistan to Syria, Iraq, Yemen, and beyond—Macron managed to bring along every major world power.

The coronavirus and its pandemic certainly spawned licenses to retreat into peoples' baser, more nationalist instincts. But it has provided the opportunity as well to remind the wider world of the benefits of multilateralism, internationalism, and liberalism, which had been so deeply under siege in the pre-coronavirus moment, but throughout recent history have proved to be the bulwark against tyranny and war. Now globalism has found an opportunity to shine through once again. In the April 21, 2020, edition of his nationally televised daily briefing, which served as a pick-me-up for much of America, New York Governor Andrew Cuomo observed:

> I believe that it's the hard times in life that actually make you better and make you who you are. If you're intelligent enough to learn from them and to get the message from them, and that's what we have to do here. We have to do it individually. We have to do it collectively. What did we learn about ourselves about the world, about the country, from this period that we're in? Sometimes you get knocked on your rear end. Okay, get up, have the strength to get up, the wisdom to learn from the experience and be a better person for it.

And be a better nation, a better society and social organization, a better world. While we may yet prove to be another species hurtling pell-mell toward our destruction as Lynn Margulis seemed to fear, we may also be the only species smart enough to engineer our own survival, if we can only get out of our own way.

NOTES

CHAPTER ONE: FLASHPOINTS

p. 3   Chad does not stand alone," Mobutu declared.
Alan Cowell, "Mobutu, on a visit to Chad, renews Zairian support," *New York Times*, August 21, 1983, https://www.nytimes.com/1983/08/21/world/mobutu-on-a-visit-to -chad-renews-zairian-support.html.

p. 5   At least 2,431,985 square miles and 278,030,000 people are today swathed in red lines.

	area	population
Mali	479,000	18,540,000
Niger	489,700	21,480,000
Chad	495,800	14,900,000
Sudan	728,200	40,530,000
South Sudan	239,285	12,580,000
Nigeria	356,667	191,000,000

p. 7   "It is a solemn moment for the American Democracy."
Winston Churchill, "The Sinews of Peace ('Iron Curtain' Speech)," March 5, 1946, International Churchill Society, accessed July 2020, https://winstonchurchill.org /resources/speeches/1946–1963-elder-statesman/the-sinews-of-peace/.

p. 9   Square miles across the Middle East.

	population	territory
Turkey	79,810.000	302,535
Syria	18,270,000	71,498
Iraq	38,270,000	168,754
Iran	81,160,000	636,400
Jordan	9,702,000	34,495
Saudi	32,940,000	830,000
Yemen	28,250,000	203,850
Total	288,402,000	2,247,532

p. 15   first red line in the form of the Monroe Doctrine.
J. D. Richardson, ed., *Compilation of the Messages and Papers of the Presidents*, vol. 2 (1907), 287, https://web.archive.org/web/20120108131055/http://eca.state.gov /education/engteaching/pubs/AmLnC/br50.htm.

p. 16   **moral impulses and crusading ideals."**
          Walter A. McDougall, "Kissinger's World Order" (speech before Foreign Policy
          Research Institute, Philadelphia, PA, October 13, 2014), https://www.fpri.org/2014
          /10/kissingers-world-order/.

p. 20   **its own arable land shrinks in the face of the ever-warming planet.**
          Kieran Cooke, "Saudi agricultural investment abroad—land grab or benign strategy?"
          Middle East Eye, October 17, 2016, https://www.middleeasteye.net/opinion
          /saudi-agricultural-investment-abroad-land-grab-or-benign-strategy.

p. 22   **threat from Iranian-backed forces in Iraq and Syria.**
          David E. Sanger, "To Contain Iran, Trump's Newest Line in the Sand
          Looks a Lot Like Obama's," *New York Times*, May 17, 2019, https://www
          .nytimes.com/2019/05/17/us/politics/trump-iran-nuclear-deal.html?smid=ny
          tcore-ios-share.

p. 16   **another, broader air strike against twice the targets.**
          Helene Cooper, Thomas Gibbons-Neff, and Ben Hubbard, "U.S., Britain and
          France Strike Syria Over Suspected Chemical Weapons Attack," *New York Times*,
          April 13, 2018, https://www.nytimes.com/2018/04/13/world/middleeast/trump
          -strikes-syria-attack.html?module=inline; and Lara Jakes, "U.S. Concludes Syria
          Used Chemical Weapons in May Attack," New York Times, Sept. 26, 2019,
          https://www.nytimes.com/2019/09/26/world/middleeast/syria-chemical
          -weapons-us.html.

p. 24   **French political scientist Bruno Tertrais.**
          Bruno Tertrais, "The Diplomacy of 'Red Lines,'" *Recherches et Documents*, Fondation
          Pour a Recherche Stratégiques, February 2016, https://www.frstrategie.org/frs
          /chercheurs/bruno-tertrais\, https://www.frstrategie.org/sites/default/files/documents
          /publications/recherches-et-documents/2016/201602.pdf.

CHAPTER TWO: ORIGINS

p. 29   **men and horses lying strewn upon the ground.**
          Mrs. Henry Duberly, *Journal Kept During the Russian War* (1855; repr., Dodo Press,
          2008), 61–62.

p. 30   **The silence was oppressive; between the cannon bursts.**
          William Howell Russell, *Russell's Dispatches from the Crimea 1854–1856* (New York:
          Hill and Wang, 1966), 123.

p. 32   **Sita steps across the line and is promptly abducted.**
          "Princess Sita's Kidnap," in *The Ramayana*, Learning Inside Story, The British
          Library, accessed July 2020, https://www.bl.uk/learning/cult/inside/ramayanastories
          /sitaskidnap/sitaskidnap.html.

p. 34   **killed his enemy with a blow from his mere.**
          S. Percy Smith, "Moremo-Nui, 1807," in *Maori Wars of the Nineteenth Century*,
          (Christchurch: Whitcombe and Tombs Limited, 1910), 46–47, http://nzetc.victoria
          .ac.nz/tm/scholarly/tei-SmiMaor-t1-body-d3.html.

p. 35   **eventually made him a very wealthy man.**
Special to *The New York Times*, "Calouste Gulbenkian Dies at 86; One of Richest
Men in the World," *New York Times*, July 21, 1955, https://timesmachine.nytimes
.com/timesmachine/1955/07/21/83363695.html?action=click&contentCollection=Arc
hives&module=LedeAsset&region=ArchiveBody&pgtype=article&pageNumber=23.

p. 36   **never had to be defended by military actions.**
Rasoul Sorkhabi, "The Emergence of the Arabian Oil Industry," *GeoExPro* 5, no. 6
(2008), https://www.geoexpro.com/articles/2008/06/the-emergence-of-the-arabian
-oil-industry.

p. 38   **military buildup, all with few consequences.**
Adam Tooze, *The Wages of Destruction: The Making and Breaking of the Nazi Economy*
(New York: Penguin, 2006), 52–53.

p. 39   **further steps we may think it necessary to take.**
Neville Chamberlain, quoted in "International Response to Anschluss,"
GCSEHitoruy.org.uk, accessed July 2020, http://www.gcsehistory.org.uk/modern
world/appeasement/anschluss.htm.

p. 41   **He waited for him at the top of the stairs."**
Santi Corvaja, *Hitler and Mussolini: The Secret Meetings*, trans. Robert L. Miller (New
York: Enigma Books, 2008), 71.

p. 42   **I have wasted my time.**
Extracts from the Minutes of the conversation between Neville Chamberlain and
Adolf Hitler at Berchtesgaden, NA, FO 371/21738, http://www.nationalarchives.gov
.uk/education/resources/chamberlain-and-hitler/source-2c/.

p. 45   **the marching orders of the German army, and I agreed."**
Corvaja, *Hitler & Mussolini*, 73–74.

p. 46   **we could now safely regard the crisis as ended."**
Conclusions of Meetings of the Cabinet, Sept. 12–Oct. 3, 1938, NA, SP 37:38–48:38,
vol. LXI, 279–289, http://filestore.nationalarchives.gov.uk/pdfs/large/cab-23-95.pdf.

p. 46   **events would not have fallen into this disastrous state.**
Winston Churchill, "Disaster of the First Magnitude, 1938," October 5, 1938, The
National Churchill Museum, accessed July 2020, https://www.national
churchillmuseum.org/disaster-of-the-first-magnitude.html.

p. 47   **the outcome of a prolonged struggle.**
Robert J. Beck, "Munich's Lessons Reconsidered" *International Security* 14, no. 2
(Fall 1989): 161–191, doi:10.2307/2538858.

p. 48   **operating against Czechoslovakia and the West."**
Willamson Murray, *The Change in the European Balance of Power, 1938–1939:
The Path to Ruin* (Princeton: Princeton University Press, 1984), 252–253.

p. 48   **The Molotov-Ribbentrop Pact.**
"The Molotov-Ribbentrop Pact, 1939," Modern History Sourcebook, Fordham
University, updated January 21, 2020, https://sourcebooks.fordham.edu/mod
/1939pact.asp.

p. 49   **has been finally disarmed and overthrown."**
"Neville Chamberlain—Resignation Speech (Full Version)—May 10, 1940,"
uploaded by Roman Styran, December 15, 2016, https://www.youtube.com
/watch?v=h7hiMKu9JCE.

p. 50   **security cannot be bought by appeasement."**
Harry S. Truman, *Public Papers of the Presidents of the United States: Harry S.
Truman, 1950*, vol. 6, December 15, 742. https://www.trumanlibrary.gov
/library/public-papers/303/radio-and-television-report-american-people
-national-emergency.

CHAPTER THREE: THE KOREAN PENINSULA: LOCKED & LOADED

For this chapter, my profound thanks to Evans Revere, whose brilliant insights and extraordinary
tales of life on the edge along the Korean peninsula enriched my understanding immensely, and
I hope that of my dear readers. Revere, with his frequent shuttle diplomacy trips into Pyongyang,
had an unparalleled front-row seat for many of the most critical turning points along the Korean
red lines for decades.

p. 52   **keep it on an even keel.**
Truman, *Public Papers,* December 15, 1950.

p. 52   **their own very specific boundaries and rulers.**
Jinwung Kim, *A History of Korea: From "Land of the Morning Calm" to States in
Conflict,* (Bloomington: Indiana University Press, 2012), 32ff.

p. 52   **Pyongyang became for its first time a national capital.**
Kim, *A History of Korea,* 36–38, 47.

p. 52   **beat back every incursion.**
Kim, *A History of Korea,* 50.

p. 53   **Commander-in-Chief of Soviet Forces in the Far East.**
"Tokyo Bay: The Formal Surrender of the Empire of Japan, USS Missouri, 2
September 1945," Department of the Navy—Naval History and Heritage Command,
accessed July 2020, https://web.archive.org/web/20141006112851/http://www.history
.navy.mil/faqs/faq69-1.htm.

p. 53   **an iron curtain has descended across the continent."**
Churchill, "Sinews of Peace ('Iron Curtain Speech')."

p. 54   **In the final document there was no mention of Korea.**
"The Yalta Conference: February, 1945," February 11, 1945, The Avalon Project,
Lillian Goldman Law Library, Yale Law School, accessed July 2020, https://avalon
.law.yale.edu/wwii/yalta.asp.

p. 55   **the thirty-eighth parallel and decided to recommend that."**
Michael Fry, "National Geographic, Korea, and the 38th Parallel: How a National
Geographic map helped divide Korea," *National Geographic,* August 4, 2013,
https://news.nationalgeographic.com/news/2013/08/130805-korean-war-dmz
-armistice-38-parallel-geography/.

p. 55   **he'd had no idea that the thirty-ninth parallel**
          "Russo-Japanese War," History.com, updated August 21, 2018, https://www.history
          .com/topics/korea/russo-japanese-war.

p. 55   **possibly the thirty-ninth as well**.
          Dean Rusk, *As I Saw It* (New York: W.W. Norton, 1990).

p. 56   **pending before Congress.**
          James I. Matray, "Dean Acheson's Press Club Speech Reexamined," *Journal of Conflict
          Studies* 22, no. 1, (Spring 2002), https://journals.lib.unb.ca/index.php/jcs/article/view
          /366/578.

p. 56   **peace and security in the area."**
          UN Security Council, Resolution 83, Complaint of aggression upon the Republic of
          Korea, S/RES/1511 (June 27, 1950), https://undocs.org/S/RES/83(1950).

p. 56   **all UN forces under American command.**
          UN Security Council, Resolution 84, Complaint of aggression upon the Republic of
          Korea, S/RES/1588 (July 7, 1950), http://unscr.com/en/resolutions/84.

p. 58   **averages two and a half miles wide.**
          "Korean Demilitarized Zone," Earth Observatory, Nasa, July 28, 2003, https://earth
          observatory.nasa.gov/images/3660/korean-demilitarized-zone.

p. 58   **prosperity being accumulated by the South.**
          Narushige Michishita, *North Korea's Military-Diplomatic Campaigns: 1966–2008*
          (Philadelphia: Routledge, 2010), 9.

p. 59   **the North Korean government exulted.**
          Chae Hui Won, "Tradition of Victory Will Go Down for Ever," Explore DPRK
          https://exploredprk.com/articles/tradition-of-victory-will-go-down-for-ever/.

p. 60   **It [was] easier to play safe."**
          Henry Kissinger, *White House Years* (New York: Little Brown, 1979), 312–321.
          This account relies heavily on Kissinger's memoir, much of which was drafted by his
          long-time aide and Harvard scholar Peter Rodman, who had access to Kissinger's
          diaries and full government archival records.

p. 62   **none of these have surfaced."**
          Minutes of Washington Special Actions Group Meeting, Washington, August
          25, 1976, 10:39 A.M., Foreign Relations of the United States, 1969–1976 E-12,
          Documents on East and Southeast Asia, 1973–1976, Office of the Historian,
          https://history.state.gov/historicaldocuments/frus1969-76ve12/d286.

p. 62   **in 2004 an agreement was finally made to end them.**
          "Koreas switch off loudspeakers," BBC News, June 15, 2004, http://news.bbc.co.uk
          /2/hi/asia-pacific/3807409.stm.

p. 63   **Seoul from building one on its own.**
          Lee Jae-Bong, "US Deployment of Nuclear Weapons in 1950s South Korea & North
          Korea's Nuclear Development: Toward Denuclearization of the Korean Peninsula,"
          The Asia Pacific Journal 1:8, no. 3 (February 17, 2009), https://apjjf.org/-Lee-Jae
          -Bong/3053/article.html.

p. 64   **to land on Seoul but not much further.**
          David C. Wright and Timur Kadyshev, "An Analysis of the North Korean Nodong
          Missile," *Science & Global Security* 4 (1994): 129–169, http://scienceandglobalsecurity
          .org/archive/sgs04wright.pdf.

p. 66   **they saw as a nest of spies."**
          Interview by the author with Evans Revere in New York City, July 24, 2019.

p. 70   **military activities on or off actual battlefields.**
          Kelsey Davenport, "Chronology of U.S.-North Korean Nuclear and Missile
          Diplomacy," Arms Control Association, May 2020, https://www.armscontrol.org
          /factsheets/dprkchron.

p. 71   **a device that could be carried by an intercontinental missile.**
          Kelsey Davenport, "North Korea Conducts Nuclear Test," Arms Control
          Association, accessed July 2020, https://www.armscontrol.org/act/2013_03
          /North-Korea-Conducts-Nuclear-Test.

p. 72   **war or instability on the Korean peninsula."**
          Michael Martina and Ben Blanchard, "China draws 'red line' on North Korea, says
          won't allow war on peninsula" Reuters, March 7, 2014, https://uk.reuters.com/article
          /uk-korea-north-china/china-draws-red-line-on-north-korea-says-wont-allow-war
          -on-peninsula-idUKBREA2703T20140308.

p. 72   **deterrence and strength, but not a bargaining chip."**
          David E. Sanger, Choe Sang-Hun, and Jane Perlez, "A Big Blast in North Korea, and Big
          Questions on U.S. Policy," *New York Times,* September 9, 2016, https://www.nytimes
          .com/2016/09/10/world/asia/north-korea-nuclear-test.html?searchResultPosition=31.

p. 73   **launching a nuclear attack on North Korea.**
          Peter Baker, "The War That Wasn't: Trump Claims Obama Was Ready to Strike
          North Korea," *New York Times*, February 16, 2019, https://www.nytimes.com/2019
          /02/16/us/politics/trump-obama-north-korea.html?searchResultPosition=2.

p. 73   **wait-and-assess doctrine or "strategic patience."**
          Gerald F. Seib, Jay Solomon, and Carol E. Lee, "Barack Obama Warns Donald
          Trump on North Korean Threat," *Wall Street Journal*, November 22, 2016,
          https://www.wsj.com/articles/trump-faces-north-korean-challenge-1479855286.

p. 73   **they want to find some pretext to attack us."**
          N. G. Sudarkiov and Pak Seong-Cheol, "From the Journal of N.G. Sudarikov, 'Record of a
          Conversation with Pak Seong-Cheol, Member of the Kwp cc Politburo, Deputy Chairman
          of The Cabinet of Ministers, And Dprk Minister of Foreign Affairs,'" April 15, 1969,
          Wilson Center Digital Archive, accessed July 2020, https://digitalarchive.wilsoncenter.org
          /document/134231. Cited in Van Jackson, *On the Brink: Trump, Kim, and the Threat of
          Nuclear War* (Cambridge: Cambridge University Press, 2018), 38.

p. 74   **a "nuclear possessing state"** (haekboyuguk or 핵보유국)
          Peter Hayes, "The DPRK's Nuclear Constitution," NAPSNet Policy Forum,
          Nautilus Institute for Security and Sustainability, June 13, 2012, https://nautilus
          .org/napsnet/napsnet-policy-forum/the-dprks-nuclear-constitution/.

p. 74   **Kim's closest entourage, eventually Kim himself.**
          "Treasury Sanctions North Korean Senior Officials and Entities Associated with
          Human Rights Abuses," US Department of the Treasury, July 6, 2016, https://www
          .treasury.gov/press-center/press-releases/pages/jl0506.aspx.

p. 74   **reentry, fall, and detonate reliably on a target.**
          Shea Cotton, "Understanding North Korea's Missile Tests," Nuclear Threat Initiative,
          April 24, 2017, https://www.nti.org/analysis/articles/understanding-north-koreas-missile-tests/.
          The full CNS North Korea missile test dataset is available in Excel format:
          https://www.nti.org/documents/2137/north_korea_missile_test_database.xlsx.

p. 75   **removal from power or assassination would be unthinkable.**
          Antony J. Blinken, "Will Rex Tillerson Pass North Korea's Nuclear Test?," *New York
          Times*, March 15, 2017, https://www.nytimes.com/2017/03/15/opinion/will-rex
          -tillerson-pass-north-koreas-nuclear-test.html?searchResultPosition=5.

p. 75   **most potent military force (after the United States, Russia, and China).**
          Michael O'Sullivan, *The End of Globalization or a more Multipolar World?* (Zurich:
          Credit Suisse Research Institute, September 2015), 56, https://web.archive.org
          /web/20180215235711/http://publications.credit-suisse.com/tasks/render/file/index
          .cfm?fileid=EE7A6A5D-D9D5-6204-E9E6BB426B47D054.

p. 75   **50,000 troops remain on duty and with a nuclear force to back them up.**
          Choe Sang-Hun and Motoko Rich, "Trump's Talk of U.S. Troop Cuts Unnerves
          South Korea and Japan," *New York Times*, May 4, 2018, https://www.nytimes
          .com/2018/05/04/world/asia/south-korea-troop-withdrawal-united-states.html.

p. 77   **to persuade China to prod North Korea back to the negotiating table."**
          Jackson, *On the Brink*, 84.

p. 78   **He is making a big mistake."**
          "Interview: Maria Bartiromo of Fox Business Interviews Donald Trump," Factbase
          April 12, 2017, soundbite 125 transcript, https://factba.se/transcript/donald-trump
          -interview-fox-business-april-12-2017.

p. 78   **Trump's resolve being not open to question**
          Roberta Rampton and Sue-Lin Wong, "Pence warns North Korea of U.S. resolve
          shown in Syria, Afghan strikes," Reuters, April 15, 2017, https://www.reuters.com
          /article/us-northkorea-usa-missile-idUSKBN17H0NL.

p. 78   **U.S. stops short of drawing a red line.**
          Mark Landler and Jane Perlez, "Pence Talks Tough on North Korea, but U.S.
          Stops Short of Drawing Red Line," *New York Times*, April 17, 2017, https://www
          .nytimes.com/2017/04/17/world/asia/trump-north-korea-nuclear-us-talks.html?search
          ResultPosition=2.

p. 79   **he was not to be trifled or tested.**
          Choe Sang-Hun, David E. Sanger, and William J. Broad, "North Korean Missile
          Launch Fails, and a Show of Strength Fizzles," *New York Times,* April 15, 2017,
          https://www.nytimes.com/2017/04/15/world/asia/north-korea-missiles-pyongyang
          -kim-jong-un.html?searchResultPosition=4.

p. 80   **They have none of that without their nuclear weapons.**
           James Clapper, "2017 J-CSIS Forum: Keynote Remarks by The Honorable James
           Clapper," Center for Strategic & International Studies, June 27, 2017, https://www
           .csis.org/analysis/2017-j-csis-forum-keynote-remarks-honorable-james-clapper.

p. 81   **places targets as far into the US as Chicago within range."**
           "The CNS North Korea Missile Test Database," Nuclear Threat Initiative, March 31,
           2020, https://www.nti.org/analysis/articles/cns-north-korea-missile-test-database/.

p. 82   **a circle thirty to forty kilometers around Guam.**
           Julian Borger, "North Korea details Guam strike plan and calls Trump 'bereft of
           reason,'" *Guardian*, August 10, 2017, https://www.theguardian.com/world/2017
           /aug/10/north-korea-details-guam-strike-trump-load-of-nonsense.

p. 82   **Trump "drew a post hoc red line."**
           Jackson, *On the Brink*, 141.

p. 82   **at least fifteen times the size of the Hiroshima bomb.**
           Joe Pappalardo, "Seismic Detective Weighs In on North Korea's Latest Nuclear Test,"
           Popular Mechanics, September 5, 2017, https://www.popularmechanics.com/military
           /weapons/news/a28057/north-korea-nuclear-test-expert/.

p. 83   **his father worked in a prisoner-of-war camp.**
           "Moon Jae-in: South Korea's president with humble roots," BBC News, April 26,
           2018, https://www.bbc.com/news/world-asia-39860158.

p. 84   **just call me directly and the problem will be solved."**
           Choe Sang-Hun, "'We No Longer Need' Nuclear or Missile Tests, North Korean
           Leader Says," *New York Times*, April 20, 2018, https://www.nytimes.com/2018/04
           /20/world/asia/kim-jong-un-hotline-korea.html.

p. 84   **meet Kim "by May to achieve permanent denuclearization"**
           "Remarks by Republic of Korea National Security Advisor Chung Eui-Yong," The
           White House, March 8, 2018, https://www.whitehouse.gov/briefings-statements
           /remarks-republic-korea-national-security-advisor-chung-eui-yong/.

p. 85   **read a statement that detailed all this.**
           Inter-Korean Summit Press Corps, Christine Kim Dahee Kim, and Heekyong
           Yang, "Panmunjom Declaration for Peace, Prosperity and Unification of the Korean
           Peninsula," Reuters, April 27, 2018, https://uk.reuters.com/article/uk-northkorea
           -southkorea-summit-statemen/panmunjom-declaration-for-peace-prosperity-and
           -unification-of-the-korean-peninsula-idUKKBN1HY193.

p. 85   **"hopefully you [reporters] will give me credit."**
           Peter Baker and Choe Sang-Hun, "With Snap 'Yes' in Oval Office, Trump Gambles
           on North Korea," *New York Times*, March 10, 2018, https://www.nytimes.com
           /2018/03/10/world/asia/trump-north-korea.html.

p. 86   **and agreed to continue lower-level meetings.**
           "Joint Statement of President Donald J. Trump of the United States of America
           and Chairman Kim Jong Un of the Democratic People's Republic of Korea at the
           Singapore Summit," The White House, June 12, 2018, https://www.whitehouse.gov

/briefings-statements/joint-statement-president-donald-j-trump-united-states-america
-chairman-kim-jong-un-democratic-peoples-republic-korea-singapore-summit/.

CHAPTER FOUR: CHINA: BY THE BEAUTIFUL SEA

Of inestimable help in researching this chapter was America's consummate expert on the South China Sea and offshore Chinese strategic interests in the region. Jan van Tol, a retired Navy captain, is senior fellow at the Center for Strategic and Budgetary Assessments. The center's mission is to "look out two to three decades to identify emerging security challenges and opportunities . . . drawing attention to a set of worrisome and profound emerging areas of concern [including] a rising China threat in the Pacific Theater . . . and has played a prominent role in the ongoing development of an AirSea Battle concept by the U.S. Air Force and Navy."

p. 90   **two guided-missile destroyers, and support vessels**
         Carrier Strike Group 1 Public Affairs, "Carl Vinson Strike Group Departs for
         Deployment to Western Pacific," United States Navy, January 5, 2018, https://www
         .navy.mil/submit/display.asp?story_id=103944.

p. 90   **I will say this: he [Kim] is doing the wrong thing."**
         Julia Limitone, "Trump on North Korea Threats: We Are Sending an Armada,"
         Fox Business, April 12, 2017, https://www.foxbusiness.com/politics/trump-on
         -north-korea-threats-we-are-sending-an-armada.

p. 90   **at least 10 artificial and highly fortified islands.**
         Stein Tønnesen, "The Paracels: The 'Other' South China Sea Dispute," *Asian
         Perspective* 26, no. 4 (2002): 145–169, https://www.jstor.org/stable/42704389?read
         -now=1&refreqid=excelsior%3A3980f9b64f2ca56f855caca0e191ff8b&seq=11#page
         _scan_tab_contents; and Dexter Watkins, "What China Has Been Building in the
         South China Sea," *New York Times*, October 27, 2015, https://www.nytimes.com
         /interactive/2015/07/30/world/asia/what-china-has-been-building-in-the-south
         -china-sea.html.

p. 91   **its southern neighbor, India, in population by 2024.**
         Hannah Ritchie, "India will soon overtake China to become the most
         populous country in the world," Our World in Data, April 16, 2019, https://our
         worldindata.org/india-will-soon-overtake-china-to-become-the-most-populous
         -country-in-the-world.

p. 91   **and 6.5% of the world's fresh water."**
         "IV. China's Path of Peaceful Development Is a Choice Necessitated by History,"
         Information Office of the State Council of the People's Republic of China,
         September 6, 2011, http://www.china.org.cn/government/whitepaper/2011-09/06
         /content_23362786.htm.

p. 92   **annual trade is estimated to be in excess of $3.4 trillion.**
         "How much trade transits the South China Sea?," China Power, Center for Strategic
         & International Studies, August 2, 2017, updated October 10, 2019, https://china
         power.csis.org/much-trade-transits-south-china-sea/.

p. 92   **multiplied into a tapestry that crisscrosses it.**
Andrew S. Erickson and Ryan D. Martinson, eds., *China's Maritime Gray Zone Operations* (Annapolis: Naval Institute Press, 2019).

p. 92   **and through the waters of the South China Sea.**
Bill Hayton, *The South China Sea: The Struggle for Power in Asia* (New Haven: Yale University Press 2014), 5.

p. 92   **little attachment to the outside world;**
David A. Andelman, "Islanders Fear Reprisals by the Indonesians," *New York Times*, May 26, 1977, https://www.nytimes.com/1977/05/26/archives/islanders-fear-reprisals -by-the-indonesians-moluccans-at-home-fear.html.

p. 92   **for the succeeding couple of centuries.**
Hayton, *The South China Sea*, 14.

p. 92   **including Sumatra, Java, Bali, Borneo, and the Philippines.**
Hayton, *The South China Sea*, 17.

p. 93   **by the time Grotius died in 1645 or Selden nine years later.**
Jonathan Ziskind, "International Law and Ancient Sources: Grotius and Selden," *The Review of Politics* 35, no. 4 (October 1973): 537–559.

p. 94   **claims for first discovery indicating lasting entitlements.**
Raul (Pete) Pedrozo, *China versus Vietnam: An Analysis of the Competing Claims in the South China Sea* (Arlington: CNA Analysis & Solutions, August 2014): 67, https://southeastasiansea.files.wordpress.com/2014/08/china-versus-vietnam-an -analysis-of-the-competing-claims-in-the-south-china-sea.pdf.

p. 94   **steaming through and around it for several weeks.**
Pedrozo, *China versus Vietnam*, 52.

p. 94   **report issued by the Chinese Embassy in the Philippines asserted.**
"Some Basic Facts on China's sovereignty over Huangyan Island," Embassy of the People's Republic of China in the Republic of the Philippines, April 13, 2012, http://ph.china-embassy.org/eng/sgdt/t922594.htm.

p. 95   **Captain D'Auvergne struck, September 12, 1784."**
Joseph Huddart, *The Oriental Navigator, or New Directions for Sailing to and From the East Indies, China, New Holland &c.*, (London, 1801): 454, https://books .google.com/books?id=FbwBAAAAYAAJ&pg=PA454#v=onepage&q&f=false. François-Xavier Bonnet, *Geopolitics of Scarborough Shoal* (Bangkok: Research Institute on Contemporary Southeast Asia 2012), http://www.irasec.com /ouvrage34.

p. 96   **scattered across 158,000 square miles of water.**
"Spratly Islands," The World Factbook, Central Intelligence Agency, updated June 3, 2020, https://www.cia.gov/library/publications/the-world-factbook/geos /pg.html.

p. 96   **land area of just under three square miles.**
"Paracel Islands," The World Factbook, Central Intelligence Agency, updated June 3, 2020, https://www.cia.gov/library/publications/the-world-factbook/geos/pf.html.

p. 96   **11 billion barrels of crude oil**
          "South China Sea Energy Exploration and Development," Asia Maritime
          Transparency Initiative, Center for Strategic and International Studies, accessed July
          2020, https://amti.csis.org/south-china-sea-energy-exploration-and-development/.

p. 96   **marginally ahead of all mainland China.**
          "Natural Gas Reserves by Country," IndexMundi, United States Energy Information
          Administration, accessed July 2020, https://www.indexmundi.com/energy/?product=g
          as&graph=reserves&display=rank.

p. 96   **claimed by China, though remain hotly contested.**
          "South China Sea Energy Exploration and Development," Asia Maritime
          Transparency Initiative.

p. 96   **P-3 Orion aircraft for maritime surveillance.**
          Valerie Insinna, "US looks to increase weapons exports to Vietnam, decrease
          Russian influence," *Defense News*, February 7, 2018, https://www.defensenews
          .com/digital-show-dailies/singapore-airshow/2018/02/07/us-looks-to-increase
          -weapons-exports-to-vietnam-decrease-russian-influence/. James Pearson and Jeff
          Mason, "Trump pitches U.S. arms exports in meeting with Vietnam," Reuters,
          February 27, 2019, https://www.reuters.com/article/us-northkorea-usa-vietnam
          /trump-pitches-u-s-arms-exports-in-meeting-with-vietnam-idUSKCN1QG1HU.

p. 97   **the ten- or eleven-dash line).**
          Pedrozo, *China versus Vietnam*.

p. 98   **scattered Chinese garrisons on some other islands."**
          "Paracel Islands," The World Factbook.

p. 100   **to use elsewhere as the international standard.**
          Henry Kissinger, *The White House Years* (New York: Little Brown, 1979), 1114.

p. 101   **"risks undermining American sovereignty."**
          "Chapter XXI: Law of the Sea," United Nations Treaty Collection, December 10,
          1982, accessed July 2020, https://treaties.un.org/pages/ViewDetailsIII.aspx?src
          =TREATY&mtdsg_no=XXI-6&chapter=21&Temp=mtdsg3&clang=_en.

p. 101   **ministry spokesman declared archly in December 2007.**
          Barry Wain, "Manila's Bungle in The South China Sea," *Far Eastern Economic
          Review* 171, no. 1 (January/February 2008): 45–48, text via *realpolitikasia* (blog),
          http://realpolitikasia.blogspot.com/2016/08/manilas-bungle-in-south-china-sea
          -barry.html.

p. 103   **little more of a threat than as obstacles to shipping.**
          "Updated: China's Big Three Near Completion," Asia Maritime Transparency
          Initiative, Center for Strategic and International Studies, June 29, 2017, https://amti
          .csis.org/chinas-big-three-near-completion/.

p. 103   **the width of the entire District of Columbia.**
          Elbridge A. Colby, "Testimony before the House Committee on Foreign Affairs
          Subcommittee on Asia and the Pacific: 'Diplomacy and Security in the South China
          Sea: After the Tribunal,'" Center for a New American Security, September 22, 2016,

https://docs.house.gov/meetings/FA/FA05/20160922/105354/HHRG-114-FA05
-Wstate-ColbyE-20160922.pdf.

p. 103 **anti-ship cruise missiles with a two-hundred-fifty-mile range,**
Humphrey Hawksley, *Asian Waters: The Struggle Over the South China Sea and the Strategy of Chinese Expansion* (New York: Abrams Press, 2018), Kindle edition.

p. 103 **an extended two-runway airfield.**
Andrew Chubb, "China's 'blue territory' and the technosphere," *southsea conversations* (blog), April 19, 2017, https://southseaconversations.wordpress.com/2017/04/19/chinas-blue-territory-and-the-technosphere/.

p. 104 **sixty other potential outposts in the Spratlys alone.**
Annual Report to Congress: Military and Security Developments Involving the Peoples Republic of China 2019 (Washington, D.C.: Department of Defense, November 14, 2019), 74–75, http://www.andrewerickson.com/wp-content/uploads/2019/05/DoD_China-Report_2019.pdf.

p. 106 **southernmost boundary of its nation.**
Hayton, *The South China Sea*, 169–170.

p. 106 **a figure that Malaysian officials would want to place in jeopardy.**
"Malaysia," The Observatory of Economic Complexity, accessed July 2020, https://oec.world/en/profile/country/mys/.

p. 106 **pseudonym for Air Force Colonel Dai Xu,**
Hayton, *The South China Sea*, 175.

p. 106 **not be taken seriously, at least for now," he concluded.**
Long Tau, "Time to teach those around South China Sea a lesson," *Global Times*, September 29, 2011, http://www.globaltimes.cn/content/677717.shtml.

p. 107 **the official Philippine census of 2016.**
Philippine Census R04B, August 1, 2016, https://www.psa.gov.ph/sites/default/files/attachments/hsd/pressrelease/R04B.xlsx.

p. 107 **build China into a maritime power."**
"Full Text of Hu Jintao's report at 18th Party Congress," Embassy of the People's Republic of China in the United States of America, November 27, 2012, http://www.china-embassy.org/eng/zt/18th_CPC_National_Congress_Eng/t992917.htm.

p. 108 **Australian military scholar. In a remarkable piece,**
Carlyle A. Thayer, "ASEAN'S Code of Conduct in the South China Sea: A Litmus Test for Community-Building?" *The Asia-Pacific Journal* 10, issue 34, no. 4 (August 19, 2012), https://apjjf.org/2012/10/34/Carlyle-A.-Thayer/3813/article.html.

p. 108 **sunny skies and a balmy seventy-two degrees,**
"Past Weather in Haikou, Hainan China—March 2017," timeanddate.com, https://www.timeanddate.com/weather/china/haikou/historic?month=3&year=2017.

p. 108 **on its maiden voyage to the Paracels.**
Ben Blanchard, "China launches new cruise ship tour in South China Sea," Reuters, March 2, 2017, https://www.reuters.com/article/us-southchinasea-china-ship-idUSKBN16A0A4.

p. 108   **to expand its offerings to air tours,**
Catherine Wong, "First cruises, now flights . . . China plans to fly tourists to
disputed South China Sea islands," *South China Morning Post*, March 7, 2017,
https://www.scmp.com/news/china/diplomacy-defence/article/2076669
/first-cruises-now-flights-china-plans-fly-tourists.

p. 109   **Chinese flag wave over waters in the Spratlys."**
Andrew S. Erickson and Conor M. Kennedy, "Trailblazers in Warfighting: The
Maritime Militia of Danzhou," Center for International Maritime Security, February 1,
2016, http://cimsec.org/trailblazers-warfighting-maritime-militia-danzhou/21475.

p. 109   **Chinese nationals and legal persons overseas.**
"IV. Supporting National Economic and Social Development," Ministry of National
Defense, The People's Republic of China, April 16, 2013, http://eng.mod.gov.cn
/Database/WhitePapers/2013-04/16/content_4442755.htm.

p. 110   **large enough to allow all five to gain a foothold.**
Bonnet, *Geopolitics of Scarborough Shoal*, 21.

p. 110   **vessels circling in the vicinity of the reef.**
Ely Ratner, "Learning the Lessons of Scarborough Reef," *The National Interest*,
November 21, 2013, https://nationalinterest.org/commentary/learning-the-lessons
-scarborough-reef-9442.

p. 110   **in an attempt to appease Hitler to prevent World War II."**
Keith Bradsher, "Philippine Leader Sounds Alarm on China," *New York
Times*, February 4, 2014, https://www.nytimes.com/2014/02/05/world/asia
/philippine-leader-urges-international-help-in-resisting-chinas-sea-claims.html.

p. 110   **to derail these critical negotiations.**
Erickson and Martinson, *China's Maritime Gray Zone Operations*, 285.

p. 110   **key shipping channels in the South and East China Seas.**
Kiyoshi Takenaka, "Philippine's Aquino revives comparison between China and
Nazi Germany," Reuters, June 3, 2015, https://www.reuters.com/article/us-japan
-philippines/philippines-aquino-revives-comparison-between-china-and-nazi
-germany-idUSKBN0OJ0OY20150603.

p. 111   **any Chinese passport decorated with this map.**
Faye Williams, "Vietnam Refuses to Stamp Chinese Passports Featuring 9-Dash Line,"
Elite Readers, accessed July 2020, https://www.elitereaders.com/vietnam-refuse-chinese
-passports/. "Philippines not to stamp China passports," United Press International,
November 29, 2012, https://www.upi.com/Top_News/World-News/2012/11/29
/Philippines-not-to-stamp-China-passports/93181354165587/.

p. 111   **China's activities across the region.**
"Hague Announces Decision on South China Sea," *New York Times*, July 12, 2016,
https://www.nytimes.com/interactive/2016/07/12/world/asia/hague-south-china-sea.
html?module=inline. Jane Perlez, "Tribunal Rejects Beijing's Claims in South China
Sea," *New York Times*, July 12, 2016, https://www.nytimes.com/2016/07/13/world
/asia/south-china-sea-hague-ruling-philippines.html.

p. 111   **arbitral awards under any circumstances."**
"中帅人民共和恐外交部牧于略菲律埠共和恐汝求建立的南海仲裁案仲裁庭所作裁决的砝明" [Statement of the Ministry of Foreign Affairs of the People's Republic of China on the Award of the Arbitration Tribunal of the South China Sea Arbitration Case Established at the Request of the Republic of the Philippines], Ministry of Foreign Affairs of the People's Republic of China, July 12, 2016, https://www.fmprc.gov.cn/web/zyxw/t1379490.shtml.

p. 111   **jurisdiction over them continuously, peacefully and effectively."**
"Full Text of Chinese govt statement on China's territorial sovereignty and maritime rights and interests in S China Sea," The State Council, The People's Republic of China, July 12, 2016, http://english.www.gov.cn/archive/publications/2016/07/12/content_281475391807773.htm.

p. 112   **not to mention aircraft landing strips.**
David Brunnstrom, "China installs weapons systems on artificial islands: U.S. think tank," Reuters, December 14, 2016, https://www.reuters.com/article/us-southchinasea-china-arms-exclusive-idUSKBN1431OK.

p. 113   **and seventy-five times the level of the Philippines.**
"Military expenditures by country, in constant (2017) US$ m., 1988–2018," Stockholm International Peace Research Institute, 2019, https://www.sipri.org/sites/default/files/Data%20for%20all%20countries%20from%201988%E2%80%932018%20in%20constant%20%282017%29%20USD%20%28pdf%29.pdf.

p. 113   **all of their South China Sea neighbors combined.**
"Military expenditure by region in constant US dollars, 1988–2018," Stockholm International Peace Research Institute, 2019, https://www.sipri.org/sites/default/files/Data%20for%20world%20regions%20from%201988%E2%80%932018%20%28pdf%29.pdf.

p. 113   **such a high-ranking officer.**
Chris Buckley, "Chinese General Visits Disputed Spratly Islands in South China Sea," *New York Times*, April 15, 2016, https://www.nytimes.com/2016/04/16/world/asia/china-south-china-sea-spratly-islands.html?action=click&module=RelatedCoverage&pgtype=Article&region=Footer.

p. 113   **facilities on the islands," according to a brief Ministry of Defense statement.**
"范欲龙峡察南沙控礁" [Fan Changlong inspects Nansha island reef], Ministry of Defense Network, People's Republic of China, April 15, 2016, http://www.mod.gov.cn/topnews/2016-04/15/content_4649514.htm.

p. 113   **the smaller patrol boats can range up to ten thousand miles.**
Erickson and Martinson, *China's Maritime Gray Zone Operations*, 115.

p. 113   **Some have helicopter decks as well.**
Erickson and Martinson, *China's Maritime Gray Zone Operations*, 5.

p. 114   **water jets cascading down their exhaust funnels.**
Erickson and Martinson, *China's Maritime Gray Zone Operations*, 109.

p. 114   **the more remote South China Sea islands.**
Liu Zhen, "Will China's new stealth amphibious drone boats guard its South China
Sea outposts?" *South China Morning Post*, April 16, 2019, https://www.scmp.com
/news/china/military/article/3006450/will-chinas-new-stealth-amphibious-drone
-boats-guard-its-south.

p. 114   **on Fiery Cross, Subi, and Mischief Reefs.**
Amanda Macias and Courtney Kube, "Chinese military conducts anti-ship ballistic
missile tests in the hotly contested South China Sea," CNBC, July 1, 2019,
https://www.cnbc.com/2019/07/01/chinese-military-conducts-missile-tests-in-the
-south-china-sea.html?__source=iosappshare%7Ccom.google.Gmail.ShareExtension.

p. 114   **trip wire for its network of red lines.**
Andrew S. Erickson, "Understanding China's Third Sea Force: The Maritime
Militia," *Fairbank Center Blog* (blog), Medium, September 8, 2017, https://link
.medium.com/Ypt2NDJDSY.

p. 114   **forces operating under a direct military chain of command."**
Andrew S. Erickson, "The South China Sea's Third Force: Understanding and
Countering China's Maritime Militia," Testimony before the House Armed Services
Committee Seapower and Projection Forces Subcommittee, September 21, 2016,
https://docs.house.gov/meetings/AS/AS28/20160921/105309/HHRG-114-AS28
-Wstate-EricksonPhDA-20160921.pdf.

p. 114   **nearly double the level of South Korea or Japan.**
United Nations Conference on Trade and Development (UNCTAD), *Review of
Maritime Transport: 2018* (New York: United Nations Publications, 2018): 38,
https://unctad.org/en/PublicationsLibrary/rmt2018_en.pdf.

p. 114   **5,512 commercial ships over 1,00 gross tons.**
"Fan Changlong inspects Nansha island reef," 29.

p. 114   **Seven of the world's top ten cargo ports are in China.**
UNCTAD, *Review of Maritime Transport*, 66.

p. 115   **only one (Los Angeles) is in the United States.**
UNCTAD, *Review of Maritime Transport*, 73.

p. 115   **a gap that will only widen going forward.**
Andrew S. Erickson, "Numbers Matter: China's Three 'Navies' Each Have the
World's Most Ships," *The National Interest*, February 26, 2018, https://national
interest.org/feature/numbers-matter-chinas-three-navies-each-have-the-worlds
-most-24653.

p. 115   **highly effective satellite communications equipment.**
Erickson and Martinson, *China's Maritime Gray Zone Operations*, 154–156.

p. 115   **Collaboration to Address Anti-Access & Area Denial Challenges."**
"Overview of the Air-Sea Battle Concept," *Navy Live* (blog), US Navy, June 3, 2013,
https://navylive.dodlive.mil/2013/06/03/overview-of-the-air-sea-battle-concept/.

p. 117   **effective response to China's expansion."**
Erickson and Martinson, *China's Maritime Gray Zone Operations*, 10.

p. 117   **"And we could build on them in 18 months."**
          Jeff Stein, "Why Beijing Isn't Backing Down on South China Sea," *Newsweek*,
          October 10, 2015, https://www.newsweek.com/why-beijing-not-backing-down
          -south-china-sea-381973.

p. 118   **an advanced P-8A Poseidon electronic surveillance plane.**
          Jim Sciutto, "Behind the scenes: A secret Navy flight over China's military buildup,"
          CNN Politics, May 26, 2015, https://www.cnn.com/2015/05/26/politics/south-china
          -sea-navy-surveillance-plane-jim-sciutto/index.html.

p. 118   **operations in the Persian Gulf and Strait of Hormuz.**
          Erickson and Martinson, *China's Maritime Gray Zone* Operations, 251.

p. 119   **in the port on a ninety-nine year lease.**
          Amy Cheng, "Will Djibouti Become Latest Country to Fall Into China's Debt Trap?"
          Foreign Policy, July 31, 2018, https://foreignpolicy.com/2018/07/31/will-djibouti
          -become-latest-country-to-fall-into-chinas-debt-trap/.

p. 119   **base of operations for US Africa Command in the Horn of Africa."**
          "Welcome to Camp Lemonnier, Djibouti," Commander, Navy Installations Command,
          US Navy, accessed July 2020, https://www.cnic.navy.mil/regions/cnreurafswa
          /installations/camp_lemonnier_djibouti.html.

p. 119   **operator of ports and related facilities in nearly fifty countries.**
          "About Us," DP World, accessed July 2020, https://www.dpworld.com/who-we-are
          /about-us.

p. 119   **In 2017, China opened its first overseas military base next door.**
          Monica Wang, "China's Strategy in Djibouti: Mixing Commercial and Military
          Interests," *Asia Unbound* (blog), Council on Foreign Relations, April 13, 2018,
          https://www.cfr.org/blog/chinas-strategy-djibouti-mixing-commercial-and-military
          -interests.

p. 120   **Chagos a vast 210,000 square mile area,**
          Adam Augustyn, "China Sea," *Encyclopaedia Britannica*, accessed July 2020,
          https://www.britannica.com/place/China-Sea.

p. 120   **its American tenant, was asserting its sovereignty.**
          Paul Rincon, "UK sets up Chagos Islands marine reserve," BBC News, April 1, 2010,
          http://news.bbc.co.uk/2/hi/science/nature/8599125.stm.

p. 120   **"classical salami-slicing strategy."**
          Erickson and Martinson, *China's Maritime Gray Zone* Operations, 269.

p. 121   **or whether he is merely bluffing."**
          Bruce M. Russett, "The calculus of deterrence," *The Journal of Conflict Resolution* 7,
          no. 2 (June 1963): 98.

p. 122   **an artificial island has been built on top of it," a US Navy official told Reuters.**
          Idrees Ali and David Brunnstrom, "U.S. warship drill meant to defy China's claim
          over artificial island: officials," Reuters, May 24, 2017, https://www.reuters.com
          /article/us-usa-southchinasea-navy/u-s-warship-drill-meant-to-defy-chinas-claim
          -over-artificial-island-officials-idUSKBN18K353.

p. 122   **"your access to those islands will not be allowed."**
"Hearing Transcript: Senate Foreign Relations Committee Hearing on the
Nomination of Rex Tillerson to be Secretary of State," January 11, 2017, https://www
.thisweekinimmigration.com/uploads/6/9/2/2/69228175/hearingtranscript_senate
foreignrelationstillersonconfirmationhearing_2017-01-11.pdf.

CHAPTER FIVE: FROM SOVIET UNION TO RUSSIAN EMPIRE

p. 123   **I first mentioned the two gentlemen in my CNN column,**
David A. Andelman, "Could World War III start here?" CNN Opinion,
November 5, 2016, https://www.cnn.com/2016/11/03/opinions/next-world-war
-andelman/index.html.

p. 124   **she launched Rahvarinne**
Olev Livik, "The Popular Front: A political mass movement in Estonia in the late
1980s," *Estonica: Encyclopedia about Estonia*, Eesti Instituut, January 3, 2010,
http://www.estonica.org/en/The_Popular_Front/.

p. 126   **a language that is of the Finno-Ugric family,**
Simon Ager, "Estonian (eesti keel)," *Omniglot: the online encyclopedia of writing
systems & languages* (blog), accessed July 2020, https://www.omniglot.com/writing
/estonian.htm.

p. 126   **roots dating back to Sanskrit,**
"Lithuanian language (*lietuviu kalba*)," Lithuanian, Atlas: A Taste of Languages at
School, University College London, accessed July 2020, https://www.ucl.ac.uk/atlas
/lithuanian/language.html.

p. 126   **Tacitus in the first century c.e., who talked briefly of the Aestii**
"Estonia (Eeesti) (Aestii)," European Kingdoms: Northern Europe, The History
Files, accessed July 2020, https://www.historyfiles.co.uk/KingListsEurope
/EasternEstonia.htm.

p. 126   **marvel at the price which they receive.**
Tacitus, "Chapter XLV: Gothones," *Germania,* United Nations of Roma Victrix,
accessed July 2020, https://www.unrv.com/tacitus/tacitusgermania.php.

p. 128   **between Churchill and Stalin alone**.
Helen Cleary, Phil Edwards, Bruce Robinson, and Victoria Cook, "Fact File: Second
Moscow Conference: 9 to 19 October 1944," WW2 People's War: An archive of
World War Two Memories, BBC, June 2003, accessed July 2020, https://web.archive.
org/web/20100820114139/http://www.bbc.co.uk/ww2peopleswar/timeline/factfiles
/nonflash/a1144874.shtml.

p. 129   **Everyone imposes his own system as far as his army can reach."**
Milovan Djilas, *Conversations with Stalin*, (New York: Harcourt Brace Jovanovich,
1962), 114.

p. 129   **closed entirely and indefinitely for unspecified "repairs."**
Michael D. Haydock, *City under Siege: The Berlin Blockade and Airlift, 1948–1949*
(Washington, D.C.: Brasseys, 2000).

p. 130   **a force of ten thousand heavily armed guards.**
Norman Gelb, *The Berlin Wall* (New York: Crown Publishing, 1986).
David Tulloch, "Berlin Wall," Encyclopedia.com, updated July 6, 2020, https://www
.encyclopedia.com/history/modern-europe/german-history/berlin-wall.

p. 131   **frontier with the free state of Austria.**
David A. Andelman, "Quiz Show: How Hungary Lures Its Youth to Party," *New York
Times*, August 1, 1978, https://www.nytimes.com/1978/08/01/archives/quiz-show
-how-hungary-lures-its-youth-to-party-negative-poll.html?searchResultPosition=4.

p. 132   **based in Dresden and lived in a building that housed the Stasi.**
Vladimir Putin, with Nataliya Gevorkyan, Natalya Timakova, and Andrei
Kolesnikov, *First Person: An Astonishingly Frank Self-Portrait by Russia's President
Vladimir Putin* (New York: Public Affairs, 2000), 66–82.

p. 133   **whoever wants it back has no brain.**
Toby Tristar Gati, "Putin's Russia," CSIS, https://csis-website-prod.s3.amazonaws
.com/s3fs-public/legacy_files/files/media/csis/pubs/0001qus_russia.pdf

p. 133   **reassemble it as best he could.**
Andrew Osborn, "Putin, before vote, says he'd reverse Soviet collapse if he could:
agencies," Reuters, March 2, 2018, https://www.reuters.com/article/us-russia
-election-putin/putin-before-vote-says-hed-reverse-soviet-collapse-if-he-could
-agencies-idUSKCN1GE2TF.

p. 133   **Russian empire he openly avowed to have admired.**
Susan B. Glasser, "Putin the Great: Russia's Imperial Impostor," *Foreign Affairs*,
September/October 2019, https://www.foreignaffairs.com/articles/russian-federation
/2019-08-12/putin-great.

p. 134   **an attack on one NATO member is an attack on all.**
"Collective defence–Article 5," North Atlantic Treaty Organization, updated
November 25, 2019, https://www.nato.int/cps/en/natohq/topics_110496.htm.

p. 134   **its vast cotton crop, much of it for consumption in Russia.**
"Uzbekistan's Forced Labor problem," The Cotton Campaign, International Labor
Rights Forum, accessed July 2020, http://www.cottoncampaign.org/uzbekistans
-forced-labor-problem.html.

p. 134   **the site of several Russian war graves.**
"Soviet Memorial Causes Rift between Estonia and Russia," Spiegel
International, April 27, 2007, https://www.spiegel.de/international/europe
/deadly-riots-in-tallinn-soviet-memorial-causes-rift-between-estonia-and
-russia-a-479809.html.

p. 135   **brick fortress on the fringes of downtown Tallinn, described the actions:**
Rain Ottis, "Analysis of the 2007 Cyber Attacks Against Estonia from the
Information Warfare Perspective," Cooperative Cyber Defence Centre
of Excellence, accessed July 2020, https://ccdcoe.org/uploads/2018/10
/Ottis2008_AnalysisOf2007FromTheInformationWarfarePerspective.pdf.

p. 136 **produced there by Georgians of the Neolithic period.**
David Keys, "Now that's what you call a real vintage: professor unearths 8,000-year-old wine," *Independent*, December 28, 2003, https://www.independent .co.uk/news/science/now-thats-what-you-call-a-real-vintage-professor-unearths -8000-year-old-wine-84179.html/. "Evidence of ancient wine found in Georgia a vintage quaffed some 6,000 years BC," *Euronews*, May 21, 2015, https://www .euronews.com/2015/05/21/evidence-of-ancient-wine-found-in-georgia -a-vintage-quaffed-some-6000-years-bc.

p. 137 **a dowry of many traditional Georgian brides.**
Giorgi Lomsadze, "Georgian government throws epic bridal shower," *Eurasianet*, November 9, 2018, https://eurasianet.org/georgian-government-throws-epic-bridal-shower.

p. 137 **absorbed into imperial Russia in the course of the nineteenth century.**
Ronald Grigor Suny, *The Making of the Georgian Nation*, 2nd ed. (Bloomington: Indiana University Press, 1994), 63ff. https://books.google.com/books?id=riW0kKz at2sC&printsec=frontcover&dq=Georgian+history&hl=en&sa=X&ved=2ahUKEw jHlM3mg6PkAhXSqFkKHQwnAl8Q6AEwAnoECAIQAg#v=onepage&q=Geor gian%20history&f=false.

p. 137 **where would they come to rest, once the parts split up?**
Stefan Wolff, "Georgia: Abkhazia and South Ossetia," *Encyclopedia Princetoniensis*, Princeton University, accessed July 2020, https://pesd.princeton.edu/node/706.

p. 139 **very much a European conflict of the twenty-first century,**
Michael Emerson, "Post-Mortem on Europe's First War of the 21st Century," *CEPS Policy Brief*, no. 167 (August 2008), http://aei.pitt.edu/9382/2/9382.pdf.

p. 139 **looked for civilian or military aid.**
Arnold van Bruggen and Rob Hornstra, "The Abkhazian Olympic Dream," The Sochi Project, accessed July 2020, http://www.thesochiproject.org/en/chapters /abkhazia-s-olympic-dream/.

p. 140 **They have fought two wars in Chechnya."**
John Thornhill and David Ibsison, "Kremlin is told that move could backfire," *Financial Times*, August 27, 2008, https://www.ft.com/content/155c31fa-745f -11dd-bc91-0000779fd18c.

p. 140 **ill-conceived boundaries maintained in poor faith.**
Independent International Fact-Finding Mission on the Conflict in Georgia, *Report*, vol. 1, September 2009, 409, https://www.echr.coe.int/Documents/HUDOC_38263 _08_Annexes_ENG.pdf.

p. 141 **sent across what existed of the frontier between Georgia and Abkhazia.**
Alexander Cooley and Lincoln Mitchell, "Abkhazia on Three Wheels," *World Policy Journal* 27, no. 2 (Summer 2010): 73–81, https://www-jstor-org.ezproxy.monroepl .org/stable/27870342?Search=yes&resultItemClick=true&searchText=%28World& searchText=Policy&searchText=Journal%29&searchText=AND&searchText=%28 Abkhazia%29&searchUri=%2Faction%2FdoBasicSearch%3FQuery%3DAbkhazia

%26amp%3Bprq%3DWorld%2BPolicy%2BJournal%26amp%3Bswp%3Don%26
amp%3Bhp%3D25%26amp%3Bso%3Drel&ab_segments=0%2Fbasic_search%2
Fcontrol&refreqid=search%3A1b74ff1324aa21860ccc1a2e0921d5c2&seq=1#meta
data_info_tab_contents.

p. 142   **through a heavily armed prism.**
Giorgi Menabde, "Georgians in Abkhazia: A Choice Between Assimilation and
Emigration," *Eurasia Daily Monitor* 16, no. 113 (August 6, 2019), The Jamestown
Foundation, https://jamestown.org/program/georgians-in-abkhazia-a-choice-between
-assimilation-and-emigration/.

p. 142   **a British correspondent writing for the Guardian.**
Andrew North, "Georgia accuses Russia of violating international law over South
Ossetia," *Guardian*, July 14, 2015, https://www.theguardian.com/world/2015/jul/14
/georgia-accuses-russia-of-violating-international-law-over-south-ossetia.

p. 144   **his farewell statement on military strategy.**
The National Military Strategy of the United States of America, 2015, Joint Chiefs of
Staff, June 2015, https://www.jcs.mil/Portals/36/Documents/Publications/2015
_National_Military_Strategy.pdf?source=GovDelivery.

p. 145   **including in its territory vast stretches of Russia and Poland.**
Michael F. Hamm, "Chapter I: The Early History of Kiev," *Kiev: A Portrait,
1800–1917* (Princeton: Princeton University Press, 1993), 3–ff. http://assets.press
.princeton.edu/chapters/s5285.pdf.

p. 145   **creeping settlement and expansion.**
Orest Subtelny, *Ukraine: A History*, 3rd ed. (Toronto: University of Toronto Press. 1988),
https://books.google.com/books?id=HNIs9O3EmtQC&pg=PA69-IA6&source=gbs_toc
_r&cad=3#v=onepage&q&f=false.
This work, which has gone through four editions, has proved especially useful for
much of this historical context.

p. 150   **according to the Central Intelligence Agency.**
"Europe: Ukraine," The World Factbook, Central Intelligence Agency, updated June
11, 2020, https://www.cia.gov/library/publications/the-world-factbook/geos/up.html.

p. 150   **demonstrated graphically the position of the peninsula.**
Harrison E. Salisbury, "Soviet Transfers Crimea to the Ukrainian Republic," *New
York Times*, February 27, 1954, https://timesmachine.nytimes.com/times
machine/1954/02/27/84109158.pdf.

p. 151   **Tarasov, member of the presidium, rose to explain the unusual action.**
Gary Goldberg, trans., "February 19, 1954: Meeting of the Presidium of the Union of
Soviet Socialist Republics," *Istoricheskii arkhiv* 1, no. 1 (1992), Wilson Center Digital
Archive: International History Declassified, https://digitalarchive.wilsoncenter.org
/document/119638.pdf?v=9c6737c4342d1343676044065d49f510.

p. 151   **the powerful leader of Ukraine's Communist Party, Alexei Kirichenko.**
Mark Kramer, "Why Did Russia Give Away Crimea Sixty Years Ago?" *Cold War
International History Project e-Dossier* 47, Wilson Center, accessed July 2020,

https://www.wilsoncenter.org/publication/why-did-russia-give-away-crimea-sixty
-years-ago.

p. 153   **came within hours of utter catastrophe.**
"Cuban Missile Crisis," John F. Kennedy Presidential Library and Museum, accessed
July 2020, https://www.jfklibrary.org/learn/about-jfk/jfk-in-history/Cuban-missile
-crisis.

p. 153   **nuclear fuel for the new nation's power plants.**
Hans M. Kristensen, Alicia Godsberg, and Jonathan Garbose, "Ukraine Special
Weapons," *The Nuclear Information Project* (blog), Federation of American Scientists,
accessed July 2020, https://fas.org/nuke/guide/ukraine/index.html.

p. 154   **The Patriarch Kirill of Moscow and All Rus'**
Interfax-Ukraine, "Patriarch Kirill to conduct prayer service in Kyiv before
Yanukovych's inauguration," *Kyiv Post*, February 20, 2010, https://www.kyivpost
.com/article/content/ukraine-politics/patriarch-kirill-to-conduct-prayer-service-in
-kyiv-60051.html.

p. 155   **visits for his first week in office to Moscow and Brussels.**
Reuters, "Ukraine Yanukovych sets visits to Moscow, Brussels," *Kyiv Post*, February 25,
2010, https://www.kyivpost.com/article/content/ukraine-politics/ukraine
-yanukovych-sets-visits-to-moscow-brussels-60426.html.

p. 155   **Yanukovych's popularity had plunged to a low of 13 percent.**
Svitlana Tuchynska, "All in the Family," *Kyiv Post*, March 2, 2012, https://www
.kyivpost.com/article/content/ukraine-politics/all-in-the-family-123517.html.

p. 155   **toward new and stronger economic ties with Russia.**
Denise Forsthuber, "From Russia Without Love," *US News & World Report*,
November 27, 2013, https://www.usnews.com/opinion/blogs/world-report/2013
/11/27/ukraines-surprising-rejection-of-the-european-union-reflects-russias-power.

p. 155   **Russia steals "Ukrainian bride" at the altar.**
Timothy Heritage and Richard Balmforth, "Russia Steals 'Ukrainian bride' at the
altar," Reuters, November 22, 2013, https://www.reuters.com/article/us-ukraine
-eu-russia/russia-steals-ukrainian-bride-at-the-altar-idUSBRE9AL0UK20131122.

p. 156   **2,500 had been injured, according to Ukrainian prosecutors.**
RFE/RL Ukrainian Service, "Ukrainians Honor Those Killed in Euromaidan
Protests," Radio Free Europe/Radio Liberty, February 20, 2017, https://www.rferl
.org/a/ukrainians-honor-killed-euromaidan-protests/28320987.html.

p. 156   **he'd been leasing for less than $40 a month,**
Irina Kasyanova and Igor Serov, "В'Межигорье' у Януковича есть зоопарк,
аэродром и оранжерея" [In "Mezhyhirya" Yanukovych has a zoo, an airfield and a
greenhouse], *Сегодня (Today)*, June 7, 2010, https://www.segodnya.ua/ukraine
/v-mezhihore-u-janukovicha-ect-zoopark-aerodrom-i-oranzhereja-200298.html.

p. 156   **in Russia, which received him with open arms.**
Alison Smale, "Just Like His Power, Ukrainian Ex-Leader Vanishes Into Thin Air,"
New York Times, February 24, 2014, https://www.nytimes.com/2014/02/25

/world/europe/just-like-his-power-ukrainian-ex-leader-vanishes-into-thin-air.
html?searchResultPosition=9.

p. 156   **we must start working on returning Crimea to Russia."**
AFP, "Putin describes secret operation to seize Crimea," Yahoo News, March 8,
2015, https://news.yahoo.com/putin-describes-secret-operation-seize-crimea
-212858356.html.

p. 157   **to back the transition underway in Kiev.**
Steven Lee Myers, "Deeply Bound to Ukraine, Putin Watches and Waits for Next
Move," *New York Times*, February 23, 2014, https://www.nytimes.com/2014/02/24
/world/europe/deeply-bound-to-ukraine-putin-watches-and-waits-for-next-move
.html?searchResultPosition=7.

p. 157   **ancestors had suffered under Stalin.**
Andrew Higgins and Steven Lee Myers, "As Putin Orders Drills in Crimea, Protestors'
Clash Shows Region's Divide," *New York Times*, February 26, 2014, https://www
.nytimes.com/2014/02/27/world/europe/russia.html?searchResultPosition=16.

p. 157   **to claim it was a "training exercise."**
Simon Shuster, "Gunmen Storm Crimea Hotel Full of Reporters on Eve of
Referendum," *Time*, March 15, 2014, https://time.com/26320/gunmen-storm
-crimea-hotel-full-of-reporters-on-eve-of-referendum/.

p. 158   **Kalashnikov Group, maker of the renowned assault rifle.**
Cory Welt, Kristin Archick, Rebecca M. Nelson, and Dianne E. Rennack, *U.S.
Sanctions on Russia* (Washington, D.C.: Congressional Research Service, January 17,
2020), 11, https://fas.org/sgp/crs/row/R45415.pdf.

p. 158   **stronger, primarily in the economic sphere."**
"Vladimir Putin: Sanctions hurt Europe more than Russia," *Deutsche Welle*, June 20,
2019, https://www.dw.com/en/vladimir-putin-sanctions-hurt-europe-more-than
-russia/a-49277071.

p. 159   **gains as the dollar appreciated in value.**
Bloomberg, "Putin's Dollar Dump Costs Russia $8Bln," *Moscow Times,* October 15,
2019, https://www.themoscowtimes.com/2019/10/15/putin-dollar-dump-costs-russia
-8-billion-a67736.

p. 159   **oil prices, which fell from $115 to $35 a barrel.**
Andrew Chatzky, "Have Sanctions on Russia Changed Putin's Calculus," *In Brief,*
Council on Foreign Relations, May 2, 2019, https://www.cfr.org/in-brief/have
-sanctions-russia-changed-putins-calculus.

p. 159   **their assets to avoid having them frozen abroad.**
Yulina Fedorinova, Ilya Arkhipov, and Evgenia Pismennaya, "U.S. Sanctions Are
Driving Russian Billionaires into Putin's Arms," Bloomberg, September 20, 2018,
https://www.bloomberg.com/news/articles/2018-09-21/u-s-sanctions-are-driving
-russian-billionaires-into-putin-s-arms.

p. 159   **1.5 percent from the nation's output.**
Welt et al., *U.S. Sanctions on Russia,* 50.

p. 159   **they have to leave the Ukrainian peninsula,"**
"New bridge cements Russia's hold in Crimea," *Euronews*, May 18, 2018,
https://www.euronews.com/2018/05/18/new-bridge-cements-russia-s-hold-on-crimea.

p. 160   **what is crossing where we can't see."**
Daniel B. Baer, "Response to Chief Observer of the Observer Mission at the Russian
Border Checkpoints Gukova and Donetsk: Statement to the PC," U.S. Mission to
the OSCE, November 17, 2016, https://osce.usmission.gov/response-chief-observer
-observer-mission-russian-border-checkpoints-gukovo-donetsk-statement-pc/.

p. 160   **one million displaced from their homes by the fighting.**
Gabriella Gricius, "The Future of the War in Ukraine," *Global Security Review*,
October 2, 2019, https://globalsecurityreview.com/future-east-ukraine-war/.

p. 160   **to call an invasion rather than a civil war.**
Nina Jankowicz, "Five myths about Ukraine," *Washington Post*, September 26, 2019,
https://www.washingtonpost.com/outlook/five-myths/five-myths-about-ukraine/2019
/09/26/9c32e3be-dfcd-11e9-b199-f638bf2c340f_story.html.

p. 160   **the damaged bridge across the line of contact."**
William B. Taylor, "Opening Statement of Ambassador William B. Taylor—October 22,
2019" (opening statement, US Congress, Washington, D.C., October 22, 2019),
https://games-cdn.washingtonpost.com/notes/prod/default/documents/542ee36f-eafc
-4f2b-a075-b3b492d981a5/note/5125c5bd-9723-4ea9-8180-7bb6fd714783.pdf.

p. 161   **sporadically but often quite lethally.**
"Ukraine Conflict: Zelensky plans frontline troop withdrawal," BBC News, October 4,
2010, https://www.bbc.com/news/world-europe-49931755.

p. 161   **assuming a non-state identity as Russia did in Crimea."**
The National Military Strategy of the United States, 4.

CHAPTER SIX: MESOPOTAMIA: CRIME & PUNISHMENT

Of inestimable value, particularly for a deep understanding of the French action and point of view
with respect to Barack Obama's red line on the use of chemical weapons in Syria, was the research
and interviews of two extraordinary French journalists: Dominique Bromberger, a longtime
anchor and political commentator for French television and radio, and Pierre Favier, who served for
years as chief of the political service and the Élysées Palace bureau chief for Agence France-Presse
during the term of President François Hollande, and who coauthored the definitive four-volume
biography of President François Mitterrand, *La Décennie Mitterrand* (Paris: Seuil, 1990–1999).

p. 162   **the powerful Safavid Dynasty in 1501.**
This map of 16th century Persia suggests the establishment of the line between
Ottomans/Arabs and the Persians: https://en.wikipedia.org/wiki/Safavid_dynasty
#/media/File:Map_Safavid_persia.png.

p. 162   **military operation ever actually took place.**
Jerome F. D. Creach, *Joshua* (Louisville: John Knox Press, 2003), https://books.
google.com/books?id=1V6ca8r3DssC&pg=PR11&hl=en#v=onepage&q&f=false.

p. 163   **its own peculiar form it took strong and deep roots.**
M. Morony, "ARAB ii. Arab conquest of Iran," *Encyclopaedia Iranica*, http://www
.iranicaonline.org/articles/arab-ii.

p. 164   **the lands Christendom considered holy.**
Thomas Asbridge, *The Crusades: The Authoritative History of the War for the Holy Land*
(New York: Ecco, 2011), 10. Much of the material on the crusades is found in this
monumental work.

p. 166   **a patchwork of tribal rulers and their often nomadic people.**
Jason Goodwin, *Lords of the Horizons: A History of the Ottoman Empire* (New York:
Henry Holt, 1999).

p. 166   **the multiplicity of such lines that crisscross the region today.**
For a more detailed discussion of this entire process, see: David A. Andelman, *A
Shattered Peace: Versailles 1919 and the Price We Pay Today* (Hoboken: Wiley, 2014).

p. 167   **when suddenly the ornate doors to the salon flew open and he was summoned inside.**
Harold Nicolson, *Peacemaking 1919: Being Reminiscences of the Paris Peace Conferenc*e
(New York: Houghton Mifflin, 1933).

p. 170   **cut off the hand of all evil foreigners and all their helpers."**
R. W. Apple Jr., "Khomeini Arrives in Teheran, Urges Ouster of Foreigners; Millions
Rally to Greet Him," *New York Times*, February 1, 1979, https://www.nytimes.com
/1979/02/01/archives/khomeini-arrives-in-teheran-urges-ouster-of-foreigners-millions
.html?searchResultPosition=10.

p. 170   **outright revolution in Iraq.**
"The Iran-Iraq War," History of Western Civilization II, OER Services, accessed July 2020,
https://courses.lumenlearning.com/suny-hccc-worldhistory2/chapter/the-iran-iraq-war/.

p. 170   **running the country for at least three years.**
"Bakr Quits in Iraq, Names Hussein," *New York Times*, July 17, 1979, https://www
.nytimes.com/1979/07/17/archives/bakr-quits-in-iraq-names-hussein-cabinet-changes
-in-iraq.html?searchResultPosition=3.

p. 170   **a particularly strategic stretch of the border.**
Werner Wiskari, "Iraq Said to Gain Its Border Aims in Iran Conflict," *New York
Times*, September 20, 1980, https://www.nytimes.com/1980/09/20/archives/iraq-said
-to-gain-its-border-aims-in-iran-conflict-iraq-is-said-to.html?searchResultPosition=4.

p. 170   **fanned by Shiite clerics in the holy city of Qom.**
Olmo Gölz, "Martyrdom and Masculinity in Warring Iran: The Karbala Paradigm, the
Heroic, and the Personal Dimensions of War," *Behemoth* 12, no. 1 (2019), https://www
.academia.edu/39134486/G%C3%B6lz_Martyrdom_and_Masculinity_in_Warring
_Iran_The_Karbala_Paradigm_the_Heroic_and_the_Personal_Dimensions_of
_War._Behemoth_12_no._1_2019_35_51.

p. 171   **American troops were based and operating in Iraq.**
"US Ground Forces End Strength," GlobalSecurity.org, last modified November 16,
2011, https://www.globalsecurity.org/military/ops/iraq_orbat_es.htm.

p. 171   **Iraq that can sustain itself, govern itself and defend itself."**
"President Bush and Iraq Prime Minister Maliki Sign the Strategic Framework
Agreement and Security Agreement," Office of the Press Secretary, The White House,
December 14, 2008, https://georgewbush-whitehouse.archives.gov/news/releases
/2008/12/20081214-2.html.

p. 172   **widows, the orphans and those who were killed in Iraq."**
Antonia Noori Farzan, "10 years ago, an Iraqi journalist threw his shoes at George W.
Bush and instantly became a cult figure," *Washington Post*, December 14, 2018,
https://www.washingtonpost.com/nation/2018/12/14/years-ago-an-iraqi-journalist
-threw-his-shoes-george-w-bush-instantly-became-cult-figure/.

p. 172   **all but unrecognized by the West, but not for long.**
"Text: Obama's Speech in Cairo," *New York Times*, June 4, 2019, https://www
.nytimes.com/2009/06/04/us/politics/04obama.text.html.

p. 173   **he set himself on fire in the ultimate act of protest.**
Yasmine Ryan, "The tragic life of a street vendor," *Al Jazeera*, January 20, 2011,
https://www.aljazeera.com/indepth/features/2011/01/201111684242518839.html.

p. 173   **from the armed killing machine of the system."**
Joshua Landis, "Free Syrian Army Founded by Seven Officers to Fight the Syrian
Army," *Syria Comment* (blog), July 29, 2011, https://www.joshualandis.com/blog
/free-syrian-army-established-to-fight-the-syrian-army/.

p. 173   **his al-Qaeda-in-Iraq organization, challenging American forces.**
Michael Weiss and Hassan Hassan, *ISIS: Inside the Army of Terror* (New York:
Phaidon Press, 2015).
Much of the material on the nexus of al-Qaeda and ISIS is drawn from this source.

p. 173   **some 42 percent of all suicide bombings in Iraq.**
Weiss and Hassan, *ISIS*.

p. 174   **The territory he was defending was much of Mesopotamia.**
Khaled Hroub, ed., *Political Islam: Context versus Ideology* (London: Saqi Books,
2012).

p. 174   **beginning in October 2006, the Islamic State in Iraq.**
"Timeline: the Rise, Spread, and Fall of the Islamic State," Wilson Center, October 28,
2019, https://www.wilsoncenter.org/article/timeline-the-rise-spread-and-fall-the
-islamic-state.

p. 174   **dispatch in May 2010 from *The New York Times* Baghdad bureau,**
Anthony Shadid, "Iraqi Insurgent Group Names New Leaders," *At War* (blog),
New York Times, May 16, 2010, https://atwar.blogs.nytimes.com/2010/05/16/iraqi
-insurgent-group-names-new-leaders/?_php=true&_type=blogs&_r=0.

p. 174   **expansion would begin in March 2013 with the capture of Raqqa.**
"Raqqah: Capital of the Caliphate," RAND National Security Research Division,
accessed July 2020, https://www.rand.org/nsrd/projects/when-isil-comes-to-town
/case-studies/raqqah.html.

p. 175   **outlawed by the world at the Geneva Convention of 1925.**
UN Office for Disarmament Affairs, Protocol for the Prohibition of the Use in
War of Asphyxiating, Poisonous or Other Gases, and of Bacteriological Methods of
Warfare, February 8, 1928, accessed July 2020, http://disarmament.un.org
/treaties/t/1925.

p. 175   **"looks like a surprise guest here."**
"Remarks by the President to the White House Press Corps," Office of the Press
Secretary, The White House, August 12, 2012, https://obamawhitehouse.archives
.gov/the-press-office/2012/08/20/remarks-president-white-house-press-corps.

p. 179   **would be in a position to launch as far as two hundred miles from their targets.**
"APACHE AP/ SCALP EG/ Storm Shadow/ SCALP Naval/ Black Shaheen," *Missile
Threat*, CSIS Missile Defense Project, December 2, 2016, updated June 15, 2018,
https://missilethreat.csis.org/missile/apache-ap/.

p. 182   **never wanted to own the problem as he told me personally."**
François Delattre, interview with the author, March 23, 2018.

p. 183   **a bitter debate that began at 2:30 P.M. and lasted until past 10:30 that evening.**
"Syria and the Use of Chemical Weapons," House of Commons Hansard Transcript,
August 29, 2013, Volume 566, https://hansard.parliament.uk/Commons/2013-08-29
/debates/1308298000001/SyriaAndTheUseOfChemicalWeapons.

p. 184   **poisoned by the Iraq episode and we need to understand the public skepticism.**
"Syria and the Use of Chemical Weapons."

p. 186   **Obama set for limited strike on Syria as British vote no.**
Mark Landler, David E. Sanger, and Thom Shanker, "Obama Set for Limited Strike
on Syria as British Vote No," *New York Times*, August 29, 2013, https://www.nytimes
.com/2013/08/30/us/politics/obama-syria.html?searchResultPosition=6.

p. 191   **President Lincoln in an often-cited historical reference, "the nays have it."**
Peter W. Rodman, "'Presidential Command,'" *New York Times*, January 16, 2009,
https://www.nytimes.com/2009/01/18/books/chapters/chapter-presidential
-command.html.

p. 193   **To armies who carry out genocide?**
"Transcript: President Obama's Aug. 31 statement on Syria," *Washington Post*,
August 31, 2013, https://www.washingtonpost.com/politics/transcript-president
-obamas-aug-31-statement-on-syria/2013/08/31/3019213c-125d-11e3-b4cb-fd7ce
041d814_story.html.

p. 193   **the only rational solution to the war.**
The Editorial Board, "Debating the Cases for Force," *New York Times*, September 2,
2013, https://www.nytimes.com/2013/09/03/opinion/debating-the-case-for-force.html.

p. 197   **"the Caliph for Muslims everywhere."**
"ISIS Spokesman Declares Caliphate, Rebrands Group as 'Islamic State,'" SITE
Intelligence Group, June 29, 2014, https://news.siteintelgroup.com/Jihadist-News/isis
-spokesman-declares-caliphate-rebrands-group-as-islamic-state.html.

p. 197   **The RAND Corporation estimates.**
Seth G. Jones, James Dobbins, Daniel Byman, Christopher S. Chivvis, Ben Connable, Jeffrey Martini, Eric Robinson, and Nathan Chandler, *Rolling Back the Islamic State* (RAND National Security Research Division, 2017), https://www.rand.org/pubs /research_reports/RR1912.html.

p. 198   **nearly to the suburbs of Baghdad.**
"Islamic State and the crisis in Iraq and Syria in maps," BBC News, March 28, 2018, https://www.bbc.com/news/world-middle-east-27838034.

p. 199   **according to US Army Colonel Steve Warren.**
Terri Moon Cronk, "ISIS Loses Control of Once-dominated Iraq Territory," *DOD News*, US Department of Defense, April 13, 2015, https://www.defense.gov/Explore /News/Article/Article/604444/.

p. 199   **a vast network of virtual red lines remains. RAND Corporation analysts.**
Patrick B. Johnston, Mona Alami, Colin P. Clarke, and Howard J. Shatz, *Return and Expand? The Finances and Prospects of the Islamic State After the Caliphate* (The RAND Corporation, 2019), chapter 6, https://www.rand.org/pubs/research _reports/RR3046.html.

p. 200   **the action spooled out at a compressed speed.**
Michael D. Shear and Michael R. Gordon, "63 Hours: From Chemical Attack to Trump's Strike in Syria," *New York Times*, April 7, 2017, https://www.nytimes.com /2017/04/07/us/politics/syria-strike-trump-timeline.html.

p. 201   **"political assassination" by any US government agency.**
"U.S. policy on assassinations," CNN, November 4, 2002, https://edition.cnn. com/2002/LAW/11/04/us.assassination.policy/.

p. 202   **Khan Sheikhoun, the same village the initial gas attack had targeted.**
Josie Ensor, "Syrian warplanes take off once again from air base bombed by US Tomahawks," *Telegraph*, April 8, 2017, https://www.telegraph.co.uk/news/2017/04/08 /syrian-warplanes-take-air-base-bombed-us-tomahawks/.

p. 202   **Barack Obama's indefensible red line.**
Tom Batchelor, "US missile strikes: Russia announces plan to bolster Syrian air defences and derides Trump over 'extremely low' effectiveness of bombing," *Independent*, April 7, 2017, https://www.independent.co.uk/news/world/middle-east /us-missile-strike-russia-syria-air-defences-bolster-donald-trump-putin-low-extremely -low-effective-a7671921.html.

p. 202   **withdrawn within a time to be fixed by the Security Council."**
James B. Reston, "Council is Divided on UNO Authority in Levant Policing," *New York Times*, February 16, 1946, https://timesmachine.nytimes.com/times machine/1946/02/16/91609408.html?pageNumber=1.

p. 202   **remaining so throughout the Cold War."**
Dmitri Trenin, "Russia's Line in the Sand on Syria," *Foreign Affairs*, February 5, 2012, https://www.foreignaffairs.com/articles/syria/2012-02-05/russias-line-sand-syria.

p. 203   **opposition forces were concentrated or held an upper hand."**
Andrew S. Weiss and Nicole Ng, "Collision Avoidance: The Lessons of U.S.
and Russian Operations in Syria," Carnegie Endowment for International
Peace, March 20, 2019, https://carnegieendowment.org/2019/03/20
/collision-avoidance-lessons-of-u.s.-and-russian-operations-in-syria-pub-78571.

p. 203   **the naval facility at Tartus.**
Alec Luhn, "Russia sends artillery and tanks to Syria as part of continued military
buildup," *Guardian*, September 14, 2015, https://www.theguardian.com/world/2015
/sep/14/russia-sends-artillery-and-tanks-to-syria-as-part-of-continued-military
-buildup.

p. 203   **bays for more than fifty military aircraft.**
"Russian airbase in Syria: RT checks out everyday life at Latakia airfield," *RT*,
October 3, 2015, https://www.rt.com/news/317528-latakia-russian-khmeimim-airbase/.
Michael Peck, "Welcome to Syria, the Russian Air Force's Battle Lab," *The Buzz*, (blog),
National Interest, September 7, 2019, https://nationalinterest.org/blog/buzz/welcome
-syria-russian-air-force%E2%80%99s-battle-lab-78671.

p. 204   **demanded that American operations cease.**
Weiss and Ng, "Collision Avoidance."

p. 204   **discuss any implementation issues that follow."**
Lisa Ferdinando, "U.S., Russia Sign Memorandum on Air Safety in Syria," *DOD News*,
US Department of Defense, October 20, 2015, https://www.defense.gov/Explore/News
/Article/Article/624964/us-russia-sign-memorandum-on-air-safety-in-syria/.
"Department of Defense Press Briefing, by Pentagon Pres Secretary Peter Cook in the
Pentagon Briefing Room, US Department of Defense, October 20, 2015,
https://www.defense.gov/Newsroom/Transcripts/Transcript/Article/624976
/department-of-defense-press-briefing-by-pentagon-press-secretary-peter-cook-in/.

p. 205   **and the coveted eurocurrency zone in 2001.**
"EU member countries in brief," European Union, accessed July 2020, https://europa
.eu/european-union/about-eu/countries/member-countries_en.

p. 206   **at a cost of $3.4 billion.**
Mustafa Kibaroglu and Selim C. Sazak, "Why Turkey Chose, and Then Rejected, a
Chinese Air-Defense Missile," Defense One, February 3, 2016, https://www
.defenseone.com/ideas/2016/02/turkey-china-air-defense-missile/125648/.

p. 206   **turned to Russian S-400s in 2017.**
Joshua Kucera, "After Abandoning Chinese Missiles, Turkey Says It's Ready to Buy
Russian," *Eurasianet*, February 23, 2017, https://eurasianet.org/after-abandoning
-chinese-missiles-turkey-says-its-ready-buy-russian.

p. 206   **in Trump's view, "a hell of a leader."**
Kathryn Watson, "Trump says he's a 'big fan' of Turkey strongman Erdogan,"
CBS News, November 14, 2019, https://www.cbsnews.com/news/trump-erdogan

-meeting-trump-says-hes-big-fan-turkey-strongman-recep-tayyip-erdogan-today
-2019-11-13/.

p. 206   **"Caliphate," will no longer be in the immediate area.**
"Statement from the Press Secretary," The White House, October 6, 2019, https://www
.whitehouse.gov/briefings-statements/statement-press-secretary-85/.

p. 207   **where it is to our benefit, and only fight to win."**
Alex Johnson, Josh Lederman, Marc Smith, and Yuliya Talmazan, "U.S. prepares to
withdraw from northern Syria before Turkish operation," NBC News, October 7,
2019, https://www.nbcnews.com/news/world/u-s-says-it-will-stand-aside-turkey
-moves-syria-n1063106.

p. 207   **We have no soldiers [there]."**
"Remarks by President Trump Before Marine One Departure," The White House,
October 10, 2019, https://www.whitehouse.gov/briefings-statements/remarks
-president-trump-marine-one-departure-69/.

p. 207   **at least twenty miles into Syrian territory.**
"Remarks by Vice President Pence and Secretary of State Pompeo in Press
Conference: Ankara, Turkey," The White House, October 17, 2019, https://www
.whitehouse.gov/briefings-statements/remarks-vice-president-pence-secretary
-state-pompeo-press-conference-ankara-turkey/?utm_source=link.

p. 207   **its view of how Turkey intended to structure its newest line.**
Paul Iddon, "How far will Turkey go with its invasion of Syrian Kurdistan," *Rudaw*,
October 11, 2019, https://www.rudaw.net/english/analysis/111020191.

p. 208   **"Operation Peace Spring will be halted entirely on completion of the
withdrawal."**
"Remarks by Vice President Pence."

p. 208   **This time, Russian units went along.**
Lara Seligman, "Turkey Advances on Kobani in Latest Broken Promise," *Foreign Policy*,
October 16, 2019, https://foreignpolicy.com/2019/10/16/turkey-advances-kobani
-syria-erdogan-trump-sdf-promise/.

p. 208   **the abandoned Tabqa military airfield.**
"Russian Troops Overtake Former U.S. Base in Northern Syria," *The Moscow Times*,
October 22, 2019, https://www.themoscowtimes.com/2019/10/22/russian-troops
-overtake-former-us-base-in-northern-syria-a67860.

p. 208   **abandoned by American forces in Aleppo province.**
Reuters, "Russia Lands Forces at Former U.S. Air Base in Northern Syria," *Moscow
Times*, November 15, 2019, https://www.themoscowtimes.com/2019/11/15/russia
-lands-forces-at-former-us-air-base-in-northern-syria-a68191.

p. 208   **meetings about how to divide up Syria.**
Anton Troianovski and Patrick Kingsley, "Putin and Erdogan Announce Plan for
Northeast Syria, Bolstering Russian Influence," *New York Times*, October 22, 2019,

updated October 24, 2019, https://www.nytimes.com/2019/10/22/world/europe
/erdogan-putin-syria-cease-fire.html.

p. 209   *The New York Times* **had already published a map.**
Ben Hubbard, Anton Troianovski, Carlotta Gall, and Patrick Kingsley, "In Syria,
Russia Is Pleased to Fill an American Void," *New York Times*, October 25, 2019,
https://www.nytimes.com/2019/10/15/world/middleeast/kurds-syria-turkey.html.

p. 209   **the internationally recognized frontier with Turkey.**

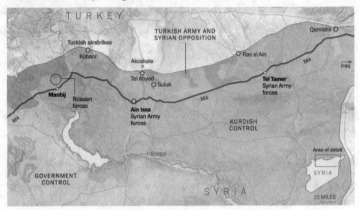

CHAPTER SEVEN: PERSIA TO IRAN AND BACK TO PERSIA

p. 211   **The village of Susa.**
Joshua J. Mark, "Susa," *Ancient History Encyclopedia*, November 12, 2018,
https://www.ancient.eu/susa/.

p. 211   **"monumental brick platforms with an apparent temple on top,"**
Gil J. Stein, "Local Identities and Interaction Spheres: Modeling Regional Variation in
the Ubaid Horizon," in *Beyond the Ubaid*, eds. Robert A. Carter and Graham Philip
(Chicago: The Oriental Institute of the University of Chicago, 2010), 25, https://oi
.uchicago.edu/sites/oi.uchicago.edu/files/uploads/shared/docs/saoc63.pdf.

p. 211   **maps of Assyria.**
Ningyou, "Map of the Assyrian Empire," *Wikipedia*, February 26, 2006, https://en
.wikipedia.org/wiki/Ashurbanipal#/media/File:Map_of_Assyria.png.

p. 211   **territories such as ancient Thrace and Macedonia."**
"Largest empire by percentage of world population," *Guinness World Records*, accessed
July 2020, https://www.guinnessworldrecords.com/world-records/largest-empire
-by-percentage-of-world-population/.

p. 212   **Columbus discovering the New World and the present.**
Matteo Compareti, "The Sasanians in Africa," *Transoxiana: Journal Libre de Estudios
Orientales* 4 (July 4, 2002), http://www.transoxiana.com.ar/0104/sasanians.html.

p. 212   **heirs of Genghis Khan, throwing gunpowder bombs.**
Arnold Pacey, *Technology in World Civilization: A Thousand Year History* (Cambridge:
The MIT Press, 1990), 45–46, https://bit.ly/2s7oyPO.

p. 213   **Safavid dynasty, which ruled the nation from 1501 to 1722.**
          Rudi Matthee, "Safavid Dynasty," *Encylopaedia Iranica*, July 28, 2008, http://www
          .iranicaonline.org/articles/safavids.

p. 214   **he killed one of his sons and blinded two more.**
          Matthee, "Safavid Dynasty."

p. 215   **a long line across Armenia into Baku.**
          Elena Andreeva, "RUSSIA i. Russo-Iranian Relations up to the Bolshevik
          Revolution," *Encyclopaedia Iranica*, January 6, 2014, http://www.iranicaonline.org
          /articles/russia-i-relations.

p. 217   **the Red Army entered Tehran with British backing.**
          Ray Brock, "Allies now hold Teheran suburbs," *New York Times*, September 18, 1941,
          https://timesmachine.nytimes.com/timesmachine/1941/09/18/issue.html.

p. 217   **a series of sanctions against the already-strapped nation.**
          Mark J. Gasiorowski, "The 1953 Coup D'etat in Iran," *Journal of Middle East Study*
          19 (1987), online August 23, 1998, http://iran.sa.utoronto.ca/coup/web_files
          /markcoup.html.

p. 218   **63 countries [were] due here for the national celebration."**
          Charlotte Curtis, "First Party of Iran's 2,500-Year Celebration," *New York Times*,
          October 13, 1971, https://www.nytimes.com/1971/10/13/archives/first-party-of
          -irans-2500year-celebration.html.

p. 218   **the Stockholm International Peace Research Institute.**
          http://armstrade.sipri.org/armstrade/page/values.php note: these figures are in TIVs,
          a SIPRI unit of Trend Indicated Value, which closely tracks US dollars. Values need to
          be entered with the years 1950 to 1979. See SIPRI factsheet: https://www.sipri.org
          /sites/default/files/files/FS/SIPRIFS1212.pdf\.

p. 218   **a small coterie of acolytes and a tape recorder.**
          Elaine Ganley, "Khomeini Launched a Revolution from a Sleepy French Village,"
          US News & World Report, February 1, 2019, https://www.usnews.com/news/world
          /articles/2019-01-31/khomeini-launched-a-revolution-from-a-sleepy-french-village.

p. 219   **adoring followers often numbering in the millions.**
          "February 1979: Ayatollah Khomeini Returns to Iran From Exile," Radio Free
          Europe/Radio Liberty, January 31, 2019, https://www.rferl.org/a/khomeini-tehran
          -iran/29739627.html.

p. 219   **the rule of the clergy as supreme over the state.**
          Imam Khomeini, *Governance of the Jurist (Velayat-e Faqeeh): Islamic Government*,
          trans. Hamid Algar (Tehran: The Institute for Compilation and Publication of Imam
          Khomeini's Works), 18–19, http://www.iranchamber.com/history/rkhomeini/books
          /velayat_faqeeh.pdf.

p. 220   **vital to the imam's mission and that of his followers.**
          R. W. Apple Jr., "Will Khomeini Turn Iran's Clock Back 1,300 Years?" *New York
          Times*, February 4, 1979, https://www.nytimes.com/1979/02/04/archives/return-from
          -exile-will-khomeini-turn-irans-clock-back-1300-years.html.

p. 221   **their own shrouds into battle, anticipating martyrdom.**
"History of Iran: Iran-Iraq War 1980–1988," Iran Chamber Society, accessed July 2020, http://www.iranchamber.com/history/iran_iraq_war/iran_iraq_war1.php.

p. 221   **terms of the United Nations–facilitated truce.**
"Background," Iran-Iraq UNIMOG, United Nations, accessed July 2020, https://peace keeping.un.org/sites/default/files/past/uniimogbackgr.html.

p. 221   **as much as $645 billion plus a million casualties.**
Pierre Razoux, *The Iran-Iraq War* (Cambridge, MA: Belknap Press, 2015), 574.

p. 222   **51 patrols along the entire border.**
"Background," Iran-Iraq UNIMOG.

p. 222   **Iran promptly convened its National Security Council.**
Reuters, "Iran Decides to Stay Neutral in Gulf Conflict," *Los Angeles Times*, January 20, 1991, https://www.latimes.com/archives/la-xpm-1991-01-20-mn-889-story.html.

p. 222   **Karim Sadjadpour of the Carnegie Endowment for International Peace wrote**
Karim Sadjadpour, *Reading Khameini: The World View of Iran's Most Powerful Leader* (Washington DC: Carnegie Endowment for International Peace, 2009), https://carnegie endowment.org/files/sadjadpour_iran_final2.pdf.

p. 223   **its dominance in the region may be challenged.**
Farzan Sabet, "Why Iran's Assembly of Experts election is the real race to be watching," *Washington Post*, February 24, 2016, https://www.washingtonpost.com /news/monkey-cage/wp/2016/02/24/why-irans-assembly-of-experts-election-is-the -real-race-to-be-watching/.

p. 223   **the split-off of Muslim-dominant Pakistan.**
"Mapping the Global Muslim Population," Religion & Public Life, Pew Research Center, October 7, 2009, https://www.pewforum.org/2009/10/07/mapping-the-global -muslim-population/.

p. 224   **65 to 70 percent of the population, (19 to 22 million people) is Shiite.**
"Mapping the Global Muslim Population."

p. 224   **the US National Defense Strategy reported in 2018.**
Jim Mattis, *Summary of the National Defense Strategy of the United States of America, 2018: Sharpening the American Military's Competitive Edge* (Washington, D.C.: Department of Defense, 2018), https://dod.defense.gov/Portals/1/Documents /pubs/2018-National-Defense-Strategy-Summary.pdf.

Much of the documentation of this section is due to the indefatigable brilliance of two remarkable researchers. First, Gary Sick of Columbia University's School of International and Public Affairs, who served on the National Security Council of Presidents Ford, Carter, and Reagan, including during the Iran Hostage Crisis. His daily e-mail blog *Gulf/2000 Project* encompasses a vast network of researchers on Iran, the Persian Gulf, and Mesopotamia. And second, Phillip Smyth, the Soref Fellow of the Washington Institute for Near East Policy. His efforts at mapping Shiism and its militias across the world has created a landmark database. His advice and counsel have proved immensely valuable as he is one of the few Western researchers to maintain regular, often daily, contact with many of the key militia leaders across the region.

p. 224 **comprising as many as 200,000 fighters.**
Sune Engel Rasmussen and Isabel Coles, "Iran's Allies Target Its Rivals, Risking Conflict," *Wall Street Journal*, May 24, 2019, https://www.wsj.com/articles /irans-allies-target-its-rivals-risking-conflict-11558690326.

p. 225 **more broadly to Afghanistan, Central Asia, Africa, even Latin America.**
Mehran Riazaty, *Khomeini's Warriors: Foundation of Iran's Regime, Its Guardians, Allies Around the World, War Analysis, and Strategies* (Bloomington: Xlibris, 2016).

p. 225 **American troops as far afield as Afghanistan, according to Congressional testimony.**
Andrew deGrandpre and Andrew Tilghman, "Iran linked to deaths of 500 U.S. Troops in Iraq, Afghanistan," *Military Times*, July 14, 2015, https://www.military times.com/news/pentagon-congress/2015/07/14/iran-linked-to-deaths-of-500 -u-s-troops-in-iraq-afghanistan.

p. 225 **who's going to replace him is a Quds Force member."**
Martin Chulov, "Qassem Suleimani: the Iranian general 'secretly running' Iraq," *Guardian*, July 28, 2011, https://www.theguardian.com/world/2011/jul/28 /qassem-suleimani-iran-iraq-influence.
Dexter Filkins, "The Shadow Commander," *New Yorker*, September 23, 2013, https://www.newyorker.com/magazine/2013/09/30/the-shadow-commander.

p. 225 **three consecutive ambassadors to Iraq beginning in 2005 have been members.**
Farzin Nadimi, "Iran Appoints Seasoned Qods Force Operative as Ambassador to Iraq," *Policy Analysis*, The Washington Institute, January 18, 2017, https://www .washingtoninstitute.org/policy-analysis/view/iran-appoints-seasoned-qods-force -operative-as-ambassador-to-iraq.

p. 225 **a tiny, impoverished village in Kerman Province.**
"Iran Guards Intelligence Chief Says Plot to Kill Soleimani Neutralized," *Iran News*, Radio Farda, October 3, 2019, https://en.radiofarda.com/a/iran-guards-intelligence -chief-says-plot-to-kill-soleimani-neutralized/30197639.html.

p. 225 **most powerful man in Iraq, no question."**
Chulov, "Qassem Suleimani."

p. 225 **And central to the entire operation is financing.**
CFR.org editors, "Iran's Revolutionary Guards," Council on Foreign Relations, updated May 6, 2019, https://www.cfr.org/backgrounder/irans-revolutionary-guards.

p. 225 **A RAND Corporation study reported in 2009.**
Frederic Wehrey, Jerrold D. Green, Brian Nichiporuk, Alireza Nader, Lydia Hansell, Rasool Nafisi, and S. R. Bohandy, *The Rise of the Pasdaran* (RAND corporation, 2009), https://www.rand.org/content/dam/rand/pubs/monographs/2008/RAND_MG821.pdf.

p. 226 **from Iran, either in the form of gifts or sales."**
Iraq: Turning a Blind Eye: The Arming of the Popular Mobilization Units (London: Amnesty International, 2017), 4, https://www.amnestyusa.org/files/iraq_report _turning_a_blind_eye.pdf.

p. 227   **absolute authority, derived from God and Mohammed.**
Phillip Smyth, "Iran Is Outpacing Assad for Control of Syria's Shia Militias," Policy
Analysis, The Washington Institute, April 12, 2018, https://www.washingtoninstitute
.org/policy-analysis/view/iran-is-outpacing-assad-for-control-of-syrias-shia-militias.

p. 227   **ridding the region of American forces.**
Matthew Levitt and Phillip Smyth, "Kataib al-Imam Ali: Portrait of an Iraqi Shiite
Militant Group Fighting ISIS," Policy Analysis, The Washington Institute, January 5,
2015, https://www.washingtoninstitute.org/policy-analysis/view/kataib-al-imam
-ali-portrait-of-an-iraqi-shiite-militant-group-fighting-isis.

p. 227   **before the Obama-era troops withdrawals.**
Michael Knights, "The Evolution of Iran's Special Groups in Iraq," *CTC Sentinel* 3,
no. 11–12, (November 2010): 12–15, https://www.washingtoninstitute.org/uploads
/Documents/opeds/4d06325a6031b.pdf.

p. 227   **advanced weaponry that could only have originated in Iran.**
James Glanz, "U.S. Says Arms Link Iranians to Iraqi Shiites," *New York Times*,
February 12, 2007, https://www.nytimes.com/2007/02/12/world/middleeast
/12weapons.html.

p. 228   **the drone attack ordered by President Trump.**
Erin Cunningham and Mustafa Salim, "Iraq's Shiites helped boost the political elite
in Baghdad. Now they want to bring it down," *Washington Post*, December 29, 2019,
https://www.washingtonpost.com/world/middle_east/iraqs-shiites-helped-boost-the
-political-elite-in-baghdad-now-they-want-to-bring-it-down/2019/12/28/7768d0e0
-20da-11ea-b034-de7dc2b5199b_story.html.

p. 228   **shortly after he formed his Imam Ali brigade.**
Phillip Smyth, photographs, The Washington Institute, https://www.washington
institute.org/uploads/Images/Books/Smyth/Combined/T-97ab.jpg.

p. 228   **Zaidi has also been photographed being transported in an Iraqi military
helicopter.**
Levitt and Smyth, "Kataib al-Imam Ali."

p. 228   **should be organized and comport themselves.**
Omar Al-Nidawi, "The growing economic and political role of Iraq's PMF,"
Middle East Institute, May 21, 2019, https://www.mei.edu/publications/growing
-economic-and-political-role-iraqs-pmf.

p. 228   **doctrine of velayat-e-faqih, would be an integral part of the Iraqi army.**
"The Prime Minister and Commander in Chief of the Armed Forces, Dr. Haider
Al-Abadi, issues regulations to adapt the conditions of the PMF fighters," March 8,
2018, Prime Minister's personal archives, https://www.pmo.iq/press2018/8-3-201803
.htm.

p. 228   **Iran and its Shiite ambitions across the region.**
"Who are Hezbollah?" BBC News, July 4, 2010, http://news.bbc.co.uk/2/hi/middle
_east/4314423.stm.

p. 229   **Hezbollah 'takeover of Lebanon is complete.'"**
          Najia Houssari and Randa Takieddine, "New government shows Hezbollah 'takeover
          of Lebanon is complete,'" *Arab News*, updated January 23, 2020, https://www.arab
          news.com/node/1616716/middle-east.

p. 229   **reaffirming militant Shia identity in the region."**
          Hanin Ghaddar and Phillip Smyth, "Rolling Back Iran's Foreign Legion," Policy
          Analysis, The Washington Institute, February 6, 2018, https://www.washington
          institute.org/policy-analysis/view/rolling-back-irans-foreign-legion.

p. 230   **"many takfiris . . . were killed and wounded by the missiles."**
          Hwaida Saad and Rod Norland, "Iran Fires a Ballistic Missile at ISIS in Syria,
          Avenging an Earlier Attack," *New York Times*, October 1, 2018, https://www.nytimes
          .com/2018/10/01/world/middleeast/iran-isis-missile-syria.html.

p. 230   **Saudi air defenses were said to have intercepted them.**
          Katie Paul and Rania El Gamal, "Saudi Arabia intercepts Houthi missile fired toward
          Riyadh; no reported casualties," Reuters, December 19, 2017, https://www.reuters
          .com/article/us-saudi-blast/saudi-arabia-intercepts-houthi-missile-fired-toward-riyadh
          -no-reported-casualties-idUSKBN1ED17Y.

p. 230   **civil war against Bashar al-Assad's government.**
          Phillip Smyth, "Lebanese Hezbollah's Islamic Resistances in Syria," Policy Analysis,
          The Washington Institute, April 26, 2018, https://www.washingtoninstitute.org
          /policy-analysis/view/lebanese-hezbollahs-islamic-resistance-in-syria.

p. 230   **as far afield as Afghanistan and Pakistan.**
          Phillip Smyth, "Iran Is Outpacing Assad for Control of Syria's Shia Militias,"
          Policy Analysis, The Washington Institute, April 12, 2018, https://www
          .washingtoninstitute.org/policy-analysis/view/iran-is-outpacing-assad-for-control
          -of-syrias-shia-militias.

p. 230   **with a vast number of social media sites.**
          Phillip Smyth, *The Shiite Jihad in Syria and Its Regional Effects*, (Washington, D.C.:
          The Washington Institute, Policy Focus 138, 2015), https://www.washington
          institute.org/policy-analysis/view/the-shiite-jihad-in-syria-and-its-regional
          -effects.

p. 230   **promote the Shiite cause and act as a potent recruiting tool.**
          Home Office of the Central Organization of Organizations in Pictures, In Pictures:
          The Central Organization Office in Kirkuk Participates in the Condolence
          Council Established by the Crowd Groups in the Daquq District, Asaib Ahl al-Haq
          Movement, January 18, 2020, https://ahlualhaq.com/post/11134.

p. 231   **The four-minute, eleven-second video.**
          Ali Falih, The martyr Mohammed Baqir Al-Bahadly, April 19, 2014, https://www
          .youtube.com/watch?v=r4U7Ow5H2Xk.

p. 231   **the family of Mohammed and Zainab al-Hawra.**
          Ali Falih, (Ibid.) The martyr Mohammed Baqir Al-Bahadly.

p. 231   **"God willing on the enemies of God."**
Ahmed Ali Hassen, Zulfiqar Brigade fighters continue to fight in Adra and insisting
on victory, Facebook, December 15, 2013, https://www.facebook.com/photo.php?fbi
d=1426283827603795&set=a.1386586404906871.1073741828.100006665737264&
type=1&theater.

p. 232   **the regime supported by Saudi Arabia's ruling Sunnis.**
Bruce Riedel, "Who are the Houthis, and why are we at war with them?" The New
Geopolitics of the Middle East, Brookings, December 18, 2017, https://www
.brookings.edu/blog/markaz/2017/12/18/who-are-the-houthis-and-why-are-we
-at-war-with-them/.

p. 232   **O Ansar Allah, so the invaders will not be safe."**
Iraqi militia volunteers to fight alongside the Houthis in Yemen (witness), arabi21,
July 7, 2018, https://bit.ly/37dPGvA.

p. 233   **this was the location of the Garden of Eden.**
Walter Reinhold Warttig Mattfeld y de la Torre, *Investigating the Pre-Biblical origins
of the Holy Bible via Archaeology*, updated November 1, 2007, http://www.bibleorigins
.net/b.html.

p. 234   **the expansion of the boundaries of Islam.**
Marta Colburn, *The Republic of Yemen: Development Challenges in the 21st Century*
(London: Stacey International, 2002), 13.

p. 234   **the Hajours remains a deadly powder keg.**
Maysaa Shuja Al-Deen, "The Houthi-Tribal Conflict in Yemen," Sada, Carnegie
Endowment for International Peace, April 23, 2019, https://carnegieendowment.org
/sada/78969.

p. 234   **millions face risks to their safety and basic rights.**
Humanitarian Needs Overview 2019: Yemen (New York: United Nations Office for
the Coordination of Humanitarian Affairs, 2019), 4, https://reliefweb.int/sites
/reliefweb.int/files/resources/2019_Yemen_HNO_FINAL.pdf.

p. 235   **Armed Conflict Location & Event Data Project.**
"Aggregated conflict, violent events and reported fatalities data bases," Armed
Conflict Location & Event Data Project, accessed July 2020, https://www.acleddata
.com/curated-data-files/.

p. 235   **85,000 children have starved to death, according to Save the Children.**
"Yemen: 85,000 Children May Have Died from Starvation Since Start of War,"
Save the Children, November 20, 2018, https://www.savethechildren.org/us/about-us
/media-and-news/2018-press-releases/yemen-85000-children-may-have-died-from
-starvation.

p. 235   **17,000 others living in areas cut off from resources by the war.**
"Hunger Crisis Set to Hit Thousands of Yemeni Children Living in Areas Cut Off from
Aid Supplies," Save the Children, November 20, 2019, https://www.savethechildren.org
/us/about-us/media-and-news/2019-press-releases/yemen-hunger-crisis.

p. 235   **half the entire population of Yemen, are at risk of famine.**
Bethan McKernan, "Yemen: up to 85,000 young children dead from starvation,"
Guardian, November 21, 2018, https://www.theguardian.com/world/2018/nov/21
/yemen-young-children-dead-starvation-disease-save-the-children.

p. 236   **Sanaa, the Houthi-controlled capital in Yemen.**
Ori Goldberg, Eigan Azani, Lorena Atiyas Lvovsky, Edan Landau, *Iran and the
Houthi in Yemen* (Herzliyah: International Institute for Counter-Terrorism, October
2019), https://www.ict.org.il/images/Iran%20and%20the%20Houthi%20in%20
Yemen-October%202019.pdf.

p. 236   **command compound where Iran was managing its military support effort in the
country.**
John Hudson, Missy Ryan, and Josh Dawsey, "On the day U.S. forces killed
Soleimani, they targeted a senior Iranian official in Yemen," *Washington Post*,
January 10, 2020, https://www.washingtonpost.com/world/national-security
/on-the-day-us-forces-killed-soleimani-they-launched-another-secret-operation
-targeting-a-senior-iranian-official-in-yemen/2020/01/10/60f86dbc-3245-11ea
-898f-eb846b7e9feb_story.html.

p. 236   **Robert O'Brien, Trump's national security advisor, told Chuck Todd on Meet the
Press**
"Meet the Press—January 12, 2020," NBC News, January 12, 2020, https://www.nbc
news.com/meet-the-press/meet-press-january-12-2020-n1113091.

p. 236   **We want you to go wisely. It is to your own benefit."**
Michael Safi, "European troops may be at risk after dispute process triggered—Iran,"
Guardian, January 15, 2020, https://www.theguardian.com/world/2020/jan/15
/european-troops-may-be-at-risk-after-dispute-process-triggered-iran.

p. 237   **Joint Comprehensive Plan of Action, agreed upon in July 2015.**
"Full text of the Iran nuclear deal," *Washington Post*, July 14, 2015, https://apps.
washingtonpost.com/g/documents/world/full-text-of-the-iran-nuclear-deal/1651/.

p. 237   **adopted in October 2015, and implemented three months later.**
"Joint Plan of Action (JPOA) Archive and Joint Comprehensive Plan of Action
(JCPOA) Archive," US Department of the Treasury, updated October 30, 2018,
https://www.treasury.gov/resource-center/sanctions/Programs/Pages/jpoa_archive.aspx.

p. 237   **191 states have joined as parties to the agreement.**
UN Office for Disarmament Affairs, Treaty on the Non-Proliferation of Nuclear
Weapons, United Nations Office for Disarmament Affairs, March 5, 1970, accessed
July 2020, http://disarmament.un.org/treaties/t/npt.

p. 237   **programmes for nuclear-weapons purposes."**
"IAEA Safeguards Overview: Comprehensive Safeguards Agreements and Additional
Protocols," IAEA Safeguards Overview, International Atomic Energy Agency,
accessed July 2020, https://www.iaea.org/publications/factsheets/iaea-safeguards
-overview.

p. 237   **hope should be shared by all."**
Ariana Rowberry, "Sixty Years of 'Atoms for Peace' and Iran's Nuclear Program,"
Brookings, December 18, 2013, https://www.brookings.edu/blog/up-front
/2013/12/18/sixty-years-of-atoms-for-peace-and-irans-nuclear-program/.

p. 238   **Iran turned to for advice, technology, and eventually fuel.**
"Iran: Iran's Nuclear Program," Institute for Science and International Security,
accessed July 2020, https://isis-online.org/country-pages/iran#1950.

p. 238   **offers of reactors and enrichment technology.**
"Iran: Nuclear," The Nuclear Threat Initiative, July 2014, accessed July 2020,
http://www.nti.org/country-profiles/iran/nuclear/.

p. 238   **moved to Natanz in 2003.**
"Implementation of the NPT Safeguards Agreement in the Islamic Republic of Iran,"
International Atomic Energy Agency, November 15, 2004, 6, https://www.iaea.org
/sites/default/files/gov2004-83.pdf.

p. 238   **nearing a critical level of 20 percent by 2010.**
"Iran: Nuclear," The Nuclear Threat Initiative, https://www.nti.org/learn/countries
/iran/nuclear/

p. 239   **Harvard's Belfer Center for Science and International Affairs.**
Kayhan Barzegar, "The Paradox of Iran's Nuclear Consensus," *World Policy Journal*
26, no. 3 (Fall 2009): 21–30.

p. 239   **nuclear weapons is forbidden and is against [our] religion."**
Ali Akbar Salehi, "Chat Room: Persian Perspective," *World Policy Journal* 29, no. 4
(Winter 2012/2013): 66–73.

p. 240   **ruled over his Persian Gulf emirate for nearly half a century.**
Tehran Bureau correspondent, "Oman sultan's Iran visit sparks hope of progress in
nuclear standoff," *Guardian*, August 30, 2013, https://www.theguardian.com/world
/iran-blog/2013/aug/30/iran-oman-nuclear-negotiations.

p. 240   **known as peacemakers for much of their existence.**
B. C., "Who are the Ibadis?" *The Economist*, December 18, 2018, https://www
.economist.com/the-economist-explains/2018/12/18/who-are-the-ibadis.

p. 240   **the power of a nation smaller than the state of Kansas.**
"Oman," Encyclopedia.com, updated July 9, 2020, https://www.encyclopedia
.com/places/asia/arabian-peninsula-political-geography/oman#LOCATION_SIZE
_AND_EXTENT.

p. 240   **"If the Iranians feel bullied or condescended to, they will walk away at once."**
John Kerry, *Every Day Is Extra* (New York: Simon & Schuster, 2018), 490.

p. 241   **'alternative' (read: military) means of preventing a nuclear-armed Iran."**
Kerry, *Every Day Is Extra*, 505.

p. 242   **throughout the various terms of this agreement.**
"The Joint Comprehensive Plan of Action (JCPOA) at a Glance," Arms Control
Association, May 2018, https://www.armscontrol.org/factsheets/JCPOA-at-a-glance.

p. 242 **what Donald Trump based his withdrawal on was a caricature of diplomatic shorthand.**
"Remarks by President Trump on the Joint Comprehensive Plan of Action," The White House, May 8, 2018, https://www.whitehouse.gov/briefings-statements /remarks-president-trump-joint-comprehensive-plan-action/.

p. 244 **Norway, and Sweden joined the INSTEX system.**
Reuters, "Six more countries join Trump-busting Iran barter group," *Guardian*, November 30, 2019, https://www.theguardian.com/world/2019/dec/01/ six-more-countries-join-trump-busting-iran-barter-group.

p. 244 **and the IAEA confirmed the cap had been breached.**
Patrick Wintour, "EU powers resist calls for Iran sanctions after breach of nuclear deal," *Guardian*, July 1, 2019, https://www.theguardian.com/world/2019/jul/01 /eu-powers-resist-calls-for-iran-sanctions-after-breach-of-nuclear-deal.

p. 245 **in the Gulf of Oman, one month after similar attacks on four tankers.**
Patrick Wintour and Julian Borger, "Two oil tankers attacked in Gulf of Oman," *Guardian*, June 13, 2019, https://www.theguardian.com/world/2019/jun/13 /oil-tankers-blasts-reports-gulf-of-oman-us-navy.

p. 245 **Soleimani at Baghdad airport shortly after midnight on January 3, 2020.**
"The Killing of Gen. Qassim Suleimani: What We Know Since the U.S. Airstrike," *New York Times*, updated January 4, 2020, https://www.nytimes.com/2020/01/03 /world/middleeast/iranian-general-qassem-soleimani-killed.html.

p. 245 **Rouhani began privately and publicly warning European leaders.**
"Rouhani warns foreign forces in Middle East 'may be in danger,'" *Al Jazeera*, January 15, 2020, https://www.aljazeera.com/news/2020/01/rouhani-warns-foreign -forces-middle-east-danger-200115090254001.html.

p. 245 **Aramco facilities that process much of that nation's crude oil output.**
Ben Hubbard, Palko Karasz, and Stanley Reed, "Two Major Saudi Oil Installations Hit by Drone Strike, and U.S. Blames Iran," *New York Times*, updated September 15, 2019, https://www.nytimes.com/2019/09/14/world/middleeast/saudi-arabia-refineries -drone-attack.html.

p. 246 **and Erbil in northern Iraq—eleven striking their intended targets.**
Dan Lamothe, "Iran's attack on U.S. forces exposes Pentagon's challenges in stopping ballistic missiles," *Washington Post*, January 11, 2020, https://www.washingtonpost .com/national-security/2020/01/11/irans-attack-us-forces-exposes-pentagons -challenge-with-stopping-ballistic-missiles/.

p. 246 **more than two thousand ballistic missiles Iran is believed to have stockpiled.**
Bel Trew and Andrew Buncombe, "Iran missile strike: Two US-Iraq bases hit by 22 rockets in revenge attacks as crisis escalates," *The Independent*, January 7, 2020, https://www.independent.co.uk/news/world/middle-east/iran-rocket-attack-iraq -missiles-us-bases-trump-soleimani-a9274546.html.

p. 246   **operations instigated by Iran, but limited to front-line states."**
          "Chapter One: Tehran's strategic intent," *Iran's Network of Influence in the Middle East* (Washington, D.C.: International Institute for Strategic Studies, 2019), 11–38, https://www.iiss.org/publications/strategic-dossiers/iran-dossier/iran-19-03-ch-1 -tehrans-strategic-intent.

CHAPTER EIGHT: AFRICA: CRADLE OF LINES

p. 249   **slave trade, the repercussions of which still reverberate today.**
          "Trans-Atlantic Slave Trades–Database," Slave Voyages, Emory Center for Digital Scholarship, accessed July 2020, https://www.slavevoyages.org/voyage/database.

p. 249   **between three and six million died in the Congo Wars.**
          Philip Roessler and Harry Verhoeven, *Why Comrades Go to War: Liberation Politics and the Outbreak of Africa's Deadliest Conflict*, (Oxford, UK: Oxford University Press, 2016).

p. 251   **this nexus of globally induced strife.**
          Emmanuel Akyeampong, Robert H. Bates, Nathan Nunn, and James Robinson, eds., *Africa's Development in Historical Perspective* (Cambridge, UK: Cambridge University Press, 2014).

p. 251   **Christopher Ehret, Department of History UCLA.**
          Akyeampong et al., *Africa's Development.*

p. 251   **the tropical zone, defined by Oxford Professor Richard J. Reid.**
          Richard J. Reid, *Warfare in African History* (Cambridge, UK: Cambridge University Press, 2012).

p. 252   **city-states that were well-fortified against intrusions.**
          Olatunji Ojo, "Silent Testimonies, Public Memory: Slavery in Yoruba Proverbs," in *African Voices on Slavery and the Slave Trade, Volume 1: The Sources*, eds. Alice Bellagamba, Sandra E. Greene, and Martin A. Klein (Cambridge, UK: Cambridge University Press, 2013), https://books.google.com/books?id=XKIaBQAAQBAJ&pg=P A150&dq#v=onepage&q&f=false.

p. 252   **clay, bronze, and terracotta that have been preserved even today.**
          Kunle Lawal, "Ife, Oyo, Yoruba, Ancient: Kingship and Art," in *Encyclopedia of African History*, ed. Kevin Shillington (New York: Taylor & Francis Group, 2005), 1–3:672, https://books.google.com/books?id=umyHqvAErOAC&pg=PA672&lpg=PA 672&dq=yoruba+kingdom+oyo+encyclopedia+african+history&hl=en#v=onepage&q =yoruba%20kingdom%20oyo%20encyclopedia%20african%20history&f=false.

p. 253   **the population might have tripled.**
          The demographics here rely heavily on the work of Angus Maddison and the Maddison Project, based at the University of Groningen.
          "Appendix B: Growth of World Population, GDP and GDP Per Capita before 1820," *Maddison Historical Statistics* (Groningen: Groningen Growth and Development Centre, 2018), 229–265, http://www.ggdc.net/maddison/other_books/appendix_B.pdf.

"Maddison Historical Statistics," Groningen Growth and Development Centre, modified January 11, 2018, https://www.rug.nl/ggdc/historicaldevelopment/maddison/.

p. 254　**according to the 1974 *Guinness Book of Records*.**
Kylie Kiunguyu, "Africa Marvels: The Walls of Benin," *This is Africa*, March 13, 2019, https://thisisafrica.me/politics-and-society/african-marvels-the-walls-of-benin/.

p. 254　**Pew Research Center's Religion & Public Life program.**
"Region: Sub-Saharan Africa," Religion & Public Life, Pew Research Center, January 27, 2011, https://www.pewforum.org/2011/01/27/future-of-the-global-muslim-population -regional-sub-saharan-africa/.

p. 255　**a territorial line that was not to be crossed.**
"Great Zimbabwe (11th–15th Century)" Heilbrunn Timeline of History, The Metropolitan Museum of Art, October 2001, https://www.metmuseum.org/toah/hd /zimb/hd_zimb.htm.

p. 255　**irrational fear of the often predatory Zimba on the east coast of Africa.**
"The Portuguse Empire (1498–1698)," Kenyalogy Safari Web, accessed July 2020, http://www.kenyalogy.com/eng/info/histo4.html.

p. 255　**and the Imbangala.**
Amy McKenna, "Imbangala," *Encyclopaedia Britannica*, accessed July 2020, https://www.britannica.com/topic/Imbangala.

p. 256　**it was left to Diego Cáo.**
"Diogo Cáo," PeoplePill, accessed July 2020 https://peoplepill.com/people/diogo -cao/.

p. 256　**limits of the early empire, was Lukeni lua Nimi.**
"Kingdom of Kongo 1390–1914," South African History Online, updated August 27, 2019, https://www.sahistory.org.za/article/kingdom-kongo-1390-1914.

p. 256　**to push inland through what is now Angola.**
Joseph C. Miller, "Nzingo of Matamba in a new perspective," *The Journal of African History* 16, no. 2 (April 1975): 201–216, https://www.cambridge.org/core/journals /journal-of-african-history/article/nzinga-of-matamba-in-a-new-perspective1/F2612 D42726E2DBCFE6B295BC5DFC33C.
Adriana Balducci and Sylvia Serbin, "Njinga Mbandi: Queen of Ndongo and Matamba," UNESCO Series on Women in African History, 2014, https://unesdoc .unesco.org/ark:/48223/pf0000230103.

p. 257　**to win its own independence from the Netherlands in 1830.**
John Obioma Ukawuilulu, "Africa: Belgian Colonies," Encyclopedia on Race and Racism, Encyclopedia.com, updated June 2, 2020, https://www.encyclopedia.com /social-sciences/encyclopedias-almanacs-transcripts-and-maps/africa-belgian-colonies.

p. 258　**few frontiers, few red lines, drawn on it.**
Hilke Fischer, "130 years ago: carving up Africa in Berlin," Deutsche Welle, February 25, 2015, https://www.dw.com/en/130-years-ago-carving-up-africa-in -berlin/a-18278894.

p. 258   **red lines that would exist, often quite toxically, until today.**
          See, for instance, Andelman, *A Shattered Peace.*

p. 259   **until the Western powers began their scramble.**
          One of the great historians of the onset of the African colonial period was Saadia
          Touval, professor at Tel Aviv University:
          *The Boundary Politics of Independent Afri*ca (Cambridge, MA: Harvard University
          Press, 1972);
          "Treaties, Borders, and the partition of Africa," *The Journal of African History* 7, no. 2
          (July 1966): 279–293, https://www.cambridge.org/core/journals/journal-of-african
          -history/article/treaties-borders-and-the-partition-of-africa/1A98887DCE0BEA908B
          747F577D35CEB2.
          Touval also made great use, as have I, of the extraordinary diaries of Lord Lugard,
          who traveled throughout Africa negotiating a whole host of treaties with African
          potentates in the late nineteenth century. *The Diaries of Lord Lugard*, in four
          volumes, are an extraordinary peek behind the curtain of a continent in chaos
          and revolution as the major powers prepared to implant their own sense of how it
          should look.

p. 260   **when the "scramble" began, the map of Africa.**
          Myles Osborne and Susan Kingsley Kent, *Africans and Britons in the Age of Empire
          1660–1980* (Abingdon: Routledge, 2015), 76.

p. 260   **French President Félix Faure lamented in 1898.**
          Barnett Singer and John Langdon, *Cultured Force: Makers and Defenders of the French
          Colonial Empire* (Madison: University of Wisconsin Press, 2004), 145.

p. 261   **France geographically taking the largest slice, followed by Britain.**
          Osborne and Kent, *Africans and Britons*, 8.

p. 261   **instability of the tribes and frequent overlappings."**
          Elliott Green, "On the Size and Shape of African States," *International Studies
          Quarterly* 576, no. 2 (June 2012): 237.

p. 261   **artificial are the contemporary state's borders."**
          Green, "On the Size and Shape of African States," 238.

p. 263   **were set by how far Lugard could walk before he had to rest.**
          Touval, *The Boundary Politics of Independent Africa*, 4.

p. 263   **to establish its frontier with Nigeria.**
          Touval, "Treaties, Borders, and the Partition of Africa," 282.

p. 263   **equally stimulated rulers and their henchmen.**
          Johannes Fabian, *Out of Our Minds: Reason and Madness in the Exploration of Central
          Africa* (Berkeley: University of California Press, 2000).

p. 263   **subsidized by the Royal Niger Company to the tune of £50 a year.**
          Lord Lugard, *The Diaries of Lord Lugard*, ed. Margery Perham and Mary Bull, vol. 4
          (London: Faber & Faber, 1963), 105–106.

p. 265   **For the French, there were the Tirailleurs Sénégalais.**
Myron J. Echenberg, *Colonial Conscripts: the Tirailleurs Sénégalais in French West Africa, 1857–1960* (Portsmouth: Heinemann, 1991), https://archive.org/details /colonialconscrip00eche/page/98.

p. 265   **British, there was the Royal West African Frontier Force.**
Julius Adekunle, *Politics and Society in Nigeria's Middlebelt: Borgu and the Emergence of a Political Identity* (Trenton: Africa World Press, 2004), 134, https://books.google .com/books?id=KkYp1Q0hYoIC&lpg=PA133&ots=-1ZcwEFATM&dq=illo%20nigeri a&pg=PA134#v=onepage&q=illo%20nigeria&f=false.

p. 266   **King's African Rifles rarely passed 2,500 men under arms.**
Reid, *Warfare in African History*, 149.

p. 266   **means of dwelling in safety within their own boundaries."**
North Atlantic Treaty Organization, The Atlantic Charter, August 14, 1941, updated July 2, 2018, https://www.nato.int/cps/en/natohq/official_texts_16912.htm.

p. 266   **at the Lord Mayor of London's luncheon at Mansion House in London, Churchill observed.**
Winston Churchill, "The End of the Beginning," speech at The Lord Mayor's Luncheon, Mansion House, November 10, 1942, The Churchill Society, accessed July 2020, http://www.churchill-society-london.org.uk/EndoBegn.html.

p. 268   **that figure had more than doubled to 762,000.**
"Lagos, Nigeria Metro Area Population 1950–2020," Macrotrends, accessed July 2020, https://www.macrotrends.net/cities/22007/lagos/population.

p. 268   **it still was only the eighth fastest growing city in Africa.**
"Lagos Population," World Population Review, accessed July 2020, http://world populationreview.com/world-cities/lagos-population/.

p. 268   **five each by Portugal and Spain, and three by Belgium.**
Alistair Boddy-Evans, "Chronological List of African Independence," ThoughtCo., updated January 25, 2020, https://www.thoughtco.com/chronological-list-of-african -independence-4070467.

p. 269   **many countries experiencing multiple forced changes in leadership.**
Monty G. Marshall, "Appendix 2b. Coups d'Etat in Africa, 1946–2004," in *Conflict Trends in Africa 1946–2004*, (Arlington: Africa Conflict Prevention Pool, October 14, 2005), http://www.systemicpeace.org/africa/ACPPAnnex2b.pdf.

p. 269   **commanded by Brigadier General Mohammedu Buhari.**
Nowa Omoigui, "History of Civil-Military Relations in Nigeria (5)*: The Second Transition (1979–83, Part 2)*," Gamji, accessed July 2020, http://www.gamji.com /nowa/nowa13.htm.

p. 269   **Twice he would become president of Nigeria.**
"Nigeria's security under Buhari," *Strategic Comments* 22, no. 6 (August 31, 2016): iii–iv, https://www.tandfonline.com/doi/10.1080/13567888.2016.1229389.

p. 270   **UN investigation was never able to establish a definitive cause.**
UN General Assembly, Report of the Commission of Investigation into the
Conditions and Circumstances Resulting in the Tragic Death of Mr. Dag
Hammarskjold and of Members of the Party Accompanying Him, A/5069 (April 24,
1962), https://www.un.org/ga/search/view_doc.asp?symbol=A/5069.

p. 270   **the Direction générale de la Sécurité extérieure (DGSE), the equivalent of the CIA.**
Count de Marenches and David A. Andelman, *The Fourth World War: Diplomacy and
Espionage in the Age of Terrorism* (New York: William Morrow and Company, 1992),
191–196.

p. 271   **top twenty-five fastest growing nations by population, twenty-three are in Africa.**
"2020 World Population by Country," World Population Review, accessed July 2020,
http://worldpopulationreview.com/.

p. 271   **annual growth rates ranging from 5 percent to 11.9 percent.**
"GDP Annual Growth Rate," Trading Economics, accessed July 2020, https://trading
economics.com/country-list/gdp-annual-growth-rate.

p. 271   **their population who are living on less than $1.90 a day.**
"Poverty headcount ratio at $1.90 a day (2011 PPP) (% of population)," The World
Bank, accessed July 2020, https://data.worldbank.org/indicator/SI.POV.DDAY.

p. 272   **proceeding to march to the center."**
Reid, *Warfare in African History*, 164.

p. 274   **volume had exploded to 738 attacks leaving 4,600 dead.**
"Numbers Show Dramatic Rise of Terrorist Attacks in Africa Over Past Six Years,
IHS Says," Business Wire, June 27, 2016, https://www.businesswire.com/news
/home/20160627005638/en/Numbers-Show-Dramatic-Rise-Terrorist-Attacks-Africa.

p. 274   **1,552 terrorist attacks left at least 3,231 dead.**
"2018 Global Attack Index: Africa/Attacks by Country," Jane's Terrorism and Insurgency
Centre, accessed July 2020, https://cdn.ihs.com/ADS/314351707/Attacks-by-Africa.html.

p. 275   **from its entry point in Borno in the northeast.**
"Islam in Nigeria," African Studies Center Leiden, updated March 4, 2020,
https://www.asceiden.nl/content/webdossiers/islam-nigeria.

p. 275   **accounting for at least half the country's population.**
"Africa: Nigeria," The World Factbook, Central Intelligence Agency, updated June 10,
2020, https://www.cia.gov/library/publications/the-world-factbook/geos/ni.html.

p. 275   **northern states of Nigeria that operate under their own form of sharia law.**
"Islam in Nigeria."

p. 276   **Society of the People of the Sunnah for Propagation and Jihad.**
John O. Voll, "Boko Haram: Religion and Violence in the 21st Century," *Religions* 6,
no. 4 (September 2015): 1182–1202, https://www.mdpi.com/2077-1444/6/4/1182/htm.

p. 277   **leaving some seven hundred dead in the fighting.**
"Boko Haram: The Emerging Jihadist Threat in West Africa," Anti-Defamation League,
December 12, 2011, http://webarchive.loc.gov/all/20120109052545/http://www.adl.org
/main_Terrorism/boko_haram.htm?Multi_page_sections%3DsHeading_2.

p. 277   **"married off" to Boko Haram fighters.**
"What now after Nigeria's Boko Haram ceasefire fiasco?," BBC News, November 3,
2014, https://www.bbc.com/news/world-africa-29881291.

p. 278   **size of Belgium and the Netherlands combined.**
David Blair, "Boko Haram is now a mini-Islamic state with its own territory,"
The Telegraph, January 10, 2015, https://www.telegraph.co.uk/news/worldnews
/africaandindianocean/nigeria/11337722/Boko-Haram-is-now-a-mini-Islamic-State
-with-its-own-territory.html.

p. 278   **rebranded itself as "Islamic State's West Africa Province."**
Lauren Ploch Blanchard, *Nigeria's Boko Haram: Frequently Asked Questions*
(Washington, D.C.: Congressional Research Service, March 29, 2016), 2, https://fas
.org/sgp/crs/row/R43558.pdf.

p. 278   **world's largest drone base just outside Agadez in Niger.**
Nick Turse, "The U.S. is building a drone base in Niger that will cost more than
$280 million by 2024," *The Intercept*, August 21, 2018, https://theintercept
.com/2018/08/21/us-drone-base-niger-africa/.

p. 278   **sandstorms and locust swarms, as well as its remote desert location.**
Jennifer H. Svan, "Air Force Begins Flight Operations at Remote Post in Niger,"
Stars & Stripes (blog), Military.com, August 16, 2019, https://web.archive.org
/web/20191219152004/https://www.military.com/daily-news/2019/08/16/air-force
-begins-flight-operations-remote-post-niger.html.

p. 278   **and mutual security interests in the region."**
Oriana Pawlyk, "US Begins Drone Operations Out of New Niger Base," Military
.com, November 1, 2019, https://web.archive.org/web/20191105134619/https://www
.military.com/daily-news/2019/11/01/us-begins-drone-operations-out-niger.html.

p. 279   **planning to pull American forces out of West Africa.**
David A. Andelman, "Trump's possible Africa withdrawal sends the wrong signal at
exactly the wrong time," Think, NBC News, February 21, 2020, https://www.nbc
news.com/think/opinion/trump-s-possible-africa-withdrawal-sends-wrong-signal
-exact-wrong-ncna1140026.

p. 279   **shut down these terrorists in Mali, Niger, and Burkina Faso.**
Eric Schmitt, "Terrorism Threat in West Africa Soars as U.S. Weighs Troop Cuts,"
New York Times, February 27, 2020, https://www.nytimes.com/2020/02/27/world
/africa/terrorism-west-africa.html.

p. 279   **which considerably reduced its operational capacity."**
"Numbers Show Dramatic Rise of Terrorist Attacks," Business Wire.

p. 279   **al-Qaeda in the Islamic Maghreb.**
"Al-Mourabitoun," Counter Extremism Project, accessed July 2020, https://www
.counterextremism.com/sites/default/files/threat_pdf/Al-Mourabitoun-03282019.pdf.

p. 280   **a UNESCO World Heritage in Danger Site.**
Amy McKenna et al., "Timbuktu, Mali," *Encyclopaedia Britannica*, accessed July
2020, https://www.britannica.com/place/Timbuktu-Mali.

p. 280   **first appearance as an independent entity in 2006.**
"Al Shabaab," Center for International Security and Cooperation, Stanford University,
last modified January 2019, https://cisac.fsi.stanford.edu/mappingmilitants/profiles
/al-shabaab.

p. 280   **Somali gunmen who took part in the attack.**
James Gordon Meek, "'Black Hawk Down,' Anniversary: Al Qaeda's Hidden Hand,"
ABC News, October 4, 2013, https://abcnews.go.com/Blotter/black-hawk-anniversary
-al-qaedas-hidden-hand/story?id=20462820.

p. 281   **seven hundred people hostage for nineteen hours, leaving twenty-one dead.**
Max Bearak, "Survivors recount nightmarish siege in Nairobi hotel attack that
killed 21," *Washington Post*, January 16, 2019, https://www.washingtonpost.com
/world/standoff-at-nairobi-hotel-attack-stretches-into-its-second-day-with-15
-confirmed-dead/2019/01/16/346597ba-1910-11e9-b8e6-567190c2fd08
_story.html.

p. 281   **declaration of al-Quds [Jerusalem] as the capital of Israel."**
Max Bearak, "Deadly Nairobi attack comes as U.S. ramps up airstrikes against
al-Shabab in Somalia," *Washington Post*, January 17, 2019, https://www.washington
post.com/world/africa/deadly-nairobi-attack-comes-as-us-military-ramps-up
-airstrikes-against-al-shabab-in-somalia/2019/01/17/ebf40936-1a6c-11e9-b8e6
-567190c2fd08_story.html.

p. 281   **government areas, including Mogadishu."**
"Somalia," In Focus, Congressional Research Service, updated January 17, 2020,
https://crsreports.congress.gov/product/pdf/IF/IF10155.

p. 282   **up from 70 in 2015 and 120 in 2017.**
Congo, Forgotten: The Numbers Behind Africa's Longest Humanitarian Crisis (New
York: Congo Research Group, New York University Center on International
Cooperation, August 2019), 3, https://kivusecurity.nyc3.digitaloceanspaces.com
/reports/28/KST%20biannual%20report%20August%2012%20%281%29.pdf.

p. 282   **Council on Foreign Relation's Nigeria Tracker.**
John Campbell, "Nigeria Security Tracker," Nigeria on the Brink, Council on Foreign
Relations, updated June 1, 2020, https://www.cfr.org/nigeria/nigeria-security-tracker
/p29483.

p. 282   **while the Yemen Data Project registered 4.13 deaths per 100,000.**
"Yemen Data Project," Yemen Data Project, accessed July 2020, https://www
.yemendataproject.org/.

p. 282   **6,555 dead from 2017 to 2019 in this region of the DRC.**
Congo, Forgotten, 5.

p. 283   **drive them out of their traditional stronghold.**
Pauline Draps, "The Evolution of the Terrorist Threat in DR Congo," Briefing,
European Strategic Intelligence and Security Center, August 15, 2019, http://www.esisc
.org/upload/publications/briefings/the-evolution-of-the-terrorist-threat-in-dr-congo
/THE%20EVOLUTION%20OF%20THE%20TERRORIST%20THREAT%20

IN%20DR%20CONGO%20-%20Growing%20evidence%20of%20Links%20
between%20the%20Islamic%20State%20and%20local%20armed%20groups.pdf.

p. 283   **child soldiers across this region.**
"DR Congo: Warlord's Conviction Reveals Trial Flaws," Human Rights Watch,
April 19, 2019, https://www.hrw.org/news/2019/04/19/dr-congo-warlords-conviction
-reveals-trial-flaws.

p. 283   **long held onto this territory as their own.**
"Movements of Rwandan rebels in South Kivu raise fears," Kivu Security Tracker,
Congo Research Group, June 21, 2019, https://blog.kivusecurity.org/movements
-of-rwandan-rebels-in-south-kivu-raise-fears/.

p. 283   **to persistent attacks by armed insurgents.**
David A. Andelman, "Ebola is back in the Congo—and America's Africa policies
aren't helping contain its spread," NBC News Think, August 23, 2019, https://www
.nbcnews.com/think/opinion/ebola-back-congo-america-s-africa-policies-aren-t
-helping-ncna1045531.

p. 283   **was freed the next day after a ransom was paid.**
"Civilian deaths set a new record," Kivu Security Tracker, Congo Research Group,
December 2019, 2–3, https://kivusecurity.nyc3.digitaloceanspaces.com/reports/30
/KST%20Report%20December%202019.pdf.

p. 284   **"organized, violent challenges to incumbent rule."**
Christopher R. Day, "The Fates of Rebels: Insurgencies in Uganda," *Comparative
Politics* 43, no. 4 (July 2011): 439–458, https://www.jstor.org/stable/23040638?seq=1.

p. 284   **mad preacher and spirit medium Alice Auma Lakwena.**
Julian Borger, "Q&A: Joseph Kony and the Lord's Resistance Army," *Guardian*,
March 8, 2012, https://www.theguardian.com/world/2012/mar/08/joseph-kony
-lords-resistance-army.

p. 284   **drowned in the Nile during World War I.**
Ruddy Doom and Koen Vlassenroot, "Kony's Message: A New Koine? The Lord's
Resistance Army in Northern Uganda," *African Affairs* 98, no. 390 (January 1999):
5–36, https://www-jstor-org.ezproxy.monroepl.org/stable/pdf/723682.pdf?ab
_segments=0%2Fbasic_SYC-5055%2Fcontrol&refreqid=search%3Aa1981dce20671a
edb15af8e89e723721.

p. 284   **provide an armored shield against any enemy bullets.**
Felix Ocen, "Alice Lakwena: From fishmonger to rebel leader," *Daily Monitor*,
October 14, 2018, https://www.monitor.co.ug/Magazines/PeoplePower/Alice
-Lakwena-fishmonger--rebel-leader-NRA-Okello-Lutwa/689844-4804780-6ewycnz
/index.html.

p. 284   **training recruits in four facilities.**
Doom and Vlassenroot, "Kony's Message."

p. 285   **immediate target zone in western Uganda.**
Christopher R. Day, "'Survival Mode': Rebel Resilience and the Lord's Resistance
Army," *Terrorism and Political Violence* 31, no. 5 (March 2017), https://enoughproject

.org/wp-content/uploads/2017/08/Survival-Mode-Rebel-Resilience-and-the-Lords
-Resistance-Army.pdf.

p. 285   **penetrating its resolutely defended perimeters.**
          Day, "'Survival Mode.'"

p. 285   **to help the Ugandan army locate Kony.**
          Ledio Cakaj and Kristof Titeca, "Bye-Bye, Kony?" *Foreign Affairs*, May 31, 2017,
          https://www.foreignaffairs.com/articles/central-africa/2017-05-31/bye-bye-kony.

p. 285   **another virulent terrorist group in that lawless region.**
          "Central African Republic: Armed Groups Target Civilians," Human Rights Watch,
          May 2, 2017, https://www.hrw.org/news/2017/05/02/central-african-republic-armed
          -groups-target-civilians.

p. 285   **as an Interpol red notice remain open.**
          "Interpol issues first Red Notices on behalf of International Criminal Court,"
          Interpol, June 1, 2006, https://www.interpol.int/en/News-and-Events/News/2006
          /INTERPOL-issues-first-Red-Notices-on-behalf-of-International-Criminal-Court.
          Abalo Irene Otto, "Ex-wife: Kony Saved My Life at Firing Squad," *The Kampala
          Post*, May 11, 2019, https://kampalapost.com/news/ex-wife-kony-saved-my-life-firing
          -squad.

p. 286   **especially given new challenges from China.**
          Helene Cooper, Thomas Gibbons-Neff, Charlie Savage, and Eric Schmitt, "Pentagon
          Eyes Africa Drawdown as First Step in Global Troop Shift," *New York Times*,
          December 24, 2019, https://www.nytimes.com/2019/12/24/world/africa/esper-troops;
          Helene Cooper, "Plan to Cut U.S. Troops in West Africa Draws Criticism from
          Europe," *New York Times*, January 14, 2020, https://www.nytimes.com/2020/01/14
          /world/africa/milley-troops-withdraw.html?searchResultPosition=1.

p. 287   **the wrong signal at precisely the worst time.**
          Andelman, "Trump's possible Africa withdrawal."

p. 287   **"Because if we let the threat flourish, it will impact us too."**
          Adam Nossiter, "France Agrees to Small Troop Increase, but Little Else at Sahel
          Summit," *New York Times*, January 13, 2020, https://www.nytimes.com/2020/01/13
          /world/africa/france-sahel-military-forces.html.

p. 288   **journalist Jean-Pierre Elkabbach in November 2019.**
          Jean-Pierre Elkabbach, "L'Interview du General François Lecointre," *La Matinale*,
          CNews, November 11, 2019.

p. 289   **Ghana's Kwame Nkrumah.**
          Joel Savage, "The Confused Moments of Nkrumah in China After the Coup,"
          Modern Ghana, August 19, 2018, https://www.modernghana.com/news/876767/the
          -confused-moments-of-nkrumah-in-china-after-the-coup.html.

p. 289   **"Drawing contours of a new world order."**
          William Wallis, "Drawing Contours of a New World Order," *Financial Times*, January
          24, 2008, http://media.ft.com/cms/e13530f4-c9df-11dc-b5dc-000077b07658.pdf.

p. 289   **three times the level of trade with the US.**
Elliot Smith, "The US-China trade rivalry is underway in Africa, and Washington is playing catch-up," CNBC, October 9, 2019, https://www.cnbc.com/2019/10/09/the -us-china-trade-rivalry-is-underway-in-africa.html.

p. 289   **take over the main port facility from Dubai's DP World.**
Abdi Latif Dahir, "A strategic port in the Horn of Africa is at the center of a $500 million lawsuit," Quartz Africa, April 10, 2019, https://qz.com/africa/1591342 /djibouti-ordered-to-pay-dubais-dp-world-533-million/.

p. 289   **allow China to build its first overseas naval base right next door.**
Max Bearak, "In strategic Djibouti, a microcosm of China's growing foothold in Africa," *Washington Post*, December 30, 2019, https://www.washingtonpost.com /world/africa/in-strategic-djibouti-a-microcosm-of-chinas-growing-foothold-in-africa /2019/12/29/a6e664ea-beab-11e9-a8b0-7ed8a0d5dc5d_story.html.

p. 289   **bases strung along the continent to spy on terrorists' hideouts.**
Craig Whitlock, "U.S. expands secret intelligence operations in Africa," *Washington Post*, June 13, 2012, https://www.washingtonpost.com/world/national-security/us-expands -secret-intelligence-operations-in-africa/2012/06/13/gJQAHyvAbV_story.html.
Lina Benabdallah, "China-Africa military ties have deepened. Here are 4 things to know," *Washington Post*, July 6, 2018, https://www.washingtonpost.com/news /monkey-cage/wp/2018/07/06/china-africa-military-ties-have-deepened-here -are-4-things-to-know/.

p. 290   **have appealed for military help from Russia.**
Eric Schmitt and Thomas Gibbons-Neff, "Russia Exerts Growing Influence in Africa, Worrying Many in the West" *New York Times*, January 28, 2020, https://www.nytimes .com/2020/01/28/world/f.

CHAPTER NINE: ETERNAL LINES

p. 293   **the Pactrians, one of the "wandering tribes."**
Herodotus, "Chapter 7," in *The Histories*, trans. George Rawlinson, https://web .archive.org/web/20061216012652/http://piney.com/Heredotus7.html.

p. 293   **Durand a member of the Afghan Boundary Commission.**
Rafia Zakaria, "What Mortimer did," *Psyche*, Aeon, July 19, 2016, https://aeon.co /essays/how-a-colonial-blunder-grew-into-a-part-of-the-war-on-terror.

p. 293   **Merv and Pul-i-Khisti during the past fortnight."**
"Russia Still Aggressive: A Reported Advance in Force to Zulfikar Pass," *New York Times*, July 16, 1885, https://timesmachine.nytimes.com/timesmachine/1885/07/16 /103063202.html?pageNumber=1.

p. 295   **Emir had renounced sovereignty beyond the line."**
Olaf Caroe, *The Pathans: 500 B.C.–A.D. 1957* (London: 1958), 382, cited in "Geographic Support Project: The Durand Line," Central Intelligence Agency,

July 1961, https://www.cia.gov/library/readingroom/docs/CIA-RDP08C01297
R000100140005-3.pdf.

p. 295   **the Palestinian territories, many controlled by Egypt at the time.**
Alexander H. Joffe, "The Rise of Secondary States in the Iron Age Levant," *Journal of
the Economic and Social History of the Orient* 45, no. 4 (2002): 425–456, https://www
-jstor-org.ezproxy.monroepl.org/stable/pdf/3632872.pdf?ab_segments=0%252Fbasic
_SYC-5055%252Ftest&refreqid=excelsior%3A4b5d64df8160a4a005f68b7044
a6ab45.

p. 295   **and Ammon (where Amman, Jordan is now located).**
Joffe, "The Rise of Secondary States."

p. 295   **containing within their walls entire palaces.**
Joffe, "The Rise of Secondary States," 443.

p. 297   **Prince of Wales anchored together off the coast of Newfoundland.**
"When History Was Made at Sea: More Views of the President and the Prime
Minister," *New York Times*, August 16, 1941, https://timesmachine.nytimes.com
/timesmachine/1941/08/16/issue.html.

p. 297   **eight points of what would become known as The Atlantic Charter.**
North Atlantic Treaty Organization, The Atlantic Charter.

p. 297   **vociferous cheers from an admiring populace."**
James MacDonald, "Churchill Sees Cabinet and King," *New York Times*, August 20,
1941, https://timesmachine.nytimes.com/timesmachine/1941/08/20/87659125
.html?pageNumber=1.

p. 298   **inseparably linked to that of its North American member countries.**
"Why was NATO founded?" NATO/OTAN, 2017, accessed July 2020, https://www
.nato.int/wearenato/why-was-nato-founded.html.

p. 299   **the three Baltic Soviet republics (Estonia, Lithuania, and Latvia).**
"NATO Member States," Eesti NATO Ühing, accessed July 2020, https://www.eata
.ee/en/nato-2/nato-member-states/.

p. 299   **the 1,500-mile Durand Line as an international boundary.**
Jayshree Bajoria, "No Man's Land," *Newsweek*, November 30, 2007, https://web
.archive.org/web/20080408113251/http://www.newsweek.com/id/73137/page/1.

p. 299   **And the Pashtuns are the core of these problems.**
Frederic Grare, "Refusing to See the Obvious in Afghanistan," Carnegie Endowment
for International Peace, February 18, 2013, https://carnegieendowment.org/2013/02
/18/refusing-to-see-obvious-in-afghanistan-pub-50982.

p. 299   **a smattering of NATO troops, invaded Afghanistan.**
"U.S.-led attack on Afghanistan begins," This Day in History, History.com, July 20,
2010, https://www.history.com/this-day-in-history/u-s-led-attack-on-afghanistan
-begins.

p. 300   **Taliban means "student" in the Pashto language.**
"Who are the Taliban?" BBC News, February 27, 2020, https://www.bbc.com/news
/world-south-asia-11451718.

p. 300   **Asia to the Middle East and Europe in the thirteenth and fourteenth centuries).**
Hassan Abbas, "Profiles of Pakistan's Seven Tribal Agencies," *Terrorism Monitor* 4,
no. 20 (October 20, 2006), https://jamestown.org/program/profiles-of-pakistans
-seven-tribal-agencies/.

p. 300   **Khalid ibn al-Walid, the storied warrior of the Prophet Mohammed.**
Bernt Glatzer, "The Pashtun Tribal System," in *Concept of Trial Society*, eds. G. Pfeffer
and D. K. Bejera (New Delhi: Concept Publishers, 2002), 265–282, http://www
.ag-afghanistan.de/files/glatzer/tribal_system.pdf.

p. 300   **Soviet republics of Turkmenistan, Uzbekistan, and Tajikistan.**
Peter Baker, "Why Did Soviets Invade Afghanistan? Documents Offer History
Lesson for Trump," *New York Times,* January 29, 2019, https://www.nytimes.com
/2019/01/29/us/politics/afghanistan-trump-soviet-union.html.

p. 300   **pledging to end its support for the Taliban resistance.**
"Soviets agree to withdraw from Afghanistan," This Day in History, History.com,
February 9, 2010, https://www.history.com/this-day-in-history/soviets-to-withdraw
-from-afghanistan.

p. 301   **died in Afghanistan since the American invasion in 2001.**
Neta C. Crawford, Suzanne Fiederlein, and SaraJane Rzegocki, "Afghan Civilians," Costs
of War, Watson Institute International & Public Affairs, Brown University, updated
January 2020, https://watson.brown.edu/costsofwar/costs/human/civilians/afghan.

p. 301   **since its activities began ten years earlier.**
"Civilian casualties in Afghanistan spike to record-high levels–UN report," UN
Assistance Mission in Afghanistan, October 17, 2019, https://unama.unmissions
.org/civilian-casualties-afghanistan-spike-record-high-levels-%E2%80%93
-un-report.

p. 302   **maintains close ties with Pakistan's ISI and al-Qaeda.**
Lindsay Maizland and Zachary Laub, "The Taliban in Afghanistan," Council on
Foreign Relations, updated March 11, 2020, https://www.cfr.org/backgrounder
/taliban-afghanistan.

p. 302   **visit by Trump that all but utterly ignored Pakistan and its leader.**
Peter Baker, Michael Crowley, and Jeffrey Gettleman, "Trump Sees Commitment to
Religious Freedom in India as Riots Break Out," *New York Times*, February 25, 2020,
https://www.nytimes.com/2020/02/25/us/politics/trump-modi.html.

p. 303   **talks with Karzai government are not possible."**
Saeed Ali Achakzai, "Taliban reject Afghan president's peace talk offer," Reuters,
September 30, 2007, https://www.reuters.com/article/us-afghan-talks-idUSISL
26606720070930.

p. 303   **come home and embrace their land."**
Ben Farmer, "Hamid Karzai reaches out to 'Taliban brothers' in Afghanistan,
Telegraph, November 3, 2009, https://www.telegraph.co.uk/news/worldnews/asia
/afghanistan/6495487/Hamid-Karzai-reaches-out-to-Taliban-brothers-in-Afghan
istan.html.

p. 303   **resume jihad against the Afghan government.**
UN Security Council, Tenth report of the Analytical Support and Sanctions
Monitoring Team submitted pursuant to resolution 2255 (2015) concerning the
Taliban and other associated individuals and entities constituting a threat to the peace,
stability and security of Afghanistan, S/2019/481, 6 (April 30, 2019), p. 6. https://www
.securitycouncilreport.org/atf/cf/%7B65BFCF9B-6D27-4E9C-8CD3-CF6E4FF
96FF9%7D/s_2019_481.pdf.

p. 304   **exporting some $400 million worth of product.**
Ibid., p. 10.

p. 304   **Russia, even China were intended to find some way forward.**
UN General Assembly/Security Council, seventy-fourth session, Agenda item 36,
The situation in Afghanistan and its implications for international peace and security,
A/74/583–S/2019/935, 4 (December 10, 2019), https://www.securitycouncilreport.org
/atf/cf/%7B65BFCF9B-6D27-4E9C-8CD3-CF6E4FF96FF9%7D/s_2019_935.pdf.

p. 304   **It finally all came together in Qatar.**
"How Qatar came to host the Taliban," BBC News, June 22, 2013, https://www.bbc
.com/news/world-asia-23007401.

p. 305   **in the days following the Arab Spring.**
Sultan Barakat, *Qatari Mediation: Between Ambition and Achievement*, Brookings
Doha Center Analysis Paper Number 12 (Washington, D.C.: Brookings Doha Center,
November 2014), https://www.brookings.edu/wp-content/uploads/2016/06/Final
-PDF-English.pdf.

p. 305   **their numbers grew from a handful to dozens.**
"How Qatar came to host the Taliban."

p. 305   **his unit in Afghanistan five years earlier.**
Ernesto Londoño, "Taliban-held U.S. soldier released in exchange for Afghan
detainees," *Washington Post*, June 1, 2014, https://www.washingtonpost.com
/world/national-security/taliban-held-us-soldier-released-in-exchange-for
-afghan-detainees/2014/05/31/8b764dac-e8db-11e3-a86b-362fd5443d19_story
.html?algtrack=cfrec-0.

p. 305   **himself an ethnic Pashtun, or at least claims Pashtun origins.**
"Khalilzad, Zalmay Dr.," Afghan Biographies, Who is who in Afghanistan?, September 10,
2009, updated February 3, 2020, http://www.afghan-bios.info/index.php?option=com
_afghanbios&id=884&task=view&total=4261&start=1964&Itemid=2.

p. 305   **quite pointedly, the Taliban Five.**
Mujib Mashai, "Once Jailed in Guantánamo, 5 Taliban Now Face U.S. at Peace
Talks," *New York Times*, March 26, 2019, https://www.nytimes.com/2019/03/26
/world/asia/taliban-guantanamo-afghanistan-peace-talks.html.

p. 305   **Baradar, described as the deputy leader of the Taliban.**
Sarah Dadouch, Susannah George, and Dan Lamothe, "U.S. signs peace deal
with Taliban agreeing to full withdrawal of American troops from Afghanistan,"
Washington Post, February 29, 2020, https://www.washingtonpost.com/world/asia

_pacific/afghanistan-us-taliban-peace-deal-signing/2020/02/29/b952fb04-5a67-11ea
-8efd-0f904bdd8057_story.html.

p. 306   **perhaps more than might ultimately be warranted:**
"Statement from the President," The White House, February 28, 2020, https://www
.whitehouse.gov/briefings-statements/statement-from-the-president-14/.

p. 306   **forty thousand square miles of territory inside Pakistan.**
Mary Schons, "The Durand Line," Resource Library, National Geographic, January 21,
2011, https://www.nationalgeographic.org/article/durand-line/.

p. 306   **territory the Taliban does not control in whole or in part.**
Dion Nissenbaum and Ehsanullah Amiri, "Pompeo Talks to Taliban, Afghan Leaders
in Bid to Settle Dispute Impeding U.S. Exit," *Wall Street Journal*, March 23, 2020,
https://www.wsj.com/articles/pompeo-arrives-in-kabul-on-a-diplomatic-rescue
-mission-11584947271.

p. 307   **he flew out of his final meeting in Doha.**
"Secretary Michael R. Pompeo Remarks to the Traveling Press," US Department
of State, March 23, 2020, https://www.state.gov/secretary-michael-r-pompeo
-remarks-to-the-traveling-press-2/.

p. 308   **By 1896, they had become a majority in the city of Jerusalem.**
Ami Isseroff, "The Population of Palestine Prior to 1948," Population of Ottoman
and Mandate Palestine, MidEastWeb, accessed July 2020, http://www.mideastweb
.org/palpop.htm.

p. 308   **form a very effective guard for the Suez Canal.**
Andelman, *A Shattered Peace*, 87.

p. 309   **pioneer work has been carried out by the Jews."**
Andelman, *A Shattered Peace*, 91.

p. 309   **leader of the British Jewish community, Lord Lionel Rothschild.**
"The Balfour Declaration Full Text," My Jewish Learning, accessed July 2020,
https://www.myjewishlearning.com/article/read-the-balfour-declaration/.

p. 310   **Faisal in the robes of a Bedouin warrior.**
"File: Weizmann and Feisal 1918: jpg," 1918, photograph, Wikimedia Commons,
https://commons.wikimedia.org/wiki/File:Weizmann_and_feisal_1918.jpg.

p. 310   **82,498 Christians and others."**
Sir John Hope Simpson, "Palestine: Report on Immigration, Land Settlement and
Development," The Question of Palestine, United Nations Information System on
the Question of Palestine, October 1930, accessed July 2020, https://unispal.un.org
/UNISPAL.NSF/0/E3ED8720F8707C9385256D19004F057C.

p. 310   **to a peak of 61,458 in 1937.**
"Demographics of Historic Palestine Prior to 1948," CJPME Factsheet 7, Canadians
for Justice and Peace in the Middle East, July 2004, https://www.cjpme.org/fs_007.

p. 310   **Jews outnumbered Arabs 716,700 to 156,000.**
"Jewish & Non-Jewish Population of Israel/Palestine (1517–Present)," Jewish Virtual
Library, The American-Israeli Cooperative Enterprise, updated April 2020,

https://www.jewishvirtuallibrary.org/jewish-and-non-jewish-population-of-israel
-palestine-1517-present.

p. 310   **the British in the course of their mandate over Palestine.**
Gideon Biger, "The Boundaries of Israel-Palestine Past, Present, and Future: A
Critical Geographic View," *Israel Studies* 13, no. 1 (Spring 2008):68–93, https://www
-jstor-org.ezproxy.monroepl.org/stable/pdf/30245820.pdf?ab_segments=0%252Fbasic
_SYC-5055%252Fcontrol&refreqid=excelsior%3A32790e805391b54f9d7579500
164f514.

p. 312   **Israel's "narrow waist" that could be used to divided Israel in half.**
Yossi Alpher, "An Israeli View: Geography or demography?" bitterlemons.org,
edition 8, February 24, 2003, http://www.bitterlemons.org/previous/bl240203ed8.html.

p. 312   **map of what it viewed as the nation's new red line.**
UN Security Council, Resolution 242, S/RES/242 (November 22, 1967), https://unispal
.un.org/DPA/DPR/unispal.nsf/0/7D35E1F729DF491C85256EE700686136.

p. 313   **a solution that is considered just by all parties.**
"Transcript of Kissinger's News Conference on the Crisis in the Middle East," *New
York Times*, October 26, 1973, https://timesmachine.nytimes.com/timesmachine
/1973/10/26/issue.html.

p. 313   **the well-being and progress of the Palestinian people."**
"Talking Points for Meeting with General Walters," The White House, October 24,
1973, declassified September 17, 2003, accessed July 2020, https://nsarchive2.gwu
.edu/NSAEBB/NSAEBB98/octwar-78.pdf.

p. 314   **He was accompanied by his principal deputy.**
"Shuttle Diplomacy and the Arab-Israeli Dispute, 1974–1975," Office of the
Historian, US Department of State, accessed July 2020, https://history.state.gov
/milestones/1969-1976/shuttle-diplomacy.
Henry Kissinger, *Years of Upheaval* (New York: Simon & Schuster, 1982).

p. 314   **as Jimmy Carter would later put it.**
"Camp David Accords: Jimmy Carter Reflects 25 Years Later," The Carter Center,
September 16, 2003, https://www.cartercenter.org/news/documents/doc1482.html.

p. 315   **21,671 square kilometers versus 5,506 square kilometers.**
Sergio DellaPergola, "Demography in Israel/Palestine: Trends, Prospects, Policy
Implications," IUSSP XXIV General Population Conference, Salvador de Bahia,
S64. Population Change and Political Transitions, August 2001, 4, https://pdfs
.semanticscholar.org/37f9/76b1ef3efc9d44daa3f00846f6ec06905efe.pdf.

p. 316   **into his second term, in June 2009, he announced the road map.**
Barak Ravid and Aluf Benn, "Netanyahu's Speech: Yes to Road Map, No to
Settlement Freeze," *Haaretz*, June 10, 2009, https://www.haaretz.com/1.5062998.

p. 316   **a highly sensitive area . . . near East Jerusalem."**
"Israeli defence minister approves 'Sovereignty Road' in occupied West Bank,"
Middle East Eye, March 9, 2020, https://www.middleeasteye.net/news
/israels-defence-minister-approves-sovereignty-road-occupied-west-bank.

p. 317 **move the American embassy in Israel from Tel Aviv to Jerusalem.**
Andy Biggs, "The day President Trump announced the US Embassy move to Jerusalem," *Times of Israel*, December 6, 2018, https://blogs.timesofisrael.com /the-day-president-trump-announced-the-us-embassy-move-to-jerusalem/.

p. 317 **along the border fence with Gaza.**
David M. Halbfinger, Isabel Kershner, and Declan Walsh, "Israel Kills Dozens at Gaza Border as U.S. Embassy Opens in Jerusalem," *New York Times*, May 14, 2018, https://www.nytimes.com/2018/05/14/world/middleeast/gaza-protests-palestinians -us-embassy.html.

p. 317 **the leading Israeli daily Haaretz, wrote in February 2020.**
Nir Hasson, "Netanyahu's Latest Election Spin Is a Point of No Return for Israeli Settlements," *Haaretz*, February 26, 2020, https://www.haaretz.com/israel-news /elections/.premium-netanyahu-s-latest-election-spin-is-a-point-of-no-return-for -israeli-settlements-1.8590666.

p. 317 **The outlines of the full 181-page plan.**
Peace to Prosperity: A Vision to Improve the Lives of the Palestinian and Israeli People (Washington, D.C.: The White House, January 2020), https://www.whitehouse.gov /wp-content/uploads/2020/01/Peace-to-Prosperity-0120.pdf.

p. 317 **in what is today the West Bank."**
"Trump's 'Conceptual Map' show Israel 'enclave communities,' 'Future Palestine,'" *Times of Israel*, January 28, 2020, https://www.timesofisrael.com/trumps-conceptual -maps-show-israel-enclave-communities-future-palestine/.

p. 319 **labeled the entire deal "utterly unacceptable and grossly unjust."**
"US Israel-Palestinian peace plan a 'mockery', upends long-standing consensus— International Conference Hears," UN News, United Nations, February 28, 2020, https://news.un.org/en/story/2020/02/1058351.

p. 319 **"talking points," which Kushner and the State Department cabled.**
"Talking Points to use with Host Government," *Politico*, accessed July 2020, https://www.politico.com/f/?id=0000016f-f245-d6d6-abff-f3473ba70000.

p. 319 **"HUGE breakthrough today!**
https://twitter.com/realDonaldTrump/status/1293922936609546240

p. 319 **As the White House put it.**
"Joint Statement of the United States, the State of Israel and the United Arab Emirates," The White House, August 13, 2020, https://www.whitehouse.gov /briefings-statements/joint-statement-united-states-state-israel-united-arab -emirates/

p. 320 **smuggle arms and explosives into this Palestinian territory from Egypt.**
Yardena Schwartz, "Israel is Building a Secret Tunnel-Destroying Weapon," *Foreign Policy*, March 10, 2016, https://foreignpolicy.com/2016/03/10 /israel-is-building-a-secret-tunnel-destroying-weapon-hamas-us-gaza/.

p. 321 **now independent nation, of Estonia.**
Ottis, "Analysis of the 2007 Cyber Attacks Against Estonia."

p. 321   **with Russia clearly the leading target.**
Bobbie Johnson, "'No one is ready for this,'" *Guardian*, April 15, 2009, https://www
.theguardian.com/technology/2009/apr/16/internet-hacking-cyber-war-nato.

p. 322   **"boost [their] joint defense capabilities."**
"Former Soviet states boost defense capability in joint drills," RIA Novosti via
Sputnik, July 22, 2008, https://sputniknews.com/world/20080722114629594/.

p. 322   **chronicling the work of the FSB at home and abroad.**
Andrei Soldatov and Irina Borogan, "Russia's Very Secret Services," *World Policy
Journal* 28, no. 1 (Spring 2011): 83–91, https://www-jstor-org.ezproxy.monroepl
.org/stable/pdf/41479271.pdf?ab_segments=0%252Fbasic_SYC-5055%252
Fcontrol&refreqid=excelsior%3Abee57d6dbf4098a002d20738fc11876a.

p. 322   **advance toward eventual NATO membership."**
"NATO Ministers affirm support for Georgia," NATO/OTAN, December 6, 2017,
https://www.nato.int/cps/en/natohq/news_149665.htm.

p. 323   **countries who are eager to enter the alliance."**
"Russian FM Lavrov supports resumption of flights to Georgia as Georgians 'realise
consequences' of June 20," Agenda.ge, September 26, 2019, https://agenda.ge/en
/news/2019/2582.

p. 323   **blatant such actions took place in August 2019 in the Norwegian Sea.**
Atle Staalesen, "30 Russian naval vessels stage show of force near coast of
Norway," *Barents Observer*, August 15, 2019, https://thebarentsobserver.com/en
/security/2019/08/30-russian-naval-vessels-stage-show-force-coast-norway.

p. 323   **nine of its own ships to monitor them as they lingered off the coast.**
Dan Sabbagh, "Royal Navy shadows Russian ships after 'high activity' in Channel,"
Guardian, March 16, 2020, https://www.theguardian.com/uk-news/2020/mar/26
/royal-navy-shadows-russian-ships-after-high-activity-in-channel.

p. 324   **he would "do his own thing."**
Uri Friedman, "Trump vs. NATO: It's Not Just About the Money," *Atlantic*, July 12, 2018,
https://www.theatlantic.com/international/archive/2018/07/trump-nato-allies/564881/.

p. 324   **Rumen Radev, described what immediately followed.**
Georgi Gotev, "Bulgarian President: Trump raised the target for NATO spending
from 2% to 4%," Euractiv, July 11, 2018, updated July 12, 2018, https://www
.euractiv.com/section/global-europe/news/bulgarian-president-trump-raised-the
-target-for-nato-spending-from-2-to-4/.

p. 325   **the United States, or by extension NATO, to assure its defense.**
Julian Borger, "Trump says Macron's call for European army is 'insulting,'"
Guardian, November 9, 2018, https://www.theguardian.com/us-news/2018/nov/09
/trump-paris-macron-peace-forum.

p. 325   **referring to the early days of the First World War.**
Nicholas Vinocur and Paul Dallison, "Donald Trump: Without the US, the French
would be speaking German," *Politico,* November 13, 2018, updated April 19, 2019,

https://www.politico.eu/article/donald-trump-without-the-us-the-french-would
-be-speaking-german/.

p. 325 **doing more together than they have done in many many years.**
"NATO Secretary General Comments to Reporters at the White House," C-Span,
November 14, 2019, video, 7:30, https://www.c-span.org/video/?466461-1
/nato-secretary-general-speaks-reporters-white-house.

p. 326 **a red line," one European diplomat told CNN.**
Alex Marquardt and Jennifer Hansler, "US push to include 'Wuhan virus' language
in G7 joint statement fractures alliance," CNN Politics, March 26, 2020,
https://www.cnn.com/2020/03/25/politics/g7-coronavirus-statement/index.html.

p. 326 **ten miles from the Hungarian frontier with Austria.**
Andelman, "Quiz Show."

p. 326 **mayor of the small border town of Ásotthalom.**
Jon Wertheim, "Subsidies for Minivans: Hungarian Government Paying Citizens
to Start Families, but Only the 'Right' Kinds of Families," *60 Minutes*, CBS News,
March 22, 2020, https://www.cbsnews.com/news/hungary-paying-citizens-to-have
-babies-60-minutes-2020-03-22/.

CODA

p. 328 **an early peak of the pandemic in March 2020.**
Kevin Rudd, "COVID-19 Trumps Nationalism," *Project Syndicate*, March 6, 2020,
https://www.project-syndicate.org/commentary/coronavirus-nationalist-response
-fails-by-kevin-rudd-2020-03.

p. 329 **world's population of some 1.6 billion.**
"1918 Pandemic (H1N1 virus)," Centers for Disease Control and Prevention,
accessed July 2020, https://www.cdc.gov/flu/pandemic-resources/1918-pandemic
-h1n1.html.

p. 329 **vastly overshadowed our perception of that era.**
Nadège Mougel, "REPERES–Module 1-0—explanatory notes—World War I
casualties," trans. Julie Gratz, Centre européen Robert Schuman, 2011, http://www
.centre-robert-schuman.org/userfiles/files/REPERES%20E2%80%93%20
module%201-1-1%20-%20explanatory%20notes%20E2%80%93%20World%20
War%20I%20casualties%20E2%80%93%20EN.pdf.

p. 329 **disease entered the continent through three seaports.**
Howard Phillips, "Influenza Pandemic (Africa)," 1914–1918 Online: International
Encyclopedia of the First World War, updated October 8, 2014, https://encyclo
pedia.1914-1918-online.net/article/influenza_pandemic_africa.

p. 331 **North Macedonia became the thirtieth member of NATO.**
"Secretary of State Michael R. Pompeo Remarks to the Press," US Department of
State, April 7, 2020, https://www.state.gov/secretary-michael-r-pompeo-remarks
-to-the-press-8/.

p. 331   **already closed its borders, especially with Italy.**
"Coronavirus: Germany latest country to close borders," BBC News, March 16, 2020,
https://www.bbc.com/news/world-europe-51905129.

p. 331   **Karsten explained. "Love is the best thing in the world."**
Patrick Kingsley, "A Closed Border Can't Stop This Elderly Couple: 'Love Is the Best
Thing in the World,'" *New York Times*, April 22, 2020, https://www.nytimes.com
/2020/04/22/world/europe/coronavirus-denmark-germany-border.html?referringSour
ce=articleShare.

p. 332   **turned into an evil caricature of himself.**
Dave Lawler, "Hungary's Viktor Orbán granted sweeping powers amid coronavirus
crisis," *Axios*, March 30, 2020, https://www.axios.com/hungary
-viktor-orban-coronavirus-powers-e438613e-6aef-458e-9ef9-720591865efa
.html?utm_source=newsletter&utm_medium=email&utm_campaign=newsletter
_axiospm&stream=top.

p. 332   **Fidesz also owns or controls most of the nation's media.**
Sarah Repucci, "Media Freedom: A Downward Spiral," Freedom and the Media 2019,
Freedom House, accessed July 2020, https://freedomhouse.org/report/freedom
-and-media/2019/media-freedom-downward-spiral?stream=top&utm_source
=newsletter&utm_medium=email&utm_campaign=sendto_newslettertest.

p. 332   **House Foreign Affairs Committee, issued a frantic statement.**
"Engel Statement on Orban's Coronavirus Power Grab," US House of Representatives
Committee on Foreign Affairs, March 30, 2020, https://foreignaffairs.house.gov
/2020/3/engel-statement-on-orban-s-coronavirus-power-grab-washington
-representative-eliot-l-engel-chairman-of-the-house-committee-on-foreign-affairs
-today-issued-the-following-statement-regarding-legislation-that-passed-through
-parliament-in-hungary-giving-the-prime-minister-sweeping-new-emergency-auth.

p. 332   **for fair and impartial administration of justice.**
Rick Noack, "Days after Brexit becomes almost certain, Poland's Supreme Court says
that country could be at risk of leaving the E.U., too," *Washington Post*, December 18,
2019, https://www.washingtonpost.com/world/2019/12/18/days-after-brexit-becomes
-almost-certain-polands-supreme-court-says-that-country-could-be-risk-leaving-eu-too/.

p. 333   **stolen cargos and defective medical masks.**
"Coronavirus: la guerre des masques," *Le Point*, April 3, 2020, https://www.lepoint.fr
/monde/coronavirus-la-guerre-des-masques-03-04-2020-2369963_24.php.

p. 333   **the world economy coming to a standstill."**
"World Health Organization COVID-19 Briefing Transcript April 3," *Rev* (blog),
April 3, 2020, https://www.rev.com/blog/transcripts/world-health-organization
-covid-19-briefing-transcript-april-3.

p. 333   **barely 16 percent disagreed with that sentiment.**
Yaroslav Trofimov and Bojan Pancevski, "Coronavirus Crisis Threatens to Split an
Already Fractured EU," *Wall Street Journal*, April 10, 2020, https://www.wsj.com
/articles/coronavirus-crisis-threatens-to-split-an-already-fractured-eu-11586525523.

p. 333   **a longstanding demand of nationalists," said Yanis Varoufakis.**
Yanis Varoufakis, "Coronavirus has sparked a perfect storm of nationalism and
financial speculation," *Guardian*, March 8, 2020, https://www.theguardian.com
/commentisfree/2020/mar/08/coronavirus-nationalism-economy-wall-street.

p. 333   **nourishing the French people has become a mission of public service.**
Beatrice Parrino, "Coronavirus: du pré à l'assiette, les coulisses de la 'voie sacrée,'"
Le Point, April 2, 2020, https://www.lepoint.fr/economie/economie-les-coulisses-de
-la-voie-sacree-02-04-2020-2369878_28.php.

p. 334   **14 deaths in the entire country.**
World Health Organization, "Coronavirus Disease (Covid-19) Situation Report-180,"
WHO, July 18, 2020, https://www.who.int/docs/default-source/coronaviruse
/situation-reports/20200718-covid-19-sitrep-180.pdf?sfvrsn=39b31718_2.

p. 334   **and recorded surges in cases and especially deaths.**
Christina Farr, "Sweden kept its country relatively open during the coronavirus
pandemic, but its elderly paid a price," CNBC, July 17, 2020, https://www.cnbc
.com/2020/07/17/how-sweden-fought-coronavirus-and-what-went-wrong.html?
__source=iosappshare%7Ccom.google.Gmail.ShareExtension.

p. 334   **France alone registered more than 82,000 new cases.**
World Health Organization, "Coronavirus disease," September 27, 2010 (Geneva),
https://www.who.int/docs/default-source/coronaviruse/situation-reports/20200928
-weekly-epi-update.pdf?sfvrsn=9e354665_6.

p. 334   **President Macron to contemplate a restoration.**
"Coronavirus: Paris dans la crainte de nouvelles restrictions, le recours contre la fermeture
des bars à Marseille et Aix rejeté," *Le Monde*, September 30, 2020, https://www.lemonde
.fr/planete/article/2020/09/30/coronavirus-paris-dans-la-crainte-de-nouvelles-restrictions
-le-recours-contre-la-fermeture-des-bars-a-marseille-et-aix-rejete_6054254_3244.html.

p. 334   **a €1.8 trillion rescue package.**
David A. Andelman, "Trump could learn from Europe's leaders, who've begun
charting a recovery from Covid-19," CNN, July 22, 2020, https://www.cnn.com
/2020/07/22/opinions/covid-19-america-european-union-andelman/index.html.

p. 334   **"This long negotiation was marked by difficulties.**
Sam Fleming, Mehreen Khan, and Jim Brunsden, "EU leaders strike deal on €750bn
recovery fund after marathon summit," *Financial Times*, July 21, 2020, https://www
.ft.com/content/713be467-ed19-4663-95ff-66f775af55"cc?shareType"=nongift.

p. 335   **plots by Iranian-backed militias.**
Tom O'Connor, "U.S. and Iran Prepare for Escalation in Iraq, Where Coronavirus
May Make Conflict Worse," *Newsweek*, April 2, 2020, https://www.newsweek.com
/us-iran-escalation-iraq-coronavirus-threat-1495810.

p. 335   **Iran was the poorest in terms of economic growth and inflation.**
Adrianna Murphy, Zhaleh Abdi, Iraj Harirchi, Martin Mckee, and Elham Ahmadnezhad,
"Economic Sanctions and Iran's capacity to respond to COVID-19," *The Lancet Public
Health* 5, no. 5 (May 2020), https://doi.org/10.1016/S2468-2667(20)30083-9.

p. 336   **doesn't have much in the way of resources."**
          "The Middle East Response to the Coronavirus," Council on Foreign Relations, April 3,
          2020, https://www.cfr.org/conference-calls/middle-east-response-coronavirus.

p. 337   **by the drafters of the Treaty of Versailles a century earlier.**
          Andelman, *A Shattered Peace.*

p. 337   **the weakest health system in our interconnected world."**
          Carol Morello, "Pandemic fuels calls to lift sanctions as Trump administration
          imposes more," *Washington Post,* March 28, 2020, https://www.washingtonpost.com
          /national-security/pandemic-fuels-calls-to-lift-sanctions-as-trump-administration
          -imposes-more/2020/03/28/552d6438-704d-11ea-96a0-df4c5d9284af_story.html.

p. 338   **Ayatollah Ali Khamenei himself, particularly in his seminal televised address.**
          Ali Khamenei, "US officials are charlatans and terrorists," Khamenei.ir, March 22,
          2020, http://english.khamenei.ir/news/7451/US-officials-are-charlatans-and
          -terrorists.

p. 338   **no cheering crowds at the Imam Reza shrine as in years past.**
          Omer Carmi, "Khamenei's Nowruz Speech in a Time of Coronavirus," Policy Analysis,
          The Washington Institute, March 23, 2020, https://www.washingtoninstitute.org
          /policy-analysis/view/khameneis-nowruz-speech-in-a-time-of-coronavirus.

p. 338   **in the Middle East, the virus only continued its spread.**
          Nada AlTaher and Henrik Pettersson, "Coronavirus surges across Middle East and
          North Africa, nations both rich and poor," CNN, July 17, 2020, https://www.cnn
          .com/2020/07/17/middleeast/coronavirus-middle-east-surge-intl/index.html.

p. 338   **to protect its right to govern as it wished.**
          Joe Lauria, "COVID-19: Devastated Saudi Royal Family Seeks to End Yemen War,"
          Consortium News, April 8, 2020, https://consortiumnews.com/2020/04/08
          /covid-19-devastated-saudi-royal-family-seeks-to-end-yemen-war/.

p. 339   **high of $63 a barrel in January 2020 to $20 three months later.**
          "Crude Oil Prices—70 Year Historical Chart," Macrotrends, accessed July 2020,
          https://www.macrotrends.net/1369/crude-oil-price-history-chart.

p. 339   **allow him to serve as president for life.**
          Andrew Higgins, "Citing Virus, Putin Suspends Vote on Keeping Him in Power,"
          New York Times, March 25, 2020, https://www.nytimes.com/2020/03/25/world
          /europe/russia-putin-coronavirus.html.

p. 339   **containing the spread of the virus and its economic impact.**
          "Coronavirus in Russia: The Latest News," *Moscow Times,* accessed July 2020,
          updated daily, https://www.themoscowtimes.com/2020/04/10/coronavirus-in-russia
          -the-latest-news-april-10-a69117.

p. 340   **"the president [was] clearly stepping back.**
          David A. Andelman, "Uh oh, Putin's following Trump's Covid-19 playbook,"
          CNN, May 11, 2020, https://www.cnn.com/2020/05/11/opinions/putin-covid-19
          -coronavirus-trump-playbook-andelman/index.html

p. 340   **virtually self-sufficient in agricultural output.**
          Andrew E. Kramer, "Thanks to Sanctions, Russia is Cushioned from Virus's
          Economic Shocks," *New York Times*, March 20, 2020, updated April 20, 2020,
          https://www.nytimes.com/2020/03/20/world/europe/russia-coronavirus
          -covid-19.html.

p. 340   **the burgeoning coronavirus crisis in Syria was high on the agenda.**
          Maxim A. Suchkov, "Intel: What was Russia's defense minister doing in Syria?"
          AL-Monitor, March 4, 2020, https://www.al-monitor.com/pulse/originals/2020/03
          /intel-russia-defense-minister-visit-syria-assad-shoigu.html.

p. 340   **medical devices including ventilators.**
          Maxim A. Suchkov, "Intel: Why Russia is getting involved in Mideast COVID-19
          fight," AL-Monitor, April 9, 2020, https://www.al-monitor.com/pulse/originals
          /2020/04/intel-russia-involve-mideast-covid19-coronavirus-syria.html.

p. 340   **with Ismail Haniyeh, head of Hamas's political bureau.**
          Suchkov, "Intel: Why Russia is getting involved in Mideast COVID-19 fight."

p. 341   **3 million containers were idle by the end of April.**
          Ryan Swift, "Container shipping lines cancel hundreds of sailings to stem losses as
          Covid-19 pandemic hits global trade," *South China Morning Post*, April 10, 2020,
          https://www.scmp.com/business/companies/article/3079234/container-shipping
          -lines-cancel-hundreds-sailings-stem-losses.

p. 341   **disadvantage its Southeast Asian neighbors in the South China Sea."**
          Kirstin Huang, "US accuses Beijing of using coronavirus as cover for South China
          Sea activity," *South China Morning Post*, April 7, 2020, https://www.scmp.com/news
          /china/diplomacy/article/3078757/us-accuses-beijing-using-coronavirus-cover-south
          -china-sea.

p. 341   **claimed by Vietnam and the Philippines.**
          Shashank Bengali, "What the coronavirus hasn't stopped: Beijing's buildup in the
          South China Sea," *Los Angeles Times*, April 10, 2020, https://www.latimes.com
          /world-nation/story/2020-04-10/coronavirus-doesnt-deter-chinas-aggression-in
          -south-china-sea.

p. 342   **the Bashi Channel east of Taiwan toward the South China Sea.**
          Tom O'Connor, "Chinese Aircraft Carrier Sails into Pacific as State Media Mock U.S.
          Navy's Coronavirus Troubles," *Newsweek*, April 13, 2020, https://www.newsweek
          .com/chinese-aircraft-carrier-sails-pacific-state-media-mock-us-navys-coronavirus
          -troubles-1497539.

p. 342   **to the Quai d'Orsay for a tongue-lashing.**
          "L'ambassadeur de Chine à Paris convoqué pour 'certains propos' liés au coronavirus"
          [The Chinese ambassador in Paris has been summoned for "certain comments"
          linked to the coronavirus], *Le Monde*, April 15, 2020, https://www.lemonde.fr/sante
          /article/2020/04/15/l-ambassadeur-de-chine-a-paris-convoque-pour-certains-propos
          -lies-au-coronavirus_6036610_1651302.html.

p. 342   **Zhao Lijian to repudiate quickly the embassy's remarks.**
"China denies criticizing France's response to Covid-19 crisis," France 24, April 15,
2020, https://www.france24.com/en/20200415-china-denies-criticising-france-s
-response-to-covid-19-crisis?ref=tw.

p. 342   **test kits were unable to yield any accurate results.**
"Coronavirus: Countries reject Chinese-made equipment," BBC News, March 30,
2020, https://www.bbc.com/news/world-europe-52092395.

p. 343   **short-range ballistic missiles (all under three hundred miles).**
Choe Sang-Hun, "North Korea Launches Two Short-Range Ballistic Missiles,"
New York Times, March 28, 2020, updated April 26, 2020, https://www.nytimes
.com/2020/03/28/world/asia/north-korea-missile-launch.html;
Choe Sang-Hun, "North Korea Fires Short-Range Ballistic Missiles, South Says,"
New York Times, March 20, 2020, https://www.nytimes.com/2020/03/20/world/asia
/north-korea-missile.html?action=click&module=RelatedLinks&pgtype=Article.

p. 343   **Trump administration sent in two aircraft carrier strike groups.**
David A. Andelman, "Trump's risky nose-to-nose challenge to China in the South
China Sea," CNN, July 7, 2020, https://www.cnn.com/2020/07/07/opinions/trump
-china-south-china-sea-andelman/index.html.

p. 343   **first two major amphibious assault ships.**
David Lague, "China expands its amphibious forces in challenge to U.S. supremacy
beyond Asia," Reuters, July 20, 2020, https://www.reuters.com/investigates/special
-report/china-military-amphibious/.

p. 343   **region in the age of pandemic, however, has been economic.**
Yan Nee Lee, "'Severe and unprecedented': IMF warns Asia's economy will not grow
at all in 2020 because of coronavirus," CNBC, April 16, 2020, https://www.cnbc
.com/2020/04/16/coronavirus-imf-forecasts-zero-growth-for-asia-economy-in-2020
.html?__source=iosappshare%7Ccom.google.Gmail.ShareExtension.

p. 344   **the most precise recent estimates suggest.**
Niall P. A. S. Johnson and Juergen Mueller, "Updating the Accounts: Global
Mortality of the 1918–1920 'Spanish' Influenza Pandemic," *Bulletin of the History of
Medicine* 76, no. 1, (Spring 2002): 105–115, https://muse.jhu.edu/article/4826/pdf.

p. 344   **the entire population of the continent was barely 150 million.**
Wm. Robert Johnston, "Historical World Population Data," last modified February 21,
2015, http://www.johnstonsarchive.net/other/worldpop.html.

p. 344   **"we must react most quickly if we want to avoid a massacre."**
Annick Cojean, "L'appel du prix Nobel de la paix Denis Mukwege: en Afrique, 'il
faut agir au plus vite si nous voulons éviter l'hécatombe,'" *Le Monde*, March 28, 2020,
https://www.lemonde.fr/afrique/article/2020/03/28/le-nobel-denis-mukwege-en-afrique
-il-faut-agir-au-plus-vite-si-nous-voulons-eviter-l-hecatombe_6034733_3212.html.

p. 345   **This was a "break the glass moment."**
David Pilling, "Officials warn Africa is at 'break the glass' moment," *Financial Times*,
March 29, 2020, https://www.ft.com/content/07716a2b-2ba5-44aa-80ff-13d5eafb4bad.

p. 345   **beds, only beds. No oxygen, no ventilators."**
          Max Bearak and Danielle Paquette, "Africa's most vulnerable countries have few
          ventilators—or none at all," *Washington Post*, April 18, 2020, https://www.washingtonpost
          .com/world/africa/africa-coronavirus-ventilators/2020/04/17/903163a4-7f3e-11ea-84c2
          -0792d8591911_story.html.

p. 345   **accompanying supplies of respiratory units.**
          Mike Woods, "Macron calls for suspension of debt to help Africa deal with coronavirus,"
          Radio France International, April 15, 2020, http://www.rfi.fr/en/africa/20200415-macron
          -calls-for-suspension-of-debt-to-africa-deal-with-coronavirus-g20-repayments-covid-19.

p. 345   **coronavirus test kits for distribution across fifty-four African nations.**
          "China's post-covid propaganda push," *The Economist*, April 16, 2020, https://www
          .economist.com/china/2020/04/16/chinas-post-covid-propaganda-push.

p. 346   **expertise that Africa would have to find elsewhere.**
          Nahal Toosi, "Trump hobbles foreign aid as coronavirus rips around the
          world," *Politico,* April 15, 2020, https://www.politico.com/news/2020/04/15
          /trump-foreign-aid-coronavirus-188659.
          "UPDATE: The United States Is Continuing to Lead the Humanitarian and Health
          Assistance Response to COVID-19," Office of the Spokesperson, US Department of
          State, April 16, 2020, https://www.state.gov/update-the-united-states-is-continuing
          -to-lead-the-humanitarian-and-health-assistance-response-to-covid-19/.

p. 346   **USAID played a central role in containment.**
          "China's post-covid propaganda push."

p. 346   **unlikely that demographics will be favorable."**
          Pilling, "Officials warn Africa is at 'break the glass' moment."

p. 347   **in a systematic way is going to be difficult.**
          Beatrice Di Caro, "COVID-19 in Africa: insights from our 16 April WHO
          media briefing," World Economic Forum, April 16, 2020, video, 1:00:46, at
          38:00–41:00 and 59:00–1:01:00, https://www.weforum.org/agenda/2020/04
          /covid-19-in-africa-insights-from-our-media-briefing-with-who-6ac4b99825.

p. 347   **as her chronicler Charles C. Mann puts it.**
          Charles C. Mann, "State of the Species," *Orion Magazine*, accessed July 2020,
          https://orionmagazine.org/article/state-of-the-species/.

p. 347   **that leads to poverty, misery, and wars.**
          Dick Teresi, "Discover Interview: Lynn Margulis Says She's Not Controversial, She's
          Right," *Discover*, June 16, 2011, https://www.discovermagazine.com/the-sciences
          /discover-interview-lynn-margulis-says-shes-not-controversial-shes-right.

p. 348   **against COVID-19, the United States retreated to the sidelines.**
          Liz Sly, Michael Birnbaum, and Karen DeYoung, "The U.S. traditionally leads in
          times of crisis. Now it's practicing self-isolation," *Washington Post,* March 26, 2020,
          https://www.washingtonpost.com/world/the-us-traditionally-leads-in-times
          -of-crisis-now-its-practicing-self-isolation/2020/03/25/1fa3f9b6-6d38-11ea-a156
          -0048b62cdb51_story.html.

p. 348   **of which he has been, for decades, the main beneficiary."**
Gilles Paris, "La panne du leadership américain dans la crise du coronavirus," *Le Monde*, March 30, 2020, https://www.lemonde.fr/international/article/2020/03/30 /la-panne-du-leadership-americain-dans-la-crise-du-coronavirus_6034856_3210.html.

p. 348   **Beasley warned the UN Security Council in April 2020.**
Edith M. Lederer, "UN food agency chief: World on brink of 'a hunger pandemic,'" Associated Press, April 21, 2020, https://apnews.com/ddf274a0521fc3047de31f56 cb71dd62.

p. 348   **Macron managed to bring along every major world power.**
David A. Andelman, "France's Macron positioning himself as leader of the world," CNN Opinion, April 15, 2020, https://www.cnn.com/2020/04/15/opinions /emmanuel-macron-world-wide-ceasefire-leader-andelman/index.html.

p. 350   **wisdom to learn from the experience and be a better person for it.**
Transcribed from recording of Andrew Cuomo as broadcast by MSNBC, 11:15 A.M. EDT, Tuesday, April 21, 2020.

Map & Illustration Credits

p. 4   United Kingdom Foreign & Commonwealth Office, Chad: Travel Advice [map], October 2016.

p. 8   WikiCommons, Cold War Europe Military Alliances Map [map], October 7, 2006, last updated May 20, 2012.

p. 29   Roger Fenton, *Henry Duberly Esq., Paymaster, 8th Hussars & Mrs. Duberly*, 1855, alamy.com.

p. 30   Crimea: location [map], 2014, *Encyclopedia Britannica*.

p. 31   Robert Gibbs, *Thin Red Line*, 1881, oil-on-canvas, National Museums Scotland, Edinburgh.

p. 57   Rishabh Tatiraju, The Demilitarized Zone in Korea [map], September 19, 2012, "Wikicommons."

p. 85   U.S. Government, North Korea Military and Economic Zone [map], "WikiCommons."

p. 98   Voice of America Vietnamese Service, 2012.

p. 99   U.S. Central Intelligence Agency, Map of the South China Sea [map], 1988, "Perry-Castañeda Map Collection, University of Texas."

p. 102   Goran tek-en, South China Sea Vector [map], January 23, 2014, "Wikicommons," last updated November 9, 2014.

p. 104   Airbus Defence and Space, *Fiery Cross Reef*, scale unknown. In: Mira Rapp-Hooper, "Before and After: The South China Sea Transformed," CSIS Asia Maritime Transparency Initiative, February 18, 2015.

p. 105   Airbus Defence and Space, *Fiery Cross Reef*, scale unknown. In: Mira Rapp-Hooper, "Before and After: The South China Sea Transformed," CSIS Asia Maritime Transparency Initiative, February 18, 2015.

p. 112   CSIS Asia Maritime Transparency Initiative/Maxar Technologies.

p. 115   Li Gang/Xinhua, "China begins naval exercise in the South China Sea," April 12, 2018, *Navy Times*.

p. 125   United States Central Intelligence Agency, The Baltic States [map], 1994, Library of Congress Geography and Map Division Washington, D.C., https://www.loc.gov/item/2005626489/.

p. 143   U.S. Central Intelligence Agency, Georgia [map], 1999, Perry-Castañeda Map Collection, University of Texas.

p. 145   Gene Thorp, Ukranian Cossack Hetmanate and Russian Empire (1751) [map], scale unknown. In: Ishaan Tharoor and Gene Thorp, "How Ukraine became Ukraine, in 7 maps," *The Washington Post*, March 9, 2015.

p. 147   Gene Thorp, Ukraine from 1654 to 1954 [map], scale unknown. In: Ishaan Tharoor and Gene Thorp, "How Ukraine became Ukraine, in 7 maps," *The Washington Post*, March 9, 2015.

p. 152   Gene Thorp, Ukraine [map], scale unknown. In: Ishaan Tharoor and Gene Thorp, "How Ukraine became Ukraine, in 7 maps," *The Washington Post*, March 9, 2015.

p. 164   Dr. Michael Izady, Islamic States in AD 985 [map], 1998, Gulf/2000, last updated 2017.

p. 165   Dr. Michael Izady, Islamic States in AD 1185 [map], 1998, Gulf/2000, last updated 2017.

p. 167   Dr. Michael Izady, Islamic States in AD 1735 [map], 1998, Gulf/2000, last updated 2020.

p. 201   Target of US, UK, France strikes in Syria [map], unknown scale. In "US, UK, France launch strikes in Syrian chemical weapons capabilities," *DW*, April 14, 2018.

p. 213   Fabienkhan, Iran Circa 1000 AD [map], September 11, 2006, "Wikicommons," last updated January 14, 2014.

p. 214   Fabienkhan, Safavid Persia [map], September 13, 2006, "Wikicommons," last updated July 14, 2011.

p. 216   Fabienkhan, Iran 1900 [map], September 24, 2006, "Wikicommons," last updated August 6, 2017.

p. 229   International Institute for Strategic Studies. (London: IISS, 2019).

p. 233   Marco Ugolini, Historical Division (1962) [map], scale unknown. In: Adam Baron, "Mapping the Yemen Conflict," European Council on Foreign Relations, 2015.

p. 235   Marco Ugolini, Houthi Expansion (2012-2015) [map], scale unknown. In: Adam Baron, "Mapping the Yemen Conflict," European Council on Foreign Relations, 2015.

p. 250   Political Map of Africa [map], Nations Online Project.

p. 258   *La Question Du Congo* (Berlin Congress 1884), December 13, 1884, illustration, Alamy.

p. 259   Eric Gaba (Wikimedia Commons user: Sting), African Colonies After the Berlin Conference of 1884 [map], November 22, 2016, "Three Acres and a Cow."

p. 260   Africa c. 1914, The Map Archives. Map code Ax0048. https://www.themaparchive.com/product/africa-c-1914/.

p. 262   Arnold Wright, *Lord and Lady Ludgard*, 1908, WikiCommons.

p. 267   Global Mapping International, The 25 Unbelievable Years: Post-Colonial Africa in 1970 [map], 2006, Mission Infobank.

p. 274   HIS Jane's Terrorism and Insurgency Centre, Militant Islamist Group Attacks in 2015 [map], scale unknown. In: "Numbers Show Dramatic Rise of Terrorist Attacks in Africa Over Past Six Years," Business Wire, June 27, 2016.

p. 275. The Sahel [map], scale unknown. In: Kim Searcy, "All Politics is Local: Understand Boko Haram," *Origins: Current Events in Historical Perspective* 9, issue 9 (June 2016).

p. 276   Nigeria: Travel Advice [map], September 2020, U.K. Foreign, Commonwealth & Development Office.

p. 286   Sam Dodge, International Military Servicemen Stationed in Africa [map], unknown scale. In: Phoebe Weston, "US, Chinese, British and French forces have troops permanently stationed in Africa to fight security threats in the region, notable piracy and the al-Shabaab militant group," *Voice of Djibouti*, July 2015.

p. 294   Peter Hermes Furian, Afghanistan and Pakistan Political Map [map], PantherMedia.

p. 296   Alexander H. Joffe, Map of the Levant in the Iron Age [map], unknown scale. In: Alexander H. Joffe, "The Rise of Secondary States in the Iron Age," *Journal of the Economic and Social History of the Orient* 45, no. 4, (2002): 433.

p. 309   *Dr. Chaim Weizman with Emir Feisal*, 1918, Beit Hatfutsot Museum of the Jewish People, Tel Aviv.

p. 311   Division of the British Mandate of Palestine [map], Ministry of Foreign Affairs, Government of Israel.

p. 312   UN Department of Public Information Cartographic Section, Territories Occupied by Israel Since June 1967 [map], June 1997, United Nations Information System on the Question of Palestine.

p. 318   Vision for Peace [map], scale not given. In: *Peace to Prosperity: A Vision to Improve the Lives of the Palestinian and Israeli People* (Washington, DC: The White House, January 2020) Appendix 1, p. 41.

INDEX